Parallel Programming Using C++

Scientific and Engineering Computation
Janusz Kowalik, editor

Data-Parallel Programming on MIMD Computers
by Philip J. Hatcher and Michael J. Quinn, 1991

Unstructured Scientific Computation on Scalable Multiprocessors
edited by Piyush Mehrotra, Joel Saltz, and Robert Voigt, 1992

Parallel Computational Fluid Dynamics: Implementations and Results
edited by Horst D. Simon, 1992

Enterprise Integration Modeling: Proceedings of the First International Conference
edited by Charles J. Petrie, Jr., 1992

The High Performance Fortran Handbook
by Charles H. Koelbel, David B. Loveman, Robert S. Schreiber, Guy L. Steele Jr., and Mary E. Zosel, 1994 ·

Using MPI: Portable Parallel Programming with the Message-Passing Interface
by William Gropp, Ewing Lusk, and Anthony Skjellum, 1994

PVM: Parallel Virtual Machine—A Users' Guide and Tutorial for Networked Parallel Computing
by Al Geist, Adam Beguelin, Jack Dongarra, Weicheng Jiang, Robert Mancheck, and Vaidy Sunderam, 1994

Enabling Technologies for Petaflops Computing
by Thomas Sterling, Paul Messina, and Paul. H. Smith, 1995

Practical Parallel Programming
by Gregory V. Wilson, 1995

An Introduction to High-Performance Scientific Computing
by Lloyd D. Fosdick, Elizabeth R. Jessup, Carolyn J. C. Schauble, and Gitta Domik, 1996

Parallel Programming Using C++
edited by Gregory V. Wilson and Paul Lu, 1996

Parallel Programming Using C++

edited by Gregory V. Wilson and Paul Lu

The MIT Press

Cambridge, Massachusetts

London, England

This book was set in Computer Modern by the editors.

Library of Congress Cataloging-in-Publication Data

Parallel programming using C++ / edited by Gregory V. Wilson and Paul Lu.
    p.   cm.—(Scientific and engineering computation)
    Includes bibliographical references and indexes.
    ISBN 978-0-262-73118-8 (pb.)
    1. C++ (Computer program language). 2. Parallel programming (Computer science). I. Wilson, Gregory V. II. Lu, Paul. III. Series.
QA76.73.C153P365   1996
005.2—dc20   96-12636
                                                    CIP

The MIT Press is pleased to keep this title available in print by manufacturing single copies, on demand, via digital printing technology.

For my mother
— GVW

For GSM
— PL

And for prisoners of conscience everywhere.

Chapter 10 Mentat   383
by Andrew S. Grimshaw, Adam Ferrari, and Emily A. West

Chapter 11 MPC++   429
by Yutaka Ishikawa, Atsushi Hori, Hiroshi Tezuka, Motohiko
    Matsuda, Hiroki Konaka, Munenori Maeda, Takashi
    Tomokiyo, Jörg Nolte, and Mitsuhisa Sato

Chapter 12 MPI++   465
by Anthony Skjellum, Ziyang Lu, Purushotham V. Bangalore,
    and Nathan Doss

Chapter 13 pC++   507
by Shelby X. Yang, Dennis Gannon, Peter Beckman, Jacob
    Gotwals, and Neelakantan Sundaresan

Chapter 14 POOMA   547
by John V. W. Reynders, Paul J. Hinker, Julian C. Cummings,
    Susan R. Atlas, Subhankar Banerjee, William F. Humphrey,
    Steve R. Karmesin, Katarzyna Keahey, M. Srikant, and
    MaryDell Tholburn

Chapter 15 TAU   589
by Bernd Mohr, Allen D. Malony, and Janice E. Cuny

Chapter 16 UC++   629
by Russel Winder, Graham Roberts, Alistair McEwan,
    Jonathan Poole, and Peter Dzwig

Contributors   671

Appendix A An Overview of C++   681

Appendix B An Overview of Parallel Computing   689

Appendix C An Overview of Polygon Overlay   701

Bibliography   709

Citation Author Index   737

Index   747

Contents

Series Foreword   xxv

A Perspective on Concurrency and C++   xxvii

Preface   xxxi

1   ABC++   1

1.1   Introduction   1

1.2   History   2
    1.2.1   Early Development   2
    1.2.2   Themes   2
    1.2.3   Experience and Change   4

1.3   Active Objects   5
    1.3.1   Synchronous Method Invocation   6
    1.3.2   Controlling Method Invocation   8
    1.3.3   Ping, Join, and Sleep   10
    1.3.4   Caveats   10
    1.3.5   Initialization, Termination, and Stack Control   11

1.4   Example: The Producer-Consumer Problem   11
    1.4.1   A Mediating Buffer   13

1.5   Processors   15

1.6   Asynchronous Method Invocation   17

1.7   Parametric Shared Regions   21
    1.7.1   The Design of PSRs   21
    1.7.2   Creating PSRs and Handles   22
    1.7.3   Caveats   23
    1.7.4   Reading and Writing Shared Regions   23
    1.7.5   Locking and Unlocking   25
    1.7.6   Read-Only Handles   26
    1.7.7   Location Inquiry   26

1.8   Example: A Shared Counter   27

1.9   More About Parametric Shared Regions   31
    1.9.1   Other Ways to Create PSRs   31

	1.9.2	Lock Shuffling	32
	1.9.3	Lock Delegation	33
	1.9.4	Versions	34
1.10	Using ABC++		34
1.11	Example: Polygon Overlay		35
	1.11.1	Performance	38
1.12	Conclusions and Future Directions		39

2   The Amelia Vector Template Library   43

2.1	Introduction		43
	2.1.1	Algorithmic Templates	45
	2.1.2	Reducing Programmer Complexity	46
	2.1.3	A Case for Standard Parallel Collections	46
	2.1.4	Library Components	47
	2.1.5	An Example	49
	2.1.6	Organization	50
2.2	AVTL Programming Model		51
	2.2.1	Two Types of Parallelism	51
	2.2.2	Granularity	51
	2.2.3	Scalar Data	52
2.3	Library Overview		52
	2.3.1	The Parallel Vector Class	52
	2.3.2	Combining Function Objects	54
	2.3.3	Element-Wise Forms	58
	2.3.4	Algorithms on Vectors	62
2.4	Example Programs		71
	2.4.1	Computing π	72
	2.4.2	Polygon Overlay	72
2.5	Related Work		83
	2.5.1	CVL	84
	2.5.2	Data-Parallel Languages	84
	2.5.3	Distributed Object-Oriented Languages	85
	2.5.4	Class Libraries	86

2.6   Difficulties and Critique   87

      2.6.1   Compiler Incompatibilities   87

      2.6.2   Debugging   88

      2.6.3   Compilation Speed   88

2.7   Summary   89

3   CC++   91

3.1   Introduction   91

3.2   Design Philosophy and Goals of CC++   91

      3.2.1   Compositionality and CC++   91

      3.2.2   Other Design Considerations   95

3.3   Overview of CC++   97

      3.3.1   Parallel Composition Operators   97

      3.3.2   Synchronization Variables   101

      3.3.3   A Producer/Consumer Program   102

      3.3.4   Atomic Functions   103

      3.3.5   Implementing a Blocking Lock   105

      3.3.6   Specifying Location in CC++   108

3.4   Implementing Other Programming Styles   116

3.5   A Programming Example: Polygon Overlay   117

      3.5.1   Shared-Memory Implementation   119

      3.5.2   Distributed-Memory Implementation   120

3.6   Implementing CC++   124

3.7   Limitations of CC++   126

      3.7.1   Thread-Local Storage   127

      3.7.2   Thread Priorities   129

3.8   Summary   130

4   CHAOS++   131

4.1   Introduction   131

4.2   Support for Distributed Arrays   134

      4.2.1   Mobile Objects   135

4.2.2	Partitioning Data Arrays	136
4.2.3	Data Movement	139
4.2.4	An Example	140

4.3	Support for Distributed Pointer-Based Data Structures	142
4.3.1	Issues in Support for Pointer-Based Data Structures	142
4.3.2	Globally-Addressable Objects	142
4.3.3	Building Distributed Pointer-Based Data Structures	144
4.3.4	Data Movement Routines	148
4.3.5	An Example	149

4.4	Implementation	151
4.4.1	Dereferencing Global References	151
4.4.2	Data Movement	152

4.5	Applications and Performance Results	155
4.5.1	Polygon Overlay	155
4.5.2	Scientific Computation: Direct Simulation Monte Carlo Method	163
4.5.3	Spatial Database Systems: Vegetation Index Measurement	166
4.5.4	Image Processing: Image Segmentation	168

4.6	Related Work	171
4.7	Critique and Conclusions	172

5	**CHARM++**	**175**

5.1	Design Philosophy	175
5.1.1	Target Domain	177
5.1.2	Evolution	177

5.2	The CHARM++ Language	178
5.2.1	Message-Driven Execution	178
5.2.2	Dynamic Object Creation: Chares and Messages	183
5.2.3	Branched Chares	190
5.2.4	Specific Information Sharing Abstractions	194

5.3   Polygon Overlay   198

5.4   Implementation   203

    5.4.1   Converse: Portability and Interoperability   205
    5.4.2   Chare Kernel   206

5.5   Tools and Libraries   207

5.6   Discussion   211

6   **COOL**   215

6.1   Introduction   215

6.2   Language Design   217

    6.2.1   Expressing Concurrency   218
    6.2.2   Mutual Exclusion   219
    6.2.3   Event Synchronization   220
    6.2.4   Task Level Synchronization   221
    6.2.5   Discussion   222

6.3   Examples   223

    6.3.1   Illustrating the Constructs   224
    6.3.2   Object Level Synchronization   226
    6.3.3   Polygon Overlay   228

6.4   Data Locality and Load Balancing   232

    6.4.1   Our Approach   233
    6.4.2   The Abstractions   234

6.5   Implementation   238

    6.5.1   Overview   238
    6.5.2   Reducing Synchronization Overhead   239
    6.5.3   Scheduling Support for Locality   241

6.6   Application Case Studies   242

    6.6.1   Ocean   243
    6.6.2   LocusRoute   247
    6.6.3   Panel Cholesky   250

6.7   Conclusions   254

7   C++//   257

7.1   Introduction   257

7.2   Basic Model of Concurrency   258

   7.2.1   Processes   259
   7.2.2   Sequential or Parallel Processes   260
   7.2.3   Communication   261
   7.2.4   Synchronization   262
   7.2.5   Sharing   263

7.3   Control Programming   264

   7.3.1   Centralized versus Decentralized Control   265
   7.3.2   Explicit versus Implicit Control   266
   7.3.3   Library of Service Routines   270
   7.3.4   Library of Abstractions   272

7.4   A Programming Method   275

   7.4.1   Sequential Design and Programming (step 1)   275
   7.4.2   Process Identification (step 2)   276
   7.4.3   Process programming (step 3)   276
   7.4.4   Adaptations (step 4)   277

7.5   Environment   278

   7.5.1   Compilation   278
   7.5.2   Mapping   278

7.6   Polygon Overlay   283

   7.6.1   Sequential Design and Programming (step 1)   283
   7.6.2   Parallel Programming   283

7.7   Implementation   288

   7.7.1   A Reflection-Based System   289
   7.7.2   A MOP for C++: Basic Classes   290
   7.7.3   Class and Member Identification   292
   7.7.4   Customization and Extension of C++//   293

7.8   Conclusion   295

8   C**   297

8.1   Introduction   297

8.2   Data-Parallel Languages   299

    8.2.1   Fine-Grain Languages   300

    8.2.2   Coarse-Grain Languages   302

    8.2.3   Large-Grain Languages   303

    8.2.4   Purely Functional Languages   304

8.3   C** Overview   304

    8.3.1   Aggregates   305

    8.3.2   Aggregate Functions   306

    8.3.3   Aggregate Constructors   306

    8.3.4   Parallel Functions   307

    8.3.5   Slices   310

8.4   User-Defined Reductions   311

    8.4.1   DSMC Example   311

    8.4.2   Syntax of User-Defined Reductions   313

    8.4.3   Semantics of User-Defined Reductions   314

    8.4.4   Extensions to User-Defined Reduction Assignments   316

    8.4.5   Implementing User-Level Reductions   317

    8.4.6   User-Defined Reduction Performance   318

8.5   C** Implementation   319

    8.5.1   LCM   320

    8.5.2   LCM Implementation   321

    8.5.3   Compiling C**   323

    8.5.4   Dynamic C** Programs   324

8.6   Polygon Overlay Example   325

    8.6.1   Naïve C** Implementation   326

    8.6.2   Grid Partitioning a Map   327

    8.6.3   Performance Tuning   331

    8.6.4   Results   333

8.7   Conclusion   337

9   ICC++   343

9.1   Introduction   343

9.2   Concurrency   344

     9.2.1   conc Blocks   345
     9.2.2   conc Loops   346
     9.2.3   Examples   347

9.3   Objects, Abstractions, and Concurrency   349

     9.3.1   Object Data Abstractions   350
     9.3.2   Concurrency Control Across Multiple Objects   352
     9.3.3   Discussion   354

9.4   Arrays, Objects, and Collections   355

     9.4.1   Defining Object Collections   355
     9.4.2   Using Collections   356
     9.4.3   Concurrent Abstractions   357
     9.4.4   Discussion   358

9.5   Unstructured Concurrency   359

     9.5.1   Spawn   359
     9.5.2   Reply   359
     9.5.3   Unstructured Idioms   360

9.6   Polygon Overlay   361

     9.6.1   Porting to ICC++   361
     9.6.2   Parallelization   363
     9.6.3   Distributing PolyOver   365

9.7   Performance   369

     9.7.1   Sequential Performance   369
     9.7.2   Parallel Performance   370

9.8   Discussion and Related Work   375

     9.8.1   C++ Compatibility   375
     9.8.2   Derivation and Concurrency   375
     9.8.3   Parallel C++ Efforts   378
     9.8.4   Other Concurrent Object-Oriented Languages   379
     9.8.5   Illinois Concert Project   380

9.9   Summary   381

9.10   Future Work   381

10   Mentat   **383**

10.1   Introduction   383

    10.1.1 The Mentat Philosophy   383

    10.1.2 Parallelism Encapsulation   384

    10.1.3 The Mentat Environment   386

    10.1.4 Roadmap   387

10.2   The Mentat Programming Language   387

    10.2.1 Mentat Classes   388

    10.2.2 Using Mentat Objects   392

    10.2.3 Choosing Mentat Classes   394

    10.2.4 Instantiation and Binding of Mentat Objects   395

    10.2.5 Return-to-Future `rtf()`   396

    10.2.6 `mselect`/`maccept`   399

    10.2.7 Compilation   400

10.3   The Runtime System   401

    10.3.1 Runtime Dataflow Detection   401

    10.3.2 Scheduling   403

10.4   Application Experience   405

    10.4.1 DNA and Protein Sequence Comparison 406

    10.4.2 Stencil Libraries   411

    10.4.3 Polygon Overlay   415

10.5   Lessons Learned   420

    10.5.1 Pure Functions   421

    10.5.2 Data-Parallel Computations   421

    10.5.3 Shallow Copying   422

    10.5.4 Virtual Functions   422

    10.5.5 Non-Preemptable Member Functions   423

    10.5.6 Object Instantiation and Scheduling 424

    10.5.7 `rtf()`   425

10.6   The Future   425

11   MPC++   429

11.1   Introduction   429

11.2   The MPC++ Approach to High Performance Computing   430

11.3   Language Overview   431
    11.3.1   Control Parallelism Facility   431
    11.3.2   Discussion of Control Parallelism Features   438
    11.3.3   Meta-level Architecture   440

11.4   Class Library and Language Extension   449

11.5   Implementation   452

11.6   Basic Performance   455

11.7   Polygon Overlay   458
    11.7.1   Implementation   458
    11.7.2   Performance   461

11.8   Concluding Remarks   463

12   MPI++   465

12.1   MPI Overview   465
    12.1.1   Summary of MPI Features   467
    12.1.2   Parallel Models Supported   468
    12.1.3   MPI++ Origins and Overview   470

12.2   Design and Implementation of MPI++   473
    12.2.1   The MPI++ Interface   473
    12.2.2   Object-Oriented Design of MPI++   477
    12.2.3   Implementation Issues   488

12.3   Example: Polygon Overlay   489
    12.3.1   Solution #1   489
    12.3.2   Solution #2   489

12.4   Performance Tests   499

12.5   Summary, Conclusions, and Future Work   500
    12.5.1   Current MPI++   501
    12.5.2   MPI-2   503

12.5.3 Conclusions   505

13   pC++   **507**

13.1 Introduction   507

13.2 History   508

13.3 Overview of pC++ Version 2.0   510
    13.3.1 pC++ Runtime System   513
    13.3.2 Tulip   514
    13.3.3 I/O   516
    13.3.4 Persistence   518

13.4 An Example: Parallel Sorting   521

13.5 The Polygon Overlay Program   526

13.6 The Self-Consistent Field Code   533
    13.6.1 The pC++ Version of the SCF Code   535
    13.6.2 Benchmark Results   537

13.7 The Particle Mesh Code   538
    13.7.1 The Particle List Collection   539
    13.7.2 The Mesh Collection   540
    13.7.3 The Main Simulation Loop   541
    13.7.4 Benchmark Results   542

13.8 Conclusion and Project Evaluation   543

14   POOMA   **547**

14.1 Introduction   547

14.2 History and Philosophy   547
    14.2.1 Why Data-Parallel Programming?   548
    14.2.2 Why a Framework?   549

14.3 Implementation   550
    14.3.1 Framework Layer Description   550
    14.3.2 Global Data Types   551
    14.3.3 Parallel Abstraction Layer   556
    14.3.4 Chained Expression Object   559

14.3.5 Component Layer   563

14.3.6 POOMA on Clustered Parallel Architectures   568

14.4 POOMA Appearance   570

14.4.1 2D Diffusion Code   570

14.4.2 Gyrokinetic Simulation   575

14.5 The Polygon Overlay Problem   580

14.5.1 POOMA Implementation Details   581

14.5.2 Performance Results   584

14.6 Critique   586

15 TAU   589

15.1 Introduction   589

15.2 Design Requirements and Goals   591

15.3 TAU Overview   592

15.3.1 TAU Architecture   593

15.3.2 TAU Implementation   595

15.4 TAU Tools   599

15.4.1 Static Analysis Tools   599

15.4.2 Dynamic Analysis Tools   601

15.4.3 Performance Extrapolation for pC++   607

15.5 Tour de TAU: The Polygon Overlay Example   609

15.5.1 Utility Tools   609

15.5.2 Static Analysis Tools   610

15.5.3 Dynamic Analysis Tools   614

15.5.4 Performance Extrapolation   621

15.6 Critique   623

15.7 Conclusion and Future Work   626

16 UC++   629

16.1 Introduction   629

16.2 History and Philosophy   630

16.2.1 The Ancient Period   631
16.2.2 The Early Period   632
16.2.3 The Middle Period   634

16.3 Overview of Current UC++   636
16.3.1 Active Objects—Overview   637
16.3.2 Active Objects—The Execution Model   639
16.3.3 Language Elements   642
16.3.4 Compiling and Running Programs   644
16.3.5 An Example: The Sieve of Eratosthenes   646

16.4 Implementation   649
16.4.1 The Translator   650
16.4.2 The Abstract Message Passing Interface   653

16.5 The Polygon Overlay Example   654
16.5.1 An Initial Solution   654
16.5.2 An Embarrassingly Parallel Algorithm   657

16.6 Critique of UC++   664

16.7 Applications of UC++   665

16.8 Conclusions and Future Work   667

Contributors   671

A   An Overview of C++   681

B   An Overview of Parallel Computing   689

C   An Overview of Polygon Overlay   701

Bibliography   709

Citation Author Index   737

Index   747

Series Foreword

The world of modern computing potentially offers many helpful methods and tools to scientists and engineers, but the fast pace of change in computer hardware, software, and algorithms often makes practical use of the newest computing technology difficult. The Scientific and Engineering Computation series focuses on rapid advances in computing technologies and attempts to facilitate transferring these technologies to applications in science and engineering. It will include books on theories, methods, and original applications in such areas as parallelism, large-scale simulations, time-critical computing, computer-aided design and engineering, use of computers in manufacturing, visualization of scientific data, and human-machine interface technology.

The series will help scientists and engineers to understand the current world of advanced computation and to anticipate future developments that will impact their computing environments and open up new capabilities and modes of computation.

This book is a collection of papers describing some of the most promising approaches to parallel programming systems based on C++.

We expect that many of the ideas presented in the book will help to construct a parallel version of C++ combining two very desirable features: high computational performance, and the ease and efficiency of sequential programming.

Janusz S. Kowalik

A Perspective on Concurrency and C++

Bjarne Stroustrup

One of the most common questions about C++ is "Why doesn't C++ support concurrency?" Sometimes, that is even phrased "Why don't you consider concurrency important enough to be supported by C++?" Those are not the right questions. Concurrency is a basic fact of life and must be supported. Better questions are "How should we support concurrency in C++?", "How do we support concurrency in C++?", and "What kinds of concurrency should we support?" This book gives many answers to these questions, and therein lies a problem and a story.

When I designed and implemented the first version of C++, concurrency was very much on my mind. I had recently completed a Ph.D. on ways of organizing software in distributed systems, I worked in a department where the local and wide-area network protocols were being designed, and I was studying the possibility of distributing operating system kernel facilities over a network. I definitely wanted to support concurrency for users of my new programming language. In fact, such support was essential. The question was simply "how?" There were—and still are—a multitude of different uses of concurrency. Operating system kernel hackers want one form of concurrency, the builders of user interface systems another, the database community needs parallelism of yet another kind, and people doing high-performance numeric computation rely on models of parallel programming that are different still. The list of application areas with apparently distinct needs is long.

In addition, hardware designers produce a steady stream of ideas for delivering better performance at lower cost by relying on new forms of parallel execution. Ideally, we would provide a single model of parallel execution for the programmer to rely on and treat the diversity of underlying models as mere implementation details. However, we have not been able to do that. The user communities appear to differ at the level of the model of concurrency needed by the programmers.

My conclusion at the time when I designed C++ was that no single model of concurrency would serve more than a small fraction of the user community well. I could build a single model of concurrency into C++ by providing language features that directly supported its fundamental concepts and ease its use through notational conveniences. However, if I did that I would favor a small fraction of my users over the majority.

This I declined to do, and by refraining from doing so I left every form of concurrency equally badly supported by the basic C++ mechanisms. I could, however, not complete my own applications without some support for concurrency. In particular, I needed support for Simula-style event driven simulations and for some real-time non-preemptable multi-threaded applications. I didn't feel that I could favor my own needs over those of the majority, so I wrote a library rather than providing direct language support. That library, the task library [Stroustrup 1980], was the first-ever C++ library, and the first-ever C++ applications relied on it. My initial implementation supported simulations only, but a few years later Jonathan Shopiro re-implemented the library to cope with multiprocessors and interrupts to make it far more widely applicable [Shopiro 1987]. Compared to today's systems, and even compared to the systems used at the time, the task library was limited and unsophisticated.

Over the years, I have occasionally felt a bit embarrassed by aspects of it and wished that it would be replaced by something better. However, it has shown a remarkable degree of resilience. It was simple and supported a significant range of uses well. I recall once trying to discourage its use locally only to find myself faced with a user who had measured it running 50 times faster than a local Ada implementation for a critical application. After that, I adopted a policy of benign neglect. The task library is still in wide-spread use today, and I receive a couple of inquiries about its use and various implementations every month. I was interested, and honored, to see that some of the much more modern and sophisticated systems described in this book count the task library among their ancestry.

C++ provides no primitives to support multiple threads of execution, no locking mechanism, no notion of collections of data being accessed in parallel, etc. Consequently, any implementation of concurrency in C++ must rely on extra-linguistic guarantees provided by convention, non-portable library functions, special treatment given to key types by modified compilers, added language primitives, etc. This book demonstrates many such alternatives. However, I still have a weakness for library-based approaches because these offer a higher degree of portability than approaches based on language extensions. Also, library-based approaches leave more choices open to application builders. If we don't know a single programming model that is sufficient for all concurrent programs, can we design a minimal set of primitives that are sufficient to act as a common base for libraries supporting the various programming models?

Many have looked for such primitives, but I'm not sure that we have yet found a set that is sufficiently primitive to serve most users without unduly biasing them towards a particular programming model. Whenever possible, we prefer not to have to deal with language dialects and must always keep an eye out for the possibility of something general enough to support everybody. However, a general-purpose language simply cannot support every specialized need well. As ever, the issues are subtle. The library approach can often approximate an ideal, but it can rarely reach it. This causes a constant pressure for some form of direct support. Also, as long as genuinely new models of parallel execution keep emerging, language dialects must inevitably emerge to serve them.

I have often wondered if I made the right choice in not supporting some form of concurrency directly in C++. After all, a good solution now is often far preferable to a perfect solution "next year". However, I did not think I had a solution that was good enough for that argument to apply. I suspect that if I had provided a concurrency mechanism in C++, I would have provided one that would have seriously annoyed many people whose livelihood or research depended on concurrency. On the other hand, I'm confident that I would have provided something that was good enough to be liked by many and also would have been minimally acceptable to many more. This could easily have become a major obstacle to experimentation with alternative and better forms of concurrency in C++. By supporting my favorite forms of concurrency well in C++, I could easily have made the task of providing other people's alternatives impractical instead of merely very difficult.

Over the years, designers of concurrent variants of C++ have struggled with the fact that C++ itself was evolving. The evolution of C++ caused two kind of problems for designers of concurrency facilities. Changes in the language required updates of compilers, and was therefore a source of extra implementation work. The emergence of new features, such as templates, exceptions, and runtime type information [Stroustrup 1994], affects tradeoffs between what is provided specifically by a parallel programming extension and what is done in the common language itself. Similarly, new language features strongly affect what can be expressed in a library, and how. Now that the standards effort is coming to a close and the features of the language and its standard library are fixed, I expect life to become easier for developers of facilities supporting concurrency. In fact, I expect the new-found stability in the language definition to cause a boom in tools and libraries in general.

No language feature can be studied in isolation from the system it is part of and the uses to which it is put. How do features for parallel computation interact with the use of multiple address spaces? How can we distribute work over multiple processors of a single computer? Over a network of computers? How do efficiencies of basic operations affect the algorithms needed for applications? How do we design algorithms to take advantage of varying degrees of concurrency? How do we design algorithms to optimize real-time response, maximize throughput, or minimize the effort needed by programmers? How can facilities supporting parallelism interact smoothly with abstraction mechanisms? What kind of concurrent programs can be widely portable? At what cost?

I suspect that much progress will come from a focus on the use of concurrency mechanisms as part of solutions to hard everyday problems. The constraints imposed by "real-world" environments can be most annoying, but part of finding a solution is exactly to discover useful constraints for the problem in hand.

Will we ever reach a grand synthesis of concurrency features for C++? That is, will we ever find a single set of facilities that essentially all non-research users can agree on? I don't know, but several of the systems described in this book have ambitions in that direction. Clearly, we must hope that some such system reaches the critical mass to succeed on the largest scale. However, the variety of systems described here shows that a grand synthesis isn't easy. Maybe it will come from a wholly unexpected angle? Whatever it is, it will be directly or indirectly based on many of the ideas presented in this book.

Preface

Gregory V. Wilson and Paul Lu

Overview

Software is generally acknowledged to be the single greatest obstacle preventing mainstream adoption of massively-parallel computing. While sequential applications are routinely ported to platforms ranging from PCs to mainframes, most parallel programs only ever run on one type of machine (if at all). One reason for this is that most parallel programming systems have failed to insulate their users from the architectures of the machines on which they have run. Those that have been platform-independent have usually also had platform-independent (i.e., poor) performance.

Many researchers now believe that the high-level mechanisms embodied in object-oriented languages will be able to cut through this Gordian knot. By hiding the architecture-specific constructs required for high performance inside platform-independent abstractions, parallel object-oriented programming systems may be able to combine the speed of massively-parallel computing with the comfort of sequential programming.

This book describes a variety of parallel programming systems based on C++, the most popular object-oriented language of today. Fourteen of these systems run on distributed-memory multicomputers, and one on shared-memory multiprocessors; one system, TAU (Chapter 15), is not a programming system *per se*, but rather a family of tools for parallel debugging and performance visualization. The systems described cover the whole spectrum of parallel programming paradigms, from data parallelism through dataflow and distributed shared memory to message-passing control parallelism.

The contributors and the editors have tried to make this book relevant to several communities. For the parallel programming community, a common parallel application is discussed in each chapter, as part of the description of the system itself. By comparing the implementations of the polygon overlay problem (Appendix C) in each system, the reader can get a better sense of their expressiveness and functionality for a common problem.

For the systems community, the chapters contain a discussion of the implementation of the various compilers and runtime systems. In addition to discussing the performance of polygon overlay, several of the contributors also discuss the performance of other, more substantial, applications. For the research community, the contributors discuss the motivations for and philosophy of their systems. As well, many of the chapters include critiques that complete the research arc by pointing out possible future research directions.

Finally, for the object-oriented community, there are many examples of how encapsulation, inheritance, and polymorphism can be used to control the complexity of developing, debugging, and tuning parallel software. Several of the systems make extensive use of C++'s templates to provide type-safe functionality; two—C++// (Chapter 7) and MPC++ (Chapter 11)—use meta-object protocols to implement extensions to C++, while POOMA (Chapter 14) uses a chained-expression object to optimize operations on user-defined data types.

To aid the reader, the editors have included overviews of C++ (Appendix A) and parallel computing (Appendix B), as well as a detailed discussion of the polygon overlay problem (Appendix C). We hope that the list of contributors and their affiliations, the unified bibliography, citation back-references, citation author index, and subject index will be helpful, and that readers will consult the on-line materials available from:

```
http://mitpress.mit.edu/mitp/recent-books/comp/ppuc.html
```

How Object-Oriented Are the Systems?

Two questions that may arise while reading this book are "How object-oriented are these parallel programming systems?" and "How well do the systems exploit the features of C++?"

Generally, an object-oriented system is one which supports encapsulation, inheritance, and polymorphism (Appendix A). Most of the systems described in this book use encapsulation to create abstractions representing either parallel processes or parallel data structures. For example, the active object model used in UC++ (Chapter 16) and other systems simplifies the task of creating and controlling a parallel process. By encapsulating the state and methods of a process within a C++

class, new parallel processes can be created as easily as passive sequential objects. Subsequent messages to the active object resemble method invocations, even if the target object resides in a separate address space.

The strengths of C++ are also brought to bear on designing parallel abstract data types. Vectors, matrices, and other collections are defined by encapsulating the (potentially) distributed data with implicitly parallel operations. This allows users to put off worrying about such things as data decomposition until the time comes to tune their programs.

Inheritance is often combined with encapsulation and polymorphism to support re-use of interfaces and code. For example, CHAOS++ (Chapter 4) uses inheritance and virtual functions to support data migration for pointer-based data structures. Also, CHARM++ (Chapter 5) uses inheritance to support its branched chare approach to implementing distributed groups of objects.

Many systems use polymorphism to implement type-specific functionality. ABC++ (Chapter 1) uses templates to implement type-specific data marshalling for method invocations, while Amelia (Chapter 2) uses them to abstract user-defined types, algorithms, and algebraic combining functions. Finally, in the spirit of C++'s streams library, pC++ (Chapter 13) uses operator overloading to provide a high-level I/O facility.

What Are the Benefits to Parallel Programmers?

The editors are, by nature, sceptical of the claims made about most parallel programming systems [Wilson et al. 1994]. However, there are some clear benefits to applying C++'s object-oriented mechanisms to parallel programming.

First, the ease with which active objects can be created and remote methods invoked is a welcome step forward. In particular, the automatic type-safe marshalling of parameters means that there is one less error-prone chore for the programmer.

Problems that are amenable to data-parallel solutions will benefit even more from the parallel abstract data types. By hiding the data distribution details, many of the systems described allow their users to think about the logical and physical aspects of the data separately. By exploiting C++'s support for operator overloading, they also provide a concise and convenient lexical notation for expressing parallelism.

It is encouraging to see object orientation exploited to deal with locality in NUMA multiprocessors (COOL, Chapter 6), and with scheduling and runtime detection of data dependencies (Mentat, Chapter 10). Also notable are MPI++'s (Chapter 12) support for the Message-Passing Interface (MPI) standard, and the more experimental work exemplified by C**'s (Chapter 8) new memory semantics, CC++'s (Chapter 3) compositional approach to parallel program construction, and ICC++'s (Chapter 9) work on compiler optimizations.

Of course, not all of the systems described in this book support all of features that we have praised. However, we feel that the systems in this book, and the others not included here, will be a rich source of inspiration from which future systems will arise.

Acknowledgments

First and foremost, we are grateful to our contributors for their time and effort. We would like to thank Karen Bennet, of IBM Canada, for allowing GVW to spend far more time on this project than was originally anticipated, and Songnian Zhou, of the University of Toronto, for allowing PL to do the same. We would also like to thank Bjarne Stroustrup for his foreword, David M. Jones for his invaluable LaTeX expertise, and Ben Gamsa and Harjinder Sandhu for their careful proofreading. Finally, we would like to thank the staff at MIT Press, particularly Bob Prior, Michael Rutter, and Deborah Cantor-Adams.

January 1, 1996

Gregory V. Wilson   Paul Lu
IBM Canada Ltd.   *Department of Computer Science*
844 Don Mills Rd.   *University of Toronto*
North York, ON M3C 1V7   *Toronto, ON M5S 3G4*
Canada   *Canada*
gvwilson@vnet.ibm.com   paullu@sys.utoronto.ca

1 ABC++

William G. O'Farrell, Frank Ch. Eigler,
S. David Pullara, and Gregory V. Wilson

1.1 Introduction

ABC++ was designed to support architecture-independent parallel programming in C++. The system consists of a class library, written in standard C++, and a runtime system which provides a uniform shared-data model on uniprocessors, networks of workstations, and massively-parallel computers.

ABC++ assumes that a single program will be executed on every processor in the machine, although different objects and/or functions may execute concurrently. ABC++ supports two commonly-used models of concurrency. The first is that of *active objects*, or actors [Agha 1986], in which C++ objects having their own independent threads of control can be created on any processor in the system. Once created, such objects are used in the same way regardless of their location. The second model is that of *shared regions* [Bal *et al.* 1992, Sandhu *et al.* 1993]. Any C++ object can be marked by the programmer as being shared; all processes have access to such shared objects, and the runtime system will guarantee the apparent consistency of all copies of such objects (so long as a few simple rules are adhered to). Such sharing does not suffer from the problem of *false sharing* that plagues page-based virtual shared memory systems [Li & Hudak 1989, Bennett *et al.* 1990].

ABC++ arose out of a research project at the Center for Advanced Studies (CAS) at the IBM Canada Toronto Laboratory. This project has involved researchers from several universities, including York, Syracuse, Toronto, and McGill. Questions and comments about ABC++ may be directed to:

abc++@vnet.ibm.com

1.2   History

1.2.1   Early Development

ABC++ originated in a project in the Centre for Advanced Studies
(CAS), at the Software Solutions Division Laboratory in Toronto. Beginning in 1992, the project, led by Bill O'Farrell, was originally intended
to explore parallelism in C, and in particular, to explore parallelization
of programs which used pointers and dynamic data structures. The reasoning here was (and is) that programmers turn to C (and C++) to deal
with problems that Fortran is not well suited for.

The project's first real research conclusion was that an approach using
C++ (versus C) would have several advantages over C. The obvious one
was that C++ was quickly supplanting C. Another was that the rich-
ness and power of the features of C++, including inheritance, operator
overloading, and templates, made it seem possible that a language-based
solution could be found. This would increase the likelihood of acceptance
in the C/C++ community, as programmers could continue to use familiar compilers and tools. Second, it would free us from the difficulties of
developing a robust compiler for a complex and evolving language, so
that we could concentrate solely on the issues of parallelization. Third,
it would reduce the time required to get a working system together, so
that we could begin experimentation quickly.

1.2.2   Themes

From our literature search came several themes. First, we wanted something more than a thread library. For example, users should not have to
explicitly create, start, and synchronize threads in order to get concurrency. Second, while we were, at first, focusing on shared-memory machines, we knew that we wanted to go beyond that to handle distributed-
memory machines in an architecture-independent way. Third, we wanted
to keep the model relatively simple, so that it would be easy to learn
and use ("as easy as ABC"). Fourth, we wanted to develop a decidedly
C++ solution, not a generic solution grafted onto C++. With these
goals in mind, we focused on developing an active objects model, where
an active object is an object which has a thread of control, and which
controls the invocation of its methods.

As identified in our original technical report, several problems with implementing active objects in a C++ class library were identified:

stack "diddling": Diddling a stack refers to the process of extracting from the stack the return address stored in the activation record of the first constructor called after object creation. This extraction of the returned address can be a problem in the presence of arbitrary levels of inheritance. If the constructor of the **Task** class is responsible for spinning-off the thread that will execute the body of the concurrent object, then the **Task** constructor must "diddle" the stack so that the original thread can return to the original program, while the new thread continues the execution of the constructors belonging to derived classes. However, if the number of levels of derivation is not known, and/or if the number of levels possessing constructors is not known, then the stack cannot be diddled in the usual way.

premature method invocation: If communication to an active object is via method invocation, its methods must not be invoked (or must not be allowed to actually execute) until its construction is complete. If a "start" routine is not used (as was our wish), C++ does not itself control when the parent task could invoke methods in a newly created concurrent object.

specification of object body: The programmer must be able to specify a routine which is to be used as the body of a concurrent object. It is the body which is executed with the object's independent thread of control. One approach used elsewhere was to use the constructor of a class as its body. However, this prevents further inheritance (even if a derived class defines its own constructor, it cannot override the previously defined constructor). Another approach is to use a member function as the body (we used a method called **main()**).

premature destruction: A concurrent object must not be destroyed until its thread of control has terminated. One idea is to have the destructor(s) for such an object wait until that happens. However, it is undesirable to force the user to include the wait code explicitly, as it could easily be forgotten, resulting in subtle race conditions.

selective method acceptance: Responding to desired method invocations, and delaying others for later processing, offers concurrent object systems power and flexibility. If a C++ based concurrent object system is to have this capability, then concurrent objects should be able to control which of their methods are invokable. C++ provides no native mechanism for this.

1.2.3 Experience and Change

Once our first system was up in 1993, several issues arose that required changes in our approach. Some users were concerned that our use of ->for both synchronous and asynchronous invocation (depending on the pointer type) was confusing, because one could not easily identify the type of call without looking up the pointer declaration. Others found that ABC++ was too unforgiving of errors. Many sorts of programming errors were not detected at compile time, and generated confusing errors at run time (typically a segmentation violation). These issues were addressed by re-thinking the way ABC++ was presented to the user. After some experimentation, it was found that by using function templates instead of an overloaded ->, most common errors could be detected at compile time, and in fact clever naming of some internal functions and variables resulted in error messages that could be comprehended by the user as ABC++ specific errors. Thus was born `ABC.h` (later renamed to the current `ABC++.h`), which contained template definitions for what would (much) later be named `Pvalue()`, `Pvoid()`, `Ppar_value()`, and `Ppar_void()`.

These function templates had another very beneficial effect. The "old" syntax had the distinct disadvantage of being somewhat fragile: when compiler versions changed, for instance, some parts of ABC++ often broke, and would have to be patched. The internal logic of parameter marshalling became so complex that it was difficult to analyze and repair such breakage, which was compounded when code optimization was attempted. The invocation templates, though uglier than the original syntax, solved all of these problems. As it stands today, ABC++ is a pure C++ class library with no "tricks" regarding virtual table pointer replacement, etc. Another of Eshrat Arjomandi's students, Henry Lee, assisted in the initial implementation of `ABC.h`.

One more issue that we found needed to be addressed was ease of programming. While active objects are certainly a way to program in an architecture independent way, we found when writing programs that we missed the ease that shared memory can provide. Consequently an architecture-independent shared-memory paradigm was developed.

Called parametric shared regions, this paradigm allowed for efficient sharing on an object-by-object basis, without the oppressive overhead often associated with distributed shared memory. It was also a purely C++ solution, as all the work in maintaining consistency is accomplished via constructors and destructors (along with a fair amount of internal machinery, all written in C++).

1.3 Active Objects

Consider the following:

```
#include <ABC++.h>
class Active : public Pabc {
    ...
};
```

By inheriting publicly from the class Pabc, defined in the library header file ABC++.h, this defines an *active object class* called Active. An active object class is one whose instances become independent light-weight threads. Class Pabc is called the *active base class* since classes derived from it become active object classes.

Process creation is done in two steps. First, a handle is declared, using the Pabc_pointer template defined in ABC++.h:

```
Pabc_pointer<Active> activePtr;
```

The template is parameterized by an active object class.

To create an active object, a program must call Pabc_create() with a handle as its first argument, and zero or more extra arguments which are passed to the active base class's constructor. Pabc_create() tells the runtime system to allocate a new instance of the type of object defined by its first argument, and to spawn a new thread to execute that object's code. The runtime system chooses the processor on which the new thread is to run. Thus:

```
Pabc_create(activePtr, 12345);
```

creates a new thread on one of the processors being used by the program, binds it to a newly-allocated instance of Active, and lets the thread run. The value 12345 is passed to the active object's constructor.

Once an active object has been created, other pointers can be turned into aliases for it. For example, after:

```
Pabc_create(ptr1);
ptr2 = ptr1;
```

both `ptr1` and `ptr2` refer to the same active object.

If an active base class contains (or inherits) a definition of a `void` method `main()`, taking no arguments, then when an instance of that class is created, its thread immediately begins executing that method. Thus, a not-particularly-interesting active base class might be:

```
class notVeryUseful : public Pabc {
 private :
  int intVal_;
 public :
  notVeryUseful(int init){
    intVal_ = init;
  }
  void main(){
    intVal_ = 0;
  }
};
```

An instance of this class would be created using:

```
Pabc_pointer<notVeryUseful> nvuPtr;
Pabc_create(nvuPtr, 12345);
```

Once the constructor had initialized `intVal_` to 12345, `main()` would immediately assign 0 to it. The active object's thread would then terminate.

If an active class does not specify how the active object is to behave, it inherits a default `main()` from the `Pabc` class. This repeatedly accepts method invocations from elsewhere in the program, invokes the specified method, and returns the results (if any) to the caller. An active object of this kind terminates when the program as a whole terminates.

1.3.1   Synchronous Method Invocation

ABC++ provides four ways for active objects to communicate directly. The first two operate *synchronously*: once a process has called one of them, its own execution is blocked until that call has completed.

Methods Returning a Value   Suppose an active object class `Active` defines a public method `methInt()`:

```
class Active : public Pabc {
 ...
 public :
  int methInt(args){
    ...
    return result;
  }
 ...
};
```

If an instance of this class has been created using `Pabc_create()` with a `Pabc_pointer` called `activePtr`, another active object can then invoke `methInt()` by calling the function `Pvalue()`. This function takes at least two arguments: a `Pabc_pointer` to an active object, and a pointer to a member function of that object's class. The value returned is the result of calling the specified method of the specified object, as in:

```
int result = Pvalue(activePtr, Active::methInt, args);
```

This call blocks the caller until the object pointed to by `activePtr` had accepted the call, executed it, and returned a value. A function call is used, rather than a method invocation, in order to trigger the templatized function expansion which ABC++ uses to implement argument marshalling and remote procedure call.[1]

If the method being invoked requires arguments, `Pvalue()` takes those arguments after the name of the method. A simple additive counter can therefore be implemented as shown in Program 1.1. Its `get()` and `incr()` methods can then be invoked using:

```
Pabc_pointer<Counter> cPtr;
Pabc_create(cPtr);
 ...
int curr = Pvalue(cPtr, Counter::get);
 ...
curr = Pvalue(cPtr, Counter::incr, 3);
```

---

[1]This is implemented by providing templates taking from zero to sixteen arguments; this upper bound may be increased in future versions of ABC++.

```
class Counter : public Pabc {
 private :
   int val_;
 public :
   Counter(){val_ = 0;}
   Counter(int init){val_ = init;}
   int incr(int amount){val_ += amount; return val_ - amount;}
   int get(){return val_;}
   void reset(){val_ = 0;}
   void reset(int resetValue){val_ = resetValue;}
};
```

Program 1.1
A Simple Counter

ABC++ also defines the function `Pvoid()` for remote method invocations which do not return anything. This also takes a `Pabc_pointer` and a method name as arguments, along with any arguments required by the method being invoked, and blocks its caller until the specified method has finished executing. The `reset()` method of the `Counter` class defined in the previous section would therefore be invoked by calling:

```
Pvoid(cPtr, Counter::reset);
```

or:

```
Pvoid(cPtr, Counter::reset, 999);
```

Note how ABC++ selects the appropriate method just as normal C++ would.

Both `Pvalue()` and `Pvoid()` may be viewed as remote procedure calls. The order in which active objects accept remote method invocations is arbitrary. However, ABC++ guarantees that each invocation is atomic, and that invocations of an object S by an object C will be served in order of receipt.

1.3.2   Controlling Method Invocation

An active object may use `Paccept()` and `Paccept_any()` to control remote invocations of its methods. (Essentially, these functions act as

```
class Signal : public Pabc {
 private :
  typedef enum {up, down} state_e;
  state_e state_;
 public :
  void raise(){state_ = up;}
  void lower(){state_ = down;}
  void main(){
    state_ = up;
    while(1){
      Paccept(lower);
      Paccept(raise);
    }
  }
};
```

Program 1.2
A Railway Semaphore

message receivers.) The first takes one or more method names as arguments. By calling it, an active object signals that it is only willing to execute those particular methods. Each call matches exactly one remote method invocation, and blocks its caller until one of the listed methods is invoked. Paccept_any() behaves like a Paccept() call with all of the calling object's methods as parameters.

For example, suppose that a class Signal is being used to simulate a railway signal. Instances of Signal have two states, up and down. When in the up state, a Signal is only willing to be lowered; when down, it is only willing to be raised. This behavior can be implemented as shown in Program 1.2.

Paccept() cannot be used while a remote method invocation is actually being handled, i.e., it is not legal to call Paccept() or Paccept_any() inside a method. Such a call causes an exception to be thrown.

ABC++ provides two macros which active objects can use to determine whether there are any invocations pending on themselves. The first, Ppending_any(), returns zero if no invocations are pending, and a non-zero value otherwise. Ppending() behaves the same way, but takes one or more method names as arguments, and only tests for invocations of those methods. These polling macros are similar to the probe functions provided by some message-passing systems.

1.3.3   Ping, Join, and Sleep

The `Pabc_pointer` template defines two methods called `join()` and `ping()`. The first blocks its caller until the active object referred to by the pointer in question has terminated. If that active object has already terminated, `join()` returns immediately. The `ping()` method returns zero if the object to which the pointer is bound has already terminated, and a non-zero value if it is still running. It is an error to call either method for an unbound active object pointer.

1.3.4   Caveats

ABC++ tries very hard to maintain the appearance of shared memory, but there are some situations it cannot handle.

Pointer Arguments: The greatest restriction ABC++ places on programmers is that pointers may not be passed to active objects during remote method invocation. Like C++, ABC++ uses by-value parameter passing, so the value of a pointer, and *not* the thing pointed to, is passed during function call. In order to prevent accidents, ABC++ traps attempts to pass pointers or references as arguments to remote method invocations during compilation. The right way to handle indirection that might go across address spaces is to use shared regions, which will be introduced in Section 1.7. Note that structures—even structures with embedded arrays—can be passed as arguments.

Static Members: If a class which derives from `Pabc` has static members, then storage for them is allocated on every processor, but not kept consistent. (This happens because the C++ compiler translates references to static members into direct accesses, so that there is nothing for the runtime system to intercept.)

Virtual Base Classes: Because of how virtual function tables are usually implemented, objects of classes derived from virtual base classes cannot presently be passed as arguments to remote method invocations. This may change in future releases of ABC++.

Invoking Methods on Oneself: Active objects are not allowed to invoke their own methods using `Pvoid()` or `Pvalue()`. The runtime system catches such attempts, and throws an exception.

1.3.5   Initialization, Termination, and Stack Control

Programs must call the initialization function `Pinit()`, with no arguments, exactly once before using any of ABC++'s other facilities. In particular, programs must call `Pinit()` before declaring any `Pabc_pointer` objects. Since C++ allows variable declarations and executable code to be mixed arbitrarily, this call is usually placed at the very top of a program's `main()` procedure.

The ABC++ termination function is called `Pexit()`. This tells the runtime system to shut down any active objects which are still executing, to free any memory which has been allocated for shared regions (Section 1.7), and then to release the processors being used by the program.

1.4   Example: The Producer-Consumer Problem

Our first full example is a producer-consumer program, in which the producer is a server for a consuming client. When constructed, the generator is told how many values to generate. When it executes, it repeatedly generates the next value in the sequence, then waits for that value to be requested. Its specification is:

```
class Generator : public Pabc {
 private :
   int _nextVal;
   int _numVal;
 protected :
   void main();
 public :
   Generator(int numVal);
   int get();
};
```

An instance of `Generator` initializes the private integer `_numVal` during construction; this indicates how many values are to be generated by the object's `main()`:

```
void Generator::main(){
  int i;
  for (i=0; i<_numVal; i++){
    _nextVal = 3 * i + 1;
    Paccept_any();
  }
}
```

The value generated is stored in _nextVal. The call Paccept_any()
then blocks the producer until some other process invokes get(), which
returns _nextVal to its caller:

```
int Generator::get(){return _nextVal;}
```

Most active classes use private member data of this kind for recording
their internal state and "communicating" between their methods.

Generator's constructor simply records the number of values to be
generated, and initializes _nextVal to a dummy value:

```
Generator::Generator(int numVal){
  _nextVal = -1;
  _numVal = numVal;
}
```

The program's main(), shown in Program 1.3, handles command-
line arguments, sets up ABC++ and the server process, processes the
integers generated by the server, and shuts ABC++ down. After system
initialization, main() calls Pabc_create() to spawn a single instance of
Generator. Its first argument, Pproc_set.pick_remote(), specifies the
processor on which the newly-spawned process is to run—in this case,
any processor other than the one on which the main program is running
(Section 1.5). The second argument acts as a handle, and gives the
creating process (or any other to which it is passed) a way of accessing
the new process. Subsequent arguments to Pabc_create() (in this case,
the number of values to generate) are constructor parameters for the
new active object.

The program's main loop is then entered. This requests numVal integers from the generator using Pvalue(). When Pvalue() is called,
main() is blocked until a value has been received. Once it has consumed numVal values, main() calls Pexit() to terminate the program.

```
int main(int argc, char * argv[]){
  Pinit();
  int numVal = atoi(argv[1]);
  Pabc_pointer<Generator> generator;
  int val, i;

  // setup
  Pabc_create(Pproc_set.pick_remote(), generator, numVal);

  // run
  for (i=0; i<numVal; i++){
    val = Pvalue(generator, Generator::get);
    cout << "main: val [" << i << "] == " << val << endl;
  }

  // takedown
  Pexit(0);
  return 0;
}
```

Program 1.3
The Producer-Consumer's `main()`

1.4.1 A Mediating Buffer

The program presented in the previous section is correct, but not very efficient, as it does not buffer the integer stream. A better approach is to put a buffer between the producer and the consumer. The first step in building such a buffer is to define the new class for it. We do this by making the class `Buffer` an abstract class so that many different classes of buffer may be derived from it:

```
class Buffer : public Pabc {
 protected :
  virtual void main()=0;
 public :
  virtual void put(int v)=0;
  virtual int get()=0;
};
```

Any actual buffer must be an instance of a concrete class derived from this abstract class. One such concrete class is `BufferQ`:

```
class BufferQ : public Buffer {
 private :
  int * _queue, _len, _num, _head, _tail;
 protected :
  void main();
 public :
  BufferQ(int len);
  ~BufferQ();
  void put(int v);
  int get();
};
```

BufferQ's put() and get() methods keep the signatures of their abstract ancestors, but have the usual array-based concrete implementations.

The main loop for BufferQ objects uses Paccept() to control which
methods can be activated when. If the buffering queue is empty, only
put() may be invoked; conversely, only get() may be invoked if the
queue is full.

```
void BufferQ::main(){
  while (1){
    if (_num == 0)        Paccept(Buffer::put);
    else if (_num == _len) Paccept(Buffer::get);
    else                   Paccept_any();
  }
}
```

A producer which can use this buffer is simple:

```
class Producer : public Pabc {
 private :
  int _numVal;
  Pabc_pointer<Buffer> _buf;
 protected :
  void main();
 public :
  Producer(int numVal, Pabc_pointer<Buffer> buf);
};
```

Its constructor and main loop are:

```
Producer::Producer(int numVal, Pabc_pointer<Buffer> buf){
  _buf = buf;
  _numVal = numVal;
}
void Producer::main(){
  int i;
  for (i=0; i<_numVal; i++){
    Pvoid(_buf, Buffer::put, 3 * i + 1);
  }
}
```

Note how a Pabc_pointer referring to the buffer is passed to the producer when it is constructed. For this to work properly, the buffer must be created *before* the producer is spawned, as the buffer's Pabc_pointer will be null otherwise.

The main program is as shown in Program 1.4. Notice how main() uses the macro Pabc_convert() to cast the type of the Pabc_pointer referring to buffer from BufferQ to Buffer when passing it as an argument during the creation of the producer. Normally, C++ pointers to objects of derived classes are automatically demoted to pointers to parent classes when the context requires it. However, buffer is not a BufferQ, but a handle on an active object. This handle is not derived in any sense from a pointer to a Buffer. Accordingly, there is no automatic type conversion of the first to the second, and so Pabc_convert() must be used to do this conversion explicitly.

1.5   Processors

By default, ABC++'s runtime system determines where new active objects will be created. However, ABC++ also overloads Pabc_create() to allow the user to specify this. Objects may be allocated anywhere, but once they have been placed, they cannot be moved.

The runtime system identifies each processor with a unique instance of the class Pproc. A program can specify a particular processor by creating a Pproc object explicitly using:

```
Pproc(n)
```

```
int main(int argc, char * argv[]){
  Pinit();
  int numVal = atoi(argv[1]);
  Pabc_pointer<Producer> producer;
  Pabc_pointer<BufferQ> buffer;
  int val, i;

  // setup (main text explains use of Pabc_convert)
  Pabc_create(Pproc_set.pick(), buffer);
  Pabc_create(Pproc_set.pick(), producer,
              numVal, Pabc_convert(Buffer, buffer));

  // run
  for (i=0; i<numVal; i++){
    val = Pvalue(buffer, Buffer::get);
    cout << "main: val [" << i << "] == " << val << endl;
  }

  // takedown
  Pexit(0);
  return 0;
}
```

Program 1.4
Another Producer-Consumer `main()`

where n is an integer. Given a `Pproc` object, a program may create
an active object on the processor it identifies by passing that `Pproc` to
`Pabc_create()`:

```
class A : public Pabc {
  ...
};
Pabc_pointer<A> aPtr;
Pproc p(3);        // better be running on at least 4 processors
Pabc_create(p, aPtr, constructor arguments);
```

This overrides whatever location the runtime system would have chosen
on its own.

The set of all processors being used in a particular run of a program
is represented by a `Pproc_set` object. Its methods are:

pick(): chooses a processor in a round-robin fashion, with the current processor chosen last. (Pproc_set's internal state keeps track of which processor to choose next.)

pick_remote(): is like pick(), except that the caller's processor will never be chosen (unless the program is only using one processor).

pick_random(): returns a Pproc identifying a randomly-selected processor.

pick_random_remote(): is like pick_random(), except that the caller's processor will not be chosen (unless the program is only using one processor).

local(): returns a Pproc identifying the processor on which the caller is executing.

num_processors(): returns the number of processors on which the program is running.

A single global Pproc_set object is automatically created at the beginning of every program.

The Pabc_pointer template defines a method proc(). This method returns a Pproc object identifying the processor on which the object referred to by the pointer is running.

1.6 Asynchronous Method Invocation

ABC++'s Pvoid() function invokes a method on a remote object, and blocks the calling process until that method completes. In contrast, Ppar_void() allows the caller to continue executing as soon as the parameters being passed to the invocation have been read. Thus, if the code:

```
Ppar_void(anAbcPtr, aClass::aMethod, args);
···following statements···
```

is executed, the calling process will execute the *following statements* as soon as ABC++ has copied the arguments to the Ppar_void() call into a safe place.

Asynchronous method invocations which cannot be serviced immediately are queued by the runtime system until the servicing object is willing to handle them. ABC++ automatically provides the buffer space needed to hold any parameters which the method invocation has been given.

The other type of asynchronous invocation supported by ABC++ is based on the *future* construct [Halstead 1985]. A future is a variable that can contain the result of an asynchronous invocation of a method which returns a value. If a process tries to read the value of a future whose computation is still running, that process is blocked until the computation's result becomes available.

A future variable is declared using the template `Pfuture`, with the base type of the variable as a parameter:

```
class C {
    ...
};
Pfuture<int> iF;
Pfuture<C> cF;
```

The variables `iF` and `cF` all have the properties of their underlying type. Once these variables have been initialized, normal expressions such as:

```
int k = iF + 3;
```

will behave as expected, unless and until the future variable becomes the target of an asynchronous computation.

A program starts such a computation by calling `Ppar_value()`. When called with a `Pabc_pointer`, a method name, and zero or more parameters, this function copies its parameters, then allows the calling program to continue executing as it invokes the specified method on the object pointed to by the `Pabc_pointer`.

`Ppar_value()` should be used in an assignment context, such as:

```
iF = Ppar_value(anAbcPtr, aClass::aMethod, args);
```

By overloading the assignment operator = on futures, ABC++ causes a flag associated with the future to be set to show that a computation for that future is outstanding. If the process which called `Ppar_value()` tries to read the value of the future variable `iF` before that computation has completed, as in:

```
int normalInt = iF;
```

then the calling process will be blocked. Once the computation has been completed, and the invisible flag associated with the future has been cleared, the process which is trying to read the future's value is allowed to proceed.

For example, suppose we wish to use two concurrent objects to perform a calculation and return the partial results to the caller. The active object class is called Calc, and the calculating method is called partialVal(). We can perform the calculation using:

```
Pabc_pointer<Calc> calc1, calc2;
Pfuture<int> res1, res2;
···use Pabc_create to spawn calculators···
res1 = Ppar_value(calc1, Calc::partialVal, args)
res2 = Ppar_value(calc2, Calc::partialVal, args)
···other calculations···
cout << "The answer is " << res1 + res2 << endl;
```

Each Ppar_value() call passes its arguments, and a request to invoke the method partialVal(), to a calculator. Once accepted, these calls run concurrently with the program's other calculations. If the caller tries to read res1 before the result of the Ppar_value() on it has been received, the caller will automatically be blocked. Once the required result is available, the caller will be re-scheduled. If res2 still does not have a value, the caller will be blocked again. Finally, with both results available, the sum is calculated, and the output statement executed.

A future variable holds either an actual value or a pointer to a container into which a Ppar_value() call will deposit its result. If a program assigns one future to another, and the first has not yet resolved, then the second is set to point at the same intermediate container being used by the first. Once the Ppar_value() call completes, the process will be able to read either.

Just as something created using:

```
Pabc_pointer<someType> tPtr;
```

is not really of type someType, the type of things created using the Pfuture template is different from that of the template argument. Because of this, the type coercion implied by:

```
Pfuture<float> fPtr;
Pfuture<int> iPtr;
```

```
...
fPtr = iPtr;
```

is a compilation error. It is possible to do explicit casting when assigning
the value of a future. However, the effect of this is to block until ip is
resolved, and then assign its value to fp.

Assigning a normal value to a future variable while a calculation is
outstanding breaks the binding between the future and its container,
and re-sets the future's status flag. For example, the code:

```
Pfuture<int> f;
int i, j;
...
f = Ppar_value(obj, meth, args);
f = i;
j = f;
```

starts a calculation, but then assigns the value of i to the variable that
was to hold that calculation's result. The subsequent assignment of f
to j is guaranteed to go through immediately, since f no longer appears
to be waiting for an outstanding calculation. The calculation itself is
not cancelled; it will run to completion, and then write its result into
the container that was allocated when Ppar_value() was called. Calling
Ppar_value() for a future when a future calculation is already running
has a similar effect.

As it is sometimes useful to be able to test a future without blocking
on its value, the Pfuture template provide a method resolved(), which
returns zero if the future has not yet completed, or a non-zero value once
it has.

Finally, the only way to get at the members of a structure or class,
or to cancel a future on a structure or class, is to use whole-object
assignment, as in:

```
typedef struct { double x, y; } Pt;
Pt normal;
Pfuture<Pt> ptFut;
...
normal = ptFut;          // block if necessary
float xval = normal.x;   // get field of future
...
ptFut = Ppar_value(args); // start future
ptFut = normal;          // cancels future
```

This is one case where ABC++ cannot completely conceal the details of its underlying implementation.

1.7 Parametric Shared Regions

ABC++ allows processes to communicate indirectly through *parametric shared regions*, or PSRs. A PSR appears to be a shared region of memory; the ABC++ runtime system makes copies of the region where processes need them, and updates these copies to maintain their consistency. ABC++ allows any C++ object to be used as a PSR, which reduces the problem of false sharing.

1.7.1 The Design of PSRs

PSRs are implemented on a shared-memory machine using the native shared memory hardware directly. In this case, the ABC++ library provides the user with the automatic structured locking and unlocking that occurs via use of the shared region handles described below.

When ABC++ runs on a distributed-memory platform, the copy constructors and destructors it defines for apparently-shared regions of memory also take care of coherence management. When updates to shared regions are made, they are made within a block associated with the construction and destruction of a write-locking handle. When the block is exited, the handle is destroyed. This causes any updates which have been made to be sent asynchronously to all other processors which currently have a replica of the region. Thus, the unit of coherence for PSRs is exactly the C++ object that is within the region. Because replication is based on need, copies only exist where they have been needed, and therefore where there is a good chance that they will be needed again.

PSRs are well-suited to programs which share dynamic or irregular data structures. ABC++ permits unlocked PSR handles to be stored in other data structures and objects, just as the regions themselves may contain arbitrary data structures and objects. Consequently, irregular data structures can be created at run time, and made accessible to active objects on arbitrary processors. As those active objects "touch" parts of the dynamic data structure, those parts are replicated automatically on the appropriate processors.

1.7.2   Creating PSRs and Handles

A PSR is created by declaring a handle for referring to the region, and then using `Psr_create()` to associate a newly-created object with that handle. This is analogous to declaring a `Pabc_pointer` of some type, and then using `Pabc_create()` to create a new active object and associate it with that `Pabc_pointer`.

The basic type of handle in ABC++ is an unlocked read-write handle. To declare such a handle, a program uses the `Psr_rwU` template with the type of shared data to which that handle can be bound as a parameter:

```
class C {
  ...
};
Psr_rwU<int> iH;      // declare unlocked read-write handles
Psr_rwU<C> cH;
```

Given a handle, a program binds it to a new object of the appropriate type by calling `Psr_create()`. In its simplest form, this takes the handle as its first argument, followed by any constructor arguments that the object requires. The code:

```
Psr_create(iH);
```

therefore allocates one new integer-sized region of memory and binds it to the handle iH: Similarly, if the class C has a constructor which takes two integers as arguments, a single shareable instance of that class can be created using:

```
Psr_create(cH, 123, 45);
```

By giving a `Pproc` as the first argument to `Psr_create()`, the user can control where this initial copy of the PSR is put. Because lock management is then done on that processor, controlling the placement of PSRs can be important when tuning program performance.

A program can create a PSR which contains a block of objects by including a positive integer argument in the call to `Psr_create()`. This argument specifies how many objects of the type parameterized by the handle the system is to create. For example, the following code creates a single PSR holding a vector of six structures of type S, and associates a single handle with the whole vector:

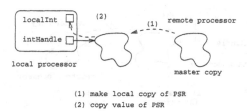

(1) make local copy of PSR
(2) copy value of PSR

Figure 1.1
Reading Value of Shared Region

```
typedef struct {···} S;
Psr_rwU<S> sH;
Psr_create(6, sH);
```

1.7.3 Caveats

The single most common mistake made with PSRs arises from the use
of embedded pointers. For example, consider a structure such as:

```
typedef struct {int * p;} S;
```

If this is used to create a PSR, as in:

```
S.p = new int[100];
Psr_rwU<S> sH;
Psr_create(sH);
```

then the pointer field **p** is put into a shared region, but *not* the vector
of 100 integers.

1.7.4 Reading and Writing Shared Regions

Once a handle has been bound to a region of memory of type T, a process
can access that memory by treating the handle as a pointer of type T.
For example, suppose **intHandle** has been passed as a parameter to an
active object **foo**, and **foo** then executes the following:

```
int localInt = * intHandle;
```

This assignment causes an implicit conversion of the handle to an
int* (Figure 1.1). As this happens, the runtime system checks to see
whether there is a local copy of the region referred to by **intHandle**. If

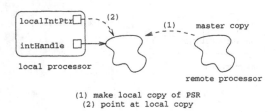

(1) make local copy of PSR
(2) point at local copy

Figure 1.2
Accessing Shared Region

there is not, it creates one by copying an instance of the shared region
from another processor. Once this is done (or if such a copy already
exists), the runtime system assigns the value of the local copy of the
shared region to the local variable `localInt`.

The behavior of assignment from a handle to a pointer is somewhat
more complicated, but can be exploited to increase program efficiency.
Suppose once again that `intHandle` is a handle for a shared region
containing a single integer, and that a program contains:

```
int * localIntPtr = intHandle;
```

When this is executed, the runtime system ensures that the caller's
processor has a copy of the shared region, and then assigns a pointer to
that local copy to `localIntPtr` (Figure 1.2). A process can then read the
value of that region of memory directly by de-referencing `localIntPtr`.
The performance gain can be substantial when the shared region of
memory contains a large structure: where the first form would copy the
whole structure, the second gives the program a way to reference fields
of the shared structure directly.

Programmers must be very careful *not* to use the shared data pointed
to by such a pointer, or write to it, unless they are sure that the region
referred to is up-to-date. As described in the next section, ABC++ does
not propagate writes to a copy of a shared region until it is implicitly
or explicitly told to do so. Programs can therefore see "stale" data in a
region unless they obey the simple rules given in the next section.

1.7.5 Locking and Unlocking

Just as the `Psr_rwU` template creates an unlocked read-write handle, the `Psr_rwL` template creates a locked read-write handle. The distinction between these two types of handle is the key to ABC++'s consistency mechanism.

Suppose a process has an unlocked read-write handle U on a shared region R. When it tries to convert U to a locked handle L, the runtime system checks to make sure that no other process currently holds a locked handle on R. If there is such a handle, the process which is trying to convert U is blocked until that other lock is released. Once no other lock on the region exists, the runtime system grants the lock on R to the process holding U. That process is then free to write to its local copy of R. However, its writes are not immediately visible in other processors' copies of the region. Instead, the runtime system only propagates the effects of the process's writes when the process releases its lock on the region. This is called *release consistency* [Adve & Gharachorloo 1995].

Getting a lock on a region is simply a matter of assigning the value of an unlocked handle to a locked one:

```
Psr_rwU<int> iH;          // Create unlocked handle
Psr_create(iH, 0);        // Create/bind shared region with value 0
...
{                         // Open lock-scoping block
    Psr_rwL<int> iL = iH; // Get lock on region (constructor)
    ···operations on shared integer···
}                         // Automatically release lock (destructor)
```

Doing this invokes the copy constructor defined by ABC++ on handles. This constructor in turn causes the runtime system to execute its locking protocol.

The creation of a small code block whose first statement is the declaration and initialization of a locked read-write handle is an important idiom in ABC++. This block defines the lifetime of the lock. When a process exits the block, the locked handle's destructor is automatically called, and the shared region automatically released. Any changes the process has made to that region are then propagated to any other copies of the region that exist.

To change the region of memory referred to by a handle, a program must convert a locked handle to a pointer, and then write to whatever that pointer references, as in:

```
Psr_rwU<int> iH;
Psr_create(iH, 0);
...
{
    Psr_rwL<int> iL = iH;
    int * rPtr = iL;        // Point to copy of shared region
    *rPtr = 12345;          // Assign to shared region
}                           // Release lock
                            // (destructor propagates changes)
```

Assigning to what the pointer `rPtr` references overwrites the contents of the local copy of the shared region. When the block is exited, and the lock released, those changes are then broadcast to other processors which hold a copy of the shared region.

1.7.6   Read-Only Handles

Read-write handles are truly exclusive, in that only one thread can hold a locked read-write handle on a region at any time. For the sake of efficiency and safety, ABC++ also supports read-only handles with the templates `Psr_roU` and `Psr_roL`. The differences between these and read-write handles are that (a) a thread holding a read-only lock may read a region, but cannot write to it; and (b) any number of threads may hold read-only locks at any time. While any read-only locks are held, no read-write lock will be granted; conversely, while a read-write lock exists, no read-only locks will be granted. This behavior allows a programmer to let many threads read from a database securely, or to let a single thread update it.

In an effort to enforce the read-write versus read-only distinction, ABC++ allows conversion of read-only handles only to `const` pointers. For example, while a `Psr_rwU<int>` may be cast to `int *` or `const int *`, a `Psr_roU<int>` may only be cast to `const int *`.

1.7.7   Location Inquiry

As mentioned earlier, all four PSR handle templates define a method `proc()`. This returns a `Pproc` object whose value identifies the processor

```
class Incr : public Pabc {
 private :
  Psr_rwU<int> counter_;
  int * store_;
 protected :
 public :
  Incr(Psr_rwU<int> c){
    counter_ = c;
    store_ = counter_;
  }
  int use(int n){
    int i, sum = 0;
    for (i=0; i<n; i++){
    // Lock lifetime determined by scope of loop body
      Psr_rwL<int> lock = counter_;
      sum += *store_;
      *store_ += 1;
    }
    return sum;
  }
};
```

Program 1.5
A Simple Incrementable Object

on which the master copy of the PSR is kept, and which is responsible for managing locks on that PSR.

1.8 Example: A Shared Counter

Section 1.3.1 described an active object which implemented a simple integer counter. In many situations, it may be simpler or more efficient to make the counter variable a PSR. The following program does this by defining a class of active objects called Incr (Program 1.5).

When an Incr is constructed, it takes an unlocked read-write handle on the integer PSR which is to act as the counter variable, and caches this in its private memory (the member counter_). It also converts this handle to an integer pointer, and caches the result in store_. During this conversion, the runtime system returns a pointer to the memory which will be used to store the local copy of the shared region. Thereafter, the active object can look at this copy simply by de-referencing the pointer. This may or may not be what the "current" value of the shared region is, since the system only updates that copy as other active objects relinquish locks on the PSR.

Incr's use() method takes a single argument, which tells it how many times to access the counter. Inside its loop, it repeatedly converts the unlocked handle cached in counter_ to a locked handle. The statements:

```
sum += *store_;
*store_ += 1;
```

add the value of the local copy of the PSR to sum, and then increment the value of the local copy. Finally, as execution reaches the end of the block which makes up the body of the for loop, the locked handle lock falls out of scope, and its destructor is automatically called. This destructor forces the system to flush the recent changes to the region, so that they become visible to other processors. Because the lock variable is stack-allocated, the cost of this idiom is simply the cost of the underlying locking protocol.

The main program which drives this example, shown in Program 1.6, is straightforward. A future is used to store the result of the Ppar_value() invocation of the incrementor's use() method; its value is printed out at the end of main().

This shared counter is straightforward, but rather messy; in particular, its behavior is not as neatly encapsulated as it should be, given the object-oriented nature of C++. Since a PSR handle is just another C++ data structure, we can create a counter class which has a PSR as a member, and hide its fetch-and-increment update protocol inside that new class.

We begin by defining the counter class itself:

```
class Counter {
 private :
  Psr_rwU<int> handle_;
 public :
  Counter(){
    Psr_create(handle_, 0);
  }
  int incr(){
    Psr_rwL<int> lock = handle_;
    int * loc = lock;
```

```
int main(int argc, char ** argv){
  Pinit();
  Psr_rwU<int> counter;
  Pabc_pointer<Incr> incr;
  int num = atoi(argv[1]);
  int i, sum = 0;
  Pfuture<int> incrSum;
  Psr_create(counter, 0);
  Pabc_create(incr, counter);
  incrSum = Ppar_value(incr, Incr::use, num);
  for (i=0; i<num; i++){
    Psr_rwL<int> lock = counter;
    int * loc = lock;
    sum += (*loc)++;
  }
  cout << "main sum is " << sum << endl;
  cout << "child sum is " << incrSum << endl;
  Pexit(0);
  return 0;
}
```

Program 1.6
Driving Program for Incrementor

```
      return (*loc)++;
    }
};
```

During construction, an instance of this class creates a PSR which only
it can access. Its **incr()** method performs the conversion necessary to
get a lock on this PSR, then fetches and increments the value it stores.

After these changes, an active object which uses a counter of this type
can be unaware of the lock-and-update protocol (Program 1.7). The
main program (Program 1.8) is equally improved. Note that **main()**
passes **counter** by value, and not a pointer to **counter**, as a constructor argument to **Pabc_create()** when spawning the incrementor. This
works because the embedded handle is copied automatically.

```
class Incr : public Pabc {
 private :
  Counter counter_;
 public :
  Incr(Counter c){
    counter_ = c;
  }
  int use(int n){
    int i, sum = 0;
    for (i=0; i<n; i++){
      sum += counter_.incr();
    }
    return sum;
  }
};
```

Program 1.7
Client of Incrementor

```
int main(int argc, char ** argv){
  Pinit();
  Counter counter;
  Pabc_pointer<Incr> incr;
  int num = atoi(argv[1]);
  int i, sum = 0;
  Pfuture<int> incrSum;
  Pabc_create(incr, counter);
  incrSum = Ppar_value(incr, Incr::use, num);
  for (i=0; i<num; i++){
    sum += counter.incr();
  }
  cout << "main sum is " << sum << endl;
  cout << "child sum is " << incrSum << endl;
  Pexit(0);
  return 0;
}
```

Program 1.8
Modified **main**() Program for Incrementor

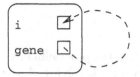

Figure 1.3
Binding a PSR Handle to Local Memory

1.9 More About Parametric Shared Regions

This section shows some of the other ways in which shared regions can be created, and describes several ways to implement a shared buffer, which illustrate some of the more advanced features of PSRs.

1.9.1 Other Ways to Create PSRs

So far, creating a PSR has been a two-step process. ABC++ also allows programs to create "immediate" PSRs, either by providing a region of memory to be copied, or by providing the memory itself. Both of these rely on the function Psr().

In its simplest form, Psr() takes a value as an argument, and returns a Psr_rwU handle specialized to its argument's type. For example, the code:

```
Psr_rwU<int> fred = Psr(3);
```

creates an integer-sized PSR, copies the value 3 into it, and assigns a handle on that region to the variable **fred**.

Psr_bind() is a relative of Psr() that uses local memory for storing the local copy of a PSR. It takes as an argument a pointer to a block of memory of some type, and returns an unlocked read-write handle for a PSR which uses that memory. Thus, the code:

```
int i = 456;
Psr_roU<int> gene = Psr_bind(&i);
```

actually uses the integer i to store the local copy of the shared region created by the Psr() call (Figure 1.3).

If Psr_bind() is given a pointer p as its first argument, and a count n as its second, it uses the n items starting at address p as the shared region. The call:

```
int p[100];
Psr_rwL<int> jake = Psr_bind(p, 100);
```

therefore turns the vector p into a shared region. It is the programmer's
responsibility to ensure that the size given to Psr_bind() is correct. Just
like Pabc_create() and Psr_create(), Psr() may take a Pproc as an
optional first argument.

The difference between a Psr_bind() on a pointer and a Psr_create()
call is important when classes, rather than scalar types or structures, are
being used as PSRs. When Psr_create() is used to create a PSR, all
copies of the PSR are constructed and destructed by the runtime system.
When Psr_bind() is used, on the other hand, the runtime system frees
replicas of the shared region which it has created on other processes, but
does *not* delete the region of memory given to it originally. It is the user's
responsibility to make sure that this object is eventually cleaned up. The
best way to distinguish between Psr_create() and Psr_bind() with a
pointer argument is that in the former, the shared region of memory is
"owned" by the runtime system, while in the latter the shared region is
"owned" by one of the processes, which makes it available for sharing.

Parallel programs often contain flag variables, with which one process signals others that some event has occurred. An ABC++ program
can implement such structures using the locking protocols for PSRs discussed in the preceding sections. However, in the right circumstances,
a program can use the ! (pronounced "bang") operator instead. When
applied to a read-write PSR handle, this operator forces the runtime
system to flush any changes which the banging process has made to its
copy of a shared region. This is what would happen if that process ac-
quired and then released a lock on a region, but does not incur the same
overheads. An example of the use of ! is given in Section 1.9.3.

1.9.2   Lock Shuffling

Locked handles are usually created and initialized from unlocked handles. It is also possible to assign to a locked handle which already has
a value. The effect of this is to relinquish the lock already held, and
acquire a lock on the region associated with the unlocked handle, in one
atomic step.

The semantics of assigning one locked handle to another are similar.
If **left** and **right** are both locked handles, then:

```
left = right;
```

releases the lock which **left** holds, and makes **left** an alias for **right**. When **left** is destroyed (e.g., by falling out of scope), the lock value is restored to **right**. This mechanism breaks ABC++'s block-structured locking rules, since the lock on **left** may be given up at any time.

It is never legal to assign a handle, locked or otherwise, to another handle which is bound to the same region. If a program needs to assign an unlocked handle to another unlocked handle, possibly on the same shared region, the target handle must be voided manually using the ~ (negation) operator. This operator cannot be applied to a locked handle, since locked handles are always bound to shared regions.

1.9.3 Lock Delegation

PSR handles may be passed as arguments to functions just like any other pointer. However, when an active object C passes a locked handle to another active object S as a method argument, the runtime system gives C's privileges to S for the duration of the invocation. The lock is thereby "delegated" to the active object servicing the method. While this makes no difference if **Pvoid()** or **Pvalue()** was used to invoke the method, it increases the safety of **Ppar_void()** or **Ppar_value()** calls. Locked handles may be thought of as tokens, which can either be created (from unlocked handles) or passed around, but not duplicated. Passing locked handles to new active objects during a **Pabc_create()** call has the same semantics. The privileges associated with the lock only return to the parent process when the child terminates.

Lock passing does create one small loophole in ABC++'s coherence mechanisms. If an active object has a read-write lock on a PSR P, and passes it as an argument to a remote method invocation, then any changes made by the process holding the lock will not be flushed before the remote method invocation begins. This behavior is easily remedied by using ! on the lock as it is passed to the child:

```
Psr_rwL<type> lockedRW = ···;
Pvoid(activePtr, Class::method,
        ! lockedRW);                    // force update using !
...
class Class : public Pabc {
  void method(Psr_roL<type> lockedRO){
```

  operations on read-only handle
```
  }
};
```

1.9.4 Versions

ABC++ associates a *version number* with every shared region created in a program. Version numbers are initialized to 1 when the region is created, and incremented every time the region is updated, either by the destruction of a locked handle or explicitly using the ! operator.

 Given a PSR handle h, the method h.version() returns an integer, which is the version number of the region currently on this processor. The method h.wait(n) blocks the caller (implicitly doing a Pyield()) until the version of the shared region on the caller's processor is version n or higher. In both cases, if the calling process's processor does not have a copy of the shared region, one is fetched. These two methods are most often used to synchronize iterative computations.

1.10 Using ABC++

ABC++ programs are run using a command script called Prun. This loads one instance of the specified program onto each of the processors that the program is to use. The executable must therefore be located in a file system which all of those processors can access. The three ABC++ runtime systems currently supported are TCP/IP, POE on top of UDP/IP, and CSS. The first two will run on LANs, while the third requires the fast switch in the IBM SP-2.

 When an ABC++ program is run, the execution manager looks for a file containing the names of machines which the program is allowed to use. Once a program is running, the runtime system installs signal handlers for SIGUSR1 and SIGUSR2. If SIGUSR1 is caught, the runtime system prints a page of statistics on PSR usage; if SIGUSR2 is caught, it prints an immediate stack traceback. To facilitate debugging, Prun can be used to run a debugger instead of running the user's program directly,

 ABC++ throws an exception when it detects a fatal error. All of these are derived from P_exception, so that programs can catch all ABC++ exceptions in a single statement:

```
try{
  ···user code···
} catch(P_exception e){
  cerr << e;
}
```

1.11 Example: Polygon Overlay

The ABC++ version of the polygon overlay problem is very similar to the sequential version described in Appendix C, and makes the same assumptions as the sequential version with respect to input files, polygon dimensions, etc. The two major differences are parallelization, and use of the Standard Template Library (STL) [Stepanov 1994] to simplify the code. We rely on the fact that the version of the STL `vector` container which we use allocates contiguous memory for its contents.

Our program uses geometric decomposition: each processor acts on a subset of the input maps, so that generation of the output map is distributed among the processors. The algorithm used is:

1. Geometrically decompose the map space into one "territory" for each of the P processors in the machine.

2. Partition the first input map on the basis of territory.

3. Partition the second input map on the basis of territory.

4. Generate partial overlays on each processor in parallel.

5. Collect and merge the partial overlays.

We partition the first input map (Step 2) by assigning each polygon to one of the territories defined in Step 1. A polygon from the first map is therefore sent to processor P_i if, and only if, it has been identified with territory t_i.

In our implementation, a polygon is identified with territory t_i if the polygon lies completely within the boundaries territory t_i. Those polygons which cross a territory boundary are kept on the local processor. In order to maintain completeness in the maps on remote processors, the portion of the polygon which lies within each territory is sent to its respective processor. These partial polygons are marked as being "trimmed". We partition the second map in exactly the same way. For efficiency, the main process accumulates the polygons to be sent to each processor, and then sends them as a block.

At this point each processor has two input maps which have the same properties as the original maps, except for their smaller size and the presence of the trimmed polygons. The trimmed polygons are essential in maintaining the property of completeness in the map, otherwise the area-depletion overlay algorithm would lose its efficiency. The overlay process begins on each processor, including the main process where those polygons left behind are overlaid. On remote processors, the overlay of two trimmed polygons is discarded, since trimmed polygons represent polygons crossing a territory boundary and will be overlaid at the main processor.

We implement this algorithm in several stages. To begin with, the first input map is read into memory and its extent determined. This area is then divided into $P - 1$ equal-sized territories, and one worker process is created to handle each. Each worker w_i is an instance of the class Worker, and performs the following sequence of operations:

- Wait for the input polygons.
- Perform the overlay on the given input.
- Wait for the collector to request the output polygons.
- Terminate.

The main() method of class Worker is therefore:

```
void main()
{
    // Wait for the input polygon lists
    Paccept(recvPolygons);
    Paccept(recvPolygons);

    // Overlay the two input lists
    overlay(inmap1, inmap2, outmap);

    // Prepare the output list for transmission
    prepareSharedRegion();

    // Wait for request for our output list
    Paccept(sendPolygons);
    // terminate
}
```

The main methods of ABC++ active objects are often structured as simple state machines in this way; control over actions is represented as conditionals in the main procedure, rather than as guards on individual actions.

After worker processes have been created, the first input map is partitioned into separate vectors of polygons. Each of these vectors is then bound to a separate shared region, for point-to-point delivery to its worker. Those polygons which crossed a territory boundary are kept in a separate vector, one for each input map, and hence not sent to workers.

Note that the shared region handles given to the workers for this purpose are read-only handles. If read-write handles were used, then when the worker released its lock on the region after reading the region's contents, the runtime system would assume that the region had been changed, and would copy the region's data back to the processor on which the main process was running. Since each worker only ever reads its input vector, by using a read-only handle, the worker indicates that no changes have been made and that copy-back is unnecessary. (Copy-back could also be avoided by using the bang operator; however, we consider this inappropriate for this problem.)

A further performance optimization is the use of Ppar_value() to permit transmission to workers to be overlapped. We use futures to ensure all workers have received the data before proceeding.

Once the second input map has been read into memory, vectors of polygons for each worker are once again collected and distributed, in the same manner as the first map. The main program then performs an overlay of the local polygons, and then requests the output polygons from each worker. These requests block until each worker has finished overlaying and is ready to reply. The output polygons are retrieved from each processor using the class Collector. For every w_i, a collector c_i is created to retrieve the output polygons via the sendPolygons() method provided by the worker objects. Collectors use Ppar_value() calls for retrieving the polygons so that broadcasts are overlapped. Requests for data from a collector are blocked until the data has actually arrived.

Finally, for every $c_i, i = 0 \ldots P - 1$, the contents of collector c_i are written to the output file, along with the output from the local overlay. In this implementation the collector receives all the polygons from its designated processor in one block.

1.11.1   Performance

The performance of the ABC++ polygon overlay program was measured using two sets of maps: one containing approximately 60,000 polygons per map, and one containing approximately 638,000 polygons per map. Maps of the first size are too small to be suitable for parallelization, but results for them are included here for comparison purposes. The large maps, on the other hand, require enough work that modest parallelization is effective.

As described above, our parallelization technique involves inserting "placeholder" polygons along the jagged edges that results from partitioning the input maps. These placeholders ensure perfect "bleed-off" of the polygons in each section, while still guaranteeing correct results. We handle overlay of boundary polygons (i.e., those that straddle the boundary lines of partitions) on processor 0, which is also used as a regular worker processor. Although this boundary computation increases the serial fraction of the computation, the overall trade-off is beneficial. We also use two worker processes per processor, including processor 0, so that commmunication and computation are overlapped. Doing this required no change to the source code for the workers, and only a minimal change in the main process.

The performance of our parallel implementation is highly superlinear. The reason for this is that the underlying algorithm has an N^2 behavior, where N is the number of polygons in each input map. As we reduce N on the worker processors, work decreases even faster. Because computation on the workers is so fast, we can only use a few processors (3 to 4, depending on problem size) before the costs of shipping data dominate total execution time, and our speedups start to decline. We note that these results suggest that a sequential divide-and-conquer algorithm for polygon overlay might outperform the sequential algorithms given in the original ANSI C program.

Version 1.1 of ABC++ was used for parallelization. In the following timings, we compiled our program using IBM's CSet++ compiler with -O3 optimization, and ran on an IBM SP-2. The times are real elapsed times; they do not include file I/O time, or the time required to sort the output map, but do include the time required to send data to worker processors, and to collect the results.

Processors	Time (sec)	Speedup	Efficiency
1	8.721	1.0	100%
2	2.691	3.24	162%
3	1.731	5.04	168%
4	1.878	4.64	116%
5	2.200	3.96	79%
6	2.625	3.32	55%

(a) 60K polygons per input map, 203K polygons in output map

Processors	Time (sec)	Speedup	Efficiency
1	288.723	1.0	100%
2	63.131	4.57	229%
3	35.852	8.05	268%
4	25.650	11.25	281%
5	27.354	10.56	211%
6	28.493	10.13	169%

(b) 638K polygons per input map, 2.28M polygons in output map

Table 1.1
Polygon Overlay Results

The times quoted for the single-processor case were obtained by running the parallel code with a single worker process on the same processor as the main process. Since ABC++'s threads are non-preemptive, the worker runs to completion once work is available, so scheduling overheads are negligible. In addition, since PSRs are managed on a per-processor basis, running the parallel program on a single processor does not force any data copying that would not be done by a "pure" sequential program.

1.12 Conclusions and Future Directions

Over the last two years, ABC++ has matured from a collection of interesting ideas glued together experimentally, into a robust object and template-oriented class library for concurrency. While we believe that the approach taken by ABC++ is applicable to many problems, we also believe that many other paradigms are also useful. The model embodied in ABC++ is well-suited to solving problems involving irregular or dynamic data structures. However, as the current version of ABC++ does not incorporate parallel array or container classes, it is less well-suited to data-parallel problems.

We recognize that it would be desirable to add a notion of groups of active objects, such that certain operations could be performed efficiently on the group in a single operation. Groups could optionally be given a topology suitable to the problem space, and could be created and destroyed collectively. This would eliminate the necessity for loops (which appear at the beginning of most ABC++ programs) that create active "worker" objects. ABC++ could also possibly be integrated with one of the several parallel array libraries. The issue to be dealt with in that case is the apparent mismatch between ABC++'s multithreading and the more constrained SPMD paradigm required by most array libraries.

The specific issue that arises when attempting to design a combined library is that of control flow. Array libraries require a form of SPMD programming, in which every processor participates in every array operation more or less at the same time. For instance, a reduction operation must be executed by every processor, with every processor receiving the reduced value, or else no processor will receive a value, and those processors which executed the reduction will be permanently blocked. This requirement for control uniformity closely follows the programming model usually required by collective communication operations on parallel machines. Such operations achieve high efficiency by employing logarithmic tree-based algorithms, and hence need the participation of all processors to proceed. Contrast this to the "stealth" broadcast employed by ABC++. When a PSR updated, the other processors are not overtly aware of the fact. Certainly the user's program does not need to contain explicit calls to broadcast routines at specific points in the code. This flexibility is accomplished in the current version of ABC++ by an invisible system thread which receives PSR data, and deals with it appropriately. Currently we do not employ a tree-based algorithm for broadcast, but that is principally because of our perception that for most programs, most regions will be shared by only a few processors. Consequently, a simple linear processor-by-processor send is actually faster than the set-up and synchronization time required for tree-based broadcast.

Another future direction is to enhance the current paradigm. For instance, there could be richer PSR semantics, including a `discard()` primitive to remove replicas, or tuning hooks (like the `touch()` method described in the full ABC++ documentation) to force the runtime system to update PSRs on demand. There could also be enhancements to enable heterogeneous computing, or possibly Parametric Unshared Regions, which would function simply as messages.

In regard to active objects, one feature that would likely prove useful is guards on methods. The current `Paccept()` statement is simple to learn and use, but has problems with inheritability. In particular, a user-defined `main()` probably has to be re-written in derived classes, because it must mention additional methods when such are defined in the derived class (this is a manifestation of the inheritance anomaly [Matsuoka & Yonezawa 1993]). Our current thinking on this is to have a `Pguard` template which matches a Boolean method to a corresponding value method, where the Boolean method determines if the value method is acceptable given the current parameters. `Pguard` calls would typically occur in constructors.

A pressing question is whether active objects should be implemented with preemptive, or non-preemptive, threads. They currently employ non-preemptive threads because of the performance advantages of these, but preemptive threads would provide behavior more consistent with traditional notions of threading. Right now, long-running sections of code must include an occasional call to `Pyield()` in order to allow pending communication to proceed, and to allow other threads to run.

In conclusion, it is important to note that whenever talking about future extensions to ABC++, we have uniformly been referring to additional classes or additional functionality for current classes. Never have we discussed language extensions. We firmly believe that extending C++ is the wrong way to achieve parallelism at this time, because the language is rich enough to extend itself, and because it is big enough to make extending it inappropriate. Most compiler writers will confirm that the C++ represented by the current working paper is sufficiently large as to make writing a correct and complete sequential compiler a significant challenge. Getting a correct and complete extended C++, and getting that extension standardized represent formidable tasks. We feel all of that is unnecessary, given the capabilities of templates, operator overloading, and inheritance.

Acknowledgments

ABC++ would not have been possible without the hard work of many people. Eshrat Arjomandi, of York University, was instrumental in helping us tackle the seemingly vast literature on object-oriented concurrency. This survey resulted in a paper [Arjomandi *et al.* 1994], which drew on systems as diverse as the AT&T task coroutine library [AT&T 1989], Doeppner's task library [Doeppner & Gebele 1987], PRESTO [Bershad *et al.* 1988], AWESIME [Grunwald 1991], Gautron's task library [Gautron 1991], Amber [Chase *et al.* 1989], Panda [Assenmacher *et al.* 1991], ES-Kit [Chatterjee *et al.* 1991], pC++ (Chapter 13), CC++ (Chapter 3), Concurrent C [Gehani & Roome 1988], Orca [Bal *et al.* 1992, Bal 1991], CHARM++ (Chapter 5), ACT++ [Kafura & Lee 1990], Mentat (Chapter 10), COOL (Chapter 6), UC++ (Chapter 16), and Versioned Objects [Feeley & Levy 1992].

Many other people also contributed, including Nancy McCracken and Pankaj Kumar (Syracuse University), Harjinder Sandhu, Susan Sim, and Fernando Nasser (University of Toronto), Peter Milley and Ilene Seelemann (University of Waterloo), Ali Ghobadpour, Henry Lee, and Cassandra Lui (York University), Ivan Kalas (IBM Canada), Howard Operowsky (IBM T.J. Watson Research Laboratory), and Young-il Choo (IBM Poughkeepsie). Karen Bennet, Jacob Slonim, and Nick Cooper, of IBM Canada, provided invaluable support for this project as it developed.

2 The Amelia Vector Template Library

Thomas J. Sheffler

The Amelia Vector Template Library (AVTL) is a polymorphic collection-oriented library for distributed-memory parallel computers. The library provides a data-parallel programming model for C++ through three main generic components: a collection class, algorithms over collections, and algebraic combining functions for collections. The collection elements themselves are application-specific and may be either built-in C types or user-defined types.

Many ideas in the AVTL are borrowed from the Standard Template Library (STL) of C++. However, a restricted programming model is proposed because of the distributed-memory model. Whereas the STL provides collections and implementations of algorithms for uniprocessors, the AVTL presents an interface that may be implemented on different parallel computers. Just as the STL attempts to increase programmer productivity through code re-use, a similar strategy for parallel computers could provide programmers with a standard set of high-performance algorithms portable across many different architectures. Experience with a variety of applications, including the NAS Conjugate Gradient benchmark, show that programs using the AVTL can obtain high performance.

The current version of the AVTL library is available at:

ftp://riacs.edu/pub/Excalibur/avtl.html

2.1 Introduction

The data-parallel programming paradigm has proven to be popular because of its power and simplicity. While it is not suitable for all parallel applications, a large number of applications are easily expressed in it. The acceptance of High Performance Fortran (HPF), with its large core of data-parallel array operations, shows that many computer and compiler vendors are committed to providing support for this model in the future [Koelbel et al. 1994].

The concept of collections lies at the center of most data-parallel programming languages [Sipelstein & Blelloch 1991]. In these languages, there are two types of parallelism that can be understood in terms of collections. Simple *element-wise* parallelism is expressed by applying an operation to all of the members of a collection in parallel. No communication is allowed in an element-wise operation. *Aggregate* parallelism is expressed as a parallel algorithm defined over an entire collection. Communication is usually part of an aggregate operation. The collections are typically arrays or vectors, but other collections are possible.

There is a link between collection-oriented programming and object-oriented systems that is often not recognized. Most object-oriented systems provide polymorphic collection classes that manage heterogeneous sets of objects [Goldberg & Robson 1983]. Traditionally, polymorphism is implemented through a class hierarchy using inheritance (although other mechanisms are possible). Common functionality is provided for a group of types by inheriting the functionality from a base class. All classes derived from this base class then have a minimal set of member functions that a collection class can use to manage its elements.

The Standard Template Library (STL) uses generic classes and functions to provide polymorphic collections. Along with the definition of a small number of collection classes, the STL provides algorithms for those collections whose implementations run as fast as hand-coded C for many applications [Stepanov 1994]. Instead of using classes to inherit common functionality, generic functions define operations that the compiler can instantiate for any type.

There are two advantages to using generic functions, instead of inheritance, to describe polymorphism. First, if generic functions are carefully written, they may avoid the overhead of calls to member functions, leading to improved performance. Second, generic functions can provide new functionality for the built-in types of C, which are not classes in C++ [Stroustrup 1991]. These two capabilities mean that programmers can write functions for generic collections that obtain the performance of hand-coded C functions for collections of the built-in types of C.

The Amelia Vector Template Library (AVTL) is a polymorphic collection-oriented library for distributed-memory parallel computers. Like the STL, it is template-based rather than inheritance-based. However, because a distributed-memory model is assumed, significant restrictions must be placed on the programming model. For example, the full generality of STL's iterators is not permitted. Instead, a restricted form of access to elements, through `elementwise()` functions provides the necessary safety.

Many collection types exist in data-parallel programming languages. The AVTL, as it currently stands, targets only the simplest distributed data type: the vector. Even with only one collection type, there is a significant amount of complexity to be considered when specializing algorithms for different element types. For example, algorithms on vectors often employ algebraic combining functions (e.g., addition in a parallel prefix algorithm). It is necessary to consider how users want to specialize combining functions for new types. As a result, the AVTL has been designed so that all algorithms are generic with respect to element types and algebraic combining functions. The generic framework links algebraic combining functions with their identity values, and readily extends to new data types.

The remainder of this section introduces some of the concepts embodied by the library and then presents a simple example of how the library extends to new data types.

2.1.1   Algorithmic Templates

A standardized library of algorithms enhances programmer productivity by raising the level of abstraction, while simultaneously providing program portability. By re-targeting the library for a new architecture, all programs written in terms of the library may be run on the new architecture simply by recompiling the sources.

Standard subroutine libraries, such as the BLAS [Lawson 1979] and LAPACK [Anderson *et al.* 1992], are an attempt to provide a standard set of algorithms that are portable to many architectures. The limitation of subroutine libraries is that they are restricted to a fixed number of data types (e.g., arrays of floating point values) and operations on those types. Specifically, subroutine libraries do not support polymorphism and function specialization. These capabilities have been lacking in the past because there has not been a widely-available programming language that allowed the specification of generic algorithms. In contrast, the C++ template mechanism provides a way to specify algorithms that are generic to many types and functions.

Templates are algorithms that may be parameterized by type. By linking specific functions with classes, templates may also be parameterized by function. For example, an algorithm to sort requires knowledge of an element type and comparison function. An algorithm to find transitive closure requires specification of the element type as well as the addition and multiplication functions of the mathematical ring over which to find closure.

Subroutine libraries have been designed that allow such parameterization by requiring users to register pointers to functions to provide various services for a new type. For example, MPI [MPI 1994] uses such a mechanism to extend parallel reductions to user-defined types. The drawback with this approach is that the runtime overhead of the function invocation may seriously degrade performance. In contrast, the C++ template mechanism can be used to move such parameterization into the type system, thereby giving the compiler the ability to generate code for the services required of a new type. Because C++ templates do not necessarily impose a runtime penalty, they provide a good foundation for the encapsulation and specification of generic algorithms.

2.1.2   Reducing Programmer Complexity

A template library enables a programmer to place the burden of maintaining many different versions of similar functions on the compiler rather than on the programmer.

Consider the task of maintaining a base set of A algorithms for T element types and F different combining functions. The total number of combinations is $(A \times T \times F)$. The programmer of a subroutine library would have to provide all of these combinations.

Using templates, a programmer merely writes each algorithm and combining function once. The total maintenance complexity is $(A + T + F)$. More importantly, the effort required to extend the library with a new algorithm, element type, or combining function is localized to the new component. A new algorithm, element type, or combining function may be added with the assurance that it will work with all existing components; adding a single new component in any of these classes increases the total number of combinations by a multiplicative factor. The template mechanism makes it possible for the AVTL to use the concept of orthogonality of algorithms, element types, and combining functions both to explain the functionality it offers and to reduce code complexity.

2.1.3   A Case for Standard Parallel Collections

The AVTL is proof that a standard a set of generic collections and algorithms can provide a convenient programming environment for distributed-memory parallel computers. To a limited extent, such a library replaces some of the functionality of current data-parallel compilers. Compilers for data-parallel languages, such as HPF, are responsible for the instantiation of parallel algorithms on collections. A simple example is HPF's **reduce** function on arrays. C++ templates provide a way to move this functionality out of the compiler and into a library without sacrificing performance in the way that subroutine libraries often do. By establishing standard interfaces to parallel collections, it should be possible to experiment with and add new collection types in the future without modification to the underlying compiler.

Of course, many low-level optimizations are beyond the scope of a template library. For example, loop fusion and array blocking optimizations must be handled at a lower level. While many current C compilers do not perform these and other optimizations common in Fortran compilers [Cray 1993, IBM 1993], it is reasonable to expect that such optimizations will become commonplace over the next few years. In much the same way that programmers write vectorizable code for vector computers, algorithms in the template library could be written in a scalable style to allow compilers to recognize appropriate optimizations.

Whereas the STL standardizes both interfaces and algorithms, this is not possible in general for distributed-memory parallel computers. The interfaces may be standardized, but separate implementations may have to be provided for different classes of machines. The initial implementation of the AVTL is written in standard C++ and uses MPI for communication [MPI 1994]. It is therefore portable to a wide variety of current distributed-memory parallel computers.[1] However, shared-memory multiprocessors and vector multiprocessors present architectures for which an entirely different implementation would be necessary.

2.1.4 Library Components

AVTL provides three integrated software components that can be applied to built-in and user-defined data types:

1. A generic distributed collection class: the vector. It is implemented as a template class.

---

[1]Programs written using the AVTL have been run on an IBM SP-2, a cluster of DEC Alphas, an Intel Paragon, and a Thinking Machines CM-5.

2. Generic algorithms on vectors. These are implemented as template functions. Standard algorithms include element-wise operations, vector permutations, scan and segmented scan operations, reductions, segmented reductions, and combining sends and fetch-and-add communication functions.

3. Generic function objects. These parameterize the vector algorithms to vary the way in which vector elements are combined.

The generic distributed vector is simply a parallel vector that is parameterized by a type. The algorithms defined on vectors are parameterized both by element type and, if necessary, a combining function type. Generic function objects provide default combining functions for standard types of arithmetic operations.

The use of C++'s function objects with template algorithms ensures high performance by allowing user-defined functions to be inlined, avoiding the overhead of a function call for the application of the function. Function objects are used uniformly in the library to specify algebraic combining operations for arbitrary data types. For example, the vector library provides parallel prefix (or scan) algorithms for vectors of any homogeneous type. For any binary associative operator $\oplus$ with an identity element $\mathbf{0}$, and a vector a, a scan computes a result b defined by:

$$
\begin{aligned}
b_0 &= \mathbf{0} \\
b_i &= b_{i-1} \oplus a_{i-1}
\end{aligned}
$$

The AVTL contains a single **scan** algorithm template; the binary operator and identity element are parameters of the algorithm. Other parallel vector libraries have offered one of two approaches to providing scan functions. To ensure high performance, libraries such as CVL provide specialized scan algorithms for a limited number of data types and operators [Blelloch *et al.* 1993]. The limitation of this approach is that it does not generalize to user-defined types. More general subroutine libraries parameterize binary associative operators by using function pointers [MPI 1994]. This approach suffers a performance loss because the function call may be unacceptably expensive.

Function objects are like function pointers except that the compiler may have complete information about the function, and inline it at compile time. The template-based approach offers the benefits of genericity, efficiency and extensibility.

2.1.5 An Example

Before we delve into the details of the AVTL, a short example will demonstrate some of the features of the library. The vector collection template class is called **pvect** (for "parallel vector"). The vector constructor accepts a length argument, and an optional value with which to initialize the elements of the vector. By default, the elements are distributed in equal-sized blocks over the available processors.

```
pvect<int>    ones(10, 1);      // length 10, elements set to 1
pvect<double> twos(10, 2.0);    // vector of doubles
```

A vector that enumerates its sites from 0 is called an *index vector*. An index vector may be computed from the **ones** vector by using the scan algorithm with addition as the operator. The AVTL provides a set of standard generic binary associative operators in the form of function objects. These function objects are parameterized by type. An index vector could be created by applying the scan algorithm with the addition function object for integers:

```
pvect<int> index = op_scan(add_op<int>(), ones);
```

A user-defined data type may be used with the AVTL as easily as a built-in type. The following class defines a type that represents a point in the plane in polar coordinates. The class also defines the addition operator for objects of type **polar** as an inlined member function:

```
class polar {
  double theta, rho;
  public:
    polar (double init)     { theta = 0.0; rho = init; }
    polar operator+(polar a) { ··· }
};
```

The user-defined type **polar** can be used to parameterize the **pvect** template:

```
pvect<polar>    a(100, polar(1.0)); // initialized to 1.0
pvect<polar>    prefixsum = op_scan(add_op<polar>(), a);
```

Given the definition of this new data type, it is reasonable to perform an add_scan() on vectors of polar elements, since addition is defined for this type. The call to op_scan() will produce the prefix sum of a vector of polar coordinates. The generic combining function add_op() may be applied because addition is defined for the polar type. Because the addition operator is an inlined member function of class polar, the compiler will inline its code body in the instantiation of the add_op() combining function, which is itself inlined in the op_scan() algorithm produced for this type. Since the resulting scan function will not have any function call overhead, its performance on polar types will equal that of a hand-written scan function.

2.1.6   Organization

The rest of this chapter is organized as follows. Section 2.2 describes the programming model provided by the library. It is essentially data-parallel, with the member and friend functions of vector elements defining the granularity of computation.

Section 2.3 provides a grand tour of the library and its components. It begins by describing the requirements placed on classes that are to be used as parallel vector elements. From there, it describes function objects and why they are important to the library both for expanding its functionality and to ensure high performance. The large number of predefined generic function objects provided by the library make it useful for all of the built-in data types of C++, but it is its extensibility through function objects that makes it interesting. Most of this section is devoted to describing the generic algorithms provided by the library. These fall into two main classes: element-wise forms, and generic parallel algorithms.

A number of example applications are shown in detail in Section 2.4. Running times for the polygon overlay example are presented, as are execution times for an implementation of the NAS Conjugate Gradient benchmark. These results illustrate that the template-based approach yields performance on par with that of hand-coded C. Section 2.5 discusses the relationship of the AVTL to other parallel C++ languages and libraries. Finally, two concluding sections offer advice to users of the library and summarize some of the points made in this chapter.

2.2 AVTL Programming Model

The AVTL implements a data-parallel programming model on distributed-memory parallel computers. In this model, each program expression describes a parallel operation across all of the elements of a collection. Synchronization occurs after each operation. The data-parallel model of AVTL offers the advantage that there is a single thread of control: race conditions, deadlock, and non-determinism are impossible.

2.2.1 Two Types of Parallelism

As discussed before, data-parallel programming models are based on the concept of element-wise and aggregate operations on collections. The AVTL offers only one collection: the vector.

The AVTL provides the `elementwise()` template function for element-wise parallel operations. It applies a friend function or function object to each set of elements at the same sites in its argument vectors. The result of the `elementwise()` function is a vector of the results computed at each site.

Aggregate parallel operations are defined by the algorithmic templates of the library. Users may define higher-level generic parallel operations by writing template functions of their own that invoke the base parallel algorithms. In fact, some of the standard set of algorithms (`minloc()`, for example) are implemented this way in the current version of the library.

2.2.2 Granularity

Data-parallel models based on SIMD architectures ensure that synchronization occurs at the *instruction* level. That is, in an element-wise construct, the instructions are executed on each element in parallel. In contrast, the AVTL ensures only that the statements of an element's member or friend functions in an element-wise construct execute without interruption. This model of execution is the same as that of pC++ (Chapter 13), where it is termed a *collection-parallel* model [Bodin 1993a].

The advantage of this model is that it gives programmers the ability to choose the level of granularity appropriate for a particular problem. An element operation could be as small as a single machine instruction, or as complicated as the update of a large data structure. The AVTL allows the programmer to select an appropriate granularity. This capability is especially important in the definition of the combining functions that are used with combining-send and fetch-and-op functions. The user can define combining functions on large structures or arrays with the knowledge that within one of these functions there will be no interruption of control flow.

2.2.3 Scalar Data

The AVTL differentiates between two types of data: scalar and parallel. Currently, the only parallel type is the distributed vector provided by the library. Scalar types may be combined with distributed vector elements through *scalar extension* as expressed with the `scalar` template type. Scalar extension makes it possible to add a value to each site in a vector without having to first create a vector of copies of the value followed by an element-wise addition.

Depending on the target architecture, the library may implement scalars in one of two ways: they may either reside on a master processor in a master-slave configuration, or may be replicated across all processors in a peer configuration. For example, on the CM-2 a scalar would reside on the host. On a CM-5, a scalar value would be replicated on each physical processor. In either case, the AVTL maintains a consistent view of scalar data.

2.3 Library Overview

The AVTL provides three generic components: the parallel vector, combining function objects and algorithms on vectors. This section discusses the role of each component, their code interfaces and how the components can be combined in different ways to create data-parallel programs.

2.3.1 The Parallel Vector Class

The primary responsibility of the `pvect` vector class is coordinating the allocation and freeing of vector memory. Each instance of a parallel vector is actually a pointer to a hidden vector descriptor that maintains information about the vector's type, length, and location in vector memory. Two or more vectors may share the same descriptor, and thus refer to the same location in vector memory. The constructors and destructors of the class maintain reference counts on vector descriptors to determine when vector memory may be released by the memory manager.

The reference counting scheme minimizes the copying of vector data. When passing vectors as arguments to functions, the only thing that is copied in as an argument, or out as a result, is a pointer to the descriptor. Vector assignment is likewise defined through the aliasing of descriptors. Most vector operations return a new vector so that application of one function does not cause a side effect in another shared vector elsewhere.

Four constructors are defined for **pvects**. The default constructor does not allocate any vector memory, but merely declares a vector pointer. With a single integer argument, vector memory is allocated;[2] an optional second argument specifies an initial value for each element of the vector. The copy constructor for a **pvect** shares the descriptor of the argument and increments the reference count.

The following example illustrates the four different constructors. The destructor for a vector decrements the reference count of the descriptor and frees the allocated vector memory when the count reaches zero:

```
pvect<int> a;              // no vector memory allocated
pvect<int> b(100);         // allocated
pvect<int> c(100, 5);      // allocated, initialized
pvect<int> d = c;          // c and d share same vector memory
```

An outline of the definition of the **pvect** class appears below. The member functions **replace()**, **dist()**, and **send()** actually modify the contents of the vector without creating a new copy. Thus, these member functions can modify vectors that are potentially shared. The other member functions of the **pvect** class are listed below.

```
template <class T>
class pvect {
 public:
  pvect<T> copy();                    // produce a copy of the vector
  T        get(int pos);              // retrieve a value from a position
  int      len();                     // get the length of the vector
  void     replace(int pos, const T val); // overwrite at a site
  void     dist(const T val); // overwrite entire vector
```

---

[2]In the current implementation, constructors are not called for vector elements at the time of their allocation. This is a deficiency of the library, and will be rectified when the memory management is redesigned to be more compliant with the C++ model.

```
    void       send(pvect<T> vals, pvect<int> positions);
                            // overwrite selected
};
```

The actual class definition includes other member functions, but those are used internally by the library.

Requirements for Element Types   The pvect template class makes very few assumptions about element types, but users designing element classes must be aware of them. A pvect vector is a homogeneous collection of fixed-size types: the size of an element must be known at compile time. Internally, the library uses the sizeof() operator when allocating space for vector elements, and the assignment operator of the element moves the contents of individual elements. Programmers should not redefine the assignment operator to mean anything other than a simple byte-wise copy of the data of the element.

While it would be desirable to allow element types whose size is fixed but not known until run time, such a view is not particularly compatible with the programming model provided by C++. In many ways, the pvect of the AVTL resembles regular vectors in C++. There is no precedent in C++ for the definition of vectors of heterogeneous or varying-sized elements.

The assignment operator is used for data movement (as opposed to a call to bcopy(), for example) because most compilers generate efficient code for copying the bytes of an element. In the future, special sizeof() and copy() template functions might be used by the library, allowing users to specialize these for types whose size is not known until runtime. Experimentation will help to evaluate whether such a capability is necessary or useful.

2.3.2   Combining Function Objects

A function object is an object with an operator()() method defined. Functions objects are used in C++ template libraries in the same situations where a pointer to a function might be used in C library routines. Algorithmic templates expecting function objects may also be used with regular function pointers too. However, function objects offer the advantage that inlined member functions do not incur the overhead of a function call.

Because function objects are instances of a class, they may also store state information in their members. This capability is useful for creating specialized functions, similar to curried functions in functional languages [Peyton Jones 1987], or closures in Lisp and Scheme [Steele 1990b, Abelson & Sussman 1985].

The STL provides a standard algorithm, find_if(), that locates the first element satisfying a predicate. The predicate may be either a function or a function object. This algorithm may be used to find the first element in a vector smaller than some value by instantiating a function object with the comparison value bound when it is defined. Because the member functions of class compar are inlined, the code generated for the find_if() function will not include any function call overhead. The following code shows an example of the definition and use of a function object to find the first value in a vector less than 10:

```
class compar {
  int thresh;
 public:
  compar(int t) : thresh(t) { }
  int operator()(int val)   { return val < thresh; }
};
int vector[N];
int *p = vector;
int *found;
found = find_if(p, p+N, compar(10));
```

Binary Associative Operators and Identity Values Efficient parallel algorithms are well known for scans and reductions using arbitrary binary associative operators (or *binops*) [Blelloch 1990, Wyllie 1979]. Most of these algorithms require the specification of the identity element associated with the binary operator. In AVTL, a binary associative operator is an object with two required member functions:

1. operator()() is a member function of two arguments performing the binary associative operation.

2. identity() is a member function of no arguments that returns the identity element of the appropriate type for the binary associative operator.

A suitable binary associative operator for the addition of integers is:

```
class add_op_int {
 public:
   int operator()(int a, int b) { return a + b; }
   int identity()              { return 0; }
};
```

Binary associative operators are used uniformly throughout the library to parameterize:

- segmented and unsegmented exclusive scans,
- segmented and unsegmented inclusive scans,
- segmented and unsegmented reductions,
- combining-sends (like the add_scatter of HPF), and
- fetch-and-op operations (e.g., fetch-and-add).

A large number of binops are predefined as generic template classes. These merely give names to standard element-wise algebraic operations: add, mul, max, min, and, or, and xor, fst (return the first argument) and scd (return the second). For example, the addition binop is defined as:

```
template <class T> class add_op {
 public:
   T operator()(T a, T b) { return a + b; }
   T identity()           { return zero_val<T>(); }
};
```

Because it invokes operator+, this binop is defined for any type for which the addition operator is defined. Note too that if the operator+ of the element type is inlined by the compiler, the entire body of the function object will be inlined when it is used.

The preceding template class introduced yet another template class without mentioning it: an identity value. The predefined binops require knowledge of four special values of each type. These are the zero value (identity for addition), the one value (identity for multiplication), the minimum value of the type (identity for maximum) and the maximum value of the type (identity for minimum). The template class definition for the zero value is:

```
template <class T> class zero_val {
  public:
    operator T { return 0; }
};
```

Whenever any object of type zero_val<T> is used in a context where a value of type T is required, the appropriate value is returned. For most of the built-in types, an appropriate conversion exists from 0 to the built-in type (integer, character, long double, etc.).

The identity classes for all of the built-in types use template specialization and the values from the standard C include file limits.h to predefine the four identity values for each of the built-in types. Thus, appropriate identity values for all of the built-in types of C are predefined based on the storage formats of the target architecture.

Because binops in the AVTL must have an identity value, regular functions may not be used as arguments where binops are required. To circumvent this problem, the library provides an adaptor class and function that constructs a binop from a function and an identity value. The class is called binop, and the adaptor function is make_binop(). A binop object stores a pointer to the function and a copy of the identity value, and provides the necessary member functions. For example, to construct a (meaningless) "power" binop the following code would suffice:

```
binop<double(*)(double,double), double> bop =
                            make_binop(pow, 1.0);
```

The result of the make_binop() function is usually used directly as an argument to a template function so that the full type of the binop template is only dealt with by the compiler.

The structure of binops and identity classes gives users flexibility about how new types and binops are integrated into the library. For a new type, the user may explicitly create binop function objects with the required members. These may specialize some of the predefined binops (e.g., add_op()) for the new type, or may have completely new names. Alternatively, the user may simply provide definitions of the standard C arithmetic operators for the new type, as well as specializations of the identity classes for the new type. Then, the generic binop classes may be instantiated for all of the predefined binops. Note that if the binop does not have a standard name, the former approach is required.

2.3.3   Element-Wise Forms

The AVTL provides two forms to express element-wise computations.
First, it overloads the standard arithmetic operators on vectors so that
they have element-wise semantics. All other element-wise computations
are handled by the elementwise() template function.

Arithmetic Operators   All of the standard C arithmetic operators
(+, -, *, /, %, <<, >>, |, &, and ˆ) are extended to mean the element-wise
application of the operator to the elements of the vectors in parallel. For
instance, if a and b are vectors, a+b is their element-wise sum. If the
elements of a and b are of differing type, the resulting vector will have
the type of the left argument. This is not as general as the standard C
type coercion rules, but it is a workable solution.

Scalar extension is the ability to (for example) add a constant to all
elements of a vector without explicitly distributing the constant across
a new vector. The AVTL does not provide automatic scalar extension
because it is difficult to recognize scalar values with template arguments.
The user of the AVTL can specify such scalar extension, but only by
identifying scalar variables explicitly.

The scalar template class is used to indicate scalar extension for
element-wise operators. An adaptor function, called make_scalar(),
may also be used. It attempts to deduce the type of the scalar from its
argument.

The following illustrates two equivalent ways of adding 5.0 to each of
the elements of a vector. The first method explicitly creates a scalar of
type double, the second uses make_scalar() to deduce the type from
its argument, 5.0:

```
pvect<double> a(100, 4.0);
pvect<double> b = a + scalar<double>(5);
pvect<double> c = a + make_scalar(5.0);
```

Comparison Operators   The standard C comparison operators (==,
!=, <, >, <=, and >=) are similarly extended. A scalar may be either
argument in such a comparison. The result of all comparisons of vectors
is of type pvect<int>.

Assignment Operators   The assignment operators of C have not
been redefined to be meaningful for vectors. Most operations in the

AVTL produce a new vector as a result. An assignment operator would modify the value of a (potentially shared) vector. While these operators would be useful, at this point the ramifications of their inclusion are not fully understood.

The Conditional Operator   Because C++ does not permit the overloading of the conditional operator (i.e., `?:`), the AVTL provides the `merge()` function. The `merge()` function takes a mask vector and two argument vectors, and returns the element-wise application of the conditional operator. The declaration of `merge()` is:

```
template <class T>
pvect<T> merge(pvect<int> mask, pvect<T> then, pvect<T> else);
```

Element-Wise Function Application   A template function called `elementwise()` applies an arbitrary function or function object to each of the elements of one or more vectors. Because the type of the value returned by a function cannot be matched by a template argument, the user must supply an argument to specify the type of the result desired.

Nine variants of the element-wise function are provided. They apply functions of 1 to 9 arguments to the elements of the corresponding vectors. In the code below, `fn()` is an element-wise function, and the variables `a`, `b`, and `c` are vectors. The argument types of `fn()` must match the element types of the corresponding vectors:

```
pvect<T>  result = elementwise(fn, pvect<T>(), a)
pvect<T>  result = elementwise(fn, pvect<T>(), a, b)
pvect<T>  result = elementwise(fn, pvect<T>(), a, b, c)
...
```

The function argument to an `elementwise()` function may be either a function object or a function pointer. For example, the Unix cosine function may be applied to each of the elements of a vector, producing a vector of cosines:

```
pvect<double> cosines = elementwise(cos, pvect<double>(),
                                    argvector)
```

Scalar extension is defined for the `elementwise()` functions just as it is for the arithmetic operators. A `scalar` used in place of a `pvect` argument to an `elementwise()` is extended across the length of the other argument vectors. All pvect arguments to an elementwise() function must be of the same length, and at least one argument must be a pvect. For example, the following uses the standard binop add_op() to add 23 to each of the elements of an integer vector, vect:

```
pvect<int> sum = elementwise(add_op<int>(), pvect<int>(),
                             vect, scalar<int>(23));
```

Users of the library need not know about the internal workings of scalar types, but the handling of scalar values in elementwise() functions is informative. Internally, the library defines STL-style iterators for both pvect and scalar classes. Incrementing a pvect iterator causes it to reference the next value in the vector. In contrast, an iterator for a scalar type always references the same value. By adopting this approach, a single family of nine elementwise() template functions handles all possible $2^9 = 512$ combinations of pvect and scalar types that could be arguments to elementwise() functions.

Function objects used with elementwise() functions are useful for their inlining capabilities. Consider the following example, where a, b and c are three vectors and x is a scalar.

```
pvect<double> result = a * b + scalar<double>(x) * c;
```

This expression calculates the element-wise product of a and b, places it in a temporary vector, computes the other product and places it in a temporary vector and finally computes the result vector sum. Besides the overhead of allocating and freeing the temporary vectors, this operation suffers from writing the temporary vectors out to memory and then reading them back in. A more efficient solution is to use a function object and the elementwise() function. This example also demonstrates how function objects may be used to implement scalar extension.

```
class funob {
    double scal;
  public:
    funop(double x) : scal(x);
    double operator()(double x, double, y, double z)
    { return x * y + scal * z; }
};

pvect<double> result =
            elementwise(funob(x), pvect<double>(), a, b, c);
```

The resulting code is certainly less readable, because the body of the element-wise form must be written as a separate function. However, when high performance is a necessity, this technique can be used in critical regions of a program. The construct ensures that the layout of the vectors in memory remains hidden, but the use of the function object ensures that the performance meets that of a hand-coded loop.

Zipping Vectors   The AVTL borrows the `pair` template type from the STL. A `pair` is parameterized by two types and may hold two values of those types:

```
template <class T1, class T2>
class pair {
 public:
  T1 first;
  T2 second;
  pair(const T1 &x, const T2 &y) : first(x), second(y) { }
};
```

Pairs are useful in many contexts. When using the AVTL, pairs can help to speed some communication operations. For example, if permuting two vectors by the same permutation vector, it may be more efficient to pack them into a single vector of pairs and then to perform a single permutation. Of course, a user could define an appropriate structure to hold the pair, and could then load the values into a vector of pairs using the `elementwise()` function with a new function object. After the permutation, the pairs would be unpacked using another new function object.

This sequence of steps is so frequent that helper functions are included in the AVTL. The function `zip()` accepts two vectors of any type as arguments and produces a vector of pairs:[3]

```
pvect<double>   a;
pvect<complex>  b;
pvect<pair<double, complex> > c = zip(a, b);
```

A vector of pairs may be separated by using the `unzip()` functions. There are two: one returns a vector of the first elements, the other returns a vector of the second elements:

---

[3] Guy Blelloch first named this operation "zip."

```
pvect<double>   new_a = unzip1(c);
pvect<complex>  new_b = unzip2(c);
```

As discussed above, zipped vectors are useful for eliminating redundant communication. Assume that two vectors are to be permuted the same way. The naïve way to accomplish the permutation is to use two calls to the **permute()** function:

```
pvect<int>      p;    // The permutation vector
pvect<double>   perm_a = permute(a, p);
pvect<complex>  perm_b = permute(b, p);
```

Using the zip functions, a single **permute()** will suffice, but additional data movement will have to be performed locally. The tradeoff may be beneficial if communication is very expensive (as it usually is). The resulting code is only slightly uglier than the original:

```
pvect<pair<double, complex> > temp = permute(zip(a, b), p);
pvect<double>   perm_a = unzip1(temp);
pvect<complex>  perm_b = unzip2(temp);
```

2.3.4 Algorithms on Vectors

The AVTL provides a large number of standard algorithms for vectors. Most of these are provided in both segmented and unsegmented variants with function overloading used to differentiate between the two. This section begins with a brief description of segmented vectors and then presents the base algorithms of the library.

Segment Descriptors Many vector operations accept an additional argument that designates *segments* within the vector. A segmented vector is one that is partitioned into disjoint ranges. The partitioning is described by another vector called a *segment descriptor*. Segmented operations on vectors treat each segment as a separate vector, but are performed over all segments in a vector simultaneously [Blelloch 1990]. For example, a segmented scan computes a recurrence in which the running sum is reset to 0 at the beginning of each segment.

There are many ways to represent segment descriptors. The AVTL uses a vector of integers whose sum is l; each element of the *segment-lengths* descriptor gives the length of a segment. For example, the following code constructs a vector of length 12 and segments it into 3

segments of length 4. The result of the segmented add scan is shown as
a comment:

```
pvect<int>  ones(12, 1);                  // [1 1 1 1 1 1 1 1 1 1 1 1]
pvect<int>  seg(3, 4);                     // [4 4 4]
pvect<int>  scan = add_scan(ones, seg); // [0 1 2 3 0 1 2 3 0 1 2 3]
```

In the AVTL, a vector of integers may be used interchangeably as a
value or as a segment descriptor. Internally, the library computes an optimized representation for segment descriptors and caches this representation, so that re-using the same vector as a segment descriptor avoids
recomputing the internal form. The cached representation is flushed,
however, if the segment vector is modified in any way.

Users of the library need not concern themselves with the internal
caching of segment descriptors, except when evaluating the performance
of programs. Additional time may be required to compile and cache the
internal segment descriptor the first time a vector of integers is used as
a segment descriptor. After that, the internal form is used directly.

Collect/Distribute   Two algorithms are provided to distribute scalar
vector data across a parallel vector, and to gather the contents of a
parallel vector into a scalar vector. These two algorithms are called
collect and distribute. These algorithms are usually used upon program startup. For example, the matrix used in a computation may be
assembled as a scalar and then distributed over the available processors
using distribute. Of course, it is possible to achieve the same effect
by sending each element individually, but using distribute is faster.

Permutation Algorithms   The basis of data movement in the AVTL
are the send() and get() functions, which implement scatter and gather
operations on vectors. Because not all destination sites in a send() operation may receive values, a vector of default values is required. The
permute() and unpermute() functions are used when the permutation
is guaranteed to be one-to-one. Conditional forms accept an additional
argument, in the form of a mask, that marks sites excluded from partic-
ipating in the operation. The complete list of permutation algorithms
appears in Table 2.1.

Program 2.1 shows an example of using the permute() function to
implement a generic function that reverses the elements of a vector.

Algorithm	Unsegmented	Segmented	Comment
permute	X	X	One-to-one permutation within a vector or segment.
send	X	X	Scatter
cond_send	X	X	Conditional scatter
unpermute	X	X	Backwards permutation
get	X	X	Gather
cond_get	X	X	Conditional gather

Table 2.1
Generic Permutation Algorithms

```
template<class T>
pvect<T> reverse(pvect<T> v)
{
  int      len = v.len();
  pvect<int>  rindex = scalar<int>(len-1) - index(len);
  return permute(v, rindex); // return the reversed vector
}
```

Program 2.1
An Implementation of the Generic **reverse()** Algorithm

Function **index()** creates a vector that numbers its sites from 0. The reversed index, **rindex()**, is computed using element-wise subtraction.

Generic Scans and Reduction Algorithms Parallel-prefix algorithms are provided in both inclusive and exclusive forms. An exclusive scan on a vector a is defined by the recurrence:

$$e_0 = \mathbf{0}$$
$$e_j = e_{j-1} \oplus a_{j-1}$$

Inclusive scans combine the value at the current site.

$$i_0 = a_0$$
$$i_j = i_j \oplus a_{j-1}.$$

Reductions simply combine all of the values in a vector. The reduction r of an array with respect to a binop is defined as:

$$r = a_0 \oplus a_1 \oplus \cdots \oplus a_n$$

Algorithm	Unsegmented	Segmented	Description
op_scan	X	X	Exclusive scan
op_iscan	X	X	Inclusive scan
op_reduce	X	X	Reduction

Table 2.2
Generic Scans and Reduction Algorithms

Name	Uses	Identity	Comment
add_op	operator+	zero_val	Addition
mul_op	operator*	one_val	Multiplication
max_op	operator>	min_val	Maximum
min_op	operator<	max_val	Minimum
and_op	operator&	one_val	Boolean AND
or_op	operator|	zero_val	Boolean OR
xor_op	operator^	zero_val	Exclusive-OR
fst_op		zero_val	First (left) argument
scd_op		zero_val	Second (right) argument

Table 2.3
Predefined Generic Binop Classes

If the length of the vector is zero, then the value of the reduction is the identity.

The AVTL provides these three algorithms in a generic form that is parameterized by element type and binop. Segmented and unsegmented forms are also provided. These are listed in Table 2.2.

The predefined generic binops give names to the arithmetic operators of C. As described earlier, each of the standard binops makes use of an associated identity class. These listed in Table 2.3.

To simplify the use of the standard binops with the scan and reduction algorithms, the library provides predefined versions of the common variants in both segmented and unsegmented forms (Table 2.4).

Scan functions are used in many contexts to compute permutation vectors. Program 2.2 shows how to use the generic op_scan() algorithm to write a split() function. split() takes a mask and a vector and permutes it so that the sites marked with a 0 are moved to the lower half of the vector, and the sites marked with a 1 are moved to the upper half. This algorithm uses a custom binop to compute two recurrences

Exclusive Scan	Inclusive Scan	Reduction	Unsegmented	Segmented
add_scan	add_iscan	add_reduce	X	X
mul_scan	mul_iscan	mul_reduce	X	X
max_scan	max_iscan	max_reduce	X	X
min_scan	min_iscan	min_reduce	X	X
and_scan	and_iscan	and_reduce	X	X
or_scan	or_iscan	or_reduce	X	X
xor_scan	xor_iscan	xor_reduce	X	X

Table 2.4
Predefined Standard Scans and Reductions

simultaneously on both the mask and the inverse of the mask (computed with the not() function).

The idea behind the algorithm is that true and false sites in the mask must be enumerated independently of one another. The enumeration is performed in a single parallel step by the call to op_scan() with the custom binop. After this step, the two enumerations are separated using the unzip() functions. At this point, the enumeration values of the true sites must be incremented by the total number of false sites that they must follow in the result vector. This number is obtained in variable cnt. The merge() step selects the appropriate value for each of the true and false sites and the final permutation moves the data values to their new sites.

A number of other generic functions are provided whose implementations are based on the scan functions. For example, copy_scan() copies the first value in a vector or segment across the rest of the vector. Its implementation uses the generic op_iscan() algorithm with the fst_op() binop. A list of these composite scan functions appears in Table 2.5.

In a similar manner, the library provides two special reduction functions called minloc() and maxloc(). These return the index of the minimum or maximum value in a vector or segment. Both of these functions are constructed using the basic op_reduce() algorithm, along with some special function objects and the zip() and unzip() functions (Table 2.6).

The implementation of minloc() is shown in Program 2.3. The call to zip() copies each vector element into a pair structure along with its index. The generic op_reduce() algorithm is used along with a

```
class add_op_pair {
 public:
  pair<int, int> operator(pair<int, int> a, pair<int, int> b)
  {
    return pair<int,int>(a.first+b.first, a.second+b.second);
  }
  pair<int, int> identity() { ... }
};

template<class T>
pvect<T> split(pvect<int> mask, pvect<T> vect)
{
  pvect<int> zipd = zip(mask, not(mask));
  pvect< pair<int,int> > scan = op_scan(add_op_pair(), zipd);

  pvect<int> s1 = unzip1(scan);
  pvect<int> s2 = unzip2(scan);
  int cnt = s2.get(s2.len()-1); // number of false sites

  pvect<int> perm = merge(mask, s1+scalar<int>(cnt), s2);
  return permute(vect, perm);
}
```

Program 2.2
Using a User-Defined Binop to Define the Generic split() Algorithm

Algorithm	Unsegmented	Segmented	Comment
copy_scan	X	X	Copy a value across a vector or segment.
index	X	X	Create a vector that enumerates its sites.
rsh1	X	X	Right shift a vector by one position.

Table 2.5
Predefined Scan Functions

Algorithm	Unsegmented	Segmented	Comment
maxloc	X	X	Find the location of the maximum value in a vector or segment.
minloc	X	X	Find the location of the minimum value in a vector or segment.

Table 2.6
Predefined Reductions

```
template <class T>
int minloc(pvect<T> a1)
{
    pvect<int>              ind = index(a1.len());
    pvect< pair<T,int> > zipped = zip(a1, ind);
    pair<T,int>             loc = op_reduce(minloc_op< pair<T,int> >(),
                                            zipped);
    return loc.second;
}
```

Program 2.3
Implementation of the Generic minloc() Algorithm

special binop called minloc_op(). This binop returns the pair whose first field is the smaller of the two. The result of the reduction is the (value,index) pair of the minimum value in the vector. The segmented version of this function is very similar and uses the same binop.

Compiled Communication Schedules   In addition to the permutation algorithms presented earlier, the library provides two-phase communication algorithms. These separate the specification of a communication pattern from its use in a data movement algorithm. The first phase compiles a communication pattern into an internal form called a schedule. A schedule is then used with one of several algorithms to move data.

Compiled communication allows programmers to treat schedules as first-class objects, and to specify exactly when communication patterns remain the same. Compilers for parallel languages, such as HPF, often

Algorithm	Unsegmented	Segmented	Comment
send_comp	X	X	Scatter
cond_send_comp	X	X	Conditional scatter
get_comp	X	X	Gather
cond_get_comp	X	X	Conditional gather

Table 2.7
Communication Schedule Compilation Algorithms

try to re-use such communication schedules. However, the dependence analysis that must be performed to detect potential re-use is difficult.

The compilation phase may also optimize the resulting schedule by performing some additional computations. While such optimization increases compilation time, the time saved in a few uses of the optimized schedule often more than makes up for it. Such runtime optimization is necessary for sparse and irregular problems that do not lend themselves to static compiler analysis [Sheffler 1992, Dahl 1990, Sharma *et al.* 1994].

The pattern compilation algorithms are listed in Table 2.7. Each has an interface similar to the permutation function it is named after.

The result of communication compilation is a schedule whose type is am_sched. This may be used with one of four data movement algorithms. The run() algorithm moves data in the pattern specified by the schedule, combining values sent to the same destination site with a combining function object. The runrev() conceptually reverses the sense of the pattern so that data moves from destination to source.

The other type of data movement is the fetch-and-op algorithm, called fao(), and faorev(), which reverses the direction of the pattern. In the data-parallel literature, fetch-and-op is also known as multiprefix [Cohn 1990, Sheffler 1993]. The result at the destination sites is the same as a combining send, but each source site is replaced with the value of the destination *before* its value is added to the destination.

The fetch-and-op algorithm can be used to construct a simple ranking algorithm based on bucket sorting. Program 2.4 implements the algorithm and illustrates the re-use of a schedule with fao() and runrev(). This program takes a vector of positive integers, called keys, and produces a vector that permutes the keys to place them in non-decreasing order. The algorithm uses two temporary vectors called histogram and prefix.

```
pvect<int> rank(pvect<int> keys, int M) // M == max key size
{
  int N = keys.len();

  pvect<int> histogram(M, 0);
  pvect<int> prefix(N, 1);
  am_sched *S;

  S = send_comp(keys, histogram);

  fao(S, add_op<int>(), prefix, histogram);        // 1
  histogram = add_scan(histogram);                 // 2
  runrev(S, add_op<int>(), prefix, histogram);     // 3

  S->free();   // release the storage for the schedule
  return prefix;
}
```

Program 2.4
Implementing the rank() Algorithm Using Compiled Communication

Program 2.4 works as follows. The application of fao() simultaneously modifies histogram so that each destination site counts the number of keys with its value, and prefix so that each key receives a count of the number of equal-valued keys that precede it. After the add_scan(), each site in histogram gives the total number of keys whose values are lower than the index of the site. Lastly, runrev() is used to retrieve the cumulative values from histogram and to add them into the prefix values. The prefix values then reflect the ranking of each key.

Utility Algorithms   Lastly, the library provides a number of utility algorithms (Table 2.8). These may be implemented using the base algorithms, but direct implementations often run faster. Some of these utility algorithms perform complicated data movement operations that are necessary to handle sparse and irregular applications in a data-parallel framework.

Algorithm	Unsegmented	Segmented	Comment
rank	X		Rank the contents of a vector.
hash_insert	X		Insert elements into a hash vector.
hash_find	X		Find elements in a hash vector.
append	X	X	Append vectors or segments.
dist	X	X	Distribute copies of a scalar to produce vector.
distv	X	X	Distribute copies a vector.
subseq	X	X	Extract a subsequence of a vector.
shift	X	X	Shift.
cshift	X	X	Circular shift.
pack	X		Compress a vector using a mask.
unpack	X		Decompress a vector using a mask.

Table 2.8
Generic High-Level Algorithms

2.4   Example Programs

The examples in this section illustrate the simplicity and extensibility of the library. The first example computes π using a straightforward integration scheme. The second example illustrates two ways to implement polygon overlay. The last example shows how users may write generic functions using the components of the library. In this example, a generic matrix-vector multiplication routine is extended to a blocked sparse version simply by defining two new classes. The resulting sparse matrix code is then used to implement the NAS Conjugate Gradient benchmark. Performance comparisons between the implementation using the AVTL and the reference implementation from IBM show that the AVTL obtains high performance in practice.

2.4.1 Computing π

The first example computes π by integrating $f(x) = \frac{4.0}{x^2+1}$ from 0 to 1 (Program 2.5). This code makes use of an instance of the class f_of_x as a function object (sometimes called a *functor*) with internal state. The constructor for the class produces an integrand function customized for a particular rectangle width h. The function accepts an index value, computes its x coordinate, and returns the area of the rectangle at that coordinate. The rest of the program is straightforward.

The main() function of this example illustrates the initialization and termination of the AVTL runtime system. The global variable _mem is a memory manager object which allocates and frees vector memory. The default manager provided by the library has type am_mem_mgmt, but others may be added in the future.

2.4.2 Polygon Overlay

The polygon overlay problem is described in Appendix C. Its input consists of two lists of rectangles. The desired output is a list of the rectangular regions in which rectangles from the two lists overlap. This section shows two ways of computing the desired intersections. Both are strictly data-parallel in their formulation and are good examples of the ease with which programs may be written using the AVTL.

Naïve Algorithm   The polygon overlay problem may be implemented by comparing every rectangle in the first list with every rectangle in the second. If two rectangles overlap, then the rectangular region of their overlap is added to the output list. For two lists whose lengths are $O(n)$, a serial program to implement this algorithm requires $O(n^2)$ time. In the data-parallel implementation shown here, we trade time for space. The resulting naïve algorithm executes in $O(1)$ parallel steps, but requires $O(n^2)$ space.

The algorithm accepts the two input lists as vectors of rectangles. The idea behind the parallel algorithm is to create copies of the elements of the two input vectors so that each site of the intermediate vector holds a unique pair (i.e., the intermediate vector is the outer product of the input vectors). The overlap rectangles can then be calculated in a simple element-wise fashion. If two rectangles do not overlap, then

```
#include <stdlib.h>
#include "avtl.h"          // Amelia Vector Template Library

class f_of_x {             // function to integrate
 private :
  double h;
 public:
  f_of_x(double height) : h(height) { }
  double operator()(int i){
    double x = (i + 0.5) * h;
    return (4.0 * h) / (x * x + 1.0);
  }
};

double compute_pi(int n)
{
    double          h = 1.0 / n;
    pvect<int>      i = index(n);
    pvect<double>   rect = elementwise(f_of_x(h),
                                       pvect<double>(), i);
    return add_reduce(rect);
}

int main(int argc, char **argv)
{
    _mem = new am_mem_mgmt(argc, argv); // parallel runtime
    double pi = compute_pi(100000);
    printf("Pi is %f\n", pi);
    delete _mem;                        // terminate runtime
}
```

Program 2.5
Computing π Using the AVTL

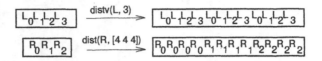

Figure 2.1
Data-parallel Calculation of Outer Product

a NULL rectangle is created. A final step identifies the non-overlapping pairs and removes the NULL rectangles.

The data-parallel idiom for calculating the outer product of two vectors L and R of length l and r, respectively, distributes r copies of vector L, and distributes l copies of the elements of vector R using a segmented distribute. This process is illustrated in Figure 2.1.

The source code for the naïve algorithm appears in Program 2.6. The first two statements implement the outer-product algorithm described above; the first element-wise statement calculates the overlap rectangles, and the second element-wise applies a predicate that determines where NULL rectangles were created. The last statement packs out the NULL rectangles and returns the result.

Execution times for the naïve algorithm on an IBM SP-2 are shown in Table 2.9. Note that the input sizes are relatively small. In fact, this algorithm is unusable for larger input sizes because there is not enough space to create the intermediate vectors. The next algorithm addresses this problem and improves the running time.

The Dart Algorithm The naïve algorithm suffers from the obvious problem that it uses too much space and compares too many pairs of rectangles. The number of comparisons can be limited by taking advantage of the fact that a rectangle can produce no more result rectangles than the area it occupies.

In this improved algorithm, each rectangle in the two lists sprays conceptual "darts" over all of the grid points it occupies. Then, element-wise over the *grid points*, each grid point compares the two darts it receives and determines an overlap rectangle. Rather than requiring $O(n^2)$ space, this algorithm requires space proportional to the grid area covered. When the input rectangles completely cover the grid, this area is $O(n)$.

```
pvect<poly>
overlay(pvect<poly> l, pvect<poly> r)
{
    // Distribute r copies of vector l
    pvect<poly> ll = distv(l, r.len());

    // Distribute l copies of each element in r
    pvect<poly> rr = dist(r, dist(l.len(), r.len()));

    // Calculate overlaps
    pvect<poly> overlap = elementwise(polyOverlay,
                                      pvect<poly>(), ll, rr);

    // Pack the ones that intersect
    pvect<int> flag = elementwise(polyIntersect,
                                  pvect<int>(), ll, rr);
    pvect<poly> result = pack(overlap, flag);

    return result;
}
```

Program 2.6
A Simple Data-Parallel Algorithm for Polygon Overlay

```
pvect<poly> dart_alg(int sizex, int sizey, pvect<poly> l,
                     pvect<poly> r)
{
    // Default vector is size of grid
    pvect<poly> dflt(sizex*sizey, poly(-1, -1, -1, -1));

    // Spray copies of polys over each grid point they occupy
    pvect<poly> gridl = spray_copies(l, dflt);
    pvect<poly> gridr = spray_copies(r, dflt);

    // Compute overlay
    pvect<poly> overlap = elementwise(polyOverlay, pvect<poly>(),
                                      gridl, gridr);

    // Save only those that intersect and that are at LL corner
    pvect<int> isect = elementwise(polyIntersect, pvect<int>(),
                                   gridl, gridr);
    pvect<int> isLL =  elementwise(isLLcorner, pvect<int>(),
                                   overlap, index(sizex*sizey));
    pvect<poly> result = pack(overlap, (isect & isLL));
    return result;
}
```

Program 2.7
Improved Dart Algorithm for Polygon Overlay

The improved algorithm is shown in Program 2.7. The first two statements spray the darts (copies of the rectangles) over the grid points they
occupy. Because the grid must be represented by a one dimensional vector, the indices of the grid are linearized in the obvious way.

The next two statements calculate the overlap rectangles and mark
the NULL rectangles as before. There is one additional problem that must
be addressed: because overlapping rectangles overlap at as many grid
points as they occupy, we must determine a unique output rectangle. For
this, we simply choose the one at the lower-left corner. The predicate
isLLcorner marks such rectangles.

Most of the work of this algorithm is done in spray_copies() (Program 2.8). The idea is to first create a copy of each rectangle for each
grid point that it occupies using a segmented distribute. Next, we calculate a grid point index for each rectangle copy using simple element-wise

```
// Spread copies of polys over area each occupies.
pvect<poly> spray_copies(pvect<poly> v, pvect<poly> grid_dflt)
{
    // Distribute copies of each poly for each grid point it occupies
    pvect<int> area = elementwise(polyArea, pvect<int>(), v);
    pvect<poly> vv = dist(v, area);

    // Enumerate grid points in each rectangle's area
    pvect<int> i = index(area);

    // Compute linearized grid point index of each point in rectangle
    pvect<int> gi = elementwise(local2glob, pvect<int>(), vv, i);

    // Send copy of poly to grid
    pvect<poly> grid = send(vv, grid_dflt, gi);

    return grid;
}
```

Program 2.8
The Spray-Copies Function Used by the Dart Algorithm

arithmetic. After this step, each copy is sent to its destination in the linearized grid using a **send()** statement.

A comparison of the running times of the naïve algorithm and the improved Dart algorithm appear in Table 2.9 and Figure 2.2. The names of the input files are given, as well as the input and output list sizes. These comparisons are limited to small input files because the naïve algorithm runs out of memory. It is clear that the improved algorithm is many orders of magnitude faster, but conclusions about its scalability are difficult to make because the times are too small.

Performance figures for the Dart algorithm with large input files appear in Table 2.10 and Figure 2.3. In addition to the fact that this improved algorithm can handle much larger input files, the running times show that the algorithm scales well with increasing numbers of processors.

This example program shows how a user-written generic function extends to new types. We begin by writing a parallel dense matrix multiplication function using AVTL algorithms. A dense matrix is be represented by a vector of type **pvect<T>**. Next, we define a serial sparse

File1 (size)	File2 (size)	Output Size	Procs	Naïve (sec)	Dart (sec)
map.00 (1049)	map.01 (1048)	(2508)	4	2.87	0.032
			8	1.48	0.023
			16	0.78	0.025
			32	0.46	0.038
map.02 (1055)	map.03 (1056)	(2528)	4	2.92	0.032
			8	1.52	0.023
			16	0.84	0.025
			32	0.52	0.040

Table 2.9
Comparison of Running Times for the Naïve Algorithm and Improved Dart
Algorithm on an IBM SP-2

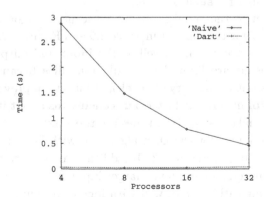

Figure 2.2
Running Times for the Naïve and Improved Dart Algorithms on an IBM SP-2

File1 (size)	File2 (size)	Output Size	Procs	Time (S)
k100.00 (60398)	k100.01 (60374)	(203006)	4	5.69
			8	2.91
			16	1.55
			32	0.85
k100.02 (60301)	k100.03 (60377)	(202498)	4	5.71
			8	2.92
			16	1.59
			32	0.82

Table 2.10
Running Times for Large Input Files Using the Improved Dart Algorithm on an
IBM SP-2

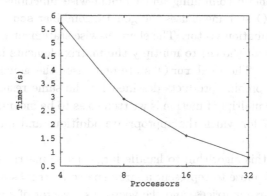

Figure 2.3
Running Times for Large Input Files Using the Dart Algorithm

matrix class, called **sparse**, and define the necessary addition and multiplication operators on this type. Finally, we define a parallel sparse matrix as a **pvect<sparse>**.

Using a segmented representation, a dense vector is stored conveniently as a vector in which each segment contains the elements of a row. To compute the matrix-vector product Ax, the elements of x are distributed down the columns of A, where an intermediate product is calculated. The sum of the products across the rows is the result vector.

With the AVTL, there are a number of methods available for performing the necessary data movement and combining operations. Here, we will use the compiled communication functions for efficiency. (This will be important when we use this sparse matrix class later in an iterative algorithm. The communication schedule is computed once, and re-used many times.)

The basic dense matrix-vector multiplication algorithm is shown in Program 2.9. It is broken into two separate functions. The first builds the communication schedules used in the main body of the multiplication algorithm. The two schedules are **schget**, used to get the elements of the vector, and **schred**, used to compute the row reduction.

The actual numeric computations are performed by **mvmult_run()**. This function completes the three main steps described above. Note the use of generic combining and element-wise functions throughout. The first **run()** statement uses the generic combiner **scd_op()** to overwrite the destination vector. The element-wise statement uses a generic **multiply()** (not shown) to multiply the matrix elements by the copies of the vector. The final **run()** statement uses the generic combiner **add_op()** to combine products destined for the same result row. This matrix-vector multiply function is written so as to be meaningful for any types **A** and **T** for which the appropriate additions and multiplications are defined.

Extending this algorithm to handle large sparse matrices is straightforward. We choose to represent a large sparse matrix as a dense array of smaller sparse matrices, and the vector as a vector of smaller blocks. The declarations below show the interface to the sparse matrix and block vector operations:

```
// global variables to hold the schedules
static am_sched *schget, *schrec;

// Block oriented algorithm assumes length of x is square root of a.
template <class A, class X>
void mvmult_setup(pvect<A> a, pvect<int> seg, pvect<X> x)
{
  int lena = a.len();
  int lenx = x.len();

  pvect<int> r, c;                // row and column index of element

  // Compute row and column of each element in a
  pvect<int> ind = index(lena);
  c = index % scalar<int>(lenx);
  r = index / scalar<int>(lenx);

  schget = get_comp(c, x);    // schedule scatters vector down columns
  schred = send_comp(r, x);   // schedule reduces rows
}

template <class A, class X>
pvect<X> mvmult_run(pvect<A> a, pvect<int> seg, pvect<X> x)
{
  // Step 1: distribute copies of vector for matrix
  pvect<X> copies(lena);
  run(schget, scd_op<X>(), x, copies);

  // Step 2: element-wise multiplication
  pvect<X> product = elementwise(multiply, pvect<int>(),
                                 a, copies);

  // Step 3: send-with-add reduction of rows
  pvect<X> result(lenx, 0);
  run(schred, add_op<X>(), product, result);
  return result;
}
```

Program 2.9
Generic Matrix-Vector Multiplication Algorithm Using Compiled Communication

```
class sparse;              // sparse matrix class
class block;               // block vector class

block operator+(block &a, block &b);
block multiply(sparse &a, block &x);
```

In terms relevant to the AVTL, the elements of the parallel vectors will be large sparse matrices and block vectors. The granularity of computation will be operations on these blocks. For instance, the element-wise multiply will multiply a sparse block by a block vector. The row reductions will add entire block vectors. The AVTL allows the programmer to choose the granularity of the parallel computation, and to express this choice in the framework of abstract data types.

NAS Conjugate Gradient Benchmark   The NAS Conjugate Gradient Benchmark [Bailey *et al.* 1994] is a sparse matrix application whose performance is tabulated for many different computers. Using the sparse matrix data type described above, it is easy to implement a version of the benchmark code based on the AVTL. This section reports on the performance obtained by an AVTL-based implementation and compares it to the best performance figures published.

Such a comparison is challenging because the reference implementation done by IBM occupied a small team of engineers for many months [Alpern 1995]: the AVTL-based implementation was coded in one day, with a few afternoons devoted to performance tuning. The comparison is shown in Table 2.11. Some numbers are missing from the two columns: the AVTL column includes smaller numbers of processors than reported by IBM, and the IBM column includes greater numbers of processors than were available for the AVTL tests.

The implementation using the AVTL is clearly not as fast as the one by IBM, and does not scale as well as the number of processors grows. However, writing the application using the AVTL was fairly easy, and high-level data types were used throughout.

Interestingly, the majority of time spent tuning performance concerned optimizing the **sparse** and **block** classes to increase node performance. Reasonable floating point performance was obtained only after unrolling most of the loops by a factor of four. Another significant performance gain was achieved by splitting a loop computing a reduction into two simultaneous reductions of the even and odd elements of a vec-

Procs	IBM Impl. Time (S)	AVTL Impl. Time (S)
2	—	40.7
4	—	22.3
8	4.91	11.8
16	3.15	10.7
32	2.45	8.6
64	1.81	—

Table 2.11
NAS Conjugate Gradient Class A Benchmark Times on the IBM SP-2

tor. This was required both to keep the functional units of the RS6000 busy and to take advantage of quad-word loads and stores. Each of these optimizations is documented [IBM 1993], but they are time-consuming to perform by hand.

None of the internal code of the AVTL has been optimized in the fashion described above. This is certainly a source of inefficiency in the performance comparisons. The IBM-written benchmark employed these types of hand optimizations throughout. At this time the AVTL does not employ architecture-specific optimizations because they may reduce the portability of the library.

2.5   Related Work

The design of the AVTL was inspired by many related projects. First and foremost, the Standard Template Library (STL) served as a model for the effective use of template classes and functions [Stepanov 1994]. The collection model of the AVTL is essentially that of pC++ [Bodin 1993b], and the base set of parallel algorithms is that of the CVL from CMU [Blelloch *et al.* 1993].

This section compares and contrasts the AVTL to various languages and libraries. When considering other parallel C++ languages we differentiate between data-parallel and distributed object-oriented dialects. The data-parallel languages use classes to define element and collection types in much the same way that the AVTL does. The focus of the distributed object languages is on using member functions as a method of controlling concurrency or the granularity of parallelism. While all of the languages considered are based on C++, their programming models are very different.

2.5.1   CVL

The CVL (C Vector Library) from CMU is a portable library of standard scan-vector functions [Blelloch *et al.* 1993]. The CVL supports vectors of four types (integer, floating point, Boolean, and character) and provides a large set of standard functions on vectors. These include a wide variety of permutation, scan, and segmented scan operations. A fixed set of element-wise operations are also defined. CVL implementations exist for the Thinking Machines CM-5, the Cray Y-MP, the MasPar MP-1, and most parallel machines that support MPI. The library was designed as a compilation target for higher-level languages; it was not designed to be used directly by programmers.

The AVTL attempts to provide the same functionality of the CVL. The main difference between the two is that the AVTL is an *extensible* library: new types may be used as element types. With regard to performance, the achieved performance on comparable machines is nearly the same [Sheffler 1995]. The CVL does currently have the advantage that it runs on more machines, but this limitation is due to the fact that C++ compilers are not available on all parallel machines. This will change as C++ compilers with full template support become available.

2.5.2   Data-Parallel Languages

pC++ (Chapter 13) is a C++-based programming language [Bodin 1993b]. It is implemented through a software translator that converts pC++ source into standard C++. pC++ has proven to be extremely portable, with implementations running on the CM-5, the Paragon, the Sequent Symmetry, the BBN TC2000, the KSR-1, and networks of workstations using PVM. pC++ uses a distributed collection programming model. Element-wise parallelism in collections is specified through special member functions of the collection that have a `MemberOfElement` designation. Similar functionality is provided in the AVTL with the `elementwise()` template function.

One of the main differences between programming with pC++ and programming with the AVTL is the level of parallelism that the two present to the user. With the AVTL, the programmer considers only element-wise and aggregate parallelism. With pC++, the user may also have to consider a third level: the processor level. While exposing this intermediate level may allow for additional optimization by the programmer, it also complicates the programming model. The AVTL hides this view by providing a base set of algorithms that are customized through function objects. The user of the library need never consider node-level code. Since pC++ does not provide a way to customize code, it must expose node-level code to the user when new element types are used with the system.

C** (Chapter 8) is an object-oriented data-parallel language whose basic collection type is the *aggregate*, or multidimensional array [Larus 1993]. The language makes array-based computations easy to express, with support for array slices and stencil computations.

Element-wise operations in C** are indicated through *parallel arguments* to member and friend functions of aggregates. This design decision was influenced by the languages C* [Rose & Steele 1987] and Dataparallel C [Hatcher & Quinn 1991]. The AVTL provides the **element-wise()** template function to do the same thing. The language also provides two types of reductions through modified C assignment operator and return statement syntax. The AVTL avoids introducing new syntax by providing generic algorithms. While the language supports aggregates of any type, it is not clear that it is extensible. For instance, how do the reductions provided by the language extend to new types? And how can a user define new reductions?

2.5.3   Distributed Object-Oriented Languages

A number of parallel programming language research projects have proposed extensions to C++ to support distributed objects. In each of the languages below, the member function is used to define a unit of synchronization. While data-parallel collections may be created in each of these languages, their focus is not primarily the support of a data-parallel programming model. These languages are mentioned here because they make use of the object-oriented features of C++ in a way significantly different from the AVTL.

Mentat (Chapter 10) is a distributed object-oriented parallel programming system designed for distributed-memory parallel computers [Grimshaw 1993]. Mentat supports some data-parallel features (arrays, for example), but its focus is distributed collections of objects. A notable feature of Mentat is that the runtime system manages scheduling and load balancing of tasks.

COOL (Chapter 6) is a concurrent object-oriented language designed for shared-memory multiprocessors [Chandra *et al.* 1994]. COOL addresses the problems of programming shared-memory parallel machines with non-uniform memory access and thus supports instantiating objects on remote processors, and migrating objects when necessary.

ICC++ (Chapter 9) supports the Concurrent Aggregates model described in [Chien & Dally 1990]. The elements of its collections are autonomous agents that each have their own thread of execution. ICC++ allows collections to be acted on as a single entity, but allows collections to have elements of heterogeneous types and supports control parallelism.

CHARM++ (Chapter 5) is another distributed object language [Kalé & Krishnan 1993]. Its message-driven model of computation attempts to hide the latency that slows down many parallel applications. The language has been ported to a large number of both shared- and distributed-memory parallel computers.

UC++ (Chapter 16) introduces concurrency into C++ by extending the object concept to allow the definition of task classes [Wei *et al.* 1993a]. A task object has an associated thread, and inherits functions for synchronizing with other tasks, and for changing its execution state. The target architectures for UC++ programs are generally shared-memory multiprocessors.

2.5.4   Class Libraries

The data-hiding features of C++ have inspired the design of many class libraries for supporting parallel programming. These libraries introduce new data types (such as arrays, or communication schedules) that ease programming parallel machines. The main difference between the AVTL and each of those mentioned below is that none of these addresses the issues of genericity or extensibility.

P++ is a library of parallel array classes and operators written by Dan Quinlan at Los Alamos National Laboratory [Lemke & Quinlan 1993]. It provides much of the functionality of array-oriented languages such as Fortran-90 through a simple class library. P++ is portable to a wide variety of machines including vector multiprocessors such as the Cray

Y-MP and distributed-memory parallel computers such as the CM-5 and networks of workstations.

LPARX is a class library for particle methods and multigrid applications [Fink & Baden 1995]. It provides classes for describing overlapping blocks for domain decompositions. LPARX is a good example of how the object-oriented features of C++ can be used to greatly simplify the programming of difficult, irregular scientific applications.

CHAOS++ is a C++ binding for the CHAOS and Parti primitives which support programming sparse and irregular scientific problems on distributed-memory machines [Sharma et al. 1994]. The applications addressed by CHAOS++ are those in which compile-time communication pattern analysis is insufficient and runtime support is necessary.

2.6   Difficulties and Critique

In addition to the usual difficulties programmers face when programming parallel computers, users of the AVTL have an additional set of problems stemming from the C++ development environment itself. This section briefly touches on problems encountered when compiling and debugging AVTL programs. As C++ matures, many of these problems will be ameliorated, but they will not disappear for a few more years.

2.6.1   Compiler Incompatibilities

C++ is an evolving language. Because of this, the compilers available support slightly different feature sets of the language or differ in their interpretation of the language standard. Unfortunately, the handling of sophisticated template features is especially inconsistent.

The AVTL makes use of template features that sometimes break compilers such as gcc. In contrast, IBM's xlC and Intel's iCC compilers seem to have correctly implemented all of the template features the AVTL exploits. Some of the incompatibilities between compilers are handled in the AVTL source code by #ifdef directives, but clearly, this is not the best solution.

For users, these incompatibilities mean that writing truly portable template-based C++ is nearly impossible. Even worse, when some of these compilers fail, they report only a terse incomprehensible message. It is difficult to discover why one compiler accepts a program that another rejects. This situation should change in the near future as more compiler vendors strive to support the STL.

2.6.2 Debugging

Debugging a template-based program can be especially aggravating if the compiler and debugger do not have integrated support for templates. Some debuggers may not allow the programmer to examine variables local to template functions, while others may not understand template classes. In developing the AVTL, `printf()` (not even `operator<<`!) was the primary debugging tool.

The AVTL attempts to offer some debugging support to its users by performing internal consistency checking on the arguments to AVTL algorithms. This checking in controlled by the `DEBUGLEVEL` compile-time flag. There are four levels of checking. `DEBUGLEVEL=0` turns off all checking: this mode is used when benchmarking programs or executing production runs. `DEBUGLEVEL=1` ensures that the lengths of vectors and segment descriptors are consistent. At `DEBUGLEVEL=2`, the contents of segment descriptors are verified. At `DEBUGLEVEL=3`, many more checks are performed: the contents of permutation vectors are verified to be within bounds, vectors are cleared upon allocation, and further assertions verify the internal consistency of AVTL algorithms. The assertions enabled by the `DEBUGLEVEL` flag can help programmers find errors early in the development cycle.

The memory manager for the library also maintains memory markers at the boundaries of allocated vector memory. If these markers are corrupted, the AVTL reports a memory error. While primitive, this simple facility points out when an errant program corrupts memory.

2.6.3 Compilation Speed

The compile time required by AVTL-based programs can be extremely long, especially at high optimization levels. For example, when compiling the NAS Conjugate Gradient benchmark code presented in Section 2.4.2, compile times of 5 minutes or more for the single main file were common. Currently, most C++ compilers for parallel computers require template definitions to be included in each translation unit in which they are used. The implication of this implementation is that the algorithms of the AVTL are recompiled every time any source file using them is recompiled. Some C++ compilers now have the ability to cache previously-compiled template functions. Such a capability would help reduce the compile time.

2.7   Summary

The AVTL is a template-based collection library for distributed-memory parallel computers. The design of the library stresses the orthogonality of element types, collection types, algorithms, and algebraic combining functions. By carefully differentiating between the roles of each of these the library achieves genericity, efficiency and extensibility to user-defined data types.

The development of quality C++ compilers has been fueled by the PC and workstation markets. Sophisticated template usage is only now beginning to be supported, largely driven by the desire for the acceptance of the STL. This technology can also be beneficially employed by high-performance parallel computer programmers for the encapsulation of generic parallel algorithms. Just as most MPPs are now using commodity microprocessors whose development was driven by the workstation market (IBM SP-2, Cray T3D, Convex Exemplar, Intel Paragon, Thinking Machines CM-5), compiler technology driven by those same large markets should be leveraged to enhance parallel programming productivity.

Acknowledgments

The work of Tom Sheffler while he was a post-doctoral scientist at the Research Institute for Advanced Computer Science (RIACS) was supported by the NAS Systems Division via Contract NAS 2-13721 between NASA and the Universities Space Research Association (USRA). His current affiliation is with Rambus Inc., `sheffler@rambus.com`.

3 CC++

Carl Kesselman

3.1 Introduction

Compositional C++, or CC++, is a general-purpose parallel programming language [Chandy & Kesselman 1992c]. By adding six new keywords to C++, CC++ enables a programmer to express many different types of parallelism. CC++ is designed to be a natural extension to C++, appropriate for parallelizing the range of applications that one would write in C++.

CC++ supports integration of different parallel programming styles in a single application. It was designed to provide efficient execution on a range of parallel computing platforms, including both shared and distributed-memory computers.

3.2 Design Philosophy and Goals of CC++

CC++ is the result of a desire to make research in compositional parallel systems available to a wider range of users than were reached with previous compositional parallel programming systems, such as PCN [Chandy & Taylor 1992]. Briefly stated, a compositional parallel system is one in which all properties of program elements are preserved when those elements execute in parallel. We will discuss compositionality in more detail shortly.

Our previous work in compositional systems was based on designing new programming languages. While starting with a clean slate has its advantages, it throws up a significant barrier to getting many people to use the resulting system, no matter how clean and elegant. Based on this experience, CC++ adds essential elements of compositional programming systems into a widely-used language. C++ was chosen as a starting point because of its widespread use and its support for library construction, code re-use and programming-in-the-large.

3.2.1 Compositionality and CC++

One of the reasons that writing parallel programs is harder than writing sequential programs is that it is difficult to reason about the behavior of a program in terms of the behavior of the pieces from which the program is constructed. A parallel programming system is said to be *compositional* if properties that hold for a part of a program in isolation still hold when that part of the program executes in parallel with any other piece of code.

To achieve compositionality, we must restrict the ways in which one component of a parallel composition can access data in another component. Consequently, parallel programming languages often limit the types of parallel computations that can be expressed. For example, parallel programs written in Mentat (Chapter 10) must follow a dataflow computational model [Böhm *et al.* 1992, Ackerman 1982]: all shared variables must have the single assignment property, and a statement in the language cannot execute until all of its input variables have been given a value. Another example is CHARM (Chapter 5) which implements a message-driven computational model [Agha 1986]. In this model, all operations on data occur locally and atomically.

The advantage of these approaches is that they guarantee compositionality. However, there are drawbacks to enforcing a compositional computational model in the design of a parallel programming language:

- There are many different models for compositional programming. Restricting a program to just one of these can make implementation more complex if the application does not map well into the model provided by the language.

- In some situations, non-compositional algorithms can yield better performance than that of their compositional counterparts.

- The pointer-based memory model of C++ can make it difficult to enforce the compositional model and to support all of C++.

For these reasons, CC++ takes a less strict approach to compositional parallel programming. There are no restrictions on how a variable can be accessed within a parallel operation, meaning that programs written in CC++ can have non-deterministic behavior. Rather than providing compositionality via a specific language-enforced mechanism, CC++ supports a wide range of compositional programming styles though language features and an approach to program design called the *proper interface* approach. The proper interface approach focuses on the properties that an interface between program components must have in order to ensure compositionality. The objective is to specify a software component clearly in terms of standard interfaces with clearly defined inputs and outputs. Features of CC++, such as interleaving semantics, explicit parallel blocks with known termination points, processor object encapsulation and synchronization variables, facilitate the use of this approach.

For the purposes of this discussion, we consider the execution of a program component to consist of a sequence of atomic actions which can read or write variables that are either local to the component or shared between components. We define the interface of an executing program component in terms of the outputs of the component and the outputs of the environment of the component. The form of the outputs—messages, shared-variables, etc.—is not important at this stage.

There are many ways of designing interfaces, but to simplify the design we will define program components and proper interfaces that satisfy the following rules:

Rule 1: An action is one of the following three types:

Inputs: The action reads shared variables as its input and (possibly) reads or modifies local variables.

Outputs: The action modifies shared variables as its output and (possibly) reads or modifies local variables.

Internal: The action does not reference shared variables.

The output actions and internal actions of a program component are non-blocking because they depend only on the state of the component (and are otherwise independent of the state of the system). Input actions can suspend.

Rule 2: If an input action B is executable at some point in a computation, then it remains executable until it is executed. This rule disallows operations such as probes [Martin 1985]. A probe checks whether an input is present and takes some action if it is not; this action can be disabled when an input arrives. Since this rule requires that an executable action remain executable until the action is taken, compositional programs may not contain probes.

This rule also prohibits the execution of a program component from changing an earlier output value; a component can add to its earlier output but it cannot change that earlier output. Thus, we have an ordering relation on the length of outputs and inputs. (In this discussion we assume that outputs and inputs are sequences of values. We can also consider other data structures, such as trees, provided their "length" is defined properly.)

Rule 3: An input to a program component consists of the output of at most one program component. If the output consists of a sequence of values, the input can be some initial sub-sequence of those values. If an input to a component is an output of two or more components, we would have to deal with interference between components writing to the same input. The input to a component may not equal the output from a component because of delays in transmission; hence, we require the input to be an initial subsequence of the output. Note that an output can feed an arbitrary number of inputs, i.e., that the output of a component x can feed the inputs of two components y and z. This is similar to the `tee` split provided in some Unix shells.

We refer the reader to [Chandy & Kesselman 1992a] for more details on the proper compositional approach to parallel programming. [Sivilotti 1994] and [Binau 1993] show how the compositional aspects of CC++ are used to prove properties of parallel programs.

CC++ extends C++   As discussed in Section 3.1, CC++ is a strict superset of C++. Any correct C++ program is also a correct CC++ program. However, this alone does not guarantee that CC++ "feels" like C++. One way we can ensure that CC++ makes sense to a C++ programmer is to apply the design philosophy of C++ to the design of CC++. Paraphrasing [Stroustrup 1991], an important aspect of C++ design is to have the language consist of a set of basic features that can be combined to achieve solutions that would otherwise have required extra, separate features. C++ is designed to support a wide range of different programming styles, without forcing any particular programming style on the user.

Just as in sequential programming, there are many different styles, or paradigms, for parallel programming. Some of the more common of these are data parallelism, task parallelism, object parallelism, and functional parallelism. Finer classifications are possible as well. For example, task parallelism can be built on shared-memory programming primitives (such as locks, monitors and semaphores) or on message passing. In turn, message passing can be point-to-point or channel-based, and be either synchronous or asynchronous.

While it is convenient to speak of task or data-parallel programs, there is no reason to restrict a program to a single programming paradigm. As the range of problems solved on parallel computers increases, we expect it to become desirable to construct *multiparadigm* programs. In their simplest form, these programs would combine task and data parallelism. It has been demonstrated that such a combination can result in performance superior to single-paradigm programs [Foster *et al.* 1994a]. We anticipate more general forms of multiparadigm programs to prove important as well.

Consequently, CC++ does not provide specialized language constructs to implement a specific parallel programming model. Rather, it consists of a small number of parallel constructs that, when combined with C++ constructs, allow us to implement a range of parallel programming paradigms. Given an appropriate set of constructs, specific parallel programming paradigms can be implemented in the language as *paradigm libraries*.

The advantage of this approach is flexibility. Parallel programming paradigms can be specialized for the requirements of specific applications. Furthermore, by combining paradigm libraries, it is straightforward to integrate multiple programming paradigms within a single application. The overall result is that the complexity of parallel program development can be reduced.

3.2.2 Other Design Considerations

A desire to support compositional programming and parallel paradigm libraries, and to be consistent with the design philosophy of C++, all had an impact on the design of CC++. Some of our other concerns were:

Execution environment: CC++ programs should be able to exploit both shared- and distributed-memory parallel computers. The abstractions in CC++ should make it possible to port a program from one parallel architecture to another without recoding. On the other hand, CC++ should also make it possible to exploit the characteristics of particular parallel computers without having to step outside the language.

Ease of learning: CC++ should be easy for C++ programmers to learn. Our goal was to make it possible for a C++ programmer to learn all of CC++ in half an hour. Learning CC++ is simplified by making most of the constructs explainable as generalizations of existing C++ concepts. Furthermore, all CC++ constructs have syntactic analogs in pure C++.

Migration path: CC++ should support migration from existing sequential applications to parallel applications. This means that all of C++ has to be included in CC++, including pointer operations, and static, file-scope, and externally linked variables. It also means that we must provide a way to encapsulate existing code in a parallel environment without change, and to introduce concurrency at arbitrary points in programs. Finally, it means that parallelism must not be tied to any specific language construct, such as an object. Not all C++ programs are written in the object-oriented style—if concurrency is tied to operations such as member function calls, the application must be rewritten in order to make it parallel.

Support for heterogeneity: We anticipate that programs written in C++ will use several parallel programming styles. In addition, we expect parallel systems to be composed of different types of modules running on different types of machines. For example, an application might wish to run its visualization component on a shared-memory workstation while its computing component runs on a multicomputer. The abstractions provided by CC++ should support this.

Safety and efficiency: Finally, it is important to keep one fact in mind: C++ is *not* perfect. The language has many safety features, but it provides users with ways to sidestep them in order to make code more efficient or to simplify an implementation. For example, a pointer to an object can be explicitly cast from a pointer to a base class to a pointer to a derived class, even if the object being pointed to is not an instance of the derived class. Similarly, CC++ allows explicit casting of global pointers (Section 3.3.6) to local pointers.

```
// parallel block
par {
   statement 1 ;
   ...
   statement n ;
}

// parallel loop
parfor (int i=0 ; i<n; i++)
   statement

// spawned function
spawn f(arg1, ..., argn);
```

Program 3.1
Parallel Control Structures in CC++

3.3 Overview of CC++

CC++ adds six keywords to C++: the parallel composition operators **par**, **parfor**, and **spawn**, the synchronization constructs **atomic** and **sync**, and **global**, which controls distribution and locality.

3.3.1 Parallel Composition Operators

CC++ programs are explicitly parallel. Parallel execution is specified by using parallel blocks (**par**), parallel loops (**parfor**), and spawned functions (**spawn**) (Program 3.1).

The parallel execution semantics of CC++ is *fair interleaving*. Consider the parallel block:

```
par {
   statement1 ;
   statement2 ;
   statement3 ;
}
```

Each statement consists of a sequence of basic operations (i.e., assembly language instructions). Under fair interleaving, the operations of any one statement must execute in sequence. However, basic operations of two or more statements can be intermingled. Further, this interleaving must be such that operations from each statement will execute eventually. For example, operations in *statement2* and *statement3* must eventually execute, even if *statement1* is:

```
while (1){
    foo();
}
```

The most basic parallel construct is the parallel block or **par** block. Its syntax is modeled after that of the **try** block, which is part of C++'s exception handling mechanism. The statements in the parallel block execute in parallel, using fair interleaving. The closing brace of the **par** block is a sequence point. This means that the statement after the **par** block does not execute until after all of the statements within the **par** block terminate.

The statements in a parallel block can be any C++ constructs except for variable declarations, **gotos**, or **returns**. Parallel blocks can contain normal compound blocks as well as nested parallel blocks. For example, the following is legal CC++:

```
par {
  {
     a();
     b();
     par {
       c();
       x = 1;
       y = x;
     }
  }
  par {
     g();
     h();
  }
  z = g(x+23);
}
```

There are no special rules on how variables can be accessed within a **par** block; all statements share the same address space. This can obviously cause problems if care is not taken. In particular, the example above suffers from a race condition on the variable **x**. Other CC++ constructs must therefore be used to ensure that **y** has a sensible value.

A parallel block only specifies when statements can execute, not where they execute. In general, the statements in a parallel block, as well as the other parallel control structures in CC++, will execute at the same location. This implies that a new thread of control may have to be created to execute each statement in a **par** block. If the parallel block is running on a shared-memory computer, fair interleaving allows each statement to be executed on a different processor to achieve speedup. On distributed-memory computers, parallel control structures are combined with constructs that control locality to obtain speedups (Section 3.3.6).

Parallel iteration in CC++ is provided by the **parfor** statement. During the execution of a **parfor**, each instance of the loop body is executed in parallel. The initialization, update and test parts of the **parfor** statement are evaluated sequentially, just as in a **for** statement, so that the execution of a **parfor** proceeds as follows:

1. Execute the initialization part of the statement

2. If the test is true, start the parallel execution of the loop body. If it is false, wait for all instances of the loop body to terminate.

3. Execute the update expression, then go to Step 2.

The semantics of the **parfor** statement is a result of the fact that C++ places no limitations on what can appear in the update, test and body of a **for** statement. Consequently, we can write:

```
parfor (list * ptr = head; ptr ; ptr = ptr->next)
  ptr->doit();
```

which iterates over a list and performs the operation **doit()** on each list element in parallel.

A consequence of the parallel execution of the loop body is that the value of the variables used to control the iteration may have changed by the time the loop body corresponding to that iteration has a chance to execute. To resolve this problem, each loop iteration is provided with a local copy of all variables declared in the initialization part of the **parfor** statement. To avoid potential errors caused by changing the value of a loop index with the expectation that the value will propagate to another iteration, these copies are made constant:

```
parfor (int i=0; i<N ; i++){
   doit(i);       // reference local copy of i
   i++;           // compilation error
}
```

Because the other loop constructs in C++ do not allow for local variable declarations, CC++ includes only a parallel for loop.

par and parfor introduce parallelism in a structured manner: the statement after par or parfor does not execute until all of the statements executed by these constructs have terminated. The spawn statement provides an unstructured alternative: it causes the specified function to execute in parallel with the rest of the program and then terminates. Termination of the spawn statement does *not* imply completion of the function being spawned. The statement after a spawn statement executes without regard to the status of the spawned function.

The execution of the spawn statement is similar to that of a regular function call. First, the function expression and argument expressions are evaluated in an arbitrary order. The evaluation of the argument expressions is used to initialize the formal arguments of the function. At this point in the execution of a normal function call, the function body would start to execute. However, in the spawn statement, the next statement in the program starts executing as soon as the arguments to the function are copied. The execution of the function body is interleaved with that of the rest of the program. Any return value from the spawned function is discarded.

The unstructured nature of the spawn statement imposes some additional responsibilities on the programmer. Consider the following example:

```
{
   int x;
   spawn f(x);   // OK, x copied before spawn terminates
   spawn g(&x);  // error: x can go out of scope
}
```

The spawned functions reference a variable that can go out of scope before either function has a chance to execute. This is not a problem in the case of f(x), as the value of x is copied before it goes out of scope. The call to g(&x), however, is dangerous, in that the pointer passed in as an argument does not necessarily refer to x when the function body executes. Note that an analogous problem can exist in a pure C++ when a pointer to a local variable is assigned to a dynamically-allocated data structure.

3.3.2 Synchronization Variables

Consider the following parallel code:

```
int x, y;
par {
  x = 1; y = x + 1;
}
```

Because of the interleaving that occurs in the parallel block, there is no way of knowing what the value of y will be. We therefore need some way to control how the operations in a CC++ program are interleaved. Synchronization, or **sync**, variables are one of two mechanisms provided in CC++ for this purpose, **atomic** functions being the other.

A **sync** variable is a single-assignment variable [Ackerman 1982]: it can be assigned a value at most once, and its value cannot be used until the assignment has taken place. Another way to view this is that a **sync** variable is just like a **const** variable with delayed initialization. Any attempt to use the value of a **sync** variable prior to initialization will cause the reading thread to block until some time after the variable has been initialized. Once the variable has been initialized, it behaves just as if it had been declared **const**. In fact, the syntax for declaring a **sync** variable is identical to that of a **const** variable.

Several examples of **sync** variable declarations are shown in Program 3.2. The first line in this example shows the normal C++ declaration for a constant integer. The declaration of a **sync** variable on the next line is similar. A **sync** variable can exist for any type that can be declared **const**; for example, the third declaration is for a **sync** pointer to an integer. In this case, we can synchronize on the existence of the pointer, but not on the object being pointed to.

The use of a **sync** variable is shown in the function **f()**. Note that the argument to **f()** is a reference to a **sync** integer. Since we are not asking for the value of the **sync** integer, calling the function **f()** will not block. Looking at the function body, the parallel block that it contains allows the statements to execute in any order. However, because of the **sync** declarations, the statement that sets the value of **sync_x** must execute

```
const int x = 23;        // constant integer
sync int sync_x;         // sync integer
int * sync iPtr;         // sync pointer to an integer

void f(sync int & sync_int){
  int y, z;
  par {
    // waits for assignment to sync_int
    y = sync_int + 1;
    // initialize the value of the sync variable
    sync_int = 23;
    // compilation error
    z = sync_x++;
  }
}
```

Program 3.2
Examples of sync Variables

before the statement that uses sync_x. Because the third statement in
the parallel block attempts to update the value of a sync variable, it is
an error.[1] While this particular error can be detected at compile time,
in the general case, such errors cannot be detected until runtime.

3.3.3 A Producer/Consumer Program

With sync variables and parallel blocks, we now have enough CC++
to implement the producer/consumer problem. Our program has two
principal components: a producer that creates a list of values, and a
consumer that uses them. As the producer and consumer run in parallel,
we must ensure that the consumer does not run ahead of the producer.

The top level of this program is shown in Program 3.3. The main()
function simply calls the functions producer() and consumer() in a parallel block. The argument to both of these functions is a sync pointer to
a list<int>. As this variable has not been initialized, the consumer()
function will block immediately. However, because the producer() uses
a reference to a sync pointer to a list<T>, it will execute.

Data is passed between the producer and consumer by building a
linked list. The pointer used to link together the elements of the list is

---

[1]The ++ operator must read before it can write.

```
// The value of the list element and the pointer to the
// next list cell are both sync variables

template <class T>
struct list {
  list(T v) : value(v) {}
  T value;
  list<T> * sync next;
}

template <class T>
void producer(list<T> * sync &);

template <class T>
void consumer(list<T> * sync);

main() {
  list<int> * sync X;
  // Run the producer and consumer in parallel.
  par {
    producer(X);
    consumer(X);
  }
}
```

Program 3.3
Main Program for Producer/Consumer Example

declared to be **sync**. This prevents the consumer from falling off the end
of the list. The implementation of the producer and consumer is found
in Program 3.4. This code is basically unchanged from what one would
expect in a sequential implementation.

3.3.4 Atomic Functions

Sometimes it is necessary to prevent certain interleavings from occurring
within a parallel execution. In CC++, this can be achieved by performing the actions within the body of an **atomic** function. An atomic
function is declared by adding the specifier **atomic** to the function's
declaration:

```
//  This function returns the value being produced
template <class T>
T producer_value();

template <class T>
producer(list<T> * sync & ptr) {
  list<T> * last_element = &ptr;
  while (1) {
    // Allocate and initialize a new list element
    list <T> * tmp = new list<T>(producer_value());
    // Add element to the list, initializing sync pointer
    (*ptr)->next = tmp;
    // Get a pointer to the next field
    ptr = &(tmp->next);
  }
}

template <class T>
consumer(list<T> * sync ptr) {
  // Iterate over the list created by the consumer.
  while (1) {
    consume_value(ptr-> value);
    // This statement will block until the next element exists.
    ptr = ptr->next;
  }
}
```

Program 3.4
Implementation of producer() and consumer()

```
class Queue {
  atomic void insert_into_queue(T);
}
```

Within an instance of a C++ class, only one **atomic** function may execute at a time. Regular C-style functions and static member functions can be declared **atomic** as well, providing atomicity within an instance of a processor object (Section 3.3.6).

The execution of an **atomic** function may be interleaved with the execution of **atomic** functions in other classes, with **atomic** functions in other instances of the same class or with non-atomic functions in the same instance of the class. In addition, an **atomic** function can directly call another **atomic** function within the same object without blocking.

An alternative to **atomic** functions would be to sequentialize access to an object and only allow a one member function at a time to execute within an instance of a class. This approach has the advantage that one does not have to be concerned with the potential interactions between member functions. One reason we choose not to take this approach is that it limits ways in which C++ classes can be used in parallel applications. Consider the following example:

```
class profiled_foo {
    foo_member() { counter++; big_function(); }
    const counter_value() { return counter; }
private:
    int counter;
};
```

In this situation, there is no reason why access to the counter should be restricted while **big_function()** is executing. If we had required sequential access to **profiled_foo**, we could not have written this type of class. Since a user can sequentialize access by making all of the public member functions of a class **atomic**, CC++ does not require sequentialization as part of the language semantics.

3.3.5 Implementing a Blocking Lock

sync variables and **atomic** functions can be combined to implement a parallel programming construct that is not part of CC++: a blocking lock. The lock is implemented as a CC++ class, and used as in:

```
Lock lock;
int i;
par {
    { lock.lock() ; i++; lock.unlock(); }
    { lock.lock() ; i++; lock.unlock(); }
}
```

The implementation of the lock contains a variable that records the lock's state. CC++ **atomic** functions are used to ensure that operations on a lock leave it in a consistent state. Because an attempt to obtain a lock that is already held must suspend, the function that implements the lock request cannot be made **atomic**. Otherwise, it would prevent

```
class Lock {
 private :
  enum lock_state {LOCKED, UNLOCKED};
  lock_state state;
  queue<sync int *> waitingQueue;
  atomic check_lock();
 public :
  void lock();
  atomic void unlock();
  Lock() { state = UNLOCKED; };
}
```

Program 3.5
Interface of CC++ Lock Class

the required unlock operation from taking place, resulting in deadlock.
Therefore, the function implementing the lock request uses an auxiliary
function, which is made **atomic**. The unlock operation, however, must
atomically test the state of the lock and either awaken a blocked thread
or reset the state of the lock to unlocked.

The declaration for this **Lock** class is given in Program 3.5. Its interface declares three functions. The use of the functions **lock()** and
unlock() should be clear. As discussed above, only **unlock()** is declared **atomic**. The class's constructor ensures that locks are always
initially unlocked.

The **private** part of the lock contains its implementation. It first
declares a private enumerated type, which is used to indicate the state
of the lock, and a variable of this type to hold its state. The variable
waitingQueue is a queue of pointers to **sync** integers, implemented using
the queue class from the Standard Template Library. Finally, we declare
that a **Lock** has an **atomic** function called **check_lock()**, which is the
auxiliary atomic function used by **lock()**.

The member functions of **Lock** are given in Program 3.6. The **lock()**
method begins by allocating the **sync** variable **got_lock**. This variable is
used to indicate when the lock is granted to this lock request. Note that
got_lock is allocated on the stack, so that its storage is automatically reclaimed when it goes out of scope at the termination of a **lock()** call. For
this memory allocation strategy to work, we need to ensure that there
are no outstanding references to this variable once the lock is granted—

```
void Lock::lock(){
  sync int got_lock;
  check_lock(&got_lock);
  // check if got_lock is initialized
  got_lock == 1;
}

atomic void Lock::check_lock(sync int * go){
  if (state == LOCKED)
    waitingQueue.push(go);
  else
    *go = locked = LOCKED;
}

atomic Lock::unlock(){
  if (waitingQueue.empty())
    state = UNLOCKED;
  else
    // Grant lock to waiting request
    *waitingQueue.pop() = 1;
}
```

Program 3.6
Implementation of Member Functions of Lock Class.

which is in fact the case in the Lock class. After allocating got_lock, the
atomic function check_lock() is then called with a pointer to got_lock
as its argument. On returning from check_lock(), we examine the
contents of got_lock. This blocks execution until got_lock has been
initialized, which indicates that this call to lock() has been granted the
lock.

The function check_lock() tests to see if the lock is already held. If
so, the pointer to the sync variable is pushed onto the waiting queue and
check_lock() returns. Otherwise, the state of the lock is set to LOCKED,
the sync variable is initialized, and check_lock() returns. Because
check_lock() is an atomic function, CC++ ensures that interleaving
will not change the state of the lock between the time the state is checked
and the time the pointer to got_lock is enqueued.

To release the lock, we must first check the waiting queue to see if any
threads are blocked. If so, we dequeue the pointer to the appropriate

got_lock and initialize it. This allows a blocked lock() call to proceed. If there are no threads waiting for the lock, we simply change the state of the lock to UNLOCKED.

3.3.6   Specifying Location in CC++

So far, all of the CC++ constructs deal with specifying when operations can take place. The remaining CC++ constructs—processor objects and global pointers—are used to specify *where* operations can execute. In addition to providing a mechanism for specifying locality, these constructs address a number of additional design issues, including:

- a means of abstracting processing resources in the programming language;

- a mechanism for separating algorithmic concerns from resource allocation issues;

- a means for describing heterogeneous computation; and

- a mechanism by which existing C++ codes can be properly composed from within a parallel block.

All of these issues are addressed by the CC++ concept of a *processor object*. In C++, a computation consists of a single instance of a program, which is constructed by linking together one or more translation units, or files. In CC++, we generalize the idea of a computation to include multiple instances of more than one program: that is, a computation can have many instances of the same program, or many instances of different programs. We call each instance of a program in a CC++ computation a *processor object*.

A processor object is defined by linking one or more translation units with a *global class* declaration. Associating a class declaration with a program enables CC++ to treat a C++ program as a regular C++ object. A processor object has a type, and can contain member functions, data members, nested class and type definitions, constructors, destructors, and so on. A processor object can by dynamically created with the **new** operator and destroyed with the **delete** operator. Program 3.7 shows that a global class definition looks like a regular class definition, except for the addition of the keyword **global**. As this file defines two different global classes, it in effect declares two different types of programs.

```
// file: global_defs.H
global class ProgramA {
 public :
  f();
}

global class ProgramB {
 public :
  f();
 private :
  g();
};
```

Program 3.7
Examples of Global Class Declarations

As with any class declaration, the global class declaration specifies the data and function members of the class. The translation units, or files that are linked together, can contain the implementation of these members. Processor object definitions are created by the CC++ compiler at link time. For example, consider the global class declarations in Program 3.7 and the source code in the file listed in Program 3.8. Using the current CC++ compiler, we could type:

```
cc++ -o program_a -ptype ProgramA file1.cc++
```

to create a processor object of type `ProgramA`. The implementation of this processor object is placed in the file `program_a`.

By executing a file containing the implementation of a processor object, we can start a CC++ computation. Initially, this computation contains a single processor object whose type is that specified by the `ptype` argument to the compiler. In our example, executing `program_a` would start a CC++ computation that contained one processor object of type `ProgramA`.

The first processor object in a computation is a special case. Once it has been created, the member function

```
int main(int, char**)
```

is run. Only the first processor object in a computation is required to have a `main()` function and the `main()` function is only run in the initial processor object in a computation.

```
//  Contents of file1.cc++
#include "global_defs.H"
int main(int, char **) { ··· }

ProgramA::f() { ··· }
```

Program 3.8
Source Code in file1.cc++

```
//  Contents of file2.cc++
#include "global_defs.H"
class A {};

ProgramB::f() { ··· }
ProgramB::g() { h() }

int x;

h() { ··· }
```

Program 3.9
Source Code in file2.cc++

Let us consider a more complicated example, shown in Program 3.9.
We can create a processor object definition from this file with the compiler command:

```
cc++ -o program_b -ptype ProgramB file2.cc++
```

Unlike the previous example, file2.cc++ contains a class declaration,
A, and a global variable, x. These declarations receive special treatment
when the complete processor object definition is constructed at link-
time. The obvious thing to do is to simply include these declarations
as members of the global class. However, this would make it difficult
to integrate existing code and libraries into a CC++ program. Even if
one had access to all of the variables and classes in a existing program,
requiring a user to manually enter all of the declarations into the global
class declaration would be awkward.

Our solution to this problem is to consider all top-level declarations
in a translation unit to be implicitly included as private members of a
processor object. Thus in Program 3.9, the class A is a private, nested

class in a processor object of type **ProgramB**, while the variable **x** is a private data member of the processor object.

One remaining issue is what to do about objects with external linkage. For example, consider the following class declaration:

```
class C {
  static int data_member;
}
```

Normal C++ semantics say that the name **data_member** refers to the same piece of storage in every instance of class **C**. Extending these semantics to processor objects would result in sharing memory between processor objects, which would be contrary to our desire to use the processor object to specify locality. Accordingly, we modify the linkage rules of C++ to state that externally-linked names are resolved to the same object within an instance of a processor object. However, between instances of a processor object, all global scoped names are treated as if there were internally linked. In other words, there is no sharing of storage between processor objects.

Creating New Processor Objects As we saw above, one way to create a processor object is to execute a file containing the implementation of that processor object. Additional processor objects can be created through the use of the **new** operator.

If we have a global class definition:

```
global class worker {
 public :
  worker();
  worker(int worker_id);
  int do_work();
  int status;
}
```

then the expression:

```
worker * global gPtr = new worker;
```

will create a new processor object of type **worker** and return a pointer to it. (We explain the use of the keyword **global** in Section 3.3.6.) In this example, the default constructor for the processor object will be

```
class worker_ptr {
 public :
  static init_workers(int n) {
     workers = n;
     for (int i=0; i<n; i++) worker_array[i] = new worker;
  }
  worker global * operator->(){
     return worker_array[next_worker = (next_worker+1)%workers];
 private :
  static int next_worker;
  static worker_array[MAX_WORKERS];
};

use_workers() {
  worker_ptr::init_workers(128);
  worker_ptr ptr;
  parfor (int i=0; i<1024; i++)
     ptr->do_it();
}
```

Program 3.10
Using Processor Objects to Achieve Parallelism

called. Note that creating a new processor object does not create a new
thread of control.

As with any other CC++ object, members of a processor object can
be accessed though a pointer to that object. Upon executing the variable
declaration shown above, the statements:

```
wPtr->status++;
wPtr->do_work();
```

will increment the value of status in the newly created **worker** processor
object and call the **do_work()** function.

We can combine C++ library-building constructs with processor objects and parallel control structures to exploit parallelism on distributed-
memory machines. Given the **worker** class above, we want to create
a collection of workers, and then call the **do_work()** function on each
worker in parallel. We would also like to hide the details of processor
objects from the end user. An implementation of this program is found
in Program 3.10.

The parallel computation is performed in the function `use_workers()`. Before we can do any work, we must create the processor objects on which the computation will take place by calling the static member function `worker_ptr::init_worker()`. This function creates processor objects of type `worker` and stores pointers to them in the static private data member `worker_array`. In practice, we will want each processor object to be located on a different physical processor; we show how this can be achieved below.

With the processor objects created, we are ready to perform a parallel computation using the function `use_workers()`. After performing the initialization, this function creates the variable `ptr`, which is of type `worker_ptr`. Within the body of a `parfor` loop, we call the `do_it()` function using `ptr` as a pointer. This expression calls the overloaded `->` operator in `worker_ptr`, which returns a pointer to a processor object. The exact processor object used depends on the number of workers and the number of times the `->` operator has been called. Thus the class `worker_ptr` not only isolates `use_workers()` from the details of processor objects, but also provides a means to separate the mapping of computation onto processor objects from the body of the function as well. Using the global pointer returned by the overloaded `->` call, the function `do_it()` is then called.

Program 3.10 demonstrates a number of interesting aspects of CC++. It shows how "where" constructs (e.g., `global`) can be combined with "when" constructs (e.g., `parfor`) to create a parallel program. It also shows how CC++ constructs can be combined with C++ constructs to encapsulate the mapping of computations to resources. While computation was distributed to processor objects in a round-robin manner in this example, more complex algorithms could be easily encapsulated in the `worker_ptr` class.

Specifying the Placement of a Processor Object As we have seen, processor objects are a convenient abstraction for talking about the distribution of computation in a CC++ program. We now discuss the method by which we can control the mapping of processor object onto physical computing resources.

The C++ `new` operator actually calls a function `new(size_t)`, where `size_t` is an implementation-defined type. Additional arguments can be passed to an overloaded **new** by using the so-called placement syntax. For example, the expression:

```
new (23) T
```

calls the function **new(sizeof(T),23)**. Placement is typically used to force the C++ runtime system to use a particular region of memory when allocating an object.

When the type of the object being allocated is defined by a global class, a function whose signature is **new(proc_t)** is called. **proc_t** is a regular C++ type defined by an implementation of CC++, just like **size_t**. However, whereas **size_t** specifies the size of an object, a **proc_t** specifies the location of an object. If no placement argument is specified, the **new** function creates a new processor object on the same processor on which the expression is being evaluated. Otherwise, the **proc_t** provided via the placement argument is passed as the first argument to the **new** function.

Returning to class **worker**, we can specify that the allocated processor objects be located on node 34 of a parallel computer named **bigboy** with the following code:

```
// Include definition of proc_t
#include <stddef.h>

// Create a proc_t that specifies node 34 on bigboy
proc_t where("bigboy#34");

// Create an instance of worker on a specific node
// Pass an argument of 10 to the constructor
worker * global gPtr = new (where) worker(10);
```

Global Pointers   In Section 3.3.6 we saw that the type of the pointer returned by a processor object allocation had the type specifier **global**. In CC++, a pointer that is used as an interprocessor object reference must have this type specifier in its declaration. We refer to such a pointer as a *global pointer*.

Declarations of global pointers look just like declarations of constant pointers:

```
// global pointer to an int
int * global p1;
```

```
// global pointer to a sync int
sync int * global p1;

// constant global pointer to a pointer to a sync int
sync int * * const global p1;
```

Global pointers give CC++ an explicit two-level locality model: objects are either close and inexpensive to reference, or (potentially) far away and expensive to reference. Note that just because a pointer is global, it does not mean that it will be costly to get to the data it references, just that it may be costly.

We can have a global pointer to any C++ object. There is an implicit conversion from a local pointer to a type to a global pointer to that type. Thus:

```
int x;
int * global iPtr = &x;
```

produces a global pointer to the variable x.

Moving Data Between Processor Objects   The final aspect of CC++ to be explained is how data is moved between processor objects. This happens whenever an operation takes place through a global pointer. For example, the following statements all have to copy data from one processor object to another:

```
class A;
class C {
 // A function with a class as its argument and return value
  C foo(A);
};

A a;
C * global cPtr;
int * global gPtr;
int x;

// copy an integer between processor objects
x = *gPtr;
*gPtr = x;

// Copy instance of classes A and C between processor objects
C retvalue = cPtr->foo(a);
```

Transferring data from one processor object to another is similar to the problem of generating copy constructors for a data type. The solution used to generate copy constructor is to perform member-wise copies, where built-in types are copied bit-wise. This approach generates a sensible copy operation as long as the data type being copied does not contain a pointer.

The CC++ compiler does the same thing to move data between processor objects. To move data between processor objects, the data must first be packed into an architecture neutral format. Conceptually, the packed data does not live on any processor, but rather in a "space" that exists between processor objects; we call this space the *void*. Data transfer consists of inserting data into the void from the source processor object and extracting data out of the void on the destination processor object. To enable this process, the compiler generates a pair of functions: an into-the-void function and an out-of-the-void function. The compiler automatically generates `void` functions by calling the appropriate `void` function on the members of the data structure.

In the situation where this is not the desired behavior, the user can specify a `void` function. For a type `T`, the `void` functions have the following signatures:

```
global void & operator << (global void & v, const T & data);
global void & operator >> (global void & v, T & data);
```

Typically, one must define a pair of void functions in the same circumstances where one has to define a copy constructor and assignment operator.

3.4   Implementing Other Programming Styles

Let us see how CC++ can be used to implement a concurrent object-based parallel programming style used by many other systems described in this book. The code presented here is just a sketch, but it should be sufficient to show how one would go about doing a complete implementation. The paradigm we will consider is one in which member function execute asynchronously and atomically. That is, the function call returns before the execution of the function completes and only one function at a time can execute in an object. Member function calls are synchronized by the use of futures. A future represents a future value of the computation. An attempt to use a future before the value is produced will block the computation that requests the value. A implementation of this programming style can be found in Program 3.11.

The class **future_int** implements a future with an integer value. In a real implementation, this class would be generalized with a template. A **sync** variable is used to signal when the value is available. By overloading the cast operator, we can make the future transparent to any expression that uses it. The key to the implementation of the future is to use the into the void function to pass a global pointer to the future when it is copied between processor objects. Thus when the value is set, by the overloaded assignment operator, we can remotely update the value as well as set the **sync** variable.

The class **async_demo** shows how to build a class that has the required semantics. The public member functions **f()** and **g()** do nothing more than copy their arguments and spawn a new thread to execute internal versions of the functions, **f_internal()** and **g_internal()**, respectively. The internal functions are all **atomic**. This ensures that only one actual member function at a time can execute. If another call is made while an internal function is still executing, then the **spawn** executes, the public function returns, but the execution of the internal function is delayed until the currently executing internal function completes.

3.5 A Programming Example: Polygon Overlay

In this section, we examine the polygon overlay example that has been used in other chapters in this book. Two different parallel implementations will be given. The first is designed specifically for shared-memory parallel computers. From this version, we will create a version of the program that can execute on distributed-memory parallel computers.

We started with an existing implementation of polygon overlay, written in ANSI C. Our approach to producing a parallel program is to make incremental changes, preserving as much of the original program as possible. The first step in this process is to ensure that the existing C code can be parsed as C++. Since the program is ANSI C, and since CC++ is a superset of C++, we were able to compile the sequential polygon overlay code with the CC++ compiler without change. With this done, we can modify the program to introduce parallelism.

```
class future_int {
 public:
  // Use value of future, wait until available
  operator int &() { if (status == 1) return value; }
  // Setting value of future is done remotely
  operator=(int v) { readPtr->set_value(v); }
 private:
  set_value(int) { value = v; status = 1; }
  int value;
  sync int status;
  future_int * global readPtr;
friend global void & operator<<(global void &,
                                const future_int &);
friend global void & operator>>(global void &,
                                const future_int &);
};

global void & operator<<(global void & v, const future_int & f) {
  v << (future_int *global) this;
}

global void & operator>>(global void & v, future_int & f) {
  v >> f.readPtr;
}

class async_demo {
 public:
  f(future_int i) { spawn f_internal(i); }
  g(future_int i) { spawn g_internal(i); }
 private:
  atomic int f_internal(future_int &i);
  atomic int g_internal(future_int &i);
}
```

Program 3.11
Sample Implementation of Asynchronous Method Invocation with Futures

```
// pl and pr point to elements in the left and right map
for (il=0, pl=left->vec; il<left->len; il++, pl++) {
  for (ir=0, pr=right->vec; ir<right->len; ir++, pr++) {
    // polyOverlayLn allocates new list cell when overlap exists
    if ((newLn = polyOverlayLn(pl, pr)) != NULL) {
    newLn->link = outList;
      outList = newLn;
    }
  }
}
```

Program 3.12
Kernel Operations in Polygon Overlay

3.5.1 Shared-Memory Implementation

The main computational kernel of the polygon overlay algorithm is shown in Program 3.12. The doubly nested loop checks every element in the first (left) map against every element in the second (right) map. Overlay regions are stored in a linked list, whose head is pointed to by the variable outList.

An obvious way to construct a parallel version of this application would be to replace the two **for** loops with CC++ **parfor** loops, modifying the body of the inner loop to ensure that concurrent updates to the output list are handled correctly. However, there is a performance problem with this solution that must be considered. Ideally, one would like to use a parallel block or loop structure whenever parallel execution is possible. However, in practice, there is a cost associated with creating a new thread of control on most current computer architectures.[2] Consequently, simply replacing the **for** statements with **parfor** statements will result in an unacceptable level of overhead.

The solution to this problem is to introduce a limited amount of parallelism by adding a single **parfor** loop around the existing sequential loops. The parallel loop slices the first map into a fixed number of sections, where calculations on the sections can execute in parallel. Within a section, the **for** loops compute the overlays sequentially.

---

[2]There are a class of multithreaded computer architectures in which thread creation is inexpensive, however, these computers are not yet widely used

We now turn to the problem of updating the output list. There are two basic methods by which concurrent updates to the output list can be made. One approach is to introduce a list class that supports atomic operations. However, requiring atomic update for every list modification can be costly. Consequently, our approach is to batch updates into a local output list, and then to atomically append the local lists together to form the overall solution. Here is an implementation of the append operation:

```
// Atomically append list l2 to list l1.
atomic atomic_append(PolyLn_p l1, PolyLn_p l2) {
  PolyLn_p end_ptr = l1;
  // Find the end of the first list.
  while(end_ptr->link != NULL) end_ptr = end_ptr->link;
  end_ptr->link = l2;
}
```

Putting everything together, Program 3.13 shows all of the changes required for a shared-memory implementation of the polygon overlay application. The variable **parallelism** controls how many overlay computations will be taking place concurrently. Each iteration of the **parfor** statement creates a local output list which it then appends into the list, **outList** to construct the final solution.

3.5.2   Distributed-Memory Implementation

In the shared-memory implementation of polygon overlay using CC++, we created multiple threads of control in a single processor object. To construct a version of this program that can execute on distributed memory computers, we must create more than one processor object. In the shared-memory polygon overlay program, parallelism is introduced by slicing the first map into sections and processing the sections in parallel. The same approach is used to introduce parallelism in the distributed-memory version as well. However, in the shared-memory code, the sections of the first map are implicitly defined by the **parfor** loop. In the distributed-memory version, the slicing is explicit as each section must be placed into a different processor object.

Notice that using more than one processor object does not prevent us from having more than one thread of control in the processor object. The shared-memory and distributed-memory versions of the polygon overlay

```
// Compute overlay on left map slices in parallel
parfor (n = 0 ; n < parallelism ; n++) {
    // List to store local overlay computation
    PolyLn_p local_outlist = NULL;
    for (il=n, pl=left->vec;
         il<left->len;
         il += parallelism, pl += parallelism) {
      for (ir=0, pr=right->vec; ir<right->len; ir++, pr++) {
        if ((newLn = polyOverlayLn(pl, pr)) != NULL) {
          newLn->link = local_outList;
          local_outList = newLn;
        }
      }
    }
    // Add local overlays to global list
    atomic_append(outList,local_outList);
}
```

Program 3.13
Shared-Memory Kernel for Polygon Overlay Application

code can be easily combined into a single application that exploits both types of parallelism. This would be appropriate for execution environments that support both shared and distributed-memory programming models. Examples include parallel computers with multiprocessor nodes, such as the Intel Paragon, or networks of multiprocessor workstations.

The top level of the distributed polygon overlay code is shown in Program 3.14. To simplify the development of this code, we use components from the standard CC++ library. This library is written completely in CC++ and contains re-usable components that implement a variety of useful parallel programming paradigms and abstractions. The declaration of class **polyoverlay_array** uses the CC++ library to define a *processor object array*, a homogeneous collection of processor objects. Each element of the **polyoverlay_array** contains a reference to an instance of class **polyOver** as well as references to the other elements of the array. Another class defined in the library is the **locations** class, which is just an array of **proc_t** objects. A **locations** object can be used when a processor object array is created to specify where the elements of a processor object array are over nodes of a computer.

```
class polyOver {
 public:
  // Interface to sequential polygon overlay computation
  polyVec_p doOverlay(polyVec_p left,polyVec_p right);
};

// Declare a array of processor objects whose
// elements are of type polyOver
global class polyoverlay_array {
  // Make this class a processor object array
  declare2(pobj_array,polyoverlay_array,polyOver)
 public:
  // Initialize processor object array
  polyobj_array_test(locations locs, const int sz) :
    array_components(locs, sz,this) {}
  polyVec_p doOverlay(polyVec_p, polyVec_p);
};

int main(int argc,char **argv)
{
  polyVec_p leftVec, rightVec;

  int nodes = atoi(argv[1]);
  // Read data from map files
  leftVec = polyVecRdFmt(argv[2]);
  rightVec = polyVecRdFmt(argv[3]);

  // Create processor objects
  polyoverlay_array array(nodes);
  polyVec_t outVec = polyover_array.doOverlay(leftVec, rightVec);

  // This sort could be parallelized as well
  qsort((void *)outVec.vec, outVec.len, sizeof(poly_t), polyCmp);

  // Write out the result
  polyVecWrFmt(argv[4], &resultpolyVec);
  return 0;
}
```

Program 3.14
Top-Level Code for Distributed-Memory Implementation of Polygon Overlay

When the distributed polygon overlay application is started, the number of nodes to use, the file names for the input maps and the output file are passed as arguments. The data from the map files is read and the contents stored into the vectors: leftVec and rightVec. We then create an instance of the processor object array polyoverlay_array, which creates **nodes** processor objects. We call the member function doOverlay(), which returns a polygon vector containing the results. After sorting the results, we can output them to a file.

The member function polyoverlay_array::doOverlay() is responsible for performing the parallel computation. Conceptually, its implementation is quite simple. It iterates in parallel over the elements of the array, calling the function polyOver::doOverlay(). This function returns the overlay of the polygon vectors passed in as arguments as a polygon vector. The first argument to polyOver::doOverlay() contains the slice of the first map to be processed by the processor object, while the second argument contains the entire second map. The calls polyOver::doOverlay() are made through global pointers created by the constructor for the processor object array. Thus into and out-of-the-void functions are used to transfer the polygon vectors between processor objects. While these must be defined as part of the parallel implementation of the parallel polygon overlay code, they are easy to construct as the polygon vector consists of a vector length and a vector of integers.

The implementation polyOver::doOverlay() contains the computational kernel from Program 3.12. As we mentioned previously, we could just as well use the version from Program 3.13, allowing our code to exploit both shared and distributed memory. With the exception of one minor modification, we use the sequential polygon overlay implementation unchanged. The alteration to the basic polygon overlay algorithm improves the performance of polyOver::doOverlay() when processing the first map in slices. The input polygon vectors are sorted by the x coordinate of the left-hand side of the polygons in the vector. Since the first argument to each instantiation of polyOver::doOverlay() only has a slice of the entire map, it does not cover the entire region. If we determine the range of the x values covered by the vector slice of the first map, an initial portion of the second map can immediately be eliminated from consideration in overlap computations. This optimization is implemented by polyOver::doOverlay().

Node	Sequential	2	4	8	16
Time	20.0	23.47	12.34	8.38	6.0
Speedup	1	0.85	1.62	2.38	3.33

Table 3.1
Performance of Polygon Overlay on an IBM SP-2

Performance results from the distributed-memory version of the polygon overlay code are shown in Table 3.1. These runs were made on an IBM SP-2. Each node has 128 Mbyte of memory. The input data were the k100.00 and k100.01 data sets, each containing approximately 60,000 polygons each. Notice that the speedup obtained is far from linear. This is because the parallel version of the program actually does more work than the sequential version. Optimizations that exploit the ordering in the maps to skip comparisons are not as effective in the parallel algorithm as the sequential one.

3.6   Implementing CC++

The current CC++ compiler is implemented as a source-to-source transformation system. CC++ code is parsed and then transformed into C++ code with calls to a specialized CC++ runtime library and calls to Nexus [Foster *et al.* 1994b], a general-purpose runtime system designed to support task-parallel computation. Beyond the obvious reasons of ease of porting and maintenance of the compiler, source-to-source transformation is used because it simplifies application porting to CC++. Many vendor's C++ compilers have differences in the exact C++ semantics they implement. For example, the lifetime of temporary variables varies from compiler to compiler. Source-to-source transformation ensures that the behavior of existing C++ code will be unchanged when passed through the CC++ compiler.

Parsing CC++ poses no particular problem. Since all of the language constructs are syntactically similar to constructs in C++, the modification of a C++ parser to accept CC++ requires a minimal number of changes. To modify an existing recursive descent CC++ parser to accept CC++ required about 400 lines of code to be added to a parser with about 200,000 lines of code.

The target of the CC++ compiler is a runtime system called Nexus. Nexus is not a runtime system for CC++, rather it was designed from the start to provide general mechanisms to support a wide range of task-parallel languages and libraries. Nexus defines five basic abstractions which can all be dynamically created or destroyed. The Nexus abstractions are:

Nodes: A locus of control. A node is a Nexus abstraction that represents a physical processing resource.

Contexts: An address space or virtual processor. Contexts are mapped onto nodes. A context is the container onto which threads of control are mapped.

Threads: Threads of control are mapped into a context. Threads of control can be created locally, via a thread creation routine, or remotely as the result of a remote service request.

Global pointers: Global pointers define a global name for arbitrary memory locations in a context. Global pointers can be passed between contexts like any other data type.

Remote service requests: Remote service requests cause a function to execute in a new thread of control in a context referenced by a global pointer. Remote service requests are asynchronous and one sided.

To simplify the compiler, it also uses a CC++ specific runtime library. This library constructs basic CC++ abstractions out of Nexus primitives. Primitives defined by this library include:

- A `sync` and `atomic` function base class implemented with Nexus thread synchronization functions.

- Processor object creation routines that use Nexus nodes and contexts.

- An untyped CC++ global pointer implemented on top of Nexus global pointers.

The compiler transforms CC++ code into C++ and Nexus calls one declaration at a time. For each declaration, the CC++ compiler makes several passes over the parse tree. Depending on the type of declaration (i.e., class, function or variable), some transformations may not apply.

A very brief summary of the transformations performed by the compiler
is:

- Class-based transformations. If the function has any atomic functions,
  a special atomic virtual base class is added. This class ensures that one
  Nexus lock is shared across all atomic functions called on an instance
  of the class. Access to a class via a global pointer is supported by the
  addition of a number of *entry* functions which provide an interface
  between a Nexus remote service request and a member function call.
  One entry function is added for each member function of the class,
  as well as an entry function to enable remote reading and writing of
  data members. The compiler also adds additional member functions
  to facilitate access to private members from a parallel block.

- Declaration-based transformations. All global pointer declarations are
  converted to be a single generic global pointer type. Primitive `sync`
  types are converted to `sync` types defined in the runtime library. The
  `atomic` keyword is stripped from function declarations and a variable
  whose constructor calls a lock function in the atomic base class is
  added to the beginning of `atomic` function definitions.

- Statement-based transformations. The thread creation interface in
  Nexus requires a pointer to a regular C function. The CC++ compiler
  must extract each statement from a parallel block or loop and encapsulate it as a static member function of a class, or make it a global
  function. In addition, detection of termination of parallel blocks must
  be added using a barrier defined in the CC++ runtime library.

  The other major statement transformation deals with expressions containing global pointers. The compiler transforms these expressions
  into a sequence of Nexus buffer operations and remote service requests. The compiler generates specialized protocols depending on if
  a function call is synchronous or asynchronous, and if the call has a
  return value.

3.7   Limitations of CC++

For the most part, CC++ is able to express a wide range of different
parallel programming styles. However, we have found two types of prob-

lems for which CC++, as currently defined, is not sufficiently expressive. The next version of CC++ will address these issues.

3.7.1 Thread-Local Storage

The first deficiency is that there is no way to associate private memory with a statement that is executing in parallel. An obvious place where this limitation shows up is in the implementation of a POSIX-style threads library in CC++ [Pthreads 1994]. Neither the self-identification route (pthread_self()), nor the routines related to thread local storage, such as pthread_setspecific() and pthread_getspecific() can be implemented in CC++.

A more interesting example of this problem has been demonstrated in the context of the P++ distributed array class library [Lemke & Quinlan 1992]. The main components in the P++ library are arrays and index sets. P++ lets users write array code like:

```
IndexSet I;
A(I) = B(I+1) + C(I-1);
```

One of the components of P++ is a WITH macro that enables one to write conditional expressions over an array:

```
WITH(2*A(I) - B(I) > 0,
  A(I) = B(I+1) + C(I-1)
)
```

A sketch of the implementation of the array class and the WITH macro is shown in Program 3.15.

The problem arises if we want to write code like:

```
IndexSet odd_elements;

array<double> a1,a2;
array<double> a3,a4;
par {
  WITH (a1 > 0,
    a2 = a1 + a2;
  )
  WITH (a3 > 0,
    a4 = a3 + a4;
  )
}
```

```
// an index set identifies a subset of array elements:
class IndexSet;

// The bitvector constructor places a one in each location
// specified by the IndexSet
class bitvector {
  bitvector(IndexSet &)
};

// a simple array class with a single operation
template <class T>
class array<T> {
  static bitvector * mask;
  // only perform operation in locations where mask == 1
  array<T> operator+(array<T> & v1){
    array<T> return_value(v1.size());
    for (int i=0 ; i<v1.size(); i++)
      if (mask && mask[i])
        return_value[i] = *this[i] + v1[i];
  }
}

#define WITH(index, statements)                       \
  mask = new bitvector(index); statements ;           \
  delete mask ;                                        \
  mask = 0;
```

Program 3.15
Simple Implementation of an Array Class with Conditional Execution

Because there is only one mask vector, the parallel block will not execute correctly. Since **operator+** only takes two arguments, we have no way to pass the mask as an additional argument. What is needed here is a way to have a global name, **mask**, reference a different object in each thread.

We have not yet determined the best way to integrate this new storage class into CC++. One way would be to simply introduce a new storage class modifier. For example, we could declare thread-local storage by combining the **static** and **auto** keywords, as in:

```
//  a globally known name
static foo;

//  name known to procedure, storage on stack
p() { auto int block_local; }

//  a globally known name, with a different value in every thread
auto static bar;
```

While this approach may make sense syntactically and semantically, there are potential implementation problems. At the time of thread creation, we will not know what thread-local variables are going to be used. We may therefore find ourselves creating and initializing all thread-local variables declared in a program for every thread.

3.7.2 Thread Priorities

CC++ does not define any means for controlling thread scheduling. In fact, fair interleaving restricts the class of schedules that can be used to implement the CC++ system. The lack of a priority mechanism clearly limits the usefulness of CC++ for real-time systems. However, the lack of control over scheduling parallel operations can also cause problems in parallel programs with no real-time requirements. In particular, there are numerical algorithms that require asynchronous operations to take place remotely. While such computations will proceed correctly regardless of when the operations take place, a delay in starting important operations can reduce the algorithm's performance. What is required in this situation is the ability to specify that certain operations are urgent, and should execute as soon as possible.

Let us consider one approach to controlling the order in which threads execute. We do not wish to alter the execution semantics of CC++ by introducing a notion of strict priority scheduling. However, we can construct a fair schedule that reflects a notion of urgency or importance of some statements over other statements. Urgent statements can execute sooner or with more frequency than non-urgent ones while still preserving a fair interleaving.

Within a program, the relative urgency of a statement can be indicated by a **pragma**. One convenient mechanism would be for a **pragma** to specify the name of a function as well as how important it is for this function to execute quickly. New threads of control created by a **spawn** statement or a global pointer operation use the information provided in the annotation to construct an execution schedule that takes into account the relative urgency of the newly created thread with respect to the rest of the computation. Other means to control thread schedule are being considered as well.

3.8   Summary

In this chapter, we have introduced CC++, a dialect of C++ extended to create a general-purpose parallel programming language. While CC++ only adds six new keywords to C++, it allows a wide range of different parallel programming styles to be expressed. The flexibility of CC++, combined with its small size and ease of learning, make CC++ a practical language for tackling a wide range of problems in both parallel and distributed computing.

Acknowledgments

The Compositional C++ language was designed in collaboration with K. Mani Chandy. We are grateful to John Garnett, Tal Lancaster, and Mei-Hui Su for their contributions to the design and implementation of the CC++ compiler. James Patton assisted in the development of the parallel implementation of the polygon overlay example.

This work was supported by the National Science Foundation's Center for Research in Parallel Computation under contract CCR-8809615, by ARPA under contract DABT63-95-C-0108, and by IBM.

4 CHAOS++

Chialin Chang, Alan Sussman, and Joel Saltz

4.1 Introduction

A large class of applications execute on distributed-memory parallel computers in single-program multiple-data (SPMD) mode in a loosely synchronous manner [Fox *et al.* 1994]. That is, collections of data objects are partitioned among processors, and the program executes a sequence of concurrent computational phases. Each computation phase corresponds to, for instance, a time step in a physical simulation or an iteration in the solution of a system of equations by relaxation. Synchronization is only required at the end of each computation phase. Therefore, once the data for a computation phase (which is typically produced by a preceding computation phase) becomes available, a collective communication phase can be performed by all processors, after which each processor will contain a local copy of the data needed to carry out the computation phase. The computation phase can then be executed completely locally on each processor.

Traditionally, parallel applications utilize multidimensional data arrays, which are often partitioned dynamically during program execution. Optimizations that can be carried out by compilers are thus limited, and runtime analysis is required [Saltz *et al.* 1991]. Good performance has been achieved by applying such runtime techniques to various problems with unstructured data access patterns, such as molecular dynamics for computational chemistry [Hwang *et al.* 1995], particle-in-cell codes for computational aerodynamics [Moon & Saltz 1994], and computational fluid dynamics [Das *et al.* 1994a].

Unfortunately, many existing runtime systems for parallelizing applications with complex data access patterns on distributed-memory parallel machines fail to handle pointers. Pointers are frequently utilized by many applications, including image processing, geographic information systems, and data mining, to synthesize complex composite data types and build dynamic complex data structures. Without proper support for pointers, existing runtime systems only allow the transfer of primitive data types, such as integers and floating point numbers, and of simple objects that contain no references to other objects. Most of these runtime systems also support either distributed arrays, or an unstructured set of named objects, and lack adequate support for pointer-based data structures.

CHAOS++ is a runtime library for object-oriented applications with dynamic communication patterns. It subsumes CHAOS [Das *et al.* 1994b], which was developed to efficiently support applications with irregular patterns of access to distributed arrays. In addition to providing support for distributed arrays through the features of the underlying CHAOS library, CHAOS++ also provides support for distributed pointer-based data structures, and allows flexible and efficient data exchange of complex data objects among processors.

CHAOS++ is motivated by the way pointers are often used in many real applications. In these applications, hierarchies of data types are defined, such that ones at higher levels serve as containers for those at lower levels. Pointers are often used by container objects to point to the objects they contain. Objects that are *solely* contained within a container object are referred to as *sub-objects*. A sub-object is effectively part of its container object, although it does not necessarily occupy memory locations within that of its container object. Objects of data types at the top of the hierarchy (i.e., objects of the outermost container class) can further be connected through pointers, forming complex pointer-based data structures. Such data structures are dynamic: their elements are often created and/or deleted during program execution, and accessed through pointer dereferences. Access patterns to such data structures cannot be determined until runtime, so runtime optimization techniques are required.

As an example, Program 4.1 shows the declaration of a set of C++ classes, which can be used to describe how pixels of an image are clustered into regions, and how regions containing pointers to adjacent regions form a map. The Region class is implemented as a container class for the Pixel class, so that a Pixel is a sub-object of a Region. Since different regions may consist of different numbers of pixels, the Region class uses a pointer to an array of its constituent pixels. A set of regions interconnected with pointers then form a graph, defined by the class Region_Map. Figure 4.1 gives an example of such a graph. When a graph is partitioned among multiple processors, the runtime system must be able to traverse pointers to support remote data accesses.

```
class Pixel {              // a single pixel of an image
  int x, y;                // x,y coordinates
};
class Region {             // a region consisting of pixels
  int    num_pixels;       // number of pixels
  Pixel  *pixels;          // an array of pixels
  int    num_neighbors;    // number of adjacent regions
  Region **neighbors;      // list of pointers to adjacent regions
};
class Region_Map {         // a connected graph consisting of regions
  Region *region;          // a pointer to some Region in the graph
};
```

Program 4.1
Pointer-Based Data Structures Containing Complex Objects

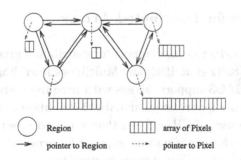

Region   array of Pixels

→ pointer to Region   ····▶ pointer to Pixel

Figure 4.1
A Graph of **Region** Objects

CHAOS++ is implemented as a C++ class library. The design of the library is architecture-independent and assumes no special support from C++ compilers. CHAOS++ currently uses message passing as its transport layer and is implemented on several distributed-memory machines, including the Intel iPSC/860 and Paragon, the Thinking Machines CM-5, and the IBM SP-1 and SP-2. However, the techniques used in the library can also be applied to other environments that provide a standard C++ compiler and a mechanism for global data accesses, including various distributed shared memory architectures [Li & Hudak 1989, Nitzberg & Lo 1991, Singh *et al.* 1993], although this has not been implemented. Throughout this chapter, we assume that there is only one process executing on each processor of the distributed-memory machines. This is simply for ease of presentation, as the techniques described can also be applied to parallel executions with multiple processes running on each processor.

The remainder of this chapter is structured as follows. In Section 4.2, we discuss how CHAOS++ supports complex objects and distributed arrays. In Section 4.3, we discuss how distributed pointer-based data structures are supported in CHAOS++. Section 4.4 describes the implementation of the library. Performance results for the polygon overlay problem and three complete applications are presented in Section 4.5. Section 4.6 discusses some related work, and we present conclusions in Section 4.7.

4.2   Support for Distributed Arrays

CHAOS++ provides runtime support for distributed arrays through use of the CHAOS [Saltz *et al.* 1995] and Multiblock Parti libraries [Sussman *et al.* 1993]. CHAOS supports arrays with irregular distributions, while Multiblock Parti supports regular data distributions. Neither library is visible to the user of CHAOS++; they are used internally to provide efficient, high-performance runtime support for arrays distributed across the processors of a distributed-memory machine.

In problems with irregular patterns of access to distributed arrays, the arrays are frequently partitioned in an irregular manner for performance reasons (e.g., to reduce communication costs or to obtain better load balance). Accesses to off-processor array elements are carried out

```
double x[max_nodes], y[max_nodes];        // data arrays
int ia[max_edges], ib[max_edges];         // indirection arrays

for (int i = 0; i < max_edges; i++)       // a parallel loop
    x[ia[i]] += y[ib[i]];
```

Program 4.2
An Example With an Irregular Loop

by message passing. Furthermore, array elements are accessed through one or more levels of indirection, as shown by the irregular loop in Program 4.2. In this example, the data access pattern is determined by the *indirection arrays* ia and ib, whose values are not known until runtime.

For loosely synchronous applications, the data access pattern of a computation phase is usually known before entering the computation phase and is repeated many times. CHAOS thus carries out optimization through two phases, the *inspector phase* and the *executor phase* [Mirchandaney *et al.* 1988, Saltz *et al.* 1991]. During program execution, the CHAOS inspector routines examine the data references expressed in the indirection arrays, given in global indices, and convert them into host processor numbers and local indices. This is done by a lookup into a *translation table* that CHAOS constructs for irregularly-partitioned arrays. Since the translation table can be large (the same size as the data array), it can be either replicated on all processors, or distributed across the processors. Duplicate irregular references are removed through simple software caching, and unique references are aggregated to reduce communication latency and startup costs. The result of these optimizations is a communication schedule, which is later used by the CHAOS data transportation routines in the executor phase to efficiently collect the data needed for the computation phase. CHAOS also provides primitives to redistribute data arrays efficiently at runtime. Special attention has been devoted towards optimizing the inspector for adaptive applications, where communication patterns are not re-used many times [Sharma *et al.* 1994].

4.2.1 Mobile Objects

CHAOS++ defines an abstract data type, called Mobject, for *mobile objects*. These are objects that may be transferred from one processor to another, so they must know how to marshal and unmarshal themselves. In general, the object model that CHAOS++ supports is one in which an object is owned by one processor, but other processors may possess shadow copies of an object, as will be discussed in Section 4.3.2. This implies that a distributed array of objects is treated by CHAOS++ as multiple objects, so that it can be distributed across multiple processors.

The Mobject class is designed as a base class for all objects that may migrate between processors, and/or will be accessed by processors other than the ones they are currently assigned to. Mobject contains two pure virtual member functions, pack() and unpack(), which CHAOS++ employs to move or copy Mobjects between processors.

An implication of requiring the user to provide pack() and unpack() functions for all Mobjects is that CHAOS++ does not allow distributed arrays of C++ base types (e.g., double, int, etc.), because C++ does not allow a user to define member functions for base types. One way for an application user to implement such a distributed array using CHAOS++ is to define a class derived from Mobject consisting solely of a member with the base type, and then provide the pack() and unpack() functions for that class. In the applications we have investigated so far, this is not a major problem, because all the distributed arrays have been arrays of complex structures.

For objects occupying contiguous memory, the pack() and unpack() functions consist of a simple memory copy between the object data and the message buffer. For a more complex object that contains pointers to sub-objects, the pack() and unpack() provided by the user must support deep copying. pack() can be implemented by deriving the classes for all sub-objects from Mobject, and having the pack() function for an object recursively call the pack() function of each of its sub-objects. On the receiving processor side, the unpack() function must perform the inverse operation (i.e., recursively unpack all the sub-objects, and set their pointer members properly).

4.2.2   Partitioning Data Arrays

The CHAOS runtime support library [Ponnusamy *et al.* 1995, Saltz *et al.* 1995] contains procedures that

- support static and dynamic distributed array partitioning;
- partition loop iterations and indirection arrays;

- remap arrays from one distribution to another; and
- carry out index translation, buffer allocation, and communication schedule generation.

The partitioning of arrays during the data distribution phase can be done with partitioners supplied either by CHAOS or by the application programmer. CHAOS provides several parallel partitioners that use heuristics based on spatial positions, computational load, connectivity, etc. The partitioners return an irregular assignment of array elements to processors. As explained earlier, this is stored in a translation table, which lists the home processor and the local address in the home processor's memory for each element of the irregularly distributed array.

A translation table lookup, which returns the home processor and the offset associated with a global distributed array index, is known as a *dereference request*. Any pre-processing for optimizing communication must perform dereferencing, since it must determine where elements reside.

Several considerations arise during the implementation of translation tables. Depending on the specific parameters of the problem, there is a trade-off involving storage requirements, table lookup latency, and table update costs. Of these, table lookup costs are of primary consideration in adaptive problems, since preprocessing must be repeated frequently, and must be efficient.

The fastest table lookup is achieved by maintaining an identical copy of the translation table in each processor's local memory. This type of translation table is a *replicated translation table*. Clearly, the storage cost for this type of translation table is $O(NP)$, where P is the number of processors and N is the array size. However, the dereference cost in each processor is constant and independent of the number of processors involved in the computation.

Due to memory constraints, it is not always feasible to replicate the translation table on each processor. In these cases, CHAOS++ distributes the translation table between processors. This type of translation table is a *distributed translation table*. Earlier versions of CHAOS could distribute translation tables between processors in a blocked fashion by putting the first N/P elements on the first processor, the second N/P elements on the second processor, etc. When an element A[m] of the distributed array A is accessed, the home processor and local offset are found in the portion of the distributed translation table stored in processor $(m \times P)/N$. The dereference requests may require a communication step, since some portions of the translation table may not reside in the local memory. Table re-organization also requires interprocessor communication since each processor is authorized to modify only a limited portion of the translation table.

As well as replicated and distributed translation tables, CHAOS also supports an intermediate degree of replication with *paged translation tables*. In this scheme, the translation table is divided into pages, which are distributed across processors. Processors that refer to a page frequently receive a copy of the page, so that subsequent references are local. A more detailed description of this scheme is presented in [Das *et al.* 1994b].

For applications with more regular data access patterns, the translation tables employed by the CHAOS library are not required. Instead, *distributed array descriptors* can be generated that contain complete information about the portions of the arrays residing on each processor. For regularly-distributed data, both the data distribution (e.g., block or cyclic) and its associated descriptor can be represented compactly, for example by using regular section descriptors [Havlak & Kennedy 1991]. This form of descriptor is used in the Multiblock Parti library [Agrawal *et al.* 1994, Agrawal *et al.* 1995, Sussman *et al.* 1993], which CHAOS++ uses to partition data and generate communication schedules for regularly distributed arrays.

Multiblock Parti has been designed to support the parallelization of applications that work on multiple structured regular grids, such as those that arise in multiblock and/or multigrid codes. Multiblock Parti produces distributed array descriptors at runtime, and therefore allows the sizes of arrays to be determined at runtime. In contrast, compilers for data-parallel languages such as Fortran-90D [Bozkus *et al.* 1993] and High Performance Fortran [Koelbel *et al.* 1994] produce such descriptors at compile time. In either case, this compact representation allows the descriptors to be replicated across all processors, so that communication schedules can be built without the additional communication required when using a CHAOS distributed translation table.

Multiblock Parti conforms to the inspector/executor model of parallel computation, i.e., builds communication schedules in an inspector phase and performing communication in an executor phase. The library supports two forms of inspectors: one for intra-array communication required because a single array is partitioned across processors, and one for inter-array communication, which handles *regular section moves* between different arrays or different portions of the same distributed array. A regular section move copies a regular section of one distributed array (e.g., as represented by Fortran-90-style triplets) into a regular section of another. This potentially involves changes of offset, stride and index permutation. Intra-array communication is handled by allocation of extra space at the beginning and end of each array dimension on each processor. These extra elements are called *overlap*, or *ghost*, cells [Gerndt 1990]. Both inspectors produce the same form of communication schedule, which can be used by the Multiblock Parti collective data movement routines.

4.2.3 Data Movement

The preprocessing, or inspector, phase of a program parallelized using CHAOS results in a data structure called a *communication schedule* [Das et al. 1992], which stores the send/receive patterns of off-processor elements. The computation, or *executor*, phase uses the schedules to carry out communication. A communication schedule is used to fetch off-processor elements into a local buffer and to scatter these elements back to their home processors after the computational phase is over. Communication schedules determine the number of communication startups and the volume of communication, so it is important to optimize them.

While communication schedules store send/receive patterns, the data transportation procedures in CHAOS actually move data using these schedules. The procedure gather() can be used to fetch a copy of off-processor elements from the processors that own the elements into a local buffer. The procedure scatter() can be used to send off-processor elements from a local buffer to the owners.

For some adaptive applications, particularly those from the particle-in-cell domain, no significance is attached to the placement order of incoming array elements. Such application-specific information can be used to build much cheaper *light-weight* communication schedules. Index translation is not required in inspectors for such applications, and a permutation list need not be generated for the schedule data structure. Besides being faster to construct, light-weight schedules also speed up data movement by eliminating the need for rearranging the order of incoming off-processor elements. Light-weight schedules were used in the parallelization of the Direct Simulation Monte Carlo code discussed in Section 4.5.2.

A set of data movement primitives has been developed to perform irregular communications efficiently using the light-weight communication schedules. While the cost of building light-weight schedules is much less than that of building regular schedules, light-weight schedules and data migration primitives still provide all the CHAOS communication optimizations, such as aggregation and vectorization of messages. Multi-block Parti also has data transportation routines similar to those in CHAOS for performing the communication specified by a schedule produced by either the ghost cell fill or regular section move routines. A more detailed description of the CHAOS procedures can be found in [Saltz *et al.* 1995].

4.2.4   An Example

Program 4.3 shows the transformed code for Program 4.2 that uses CHAOS++ to carry out inspection and execution. The arrays ia and ib contain the globally indexed reference patterns used to access arrays x and y, respectively. Because some referenced data might reside on other processors, non-local values must be transferred to local memory. However, communication between two processors involves a non-trivial startup latency on distributed-memory machines. Vectorizing communication reduces the effect of communication latency and software caching reduces communication volume. To carry out either optimization, it is helpful to have *a priori* knowledge of data access patterns.

In Program 4.2, values in array x are updated using the values in array y. Hence, a processor may access an off-processor array element of y to update an element of x. A processor may also need to update an off-processor array element of x, if loop iteration i is not assigned to the processor owning x[ia[i]]. The two localize() calls in Program 4.3 perform the inspectors for arrays x and y. This computes the schedules both to pre-fetch off-processor data items before executing the loop and to carry out off-processor updates after executing the loop. Hence, the inspector computes:

a gather schedule that can be used to fetch off-processor elements of y; and

```
// create required schedules (Inspector)
localize(dist_of_x, schedule_ia, ia, local_ia, n_local_iterations,
        &off_proc_x);
localize(dist_of_y, schedule_ib, ib, local_ib, n_local_iterations,
        &off_proc_y);
// actual computation and communication (Executor)
zero_out_buffer(&x[begin_buffer_x], off_proc_x);
gather(&y[begin_buffer_y], y, schedule_ib);
for (int i = 0;  i < n_local_edges; i++)
  x[local_ia[i]] = x[local_ia[i]] + y[local_ib[i]];
scatter_add(&x[begin_buffer_x], x, schedule_ia);
```

Program 4.3
Node Code for Simple Irregular Loop

a scatter schedule that can be used to send updated off-processor elements of x.

Copies of the off-processor elements are stored in the on-processor buffer area. The on-processor buffer for off-processor array elements immediately follows the on-processor data for that array in physical memory. For example, the buffer for array y begins at y[begin_buffer_y], and is of size off_proc_y. The value of off_proc_y is returned by the localize() function call. localize() also translates ia and ib to local_ia and local_ib, respectively, so that valid references are generated when the loop is executed. All references to off-processor elements are translated so that they point to the on-processor buffer. The communication schedule returned by localize() is used by the CHAOS gather() operation to fetch the off-processor data and store them in the on-processor buffer. The data are stored so that execution of the loop using local_ia and local_ib accesses the correct data.

CHAOS data movement routines, such as gather(), are collective operations. That is, all processors must participate to complete the operation, but synchronization occurs only through matching sends and receives between processors. No explicit barrier occurs in the CHAOS data movement routines, or needs to be inserted by the application programmer. The CHAOS scatter_add() procedure is a variant of scatter() that adds values from the on-processor buffer into the corresponding off-processor array elements, instead of overwriting them.

4.3   Support for Distributed Pointer-Based Data Structures

In addition to arrays, CHAOS++ is designed to support distributed
pointer-based structures. It is more difficult to support such structures because they usually have more dynamic behavior than arrays.
In this section, we first describe the type of runtime support required
for distributed pointer-based data structures, and then briefly discuss
how CHAOS++ provides the required functionality. The approach that
CHAOS++ takes relies heavily on class inheritance.

4.3.1   Issues in Support for Pointer-Based Data Structures

In pointer-based data structures, elements (objects) may be added to
and removed dynamically. No static global names or indices are associated with the elements, and accesses to those elements are done through
pointer dereferencing. It is therefore not feasible for the runtime system to rely on the existence of global indices. Furthermore, partitioning a pointer-based data structure may assign two elements connected
via pointers to two different processors. This raises the need for *global
pointers*. As supported by such languages as Split-C [Culler *et al.* 1993],
CC++ (Chapter 3), and pC++ (Chapter 13), a global pointer may point
to an object owned by another processor, and effectively consists of a
processor identifier and a local pointer that is only valid on the named
processor.

In CHAOS++, these problems are addressed by introducing an abstract data type, called *globally-addressable objects*, which we now discuss in detail.

4.3.2   Globally-Addressable Objects

One obvious mechanism for managing global pointers is to define a C++
class for global pointers and overload the dereference operator (*), so
that whenever a global pointer is dereferenced, the necessary interprocessor communication is automatically generated. This approach, however, does not allow collective communication, which is an important
technique for achieving high performance in a loosely-synchronous execution model. Furthermore, dereferencing a global pointer requires a
conversion between a reference to a remote object and a reference to a lo-

cal buffer. This imposes additional overhead with *every* dereference of a global pointer. It is more desirable to perform the conversion only when the binding between the global pointer and the local buffer changes.

Instead of defining a class for global pointers, CHAOS++ defines an abstract C++ base class for globally-addressable objects, or Gobjects. A Gobject is an object with ownership assigned to one processor, but with copies allowed to reside on other processors. These copies are referred to as *ghost objects*; each processor other than the one assigned ownership of the Gobject may have a local copy of the Gobject as a ghost object. Figure 4.2 shows a graph which is partitioned between two processors. The dashed circles represent ghost Gobjects. Each Gobject has a member function that determines whether it is the real object, or a ghost. The ghost object caches the contents of its remote counterpart; once the ghost object is filled with data from its real counterpart, the object can be accessed locally. The contents of ghost objects are updated by explicit calls to CHAOS++ data exchange routines. When to update a ghost object from a real object is decided by the application. This description implies that all Gobjects must also be CHAOS++ Mobjects, to support transfer of data between real and ghost objects that are owned by different processors.

In the object model supported by CHAOS++, a pointer-based data structure is viewed as a collection of Gobjects interconnected by pointers. Partitioning a pointer-based data structure thus breaks down the whole data structure into a set of connected components, each of which is surrounded by one or more layers of ghost objects. In the partitioned data structure, pointers between two Gobjects residing on the same processor are directly represented as C++ pointers. Pointers to Gobjects residing on other processors are represented as C++ pointers to local ghost object copies of the remote Gobjects. The outermost layer of ghost objects on a processor can be thought of as the boundary of the distributed data structure assigned to that processor, and are the nodes where a local traversal of the data structure terminates (Figure 4.2(b)).

Since accesses to elements of a pointer-based data structure are done through pointers, the layers of ghost objects surrounding each connected component encapsulate all the possible remote accesses emerging from that connected component. Accesses to remote objects that are more than one "link" away can be satisfied by creating ghost objects for remote objects that are pointed to by local ghost objects, and filled on

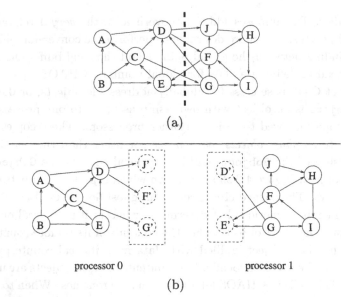

(a)

(b)

processor 0   processor 1

Figure 4.2
Partitioning a Graph Between Two Processors. (a) shows the graph to be
partitioned along the dotted vertical line, and (b) shows the two components as the
result of the partition.

demand. A *mapping structure* is constructed by CHAOS++ for each
distributed pointer-based data structure on each processor, to manage
the ghost objects residing on that processor. The mapping structure
maintains the possible remote accesses from the local processor by creating a list of all the ghost objects. The mapping structure also records
the processor number and the local address of the remote object that
each ghost object represents. The mapping structure is used during the
inspector phase of the parallel execution for translating global references
into processor and local address pairs to generate communication schedules. The CHAOS++ data exchange routines then use the schedules to
transfer data between real `Gobject`s and ghost `Gobject`s in the executor
phase.

4.3.3   Building Distributed Pointer-Based Data Structures

A distributed pointer-based data structure is defined by its nodes and
edges, as well as by how it is partitioned among the processors. Distributed pointer-based data structures are usually built in two steps: all

processors first construct their local connected components, and then compose those components to form the final distributed data structure. In general, there are two possible scenarios: one in which each node in the structure has a globally-unique identifier, and another in which no such identifier exists. In both cases, CHAOS++ provides primitives to assist in the construction of such structures, and to create their corresponding mapping structures.

Nodes with Unique Identifiers In many applications, each node in a pointer-based data structure is associated with a globally-unique identifier. In such cases, nodes can be named by their associated identifiers, the edges can be specified by the identifiers of their two end points, and partitioning information can be described by pairs of processor numbers and node identifiers. One example of this is an unstructured CFD code, in which a node table is used to record all the node information for the graph (including initial values, node identifiers and the assigned processor numbers), and an edge table is used to specify the graph's connectivity. When node identifiers are available, CHAOS++ provides a hash table on each processor that stores, for each node of the local component of the data structure, the node identifier, its local address, and its assigned processor number if known. The table's records are hashed by node identifiers, so accesses through node identifiers are fast.

Program 4.4 demonstrates how the CHAOS++ hash table assists in constructing a distributed data structure. Applications can store information about their distributed pointer-based data structures in any format. For simplicity, the application in this example uses replicated C++ arrays Node_Table and Edge_Table.

Program 4.4 consists of three steps. In the first, the program scans through the node table and registers node information in the hash table. Nodes assigned to the local processor are created and properly initialized in this step. Nodes that are not assigned to the local processor are marked by recording their assigned processor numbers. If a node is known to be remote, but the owner processor is not yet known, the constant CHAOSXX_REMOTE can be used as the owner processor. CHAOS++ uses this information to bind local copies with remote copies, in the final step of the program. Exact knowledge of the owner processors of remote nodes makes that process more efficient, since a single request suffices to locate a remote node. When the owner processor is not known to the

```
class Graph_Node : Gobject { ··· };
// declare a CHAOS++ hash table
chaosxx_hash_table<Graph_Node> htable;
Graph_Node  *node, *from_node, *to_node; // pointers to graph nodes

// assume a replicated node table and edge table
// go through the node table
for (i=0; i<num_nodes; i++){
  if (Node_Table[i].owner_processor == MY_PROC_ID)
    node = new Graph_Node(···);  // create and initialize the node
  else
    node = NULL;
  // register the node with CHAOS++ hash table
  htable.add(Node_Table[i].node_id, node,
             Node_Table[i].owner_processor);
}

// go through the edge table
for (i=0; i<num_edges; i++){
  j = Edge_Table[i].from_node_id;
  k = Edge_Table[i].to_node_id;
  if ((from_node = htable.get_local_pointer(j)) != NULL){
    // an edge from a local node
    if ((to_node = htable.get_pointer(k)) == NULL){
      // a ghost node needs to be created
      to_node = new Graph_Node(···);     // create a ghost node

      // register the node with CHAOS++ hash table
      htable.set_pointer(k, to_node);
    }

    // add a pointer from *from_node to *to_node
    from_node->neighbor[from->number_of_neighbors++] = to_node;
  }
}

// create the mapping structure for CHAOS++
TPMapping<Graph_Node> *map = htable.create_map();
```

Program 4.4
Constructing a Distributed Graph with a CHAOS++ Hash Table

runtime system, locating a remote node may require the local processor to send out multiple requests.

In the second step, the program scans through the edge table and creates the specified pointers. Only edges that originate from a node assigned to the local processor are of interest. The CHAOS++ hash table is used to find the addresses of the end nodes, specified by the node identifiers stored in the edge table. Nodes that are assigned to the local processor are created in the first step, and their addresses can be retrieved from the hash table through their node identifiers. Nodes that are not assigned to the local processor can be created as ghost objects and registered with the hash table upon their first appearances in the edge table. At the end of the second step, each processor has constructed its local component of the distributed data structure, containing both objects assigned to the local processor and ghost objects.

The final step of Program 4.4 constructs an appropriate mapping structure. The mapping structure is of type TPMapping<Graph_Node>, and records the association between ghost objects and real remote objects, using the information stored in the hash table. This is done via a collective communication, in which all processors exchange the node identifiers and the local addresses stored in their CHAOS++ hash tables.

Nodes without Unique Identifiers CHAOS++ provides another interface for applications with nodes that do not have unique identifiers. Since there is no natural way to name the nodes in distributed pointer-based data structures, the connectivity of the data structures in these applications is usually determined from application-dependent information. For example, the initial graph built by the image segmentation problem, which is discussed in Section 4.5.4, is defined by the input image. In this case, the CHAOS++ library assumes that each processor running the target application is able to build its assigned component of the distributed data structure. Furthermore, each processor is assumed to have the information necessary to order its boundary nodes in a way that is consistent with the ordering on the other processors. CHAOS++ primitives can then be used to associate the corresponding boundary nodes, to compose the local components into a global data structure, and generate an appropriate mapping structure.

To be more specific, each processor i provides, for each other processor j, two lists of node pointers, $local_{ij}$ and $ghost_{ij}$. $local_{ij}$ consists of the nodes that are owned by processor i but have ghost objects on processor j, and $ghost_{ij}$ consists of the ghost nodes residing on processor i that correspond to real objects on processor j. To compose the components between two processors correctly, node pointers in the corresponding lists must be listed in the same order. That is, node pointers in $local_{ij}$ must match exactly with the node pointers in $ghost_{ji}$, one-to-one, and those in $ghost_{ij}$ must match with those in $local_{ji}$, one-to-one. As an example, to compose the two components on processor 0 and 1 in Figure 4.2, the processors would construct the following matching boundaries:

$$processor\ 0: \quad local_{01} = \{D, E\} \quad ghost_{01} = \{J', F', G'\}$$
$$processor\ 1: \quad local_{10} = \{J, F, G\} \quad ghost_{10} = \{D', E'\}$$

The ordering of the lists implies that nodes D and E on processor 0 are associated with ghost nodes D' and E', respectively, on processor 1, and that nodes J, F, and G on processor 1 are associated with ghost nodes J', F', and G', respectively, on processor 0.

Given the information for the boundaries between every pair of processors, the CHAOS++ runtime library is able to associate real objects with their corresponding ghost objects (i.e., compute the local addresses on each processor, for later communication), through collective communication, and store that information in the mapping structure.

4.3.4   Data Movement Routines

Data transfer between real and ghost Gobjects is carried out by the CHAOS++ data movement routines. CHAOS++ allows processors either to update ghost objects with data from their corresponding remote objects on other processors (as in a CHAOS gather operation), or to modify the contents of remote objects using the contents of ghost objects (as in a CHAOS scatter operation). The data movement routines use the pack() and unpack() functions of Mobjects to enable deep copying. (Recall that all Gobjects are also Mobjects.) The communication schedules generated from the mapping structure, constructed using either of the two methods discussed in Section 4.3.3, ensure that neither polling nor interrupts are needed at the receiving processors, so that communication can be performed efficiently.

4.3.5 An Example

An example of using the CHAOS++ runtime library is given in Program 4.5. In this example, a parallel computation is applied to a distributed graph consisting of objects defined by a user-defined class, Graph_Node. The user derives class Graph_Node from the CHAOS++ Gobject base class, and provides implementations of the two virtual functions pack() and unpack().

Each Graph_Node object contains a list of pointers to other Graph_Node objects that it interacts with. The member function num_neighbors returns the number of Graph_Node objects a Graph_Node object interacts with, and the member function neighbor(i) returns a pointer to the ith neighboring Graph_Node object.

The program first constructs the distributed graphs, using either of the two methods described in Section 4.3.3, and generates a mapping structure. For simplicity, we assume that each processor is assigned one connected component, pointed to by a Graph_Node pointer root. CHAOS++ then analyzes the mapping structure and builds a communication schedule to allow efficient data transfer between real and ghost objects. The for loop traverses the local component of the distributed graph on each processor to perform computation on the graph nodes. In this example, each Graph_Node object accumulates into its member data1 the values of data2 from its neighboring Graph_Node objects. Remote data accesses are required to perform this computation over a distributed graph.

To achieve good performance, the loop body is broken into a communication phase and a computation phase. During the communication phase, all ghost nodes are filled with data from their remote objects by invoking the CHAOS++ gather() routine with the communication schedule generated before the for loop. The computation phase follows, with every processor traversing its local component of the distributed graph to apply the computation to each of the Graph_Node object it owns. Program 4.5 uses a recursive depth-first search algorithm to traverse the local graph. The local traversal of the graph terminates when encountering either the end of the graph (node == NULL), a ghost object (node->isGhostObject() == TRUE), or a node that has already been visited (node->has_visited() == TRUE). All the computations applied to the local graph nodes are performed locally, since all remote

```
class Graph_Node : public Gobject {
  ...
 public:
  int num_neighbors() const;
  Graph_Node* neighbor(int i);
  int & data1();
  int data2() const;
  void pack(Buffer &);
  void unpack(Buffer &);
};
// build partitioned graph and create appropriate mapping structure
Graph_Node *root = ...;
TPMapping<Graph_Node> *map = ...;
// inspector: build communication schedule from mapping structure
PSchedule<Graph_Node> *sched = map.schedule();
for (int i=0; i < num_iterations; i++){
  // executor: transfer data from remote real objects
  // to local ghost objects with CHAOS++ gather function
  sched->gather();

  // a local graph traversal, starting from the root of the local
  // component, to compute for every Graph_Node object,
  // the sum of data2 of its neighboring Graph_Node objects
  mark_all_nodes_as_not_visited(root);
  local_traversal(root);
  ...     // some other computation that might update the value of data2
}
void local_traversal(Graph_Node *node)
{
  if (node == NULL || node->isGhostObject() ||
      node->been_visited())      return;
  node->mark_visited();
  // computation on node data values
  for (int i=0; i<node->num_neighbors(); i++){
    Graph_Node *next = node->neighbor(i);
    node->data1() += next->data2();
    local_traversal(next);
  }
}
```

Program 4.5
Parallel Computation over a Partitioned Graph

data required by the computation was fetched during the communication phase.

4.4 Implementation

CHAOS++ provides support for efficient data transfer between remote objects and local buffers. This requires the runtime system to be able to translate a global reference into a processor number and a local reference on that processor. This process is referred to as a *dereference*, and is discussed in Section 4.4.1. After dereferencing, communication optimizations are applied to generate a communication schedule, which is later used by the CHAOS++ data transfer routines to carry out interprocessor communication. CHAOS++ communication schedules and data transfer routines will be discussed in Section 4.4.2.

4.4.1 Dereferencing Global References

The purpose of dereference operations is to determine the local address of the object that corresponds to a given global reference. For distributed arrays, the most convenient global references are global indices, which often appear as indirection arrays in programs with irregular array data access patterns. CHAOS++ uses a translation table to record the association between global indices and local addresses. However, since CHAOS++ supports global pointers implicitly through Gobjects, pointers to Gobjects that are actually ghost objects *are* the global references used by an application. CHAOS++ uses its mapping structure to carry out dereference operations for distributed pointer-based data structures.

Translation Tables A translation table stores the information that is required for dereference operations. For a regular array distribution, such as block or cyclic, a simple formula is stored that allows the dereference to be performed by local computation. For an irregular distribution, an entry is created for every element of the distributed array that lists the home processor and the local address in that processor's memory, and a dereference is performed using table lookup. Since the local addresses of array elements are described in terms of offsets from a local base address, rather than by absolute memory addresses, a translation table can be shared by multiple distributed data arrays with the same distribution.

A translation table can be replicated on all the processors, in which case a dereference can be performed locally on each processor. But with an irregular distribution, the translation table has the same size as the distributed array that it describes, so could be quite large. To minimize memory usage, a translation table can be distributed among the processors, in which case interprocessor communication is required for dereference. CHAOS++ also uses the *paged* translation table [Das *et al.* 1994b] described in Section 4.2.2. The advantage of a paged translation table is that each processor is allowed to choose which pages to replicate based on the access patterns to its distributed arrays, so that the communication cost for dereference can be minimized. [Das *et al.* 1994b] discusses the performance behavior of two applications using paged translation tables. Unsurprisingly, performance improves as more of the table entries are cached locally.

4.4.2 Data Movement

CHAOS++ provides efficient and flexible data movement routines to transfer data between remote objects and local buffers.

Communication Schedules A communication schedule for processor p stores the following information:

send list: an array of lists of references, one list per processor, to local objects that must be sent to other processors,

send size: an array that specifies the numbers of objects to be packed into each of the outgoing messages from processor p to other processors,

fetch size: an array that specifies the number of objects to be unpacked from each of the incoming messages to processor p from other processors.

permutation list: an array of references to local buffer space that specifies the placement of incoming off-processor objects,

The CHAOS++ runtime library provides communication schedules for both distributed arrays and pointer-based data structures. Both types of communication schedules have the same structure, with the only difference being the way information is represented in the schedules.

CHAOS++ uses CHAOS communication schedules for distributed arrays [Das *et al.* 1994b], which refer to local objects and buffer space using local indices. The starting addresses of the distributed arrays involved are needed only when the actual data transfer occurs. Due to the abstraction provided by local indices, communication schedules for distributed arrays can be shared by different arrays that have the same distribution and are accessed via the same indirection arrays. CHAOS++ also provides, through the underlying CHAOS library, routines to build *incremental* schedules, which for a given indirection array, only fetch additional objects that have not been brought in by previously built schedules. To minimize message startup overhead, CHAOS++ also provides the capability of merging existing schedules.

In contrast, communication schedules for distributed pointer-based data structures cannot rely on local indices. The schedules must use local pointers to refer to local objects and buffer space, and, as a consequence, they cannot be shared among different data structures, even those with the same distribution of objects. A schedule of this type can be built out of a CHAOS++ mapping structure.

Data Transfer   CHAOS++ data movement routines use the communication schedules described in Section 4.4.2 to perform the required interprocessor communication. All the data transfer routines use the same basic algorithm:

1. For each remote processor that expects data from the local processor, pack local objects specified by the communication schedule into a message.

2. Send the sizes of the outgoing messages to remote processors.

3. Allocate buffers for incoming messages.

4. Send to, and receive from, remote processors messages that contain objects packed in step 1.

5. Unpack all objects from the incoming message buffers.

The data transfer algorithm requires step 2 because it is not always possible to determine in advance the amount of space needed to hold all the packed Mobjects. This may happen, for example, because different

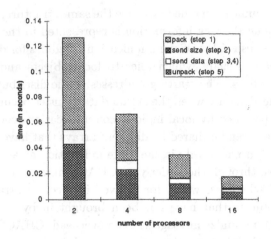

Figure 4.3
Running Time (sec) for Gathering 100,000 Integers on an IBM SP-2

objects of the same data type contain different numbers of sub-objects, and thus require different amounts of storage. If the size of each packed `Mobject` can be determined, and all `Mobject`s involved in the communication are known to have the same size, CHAOS++ replaces step 2 by a local computation to avoid one round of all-to-all interprocessor communication.

Figure 4.3 shows the time required on an IBM SP-2 to gather a total of 100,000 integers on all processors categorized by the steps in the algorithm. As can be seen, most of the time is spent marshalling and unmarshalling objects. This is in part due to the high overhead of dynamic dispatch in C++, which could be reduced by more aggressive C++ compiler optimization.

Although the CHAOS++ data exchange routines can be made quite efficient, additional optimizations are still necessary. For complex data types, objects may become quite large, and simply transporting the entire contents of the object for every communication operation may impose unnecessary overhead. CHAOS++ therefore allows an application to specify what data is to be exchanged during every communication phase. This is done by allowing applications to specify a pair of routines to override the `Mobject`'s `pack()` function in Step 1 and the `Mobject`'s unpack() function in Step 5 of the data transfer algorithm, for each function call to a CHAOS++ data transfer routine (gather or scatter). This enables CHAOS++ to transfer the minimum amount of data necessary to carry out each local computation phase. The pack() and unpack() functions of a Mobject are then only used by default, when no customized routines are provided. Furthermore, by passing different customized functions to the data exchange routine in different communication phases, the same communication schedule can be re-used, and the cost of building the schedule can be amortized.

4.5   Applications and Performance Results

To provide examples of using CHAOS++, and to evaluate the performance of the CHAOS++ library, we will present results for the polygon overlay problem discussed in Appendix C, and also for three complete applications selected from three distinct classes [Chang et al. 1995]: computational aerodynamics (scientific computation), geographic information systems (spatial database processing), and image processing. The performance results for the parallel polygon overlay algorithms were obtained on the SP-2 at the University of Maryland Institute for Advanced Computer Studies (UMIACS), using the IBM mpCC C++ compiler and the MPL communication library. The other experiments were conducted on the Intel iPSC/860 at the National Institutes of Health (NIH), compiled with the GNU C++ compiler (gcc version 2.5.8), and on the IBM SP-1s at both Argonne National Laboratory and the Cornell Theory Center, using mpCC and MPL.

4.5.1   Polygon Overlay

The sequential polygon overlay algorithm presented in Appendix C consists of a nested loop that sweeps through two input maps. Throughout this section, we will refer to the input map that corresponds to the outer loop in the sequential code as the *outer input map*, and the one that corresponds to the inner loop as the *inner input map*. Based on the sequential algorithm, we have implemented two parallel polygon overlay algorithms with the CHAOS++ library. Our basic strategy is to partition the outer input map across the processors so that iterations of the outer loop can be executed in parallel. The two implementations differ in the way the inner input map is handled.

The experiments presented in this section use sorted input maps containing 60,398 and 60,374 polygons respectively; the resulting output map contains 203,006 polygons. The reported running times do not include the time either for sorting the output or for I/O.

In the first algorithm, polygons from the inner input map are fully replicated across all processors. After reading all its assigned polygons into local memory, each processor concurrently executes the sequential overlay algorithm over its assigned polygons. Various optimizations from Appendix C that improve the performance of the sequential algorithm can be applied to this parallel algorithm without modification. Figure 4.4 gives the performance results for this implementation with the outer input map partitioned both block-wise and cyclically. Execution times are labelled according to the optimization used.

As expected, the naïve algorithm shows a linear speedup. The sorted-order optimization reduces the processing time relative to the naïve algorithm by approximately half when using a cyclic distribution, but was far less effective for the block distribution, and actually increased the processing time on 16 processors. This occurred because the sorted-order optimization reduces the workload by telling every outer polygon how early it can terminate the inner loop. This is very effective for polygons located near the beginning of the sorted outer input array, since very few polygons from the sorted inner input array need to be examined before the sorted-order optimization terminates the inner loop. However, for polygons located near the end of the sorted outer input array, the sorted-order optimization does not terminate the inner loop until most of the polygons from the sorted inner input array are examined. With a block distribution of the outer input map, this results in very imbalanced load on the processors, because the processor that is assigned the last part of the outer array cannot terminate the inner loop early to reduce its computation. That processor thus must perform more computation than the others, and becomes the bottleneck. In contrast, the work load is distributed more evenly when a cyclic distribution is used.

The area-tracking and list-deletion optimizations are less effective in the parallel than in the sequential implementation. In particular, the list-deletion optimizations make parallel execution much slower than sequential execution with the same optimization. This is because the area-

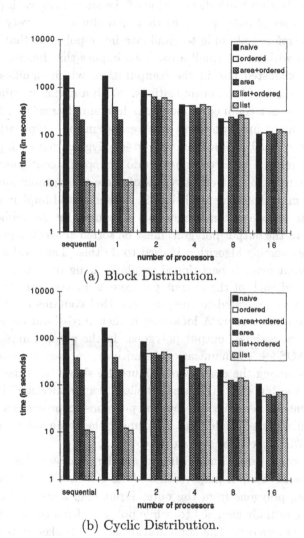

(a) Block Distribution.

(b) Cyclic Distribution.

Figure 4.4
Performance of the Replicated Parallel Implementation

tracking and list-deletion optimizations reduce computation by skipping all inner polygons that have been exhausted by the preceding outer polygons. With a block distribution of the outer map, each processor is assigned a set of outer polygons that spatially spans a very small area, and is therefore only able to eliminate inner polygons that are wholly contained within that small area. This implies that inner polygons can only be exhausted late in the computation, which significantly limits the effectiveness of the optimizations. With a cyclic distribution, each processor is not confined to polygons in a small area, and is therefore able to exhaust inner polygons much earlier in the computation, providing greater benefits. However, the outer polygons that each processor is assigned under a cyclic distribution do not span a contiguous area, significantly reducing the effectiveness of these two optimizations, so that they are much less beneficial than in the sequential implementation.

No interprocessor communication is required in the replicated algorithm until the output polygons must be sorted across the processors. A simple bin sorting algorithm is used to do this. The total area covered by the input maps is partitioned regularly along the x-axis among processors, and each of the output polygons is moved from the processor where it was generated to the processor that contains the x-coordinate of its lower left corner. A local sort is then carried out on each processor over the assigned output polygons. In the parallel implementation, the CHAOS++ communication primitives are used to scatter output polygons among the processors. Figure 4.5 shows the time required to perform the bin sort. The area labelled "communication" includes the time spent for assigning the output polygons to processors, building a communication schedule, and performing the communication, and was about 14% of the total sorting time.

The second parallel algorithm forms the processors into a ring, and partitions both input maps with a block distribution. During program execution, polygons from the outer input map stay on the processors they were initially assigned to, while polygons from the inner map move between processors. The computation is thus broken down into alternating phases of computation and communication. In the computation phase, all processors concurrently execute one of the sequential overlay algorithms. In the communication phase, each processor employs the CHAOS++ data movement routines to pack all the inner polygons it currently holds into a single message, then send the polygons to the next

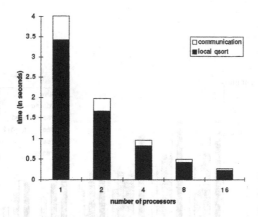

Figure 4.5
Time Spent Performing Bin Sort

processor in the ring. With P processors, exactly P computation phases and $P-1$ communication phases are required to ensure that the entire inner input map is examined by all processors. Since the communication pattern remains the same throughout the entire execution, a schedule is computed once and used for all the communication phases. The same bin sort algorithm described earlier is used for sorting the resulting map.

Figure 4.6 shows the performance of the parallel ring algorithm. The naïve ring algorithm provides the same performance and linear speedup as the naïve replicated algorithm. The sorted-order optimization, which can be applied without any modification to the parallel ring algorithm, suffers from the same load imbalance problem as it does in the replicated algorithm. The area-tracking optimization is implemented by transmitting an auxiliary area vector during each communication phase in addition to the inner input polygon vector. Area-tracking is more effective than in the replicated algorithm, since processors in the ring algorithm are able to skip inner polygons that have been exhausted by preceding processors in the ring. This effectively reduces the computational load, which did not happen with the replicated algorithm.

Figure 4.6 also suggests that the list-deletion optimization provides the greatest performance improvement over the naïve parallel ring algorithm. In the parallel implementation, the linked list that shadows the inner input map is declared as a CHAOS++ Mobject. By using

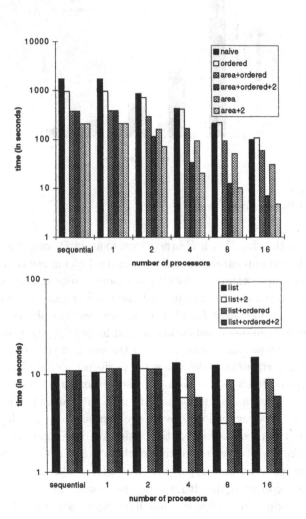

Figure 4.6
Performance of the Ring Parallel Implementation Using Block Distributions

number of processors	simple communication scheme	first communication phase	ping-pong communication scheme
2	393	393	393
4	2394	1026	1710
8	11690	2492	4025
16	50533	5244	8479

Table 4.1
Number of Polygons Sent by Ring Parallel Implementation Using the List-Deletion Optimization Under Two Different Communication Schemes. The inner map contains 60,374 polygons.

a customized `pack()` function, the runtime system is able to traverse the list during each communication phase and transmit only the inner polygons that have not yet been exhausted. This not only reduces the volume of communication, but also greatly reduces the processing time in later computation phases.

The effectiveness of the list-deletion optimization is further amplified by the fact that the two input maps were partitioned using the same distribution function. Partitioning both maps with a block distribution assigns sub-maps that are almost spatially aligned with each other to the same processor, which enables the parallel program to eliminate most of the inner polygons during the first computation phase. The first column of Table 4.1 shows the total number of inner polygons sent over all the communication phases using the simple communication scheme and the list-deletion optimization. The second column shows the number of polygons sent during the very first communication phase for the simple communication scheme. It can be seen that only a few inner polygons survive the first computation phase to be transferred through the processor ring for further processing. For comparison, the naïve algorithm (with no optimizations) transfers the whole inner map (60,374 polygons) during *every* communication phase. The third column in Table 4.1 gives the total number of polygons that need to be communicated by the ring algorithm, when using a different communication scheme that will be described shortly.

Since every processor in the ring parallel algorithm performs multiple scans over its assigned outer input sub-map, it should be useful to also apply the area-tracking and list-deletion optimizations to the outer input map. Applying these optimizations results in a significant performance improvement, as shown by the bars marked with "+2" in Figure 4.6.

However, Figure 4.6 also reveals that the parallel implementation never outperforms the sequential implementation when the list-deletion optimization is applied to the inner input map. Even with the list-deletion optimization applied to both input maps, there is a slowdown when increasing the number of processors from 8 to 16. This is because the simple rotation communication scheme does not take full advantage of the spatial locality between the two input maps. As was described earlier, the two input maps were partitioned with the same block distribution. With that distribution, every outer polygon only overlaps with inner polygons on the same processor, and possibly ones on the neighboring processors in the ring. Therefore, the ring algorithm starts with a partitioning scheme that promotes polygon exhaustion during the very first computation phase. However, the simple communication scheme consistently rotates the inner input map in one direction along the processor ring. This gradually increases the spatial mismatch between the two input maps, thereby preventing early exhaustion of inner map polygons in later computation phases.

This shortcoming can easily be fixed by adopting a *ping-pong* communication scheme. If we view the processors as forming a ring, and do arithmetic mod P, an inner input sub-map that is initially assigned to processor i would visit processor $i + 1$, processor $i - 1$, processor $i + 2$, processor $i - 2$, processor $i + 3$, etc., as illustrated by Figure 4.7. The last column in Table 4.1 shows the total number of polygons transferred over all the communication phases with the ping-pong communication scheme. Compared to the simple communication scheme shown in the first column, many fewer polygons were transferred between processors with the ping-pong communication scheme. Note that the same number of polygons are communicated during the first communication phase under both communication schemes (the second column in the table), since both schemes exhibit the same communication pattern in the first communication phase. The only modification to the parallel program is to generate a new communication schedule for every communication phase. Figure 4.8 shows that a parallel implementation using the ping-pong communication scheme scales quite well up to 16 processors.

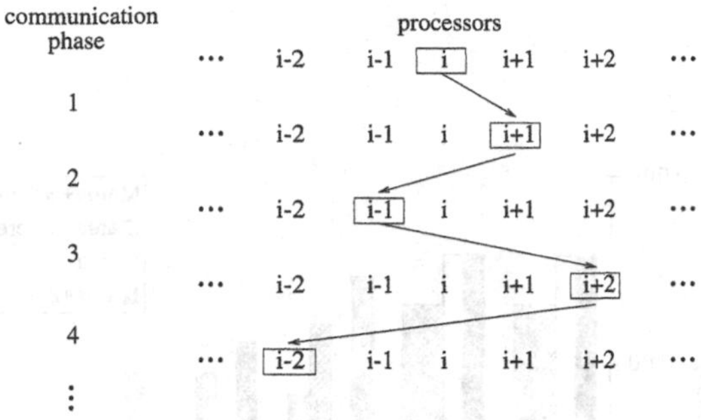

Figure 4.7
Communication Pattern of an Inner Input Sub-Map Initially Assigned to Processor *i*, Using a Ping-Pong Communication Scheme

4.5.2 Scientific Computation: Direct Simulation Monte Carlo Method

The Direct Simulation Monte Carlo (DSMC) method is a technique for computer modeling of a real gas by a large number of simulated particles. It includes movement and collision handling of simulated particles on a spatial flow field domain overlaid by a 3-dimensional Cartesian mesh [Rault & Woronowicz 1993]. Depending upon its current spatial location, each particle is associated with a mesh cell, which typically contains a few particles, and moves from cell to cell as it participates in collisions and various boundary interactions in the simulated physical space. What distinguishes the DSMC method from other Particle-in-Cell (PIC) methods is that the movement and collision processes of particles are completely uncoupled over a time step [Roache 1972].

In the parallel implementation, mesh cells are distributed irregularly among the processors to achieve a good load balance. A CHAOS++ translation table with an entry for each mesh cell is constructed to describe the distribution. Particles, which only interact with other particles in the same mesh cell, are assigned to the owner processors of the mesh cells that the particles reside in. Since particles move between mesh cells, the cells, and thus the particles, are redistributed across the processors occasionally (once every few time steps) to maintain a good load balance.

[Moon & Saltz 1994] describes a parallel implementation of the DSMC application that uses the CHAOS runtime library. Various physical

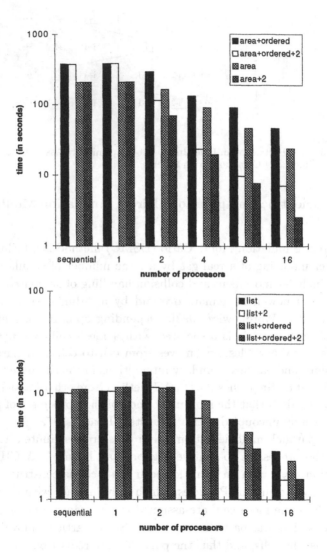

Figure 4.8
Performance Results for Ring Parallel Implementation Using Block Distribution
and Ping-Pong Communication

quantities associated with each particle, such as velocity components, rotational energy and position coordinates, are stored in separate data arrays, and the association between the Cartesian mesh cells and the particles is represented by indirection arrays. As mesh cells are re-distributed, these data arrays are also redistributed accordingly using the CHAOS data transportation primitives. Since the number of mesh cells is relatively small, the translation table for mesh cells is replicated across all the processors so that dereference requests can be resolved locally without any communication. The replicated translation table is modified only when the mesh cells are redistributed.

We have re-implemented the DSMC application using CHAOS++ to maintain the application's distributed data structures. A container class called Cell is defined for the mesh cells. Individual particles are represented as instances of the class Particle. Particle objects are stored in arrays pointed to by a data member in the Cell class, so that Cell serves as a container class, and Particles are sub-objects of Cells. Both classes are derived from the Mobject base class; Cell's pack() and unpack() functions are used to move all the particles associated with a cell, and other data for each cell, between processors.

Figure 4.9 gives the performance for both the C++/CHAOS++ and Fortran/CHAOS codes. The simulated space consists of 9,720 cells, and initially contains about 48,600 particles. 400 time steps are performed, and a chain partitioner [Moon & Saltz 1994] is used to dynamically partition the mesh cells at runtime when load imbalance is detected. The Fortran code has been shown to be a good implementation, and the C++ version takes at most 1.15 times as long as the Fortran code. As the number of processors increases, communication cost becomes a significant factor and accounts for the non-linear speedup of the Fortran code. In the C++ version, invoking the virtual functions pack() and unpack() when moving particles and cells is somewhat expensive, and is the main reason why the C++ version is slower than the Fortran version when small numbers of processors are used. (In such cases, each processor is assigned a large number of particles and cells, and therefore invokes pack() and unpack() many times.) As more processors are employed, fewer cells and particles are assigned to each processor, and so these functions are invoked fewer times. The performance of the C++ code therefore approaches that of the Fortran version.

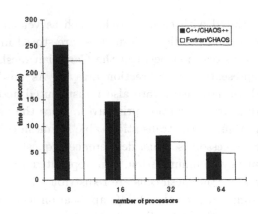

Figure 4.9
Performance of DSMC on Intel iPSC/860

4.5.3 Spatial Database Systems: Vegetation Index Measurement

Vegetation Index Measurement (VIM) is an application that computes a measure of the vegetation on the ground from a set of satellite sensor images. It has been developed as part of the ongoing Grand Challenge project in Land Cover Dynamics at the University of Maryland [Parulekar *et al.* 1994]. The overall project is developing portable, scalable parallel programs for a variety of image and map data processing applications, to be integrated with new methods for parallel I/O of large scale images and maps. The project's main focus is to apply high performance computing to the analysis of remotely sensed imagery. Initial studies are targetted at generating land cover maps of the world's tropical rain forest over the past three decades. The VIM application is an example of such analysis, and exhibits data access patterns that are often observed in these types of applications.

In the VIM application, a user specifies a query region of interest on the ground and a set of satellite images to process. The images may be images of the region taken from the same sensor over a period of time, or images from multiple sensors taken at the same time. The query region is overlaid with a 2-dimensional mesh, whose resolution is likely to be coarser or finer than that of the given images. For each mesh cell, the algorithm selects the set of data points from the given images that intersect the mesh cell, using a C++ class library of spatial operators

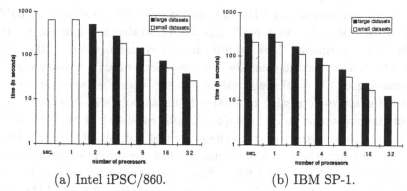

(a) Intel iPSC/860.   (b) IBM SP-1.

Figure 4.10
Execution Time for the Vegetation Index Measurement (VIM)

[Shock *et al.* 1995] currently under development as part of the Grand Challenge project, and computes a vegetation index.

CHAOS++ has been linked to this spatial operator class library to implement a parallel version of VIM. In the parallel version, a satellite image is defined as a vector of column data vectors. Each column is represented by a class derived from `Mobject`, as this allows efficient implementation of the spatial operators provided by the existing class library. For every specified sensor image, the algorithm computes a sub-image that spatially contains the whole query region, and regularly partitions the sub-image across the processors by blocks of columns of data vectors to obtain good load balance.

Routines from the Jovian I/O library [Bennett *et al.* 1994] are then invoked to read the computed sub-image from the disks and distribute the data vectors as specified. Each processor then computes the contribution of its assigned portion of the sub-image to the mesh cells of the query window. The CHAOS++ library is then used to generate the communication required to combine the results across all processors. The communication phase is necessary because each sub-image is distributed to obtain good load balance, and so computing the vegetation index of a single mesh cell may require satellite image data points assigned to different processors. Furthermore, the mesh cells may not be spatially aligned with the input satellite data, and therefore may be distributed differently from the satellite data.

The results of running VIM on both the Intel iPSC/860 and the IBM SP-1 over two different sets of data are illustrated in Figure 4.10. In the first experiment, three satellite images containing 750×100 data points each are used to compute the vegetation index for a query region consisting of 150×20 mesh points. In the second experiment, three satellite images consisting of 1200×150 data points are used to compute the vegetation index for a query region consisting of 240×30 mesh points. The execution times for the sequential code are also given. (Due to insufficient memory, we could not conduct the second experiment on a single node of the iPSC/860.) Since we are mainly concerned with the computation time for characterizing the behavior of the CHAOS++ library, the query regions in both experiments wholly contain all the input satellite images, and the I/O time is not included in these measurements. A detailed description of the I/O performance of the VIM application using the Jovian library is given in [Bennet *et al.* 1995]. The results from Figure 4.10 show that good speedup is obtained.

4.5.4   Image Processing: Image Segmentation

Another application under development is image segmentation. This application segments an image into a hierarchy of components based on the border contrast between adjacent components. Segmentation serves as a pre-processing phase for an appearance-based object recognition system developed at the University of Maryland [Rodríguez 1994]. The hierarchy is used by a high-level vision phase to heuristically combine components from various levels of the hierarchy into possible instances of objects. Further analysis by shape delineation processes select the combinations that correspond to the locally-best instances of objects.

This application first classifies all the pixels in a given image into components, based on some contrast criterion between adjacent pixels given by the user. The algorithm then collapses adjacent components into larger components, based on a series of weaker and weaker criteria on the border contrast between adjacent components. The history of component collapses is kept as a hierarchy of image segmentations for later use.

The initial image is represented in the parallel implementation as an array, which is regularly distributed by blocks of columns of pixels across the processors. On each processor, CHAOS++ routines are used to fetch non-local neighboring pixels into a local buffer, so that the computation

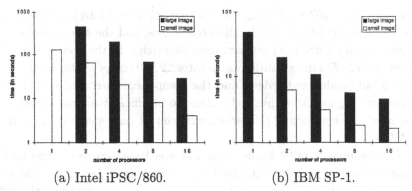

(a) Intel iPSC/860. (b) IBM SP-1.

Figure 4.11
Performance Results for the Image Segmentation Application

for clustering pixels into components can be carried out locally. A component is then created for each identified cluster of pixels. Once formed, the components are stored in a local undirected weighted graph on each processor, with nodes representing components and edges representing component connectivity. The weight associated with each edge represents the border contrast between a pair of components. A C++ class is derived from the CHAOS++ Gobject base class to represent components, which are the graph nodes in the undirected graph.

A C++ component object keeps a list of border objects, each of which contains a pointer to one of the adjacent components, along with other related information. These are the weighted edges in the undirected component graph. After the local component graphs on all the processors are built, they are used to form a distributed graph. A simple scheme is used to merge and assign overlapping components to processors to achieve better load balance. and CHAOS++ routines are invoked to compose local component graphs into a global distributed graph (Section 4.3.3). The CHAOS++ mapping structure is then constructed on each processor for the distributed graph, and used to generate a communication schedule. The communication schedule is used for efficient exchange of component data between real Gobjects and ghost Gobjects when performing graph contraction. As the graph changes during program execution, CHAOS++ primitives are invoked repeatedly to modify the mapping structure, and generate new communication schedules.

Figure 4.11 shows the performance of segmenting two different images on both the Intel iPSC/860 and the IBM SP-1. In the first experiment, the pixels of a 400×400 image are initially clustered into 7,935 components, connected by 17,816 (undirected) edges, and the components are used to build a five-level segmentation hierarchy. In the second experiment, a 512×513 image initially generates 22,100 components, connected by 49,549 (undirected) edges, and the components are used to build a nine-level segmentation hierarchy. Due to insufficient memory, there is no result for conducting the second experiment on a single node of the iPSC/860.

Our original parallel implementation was based on sequential code that has not been highly optimized. On a single iPSC/860 node, the sequential code takes 1.3 times as long as the parallel code on the 400×400 image. The parallel implementation was further optimized by changing one of the key data structures, thus eliminating the bottleneck that plagued both the sequential and parallel implementations. The performance results given in Figure 4.11 come from this optimized parallel implementation. Although the same optimization could also be applied to the sequential implementation, that was never implemented by our application collaborators. We therefore only present the execution times for the optimized parallel code.

In the current implementation, newly-formed components are allocated dynamically and inserted into the component graph. On the iPSC/860, however, allocating memory dynamically turns out to be a very expensive operation, and is responsible for almost 80% of the total running time of the application. That is the main reason why the SP-1 greatly outperforms the iPSC/860 in both experiments, especially when the number of components generated from the image is large. The cost of dynamic memory allocation on the iPSC/860 is also non-linear, meaning that as more components are allocated, the longer it takes on average to allocate one component. Since using more processors causes each processor to allocate fewer nodes in the component graph, the superlinear speed-ups shown in Figure 4.11 for the iPSC/860 are not surprising.

On the SP-1, since the data sets are relatively small, communication cost becomes a factor as the number of processors increases and the amount of work assigned to each processor decreases, and accounts for the non-linear speedup. One other significant feature of the current implementation of the segmentation algorithm is that no remapping of the distributed component graph is performed, once it is formed. Currently the input image is initially partitioned, and that partition decides how the components are distributed among processors. This results in a rather unbalanced work load among the processors, and also contributes to the non-linear speedups as the number of processors increases.

4.6 Related Work

Below, we briefly discuss other systems from the area of concurrent object-oriented programming, as well as related work on support for distributed pointer-based data structures.

Roughly speaking, there are two types of systems are relevant to our work. The first type of system augments an existing language with parallel constructs. Parallelism is exploited by both a compiler and an associated runtime system. Examples of this type of system, based on C++, include Mentat (Chapter 10), CC++ (Chapter 3), ICC++ (Chapter 9), C** (Chapter 8), CHARM (Chapter 5), and pC++ (Chapter 13). Mentat, CC++, and CHARM consider program execution as completely unstructured interactions among a set of objects, and support only asynchronous communication. This approach suffers from overhead incurred from either polling or interrupts. ICC++, pC++, and C** provide array-based collections of objects, and parallel constructs to operate on them. However, the runtime system of C** assumes a shared-memory or distributed shared-memory architecture, and data fetch is performed by page faulting through the underlying memory consistency protocol. ICC++ and pC++ are able to run on distributed memory architectures, but still rely solely on asynchronous communication. CHAOS++, in contrast, is a user-level class library, and does not assume any language or compiler support. After analyzing and optimizing communication patterns, CHAOS++ generates communication schedules to enable collective communication, which ensures that neither polling nor interrupts are needed at the receiving processors. Communication can thus be performed efficiently for loosely synchronous applications.

The second type of system is a user-level class library that assumes no special support from the compiler, just like CHAOS++. Examples include P++ [Parsons & Quinlan 1993] and LPARX [Kohn & Baden 1994]. These libraries both provide efficient management of array-based parallel constructs distributed across processors. CHAOS++, however, performs optimization through preprocessing techniques, and provides efficient support for dynamic distributed data structures, including pointer-based data structures.

Some recent work focuses on support for distributed pointer-based data structures. [Gupta 1992] suggests an approach that assigns to every element of a distributed pointer-based data structure a name known to all processors. The name is based on the position of the element in the data structure, which is registered with all processors as the element is inserted into the data structure. This naming convention restricts the way the data structure can be used. For example, new elements can only be added to the data structure one at a time, not in parallel. This is a serious restriction for efficient parallel implementations, because it could require many expensive synchronization operations.

[Carroll & Pollock 1994] proposes a composite tree model, which describes a data-parallel computation as a tree structure. The computation starts at the root of the structure, and invokes methods from its child nodes (usually in parallel). The child nodes, in turn, recursively invoke methods from their children. Parent nodes then wait for their children to complete, and combine the results returned by their children nodes to form their results. However, it is not clear how accesses through pointers of an element of a distributed pointer-based data structure can be implemented under the composite tree model, other than with fine-grain blocking sends and receives.

Olden [Rogers *et al.* 1995] is a C-based system that supports recursively defined pointer-based data structures. In Olden, an application allocates nodes of its pointer-based data structures on the heaps of different processors, and the runtime system migrates threads of computation to processors that own the heap-allocated nodes being processed. Parallelism is exploited through concurrent execution of migrating threads and their continuations. A major difference between Olden and CHAOS++ is the way work is allocated. In Olden, work follows the data, while in CHAOS++, the required data is copied so that computation can be carried out locally.

4.7   Critique and Conclusions

We have presented a portable object-oriented runtime library that supports SPMD execution of adaptive irregular applications that contain dynamic distributed data structures. In particular, CHAOS++ supports distributed pointer-based data structures, in addition to distributed arrays, consisting of arbitrarily complex data types. CHAOS++ translates global object references into local references, generates communication schedules, and carries out efficient data exchange. The library assumes no special compiler support, and does not rely on any architecture-dependent parallel system features, other than an underlying message-passing system. Integration with the CHAOS runtime library, for array-based adaptive irregular applications has already been accomplished, and integration with the Multiblock Parti runtime library, for array-based structured grid applications, is currently in progress.

We are currently working to create a more robust version of the CHAOS++ runtime library, so that it can be more effectively used by application developers. One of the major difficulties in using the current version of the library is the complexity of the user interface. A user is asked to derive classes from the Mobject base class, and provide implementations for the pack and unpack functions to support deep copies. Some of this could be automated by a compiler, perhaps with the help of annotations provided by the user. On the other hand, building a distributed graph requires some understanding of the way the runtime library works, and extra work from the user (for example, laying out the Gobjects on the boundaries of the subgraph owned by a processor in a consistent order, as described in Section 4.3.3). At this point in time, we have yet to find a more general interface for building distributed graphs. Furthermore, CHAOS++ relies heavily on C++ virtual function invocations, which are usually somewhat more expensive than normal function calls. Compiler analysis and optimization that reduces the cost of virtual function invocations could significantly improve the performance of the CHAOS++ runtime library.

CHAOS++ is targeted as a prototype library that will be used to provide part of the runtime support needed for High Performance Fortran and High Performance C/C++ compilers. We are also in the process of integrating CHAOS++ into the runtime software being developed by the Parallel Compiler Runtime Consortium. The goal of this consortium is to provide common runtime support for compilers of data parallel languages, through specification of interfaces for data structures and for routines for deriving and optimizing data movement among processors. Runtime support, such as that provided by CHAOS++, could then be used by any compiler that understands these interfaces, allowing the use of multiple runtime support packages (e.g., for coping with different array distributions) by a single compiler.

Acknowledgments

This research was supported by the National Science Foundation under Grant #ASC 9318183, NASA under Grant #NAG 11485 (ARPA Project #8874), and the Office of Naval Research under Grant #N00014-93-1-0158 (Rice University Subcontract #292122193).

The authors would like to thank Richard Wilmoth at NASA Langley and Bongki Moon at Maryland for the use of their sequential and parallel DSMC codes, Carter T. Shock at UMIACS and Samuel Goward in the Department of Geography at Maryland for their help on the VIM application, and Larry Davis and Claudia Rodríguez at the University of Maryland for many discussions on the image segmentation problem and the use of their sequential code.

The authors are also grateful to the National Institutes of Health for providing access to their iPSC/860, and the Cornell Theory Center and Argonne National Laboratory for providing access to their SP-1s.

5 CHARM++

Laxmikant V. Kalé and Sanjeev Krishnan

CHARM++ is a parallel object-oriented language based on C++. It was developed over the past few years at the Parallel Programming Laboratory, University of Illinois, to enable the application of object orientation to the problems of parallel programming. Its innovative features include message-driven execution for latency tolerance and modularity, dynamic creation and load balancing of concurrent objects, branched objects which are groups of objects with one representative on every processor, and multiple specific information-sharing abstractions. This chapter describes its design philosophy, essential features, syntax, implementation, and applications.

5.1 Design Philosophy

CHARM++ aims to reduce the complexity of parallel program development by addressing the following issues:

Portability: Portable programs are ones which can run unchanged on different machines, while maintaining performance close to native implementations. Portability is necessary for applications that need to run on multiple platforms and for protecting the investment in parallel software when the underlying parallel machine is upgraded or changed. While portability is an accepted idea now, having been achieved to some extent in several systems, achieving portability without performance loss was a novel objective when the early version of the CHARM parallel programming system was designed in 1987 [Kalé & Shu 1988]. CHARM++ programs can run today without change on most MIMD computers, including shared- and distributed-memory machines such as the Intel Paragon, Thinking Machines CM-5, IBM SP-2, nCUBE/2, Convex Exemplar, Sequent Symmetry, Encore Multimax, and workstation networks.

Latency tolerance: Remote data usually takes more time to access than local data on scalable parallel machines. Moreover, the arrival of remote data can be further delayed due to message contention, or to computations being done on remote processors. The magnitude and unpredictability of these latencies often cause significant performance loss; avoiding them often requires contorted program logic. A parallel programming system should make it possible to tolerate communication latency with minimal additional programming effort.

Support for irregular and dynamic problem structures: There has been much research into applications and languages based on the data-parallel and SPMD programming models, in which problem structures are regular and static (i.e., do not change over time). However, the best algorithms for many seemingly regular problems often involve irregular or asynchronous structures. Moreover, application domains such as irregular finite-element computations, adaptive grid refinement, discrete event and N-body simulation, AI search computations, and discrete optimization are inherently irregular. A general-purpose parallel language should therefore efficiently support irregular problem structures and asynchronous behavior. In particular, it is necessary to support dynamic creation of work and dynamic load balancing.

Modularity and re-use: The intrinsic complexity of parallel programming implies that re-use of software modules will be even more cost-effective than it has proved for sequential software. However, re-use in a parallel context is fraught with challenges:

- Modularity should not lead to a loss of efficiency. In particular, latency tolerance by overlapping computations in one module with idle time in another should be possible.

- Modules written in a parallel language must be able to interoperate with modules written in other languages.

- Modules must be able to exchange data in a fully distributed fashion flexibly, without constraining their potential for re-use.

These issues make parallel programming more complex, and hence more difficult, than sequential programming. As they have proved effective in controlling complexity in sequential programming, we believe that it is worthwhile to apply object-oriented techniques to parallel programming. Apart from the advantages of encapsulation, inheritance and polymorphism provided by object-oriented languages, the notions of state and persistence seem to make object-oriented languages naturally suited to parallel execution. A parallel program can be viewed as consisting of independently-executing objects or processes which encapsulate state, and which communicate by sending messages to methods in other objects.

5.1.1 Target Domain

Developing a parallel application involves four tasks:

decomposition: splitting the computation into parallel parts;

mapping: assigning these computations to processors;

scheduling: determining the order of execution of the computations on processors; and

machine-dependent expression: specifying the decisions made.

Various approaches to parallel programming can be characterized by the extent to which these tasks are automated by the programming system and by the generality of their approaches. A low-level portable layer such as PVM [Sunderam 1990] only provides machine-independent expression (thereby automating machine dependent expression), but is sufficiently general to be useful in most problem domains. A programming system such as HPF [Koelbel *et al.* 1994] automates scheduling, but allows the programmer to specify the mapping of computations to processors and directly supports only data-parallel applications. Parallelizing compilers attempt to automate all four tasks, but have so far proved effective only for regular problems having loop-based parallelism [Padua & Wolfe 1986].

CHARM++ is a general-purpose language that provides portability, automatic mapping, and scheduling. This enables a division of labor between the programmer and the system: programmers, with their understanding of the application and algorithm, specify the decomposition of the computation into parallel actions, while the system implements resource management and scheduling. Although CHARM++ automates these tasks, it allows programmers to override mapping explicitly and lets them influence scheduling via prioritization.

5.1.2 Evolution

The parallel programming concepts in CHARM++ were first developed in the CHARM language and the Chare Kernel runtime system between 1987 and 1991 [Kalé 1990, Fenton *et al.* 1991, Kalé 1992]. CHARM is an extension of C which supports parallel objects, called *chares*. It was one of the first parallel languages to support a message-driven style of programming. The Chare Kernel runtime system supported dynamic object creation, dynamic load balancing, and prioritized message-driven scheduling in a portable manner. CHARM++, an extension of C++, was developed in 1992–93. CHARM++ retains the essential parallel concepts in CHARM, which are described in detail in [Kalé et al. 1995a, Ramkumar et al. 1995]. This chapter describes the CHARM++ language and illustrates it with programming examples. CHARM++ fully incorporates object-oriented features such as inheritance and polymorphism into the CHARM model [Kalé & Krishnan 1993]. Recently, the Chare Kernel was modified to operate on top of Converse [Kalé et al. 1995b], a machine-independent layer (described in Section 5.4.1) which supports interoperability by allowing modules from multiple languages to co-exist in a single application.

5.2   The CHARM++ Language

In this section we discuss the essential features of CHARM++. The first two features—message-driven execution and dynamic object creation— had been defined and explored in work on *actors* [Agha 1986] done prior to CHARM++. The contribution of our work was in developing one of the first pragmatic and portable implementations of message-driven execution and the development of a suite of dynamic load balancing strategies to support dynamic object creation. The next two features, branched chares and specific information-sharing abstractions, originated in CHARM, and thus represent our point of departure from the Actors model.

5.2.1   Message-Driven Execution

CHARM was one of the first systems implemented on distributed-memory multicomputers which used message-driven execution to deal with the problem of communication latency. In message-driven execution, all computations are initiated in response to the availability of messages. In CHARM++, messages are directed to a method inside an object. Messages received by a processor are stored in a pool; the system scheduler repeatedly chooses a message from this pool, then invokes the indicated method within the destination object. It allows the method to run to completion before selecting another message from the pool. Note this dictates that the code in the methods be non-blocking. Sending a message to an object thus corresponds to an asynchronous remote method invocation.

Combined with an asynchronous (non-blocking) model of communication, message-driven execution enables latency tolerance by overlapping computation and communication adaptively and automatically. Each processor is responsible for multiple active objects, some of which have messages waiting for them in the runtime system. Remote operations (such as fetching remote data) are done in a split-phase manner as follows: an object initiates the remote operation from code within a method by sending a request to the remote processor and returns control from the method to the runtime system. The runtime system can then schedule any of the other objects on the processor, ensuring that the processor does not idle while there is still work to be done. When the requested remote data finally arrives (in the form of a message directed to a method), the runtime system can schedule the target method in the requesting object. Message-driven execution also allows a single server-like object to initiate several remote operations and process them in the order in which remote data becomes available, thus allowing the programmer to use careful non-determinism to improve efficiency. Message-driven execution thus has advantages over communication based on blocking receives and yields better performance by adaptively scheduling computations.

Message-driven execution also helps to promote modularity and re-use in parallel programs without loss of efficiency, by allowing the overlap of computations across modules. In Figure 5.1a, A, B, and C are each parallel modules running on all the processors. A wishes to invoke B and C, while there are no dependencies between B and C. However, modules B and C cannot be overlapped in an SPMD system based on blocking receives because control transfers from B to C only after B has completed. B cannot transfer control to C in the middle of its own execution because in a modular parallel program, B does not even know about the existence of other modules such as C. Thus, when B waits on a remote operation, the processor idles.

On the other hand, in the message-driven model shown in Figure 5.1b, the scheduler determines the transfer of control between modules. B does some work, but instead of waiting on a remote operation, it returns control to the scheduler, which can then transfer control to C if there is a message (work) waiting for it. Thus, message-driven execution makes it possible to overlap computations across modules and prevent processor idling as long as there is work to be done in some module.

Libraries constitute an important part of the software development process. They provide re-usable, portable code, and they hide details from application programmers. There are many SPMD parallel libraries available for commonly used kernel operations, such as numerical solvers, FFT, etc. However, the SPMD style does not encourage use of multiple concurrent libraries. When faced with performance loss in a situation, such as in Figure 5.1a, an SPMD programmer typically breaks the library abstraction by combining modules B and C with A. CHARM++ alleviates this problem by providing system support for a message-driven scheduler which receives messages and forwards them to the correct object and by supporting multiple independent objects on each processor.

In summary, the message-driven style of programming encourages creation of smaller and more re-usable modules. Therefore, we expect libraries to be a major strength of message-driven systems in the future. These issues, and empirical studies of the performance advantages of message-driven execution, are discussed in [Gursoy 1994].

Related Concepts   Research on dataflow systems [Arvind & Brobst 1993] represents some of the earliest exploration of the idea of scheduling work adaptively based on the availability of data. This work was largely focused on fine-grained parallelism and involved construction of special-purpose machines. Later research on macro-dataflow [Evripidou & Gaudiot 1990, Grimshaw 1993] is more directly related to our approach.

Actors are also a close antecedent to message-driven execution in CHARM++; the semantics of actor systems was explored extensively in [Agha 1986]. Actors allow concurrency within a parallel object while CHARM++ takes the view that objects define the border between parallelism and sequentiality: multiple actions within an object are not allowed to run in parallel. Message-driven execution is also used in the implementation of many parallel functional and logic languages [Keller et al. 1984, Kalé 1987, Conery 1987].

The active message model [von Eicken et al. 1992] is a recent concept with some relation to CHARM. An active message is simply an efficient

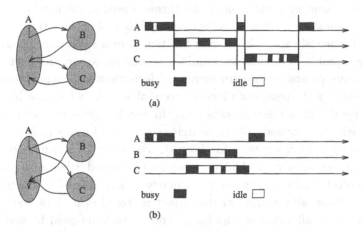

(a) SPMD Modules Cannot Share Processor Time
(b) Message-Driven Modules can Overlap Computations
in One Module with Idle Times in Another

Figure 5.1
Overlapping Computations

user-level interrupt generated by the arrival of a message. The interrupt handler function for the message is specified by the message itself. The computation running on the receiving processor is interrupted to process the message; the handler code is usually constrained not to carry out certain communication operations. No scheduling of messages from a pool is possible.

Using multithreading in conjunction with message-passing is an alternative mechanism for tolerating communication latencies without losing modularity. In such a formulation, each node of a distributed-memory machine runs multiple threads, which can communicate via messages with threads on other processors. A thread may relinquish control to another when the first has to wait for a message. Although both threads and message-driven objects adaptively overlap communication and computation, they present different tradeoffs:

Memory requirements: Threads require memory for stacks for each individual thread, hence the number of threads per processor in a thread-based language will be limited by the available memory and

virtual memory performance. In thread based systems which associate one stack with each object, the number of objects that can be
simultaneously active is severely limited. It may seem unlikely that a
large number of threads are required on one processor. However, in a
medium- or fine-grained concurrent object-oriented system, there are
potentially thousands of objects active at a time, which are blocked
for results from other objects (e.g., in parallel game-tree search applications, each node of the search tree is an object which is waiting for results from its child objects). For message-driven objects in
CHARM++, only one stack per processor is needed; when a method in
an object finishes execution, it explicitly *returns* control to the scheduler. Thus, all the state of the object is stored in its local variables
(which are allocated on the heap) and there is no need to save the
stack between two method invocations of an object. In other words,
the memory requirements of a CHARM++ program with N objects
is much less than a thread-based program with N threads.

Handling shared variable accesses: As threads share memory and
can interleave their execution, accesses to shared variables must be
protected using locks and critical sections. In contrast, CHARM++
does not provide a shared-memory model across processors (except
for the shared object types described in Section 5.2.4) and within a
processor although objects may share data, only one method of any
object executes at a time (if method invocations are medium- or fine-
grained, this does not usually lead to a loss of concurrency). Combined
with the encapsulation provided by objects, this ensures that critical
sections and locks are not needed, thus avoiding a potential source
of programming errors and making it easier to write correct parallel
programs.

Context switching overhead: This is higher for threads than for dis-
patching objects.

Expressing flow of control: Threads have the advantage of representing the flow of control in a function in a linear fashion, as compared
to message-driven objects which have to use a less clear split-phase
flow of control.

Further problems arise when threads are used in conjunction with
message-passing systems [Haines *et al.* 1994] such as MPI, particularly

with blocking global operations. For example, consider what happens when two sets of threads A and B, each consisting of one thread per processor, wish to perform separate, independent global sums. If the global sum operation is blocking (as in MPI), all threads in set A must arrive at the sum operation before any thread in set B (or vice versa), otherwise a deadlock results.[1] Since threads are independently scheduled, it is difficult to prevent the deadlock. This problem has led to the introduction of cross-processor scheduling constraints on thread scheduling [Mehrotra & Haines 1994]. We believe that threads should instead be used *in conjunction* with message-driven execution. In such a formulation, even global operations are asynchronous; threads in separate processors do not have to arrive at the global operations in the same order. The Converse framework described in Section 5.4.1 provides such message-driven threads [Kalé *et al.* 1995b].

5.2.2 Dynamic Object Creation: Chares and Messages

In order to support irregular computations in which the amount of work on a processor changes dynamically and unpredictably, CHARM++ allows dynamic, asynchronous creation of parallel objects (chares), which can then be mapped to different processors to balance loads. Chare creation is a relatively low-cost operation: tens of thousands of chares can be created per second on a single current-generation processor, so chares may be thought of as medium-grained objects. A chare is identified by a *handle*, which is a global pointer; CHARM++ therefore provides a shared object space for chares.

Chares communicate using messages. Sending a message to an object corresponds to an asynchronous method invocation. Message definitions have the form:

```
message class MessageType {
  // List of data and function members as in C++
};
```

---

[1]It is possible that future versions of MPI may provide asynchronous global operations. However, given the resistance to incorporating an asynchronous broadcast, which requires similar capabilities, this may be difficult.

Chare definitions have the form:

```
chare class ChareType {
  // Data and member functions as in C++.
  // One or more entry functions of the form:
  entry:
  void FunctionName(MessageType *MsgPointer)
  {
    ···C++ code block···
  }
};
```

In the above definitions, message, chare, and entry are keywords.

An entry function definition specifies code that is executed *without interruption* when a message is received and scheduled for processing. Only one message per chare is executed at a time. Thus, chare objects define a boundary between sequential and parallel execution: actions within a chare are sequential, while actions across chares may happen in parallel.

Entry functions are defined exactly as sequential functions, except that they cannot return values and they must have exactly one parameter. This parameter must be a pointer to a message. The handle of a chare ChareType is of type ChareType handle (analogous to object pointers in C++, which have the type ObjectType *) and is unique across all processors. Just as C++ supports multiple inheritance, dynamic binding, and overloading for sequential objects, CHARM++ supports these concepts for chares, thus permitting inheritance hierarchies of chare classes. Dynamic binding is also supported by allowing runtime determination of the type of a remote parallel object whose method is to be executed.

Every CHARM++ program must have a chare type named main, which must have the function main(). There can be only one instance of this chare type, which usually executes on processor 0. Execution of a CHARM++ program begins with the system creating an instance of the main chare and invoking its main() function. This function is typically used by programmers to create chares and branched chares (Section 5.2.3) and to initialize shared objects.

Chares are created using the operator newchare, similar to C++'s new memory allocator. Its syntax is newchare ChareType(MsgPointer), where ChareType is the name of a chare class and MsgPointer is a message which can be accepted by the constructor entry-function of the chare class. The **newchare** operator deposits the *seed* for the new chare in a pool of seeds and returns immediately. The runtime system actually creates the chare at a later time on a processor selected by the dynamic load balancing strategy. When the chare is created, it is initialized by executing its constructor entry function with the message contained in the **MsgPointer** argument given to **newchare**. The user can also specify the processor on which to create the chare, through use of an optional argument, and thereby override the dynamic load balancing strategy.

newchare does not return any value. The user may, however, obtain a *virtual handle*—virtual because the chare has not yet been created. A chare can also obtain its own handle once it has been created. Chare handles may be passed to other objects in messages.

Messages are allocated using the C++ **new** operator. Messages are sent to chares using the notation **ChareHandle=>EF(MsgPointer)**. This sends the message pointed to by **MsgPointer** to the entry function **EF()** of the chare referenced by the handle **ChareHandle**. **EF()** must be a valid entry function for that chare type. This syntax is intentionally different from the method invocation syntax for sequential objects in C++ so that programmers can clearly distinguish the semantics of parallel objects. A new token "**=>**" is used for sending messages instead of "**->**" to emphasize the difference between message sending and sequential method invocation: the former is non-blocking.

Dynamic Load Balancing   Dynamic object creation is supported by dynamic load balancing libraries, which help to map newly created chares to processors so that the work is balanced. Since the pattern of object creation varies widely between applications and the characteristics of the underlying parallel machine also vary, different dynamic load balancing strategies are suitable in different circumstances. CHARM++ provides many generic libraries for this purpose; a user may select a particular library at link time [Sinha & Kalé 1993] to match the requirements of her application. These libraries are implemented as modules on top of the basic runtime system. Since chare creation is asynchronous, some of these strategies can delay the mapping of chares to processors until the chares actually start executing. This allows a greater degree of adaptation to varying load conditions. Chare migration (i.e., relocation of a chare after it has started execution) has also been explored [Doulas & Ramkumar 1994].

Prioritized Execution CHARM++ provides many user-selectable strategies for managing queues of messages waiting to be processed. Some of them, such as FIFO and LIFO, are based solely on the temporal order of arrival of messages. However, in applications such as search-based algorithms and discrete event simulations, it is necessary to allow the application to influence the order of processing of messages by assigning message priorities. CHARM++ supports integer priorities as well as bit-vector priorities that use a lexical comparison of bit-vectors to determine the order of processing. These are especially useful for prioritizing combinatorial search algorithms [Saletore & Kalé 1990].

Conditional Message Packing CHARM++ allows arbitrarily complex data structures in messages. On private memory systems, pointers are not valid across processors, hence it is necessary to pack pointer-linked structures into a contiguous block of memory before sending the message. However, packing is wasteful on shared-memory systems, or if the message is being sent to an object on the same processor as the sender. To allow optimal performance in these cases for messages involving pointers, the user is required to specify packing and unpacking methods called `pack()` and `unpack()`. These are called *by the system* just before sending and after receiving a message, respectively. Thus, only messages that are actually sent to other processors are packed.

Related Work in Concurrent Objects Dynamic object creation is provided in ICC++ (Chapter 9), Mentat (Chapter 10), UC++ (Chapter 16), C++// (Chapter 7), ABCL/1 [Yonezawa 1990], and COOL (Chapter 6), among others. Mentat supports coarse-grained objects, while ICC++ and languages such as Cantor [Athas & Boden 1989], HAL [Houck & Agha 1992], and CA [Chien 1993] support fine-grained objects. Compilers for fine-grained languages typically coalesce multiple objects and operations into coarser ones in order to achieve acceptable performance on available parallel machines.

While CHARM++ does not allow parallelism within an object (i.e., all methods are atomic), CC++, ICC++ and others, including actor-based languages, allow parallelism within an object. These languages usually ensure consistency of shared variable access by supporting spe-

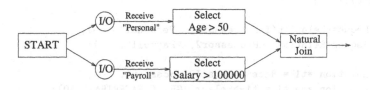

Figure 5.2
Macro-Dataflow Diagram for Query Object

cial program constructs such as locks, monitors, and single-assignment variables, or through data-dependence analysis in the compiler.

Automatic mapping of objects to processors is supported to some extent in Mentat, which allows the programmer to specify object location hints, and in ICC++, which supports a simple randomized load balancing scheme. CC++, which uses a thread-based model along with logical processor objects for encapsulating address spaces, requires programmers to manage locality and load balance explicitly, and does not support dynamic mapping of objects to processors. Most other languages require programmers to specify object-to-processor mappings explicitly.

A Database Query Processing Object This section presents a simplified example of how message-driven execution and dynamic object creation can improve performance by doing work adaptively as remote data become available.

In parallel database applications, it is often beneficial to introduce intra-query concurrency to improve query response times. For example, consider an employee database having two relations: **Personal**, whose fields include **Name** and **Age**, and **Payroll**, whose fields include **Name** and **Salary**. Assume that the two relations are stored on separate disks, each served by an I/O processor, and that the query processor must request the two relations from the I/O processors before it can start processing them. The query processor is required to answer a query of the form "Find all employees over the age of 50 who are earning more than $100,000." The macro-dataflow diagram for this query is given in Figure 5.2.

A program for this query using blocking receive calls implemented using standard message-passing libraries can be expressed as:

```
Query()
{
  RequestRelation(IOProcessor1, "Personal", ···);
  RequestRelation(IOProcessor2, "Payroll", ···);

  Relation *t1 = ReceiveData(IOProcessor1, ···);
  Relation *newt1 = t1->Select(AGE, GREATERTHAN, 50);

  Relation *t2 = ReceiveData(IOProcessor2, ···);
  Relation *newt2 = t2->Select(SALARY, GREATERTHAN, 100000);

  Relation *result = newt1->NaturalJoin(newt2);
  ··· return result relation to requester ···
}
```

The disadvantage of this program is that it will often have significant idle times. This is because the delays at the I/O processors are unpredictable, which means that the two relations may be received in any order. However, the code above enforces a fixed order of execution: if the Payroll relation is received first, the processor will idle while it waits for the Personal relation, degrading the query response time. The following CHARM++ code solves this problem:

```
chare class Query {
  int DonePersonal, DonePayroll;
  Relation *newt1, *newt2;
 entry:
  Query(QueryData *q)
  {
    IOChare1=>RequestRelation("Personal", thishandle,
                         &(Query::SelectPersonal));
    IOChare2=>RequestRelation("Payroll", thishandle,
                         &(Query::SelectPayroll));
    DonePersonal = DonePayroll = FALSE;
  }
  void SelectPersonal(Relation *t)
  {
    newt1 = t->Select(GREATERTHAN, AGE, 50);
    DonePersonal = TRUE;
    if (DonePayroll) JoinRelations();
  }
  void SelectPayroll(Relation *t)
  {
    newt2 = t->Select(GREATERTHAN, SALARY, 100000);
```

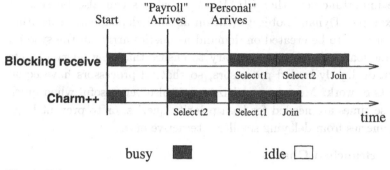

Figure 5.3
Performance of Query Object

```
    DonePayroll = TRUE;
    if (DonePersonal) JoinRelations();
  }
 private:
  void JoinRelations()
  {
    Relation *result = newt1->NaturalJoin(newt2);
    ··· return result relation to requester ···
  }
};
```

In this CHARM++ code, the SelectPersonal() and SelectPayroll()
methods in the Query chare receive input from the I/O processors. These
methods are invoked by the message-driven scheduler on the query processor, in the order the relations are received. If the Payroll relation
arrives before the Personal relation, the blocking receive-based code will
continue to wait for the Personal relation to arrive, while the message-
driven code will execute the appropriate select operation automatically.
This prevents the processor from idling while there is work to be done.
Thus the CHARM++ code above is likely to have a better query response time (Figure 5.3). Note that thishandle specifies a chare's own
handle and is similar to this in C++.

The advantages of message-driven execution are even more apparent
when there are multiple objects active on a processor (e.g., when the
processor is computing many complex queries simultaneously). Each
query object is scheduled for execution as its data becomes available,
which minimizes idle time and improves query response times.

The importance of other CHARM++ features can also be seen in this example. Dynamic object creation allows independently-executing query objects to be created on demand as queries arrive in the system. Dynamic load balancing is necessary to ensure that new query objects are run on lightly-loaded processors, so that all processors have equal amounts of work. Message prioritization is also very useful when quick response times are needed for high priority queries, or to prevent large batch queries from delaying smaller interactive ones.

5.2.3   Branched Chares

A branched chare is actually a group of chares with a single name. A branched chare has one representative of the group (a branch) on each processor, but has a single global group identifier.[2] A program can asynchronously invoke a method in a representative of a branched chare, i.e., send a message to it, by specifying its group identifier as well as the processor. In addition, one can synchronously invoke a method within the *local* representative of a branched chare. This behaves exactly like a sequential function call.

Branched chares are a versatile construct. They can be used to implement distributed services, such as distributed data structures, global operations, and high-level information-sharing abstractions, thereby encapsulating concurrency. They can be used for static load-balancing in object-parallel computations by having each representative perform the same computation on the data owned by it. They also provide a convenient mechanism for distributed data exchange between modules: the group identifier allows each representative of a branched chare in one module to hand data over to the representative in the other module on its own processor. For example, in a molecular dynamics application, branches of the main module might hand over the coordinates and velocities of all atoms to the corresponding branches of a "kinetic energy calculator" branched chare. In a pure actor model, finding the corresponding branches on each processor would be somewhat clumsy. Finally, branched chares can also be used to encapsulate variables whose value is specific to every processor (e.g., a list of neighbors in a grid

---

[2]Branched chares are derived from the branch-office chares of CHARM, whose design and use are described in detail in [Kalé *et al.* 1995a]. Here we briefly summarize the utility and syntax of branched chares in CHARM++ and illustrate it with an example.

computation, or statistics of program execution for a performance measurement module).

Branched chares are defined with a syntax similar to normal chares, except that branched chare classes are required to inherit from the system-defined class **groupmember**. It is possible to create multiple instances of a branched chare type. The group identifier of a branched chare instance is available from the variable **thisgroup**; the chare handle of the particular branch is available, as usual, from **thishandle**. The group identifier for a branched chare class **BChareType** has the type **BChareType group** and can be thought of as referring to an array of chare handles.

Branched chares are created with the **newgroup** operator, whose syntax is similar to **newchare**. When a branched chare is created, the runtime system creates a branch on every processor and initializes it by executing the class's constructor entry function. Branched chares are usually created in the **main()** function of the **main** chare, in which case **newgroup** returns the identifier of the newly created branched chare. When **newgroup** is used outside **main::main()**, it does not return the identifier immediately, but requires the programmer to specify a chare to which the identifier is later returned, after the new branched chare has been initialized on all processors. If **ChareGroup** is the group identifier for a branched chare, then the notations:

```
ChareGroup[LOCAL]->DataMember
```

and:

```
ChareGroup[LOCAL]->FunctionMember()
```

can be used to access data and function members of the local branch of a branched chare;

```
ChareGroup[P]=>EF(MsgPointer)
```

sends a message to the function **EF()** in the branch of a branched chare on the processor P. Finally:

```
ChareGroup[ALL]=>EF(MsgPointer)
```

results in a message being broadcast to all branches of a branched chare (i.e., to all processors).

Global Sum Using Branched Chares   The branched chare shown
below forms the global sum of values resident in each processor, without
creating a barrier.

```
message class IntegerMessage {
   int value;
};

chare class Sum : public groupmember {
   int total, numResponses;
   ClientFnType clientfunction;
   Client group client;   // Client is the superclass for all clients
 entry:
   Sum(EmptyMessage *);   // Initialize local variables
   void FromChild(IntegerMessage *m)
   {
      total += m->value;
      if (++numResponses == CNumPes()) {
      // CNumPes() returns the number of processors
         m->value = total;
         client[ALL]=>clientfunction(m);
      } else {
         delete m;
      }
   }
 public:
   void DepositNumber(int n, Client group c, ClientFnType f)
   {
      clientfunction = f;
      client = c;
      IntegerMessage *m = new IntegerMessage;
      m->value = n;
      thisgroup[0]=>FromChild(m);
   }
};
```

The client on each processor gives its value to the local representative of Sum, which forwards it to the branch on processor 0. When the
number of branches that have sent their values equals the number of
processors, the branch on processor 0 broadcasts the global sum result
to all branches of the client.

   A scalable version of Sum avoids the bottleneck at processor 0 by using
a spanning tree:

```
chare class AnyClient : public Client {
  Sum group sum;
  AnyFunction()
  {
    int number ;
    ···compute this processor's number···
    sum[LOCAL]->DepositNumber(number, thisgroup,
                              &(AnyClient::ReceiveSum));
    ···do other work···
  }
entry:
  void ReceiveSum(IntegerMessage *m)
  {
    // Sum is in m->value
  }
};
```

Note the use of the group identifier and entry function pair in the parameters to DepositNumber(): this provides a "return address" which is used by the FromChild() method in the Sum object to broadcast results back to the client, or possibly delegate another object to do the work and return results directly to the client.

If multiple concurrent client objects (i.e., with overlapping executions) need to compute global sums, they can do so by creating and using multiple instances of the Sum branched chare. A simple function call interface (via the DepositNumber() function) to a global sum module without using branched chares does not provide the same flexibility. The ability of branched chares to link together a group of branches created via a single creation call is crucial for such applications involving multiple clients.

Related Concepts   The notion of branch-office chares in CHARM has similarities with that of Concurrent Aggregates [Chien 1993], which was developed independently at about the same time. Aggregates are not required to have exactly one representative on each processor. Moreover, a client cannot invoke a method in a specific representative: invocations are addressed to the aggregate as a whole. The collections of pC++ [Lee & Gannon 1991] are also similar to branched chares. However, collections are synchronous objects mainly suited for data-parallel computations: a method invoked on a collection results in it being invoked on every member of the collection synchronously.

5.2.4   Specific Information Sharing Abstractions

Most parallel programming languages provide a single mechanism for sharing information between processes or objects. For example, the sole information-sharing mechanism in PVM [Sunderam 1990], MPI [MPI 1994] and Actors is message passing, while Linda's only mechanism is a shared tuple space [Carriero & Gelernter 1989]. However, any single mechanism can be too restrictive and awkward for expressing the diverse needs of all applications. A shared variable, supported by a shared address space, provides unrestricted sharing. However, it is difficult to support arbitrary shared variables in an efficient, scalable way in hardware or software, and the programming overhead of ensuring correctness by locks, monitors, etc. is large. Moreover, a shared variable is too general an abstraction: one rarely needs a variable that any process/object can read or modify in an arbitrary way at any point in time.

Providing only a single generic means of information sharing leads to a loss of expressiveness because the programmer is forced to express all modes of information exchange using only one mechanism. It may also lead to a loss of efficiency because the most efficient implementation of a given mode of sharing information may be different on different machines (e.g., shared vs. distributed memory). For example, a read-only variable whose value does not change after initialization, might be implemented as a truly shared variable on shared-memory machines, but by replication on distributed-memory machines. Implementing it in only one way would be cumbersome or inefficient.

CHARM++ provides specific abstract object types for sharing information [Sinha & Kalé 1994]. Each abstraction for information sharing may be thought of as a template of an abstract object, with methods whose code is to be provided by the user. These shared objects have global handles, or names, and can be accessed on all processors, but only through their specific methods. These abstractions may be implemented differently on different architectures by the CHARM++ runtime system to ensure efficiency. A brief description of some of these abstractions is given below. More details can be found in [Kalé *et al.* 1995a]. Additional abstractions may be added as libraries as need for them arises.

Read-Only and Write-Once Objects: These objects hold information such as problem parameters, which does not change after they are initialized. Read-only objects are initialized in the `main::main()` function immediately after the program begins execution, while write-once objects can be initialized at any time. Either can be accessed from any chare on any processor; since such accesses are local, their overhead is low.

Distributed Tables: A distributed table is a set of records, each of which has a key and a data field. A distributed table type can be defined for any particular data type. Access to records is provided through asynchronous calls which `Insert()`, `Find()`, and `Delete()` records in a particular table.

Accumulator Objects: An accumulator object has two operators defined on it: `add()`, which adds to the object in some user defined manner and `combine()`, which combines two objects. These operators must be commutative and associative. The accumulator template is predefined by the system; however, the code for the `add()` and `combine()` operations for each particular type must be provided by the user. Any chare can "add" to an accumulator variable. The final value can be accessed once for each accumulator variable. Accumulators thus provide a "write-many, read-once" abstraction and are optimized for fast updates.

Monotonic Objects: Monotonic objects provide a "write-many, read-many" abstraction, subject to the restriction that the object's values must be monotonically increasing in order to ensure consistency. A monotonic object is updated by an operation that is idempotent as well as commutative and associative. Like accumulators, the monotonic template is predefined, but the user must provide code for the update operation. The value of a monotonic variable available at a processor is not guaranteed to be the globally latest value, but the system propagates the best value as soon as possible. Monotonic objects are useful in branch-and-bound search computations, where they are used to store the value of the best solution seen so far.

Read-only variables are declared by using the type modifier `readonly`, which is similar to `const` in C++. They can be accessed just like local variables on all processors. Large data structures containing pointers can be made available as read-only variables using "read-only messages". The packing functions associated with messages are used by the system to copy these data structures to other processors.

```
accumulator class SolutionCount {
  CountMessage *m;
 public:
  SolutionCount(CountMessage *msg) { m = msg; }
  void Accumulate()               { (m->value)++; }
  void Combine(CountMessage *msg) { m->value += msg->value; }
};

readonly SolutionCount handle counter;
table nodetable;
```

Program 5.1
State-Space Search Using Shared Objects (continues over page)

An example is:

```
readonly int x;
readonly MessageType *msgpointer;
```

Distributed tables are declared using the predefined class `table`, as in:

```
table TableName;
```

Its three member functions—`Insert()`, `Find()`, and `Delete()`—are all non-blocking; the calling chare specifies a destination to which the results of the call are to be returned. For example, the function:

```
TableName.Find(key, returnFn, returnHandle, option)
```

is used to determine if a particular record (identified by a key) exists in the table. If it does, it is sent in a message to `returnFn()` entry function of the chare specified by `returnHandle`. Alternatively, the `Find()` request may be queued and the record is returned when it becomes available, depending on the `option` specified.

State-Space Search The example in Programs 5.1 and 5.2 demonstrates how information-sharing abstractions are useful in an exhaustive state-space search program. The computation specified by the program is tree-structured: a tree of chares of type `TreeNode` is created to explore the search tree and the chares are dynamically load balanced. The accumulator type `SolutionCount` counts the number of solutions found,

```
chare class TreeNode {
  int nodeid, statesize;
  State *state;
 entry:
  TreeNode(StateMessage *m)
  {
      ···copy the state of this node from m into state···
      delete m ;
      // Insert state into nodetable; report back to ReturnData method
      // If state already existed, the exists flag in reply message is set
      nodetable.Insert(nodeid, state, statesize,
                       &(TreeNode::ReturnData), thishandle,
                       TBL_RETURN_FLAG);
  }
  void ReturnData(TableMessage *t)
  {
    if (t->exists)        // This state already existed in table
      return;
    else if (ThisIsASolution())
      counter->Accumulate();
    else {                // Create the two child nodes
      StateMessage *m = new StateMessage;
      ··· fill state of first child node in m ···
      newchare TreeNode(m);
      m = new StateMessage;
      ··· fill state of second child node in m ···
      newchare TreeNode(m);
    }
  }
  int ThisIsASolution();
};
```

Program 5.2
State-Space Search (continued from previous page)

and a handle to an instance of the accumulator is held in the read-only variable `counter`. Since the same search node can occur at more than one place in the search tree, a distributed table `nodetable` keeps track of already existing nodes. Each chare does a table lookup to confirm that the node corresponding to it has not already been created.

5.3   Polygon Overlay

The CHARM++ implementation of polygon overlay uses a spatial decomposition of the grid over which the polygons are defined. The grid is first partitioned into a large number of sub-regions of identical area. Each processor is given a group of adjacent sub-regions, forming a rectangular region, and is responsible for overlaying all of the polygons which are in its group.[3] Partitioning the grid into sub-regions in this way also increases sequential performance, since each sub-region only considers polygons which are in its area.

Since our implementation does not assume a parallel I/O facility, all input must be performed by on one processor (processor 0 in our program). An obstacle to efficient parallelization is partitioning the input and distributing it to all processors. Two ways to do this are:

- Processor 0 partitions the input and sends each processor only those polygons which are in its sub-regions. Each processor then has to do only the sequential overlay. This method has the disadvantage of causing a sequential bottleneck at processor 0.

- Processor 0 broadcasts the entire input to all processors. Each processor removes input polygons that are not in its own sub-regions, and then does the sequential overlay. This method alleviates the sequential bottleneck to some extent, but increases the volume of communication handled by processor 0, which can cause a loss of performance due to a communication bottleneck.

The CHARM++ program below uses the second approach, with enhancements to allow for irregular polygon densities (i.e., input sets which

---

[3] Rectangles on the boundary between two sub-regions are processed by both sub-regions; a simple duplication removal pass is used to prevent the same output polygon from being generated by two sub-regions. Each sub-region only retains those resultant polygons whose bottom left corner is within its area. The code and performance numbers include this duplication removal pass.

```
readonly int NUMREGIONS; // total number of subregions
readonly int Xmax, Ymax; // size of input grid

message class OutPolyMsg {
 public:
  int len;
  // VARSIZE allows variable-size arrays to be defined inline
  // (i.e., without pointers) in a contiguous message buffer.
  poly_t vec[VARSIZE];
  OutPolyMsg(polyVec_t *);
};

message class InputPolyMsg {
 public:
  int region, leftlen, rightlen;
  poly_t left[VARSIZE];
  poly_t right[VARSIZE];
  InputPolyMsg(polyVec_t **, polyVec_t **, i);
};

polyVec_t *SeqPolyOverlay(polyVec_t *, polyVec_t *);
void ReadPolygons(int, char **, int *, int *, InputPolyMsg *);
void GetInputSize(int, char **, int *, int *);
void OutputPolygons(OutPolyMsg **);
```

Program 5.3
Message Declarations and Prototypes for Polygon Overlay

lead to some processors getting more polygons, and therefore more work, than others), or for varying speeds of individual processors. Each subregion is assigned to a chare object, which can be dynamically re-mapped to a less-loaded processor by the dynamic load-balancing strategy. For uniform load distributions, this load balancing strategy keeps objects on the processor which created them, thus preventing unnecessary communication.

In the CHARM++ program below (Programs 5.3 and 5.4), execution starts at the main::main() function, which reads in the input, initializes read-only variables, and creates the branched chare PolyBChare. This last action broadcasts the input to the branches of the chare on all processors.

```
chare class main {
  int begintime;
  int count;
  OutPolyMsg **msgvec;

 public:
  main(int argc, char *argv[])
  {
    // This CHARM++ program starts here
    int lengths[2];
    GetInputSize(argc, argv, lengths, &NUMREGIONS);

    // Allocate the message carrying input.
    // lengths specifies sizes of VARSIZE arrays in InputPolyMsg
    InputPolyMsg *m = new (lengths) InputPolyMsg;
    ReadPolygons(argc, argv, &Xmax, &Ymax, m);
    // CTimer() returns the current system time in milliseconds
    begintime = CTimer();

    // Create branched chare, implicitly broadcast input
    newchare PolyBChare(m);

    // Some initialization for receiving results
    count = 0;
    msgvec = new OutPolyMsg *[NUMREGIONS];
  }
 entry:
  void RecvOutputPolys(OutPolyMsg *msg)
  {
    // The output from all chares is received here
    msgvec[count++] = msg;
    if (count == NUMREGIONS){
      // CPrintf() provides atomic terminal I/O
      CPrintf("Total time %d msec", (int)CTimer()-begintime);
      OutputPolygons(msgvec);
      CharmExit();                    // end execution of program
    }
  }
};
```

Program 5.4
main Chare Declaration for Polygon Overlay

The input is received at the `PolyBChare` entry function (program Program 5.5), in `PolyBChare`, where it is first pruned to retain only those polygons assigned to the current processor. The remaining polygons are further partitioned among the sub-regions. Note that this partitioning takes only $\mathcal{O}(NA)$ time, where N is the number of polygons and A is the average number of sub-regions each polygon falls in. Each sub-region is assigned to an instance of the chare type `SubRegion`.

The `SubRegion` object (program Program 5.6) begins execution at its `SubRegion` entry function, computes the sequential overlay using the sequential ANSI C code, and sends the output polygons back to the `main` chare. The `main` chare receives output polygons at the `RecvOutput-Polys()` function and outputs them to a file.

Table 5.1 shows execution times (in seconds) for this program on the Intel Paragon for input maps containing 60,000 polygons each, which leads to an output of 200,000 polygons. The total number of sub-regions, which is independent of the number of processors, is 1024. Our program has considerably better sequential performance than the original sequential code (which took 29.26 seconds on this input set, as compared to 8.03 seconds for our code), because of the sub-region partitioning scheme.

Although the sequential speed of this formulation is good, in its parallel execution there exists a communication bottleneck at processor 0 caused by centralization: broadcast of input data and the collection of the output polygons. This bottleneck is inevitable in any parallel program for polygon overlay unless the machine supports concurrent I/O (or the problem specification allows us to assume that the input data is available on all processors and the output polygons do not need to be collected on one processor). Due to this, no significant speedups are observed beyond 16 processors. The existence of the bottleneck was also confirmed using the Projections [Kalé & Sinha 1993] performance analysis tool for CHARM++.

To demonstrate the performance of the essential algorithm, the second row of Table 5.1 provides timings for the essential computation without the input broadcast and output collection times. Note that these times include the rest of the overhead of parallelism: each processor must examine *all* input polygons to prune polygons that are completely outside its domain and each chare must eliminate duplicates that are counted by other chares.

```
chare class PolyBChare : public groupmember {
 entry:
  PolyBChare(InputPolyMsg *msg)
  {
    polyVec_t *leftVec =
      new polyVec_t(msg->leftlen, msg->left);
    polyVec_t *rightVec =
      new polyVec_t(msg->rightlen, msg->right);
    // Remove polygons not owned by this processor
    leftVec->prune();
    rightVec->prune();

    // Partition input polygons among subregions
    polyVec_t **leftvecs = leftVec->partition();
    polyVec_t **rightvecs = rightVec->partition();

    // Create a chare object for each subregion
    for (int i=0; i<NUMREGIONS/CNumPes(); i++){
      int lengths[2] = {leftvecs[i]->len, rightvecs[i]->len};
      InputPolyMsg *im =
        new (lengths) InputPolyMsg(leftvecs, rightvecs, i);
      newchare SubRegion(im);
    }
    delete leftVec;
    delete rightVec;
    delete msg;
  }
};
```

Program 5.5
Branched Chare Code for Polygon Overlay

```
chare class SubRegion {
 entry:
  SubRegion(InputPolyMsg *msg)
  {
    polyVec_t *leftVec =
      new polyVec_t(msg->leftlen, msg->left);
    polyVec_t *rightVec =
      new polyVec_t(msg->rightlen, msg->right);
    polyVec_t *outVec = SeqPolyOverlay(leftVec,rightVec);
    outVec->RemoveDuplicates(msg->region);

    // Create message for sending results back
    OutPolyMsg *outmsg = new (&(outVec->len)) OutPolyMsg(outVec);

    // Send output back to main chare
    mainhandle=>RecvOutputPolys(outmsg);

    delete leftVec; delete rightVec;
    delete outVec;
    delete msg;
  }
};
```

Program 5.6
SubRegion Chare Code for Polygon Overlay Program

Figure 5.4 shows the speedups for the total program execution and the essential part of the execution. It can be seen that although the centralization bottleneck flattens the speedups for the overall execution curve, the essential algorithm scales up well.

5.4 Implementation

CHARM++ has been implemented using a translator and a runtime system. The translator converts CHARM++ constructs into C++ constructs and calls to the runtime system. The runtime system consists of a language-independent portable layer called Converse [Kalé *et al.* 1995b], on top of which is the Chare Kernel layer [Fenton *et al.* 1991, Ramkumar *et al.* 1995].

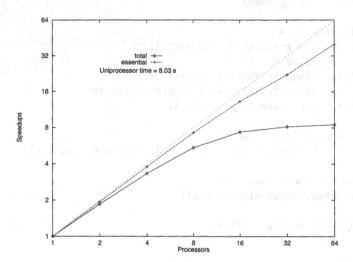

Figure 5.4
Speedups for Polygon Overlay on an Intel Paragon. (Speedups for essential part of
execution exclude input broadcast and output collection times.)

Processors	1	2	4	8	16	32	64
Total time (s)	8.03	4.34	2.41	1.48	1.09	0.98	0.94
Essential time (s)	7.99	4.13	2.11	1.10	0.60	0.36	0.20

Table 5.1
Total and Essential Time for Polygon Overlay on an Intel Paragon

5.4.1   Converse: Portability and Interoperability

The Converse layer provides a portable machine interface which supports essential parallel operations on MIMD machines. These include synchronous and asynchronous sends and receives, global operations such as broadcast, atomic terminal I/O, and other advanced features.

Converse is designed to help modules from different parallel programming paradigms to interoperate in a single application. In addition to common components, such as the portable machine interface, it provides paradigm-specific components, such as message managers and thread objects, that can be customized and used to implement individual language runtime layers.

Some important principles that guided the development of Converse include:

need-based cost: Since Converse is intended to be an underlying interoperable layer, it should not require upper layers of software to incur a cost for functionality they do not need. For example, Converse should not require all messages to go through a tag-based receive mechanism and its associated overhead (which exists in most message-passing libraries supported by vendors), since a message-driven system such as CHARM++ does not need it. Similarly, Converse should not require all messages to go through a scheduler with its corresponding overhead, since a simple message-passing library does not need it.

efficiency: the performance of programs developed on top of Converse should be comparable to native implementations; and

component-based design: the Converse layer is divided into components with well-defined interfaces, and possibly multiple implementations, which can be plugged in as required by higher layers.

Converse supports both SPMD-style programs (which have explicit control flow as specified by the programmer and no concurrency within a processor) and message-driven objects and threads (which have concurrency within a processor and implicit, adaptive scheduling).

The Converse machine interface has been ported to a large number of parallel machines. Languages implemented on the Converse framework include CHARM, CHARM++, PVM message-passing primitives, threaded PVM, a simple messaging layer called SM, and DP [Kornkven

& Kalé 1994], an HPF-based data-parallel language developed on top of CHARM.

5.4.2   Chare Kernel

The Chare Kernel was originally developed to support CHARM, but was then modified to support the C++ interfaces required by CHARM++. It implements functions such as system initialization, chare creation, message processing (including identification of target objects and message delivery), performance measurements, quiescence detection, and so on.

One important function of the Chare Kernel is to map parallel class and function names into consistent integer IDs, which can be passed to other processors. This is required because function and method pointers may not be identical across processors, especially in a heterogeneous execution environment. The CHARM++ translator cannot assign unique IDs to classes and methods during compilation because CHARM++ supports separate compilation, and the translator cannot know about the existence of other modules. Also, this mapping must be implemented so as to support inheritance and dynamic binding while passing IDs for methods across processors. When a sender sends a message to a chare C at an entry function E defined in C's base class, C must call its own definition of E if it has been redefined, but its base class's definition of E otherwise.

To meet these requirements the Chare Kernel provides a function registration facility, which maintains the mapping from IDs to pointers. The translator-generated code uses this registration facility during runtime initialization to assign globally unique indices to chare and entry function names. These unique IDs can be passed in messages between modules. The translator also generates a stub function for every entry function in every chare class. When a message is received and scheduled for processing, the Chare Kernel uses this stub function to invoke the correct method in the correct chare object. To make dynamic binding work, the stub function invoked is the one corresponding to the static type of the chare handle at the call site; the C++ virtual function mechanism then invokes the correct method depending on the actual type of the chare object.

The Chare Kernel uses a scheduler (defined as a component of Converse) which picks up incoming messages from the Converse message buffer, enqueues them by priority according to a user-selected queueing strategy, and then chooses the highest-priority message from the queue for processing.

Finally, the Chare Kernel also manages chare handles (which are essentially global pointers) and handles the mapping between local object pointers and chare handles. Branched chare identifiers need to be managed slightly differently, since they have a single global identifier for a group of chares; the Chare Kernel ensures that a consistent identifier is used on all processors.

5.5 Tools and Libraries

The CHARM++ system is supported by a variety of program development tools, which offer such functionality as performance feedback, graphical performance visualization, expert system-based performance analysis, program development, visual specification, performance prediction via simulation, and debugging. Many of these are mature and well-established, while research continues on others. The tools and some of their interesting features are made possible by the language features in CHARM++.

While message-driven execution has performance benefits, the asynchronous or split-phase communication style it imposes can interfere with a clear expression of control flow within an object [Gursoy 1994]. An example of this is the use of flags and the somewhat awkward expression of control flow in the query object of Section 5.2.2 to enforce dependencies. Visual Dagger is a GUI-based tool that depicts the dependencies between messages and methods graphically, thus allowing the user to view the high-level structure of a CHARM++ program easily. A user draws a macro-dataflow graph (Figure 5.5) in which rectangles represent methods in a CHARM++ object (which execute atomically), circles represent message reception events, and edges represent dependences. This graph specifies the possibilities for overlap between concurrently executing methods on a processor, by allowing methods to execute in an adaptive, data-driven sequence while maintaining dependencies. The visual language editor allows the user to build and edit the graph for a chare, and to edit the CHARM++ code attached to the rectangle nodes. It then automatically generates code to enforce de-

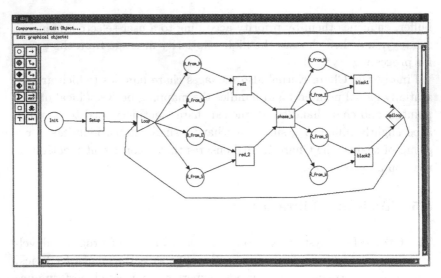

Figure 5.5
Visual Dagger Display for Red-Black Squares Program

pendencies. Figure 5.5 shows a Visual Dagger display in a program for
an iterative method for solving partial differential equations using the
red-black coloring scheme. The rectangles **red1** and **red2** represent, for
example, two methods which can be executed in either order depending
on the arrival of messages (**B_from_N**, etc.) from other objects. The
messages at **R_from_N**, **R_from_E**, etc. cannot be processed until method
phase_b() completes. Visual Dagger will be incorporated in future into
an integrated programming environment.

It is often useful to be able to predict the performance of a program
on a specific parallel machine, without actually running the program on
such a machine. Also, one may wish to study how the performance of a
program will vary as some machine parameter (such as communication
latency) is varied. An emulator provided with the uniprocessor version
of CHARM++ can be used for this purpose. The emulator embodies a
machine model parameterized by user-specified control parameters. It
allows the user to specify the number of processors to emulate, then
runs the user's program and estimates the execution times that would
be achieved on the emulated machine.

Language-specific information provided by chares, branched chares,
multiple information-sharing abstractions, and support modules, such

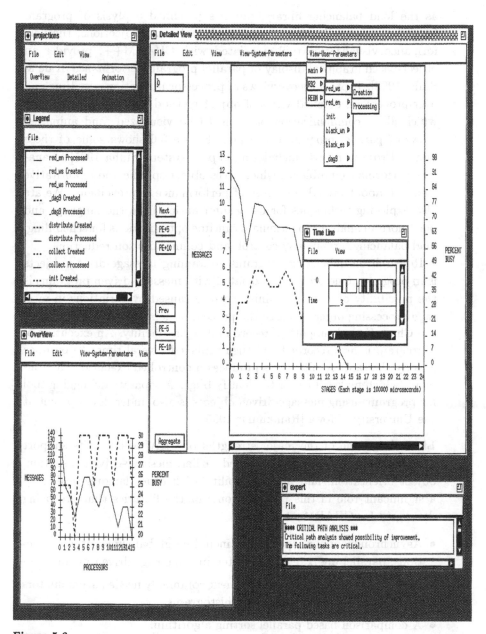

Figure 5.6
A Sampling of Projection Views

as the load balancing library, permits a refined analysis of program behavior and possibly even automated analysis. Projections, the performance visualization tool associated with CHARM++, provides an object-based graphical display of parallel program performance [Kalé & Sinha 1993]. It provides overviews of processor utilization over time and over processors, detailed views of object method invocations, timelines which allow communication patterns to be visualized, and animated views of parallel program execution. Figure 5.6 shows some of these views. Projections also includes an expert system [Sinha 1995] to analyze performance problems, which gives object-specific and quantitative feedback about probable sources of performance improvement. We are also exploring techniques for using information from the language and post mortem analyzer to automate runtime optimizations for scheduling, load balancing, granularity control, and communication reduction.

Research on debugging programs containing message-driven objects is in progress. One problem associated with message-driven programs is the possibility of non-deterministic errors caused by variations in message processing order. To ease the process of debugging such problems, the Chare Kernel supports a record and replay facility. An execution of a program is first recorded and then replayed several times to produce exactly the same results. This produces a controlled execution environment, which makes it easier to identify bugs. A separate debugging tool for programs using message-driven objects is also under development at the University of Iowa [Ramkumar 1995].

Libraries One of the major strengths of CHARM++ is its support for modularity and re-use. As argued earlier, message-driven execution, object orientation, and interoperability with other languages all play a significant role in this regard. Some of the libraries that are being developed for CHARM++ include:

- Asynchronous global operations, including global sums, other reductions, parallel prefix, etc, all written in a message-driven manner.
- Accumulator libraries that implement commonly needed accumulators such as distributed counters and histograms.
- A comparison based parallel sorting algorithm.
- Processor groups and virtual processors.

- Quiescence Detection: this is useful for detecting program termination since the CHARM++ model provides independently-executing parallel objects, and there is no single global thread of control. This library detects quiescent situations in which no object is executing any computation and all messages that were sent have been processed. The programmer may then choose to exit the program or start its next phase.

5.6 Discussion

CHARM++ provides a rich set of facilities that make it suitable for a broad range of applications. Some of the features that distinguish CHARM++ from other approaches to parallelizing C++ include:

- support for irregular (non data-parallel) computations through dynamically creatable parallel objects (chares), dynamic load balancing and message prioritization; and regular computations through groups of objects (branched chares);
- support for modularity, without loss of efficiency, through its message-driven execution model;
- support for specific information-sharing abstractions through templates for shared objects;

CHARM++ and CHARM have been used for several parallel applications. Notable examples include a series of results in the area of VLSI-CAD [Ramkumar & Banerjee 1994]. A novel parallel molecular dynamics program NAMD [Nelson *et al.* 1995] has been developed for production use. CHARM++ is well-suited for parallel discrete event simulations and a project is under way to develop a parallel simulation language based on CHARM++. Other application areas in which CHARM++ programs have been written include N-body simulations, computational fluid dynamics, and state-space search.

Two lessons learned are worth further note. First, while it is syntactically close to C++, the extra syntax introduced by CHARM++ requires us to fully parse input programs. Partly due to the complex syntactic structure of C++, the lack of robust compilers for it on several parallel computers (some do not provide the latest versions of the compilers, or

the available compilers are unable to handle the legal syntactic structures generated by the CHARM++ translator) and the variations among
compilers and vendors' libraries, keeping our parser up-to-date has taken
a substantial effort in a resource-limited project. In retrospect, simplifying the language's syntax to avoid full parsing would have been a better
path.

The second lesson involves the inherent dichotomy between the concepts of message sending and method invocation. In the former, a message object is sent to a remote parallel object and can be viewed as an
instance of a communication class. In the latter, the parameters in a
method invocation are sent to the remote object; this naturally leads to
automatic parameter marshalling. The former view has the advantage
that one can define inheritance hierarchies of communication classes.
Compared to marshalling, it can also provide runtime efficiency—an object can simply take an incoming message, modify some fields, and send
it off to another object, without incurring the allocation and copying
costs incurred by parameter marshalling. However, the syntactic convenience and brevity afforded by automatic parameter marshalling cannot
be ignored. As a result, we plan to provide optional automatic parameter marshalling in future versions of CHARM++, possibly based on the
IDL standard defined in CORBA [OMG 1993].

Interoperability with other languages represents an important ongoing concern. Because CHARM++ is developed on top of the Converse
framework, CHARM++ modules can co-exist in a single application
program with PVM, MPI, and thread-based systems. We also expect
CHARM++ modules to co-exist with modules written in other languages from the CHARM family, including CHARM itself and DP [Ko-
rnkven & Kalé 1994], an HPF-based data-parallel language implemented
using the message-driven model. This will allow one to develop individual modules using the appropriate tool for each task. It will also
encourage re-use of modules written in different languages that might
otherwise not be re-used.

We plan to leverage the support in CHARM++ for modularity and re-
use and build a substantial collection of parallel libraries. CHARM++
also supports separate compilation and therefore facilitates distribution
of libraries in object code format. Thus, we hope that CHARM++
will be a useful medium for algorithm developers and library builders.
They can use the CHARM++ infrastructure to develop and test efficient

implementations of their algorithms while being assured that they can be re-used in applications written in many different languages.

Acknowledgments

This work would not have been possible without the research on the CHARM runtime system over the past several years by the current and past members of the Parallel Programming Laboratory at the University of Illinois, including Wennie Shu, Kevin Nomura, Wayne Fenton, Balkrishna Ramkumar, Vikram Saletore, Amitabh Sinha, Attila Gursoy, Narain Jagathesan, Josh Yelon, and Milind Bhandarkar.

6 COOL

Rohit Chandra, Anoop Gupta, and John L. Hennessy

6.1 Introduction

While parallelizing compilers can restructure programs automatically to extract simple loop-level parallelism, many codes are not amenable to such compiler-based parallelization. They require the exploitation of unstructured task-level parallelism which must be indicated by the programmer. However, exploiting task-level parallelism requires language mechanisms to specify both concurrent execution as well as the communication and synchronization between the parallel tasks. Furthermore, obtaining high speedups requires good data locality and load balance in the execution of the program. In this chapter we describe how these requirements are addressed by the COOL parallel programming language (Concurrent Object Oriented Language), designed to exploit coarse-grained parallelism at the task-level in shared-memory multiprocessors.

The primary design goals for the language are efficiency and expressiveness. Efficiency is important in that the language constructs should be implementable with low overheads, and a parallel program should not incur the overheads of features that it does not use. These goals often conflict with each other, and the design of a language is usually a balancing act between these goals. Since COOL is meant for high-performance parallel programming, we have chosen to emphasize efficient execution, sometimes at the cost of ease of use. COOL therefore provides simple and efficient constructs that allow straightforward applications to be expressed easily yet enable the programmer to get full control over the parallel execution of applications that have more complex requirements.

COOL is designed to explore the benefits of an object-based approach to writing parallel programs. Object-oriented programming has been shown to offer many benefits—it enhances the expressiveness of programs and makes them easier to understand and modify. However, organizing concurrency and synchronization around the objects in a program also has advantages that are particular to parallel programming. For instance, it enables us to build abstractions that encapsulate concurrency and synchronization within the object while providing a simple interface for its use, thereby enhancing the expressiveness of the language. Second, the synchronization operations (and the data protected by the synchronization) can be clearly identified by the compiler, enabling optimizations for efficient synchronization support. Finally, by associating tasks with the objects they reference (either automatically or through programmer supplied information), the runtime system can move tasks and/or data close to each other in the memory hierarchy, and thereby improve both data locality and load balance. An object-based approach, therefore, has the potential to improve both the expressiveness and the efficiency of a parallel program.

COOL is an extension of C++ [Stroustrup 1991]. C++ was chosen as a starting point because of its support for defining abstract data types and its widespread use. Extending an existing language also has the advantage of offering concurrency features in a familiar programming environment. The constructs in COOL are provided within the class mechanism of C++, and thereby exploit the object structure of a C++ program. Concurrent execution in COOL is expressed through the invocation of *parallel functions* that execute asynchronously when invoked. Parallel functions execute in the same address space and therefore communicate through load/store references to shared data. Synchronization between parallel functions is through monitors and condition variables [Hoare 1974] for mutual exclusion and event synchronization respectively.

The majority of the individual constructs in COOL are not novel; rather, we have tried to put together a simple set of features that mesh well together affording the programmer flexibility and control, and that can be implemented efficiently. Thus we view COOL as a vehicle through which we can gain experience with parallel applications, and study the issues that arise in writing parallel programs and having them perform well.

COOL is designed for programming shared-memory multiprocessors only. Compared to message-passing systems, where communication between processors must be specified through explicit messages between processors, shared-memory architectures are easier to program since interprocessor communication can be specified implicitly through load/ store operations to shared memory locations. In addition, concerns regarding the scalability potential of shared-memory architectures have been successfully addressed by recent research prototypes such as the

Stanford DASH [Lenoski *et al.* 1992a], the MIT Alewife [Agarwal *et al.* 1995, Agarwal *et al.* 1990], and commercial machines such as the Convex Exemplar [Convex 1994].

An implementation of COOL has been operational for over four years at Stanford University on several shared-memory multiprocessors, including the DASH, the SGI 4D-340 multiprocessor workstation, and the Encore Multimax. We have written several parallel applications in COOL, including applications from the SPLASH [Singh *et al.* 1992] parallel benchmark suite. COOL has been used in research projects by several undergraduate and graduate students, and in a graduate class that attracts students from many engineering departments and requires a significant parallel programming project. COOL has also been distributed to other university and industrial sites.[1]

In this chapter we describe the language constructs in Section 6.2 and illustrate them through some example programs in Section 6.3. Next, in Section 6.4 we describe the support provided in COOL to address data locality and load balancing. In Section 6.5 we provide a brief overview of the COOL implementation, including several compiler optimizations to reduce the overhead of synchronization operations on monitors. We present a detailed case study of three different applications expressed in COOL in Section 6.6, and offer some concluding remarks in Section 6.7.

6.2 Language Design

Concurrency in a COOL program is expressed through parallel functions; communication between parallel functions is through shared variables; and the two basic elements of synchronization—mutual exclusion and event synchronization—are expressed through monitors and condition variables respectively. In addition, for convenience, we also provide a construct to express fork-join style synchronization at the task level.

Before presenting the language constructs, we briefly describe the runtime execution model for a COOL program. The COOL runtime system implements user-level (or light-weight) threads: this is a runtime layer that manages units of work called tasks entirely within user space, analogous to the management of processes by the operating system. Tasks are

---

[1]An implementation of COOL for SGI multiprocessor workstations, as well as related papers, are available over the World Wide Web from:
http://www-flash.stanford.edu/cool/cool.html.

typically coarse-grain (several hundreds to thousands of instructions), and are managed efficiently since they are highly streamlined and execute in user space. An executing task (or process) is commonly referred to as a thread of execution. The programmer can therefore identify the concurrency in the program, and depend on the runtime system to efficiently take care of the details of task management and scheduling.

6.2.1   Expressing Concurrency

The only way to specify concurrent execution in a COOL program is through the invocation of **parallel** functions. Both C++ class member functions, and C-style functions can be declared parallel by prefixing the keyword **parallel** to the function header. An invocation of a parallel function creates a task to execute that function; this task executes asynchronously with all other tasks including the caller. In addition, the task executes in the same shared address space as all other tasks and can access the program variables like an ordinary sequential invocation. The COOL runtime system automatically manages the creation and scheduling of user-level tasks. Since tasks are light-weight threads of execution, they can be dynamically created to express relatively fine-grained concurrency, making it easier to specify parallelism at a level natural to the problem.

It is useful to have certain invocations of a parallel function execute serially within the caller when the default of parallel execution results in unnecessary parallelism. For instance, in an implementation of merge-sort, one may wish to invoke the sort on the left half of the array in parallel, while the sort on the right half is invoked serially. We therefore allow a parallel function to be invoked serially by specifying the keyword **serial** at the invocation.

To enable synchronization for the completion of a parallel function, all parallel functions implicitly return a pointer to an event of type **condH** (Section 6.2.3). When the parallel function is invoked an event is automatically allocated, and a pointer to it returned immediately to the caller. To synchronize for the completion of the parallel function, the caller can store this pointer and continue execution, and later wait on this event (when necessary) for the parallel function to complete. The called parallel function automatically broadcasts a signal on this event upon completion, resuming any waiting tasks.

Parallel functions cannot return a value other than a pointer to an event. This restriction is necessary because of the complex semantics of returning a value that may be read (or even modified) by the calling task while a parallel function is executing to produce the return value. Therefore, the results produced by a parallel function must be communicated through global variables and pointer arguments to the function. Returning a pointer to an event is a simple mechanism to synchronize for the completion of parallel functions. Synchronization is automatically provided by the implementation within the caller, without requiring the programmer to modify the called function.

6.2.2 Mutual Exclusion

Parallel functions communicate through objects in shared memory. With traditional monitors [Hoare 1974], synchronization for a shared object (an instance of a class) is expressed by specifying the class to be a monitor. All the operations on that class are assumed to modify the object and must acquire exclusive access to the object before executing. Instead of specifying a class to be a monitor, in COOL synchronization for a shared object is expressed by specifying an attribute, either **mutex** or **nonmutex**, for the individual member functions of that class. A function so attributed must appropriately acquire access to the object while executing, thereby serializing concurrent accesses to the object. A **mutex** function requires exclusive access to the object instance that it is invoked on; it is therefore assured that no other **mutex** or **nonmutex** function executes concurrently on the object. A **nonmutex** function does not require exclusive access to the object; it can therefore execute concurrently with other **nonmutex** functions on the same object but not with another **mutex** function. Functions with neither attribute execute without synchronization like ordinary C++ functions, and are discussed later in this section.

Typically, functions that modify the object are declared **mutex** while those that reference the object without modifying it are declared **nonmutex**, automatically providing multiple-reader/single-writer synchronization for the shared object. Synchronization occurs between functions on the same object, and is unaffected by functions on other instances of the class. Since this synchronization is based on objects, C-style functions cannot be declared **mutex** or **nonmutex**. A function can have only one of the **mutex** and **nonmutex** attributes. However, these two attributes

are orthogonal to the parallel attribute. A function that is both parallel
and mutex/nonmutex executes asynchronously when invoked and appropriately locks the object before executing.

Often the programmer may know that certain references to a shared
object can be performed safely without synchronization. In such cases,
we allow the programmer to reference the object directly without regard
for executing mutex and nonmutex functions. For instance, a task may
wish to simply examine the length of a queue object to decide whether to
dequeue an element from this queue or to move on to another queue. Although unsynchronized accesses violate the synchronization abstraction
offered by the mutex and nonmutex attributes, they avoid the synchronization overhead and serialization when they can be performed safely.

We permit unsynchronized accesses in two ways. First, we do not
require functions to have a mutex/nonmutex attribute. Those without an
attribute can execute on the object without regard for other concurrently
executing functions. Second, we maintain the C++ property that allows
the public fields of an object to be accessed directly rather than through
member functions alone, again independently of executing functions.
When performed safely, these unsynchronized references can avoid the
synchronization overhead and enable additional concurrency. Although
the burden for determining when these unsynchronized references are
safe is left entirely to the programmer, we believe that such compromises
are frequently necessary for efficiency reasons.

6.2.3   Event Synchronization

Waiting for an event (such as waiting for some data to become available) is expressed through operations on condition variables. A condition variable is an instance of a predefined class cond in the language.
Operations on condition variables allow a task to wait for or signal the
event represented by the condition variable. The main operations on
condition variables are wait(), signal(), and broadcast(). A wait()
operation always blocks the current task until a subsequent signal()
on that condition variable. A signal() wakes up a single task waiting
on the event, if any (it has no effect otherwise). A broadcast() wakes
up all tasks waiting for that event, and is useful for synchronizations like
barriers that resume all waiting tasks.

Within a mutex/nonmutex function, waiting for an event that is signaled by another function on the same object is done using a release()

operation. Invoking a **wait()** operation may lead to deadlock since the function has locked the object, preventing the signaling function from acquiring access to the object. The **release()** operation atomically blocks the function on an event and releases the object for other functions. When the event is signaled the function resumes execution at the point that it left off after waiting for the signaling function to complete, and re-acquiring the appropriate lock on the object. Thus the synchronization requirements of **mutex** and **nonmutex** functions are maintained.

Notice that a **wait()** operation is resumed by subsequent signals only—i.e., condition variables do not have history. In some situations, such as a **wait()** operation on the event returned by a parallel function, the **wait()** should obviously continue without blocking if the event had been signaled before the **wait()** operation. Although this functionality can be implemented with the existing mechanisms in the language, for convenience we provide the class **condH** (condition-plus-history) in which a **signal()** operation is never lost; if a task is waiting then it is resumed, otherwise the signal is stored in the condition variable. A **wait()** operation blocks only if there is no stored signal, otherwise it consumes a signal and continues without blocking. The broadcast operation is equivalent to infinitely many signals; all subsequent wait operations continue without blocking. We provide an **uncast()** operation to reset the stored signals to zero, and a non-blocking **count()** operation that returns the number of stored signals. The latter operation is useful while writing a non-deterministic program that tests an event and takes a different action depending on whether the event has been signalled or not.

In contrast to COOL, condition variables in traditional monitors are restricted to be only private variables within a monitor. Their **wait()** operation is like our **release()**—it releases the monitor and blocks until a subsequent signal is performed. However, we allow condition variables to be used outside a monitor as well, for general event synchronization between tasks. The **release()** operation is therefore distinct from a **wait()**—both operations block on the event while a **release()** unlocks the object as well.

6.2.4   Task Level Synchronization

Programs often have clearly identifiable phases that are performed in parallel (e.g., a time step in a simulation program). Rather than synchronize for each individual object to be produced by the different parallel tasks in the phase, it is often simpler and more efficient to wait for the entire phase to complete. In COOL, this task-level synchronization can be expressed using the `waitfor` construct, by attaching the keyword `waitfor` to a scope wrapped around the block of statements of that phase. The end of the scope causes the task (that executed the scope) to block until all tasks created within the scope of the `waitfor` have completed. This is precisely the dynamic call graph of all functions invoked within the scope of the `waitfor`, and includes all parallel functions invoked directly by the task, or invoked indirectly on its behalf by other functions.

Using a `waitfor` wrapped around a phase in a COOL program is similar to using barriers at the end of a phase in programming models without light-weight threads, such as the ANL macros [Boyle *et al.* 1987]. However, a barrier is tied to the number of processes that participate in the barrier. In contrast, since the computation within a phase is usually expressed by calling parallel functions in COOL, synchronization for the phase to complete is the same as waiting for the various parallel functions to complete.

6.2.5 Discussion

The COOL constructs are summarized in Table 6.1; We now briefly elaborate on three issues that we have side-stepped so far. The first concerns events returned by a parallel function, while the other two deal with the semantics of monitor operations, i.e., `mutex` and `nonmutex` functions.

First, it is the programmer's responsibility to free the storage associated with the event returned by a parallel function once it is no longer required. The compiler performs simple optimizations such as not allocating the event at all for invocations of parallel functions where the return value is ignored, and deallocating the event once it is no longer accessible in the program (e.g., exiting the scope of an automatic variable that stores the only pointer to the event). The compiler performs the optimizations safely, i.e., it ensures that an event is not deallocated by both the programmer and the compiler. However, although the compiler can optimize simple situations, the ultimate responsibility for deallocating the event rests with the programmer.

Second, in a traditional monitor, recursive monitor calls to the same object by a task result in deadlock, since the task is trying to re-acquire an object. However, in COOL such recursive monitor calls (both direct and indirect) proceed without attempting to re-acquire the object, since the task has already satisfied the necessary synchronization constraints. This semantics for monitor functions is more reasonable since it avoids obscure deadlock situations when the program has already performed the desired synchronization. However, note that deadlock is still possible in a COOL program when two tasks attempt to acquire multiple objects in a different order. This is a common problem when acquiring multiple resources; well structured programs solve it by acquiring the resources in a specific total order. Finally, invocations of monitor operations can rely on not being starved. The implementation guarantees that a blocked monitor operation is not indefinitely overtaken by subsequent monitor operations, and is ultimately serviced.

Notice the allowances made in the language design for programmers to leverage their knowledge of the code for additional expressiveness and/or performance benefits. The features that relate to monitor operations include specifying different kinds of synchronization for functions on shared objects, permitting unsynchronized access to an object, and supporting recursive monitor calls without deadlock. Other features include condition variables with history, general event synchronization through condition variables, and task-level synchronization. Some of these allowances are not desirable from safety concerns, but we believe that they offer sufficient performance benefits to justify offering them in a controlled manner.

6.3   Examples

As we have seen, the concurrency and synchronization constructs in COOL are integrated with data abstraction; we now illustrate the benefits of this design through some example programs. We first illustrate the basic concurrency and synchronization features of COOL with a particle-in-cell code (PSIM4 [McDonald 1991]). We then illustrate the ability to build synchronization abstractions in COOL with an example that implements synchronization for multiple values produced by a parallel function (taken from the Water application [Singh *et al.* 1992]). Finally we describe the polygon overlay example expressed in COOL.

What	Construct	Syntax
Concurrency	Parallel functions	**parallel** **condH*** egc::f()
Mutual exclusion	Mutex/Non-Mutex Functions	**mutex int** egc::g()
Concurrency and mutex	Parallel mutex functions	**parallel mutex** **condH*** egc::h()
Event synch.	Condition variables	**condH** x; **cond** y;
	Wait for an event	x.**wait**()
	Signal an event	x.**signal**()
	Wait and release monitor	x.**release**()
	Broadcast an event (**condH**)	x.**broadcast**()
	Reset an event (**condH**)	x.**uncast**()
	Num. stored signals (**condH**)	x.**count**()
Task-level synch.	Waitfor	**waitfor** { ... }

Table 6.1
Summary of COOL Constructs

6.3.1 Illustrating the Constructs

PSIM4[2] is a three dimensional particle-in-cell code that is used to study the pressure and temperature profiles created by an object flying through the upper atmosphere. The program contains particle objects that represent air molecules and space cell objects that represent the wind tunnel. It evaluates the position, velocity, and other parameters of every particle over a sequence of time steps. The main computation consists of a move and a collide phase. The move phase calculates a new position of the particle using the current position and velocity vectors, and moves the particles to their destination cell based on their new position. The collide phase models collisions among particles within the same space cell.

Concurrency is organized around space-cell objects in the parallel version of the algorithm, as shown in Program 6.1. Within the move phase, particles in different space cells can be moved concurrently, expressed through the parallel move() function on a space cell. In the collide phase only particles in the same space cell may collide with each other so collisions in different space cells can be modeled concurrently through the parallel collide() function on a space cell.

---

[2] An improved version of the better known SPLASH benchmark program, MP3D.

```
class ParticleList_c {
  ...
 public:
  mutex void add (Particle*);
};
class Cell_c {
  ...
  ParticleList_c incomingParticleList;
 public:
  // Perform the move phase for particles in this cell.
  parallel condH* move(){
    ...
    Cell[dest].addParticle (p); // Move particle p to cell dest
  }
  // Model collisions for particles in this cell.
  parallel condH* collide(){
    // Transfer particles from the incomingParticleList
    // and add them to the list of particles in this cell.
    // Access incomingParticleList without synchronization.
  }
  void addParticle (Particle* p) {
    incomingParticleList.add (p);
  }
} Cell[N];
main(){
  for (each time step) {
    // Move particles in different cells concurrently.
    waitfor {
      for (i=0; i<N; i++) Cell[i].move();
    } // Wait for the move phase to complete.
    // Model collisions in different cells concurrently.
    waitfor {
      for (i=0; i<N; i++) Cell[i].collide();
    } // Wait for the collide phase to complete.
  }
}
```

Program 6.1
Expressing parallelism in PSIM4

During the simulation, particles that move from one space cell to another are removed from their present space cell and added to the destination space cell, by invoking the addParticle() function on the destination cell. Each cell maintains a list of incoming particles that provides the mutex function add(); the addParticle() function calls the add() function to enqueue particles on this list. The incoming particles are incorporated with the other particles in the space cell in the beginning of the collide phase. While transferring the new particles, the incomingParticleList can be manipulated directly without synchronization since all cells have already completed their move phase. Finally, since each phase must complete before going on to the next phase, the synchronization is naturally expressed by wrapping the waitfor construct around each phase.

6.3.2 Object Level Synchronization

We use the Water code [Singh *et al.* 1992] to illustrate object-level synchronization in COOL. The water code is an N-body molecular dynamics application that evaluates forces and potentials in a system of water molecules in the liquid state. The molecules are partitioned into groups, with a parallel function stats() on a molecule group to compute various internal statistics like the position, velocity, and potential energy of the molecules in that group. In this example we show how to synchronize for individual values produced by a parallel function as they become available rather than waiting for the entire function to complete, thus enabling the caller to exploit additional concurrency.

In Program 6.2 we show the synchronization for PotEnergy, representing the potential energy of a molecule group. This example exploits the ability in C++ to define type conversion operators, that are automatically invoked to construct values of the desired type. We define a class double_s that adds a condition variable for synchronization to a double. This class has two operators. The first is an assignment operator which is invoked when a value of type double is assigned to a variable of type double_s. The operator stores the value in the variable and broadcasts a signal on the condition variable. The second is a cast operator invoked when a value of type double_s is used where a double is expected. The operator waits for the event to be signaled and then returns the value. With these operators a double can be safely used in place of a double_s and vice versa.

```
class double_s {
  double value;
  condH x;
 public:
  // Initialize the value to be unavailable.
  double_s(){ x.uncast(); }
  // Operator to cast a double to a double_s
  void operator= (double v) { value = v; x.broadcast(); }
  // Operator to cast a double_s to a double
  operator double(){ x.wait(); return value; }
};
// Compute internal statistics of molecules (e.g., position, energy)
parallel condH* moleculeGroup::stats (double_s* poteng, ···) {
  ···Compute local potential energy···
  *poteng = local potential energy;
  ···Continue - compute position, velocity etc···
}
main(){
  moleculeGroup mg; double totalEnergy = 0; double_s potEnergy;
  ···
  mg.stats (&potEnergy, ···other arguments···); // Parallel invocation
  ···perform other useful computation···
  // Use potEnergy - block if the value has not been computed yet
  totalEnergy += potEnergy;    // Continue after value becomes available
}
```

Program 6.2
Object-Level Synchronization in the Water Code

The caller passes the address of PotEnergy to the stats() function and continues execution. When it later references the value of PotEnergy it invokes the cast operator which automatically blocks until the value is available. The pointer to PotEnergy can be passed to other functions without blocking, thus exploiting additional concurrency. The called function computes the potential energy and stores it in the supplied variable; this assignment invokes the assignment operator which stores the value and signals all tasks waiting on the condition variable. The function stats() continues execution to compute the other parameters.

As the example shows, the desired synchronization is expressed naturally at the object level. It allows the caller to execute asynchronously until it needs the value, and allows the called function to execute independently, making the various parameters available as they get computed. In addition, we use the ability to define operators in C++ to build a double_s abstraction; this abstraction encapsulates synchronization within the object, and can be used like an ordinary double. This enables us to integrate synchronization as a property of the shared object, similar to futures in Multilisp [Halstead 1985]. However, a future in Multilisp is a single mechanism that expresses both parallelism as well as synchronization for the completion of the parallel activity. In contrast, COOL provides separate mechanisms for spawning concurrency and expressing synchronization. As a result the individual mechanisms in COOL are simple and efficiently implemented (Section 6.5.2), yet expressive enough to build abstractions with future-like synchronization as shown in this example.

6.3.3 Polygon Overlay

We next discuss the polygon overlay example expressed in COOL. In this problem we are given two rectangular maps, each partitioned into a set of non-overlapping polygons, and are required to find their intersection, which is the map consisting of the pair-wise intersection of the constituent polygons within each map.

The basic computation in this problem consists of computing the intersection of two polygons (one from each map) and adding the resultant overlap polygon (if any) into the output map. This computation is performed for each pair of polygons, and is essentially fully parallel— multiple such computations can proceed concurrently without conflict since the computation only reads the two polygons. The only synchronization required is to serialize multiple insertions into the output map.

The COOL code for this example is shown in Program 6.3, and has two main objects: polygons and vectors of polygons (or maps). The poly class represents a polygon by its x and y coordinates, and offers methods to compute the intersection of the polygon with either another polygon (polyOverlay) or with an entire map (polyVecOverlay()). The polyVec class represents a map as a vector of polygons, and offers methods to insert and fetch a polygon. Parallel execution is expressed by labelling the polyVecOverlay() method to be parallel—as a result different polygons in the left map are processed concurrently. (Since each polygon overlaps with only a few polygons from the other map, creating a task for each pair-wise overlap results in wasted concurrency). Multi-

```
class polyVec {
  poly* vec;  // vector of polygons
 public:
  mutex void insert (poly* pg);      // Insert a polygon one at a time
  poly* GetPoly (int index);         // Get a polygon (no synchroniza-
tion)
};
class poly {
  int xl, xh, yl, yh;
 public:
  // compute single intersection of this and pg
  void polyOverlay (poly* pg, polyVec* output) {
    if ((xh >= pg->xl) && (xl <= pg->xh) && (yh >= pg->yl) &&
        (yl <= pg->yh)) {
      // they do overlap; construct the overlap polygon and insert
      output->insert (new poly (max(xl, pg->xl),max(yl, pg->yl),
                                min(xh, pg->xh),min(yh, pg->yh)));
    }
  }
  // compute all intersections involving this polygon with the given map
  parallel condH* polyVecOverlay(polyVec* right, polyVec* output){
    for (all polygons pg in right) polyOverlay (pg, output);
  }
};
main(){
  polyVec *left, *right, *output;
  waitfor {
    // process each polygon in the left map in parallel
    for (all polygons pg in left) pg->polyVecOverlay (right, output);
  } // wait for all the overlays to be computed
}
```

Program 6.3
Computing Polygon Overlay

ple insertions into the output map are serialized by labelling the insert method to be mutex.[3] However, since the GetPoly() method is invoked only on the input maps which are read-only, we exploit the flexibility of monitors in COOL and allow the GetPoly() method to execute without synchronization. We wait for the overall computation to complete by wrapping the code within a waitfor in the main() procedure. Overall, both concurrency and synchronization in this example are easily expressed in COOL.

The implementation described above can be quite wasteful since it performs each pair-wise comparison of polygons from the two maps. We now show how two optimizations to prune the number of useless comparisons are incorporated within the COOL code (see Program 6.4). The first optimization is possible only if the polygons within each input map are sorted along (say) the xl values (the x coordinate of the lower left corner). Since two polygons cannot overlap if the xl value of one exceeds the xh value of the other (x coordinate of the upper right corner), the vecPolyOverlay() method performs a binary search along the polygons of the right map to find the first polygon that has an xl value greater than the xh value of the current polygon. All polygons to the right of this polygon cannot overlap with the current polygon, and need not be examined. The second optimization maintains (within each polygon) the area of the portion of the polygon that has not been overlapped so far. This area is decremented as each overlap is computed, and once the area reaches zero, no further comparisons are necessary since there can be no further overlap with another polygon. As shown in Program 6.4, the COOL code is easily extended to include both these optimizations.

Having expressed the concurrency and synchronization in COOL, we briefly discuss the performance considerations in this application. Since there are hundreds to thousands of polygons in a map, the above code is likely to have good load-balancing. Regarding data locality, nearby polygons within a map are likely to overlap with the same set of polygons from the other map, and processing them on the same processor can improve cache re-use. In the following section we describe the support provided in COOL to guide the scheduling of tasks across processors. As we shall see, these scheduling mechanisms enable us to easily experiment

---

[3] A further optimization is for each processor to perform its insert in a local map without synchronization, and merge the multiple maps from each processor at the end.

```
class synch_int {
  int value;
 public:
  mutex int decr (int delta)
              { value -= delta; } // synchronized update
  operator int(){ return value; }   // unsynchronized read
};
class poly {
  ...

  synch_int area;
 public:
  void polyOverlayLn (poly* pg, polyVec* output) {
    if (this and pg overlap) {
      poly* np = new poly (···);
      area->decr (np->area);  pg->area->decr (np->area);
      output->insert (np);
    }
  }
  parallel condH* vecPolyOverlay(polyVec* right, polyVec* output){
    // find the first polygon with xl greater than my xh (do a binary search)
    int lower = 0, upper = right->length(), middle;
    while (upper > (lower+1)) {
      middle = (lower+upper)/2;
      if (right->GetPoly(middle)->xl < xh) lower = middle;
      else upper = middle;
    }
    for (int i=0; i<=middle, poly* pg = right->GetPoly(i); i++)
      // prune: compare only if the area is non-zero
      if (pg->area != 0) {
        polyOverlayLn (pg, output);
        if (area == 0) break;
      }
  }
};
```

Program 6.4
Optimized Version of Polygon Overlay

with different partitions of a rectangular map and schedule tasks from a partition onto the same processor.

6.4   Data Locality and Load Balancing

Expressing the concurrency and the accompanying coordination in an application does not automatically ensure great speedups; obtaining good performance on a multiprocessor requires good load balance so that processors do not sit idle for lack of available work, and good data locality so that individual processors do not waste time waiting for memory references to complete. The latter problem is particularly severe on modern multiprocessors where the latency of memory references can range from tens to hundreds of processor cycles. Therefore, any parallel programming system must address these performance issues.

For this study, we assume a three-level memory hierarchy consisting of per processor caches, local portion of shared memory, and remote shared memory (Figure 6.1). We believe this captures the essential components of the memory hierarchy found in modern multiprocessors (e.g., the Stanford DASH, MIT Alewife, and Convex Exemplar). The primary mechanisms to improve data locality in such architectures are task scheduling and object distribution. For instance, we can exploit cache locality (i.e., re-use in the cache) by scheduling tasks that reference the same objects on the same processor. Cache locality can be further enhanced by scheduling these tasks back-to-back to reduce possible cache interference caused by the intervening execution of other unrelated tasks. When cache locality alone is insufficient, we can exploit memory locality by identifying the primary object(s) referenced by a task and executing the task on the processor that contains the object(s) in its local memory. Thus, references to the object that miss in the cache will be serviced in local rather than remote memory, resulting in lower latency.

Along with task scheduling, object placement is often necessary as well. For example, exploiting memory locality and simultaneously ensuring a good load balance requires both task scheduling and an appropriate distribution of objects across processors (local memories). Thus, it is important to provide mechanisms to distribute and dynamically migrate objects across the processor memories.

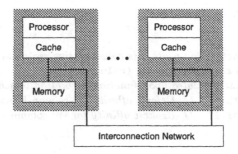

Figure 6.1
Multiprocessor Architecture and Memory Hierarchy

6.4.1 Our Approach

Determining an efficient task and object distribution requires knowledge about the program that is often beyond the scope of a compiler, but may be readily known to the programmer. In COOL, therefore, we provide abstractions for the programmer to supply hints about the data objects referenced by parallel tasks. These hints are used by the runtime system to appropriately schedule tasks and migrate data, and thereby exploit locality in the memory hierarchy; they do not affect the semantics of the program. This approach provides a clear separation of functionality: the programmer can focus on exploiting parallelism and supplying hints about the object reference patterns, leaving the details of task creation and management to the implementation.

Since our approach depends on programmer participation, it is important that the abstractions be intuitive and easy to use. At the same time they should be powerful enough to exploit locality at each level in the memory hierarchy without compromising performance. We address these goals through the following key elements of our design. First, the abstractions are integrated with the task and object structure of the underlying COOL program so that the hints are easily supplied. Second, the abstractions are structured as a hierarchy of optional hints so that simple optimizations are easily obtained as defaults while more complex ones require incremental amounts of programmer effort. Finally, the abstractions are designed to enable experimentation with different optimizations, and address locality at each level in the memory hierarchy.

For simplicity, we currently leave the burden of distributing and migrating objects across processors' memories to the programmer, and

```
class  column_c {
  ...
 public:
   // Parallel function to update this column using src column.
   parallel mutex condH* update (column_c* src)
   // Affinity hints: executed upon function invocation to schedule task.
   [ affinity (this); // Default affinity for column being reduced (this).
     affinity (src);  // Explicit affinity for src column reducing this. ];
} *column;
main(){
  for (int i=0; i<N; i++)
    for (int j=0; j<i; j++)
      // Invoke the parallel function, scheduling the corresponding
      // task based on the specified affinity hints (or default).
      column[i].update (column+j);
}
```

Program 6.5
Illustrating Affinity Hints

simply provide constructs to allow this to be expressed in the language.
Ongoing compiler research to automatically determine a good object
distribution has enjoyed some success for regular data access patterns,
and could reduce this burden on the programmer.

6.4.2   The Abstractions

In COOL, information about the program is provided by identifying
the objects that are important for locality for a task. Along with a parallel function, the programmer can specify a block of code that contains
affinity hints (Program 6.5). This block of code is executed when the
parallel function is invoked and a corresponding task is created. The
affinity hints themselves are simply evaluated by the runtime system to
determine their effect on the scheduling of the task; they do not affect
the semantics of the program. The hierarchy of the affinity abstractions
in COOL is as follows.

Default Affinity: Parallel functions in COOL have a natural association with the object that they are invoked on. So, by default, tasks
created by invocations of this function are scheduled on the processor
that contains that object in its local memory. The task is therefore likely
to reference the object in local rather than remote memory. In addition,

```
class column_c {
  ...
 public:
  parallel mutex condH* update (column_c* src)
  [ // Exploit memory locality on the destination column
    // using object affinity for this
    affinity (this, OBJECT);
    // Exploit cache locality on the source column
    // using task affinity for src
    affinity (src, TASK);
  ];
};
```

Program 6.6
TASK and OBJECT Affinity in Gaussian Elimination

if there are several tasks that operate on that object, then the runtime system executes such tasks back-to-back on that processor to further improve cache locality.

Simple Affinity: When a parallel function would benefit from locality on object(s) other than the default object, the programmer can override the default by explicitly identifying the object through an affinity specification for the function. When affinity for an object is explicitly identified, the runtime system schedules the task in a manner similar to the default described above, except that the scheduling is based on the specified object rather than the default object.

Task and Object Affinity: It is often useful to simultaneously exploit memory locality on one object and cache locality on a different object. To illustrate this we consider a column-oriented Gaussian elimination on a matrix. In the algorithm, each column of the matrix is updated by the columns to its left to zero out the entries above the diagonal element. Once the column has received all such updates (i.e., all entries above the diagonal element are zero), it is used to update other columns to its right in the matrix. A task in this algorithm is an invocation of the parallel function **update()** (Program 6.6), which updates a destination column by a given source column. A desirable execution schedule and object distribution for this column-oriented algorithm are as follows [Rothberg & Gupta 1990]. The algorithm executes an update on the processor where the destination column is allocated, thereby exploiting memory locality on the destination column (the number of columns per processor is so large that they are not expected to fit in the cache). Distributing the columns across processors in a round-robin fashion results in good load distribution. In addition, each processor executes multiple updates that involve the same source column; by executing these updates in a back-to-back manner the algorithm exploits cache locality on the source column as well.

Given the above need for exploiting different kinds of locality, we allow the keywords TASK and OBJECT to be specified with an affinity statement. The TASK affinity statement identifies tasks that reference a common object as a *task-affinity set*; these tasks are executed back-to-back to increase cache re-use. The OBJECT affinity statement identifies the object for memory locality; the task is co-located with the object. As shown in Program 6.6, we can simultaneously exploit cache locality through task-affinity on the source column, as well as memory locality through object-affinity on the destination column. This exactly captures the way the algorithm was hand-coded using ANL macros [Boyle *et al.* 1987] to run on the Stanford DASH multiprocessor; the same scheduling is simply expressed in COOL.

Processor Affinity: For load balancing reasons it sometimes becomes necessary to directly schedule a task on a particular processor (in practice the corresponding server process), rather than indirectly through the objects it references. We therefore provide *processor affinity* through the PROCESSOR keyword that can be specified for an affinity declaration. An integer argument is supplied instead of an object address, and its value (modulo the number of server processes) becomes the server number on which the task is scheduled.

If affinity is specified for multiple objects, the runtime system simply schedules the task based on the first object. It is the programmer's responsibility to supply appropriate affinity hints for tasks that would benefit from locality on multiple objects. For instance, to exploit memory locality on multiple objects, the programmer could allocate all the objects from the memory of one processor, and supply an object-affinity hint for any of those objects. To exploit cache locality on multiple objects, the programmer could pick one of the several objects, and supply a task-affinity hint for that particular object consistently across the various tasks. We are evaluating heuristics that would automatically make an intelligent scheduling decision when multiple affinity hints are sup-

Affinity Construct	Description and Effect
affinity (*address*)	Simple affinity: Co-locate with object, schedule back-to-back
affinity (*address*, **OBJECT**)	Object-affinity: Co-locate with object
affinity (*address*, **TASK**)	Task-affinity: Schedule tasks in task-affinity set back-to-back
affinity (*num*, **PROCESSOR**)	Processor-Affinity: Schedule on specified processor
x = **new** (*P*) *type*	Allocate object from the memory of processor P
migrate (*address*, *P*)	Migrate object to the memory of processor P
migrate (*address*, *P*, *size*)	Migrate an array of 'size' objects to memory of processor P
home (*address*)	Return processor that contains object object in its local memory

Table 6.2
Summary of Affinity Specifications and Data Distribution Constructs

plied, such as determine the relative importance of objects based on their size, and schedule the task on the processor that has the most objects in its local memory.

Object Distribution: In addition to the affinity hints for a task, we also allow the programmer to distribute objects across memory modules, both when they are allocated, as well as by dynamically migrating them to another processor's local memory. Unless specified otherwise, memory is allocated from the local memory of the requesting processor. For dynamic object distribution we provide a `migrate()` function that takes a pointer to an object and a processor number, and migrates the object to the local memory of the specified processor (modulo the number of server processes). An optional third argument that specifies the number of objects to be migrated is useful to migrate an array of objects.[4] Finally, the `home()` function returns the number of the processor that contains the given object allocated in its local memory.

---

[4]The operating system on the SGI and DASH multiprocessors supports data allocation at the page level only, therefore the migrate call on these machines is implemented through the migration of entire pages spanned by the object, rather than the object alone.

The affinity hints are summarized in Table 6.2. They are used by the runtime scheduler to schedule tasks as described above. In addition to scheduling tasks for good locality, the scheduler employs several heuristics to maintain good load balancing at runtime. For instance, an idle processor steals tasks from other processors. An idle processor will also try to steal an entire task-affinity set, since the set can execute on any processor and benefit from cache locality. Several processors can execute tasks from the same task-affinity set if the common object is not being modified; modifications to the object will invalidate it in other processors' caches.

In summary, we have described the support provided in COOL for the programmer to supply information about the program, which is used by the runtime to schedule tasks for better data locality. The hints are supplied in terms of objects referenced by tasks, thereby exploiting the natural structure of a COOL program. Programmer participation is an important component of our approach; however, a hierarchy of abstractions, and smart runtime defaults, help to reduce the burden on the programmer.

6.5 Implementation

We have implemented COOL on several multiprocessors, including a 32-processor Stanford DASH. Here we give a brief overview of the implementation, present some compiler optimizations, and describe the runtime task queue structures to support task scheduling for better data locality.

6.5.1 Overview

A COOL program is translated to a C++ program by a yacc-based source-to-source translator. The generated C++ program can then be compiled by a C++ compiler and linked with the COOL runtime libraries. When a COOL program begins execution, several server processes are created, usually one per available processor. Each server process is assigned to a processor; it executes on that processor without migrating. Server processes correspond to traditional heavy-weight Unix processes, but share the same address space. They are created initially and execute for the entire duration of program's execution. An invocation of a parallel function creates a task. Tasks are implemented entirely within the COOL runtime system. They have their own stack and execute in the shared address space. Each server continually fetches a task and executes it without preemption until the task completes or blocks (perhaps to acquire a `mutex` object or wait on an event). The program finishes execution when all tasks have completed.

6.5.2   Reducing Synchronization Overhead

A naïve implementation of monitors can incur high overheads. We now present some optimizations that help eliminate most of these overheads. These optimizations also illustrate the benefits of integrating monitors with the object structure. This integration enables the compiler to identify the data associated with the monitor synchronization, and identify the synchronization operations on an object. The compiler can therefore analyze the synchronization operations and optimize their implementation in various ways that we outline below.

We first describe the basic implementation of monitors and identify the major sources of overhead, and then describe how they may be optimized. Monitor operations are implemented by first executing some entry code to acquire access to the object, then executing the user function code, and finally executing some exit code to surrender the object to a waiting operation, if any. If another monitor operation is already executing on that object, then the task executing the entry code must wait until the object becomes available. This waiting must be implemented by blocking the task that executes the entry code, so as to free the underlying processor to fetch and execute other tasks. Implementing the waiting with busy waiting can lead to deadlock in some programs.

The primary overhead in this scheme occurs when it blocks a task and switches to another context. Although blocking immediately on an unavailable monitor is efficient in situations where the operations execute for long durations, it has excessive overhead for shared objects with small critical sections. We therefore implement the entry to a monitor operation with a two-phase algorithm, in which the entry code busy-waits for a 'while' (heuristically chosen by the runtime system) and then blocks if the monitor object is still unavailable.[5] Furthermore,

---

[5]Note that this context switch is between user level tasks, and is analogous but orthogonal to the implementation of locks in the context of operating system scheduling, where locks can be implemented with pure spin or with blocking.

we have developed compiler techniques to automatically identify those monitors that are suitable to implement with pure busy-wait semantics (called a *spin monitor*). A monitor can safely be implemented with busy-wait alone if none of the monitor functions call an operation that could block, i.e., a monitor operation on another object or a wait on an event. In addition, a monitor is worthwhile to implement as a spin monitor if all the monitor operations have a 'small' body (determined heuristically). Spin monitors are protected by a simple lock which must be held for the duration of the monitor function; they are therefore attractive for small shared objects since they have minimal runtime and storage overhead.

In several of the applications that we have programmed in COOL, the synchronizations built using monitors meet our heuristic criteria for spin monitors, such as synchronization for shared objects. In Figure 6.2 we show the performance impact of these optimizations on the Water code, executing on a thirty-two processor DASH multiprocessor. As we can see, a two-phase implementation of monitors performs better than a blocking monitor. In addition, this program has a shared object that meets our criteria for a spin monitor. Implementing this object as a spin monitor further improves performance by over 20% as compared to a blocking monitor.

Monitor implementations incur other overheads that can frequently be optimized by a compiler. For instance, a monitor often has only **mutex** and no **nonmutex** functions. A compiler can identify such monitors and entirely discard the support for **nonmutex** functions, reducing both storage and runtime overhead. Second, all monitor calls require a runtime check to detect if they are recursive calls, in which case they should proceed without synchronization. A compiler can often identify recursive calls statically, again doing away with the storage and runtime check altogether. Finally, synchronization abstractions are frequently built with a condition variable declared private within the monitor class. In such situations, accesses to the condition variable need not be protected by a separate lock, since accesses to the variable are automatically serialized through the **mutex** functions on the object.

In the last few paragraphs, we have suggested many of the optimizations possible when monitors are integrated with the object structure. We have implemented two-phase monitors and the optimization of recursive monitor operations. Automatically identifying spin monitors,

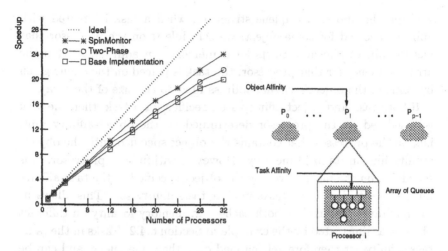

Figure 6.2
Effect of Synchronization Optimizations in the Water Code (left), and Task Queue
Structure to Support Task and Object Affinity (right)

private condition variables, and classes without **nonmutex** functions, are
not implemented in our current system since they require a two-pass
compiler. However, these techniques are highly effective at optimizing the overheads associated with most common synchronizations built
using monitors, and are therefore necessary for any monitor based environment. Finally, note how the integration of monitors with the object
structure enables the analysis required for these optimizations; this analysis would not be possible if monitors were provided in a runtime library.

6.5.3   Scheduling Support for Locality

Object-affinity requires that tasks be executed on the processor that
contains the object allocated in its local memory, while task-affinity requires that tasks be executed back-to-back on a processor. To support
task scheduling for object-affinity, there is a task queue for each server
process and a task with object-affinity is co-located with the object (Figure 6.2). To support task-affinity sets, each processor must distinguish
tasks belonging to different sets. Therefore each server actually has
an array of queues, with each element of the array corresponding to a
task-affinity set.

Given the above task queue structure, when a task is created with affinity specified for some object, we schedule it on the processor that has the object allocated in its local memory. In addition, within the array of queues for that processor, the task is placed on the queue given by value of the object's virtual address modulo the size of the array.

If both task and object affinity are specified for a task, then the task is scheduled on the processor determined by the object-affinity hint, i.e., on the processor that contains the object specified with the object-affinity hint in its local memory. However, within that processor, it is scheduled on the queue given by the object specified in the task-affinity hint, thereby identifying tasks in that task-affinity set. This allows us to simultaneously exploit both cache and memory locality on different objects, as illustrated by the example in Section 6.4.2. Tasks in the same task-affinity set therefore get mapped onto the same queue, and can be serviced back-to- back. Collisions of different task-affinity sets on the same queue can be minimized by choosing a suitably large array size.

This task queue structure is implemented efficiently. Determining where to schedule a task simply requires two modulo operations. Within the task queue structure of each processor, the non empty queues in the array are linked together to form a doubly linked list and provide fast enqueue and dequeue operations.

6.6   Application Case Studies

Sections 6.2 and 6.4 illustrated the COOL constructs with some simple examples. For a more thorough evaluation of the language, we have rewritten several of the SPLASH [Singh *et al.* 1992] applications in COOL. The SPLASH suite is a collection of large scientific and engineering applications (ranging from 3000 to 9000 lines of code) that have been explicitly hand-parallelized. They are therefore good candidates to evaluate both the programmability and performance of COOL.

We now provide a brief description of our experience with three of these applications in COOL—Ocean, LocusRoute, and Panel Cholesky. A detailed discussion of these and other applications can be found in [Chandra 1995]. For each application we describe how the COOL constructs were used to express the desired concurrency and synchronization as well as address the locality and load balancing concerns. We present

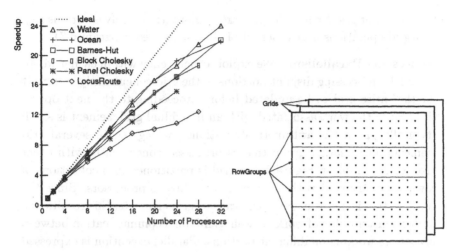

Figure 6.3
Absolute Speedup on 32-Processor DASH (left), and Grid Structure in the Ocean
Code (right)

performance results running on a 32-processor Stanford DASH (organized into eight clusters each with four processors and some physical
memory). On DASH references that are satisfied in the cache take one
processor cycle. Memory references to data in the local cluster memory
take nearly 30 cycles, while references to the remote memory of another
cluster take about 100-150 cycles. In addition to measuring program performance, we use the hardware performance monitor on DASH [Lenoski
et al. 1992b] to monitor the bus and network activity in a non-intrusive
manner. In particular, the performance monitor allows us to track the
number of local and remote cache misses incurred during the execution
of an application.

Figure 6.3 presents overall performance results of some COOL programs. As we can see, the speedups are as high as 24 on 32 processors.
Overall, the COOL overhead is low—a COOL parallel program on one
processor runs about 2-3% slower than the original serial program.

6.6.1   Ocean

Ocean [Singh & Hennessy 1992] is a program to study the influence
of eddy and boundary currents on large-scale ocean movements. The
main data structures in the application are twenty-five double-precision

floating-point grids, while the primary computation involves various regular grid operations over a period of time steps (see Program 6.7).

Expressing Parallelism   We exploit concurrency within each grid operation by processing disjoint portions of the grid concurrently, and wait for the entire grid to be updated before proceeding to the next operation. Since the work associated with an individual grid element is small (typically just a few arithmetic operations), we aggregate several grid elements into a larger group that is processed concurrently with other groups. As shown in Figure 6.3, a grid is partitioned into collections of rows or `rowGroups`,[6] with as many rowGroups as processors. Since the computation is uniform across the various grid elements, this results in a uniform distribution of work, as well as minimal communication between processors working on different portions. Parallel execution is expressed by invoking a parallel function on a rowGroup, illustrated by the function `laplace()` in Program 6.7. Synchronization for a grid operation to complete is expressed by wrapping the parallel rowGroup operations within a `waitfor`. This is the only synchronization requirement—the operations on individual grid elements are fully parallel and can proceed without synchronization.

The grid operations include both intra-grid and inter-grid operations. The former only reference the grid that they are invoked upon, while inter-grid operations—such as adding two grids and storing the result in a third—must reference one or more additional grids along with modifying the grid that they are invoked upon. We allow the functions to directly access the internals of other grids in an inter-grid operation. Although this compromises the modularity of grid objects, it is useful when objects are shared at a fine-granularity, as in this application.

Performance   We ran the program as coded above on a 194x194 grid, but achieved a speedup of only about 12 on 32 processors (see Figure 6.4). Using the hardware performance monitor (see the results below), we found a high number of cache misses to remote memory. As part of initialization, therefore, we explicitly distributed the rowGroups of the grids across the memories of the processors, so that corresponding rowGroups of different grids are allocated within the same local memory

---

[6]For larger numbers of processors other partitionings such as a blocked decomposition of the grid may be more appropriate.

```
class row_c {
  double element[numElements];
};
class rowGroup_c {
  row_c myrow[numRows];
  ···other data, such as row indices···
public:
  parallel condH* laplace (rowGroup_c*);
  parallel condH* sub (rowGroup_c*, rowGroup_c*);
  parallel condH* jacobi (rowGroup_c*);
  ...
};
class grid_c {
  rowGroup_c rowGroup[numGroups]; // grid composed of rowGroups
 public:
  void distribute(){
    for (i=0; i<numGroups; i++) migrate (rowGroup+i, i);
  }
  void laplace (grid_c* p) {
    waitfor {
      // Process all the rowGroups in parallel.
      for (all rowGroups i)
          rowGroup[i].laplace (&(p->rowGroup[i]));
    } // wait for the operations to complete over all rowGroups.
  }
  ···other grid operations···
};

main(){
  grid_c  A, B, C, D;
  A.distribute(); B.distribute(); C.distribute(); D.distribute();
  ...
  for (all time steps){
    A.laplace(B);
    C.jacobi(D);
    ···other grid operations···
  }
}
```

Program 6.7
Concurrency and Affinity in the Ocean Code

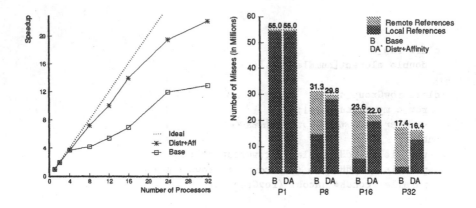

Figure 6.4
Performance Improvements (left) and Cache Miss Statistics Before and After
Affinity Hints in the Ocean Code

(see the `distribute()` function in Program 6.7). With this distribution,
the COOL runtime automatically schedules tasks for locality on the row-
Group objects, based on their default affinity. The grid operations are
therefore likely to find the data they reference in local memory. As shown
in Figure 6.4, performance improved dramatically (75-100%) with these
hints, achieving a speedup of over 22 on 32 processors.

The statistics gathered with the hardware performance monitor on
DASH are shown in the bar charts in Figure 6.4. The figure plots the
total number of cache misses before (labelled B) and after optimization (labelled DA) during the execution of the parallel portion of the
program, for different number of processors. Each bar corresponds to
the total number of caches misses and is partitioned into two regions.
The dark region represents the cache misses that were serviced in local
memory while the light region corresponds to misses that were to data
in remote memory. As shown in the figure most misses are to remote
memory before optimization, but with the optimizations nearly all (80-
90%) of the cache misses are satisfied in local memory. Thus the primary
performance gains are due to the objects being referenced in local rather
than in remote memory.

To summarize, the data structures in this application were organized
into a hierarchy of objects, and concurrency was expressed with little
additional COOL code. A simple object distribution together with the

default affinity improved both cache and memory locality. Explicit distribution of objects was required of the programmer, but easily expressed through the migrate statement. Furthermore, experience with this example suggests an automatic object distribution strategy in which the objects associated with a parallel function are distributed in a round-robin manner across the local memories of processors. This default would be sufficient for programs with a regular structure, and could always be overridden with explicit object distribution by the programmer for more complex programs.

6.6.2 LocusRoute

LocusRoute [Rose 1988] is a parallel algorithm for standard-cell placement and routing in integrated circuits. Given a placement of circuit modules, it tries to determine the paths of the connecting wires that minimize the area of the circuit. The two main data structures are `Wires` and the `CostArray`. A wire object contains the list of pin locations to be joined while `CostArray` keeps track of the number of wires running through each routing cell. The cost of a route is given by the sum of the `CostArray` values for all the routing cells that it traverses. The program iteratively converges to a route for each wire. Within each iteration, LocusRoute invokes the function `Route()` on each wire object (see Program 6.8). This function rips out the previous route of a wire, generates the possible alternate routes, and chooses the lowest-cost route. After all wires have been routed in an iteration, this process is repeated in the next iteration.

Expressing Parallelism The primary source of parallelism in the program is to route different wires concurrently within an iteration, expressed by annotating the Route function to be parallel. In contrast to the previous application, exploiting wire parallelism is appropriate from both granularity and load-balancing viewpoints—routing a wire is a coarse-grained operation, and typical input circuits contain thousands of wires thereby generating sufficient parallelism. The only synchronization required is that all wires be routed in an iteration before proceeding to the next iteration; this is expressed by wrapping a `waitfor` around an iteration. Although routing multiple wires concurrently may generate simultaneous updates to `CostArray`, the algorithm is robust enough that it converges in spite of some inconsistencies in `CostArray`.

```
struct {
  int xcost, ycost;
} CostArray [XMAX][YMAX];
// Function to determine the CostArray region that the
// wire lies in, based on the mid-point of the wire.
int Region (Wire*);
class  Wire {
  ...
 public:
  int findCost();            // Determine the cost of a route.
  parallel condH* Route()    // Parallel function to route a wire.
  [ affinity (Region (this), PROCESSOR); ];
};
main(){
  ...
  while (not converged) {
    waitfor {
      for (all wires w)  w->Route(); // route the wires in parallel
    } // Wait for all wires to be routed.
  }
}
```

Program 6.8
LocusRoute in COOL

Performance   The algorithm spends most of its time in evaluating the
cost of different routes for a wire, so locality in CostArray is important.
We can express this by viewing CostArray as partitioned into geographical regions that correspond to a spatial partitioning of the circuit and
have each processor route wires that lie within its region of CostArray,
thereby reusing that region of CostArray in the cache. To distribute the
load uniformly across processors we actually exploit this locality using
processor-affinity: each region of CostArray is (conceptually) assigned
to a processor, and tasks within that region are directly scheduled on the
corresponding processor. Besides reusing the same region in the cache,
each region is likely to be referenced by only one processor, thereby
reducing the invalidations of CostArray in caches of other processors.
Finally, depending on the degree of re-use, physically distributing the
regions of CostArray across the memories of different processors may

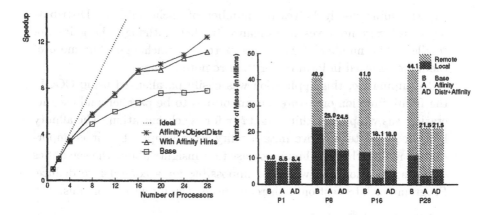

Figure 6.5
Performance Improvements (left) and Cache Miss Statistics (right) in LocusRoute
with Affinity Hints

further improve performance, since the misses to `CostArray` will be to
local rather than remote memory.

The code to express these hints is shown in Program 6.8. The function
`Region(CurrentWire)` returns the region number that the midpoint of
the wire lies within, which is then used in the processor-affinity hint.
Task stealing corrects any load imbalance across regions. Partitioning
`CostArray` into a few large regions (say one per processor) will have
better locality but poorer load balance, while larger numbers of smaller
regions will have better load balance at the expense of data locality.
These tradeoffs can be easily explored by varying the `Region()` function.

Since we had only small input circuits available, we demonstrate our
technique using a synthetically constructed input consisting of a dense
network of wires within the regions of the circuit (8160 wires uniformly
distributed in a circuit 1760 cells wide and 20 channels deep). The performance results in Figure 6.5 show the Base version in which tasks are
scheduled in a round-robin fashion across processors, the Affinity version in which tasks are scheduled based on the processor-affinity hint,
and the Affinity+ObjectDistr version in which the regions of `CostArray`
are physically distributed across processors' memories as well. Overall speedups are small due to the high degree of communication of
shared data. However, performance improves significantly with the affinity hints. As shown by the cache miss statistics in Figure 6.5, affin-

ity scheduling nearly halves the number of cache misses. Distributing `CostArray` improves performance further, although the gains are smaller. The number of cache misses remain unchanged but more of them are serviced in local rather than remote memory.

To summarize, this application was easily parallelized using COOL: the Route function on a wire was annotated to be parallel, and each iteration was wrapped within a `waitfor` for synchronization. The affinity hints required to improve data locality were simple, but it is important to realize that the hints are based on insights about the semantics of the application and would be impossible for a compiler to deduce. Programmer intervention is therefore necessary for such programs.

6.6.3   Panel Cholesky

The last application, Panel Cholesky, performs parallel Cholesky factorization of a sparse positive definite matrix. Given a sparse matrix A, the program finds a lower-triangular matrix L, such that $A = LL^T$. Rothberg and Gupta have suggested a matrix representation in which columns with identical non-zero structure are organized into panels [Rothberg & Gupta 1990]. Operations are performed between panels—each panel has updates performed to it by relevant panels to its left, and once all the updates to a panel have been performed, the panel becomes 'ready' and can be used to update other panels to its right.

Expressing Parallelism   Parallelism in this algorithm consists of performing the panel-panel updates concurrently. Typical inputs have thousands of panels, and this concurrency is suitable from both a granularity and a load-balancing perspective. The COOL code expressing this computation is shown in Program 6.9. The main data structures are panel objects that offer two methods of interest, `updatePanel()` and `completePanel()`. `updatePanel()` updates a destination panel using the supplied source panel and invokes `completePanel()` if all updates have completed. `completePanel()` performs internal completion on a panel and generates updates that use this panel as a source. Concurrent execution is expressed by labelling both these functions to be parallel. The computation is initiated in `main()` by calling `completePanel()` on those panels of the matrix that are initially ready.

The concurrent execution of multiple updates is subject to the following synchronization constraints: since an update modifies the destina-

```
class panel_c {
  int remainingUpdates;
  ...
 public:
   // Update this panel by the given source panel.
   parallel mutex condH* updatePanel (panel_c* src)
   [ affinity (src, TASK); affinity (this, OBJECT);] {
     ···Update this panel by the given src panel···
     if (--remainingUpdates == 0) completePanel(); // Panel ready
   }
   // Perform internal completion of the panel.
   parallel condH* completePanel(){
     ···perform internal completion···
     // Produce updates that need this panel.
     for (all panels p modified by this panel)
       panel[p].updatePanel (this);
   }
} *panel;
main(){
  ...
  // Distribute panels across processors memories in a round robin fashion.
  for (i=0; i<MaxPanels; i++) migrate (panel+i, i);
  waitfor {
    // Start with the initially ready panels.
    for (all panels p that are initially ready)
      panel[p].completePanel();
  } // Wait for all updates to complete.
}
```

Program 6.9
Panel Cholesky in COOL

tion panel, only one update can proceed on a destination panel at any time; all updates that are due to be performed on a panel must complete before that panel can itself be used to perform other updates; and the overall computation finishes when all the updates have completed.

These synchronization requirements are expressed as follows. Multiple updates to a destination panel are serialized by annotating the updatePanel() function to be mutex; it therefore has exclusive access to the panel being modified. For the second synchronization requirement, as part of initialization the algorithm counts the number of updates that must be performed on each panel and stores that number within each panel object. This number is decremented by each update operation. Once it reaches zero then all updates have been performed and the panel is ready. Although this is a specialized synchronization scheme that is explicitly constructed by the programmer, it is very efficient and easily coded in COOL. Finally, synchronization for the overall computation is expressed using the waitfor construct as shown.

Synchronization for a panel is necessary only when it is being updated; after all the updates have been performed, the panel can be read without any synchronization. We therefore enforce synchronization for the panels being updated, and bypass it for the ready panels.

Performance   Most of the work is done in updatePanel(), which reads the source panel and modifies the destination panel. By default, tasks corresponding to updatePanel() have affinity for the panel that they are invoked on (the destination panel) and are automatically scheduled to exploit both cache re-use and memory locality on the destination panel. By distributing the panels across processors' memories we can achieve a uniform distribution of work across processors as well. Finally, similar to the column-oriented Gaussian elimination example discussed in Section 6.4.2, we can simultaneously exploit cache re-use on each source panel by identifying tasks with the same source panel as a task-affinity set. Since each processor usually has multiple panels assigned to it that need to be modified by any given source panel, executing these updates back-to-back on the processor will re-use the source panel in the cache.

The performance results are shown in Figure 6.6. We use the matrix BCSSTK33 from the Boeing-Harwell set of sparse matrix benchmarks [Duff *et al.* 1989]. This matrix has 8738 columns organized into 1201 pan-

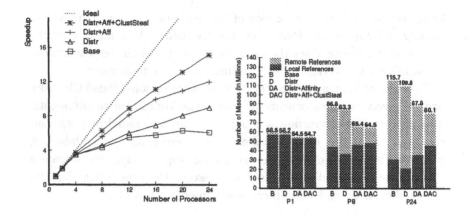

Figure 6.6
Performance Improvements (left) and Cache Miss Statistics (right) with Affinity Hints for Panel Cholesky (matrix BCSSTK33)

els. The Base version has no optimizations. Distr includes round-robin distribution of panels across processors, but with random task distribution. The improvement in performance is due to a better distribution of the memory bandwidth requirements. Performance further improves with scheduling tasks with affinity for the source and destination panels as described above, shown by the plot Distr+Aff.

We now discuss an experiment we did with cluster-based scheduling. Recall that although tasks are co-located with the destination panel on a particular processor, all processors within that cluster (in DASH) share the local memory containing the destination panel. We restricted an idle processor to steal tasks only from other processors within the same cluster; the stolen tasks would therefore continue to reference the destination panel in local rather than remote memory. As shown by the plot Distr+Aff+ClustSteal, stealing only within a cluster further improves performance.

Although we directly manipulated cluster scheduling in these experiments, the runtime scheduler could automatically try to steal tasks from processors within the same cluster before stealing tasks from remote processors. However, more experience is required before good defaults and automatic strategies can be developed.

Figure 6.6 displays the effect of the optimizations on the cache miss behavior of the program. Simply distributing the panels improves performance due to better utilization of the available memory bandwidth. Affinity and cluster scheduling significantly reduce the number of cache misses. Furthermore, since the tasks are co-located with the panel, more of the misses are serviced in local rather than remote memory.

To summarize, compared to the previous applications, Panel Cholesky had relatively complex concurrency and synchronization requirements. The important computation was organized around panel objects, and concurrent execution and mutual exclusion were expressed by labelling methods on panels to be `parallel`/`mutex` respectively. While panels were explicitly distributed across processors, the scheduling defaults were sufficient to exploit both cache and memory locality.

6.7   Conclusions

In this chapter we have described the parallel programming language COOL, that integrates concurrency and synchronization with the object structure of a C++ program. We show how we exploit this support for data abstraction to improve both the expressiveness and efficiency of COOL programs. The underlying data abstraction provides the programmer the facility to build object level abstractions that encapsulate concurrency and synchronization within the object. In addition, providing synchronization integrated with objects enables compiler analysis and optimizations that significantly reduce the synchronization overhead in a COOL program.

We have shown how the structure of COOL program, decomposed into tasks and objects, provides an attractive framework to address data locality and load balancing. We provide abstractions for the programmer to supply information about the objects referenced by tasks; this information is used to distribute tasks and objects appropriately across processors. Our experience in using these hints, and the ensuing performance improvements lead us to conclude that a combination of simple programmer hints and smart runtime strategies is a highly effective approach for improving data locality and load balance.

We have implemented COOL on several shared-memory multiprocessors, and programmed a variety of application programs in the language. Our experience in writing programs in COOL, as well as the performance of the programs on actual multiprocessors, has demonstrated the benefits of data abstraction in expressing concurrency and synchronization, and in exploiting data locality.

Acknowledgments

Arul Menezes and Shigeru Urushibara helped with the initial COOL implementation. Avneesh Agrawal, Maneesh Agrawala, Denis Bohm, Robert Wilson, and Kaoru Uchida provided valuable programming feedback. Kourosh Gharachorloo and J.P. Singh offered many useful comments. This research has been supported by the Defense Advanced Research Projects Agency under DARPA contract #N00039-91-C-0138.

7   C++//

Denis Caromel, Fabrice Belloncle, and Yves Roudier

7.1   Introduction

The C++// language (pronounced "C++ parallel") was designed and implemented with the aim of importing re-usability into parallel and concurrent programming, in the framework of a MIMD model. C++// defines a comprehensive and versatile set of libraries, using a small set of simple primitives, without extending the syntax of C++. The libraries are themselves extensible by end users, making C++// an open system.

Information on our system is available through the World Wide Web at:

http://www.inria.fr/sloop/c++ll

while queries and comments can be sent via e-mail to:

c++ll@unice.fr

Re-usability has been one of the major contributions of object-oriented programming; bringing it to parallel programming is one of our main goals, and it would be a major step forward for software engineering of parallel systems. Part of the challenge is to combine the potential for extensive re-use with the high performance which is usually required of parallel and real-time systems.

Working mainly within the framework of physically-distributed architectures, we are concerned with both explicit and implicit parallelism in both the problem and solution domains. Our applications include parallel data structures, computer-supported cooperative work (CSCW), and fault tolerance and reliability in safety-critical and real-time systems.

We are part of the *SLOOP* (Simulation and Parallel Object-Oriented Languages) project, a recently-formed research team with approximately 15 members at I3S-CNRS, the University of Nice, and INRIA Sophia Antipolis. This team is investigating three research areas: parallel and distributed discrete event simulation, parallel object-oriented languages, and communication and interconnection networks. These three domains are not independent: each level needs and uses the primitives and capabilities of the layer beneath it. As a member of this group, supporting distributed simulations [Mallet & Mussi 1993] is of first importance for our system.

To achieve this, we began the design and implementation of C++// in early 1994. While a recent development, C++// owes a significant part of its design and implementation techniques to previous research, which led to the definition of Eiffel// [Caromel 1989, Caromel 1993a, Caromel 1993b], a parallel extension of Eiffel [Meyer 1988, Meyer 1992]. In particular, C++// defines a reduced set of simple primitives: these can then be composed to create comprehensive and versatile libraries, which—most importantly—can then be extended by end users.

Another important characteristic of our system is the complete absence of any syntactical extension to C++. C++// users write standard C++ code, relying on specific classes to give programs a parallel semantics. These programs are then passed through a pre-processor, which generates new files. The original and new code are finally compiled and linked with a standard C++ compiler. When appropriate, all names related to the C++// system include the 11 root in their name (for "parallel").

This chapter begins by describing the basic features of our programming model, which is a distributed-memory MIMD model. Section 7.3 deals with the control programming of processes (i.e., the definition of concurrent process activity). A recommended method for parallel programming in C++// is outlined in Section 7.4. Those parts of the programming environment which handle compilation and mapping are described in Section 7.5. We then present our implementation of polygon overlay in Section 7.6. Finally, an overview of the implementation techniques which make the system open and user-extensible is given in Section 7.7; we present our concluding remarks in Section 7.8.

7.2   Basic Model of Concurrency

This section describes four important characteristics of our parallel programming model: parallel processes, communication between them, synchronization, and data sharing. As mentioned above, we adopt a distributed-memory MIMD model, which means that there are no directly-shared objects in our system.

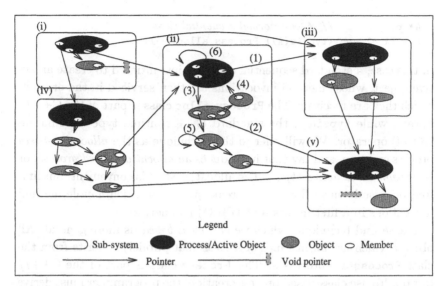

Figure 7.1
Processes and Objects at Runtime

Along with simplicity and expressiveness, re-usability is one of our major concerns. More specifically, we want to allow users to take an existing C++ system and transform it into a distributed one, so that they may derive parallel systems from sequential ones [Caromel 1990b].

7.2.1 Processes

One of the key features of the object-oriented paradigm is the unification of the notions of module and type to create the notion of class. When adding parallelism, another unification is to bring together the concepts of class and process, so that every process is an instance of a class, and the process's possible behavior is completely described by its class. However, not all objects are processes. At runtime, we distinguish two kinds of objects: *process objects* (or active objects), which are active by themselves, with their own thread of control, and *passive objects*, which are normal objects. This second category includes all non-active objects. An example of the arrangement of processes and objects at runtime is given in Figure 7.1.

At the language level, there are two ways to generate active objects. In the first, an active object is obtained by instantiating a standard sequential C++ class using `Process_alloc`:

```
A* p;           // A is a normal sequential class
p = (A *) new (typeid(A)) Process_alloc(···);
```

In this case, a standard sequential class A is instantiated to create an active object, whose method invocations are then serviced in the order in which they are received. The Process_alloc class is part of the C++// library, while typeid is the standard C++ runtime type information (RTTI) operator. We will refer to this technique as the *allocation-based* process creation, and say that it produces an *allocation-based process*, or *allocation-based active object*. The allocation style is convenient, but limited because it only allows us to create processes which handle method invocations in a first-in, first-out (FIFO) manner.

The second technique, which we call *class-based*, is more general. All objects which are an instance of a class that publicly inherits from the class Process are processes. This Process class is part of the C++// library. To use class-based process creation, the programmer must derive a specific class, called a *process class*, from Process, as in:

```
class Parallel_A : public A, public Process {
  ...
};
...
Parallel_A* p;
p = new Parallel_A(···);
```

As with the allocation-based technique, instances of subclasses of Process have a default FIFO behavior. However, as we will see in the following sections, it is possible to change this to create other behaviors. We say that the class-based technique generates *class-based processes*, or *class-based active objects*.

As shown on Figure 7.1, passive objects (i.e., objects which are not active) belong at runtime to a single process object. This organizes a parallel program into disjoint sub-systems, each of which consists of one active object encapsulating zero or more passive objects. Figure 7.2 presents the two styles of active object definition.

7.2.2   Sequential or Parallel Processes

A major design decision for any concurrent programming system is whether processes are sequential (i.e., single-threaded) or able to support internal concurrency (i.e., multithreaded). Because our system is

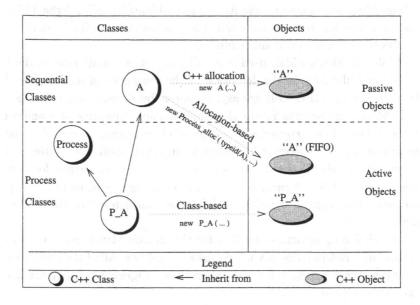

Figure 7.2
Allocation-Based and Class-Based Active Objects

oriented towards re-use and software engineering of parallel systems, rather than operating systems programming, we chose to make processes sequential. We believe that single-threaded processes are easier to re-use, and easier to write correctly.

The model does not allow the user to program multithreaded processes, but this does not prevent multithreading at the operating system level. As we will see in Section 7.5.2, several sequential processes can be implemented with one multithreaded operating system process for the sake of light-weightness.

7.2.3 Communication

Since a process is an object, it has member functions. When an object owns a reference to a process, it is able to communicate with it by calling one of its public members. This is C++//'s interprocess communication (IPC) mechanism: all communication towards active objects appear syntactically as member function calls:

```
p->f(parameters);
```

This idea, introduced by the Actors model [Hewitt 1977, Agha 1986], means that what is sometimes called a process entry point is identical to a normal routine or member function.

While this idea is widely used in parallel object-oriented systems, there are many differences in the definition of the semantics of method-based IPC. In C++//, IPC calls are asynchronous by default, while function calls to passive objects retain the synchronous semantics of standard C++. This choice encourages the parallel execution of objects, and makes each process more independent from other parallel activities and more self-contained. As we will see, it is also very important for supporting re-usability. Synchronous function calls are possible in C++//, but must be specified explicitly in either the function call or the process definition.

The choice of asynchronous IPC for the default structures a C++// system into independent asynchronous *sub-systems*: all of the communication between sub-systems is asynchronous. Figure 7.1 illustrates five such sub-systems.

7.2.4   Synchronization

Asynchronous communication can be difficult for programmers to manage. For example, since function calls to processes are asynchronous, one needs to explicitly synchronize before using result values, to make sure they have been returned by the processes. Commonly, such models lack the implicit synchronization usually provided by a synchronous communication semantics.

We use a simple rule, called *wait-by-necessity*, to address this problem. In C++//, a process is automatically blocked when it attempts to use the result of a parallel member function call that has not yet been returned. Thus, a caller does not wait for the result of an asynchronous function call until that value is explicitly used in some computation. Should a value not have been returned at that point, the caller is automatically blocked until the value becomes available. This mechanism implicitly synchronizes processes; the two primitives `Wait()` and `Awaited()` are provided for explicit synchronization.

Program 7.1 summarizes the semantics of wait-by-necessity. The result of a function call not yet returned is called an *awaited object*. Our semantics define that no wait is triggered by assigning a pointer to such an object to another variable, or by passing such a pointer as a param-

```
v = p->f(parameters);        // asynchronous call
...
v->foo();                    // implicitly triggers a wait
                             // if v is awaited
...
if (Awaited(v)) {            // test the status of v
  ...
}

Wait(v);                     // explicitly triggers a wait
                             // if v is awaited
...
obj->g(v);                   // no wait if pointer access
v2 = v;
```

Program 7.1
Wait-by-Necessity

eter. A wait occurs only when the program accesses the awaited object itself (which is syntactically a pointer access to the object) or transmits (copies) the object to another process.

Wait-by-necessity is a form of future [Halstead 1985], and is related to concepts found in several other languages: the Hurry primitive of Act1 [Lieberman 1987], the CBox objects of ConcurrentSmalltalk [Yokote & Tokoro 1987], and the future-type message passing of ABCL/1 [Yonezawa et al. 1987]. However, an important difference is that the mechanism presented here is systematic for all asynchronous function calls and automatic, which is reflected in the absence of any special syntactic construction. This has a strong impact on re-usability.

In order to avoid the runtime overhead involved in the implementation of wait-by-necessity, programmers can use explicit synchronization primitives instead of implicit synchronization. This is a tradeoff between programming ease and re-usability on the one hand, and efficiency and speedup on the other.

7.2.5 Sharing

If two processes refer to the same passive object, method calls to that object may overlap, which raises all of the problems usually associated with shared data. To address this issue, each non-process object in

C++// is a private object, and is accessible to only one process. We say that a private object belongs to its process's sub-system.

The programming model ensures that sharing does not occur: the communication of passive objects between processes uses a copying semantics. Passive object parameters of a call are automatically transmitted by value from one process to another. A deep copy of these objects is achieved: when an object X is copied, all the (also passive) objects referred to by pointers in X are deep-copied as well. The implementation automatically and transparently handles the required marshalling of data and pointers, as well as circular object structures. Of course, process parameters are always passed by reference.

Figure 7.1 illustrates the absence of passive objects shared by processes in C++// programs. Each passive object is accessible to exactly one active object; each of the five sub-systems in this program consists of one active object and all the passive objects it can reach. The arcs labelled (1) and (2) are always activated as asynchronous communication (IPC), while the arcs labelled (3) to (6) are activated as normal function calls. As a consequence of the absence of shared objects, synchronization between sub-systems only occurs when one sub-system waits for a result value from another process.

Prohibiting shared data also has important methodological consequences. As we shall see in Section 7.4.3, the features of C++//, together with object-oriented techniques such as polymorphism and dynamic binding, permits the derivation of parallel systems from sequential ones. The absence of shared objects allows either an immediate re-use (the default automatic copy of parameters is the correct semantics), or the identification of new processes to program in order to implement semantically shared values. Finally, due to the absence of interleaving of operations inside sub-systems, it helps to ensure the correctness of the parallel applications derived from sequential ones.

The basic characteristics of our programming model are summarized in Figure 7.3.

7.3   Control Programming

So far, we have only examined and defined the features of C++// which deal with the global aspects of the programming model, such as the

- A process is an active object, sequential and single-threaded.

- Communication to active objects are syntactically programmed as member function calls, and are asynchronous.

- An object is automatically blocked when it attempts to use the result of a member function call that has not been returned yet (wait-by-necessity).

- There are no shared passive objects.

- Passive objects parameters are passed by value (copy).

Figure 7.3
Basic Features of the C++// Model

nature of processes and their interactions. This section describes how the control flow of processes is specified, i.e., how behavior, communication, and synchronization of active objects is programmed. Here and later, we use *request* to mean a call issued to a process member function. Since communication is asynchronous, the process to which the request was issued will later *serve* the request: that is to say, it will execute the member function being invoked.

7.3.1 Centralized versus Decentralized Control

Decentralized control is distributed throughout a program. Each routine, public or otherwise, may contain a part of the control. An example of this is the **uses** clause of the Hybrid language [Nierstrasz 1987]:

```
type buffer of (···);
...
private {
put: (item: item_type) ->;
  uses not full;
  { ··· }
get:->item_type;
  uses not empty;
  { ··· }
```

Alternatively, control can be centralized (i.e., gathered into one place in the definition of a process), independent of the function code. An example of this is the CONTROL construct of Guide [Decouchant *et al.* 1989]:

```
CLASS buffer IS

METHOD put(···); BEGIN
  ...
END put;

METHOD get(···); BEGIN
  ...
END get;

CONTROL
  put: ((completed(put) - completed(get)) < size )
       and (current(put) = 0);
  get: (completed(put) < completed(get))
       and (current(get) = 0);
END buffer
```

Decentralized control makes the re-use of member functions difficult for two reasons. First, functions designed in a sequential framework cannot be re-used in a parallel one just as they are, as elements of control must be added to them. Second, when a new process class is obtained through inheritance of another process class, the new class often needs to change the synchronization scheme used in the original class. If control is embedded in function bodies, this may not be feasible. This led us to decide to use centralized control in C++//, as it allows function re-use for both sequential and process classes.

Program 7.2 presents partial code for the library class **Process**. After creation and initialization, a process object executes its **Live()** routine. This routine describes the sequence of actions which that process executes during its lifetime. The process terminates when the **Live()** routine completes.

7.3.2   Explicit versus Implicit Control

Another design decision that must be made in concurrent object-oriented systems is whether process control is implicit or explicit. Control is explicit if its definition consists of an explicitly programmed thread of control (e.g., as in Hybrid). Otherwise, control is implicit, which in practice usually means that it is declarative (e.g., as in Guide).

```
class Process {
 public:
  Process (···) {      // process creation
   ...
  }

  virtual void Live() {     // process body
   ··· // default FIFO behavior
  }
  ...
};
```

Program 7.2
The Process Class

Implicit control is a high-level concept. Thanks to its declarative nature, it is an effective way to express synchronization. It usually provides programmers with a consistent framework, in which they can forget implementation details and describe the synchronization constraints in a very synthetic manner. Implicit control has also the advantage of promoting synchronization re-use [Matsuoka *et al.* 1990, Neusius 1991, Decouchant *et al.* 1991, Shibayama 1991, Frolund 1992, Lohr 1992].

However, many implicit control frameworks (i.e., abstractions for concurrency) exist, including synchronization counters [Robert & Verjus 1977, McHale *et al.* 1990], path expressions [Campbell & Haberman 1974], behavior abstractions [Kafura & Lee 1990], and synchronizers [Agha *et al.* 1993]. Each has a different expressive power, and different properties regarding re-usability of synchronization constraints. None is universal: within each, some problems are difficult to describe, and some problems cannot be described at all. Nevertheless, for its abstract nature and its re-use potential [Kafura & Lee 1989, Frolund 1992], we believe that implicit control should be used as often as possible.

Synchronization expressed using explicit control is not defined declaratively, but is instead programmed. The languages CSP [Hoare 1978, Hoare 1985], Ada [Burns 1985, Gehani 1984b, Ichbiah *et al.* 1979], Occam [Inmos 1988], ABCL/1 [Yonezawa *et al.* 1987], POOL2 [America 1988], Concurrent C [Gehani & Roome 1989], and Eiffel// [Caromel 1993a] all use explicit control. Its first advantage is that, since the programmer actually programs a thread of control, all the expressive power associated with imperative language can be used. The detailed behavior of an active object can be specified, and fine tuning of policies is possible.

The second advantage of explicit control is that it allows programmers to describe the internal actions of processes, i.e., operations that are to execute independently of external requests. This kind of activity is difficult, or even impossible, to program with implicit control, since there is usually no place to mention the activation of personal actions. In any case, it is very hard to finely control the time spent executing such actions, and the time spent servicing externally-visible routines.

The third (and, to our group, decisive) advantage of explicit control is that under some conditions, it permits the design and construction of implicit control frameworks. Such abstractions can be put into libraries, from which programmers can chose the most appropriate for their needs [Caromel 1990c]. Then, within one language, one can always choose the type of control programming that best fits a given problem. In fact, explicit control may be viewed as a low-level mechanism, allowing either the definition of complex and precise synchronization, or the construction of a particular abstraction to be used for higher-level implicit control.

In summary, our argument is that:

1. programmers sometimes need explicit control;

2. implicit control permits the re-use of synchronization;

3. no universal implicit control abstraction exists; and

4. explicit control allows us to build implicit control abstractions.

As a consequence, the basic mechanism for programming process behavior in C++// is explicit control. Explicit control programming consists of defining the **Live()** routine of the **Process** class and its derived classes (Program 7.2) using the sequential control structures of C++. All of the expressive power of C++ is available, without any limitation. For example, the process body of a bounded buffer can be defined as:

```
class Buffer1 : public Process {
   ...
   virtual void Live()
   {
      while (executing) {
         if (!full())
```

```
        explicit service of put
    if (!empty())
        explicit service of get
    }
    }
};
```

Besides explicit control, other features are needed in order to construct abstractions for concurrent programming. These features also provide C++// with a mechanism to explicitly service requests, the two instructions left unspecified in the example above.

First, defining a process's thread of control often consists of defining the synchronization of its public member functions. Since such an activity requires dynamic manipulation of C++ functions, we need to represent member functions as first-class objects. (In practice, only some limited features, such as the ability to use routines as parameters, and system-wide valid function identifiers, are needed.)

To fill that need, we provide the function mid() (for "method ID") to return function identifiers. Its usage is:

```
member_id f;
f = mid(put);
f = mid(A::put);
f = mid(A::put, A::get);
f = mid(A::put(int, P *));
```

In order to deal with overloading, this function returns either a single identifier, or a representation of all adequate functions. Related functions are defined in Section 7.7.3.

In the same way, because we need to explicitly program request servicing, we must be able to manipulate requests as objects (i.e., to pass them as parameters of other functions, to assign them to variables, and so on). In C++//, the class Request models requests. As shown below, every request is an instance of this class:

```
class Request {
 public:
   member_id m;              // member to be called
   List<Any> eff_params;     // effective parameters
   Any object;               // target object
   request_id id;            // ID of the request
   ...
};
```

A request object holds the identifier of the function to be invoked, the actual parameters of the invocation, a reference to the target object, an ID of the request, and information needed in order to implement the remote invocation. The class **Any** is used to manipulate any basic type of C++, and any pointer to a class or a structure. Since **Any** is implemented in standard C++, the basic type conversions are implicit, while conversions to class pointers must be explicit.

Finally, to be able to fully control request servicing, programmers must have access to the list of pending requests. This is given through the **Process** class, with a specific member named **request_list** that contains the list.

With these three facilities in place, it is possible to program the control of processes in diverse and flexible ways presented in the two next sections.

7.3.3   Library of Service Routines

Service primitives are needed to allow programmers to program control explicitly. Usually, programmers are given only a few such primitives, mainly because they are made part of the language itself as syntactical constructions (e.g., the **serve** instruction of Ada). With the primitives we define, it is possible to program a complete library of service routines [Caromel 1990a]. Some of these are shown in Program 7.3, where f and g are member identifiers obtained from the function **mid()** introduced in the previous section.

These functions are defined in the class **Process**, and can be used when programming the **Live()** routine. There are no limitations on the range of facilities that can be encapsulated in service routines. Timed services are an example of such expressiveness; selection based on the request parameters is another. Moreover, if a programmer does not find the particular selection function she needs, she is able to program it. Thus, libraries of service routines, specific to particular programmers or application domains, can be defined.

Another important point concerns efficiency: concurrency policies are determined within the context of each process, based on local information, rather than by using IPC. This avoids problems like polling bias [Gehani 1984a]. This is an important advantage in distributed programming.

```
// Non-blocking services
serve_oldest();          // Serve the oldest request of all
serve_oldest(f);         // The oldest request on f
serve_oldest(f, g, ···);   // The oldest of f or g
...

serve_flush();           // Serve the oldest, wipe out the others
serve_flush(f);          // The oldest on f
...

// Blocking services: wait until there is actually a request to serve
bl_serve_oldest(f);      // blocking version of serve_oldest on f
bl_serve_flush();        // blocking version of serve_flush
...

// Timed blocking services: block for a limited time only
tm_serve_oldest(t);      // Serve the oldest, wait at most t
...

// Information retrieval
exist_request()          // true if a pending request exists
exist_request(f)         // True if a pending request exists on f
...

// Waiting primitives
wait_a_request();        // Wait until there is a request to serve
wait_a_request(f);       // Wait a request to serve on f
```

Program 7.3
A Library of Service Routines

```cpp
class Buffer: public Process, public List {
  ...
 protected:
  virtual void Live()
  {
    while (!stop) {
      if (!full())
        serve_oldest(mid(put));
      if (!empty())
        serve_oldest(mid(get));
    }
  }
};
```

Program 7.4
An Explicit Bounded Buffer Example

To illustrate the use of explicit control programming, Program 7.4 presents a C++// implementation of a bounded buffer. This definition implements a specific policy: when the buffer is neither full() nor empty(), the buffer alternates service on put() and get(). This policy is clearly not the only possible one. For example, some situations might require requests to be processed in the order of their arrival. Such a policy can be programmed as follows:

```
virtual void Live() {
  while (!stop) {
    if (full())
      serve_oldest(mid(get));
    else if (empty())
      serve_oldest(mid(put));
    else
      serve_oldest(mid(put), mid(get));
  }
}
```

This is an example of explicitly fine-tuning the synchronization of processes. While this might be important in some contexts, in other contexts we might want to program within a more abstract framework, and ignore the implementation details. The next section shows how we allow such programming.

7.3.4 Library of Abstractions

Again, using the basic features defined in Section 7.3.2, it is possible to program the abstractions for concurrency control that are usually built into parallel languages [Caromel 1990c, Caromel 1991, Caromel 1993c]. In order to define a new abstraction, one inherits from the Process class, and creates the desired synchronization behavior framework. In order to exploit the abstraction, users inherit from this class instead of from the Process class when defining an active object.

For example, we can program a simple abstraction in which: a blocking condition (i.e., a function returning true or false) is associated with each public function, and a public function whose blocking condition is true is not served. The class Abst_Process, shown in Program 7.5, defines this framework. The function associate() permits users to specify blocking conditions for public functions; these associations are to be defined in the user class within the synchronization() function.

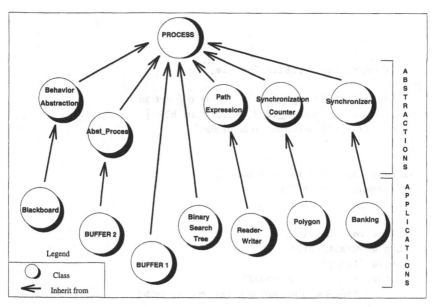

Figure 7.4
Library of Abstractions

The process body, which overrides the generic `Live()` routine, calls the `synchronization()` function once, and then loops to scan the pending request list, serving a request when its blocking condition is false. This `synchronization()` function is empty in the class `Abst_Process`, thus providing a default FIFO policy (no blocking condition).

This abstraction can be used to program a bounded buffer in an implicit style, as shown by the class `Buffer` in Program 7.6. Instead of inheriting from `Process`, this class uses the `Abst_Process` abstraction and, as previously, also inherits from the data structure `List`. The routine `synchronization()` defines the class's concurrency control; the functions `full()` and `empty()` are the blocking conditions of the public functions `put()` and `get()` respectively.

The definition of the buffer given in Program 7.6 is much more abstract than the one given in Program 7.4. In the former, control is specified declaratively, and is also non-deterministic, in that we have not specified whether the order of service respects the order of request arrival. In languages with explicit control, a specific instruction is usually needed in order to obtain non-determinism, such as the `select`

```
class Abst_Process: public Process, ··· {
 public:
  // associate a blocking condition bl with a function f
  void associate(member_id f, member_id bl) {
    ···    // synchronization to be defined
  }

  virtual void synchronization() {
    // empty: FIFO policy
  }

  virtual void Live() {
    synchronization();
    while (!stop)
      for (each pending request)
        if (blocking function is false) service request
  }
};
```

Program 7.5
An Example of Abstraction

```
class Buffer2: public Abst_Process, public List {
  ···
 protected:
  virtual void synchronization() {
    associate(mid(put), mid(full));
    associate(mid(get), mid(empty));
  }
};
```

Program 7.6
An Implicit Bounded Buffer

- Processes have centralized and explicit control programming.
- Member functions and requests are first class objects.
- The list of pending requests is accessible.
- A library of service routines provides for explicit control programming.
- A library of abstractions allows for implicit and declarative control.

Figure 7.5
Control Programming in C++//

instruction in Ada. This important capability is sometimes very much desirable for its abstraction, sometimes not. For example, it can be useful for a simple and concise specification of the next service over a set of member functions. In our framework, non-determinism is obtained, when needed, by normal programming, and made available through the library of abstractions (Figure 7.4), which can be specific to particular programmers or to application domains, and are extensible by final users. Figure 7.5 summarizes the basic features of the C++// model for control programming.

7.4 A Programming Method

This section presents how to use C++// to program parallel and distributed applications. Because it is rather difficult to evaluate performances of distributed systems before they actually run, we believe that definition of processes has to be postponed as much as possible, and should be flexible and adaptable.

7.4.1 Sequential Design and Programming (step 1)

The first step is a standard, sequential, object-oriented design [Booch 1986, Booch 1987, Halbert & O'Brien 1987, Meyer 1988]. The only thing that matters is, before defining parallel activities, to have a fully sequential implementation: we are then able to conduct tests to ensure the correctness of the sequential algorithms and implementation. The next three steps deal with parallel design and are specific to C++//.

7.4.2 Process Identification (step 2)

Processes are a subset of classes. Object-oriented design usually gives a finer-grained decomposition than structured design, so there is no need for restructuring. This step is therefore defined by two successive phases.

(2.1) Initial Activities: In a concurrent system, there are points where the activity starts. Our method uses these sources of *initial activity* to structure a system into processes. The objects where an activity takes place will be the initial processes.

There are various cases, heavily depending on the application domain: *active objects* for parallelization, *control objects* that continuously ensure their function of control, *event dependent objects* that need to be activated at dedicated speed or asynchronously, all the periodic or asynchronous I/O, etc.

(2.2) Shared Objects: At this point, a set of classes are defined to be processes and we know the system topology. The concurrent model focuses on each object referred to by at least two processes. If the object can be passed by copy, there is nothing to change, the model automatically ensures this behavior. If it appears that the object really needs to be shared, a process class has to be programmed. This rule leads to identification of new processes.

7.4.3 Process programming (step 3)

In this section we program the processes identified during the previous step. The classes that remain passive are commonly used without any changes.

(3.1) Define Process Classes: The method to directly program the processes relies on the fact that each class is a potential process.

First, it has to be decided which technique is the most appropriate for programming the concurrency control of the process: explicitly (using the basic **Process** class), or implicitly (choosing and using one abstraction). Then, the new process class is a new class that derives from the corresponding passive class and either the class **Process**, or the selected abstraction.

Because IPCs are unified with member function calls, we are able to use the methods defined in the ancestor. However, not every original public operation will be used. Since we program the process class, new interfaces reflecting the concurrent activities can be defined.

(3.2) **Define the Activity:** A process class is given a default FIFO body. There are mainly two, possibly simultaneous, cases where we need to change the process body by redefining the control method: the *synchronization* is not FIFO, or the process carries on *internal activities* besides the request services. This is not a problem since the programmer has all the control to tune up fine policies regarding the relative time to spend among the different activities.

(3.3) **Use the Process Classes:** In order to use the process classes defined previously, all the objects identified in step 2. as processes need to be assigned with an instance of the corresponding process. An entity a declared as: A* a; has to be assigned with a process object of type P_A (derived class of A): a = new P_A (···). A function call on a is now executed on an asynchronous basis (the caller does not wait for its completion). This automatic transformation of synchronous calls into asynchronous ones is crucial to avoid method redefinition. An inherited method may use the result of a function call issued to the process:

```
res = a->fct(parameters);
...
res->g(parameters);
```

In this case, the *wait-by-necessity* handles the situation. Without this automatic *data-driven synchronization* one would have to redefine the routine in order to add explicit synchronization.

7.4.4 Adaptations (step 4)

At this stage, the system starts running and efficiency tests are realized. This last step is a system refinement in order to match parallel specifications.

(4.1) **Refine the Topology:** If a value is kept in another process context, it can be obtained in two different ways: (1) by requesting the object that holds the data, (2) by receiving the data asynchronously through a public method. Generally a refinement in the topology will transform a situation (1) into a situation (2). The aim is usually to globally minimize the number of interprocess communications. Such a modification leads to design new classes by inheritance. A process will receive the value it needs through a new public method.

(4.2) **Define New Processes:** There are various reasons leading to define new processes: *buffering processes* can be useful (even if the model is asynchronous), *secretary* process can trim the workload of another process, an object detected to be *computationally intensive* may need to be transformed into a process to map it onto another processor, etc. Since this phase identifies new processes, we again apply rule 2.2 about shared objects. Finally, we apply step 3 in order to program the new process classes. Step 4 (*Adaptation to constraints*) is realized repeatedly.

7.5 Environment

This section describes the facilities that support the development of C++// programs, including compilation of source code, executable generation, and a mechanism for mapping active objects onto machines.

7.5.1 Compilation

Compilation is achieved by pre-processing a program's source files using the command c++11. The pre-processor does not modify the user classes, but instead generates extra code in separate files. For each user file, a corresponding C++ file is generated by the C++// system. These generated files and the original user files are then compiled with a standard C++ compiler. All files are finally linked together with the C++// library (Figure 7.6).

For each source file, `file.cc`, code generation is achieved in two phases, which are transparent to the user. The first phase analyses the source code and generates an information file named `file-11` in a directory called `.c++11` below the directory of the original file. The second phase generates a C++ file (`file-11.cc`).

The file `.c++11-config` contains general information regarding the user's personal settings of the C++// installation. Information specific to each C++// system is specified in the file `.c++11-system` in order to produce an executable from a set of files.

7.5.2 Mapping

Mapping assigns each active object created during the execution of a C++// program to an operating system process on an actual machine or processor. In order to avoid confusion, we call the sub-system consisting of one active object and all its passive objects a *language process*, and

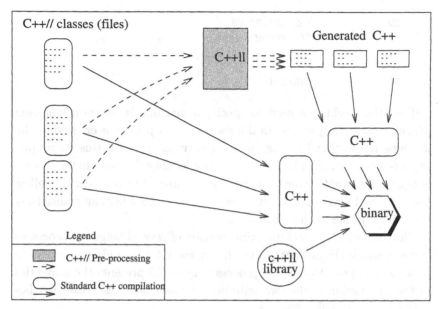

Figure 7.6
Compilation of a C++// System

use the term *OS process* for the usual notion of an operating system process.

The mapping of a language process to an OS process on a particular processor is controlled by the programmer through the association of the machine where the process is to be created, and its light-weight or heavy-weight nature. The machine itself can be specified in two ways. The first method is to specify a virtual machine name, which is simply a string. This name is related to an actual machine name by a translation file called .c++ll-mapping. The C++// system looks for this file first in the directory in which the process is running, and, if it is not found there, in the user's home directory. An example of such file is:

```
// .c++ll-mapping
// virtual name   actual name
   Mach_A         Nice
   Mach_B         cannes.unice.fr
   Mach_C         alto.unice.fr
   Names          monaco
   Server         Inria.Sophia.fr
   S1             wilpena.unice.fr
```

S2	192.134.39.96
S3	// *current machine*
P1	I3S-1
...	...
P6	INRIA-1

The other technique used to specify a machine is to use a language
process that already exists. In this case, the new process is created on the
machine where that language process is running. With this technique,
processes can be linked together to ensure locality. We say that a process
is *anchored* to another one, because its mapping will automatically follow
that specified for the process it is anchored to. An anchor can transitively
reference another anchored process.

The *light-weight* switch permits creation of several language processes
inside a single OS process. In the *heavy-weight* case, only one language
process is mapped to each OS process. Figure 7.7 presents the semantics
of the association of the two criteria. The user accesses these switches
through a class called `Mapping`:

```
class Mapping {
 public:
   virtual void on_machine(const String& m); // virtual machine
   virtual void with_process(Process* p);
     // set the machine to be the same as for the existing process p

   virtual void set_light();    // set to light-weight process
   virtual void set_heavy();    // set to heavy-weight (OS) process
};
```

When a program creates a language process, an object of type `Mapping`
can be passed to the allocator (`new()`) in order to specify the desired
mapping of the new process. Program 7.7 presents the syntax used for
this. With the `.c++11-mapping` file taken from above, Program 7.7
produces the mapping presented in Figure 7.8. Note that a language
process, even created as heavy-weight, becomes light-weight if a new
language process is mapped onto its OS process; this is the case for the
p1 process.

Besides this local control of mapping, there is a global variable that
is valid within each C++// sub-system:

```
Mapping* mapping;
```

```
A *p1;      // A is a normal sequential class: allocation-based style
P_A *p2, *p3;          // P_A is a process class: class-based style
Mapping *map1, *map2; // mapping objects
...
map1->set_heavy();
map1->on_machine("Server");
p1 = (A *) new (typeid(A), map1) Process_alloc(...);
                       // p1 on a new OS process,
                       // on machine with actual name "Server"
...
map2->set_heavy();
map2->with_process(p1);
p2 = new (map2)  P_A(...);
                       // p2 on a new heavy-weight process,
                       // same machine as p1
map2->set_light();
p3 = new (map2)  P_A(...);
                       // p3 on a light-weight process,
                       // same machine as p1,
                       // inside the same OS process as p1
map2->on_machine("P1");
for (int i=0; i < 100 ; i++)
   t[i] = new (map2) P_A(...);
                       // t[i] on a light-weight process,
                       // on machine with actual name "P1",
                       // all within the same OS process
```

Program 7.7
Mapping Processes to Machines

Machine

		Virtual machine M	Machine where the language process p is running
P **r** **o** **c** **e** **s** **s**	Light	On machine actual_name (M) On an arbitrary existing OS process (a new one if none)	Same machine and OS process as p
n **a** **t** **u** **r** **e**	Heavy	On machine actual_name (M) On a new OS process	Same machine as p On a new OS process

Figure 7.7
Combination of the Mapping Criteria

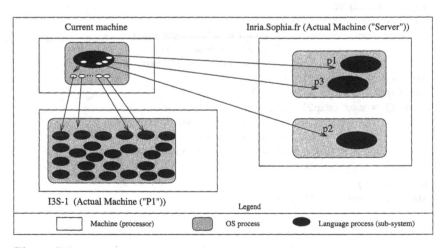

Figure 7.8
Example of Mapping

which permits the establishment of a global mapping strategy. This variable is accessible to all the objects of the sub-system, and is used by default during process creation when no mapping object is passed. The scope of **mapping** is the process sub-system; each sub-system has its own copy of this variable. Using this functionality, a global mapping strategy accessible throughout a program can be implemented by constructing a centralized server (a C++// process) which on request returns a mapping object to be used for subsequent process creation.

Our intention is to develop more sophisticated mapping strategies by deriving new classes from the **Mapping** class. For example, we are currently defining **Cluster** classes to allow processes to be grouped and managed in a more abstract manner. In the longer term, we aim to develop automatic or semi-automatic load-balancing classes that will rely on modelling and evaluation of machine and network load.

7.6 Polygon Overlay

7.6.1 Sequential Design and Programming (step 1)

We implement the overlay of two polygon maps using a simple pipeline. We define the class **polygon** (Program 7.8), whose objects can test their intersection with other polygons. The pipeline is a list of objects of class **polygon**. It is initialized with the contents of the first map, and is fed with polygons from the second map.

This algorithm is enhanced by the addition of an **area** field to the class **polygon**. This permits us to stop propagating a polygon from the second map through the pipeline whenever it has been completely accounted for by the polygons of the first map. Symmetrically, it allows us to remove a polygon from the first map when its area has been totally consumed.

The construction of the pipeline is straightforward: polygons from the first map are read and linked together, and then polygons from the second map are passed to the pipeline (Program 7.9).

7.6.2 Parallel Programming

Light-Weight Processes Once the sequential polygon pipeline has been written and debugged (method step 1), it can be parallelized. The pipeline polygons can be identified as active (step 2). The simplest

```
class polygon {
public:
  polygon (int x1, int y1, int x2, int y2, polygon* n=0) :
    xl(x1), yl(y1), xh(x2), yh(y2), next(n)
    { area = (x2-x1) * (y2-y1); }

  virtual polygon* get_next () { return next; }

  // set_next call will be polymorphic (polygon) in the parallel classes
  virtual void set_next (polygon * n) { next = n; }
  ...
  virtual void overlay (polygon * map2_polygon) {
    if (map2_polygon->get_area())
      if (!area) next->overlay(map2_polygon);
      else if (!intersection(map2_polygon))
             next->overlay(map2_polygon);
           else {
             produce_intersection(map2_polygon);
             if (map2_polygon->get_area())
               next->overlay(map2_polygon);
           }
  }
protected:
  int xl, yl, xh, yh, area;
  polygon * next;
};
```

Program 7.8
Polygon Class

```
#include "polygon.h"

polygon * tmpPoly;
polygon * map1 = 0;

void read_map1(void) {
  for(int i=0; i<nbpoly1; i++) { ··· // read from file
    map1 = new polygon(xl, yl, xh, yh, map1);
  }
}

void read_and_overlay_map2(void) {
  for(int i=0; i<nbpoly2; i++) { ··· // read from file
    tmpPoly = new polygon(xl, yl, xh, yh, 0);
    map1->overlay(tmpPoly);      // possible stack overflow!
  }
}

// the first process
int main(int argc, char * argv[]) {
  read_map1();
  read_and_overlay_map2();
}
```

Program 7.9
Pipeline Construction

parallel version can be obtained by deriving a new class (Program 7.10) from the sequential class **polygon** and the system class **Process** (step 3.1). In this version, each method call to a pipeline polygon object will be transformed into a request to a polygon process; its service policy needs only be FIFO (step 3.2).

Of course, this parallelization option is practical for large data sets only if the environment is multithreaded.

We must also redefine the construction of the polygons of the first map (i.e., create process polygons). Program 7.11, maps light-weight processes to three different virtual machines.

Heavy-Weight Processes If the underlying system only provides heavy-weight processes, parallelization is still possible, but will be best

```
#include "Process.h"
#include "polygon.h"

class ppolygon : public polygon, public Process {
 public:
  ppolygon (int x1, int y1, int x2, int y2, ppolygon2* n=0) :
    Process(), polygon(x1, y1, x2, y2, n)   { }
};
```

Program 7.10
Ppolygon: a Light-Weight Process Polygon Class

```
Mapping* light_mapping = new Mapping;
char *machines[3] = {"Mach_A", "Mach_B", "Mach_C"};
int current_machine=0;
...
void read_map1(void) {
  light_mapping->set_light();
  for(int i=0; i<nbpoly1; i++) { ...
    light_mapping->set_machine(machines[current_machine]);
    if (current_machine < 2) current_machine++;
      else current_machine = 0;
    // polymorphic assignment of result
    map1 = new(light_mapping) ppolygon(xl, yl, xh, yh, map1);
  }
}
```

Program 7.11
Modifications to the Main Routine

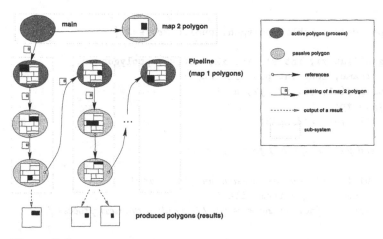

Figure 7.9
Heavy-Weight Polygon Process Pipeline

done by combining active parallel polygons (Program 7.12) and passive sequential polygons to program the pipeline (steps 2 and 3).

In Figure 7.9, we show the system of active and passive objects created by this program and the passing of a polygon from the second map to the pipeline. This polygon will be forwarded through the pipeline until its area has been consumed by all its intersections. In the figure, for example, the polygon from the second map is not forwarded beyond the second language process.

Note that the same **Process** class should serve for both the light-weight and heavy-weight versions, since it only denotes a language process. However, the mapping description is different in the two main programs. Mapping should be the only place where we have to indicate whether the language process should be mapped onto the same OS process.

Note also that the sequential version is programmed with terminal recursion. With large input maps, this can produce a stack overflow during the execution. Therefore, we have also programmed a recursion-less version. It is a little less natural, but is able to process large maps. The parallel version, although normally suffering from the same problem, is able to handle big maps: indeed, when the pipeline is split between several processes, the stack is partially split between pending requests

```
class ppolygon2 : public polygon, public Process {
public:
  ppolygon2(int x1, int y1, int x2, int y2, ppolygon* n,
    char *fname, long int pos, int nb) :
      polygon(x1, y1, x2, y2, n) {
      polygon *p;
      int xa1, ya1, xa2, ya2;

      // Read portion of map1 from file fname

      if (nb) {    // read last passive polygon (if any):
        p = read_polygon_from_file();
        p->set_next(next); next = p; // point to the next process
      }

      // read other passive polygons (if any):
      for(int i=1; (i<nb) && !feof(f); i++) {
        p = read_polygon_from_file();
        p->set_next(next); next = p;
      }
      area = (xa2-xa1) * (ya2-ya1);
  }
};
```

Program 7.12
Ppolygon2: a Heavy-Weight Process Polygon Class

lists. For the same reason, there are no restrictions about stack size on the size of maps in the light-weight process version.

For performance figures, we refer the reader to the WWW pages mentioned earlier.

7.7 Implementation

C++// currently runs on the following platforms: DEC AlphaStation 200 4/166, Sun SPARCStation 4C (IPC), Sun SPARC 4D (multiprocessor), and PC ix86. Operating systems supported include DEC Unix 3.0 (formerly DEC OSF/1), SunOS 4.1.3, Solaris 2, and Linux 1.2.8. We are using the GNU compiler and library version 2.7.0; PVM 3.3.7 and PVM 3.3.8 for interprocess communication [Furmento & Baude 1995], and are running on a 10 Mbit/s Ethernet. The system will be ported to other platforms in the near future, since its only requirements are a C++ compiler supporting RTTI and a PVM library (though the language is not tied to PVM, and could use a simpler communication library).

Below, we describe the construction of the C++// environment. This presentation goes beyond implementation details since the technique we use—reification—also supports the customization and extension of our system, as laid out in Section 7.7.4.

7.7.1   A Reflection-Based System

The C++// system is based on a meta-object protocol (MOP) [Kiczales *et al.* 1991]. There are various MOPs for different languages and systems, with various goals, compilation and runtime costs, and various levels of expressiveness. Within our context, we use a reflection mechanism based on reification. Reification is simply the action of transforming a call issued to an object into an object itself; we say that the call is "reified". From this transformation, the call can be manipulated as a first class entity (i.e., stored in a data structure, passed as parameter, sent to another process, etc).

A *meta-object* (Figure 7.10) captures each call directed towards a normal *base-level* object; a meta-object is an instance of a *meta-class*. In some ways, a local object that provides a remote object with local access, i.e., a *proxy* [Shapiro 1986, Edelson 1992, Makpangou *et al.* 1994, Dave *et al.* 1992, Birrell *et al.* 1995], is a kind of meta-object.

MOP techniques have been used in many contexts to provide an elegant model of various concepts, and an extensible design and implementation of various language features or extensions (such as remote objects). An important work has been the CLOS MOP [Bobrow *et al.* 1988]. In that case, even the semantics of inheritance is extensible through meta-object programming (something which we do not support). The Eiffel// language [Caromel 1990a, Caromel 1993b] also used a meta-level for reification. MOPs have a wide scope of applications, and are an active field of research for parallel and distributed programming [Chiba & Masuda 1992, Watanabe & Yonezawa 1998, Yokote & Tokoro 1986, Madany *et al.* 1992, Buschmann *et al.* 1992, McAffer 1995, Chiba 1995]. Work using more traditional methods, such as *proxy generators*, are closely related [Birrell *et al.* 1995].

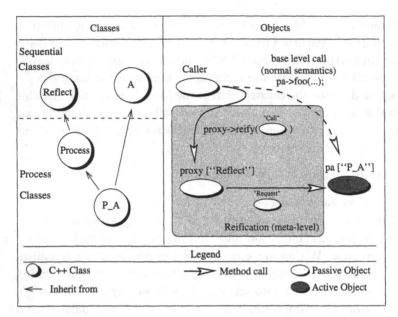

Figure 7.10
Reification of Calls

7.7.2   A MOP for C++: Basic Classes

The first principle of our MOP for C++ is embodied in a special class, called **Reflect**. All classes inheriting publicly from **Reflect**, either directly or indirectly, are called *reified classes*. A reified class has *reified instances*; all calls issued to a reified object are reified. This last requirement is important for re-usability, as it permits users to take a normal class, and then globally modify its behavior, in order to transform it into a process.

The **Reflect** class implements the reflection mechanism with reification:

```
class Reflect {
 public:
   virtual void reify(Call* c) {
     c->execute();    // a call reification
   }
   void* operator new (size_t s, type_info& t) {
     ...
   }
```

```
Reflect(···) {
  ...
}
};
```

The creation of an instance of a **Reflect** class returns a meta-object (in our case, a proxy) for the type being passed in as a parameter of the allocator. **type_info** is the standard RTTI class of C++.

All calls issued to instances of the **Reflect** class and its derived classes will trigger the execution of the member function **reify()** with the appropriate object of type **Call** as a parameter:

```
class Call {
public:
  virtual void execute();
  List<Any> eff_params;        // effective parameters
  member_id m;                 // member to be called
  Any object;                  // target object
  Any result_place;            // result address
};
```

Instances of the **Call** class are reified calls (i.e., objects which represent the reification of calls). Figure 7.10 illustrates reification.

From this mechanism, we implement the basic classes of our programming model described in Section 7.2.1. For example, the class **Process_alloc** inherits from **Reflect**, and redefines the **reify()** function as:

```
class Process_alloc: public Reflect {
public:
  virtual void reify(Call* c) {
    ...                  // send the request to the remote process
  }
  void* operator new (size_t s, type_info& t) {
    ...                  // process creation
  }
  Process_alloc(···) : Reflect (···) {
    ...
  }
};
```

It is at this point, within such routines, that a mapping between the primitives needed to implement a specific model of parallel programming (such as point-to-point communication or broadcasting) and the actual platform primitives will take place. This permits our system to use the most efficient primitives available on a given architecture.

7.7.3   Class and Member Identification

Within the framework of multiple address spaces, the need for class and member identifiers is inescapable. While the classes presented in the previous section can have simple and low-cost representations in a shared address space, more sophisticated policies are needed in a distributed environment.

Another issue is the capability to automatically marshal and unmarshal objects between processes and address spaces. The `Class_info` and `Member_info` classes respond to these specific issues:

```
class Class_info {
 public:
   class_id id;              // system-wide valid identification
   structure s;              // information on the class structure
                             // for (un)marshalling of objects
   List<Any> flat(Any obj);  // flattening an object
   Any build(List<Any> l);   // building an object
   ...
};

class Member_info {
 public:
   member_id id;             // system-wide valid identification
   Class_info* return_type;  // information on the member
   ...
};
```

These meta-classes represent information on C++ classes. They conform to the design principle of the standard class `type_info`, which provides some basic information, and which was designed with the intention of being extended according to specific needs [Stroustrup 1994].

Two functions are used to obtain the class and member IDs:

```
class_id  cid(A);    // class Id
member_id mid(put);  // member Id
```

The `mid()` primitive was presented in Section 7.3.2 for member manipulation, and used in Sections 7.3.3 to 7.3.4 for programming the control of processes. By construction, **class_id** and **member_id** have system-wide validity (i.e., can be passed as parameters between processes), while the **Class_info*** and **Member_info*** pointers have a specific value within each address space. Two functions:

```
Class_info*  cid_class(class_id c);     // from cid to class
Member_info* mid_member(member_id m);   // from mid to member
```

provide a mapping in a given address space between class and member identifications and local **Class_info*** and **Member_info*** addresses. For convenience, two other functions provide direct access to the objects representing a class and a member function, respectively:

```
Class_info*  typeid_ll(A);      // class representation
Member_info* memberid_ll(put); // member representation
```

These are similar to the RTTI **typeid()** operator of standard C++. Finally, the following function allows direction translation from RTTI class representation to C++// class identifiers:

```
class_id  rtti_ll(type_info& t); // RTTI to class id
```

In our distributed framework, the class **Request** (introduced in Section 7.3.2) is implemented through inheritance from the MOP class **Call**, and defines only the new members corresponding to the specific information which is needed:

```
class Request: public Call {
 public:
  virtual void execute();    // new definition
  request_id id;             // ID of the request
  ...
};
```

An instance of this class is then sent to the remote process, which executes the call by calling the **execute()** function on it.

7.7.4 Customization and Extension of C++//

The MOP presented above is independent of any parallel programming model. The MIMD model we described in this paper is programmed on top of the MOP, without any compiler modification. All the classes described in the model, such as **Process** and **Process_alloc**, are defined as

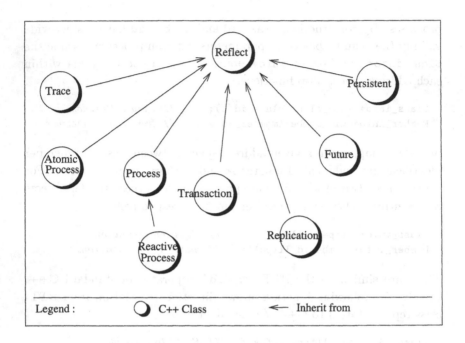

Figure 7.11
Customization and Extension of C++//

library classes using the basic **Reflect** and **Call** classes and the class and
member identification primitives. An important consequence of this is
that other parallel programming models, such as shared-memory MIMD
or SPMD, can be defined on top of the MOP.

As well as supporting libraries of concurrent programming models, this
technique also permits us to address extension issues. We might provide
a debugging environment and tracing, or use efficient platform-specific
primitives for communication (e.g., broadcast and multicast communication), since specific behaviors can be added at the reification stage.
It is also worth noting that this mechanism allows us to handle issues
such as persistent objects, atomicity, replication, and fault tolerance
(Figure 7.11). Wait-by-necessity, for example, is implemented through a
class **Future**, which uses reification by inheriting from **Reflect**. Such an
open system, or open implementation [Kiczales *et al.* 1991], is extensible
by the end user, and adaptable to various needs and situations.

7.8   Conclusion

Our system currently has several limitations. First, basic types are not subject to wait-by-necessity; this can only be achieved by encapsulating them in classes. While this can be a problem regarding re-usability, the runtime cost of adding synchronization to basic types was felt to be too high.

The fact that data members cannot be accessed transparently on a process object is a partial limitation of our model. However, since C++ does not provide uniform access to data or function members, this constraint is unlikely to be removed in the future.

Light-weight language processes and reflective template classes are not yet implemented. We are currently working on these important features.

Finally, to support the use of polymorphism between standard passive objects and process objects, all public functions have to be virtual; otherwise, non-virtual function calls will not be transformed into IPCs. This limitation comes directly from C++, which does not provide dynamic binding by default on all members. This drawback can be alleviated if the C++ compiler provides an "all-virtual" option. The choice here is between re-usability, and paying the price of having all functions virtual. Of course, making such a change requires recompiling all of files involved, but this is a small price to pay compared to the benefits of code re-use.

Our work focussed on re-use, flexibility, and extensibility. At different levels—service routines, abstractions for control programming, and libraries defining specific programming models—the system we propose tries to both conform to information hiding principles, and to be open for customization and extension. We feel this approach is at least a partial solution to the complexity and diversity of parallel programming.

Granularity is another crucial point of parallel programming. Achieving an appropriate match between the granularity of program activities, and the capability of the underlying parallel architecture, is a challenging part of high-performance programming. We believe that the re-usability and flexibility of object-oriented languages allows us to address this problem.

Finally, another important aspect of distributed programming is the correctness issues it raises. These were not addressed in this chapter, but this is another area of investigation for our group [Attali *et al.* 1993,

Attali & Caromel 1995]. We hope formal techniques, together with parallel object-oriented programming, will permit advances to be made.

Acknowledgments

The authors gratefully acknowledge the help and support of the SLOOP project members. The work of Françoise Baude and Ph.D. student Nathalie Furmento on interprocess communication was decisive to the current system. Discussions, and joint work with collaborators Jean-Claude Bermond, Bruno Gaujal, Philippe Mussi, and Michel Syska, and Ph.D. students Olivier Dalle, Olivier Delmas, Stéphane Perennes, and Günther Siegel have been of first importance.

8 C**

James R. Larus, Brad Richards, and Guhan Viswanathan

8.1 Introduction

C** is a large-grain data-parallel programming language. It preserves the principal advantages of SIMD data parallelism—comprehensible and near-determinate parallel execution—while relaxing SIMD's constricted execution model [Larus 1993]. We have used C** as a vehicle for experimenting with parallel language features and with implementation techniques that exploit program-level control of a parallel computer's memory system [Larus et al. 1994]. This paper both describes the language and summarizes progress in language design and implementation since the previous C** paper [Larus 1993].

Data-parallel programming languages originally evolved on fine-grain SIMD computers [Flynn 1966], which execute individual instructions in lockstep on a collection of processing units. Early data-parallel languages, such as C* [Rose & Steele 1987], mimicked this execution model by executing each parallel operation in lockstep. Both the machines and languages benefited from the simplicity of a single thread of control and the absence of data races. However, both suffered from SIMD's intrinsically inefficient conditional statements—in which each processing unit steps through both arms of a condition—and inefficiencies introduced by the synchronization necessary to run SIMD programs on the more common MIMD processors.

Section 8.2 outlines several alternatives to SIMD execution of data-parallel languages. Most of these languages take a pragmatic approach and run data-parallel operations in MIMD style, i.e., asynchronously. This approach causes no problems for simple operators, such as whole-array arithmetic, and offers the notational convenience of structuring a program with data-parallel operators. However, uncontrolled sharing allows data races, and these data-parallel languages provide few, if any, mechanisms for serializing conflicts. In effect, these languages trade a higher-level programming model for implementation ease and the siren's lure of high performance.

C** follows a different approach. It defines a clear semantics for conflicting memory references in asynchronously-executed data-parallel op-

erations (Section 8.3). In C**, invoking a data-parallel operation on a
data aggregate asynchronously executes the operation on each element in
the collection. However, C**'s semantics require that invocations appear
to execute simultaneously and instantaneously, so that their memory
references cannot conflict. This semantics is similar to the copy-in-copy-
out semantics of primitive operations in other data-parallel languages.
However, unlike other languages, C**'s semantics is not limited to a
few arithmetic operations on dense matrices. Instead, C** defines and
implements this semantics for arbitrary C++ code.

C** prevents conflicts within a data-parallel operation by deferring
the delivery of values until after the operation completes and by providing a rich and extensible collection of reduction operators to combine
conflicting values. A data-parallel operation can modify memory, but
changes do not become globally visible until the operation completes. At
that point, modifications from different invocations are reconciled into a
globally consistent state for the next data-parallel operation. This mechanism works well for one-to-one and one-to-many communication, but is
insufficient for many-to-one or many-to-many communication since providing a semantics for conflicting writes to the same location is difficult.
Instead, C** supports the latter forms of communication with a rich
variety of reductions, including reduction assignments and user-defined
reduction functions (Section 8.4).

Of course, a clear semantics is no substitute for high performance.
Our C** implementation exploits Tempest [Hill *et al.* 1995, Larus *et al.*
1994], an interface which provides user-level code with the mechanisms
to implement a shared-address space and a custom coherence policy.
LCM, C**'s memory system, allows shared memory to become inconsistent during data-parallel operations. When a data-parallel operation
modifies a shared location, LCM uses a fine-grain, copy-on-write coherence policy that matches C** semantics to copy the location's cache
block (Section 8.5). When the data-parallel operation finishes, LCM
reconciles copies to create a consistent global state.

As an extended example, Section 8.6 contains our solution to the polygon overlay problem (Appendix C). The first version is an inefficient,
but concise, data-parallel program, which is greatly improved by using a
better algorithm. This algorithm's performance is in turn improved by
using high-level C** mechanisms—in particular, user-level reductions—
to improve communication. Other benchmarks also show that, although

high-level and concise, C** programs can run as fast, or faster than low-level, carefully-written and tuned programs.

It is a commonplace that parallel programming is difficult, and that parallel machines will not be widely used until this complexity is brought under control. If true, the programming languages community bears responsibility for this failure. It has invested more effort in packaging hardware-level features, such as message passing, than in exploring new languages that raise the level of programming abstraction, such as HPF.

Parallel languages with a higher-level semantics may not please all programmers or solve all problems, but they do make parallel programming easier. The architecture community draws a clear distinction between mechanisms, which hardware should provide, and policy, which software should implement [Wood *et al.* 1993, Wulf 1981]. The languages community should look at hardware mechanisms as a means to an end, not an end in itself.

8.2   Data-Parallel Languages

A *data-parallel* programming language expresses parallelism by evaluating, in parallel, operations on collections of data [Hillis & Steele 1986]. The key features of such a language are: a means for aggregating data into a single entity, which we will call a *data aggregate*; a way to specify an operation on each element in an aggregate; and a semantics for the parallel execution of these operations. Data-parallel languages should be distinguished from the data-parallel programming style [Fox 1988], which can be used even in languages that do not claim to support data parallelism.

Unfortunately, the definition of data parallelism is a bit fuzzy around the edges. For example, languages such as Fortran-90 [Adams *et al.* 1992] and HPF [Koelbel *et al.* 1994] mix other programming models with a limited collection of data-parallel operations. A sub-language can be data parallel, even though its parent language is not. In addition, functional languages provide data aggregates and operations [Backus 1978], but typically do not consider parallel execution. However, since these languages do not permit side effects, extending their semantics to permit parallel execution is straightforward.

Data-parallel languages differ widely in the operations and semantics that they provide. We choose to classify data-parallel operations into four categories: fine grain, coarse grain, large grain, and functional. The discussion below is organized around this classification, since these categories strongly affect semantics. Techniques for specifying data aggregates differ mainly in syntactic details and are not discussed further.

8.2.1   Fine-Grain Languages

As discussed earlier, *fine-grain* data-parallel languages originally evolved from the model of fine-grain SIMD machines, such as the ICL DAP and Thinking Machines CM-1 [Hillis 1985]. Beyond hardware simplicity, a fine-grained SIMD model offers several programming advantages. Since each SIMD processor executes the same instruction simultaneously, a parallel program has a single thread of control and is easier to understand. In addition, read-write and write-read data races cannot occur since a parallel instruction reads its input before computing and writing its output. The only possible conflicts are output dependencies in which two instructions write to a memory location. Some machines (e.g., CM-2) provide an elaborate collection of mechanisms for combining values written to a memory location.

Unfortunately, SIMD execution has a fatal disadvantage for many programs. In particular, lockstep execution is extremely costly for programs with conditionals, since each processor must step through both arms of a conditional, although it only executes code from one alternative.

Several languages, such as C*[1] [Rose & Steele 1987], directly implement a SIMD model and consequently inherit its advantages and disadvantages. In C*, a *domain* is a collection of data instances, each of which is associated with a virtual processor. The virtual processors for a domain execute operations on their instance in lockstep. The granularity of a lockstep operation is a language operator, rather than a machine instruction (a distinction which makes little difference in C). Although it was designed for SIMD machines, Quinn and Hatcher successfully compiled C* for MIMD machines by eliminating unnecessary synchronization and asynchronously executing sequences of non-conflicting instructions [Hatcher & Quinn 1991, Seevers *et al.* 1992].

---

[1] Version 5 of C*. Version 6 changed the language significantly; this section considers only the older version.

```
domain point {
  float x;
} A [N][N];

[domain point].{
  int offset = (this - &A[0][0]);
  int i = offset / N;                /* Compute row and column */
  int j = offset % N;
  if ((i > 0) && (j > 0) && (i < N) && (j < N))
      x = (A[i-1][j] + A[i+1][j] + A[i][j-1] + A[i][j+1]) / 4;
}
```

(a) Point-Based Stencil in C* (version 5)

```
A(1:N, 1:N) = (A(0:N-1, 1:N) + A(2:N+1, 1:N) +
               A(1:N, 0:N-1) + A(1:N, 2:N+1)) / 4
```

(b) Array-Based Stencil in HPF

Program 8.1
5-Points Stencils in C* and HPF

Fine-grain data parallelism has other manifestations as well. Lin and Snyder distinguish point-based data-parallel languages, such as C*, from array-based ones [Lin & Snyder 1994]. Array-based languages, such as ZPL [Lin & Snyder 1994] or parts of Fortran-90 [Adams et al. 1992] and HPF [Koelbel et al. 1994], overload operators to apply to data aggregates—for example, add arrays by adding their respective elements—and provide array shift and permutation operations. This approach expresses parallelism through compositions of the initial parallel operators. For some application domains, such as matrix arithmetic, point-based languages produce clear and short programs.

To contrast these approaches, compare the two programs in Program 8.1. which contains a point-based stencil written in C* and in HPF.

Both types of fine-grain languages communicate by reading and writing memory. SIMD and whole-array operations share a read-compute-write semantics in which a parallel operation reads its input values before modifying a program's state. For example, in both stencils, the computations average neighboring values from the previous iteration.

These semantics prevent read-write, but not write-write, conflicts. Some fine-grain languages allow reduction functions to combine colliding values into a single value. We refer to this process as a *reduction assignment*. An alternate view of a parallel assignment operator treats it as a *mapping* [Sabot 1988, Steele & Hillis 1986], which is a restricted many-to-many communication operator.

8.2.2   Coarse-Grain Languages

Fine-grain data parallelism shares SIMD's inefficient execution model, which requires excessive synchronization on non-SIMD hardware. An obvious generalization is to execute data-parallel operations asynchronously, so that each invocation of an operation runs independently of other ones. Although this change eliminates inefficient conditional statements, it also raises new problems with memory conflicts between parallel tasks. The original SIMD data-parallel model requires no locks, barriers, or other explicit synchronization. Asynchronous data-parallel languages, for the most part, ignore the possibility of conflict and allow these error-prone features of MIMD programming.

Coarse-grain data-parallel languages allow data-parallel operations to execute asynchronously. For example, HPF's INDEPENDENT DO loops [Koelbel *et al.* 1994] or pC++'s parallel member functions [Lee & Gannon 1991] execute arbitrary code as a data-parallel operation. These languages provide no guarantees about conflicting memory accesses, so a programmer must ensure that parallel operations are independent. For example, an HPF stencil operation (Program 8.2) needs two copies of an array to ensure that updates do not interfere with reads. The real cost of coarse-grain data parallelism is the time and effort required to write, understand, and debug the complex code and not the storage or time overheads.

Communication in coarse-grain data-parallel languages again occurs through assignment to memory. Assignments may cause conflicts, and a programmer must ensure that parallel operations are data race-free by avoiding conflicting data accesses or by resolving collisions with reductions. Most coarse-grain languages limit reductions to a predefined set of operators, but some, such as HPF, are considering adding user-defined reductions.

```
!HPF$ INDEPENDENT
DO 10 I=1,N
  !HPF$ INDEPENDENT
  DO 10 J=1,N
    A1(I, J) = (A2(I-1, J) + A2(I+1, J) +
                A2(I, J-1) + A2(I, J+1)) / 4
10 CONTINUE

!HPF$ INDEPENDENT
DO 20 I=1,N
  !HPF$ INDEPENDENT
  DO 20 J=1,N
    A2(I, J) = (A1(I-1, J) + A1(I+1, J) +
                A1(I, J-1) + A1(I, J+1)) / 4
20 CONTINUE
```

Program 8.2
Coarse-Grained Stencil in HPF

```
A[#0][#1] = (A[#0-1][#1] + A[#0+1][#1] +
             A[#0][#1-1] + A[#0][#1+1]) / 4;
```

Program 8.3
Large-Grained Stencil in C**

8.2.3   Large-Grain Languages

Large-grain data-parallel languages allow coarse-grain parallelism, but provide a clearly defined semantics for conflicting memory accesses. For example, C** [Larus 1993] specifies that each invocation of a data-parallel operation runs as if it were executed simultaneously and instantaneously, so that all invocations start from the same memory state and incur no conflicts. When an invocation updates a global datum, only that invocation sees a change to the memory state until the data-parallel operation completes. At that point, all changes are merged into a single consistent view of memory. Program 8.3 shows how a stencil operation can be written in C**. The pseudo-variables, #0 and #1, are bound to each invocation's i^{th} and j^{th} coordinates, respectively. Since it is written with only one copy of the array, this code is similar to the point-based stencils described earlier (Program 8.1).

Large-grain languages permit conflict-free execution of coarse-grain programs, at the expense of considerable compiler analysis or runtime complexity. However, as discussed below, this complexity is manageable and the semantic clarity is beneficial to programmers.

8.2.4 Purely Functional Languages

The final data-parallel languages are purely functional (e.g., NESL [Blelloch 1993]) and offer advantages of data parallelism and functional programming. Conflicts do not occur because these languages do not permit imperative updates. As a result, the languages need not limit grain size or define new memory semantics to guarantee deterministic execution. On the other hand, these languages present all of the implementation difficulties of conventional functional languages [Peyton Jones 1987].

Data communication in purely functional languages occurs through function arguments and return values. Functional languages heavily use reductions to combine values returned from parallel functions, thereby providing powerful many-to-one communication mechanisms. Reductions, unfortunately, do not extend easily to many-to-many communication, so programmers must build and decompose intermediate structures.

8.3   C** Overview

> This section is a revised version of [Larus 1993], and appears
> with the permission of Springer-Verlag.

C** is a large-grain data-parallel language (to use the taxonomy and concepts introduced in Section 8.2). It was designed to investigate whether large-grain data parallelism is both useful as a programming paradigm and implementable with reasonable efficiency. After several years of effort, the answer to both questions appears to be "yes".

C** introduces a new type of object into C++. These objects are *Aggregates*, which collect data into an entity that can be operated on concurrently by parallel functions. C** also introduces *slices*, so that a program can manipulate portions of an Aggregate. These concepts are extensions to C++, so a C** program can exploit that language's abstraction and object-oriented programming facilities.

8.3.1   Aggregates

In C**, Aggregate objects are the basis for parallelism. An Aggregate class (Aggregate, for short) declares an ordered collection of values, called Aggregate elements (elements, for short), that can be operated on concurrently by an Aggregate parallel function (parallel function, for short). To declare Aggregates, C** extends the class definition syntax of C++ in two ways. First, the programmer specifies the type of the Aggregate element following the name of the Aggregate. Second, the number of dimensions and their sizes follow the element type. For example, the following declarations define 2-dimensional matrices of floating point elements of an indeterminate and two determinate sizes:

```
class matrix(float) [] [] {···};
struct small_matrix(float) [5] [5] {···};
class large_matrix(float) [100] [100] {···};
```

Like C++ classes, Aggregates use either the keyword **class** or **struct** to declare a new type of object. Unlike C++ classes, Aggregates have a rank and cardinality that is specified by their declaration. An Aggregate's data members can be either basic C++ types or structures or classes defined by the programmer. An Aggregate's *rank* is the number of dimensions specified in its class declaration. Rank is defined by the declaration and cannot be changed. The *cardinality* of each dimension may be specified in the class declaration. If omitted from the class, the cardinality must be supplied when the Aggregate is created. Each dimension is indexed from 0 to $N - 1$, where N is the cardinality of the dimension. For example, indices for both dimensions of a **small_matrix** run from 0 to 4.

An Aggregate object looks similar, but differs fundamentally, from a conventional C++ array of objects:

- An Aggregate class declaration specifies the type of the collection, not of the individual elements. This is an important point: **matrix**, which is an Aggregate, is an object consisting of a two-dimensional collection of floating point values, not a two-dimensional array of objects.

- Aggregate member functions operate on the entire collection of elements, not individual elements (Section 8.3.2).

- Elements in an Aggregate can be operated on in parallel, unlike objects in an array.

- Aggregates can be sliced (Section 8.3.5).

However, Aggregate elements can be referenced in the same manner as objects in an array. For example, if A is a small_matrix object, A[0][0] is its first element.

8.3.2   Aggregate Functions

Aggregate member functions are similar to class member functions in most respects. A key difference, however, is that Aggregate member functions are applied to an entire Aggregate, not just an element, and that the keyword this is a pointer to the entire Aggregate. For example, in:

```
class matrix (float) [] []{
   friend ostream& operator<< (ostream&, matrix&);
};

ostream& operator<< (ostream &out, matrix &m) {
   for (int i = 0; i < cardinality (0); i++) {
     for (int j = 0; j < cardinality (1); j++)
        out << m[i][j] << " ";
     out << '\n';
   }
}
```

the operator << is a friend function that prints a matrix to a stream.

All Aggregates automatically have the following two member functions:

> int rank ()   *Return number of dimensions*
> int cardinality (int dim) *Return cardinality of dimension* dim

8.3.3   Aggregate Constructors

As in C++, Aggregates may define constructors and destructors. An Aggregate constructor initializes the entire collection of elements, not the individual elements. By contrast, each element in an array is initialized by a call to the type's default constructor. For example:

```
class matrix (float) [] [] {
  matrix (float initial_value) {
    int i, j;
    for (i = 0; i < cardinality (0); i++)
      for (j = 0; j < cardinality (1); j++)
        (*this)[i][j] = initial_value;
  };
};
```

defines an Aggregate matrix of floating point values whose constructor initializes all matrix elements to a specified value, so that

```
new matrix [100][100] (1);
```

creates a 100×100 matrix of 1's.

8.3.4 Parallel Functions

Aggregate member and friend functions are sequential by default. A *parallel function* is a member or friend function in an Aggregate class that can be invoked simultaneously on each element of the Aggregate. A parallel function (either a member or friend function) is identified by keyword **parallel** after its argument list. For example:

```
class matrix (float) [] [] {
  float checksum () parallel;
  friend transpose (parallel matrix) parallel;
};
```

declares **checksum()** and **transpose()** to be parallel functions.

In a parallel member function, the *parallel argument* is the Aggregate object to which the function is applied. In a parallel friend function, the parallel argument must be prefaced by **parallel** (for example, the first argument in **transpose()**).

Analogous to the variable **this**, which points to the entire Aggregate, parallel functions may also use the **self** pointer, which points to the element the invocation operates on.

A parallel function behaves as if it were invoked simultaneously on all elements of its parallel argument. An invocation of a function on an Aggregate element can determine the coordinates of its element from the pseudo variables:

#0	1st coordinate
#1	2nd coordinate
...	
#$n-1$	nth coordinate

Semantics of Parallel Functions   To explain parallel functions more precisely, we must define a few terms. A parallel function *call* is the application of a parallel member or friend function to an Aggregate. A parallel function *invocation* is the execution of the function on one Aggregate element. Hence, calling a parallel function starts many function invocations, all of which appear to execute simultaneously. A function invocation's *state* is the collection of memory locations read or written during the invocation.

"Applied atomically" means that while a parallel function is executing, its state is only modified by the function itself, not by other concurrently executing tasks. In other words, the function appears to execute instantaneously and is unaffected by anything else running at the same time. In effect, the semantics are as if each invocation executed as follows:

- Atomically copy all referenced locations into a purely local copy.

- Compute using local copies.

- Write all modified copies back to global locations.

Since a parallel function is applied *simultaneously* to an Aggregate's elements, all invocations begin with identical state (except for the pseudo variables, #0, #1, etc., which differ in each invocation).

As an example, consider a stencil computation on a matrix:

```
friend void stencil (parallel matrix A) parallel
{
  A[#0][#1] = (A[#0-1][#1] + A[#0+1][#1]
             + A[#0][#1-1] + A[#0][#1+1]) / 4.0;
}
```

The computation is applied simultaneously to each element of the matrix, so the new values are entirely a function of the old.

If invocations of a parallel function modify global state, C** only guarantees that each modified location will contain a value computed by some invocation. If an invocation modifies more than one location, only a portion of its modifications may be visible after the parallel call.

Part of a modification of multiple locations can be overwritten by other invocations.

Results From Parallel Functions If a parallel function's result type is the same as its parallel argument's type, the parallel function allocates a new Aggregate of the same size and type as the parallel argument and initializes it with results returned from the corresponding invocations. The function invoked on the first element of the parallel argument computes the value for the first element of the result, and so on. Since the parallel function initializes the result Aggregate, the Aggregate's constructor, if any, is not invoked.

On the other hand, if the result type is a scalar, the values returned by the parallel function must be returned in reduction return statements (Section 8.3.4) that combine results from the invocations into a single value of the specified type.

For example:

```
friend matrix operator* (parallel matrix A, matrix B) parallel
    {return (A[#0][] * B[][#1]);}

friend float operator* (parallel mrow R, mcol C) parallel
    {return%+ (R[#0] * C[#0]);}
```

is a matrix multiplication routine that creates and returns a new parallel matrix of the same size as the parallel matrix A. The invocation associated with element (i, j) of A computes the dot product $A(i, *) \cdot B(*, j)$.

Reductions Reductions are a basic operation in data-parallel programming because they provide a conflict-free and efficient way of combining results from independent computations. A reduction applies an associative binary operator, pair-wise, to a sequence of values. For example, if $\circ$ is the operator, the reduction of the sequence v is $v_1 \circ v_2 \circ v_3 \ldots \circ v_n$. Given n processors, this reduction can be applied in parallel in $\lg n$ steps.

C** supplies two types of reductions. The first combines values assigned to a location to avoid conflicts between concurrent writes. The second combines values returned from the multiple invocations of a parallel functions.

Reduction Assignment Reduction assignments are legal only within parallel functions. A reduction assignment uses the operator specified

to the right of the % to combine the values assigned to the location in
different invocations. Reduction assignments are necessary because an
ordinary assignment permits only one invocation to modify the location.
Changes to the location are not visible until the parallel function call
completes.

For example:

```
float sum = 0.0, pos_sum = 0.0;

matrix::sum_elements () parallel {
  sum =%+ *self;
  if (*self > 0)
    pos_sum =%+ *self;
}
```

computes two sums. The first is the sum of all elements in a matrix.
The second (pos_sum) is the sum of the positive elements in the matrix.

Reduction Returns   A parallel function with a scalar result must
combine the results from each invocation with a reduction return. This
return combines multiple values using the operator specified to the right
of the %.

For example:

```
friend float sum (parallel mrow A) parallel
  {return%+ (A[#0]);}
```

8.3.5   Slices

A *slice* selects a subset of an Aggregate along an axis. A slice is not a
copy. It shares all selected elements with the larger Aggregate. Slices are
particularly valuable when they themselves are also Aggregates and consequently can be manipulated in parallel. Slices permit effective specification of parallel computations on pieces of an Aggregate. For example,
many matrix computations are naturally described in terms of operations on rows and columns. If the row and column slices are Aggregates,
the operations can be data parallel.

In C**, omitting an index expression from a dimension of an Aggregate reference produces a slice that includes all elements along that
dimension. This slice differs from the pointer to an array element that
results from omitting a subscript in a C++ array reference. Trailing

empty braces may be omitted, so that `A[1][]` is equivalent to `A[1]`. For example, the following three expressions are slices of a matrix:

```
matrix A;
```

`A[i]` i^{th} *row of A*
`A[i][]` *equivalent to the above*
`A[][j]` j^{th} *column of A*

Subclassing and Slices   In C**, the type of a slice is a subclass of the Aggregate's class, in all respects except inheritance of functions. The declaration of a slice's subclass both names the new subclass and describes which indices must be specified in computing the slice. `#n` denotes the nth index in a reference to the slice. For example, consider the following matrix slices:

```
class mrow : matrix[.];    // row slice of matrix
class mcol : matrix[][.];  // column slice of matrix
```

`mrow` is a row from a matrix that is computed by omitting the column index.

8.4   User-Defined Reductions

Since C** was first defined, the principal change to it has been the addition of user-defined reductions. This feature permits efficient many-to-one communication by providing a well-defined semantics for conflicting writes. Existing data-parallel languages typically resolve collisions with a limited collection of reduction functions. C** provides *user-defined reductions*, which are arbitrary binary functions that combine colliding values. This feature extends reduction functions to user-defined data types and enables programmers to combine values in many more situations.

8.4.1   DSMC Example

To motivate user-defined reductions, consider DSMC, a particle-in-cell code that simulates particle movement and collision using discrete Monte Carlo simulation [Sharma *et al.* 1994]. DSMC divides space into cells in a

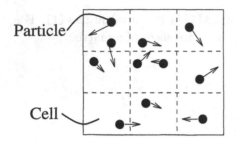

Figure 8.1
DSMC Schematic Diagram

static Cartesian grid and distributes molecules among cells (Figure 8.1). Molecular interactions create forces that move molecules. DSMC simulates the movement and collision of molecules over many time steps, each of which comprises three phases:

move: molecules change position based on their velocities.

enter: new molecules enter the domain from a jet stream.

collide: molecules collide with others in the same cell.

Parallelism in DSMC can be expressed as data-parallel operations on either cells or molecules. The latter technique is more complex as the collide phase requires an extra mapping to associate molecules with cells. The discussion below is based on the cell approach, which is used in practice [Sharma *et al.* 1994, Mukherjee *et al.* 1995].

The move phase requires many-to-many communication since it updates the positions of all molecules. In the process, molecules may move from one cell to another (usually neighboring) cell. Inter-cell molecule transfer results in many-to-many communication, since each cell exports molecules to different destinations and receives molecules from many other cells.

Consider expressing this pattern in a fine-grain data-parallel language. A fine-grain language can transfer molecules between cells through parallel assignment. Let *Leave* and *Enter* be the maximum number of molecules leaving and entering a cell in a time step, respectively. A parallel assignment can transfer only one molecule at a time. Therefore, a fine-grain language requires *Leave* repetitions of the assignment to transfer all molecules. Furthermore, unless the language provides reductions capable of resolving conflicts, these parallel assignments would fail when two molecules are simultaneously transferred to the same cell. To handle this case, the transfer must become a two step process. In the first step, senders to a cell choose a winner. In the second step, the winner transfers a molecule. In the worst case, this algorithm requires *Leave* × *Enter* parallel steps, each of which involves two synchronizations. User-defined reductions or a parallel prefix operation to enumerate incoming molecules reduces the cost of combining colliding molecules, however, the algorithm still require *Leave* steps in a fine-grain language.

In a coarse-grain language, this algorithm is typically implemented using low-level synchronization primitives, such as locks or monitors. These constructions are undesirable since they introduce explicit synchronization, which destroys the data-parallel abstraction. In addition, their high cost, and the serialization they induce, can prevent parallel speedup [Mukherjee *et al.* 1995].

By contrast, user-defined reductions capture the many-to-many communication pattern of molecule transfer. In a language that supports them, such as C**, DSMC can use an `append()` function to resolve conflicts between molecules entering a cell by merging lists of them. This approach leads to good performance. For example, on a 32-processor CM-5, a version of DSMC written in C** using user-defined reductions ran 1.1 times faster than the hand-coded C version of the program.

8.4.2 Syntax of User-Defined Reductions

User-defined reductions combine colliding values in a parallel assignment. These reductions are specified by a function name in a reduction operation. For example, the polygon overlay C** code (Program 8.6) uses the combining function `merge()` in the statement

```
return %merge theList: nullList;
```

The `nullList` argument is initial value of the accumulator.

In general, the reduction function for values of type α has type $\alpha \times \alpha \to \alpha$. For example, the `merge()` function in Program 8.6 has type `polyList_s` × `polyList_s` → `polyList_s`. The current C** compiler uses a variant of this typing rule in which the first parameter serves as both input and output (e.g., type `(polyList_s *)` × `polyList_s` → `void`).

8.4.3   Semantics of User-Defined Reductions

Although the concept of user-defined reductions is not new, they have not been implemented in another parallel programming language (to the best of our knowledge). However, the MPI message-passing library does provide for user-defined reductions [MPI 1994]. In the process of implementing user-defined reductions, several questions arose about their semantics. The discussion below describes these choices and how we resolved them in C**.

Conflicts If they are used in reduction assignments, user-defined reduction functions are invoked during execution of a parallel function, which, in languages such as C**, has a well-defined semantics for conflicting memory accesses. What restrictions (if any) should be placed on memory accesses in reduction functions?

The most severe restriction is to require that reduction functions be side-effect free, so their output is a pure function of their input.[2] This approach has many advantages (and is used by SIMD hardware and fine-grain languages) since pure functions do not introduce new conflicts. Although this restriction may be reasonable for atomic data, such as numbers, it can impede reductions on structured data, since it demands a functional style that may introduce considerable overhead. Consider, for example, using user-defined reductions to add new nodes to an oct-tree in a Barnes-Hut algorithm [Barnes & Hut 1986]. Without side-effects, each insertion requires copying all nodes along the path from the root to the leaf. Even this approach is problematic in languages like C, that separate memory allocation from initialization since, without an effect system [Lucassen & Gifford 1988], assignments will appear as side effects.

Alternatively, a language may permit compiler directives, such as HPF's INTENT directive, to declare safety properties that a compiler cannot prove. This approach allows reduction functions that have side effects but do not cause conflicts. However, erroneous directives may lead to subtle conflict errors.

A third alternative requires a runtime system to identify data access conflicts due to unsafe user-defined reductions, as in Steele's Parallel

---

[2]Note that side effects and associativity are independent properties since a routine with side effects can easily be associative.

Scheme [Steele 1990a]. This approach identifies all errors at runtime, but is complex and expensive.

In the end, we decided not to restrict user-defined reduction functions and to trust programmers to use this powerful feature carefully, since it could easily subvert the language semantics. This decision was in part necessary because of the difficulty of determining if an arbitrary piece of C++ code is side-effect free and in part desirable so programmers had the freedom to experiment with this new language feature.

Reduction Assignment Result Availability If a parallel function references the target location of a reduction assignment, what value does it see after the assignment? With the original C** semantics, a parallel function sees only its update, as if it runs sequentially. Although this provides a simple semantic model, it can be difficult to implement, so we considered several alternatives.

The first is to prohibit non-reduction accesses to a location used for reduction assignments, as in Fortran D [Fox *et al.* 1990]. This method's advantage is that it provides a runtime system with the flexibility to determine when and how a reduction should be carried out. However, this method has two major disadvantages. First, it burdens a programmer unnecessarily. For example, in DSMC's move phase, the parallel function for a cell reads its molecule list and moves molecules to other cells' lists. The restriction requires a programmer to maintain a separate "incoming" list for each cell, and merge it with the cell's molecule list in a separate phase. Second, static analysis cannot identify all erroneous accesses. More complex and expensive runtime disambiguation is necessary to detect all errors.

The second approach is to retain the original value of a location, even after a reduction assignment. When a data-parallel operation completes, the runtime system combines colliding values and updates locations. In effect, this approach performs reductions after the data-parallel operation (although a system has the freedom to perform the two phases concurrently, so long as a reduction does not conflict with a data-parallel operation).

The final approach combines the two and is suitable for a language like C**. Like the second alternative, it defers reductions, but it also updates a local copy of a location to merge the local contribution. This approach ties reductions closely to C**'s semantics and may not be appropriate for coarse-grain languages in general.

Combining Order   Since primitive reduction functions are associative and commutative, the order in which values are combined does not affect the result. This freedom provides a runtime system with flexibility to implement reductions efficiently. For example, a runtime system can use a combining tree to implement reductions in logarithmic parallel time. User-defined reductions, on the other hand, are not necessarily associative or commutative, but are usually effectively associative. *Effectively associative functions* are reduction functions whose lack of associativity does not affect a program's results [Sabot 1988]. For example, consider using an append() function as a set union operator for a set in which the order of items is semantically unimportant.

Arbitrary reduction order is a reasonable choice for user-defined reductions for two reasons. First, a programmer can implement a specific ordering by collecting all values into a list (e.g., using append()), sorting the list, and combining values explicitly. More importantly, the absence of ordering allows optimizations that improve the performance of user-defined reductions.

8.4.4   Extensions to User-Defined Reduction Assignments

A reduction assignment is actually two actions, combining conflicting values and updating the target with the value. By default, the update operation is simple assignment. C** generalizes the update with a user-defined *update* function. An update function can store the combined value in the target in non-trivial ways. For example, in DSMC (Section 8.4.1), an update function merges the list of incoming molecules with a cell's list of molecules. A user-defined update is only syntactic sugar and adds no power to the language. To continue the DSMC example, without user-defined updates, the programmer must store the incoming list in a temporary and append it to the cell's list later. Semantically, an update function satisfies the same restrictions as a combining function (Section 8.4.3). The insertPoly() function in Program 8.4 (reproduced below from the polygon overlay code in Program 8.9) is a example of an update function. insertPoly() adds incoming polygons to a grid cell's polygon list.

```
void insertPoly(polyNode_p *result, poly_s thePoly)
{
  polyNode_p ptr = new polyNode_s;// allocate new node
  ptr->poly = thePoly;            // fill it in
  ptr->next = *result;            // link node into list
  *result = ptr;                  // return result
}
```

Program 8.4
Code to Partition a Polygon Vector

Another option is to omit a combining function and only specify an update function. The C** runtime system uses the update function to insert colliding values, one by one, in the target location. The function `polyVec::partitionVec()` in Program 8.9 uses the update function `insertPoly()` (in Program 8.4), in this manner, to add incoming polygons one by one. Updates without combining are analogous to integrated reductions [Yang *et al.* 1994].

8.4.5   Implementing User-Level Reductions

User-defined reductions can be implemented on a message-passing machine or by using the Tempest interface with minimal runtime system support. Furthermore, the semantics of reductions provide a compiler with opportunities for optimization. This section describes the implementation of user-defined reductions in the C** compiler. In C**, reductions follow the deferred reduction model that retains old values. Currently, C** does not specify methods to identify or prevent conflicts between independent reductions. All mechanisms described in this section extend easily to other data-parallel languages. The description has three stages. The first describes basic mechanisms that the compiler uses to implement reductions. The second shows how the compiler can vectorize messages to improve performance. The third describes how local combining allows the compiler to reduce the amount of data communicated between processors.

Basic Reductions   A reduction assignment updates its target with the combined value of colliding right-hand-side values. The C** implementation involves two processors: the processor that executes the reduction assignment (processor A) and the processor that owns the target location (processor B). Processor A, which executes the reduction, sends processor B a message containing three items: the right-hand-side value, the combining function descriptor, and the target location pointer. At the end of the parallel phase, Processor B collects incoming reduction messages, combines colliding values and updates target locations. To implement update reductions (Section 8.4.4), processor B replaces the combining function with an update function.

The "owner-updates" model is simple to implement and requires minimal runtime system support. It depends on the runtime system to support target location queries, which is usually available in languages that provide a global name space.

Bulk Reductions   During a data-parallel operation, a processor may execute multiple reductions for two reasons. First, the number of elements in a collection is typically much larger than the number of processors, so each processor executes multiple invocations. Second, each invocation may itself execute multiple reduction assignments. The deferred reduction model allows the compiler to defer sending reduction messages until the end of the parallel phase. This permits several messages to the same destination processor to be bundled into a single message, which is typically far more efficient to send and receive.

Local Combining   Local combining further enables the compiler to reduce the amount of data communicated in messages. If different invocations perform reductions on the same target, values can be combined locally, before global combining. C**'s runtime system uses a per-processor hash table to track common targets. Probing this table increases the overhead of the reduction, but allows for a decrease in communications cost. This is a good example of an optimization that trades off worse sequential performance for better communication (and therefore parallel) performance.

8.4.6   User-Defined Reduction Performance

We evaluated our reduction implementation by comparing C** versions of five benchmarks (one small and four medium-size applications) against highly optimized hand-coded SPMD versions of the programs on a 32-processor CM-5. All of these programs' communication patterns were fully captured by reduction assignments (both user-defined

Program (Domain)	Compared to	C**	SPMD	SPMD/ C**
DSMC (Particle-in-cell)	Hybrid SM-MP	74.2	82.7	0.90
EM3D (Electromagnetics)	Hybrid SM-MP	10.7	5.0	2.14
Water (Mol. dynamics)	SM	13.0	13.6	0.96
Moldyn (Mol. dynamics)	Hybrid SM-MP	27.0	26.7	1.01
FFT	SM	2.0	8.5	0.11

Table 8.1
Comparative Benchmark Execution Times (in seconds on 32-processor CM-5)

and primitive). Table 8.1 summarizes our results. In the worst case, the C** version was 2 times slower than the message-passing EM3D code. It was between 1% slower and 10% faster on DSMC, Moldyn and Water, and 4.25 times faster on the communication intensive FFT code. Given the complexity and effort in tuning the SPMD codes, the C** programs are far more attractive.

8.5 C** Implementation

This section is a shorter version of [Larus *et al.* 1994], and appears with the permission of the IEEE.

Efficiently compiling parallel languages for parallel computers is difficult. Most languages assume a shared address space in which any part of a computation can reference any data. Parallel machines provide either too little or too much support for many languages [Larus 1994]. On one hand, message-passing machines require a compiler to statically analyze and handle all details of data placement and access, or pay a large cost to defer decisions to run time. On the other hand, shared-memory machines provide more dynamic mechanisms, but generally use them to implement a fixed cache-coherence policy that may not meet a language's needs.

In C**, the compiler exploits control over the memory system of a parallel computer to construct a language-specific address space for a high-level parallel language. Because the semantics of memory match the semantics of a language, a compiler can generate efficient code, with assurance that the memory system will detect unusual cases and errors so that a runtime system can handle them.

The hardware base is a parallel computer with a Tempest-like interface, which provides mechanisms that permit user-level software to implement shared-memory policies [Kranz *et al.* 1993, Reinhardt *et al.* 1994]. A Tempest memory system is possible on a wide range of parallel systems, including those without shared-memory hardware [Schoinas *et al.* 1994]. Tempest offers a program control over both communications and data placement, as is possible with message passing, and the dynamic fine-grain policies possible with shared memory.

Reconcilable Shared Memory (RSM) provides a global address space and basic coherence policy whose two key policies governing memory system behavior are under program control. The first is the system's response when a processor requests a copy of a cache block. The second is the system's response when a processor returns a cache block in response to a request. Unlike most shared-memory systems, RSM places no restrictions on multiple outstanding writable copies of a block and permits non-sequentially consistent memory models. A language-specific coherence protocol uses RSM mechanisms to support a language's semantics directly. Custom coherence policies can also improve the performance of shared-memory programs written in any language. For example, global reductions and stale data fit naturally into the RSM model. Finally, RSM can help detect unsynchronized data accesses (data races).

8.5.1 LCM

RSM systems can aid the implementation of parallel programming languages, particularly higher-level languages such as C**. A natural way to implement C**'s semantics is a copy-on-write scheme, in which each parallel invocation obtains and modifies its own copy of shared data. We implemented this policy in an RSM system called Loosely Coherent Memory (LCM). LCM and the C** compiler cooperate to detect the need for shared data and to copy it, instead of the conventional approach in which a compiler generates conservative code to copy shared data. LCM's copies, although they share the address of the original, are private to a processor and remain inconsistent until a global reconciliation returns memory to a consistent state.

RSM offers several advantages over explicit copying. A compiler can produce code optimized for cases in which no copying is necessary; these predominate in many programs. Compiler-produced copying code is conservative and incurs unnecessary overhead either by copying too much data or by testing to avoid unnecessary copying. The LCM copy-on-write scheme defers copying until a location is actually accessed, which reduces the quantity of data that must be copied. The Myrias machine [Beltrametti *et al.* 1988] implemented, in hardware, a similar copy-on-write mechanism for parallel DO loops. It, however, used a fixed reconciliation policy and copied entire hardware pages.

A compiler's control of LCM permits optimizations when analysis is possible. For example, not all modifications to shared data need cause a copy. Only items which might be shared between processes must be copied. If compiler analysis determines that no other process will access a location, it need not be copied, which avoids the overhead of making and reconciling a copy. However, this approach requires close cooperation between the compiler and memory system to select—at a fine grain—policies governing portions of data structures.

Computation in C** alternates between parallel and sequential phases. Memory becomes coherent at the end of a parallel phase as processors reconcile their modified memory locations. C**'s semantics dictate how copies are reconciled. In general, C** requires only that the coherent value left in a memory location modified by a parallel function call be a value produced by some invocation of the call. LCM discards all but one of the modified copies. However, values written by C**'s reduction assignments require different reconciliation functions that combine values.

8.5.2   LCM Implementation

We built an LCM system on the Blizzard implementation of Tempest. Blizzard is a fine-grain distributed shared memory system that runs at near shared-memory hardware speeds on a CM-5 [Schoinas *et al.* 1994]. We compared the performance of four C** programs running under both the unmodified Stache protocol [Reinhardt *et al.* 1994] and LCM (implemented using the Tempest mechanisms provided by Blizzard). We found that the LCM memory system improved performance by up to a factor of 4 for applications that used dynamic data structures. LCM's performance was slightly slower than transparent shared memory for applications with static data and sharing patterns, which a compiler can analyze and optimize directly without using LCM.

LCM is a user-level Tempest protocol that runs on a CM-5. We started with the user-level Stache protocol [Reinhardt *et al.* 1994], which provides cache-coherent shared memory and uses a processor's local memory as a large, fully associative cache. This cache is essential to ensure that a processor's locally modified (inconsistent) blocks are not lost by being flushed to their home node. When a modified cache block is selected for replacement (either because of a capacity or conflict miss), the block is moved to the Stache in local memory. On a cache miss to the block, its value comes from the Stache, rather than the block's home processor.

LCM provides the C** compiler with three directives. The first of these, mark_modification(addr), creates an inconsistent, writable copy of the cache block containing addr. If the block is not already in the processor's cache, it is brought in. The second, reconcile_copies() appears as a global barrier executed by every processor. When it finishes and releases the processors, the memory has been reconciled across all processors and is again in a coherent state. This directive flushes all modified blocks back to their home processors to be reconciled. Outstanding read-only copies of these blocks are then invalidated throughout the system. The third, flush_copies(), performs a partial reconciliation by flushing a processor's modified cache blocks back to their home processors. The next section illustrates how the C** compiler uses these directives.

C** parallel function invocations start execution with the original (pre-parallel call) global state. LCM retains an unmodified copy of global data throughout a parallel call. At the first write to a cache block managed by the copy-on-write policy, the block's home node creates a *clean copy* of the block in main memory. The node uses a clean copy to satisfy subsequent requests for unmodified global data.

Another complication is that each processor typically runs many distinct invocations of a parallel function. The system must ensure that a new invocation does not access local cache blocks modified by a previous invocation. To avoid this error, LCM's flush_copies() directive removes modified copies of global data from the Stache. If a compiler cannot ensure that invocations access distinct locations, it issues this directive between invocations. This directive flushes cache blocks to their home processor, where they are reconciled. A subsequent read of one of these blocks returns its original value from the clean copy. Cache flushing, although semantically correct, performs poorly for applications that re-use data in flushed blocks. In another approach, each processor keeps a clean copy of every block it modifies. In this case, the flush_copies()

directive returns modified values to their home node and replaces the cached value with the clean copy, so it remains local for a subsequent reference.

LCM's memory usage depends on the number of potentially modified locations. At a location's first mark_modification() directive, LCM creates a clean copy in memory. Cached copies resulting from this directive require slightly more state information than ordinary cached blocks. Clean copies exist only during a parallel function call and are reclaimed at the reconcile_copies() directive.

8.5.3 Compiling C**

Compiling a C** program to run under LCM is straightforward. To ensure the correct semantics for parallel functions, the C** compiler inserts memory system directives, described above, in parallel functions. Alternatively, the compiler could guarantee these semantics with runtime code that explicitly copies data potentially modified in a parallel function invocation. Explicit copying works well for functions with static and analyzable data access patterns. However, it becomes complicated and expensive for programs with dynamic behavior, since the generated code must either perform runtime checks or copy a conservative superset of the modified locations. This section illustrates both approaches with a static parallel function (the stencil function) and a dynamic parallel function (an adaptive mesh) and compares the performance of LCM against the explicit copying strategy.

Stencil Example As a first example, consider a simplified version of the code generated by the C** compiler for a stencil function to run under LCM:

```
void stencil_SPMD(matrix &A)
{
  for(all invocations assigned to me)
  {
    set variables #0 and #1;

    // Function body:
    mark_modification(A[#0][#1]); // LCM directive

    A[#0][#1] = (A[#0-1][#1] + A[#0+1][#1] +
                 A[#0][y-1] + A[#0][#1+1]) / 4.0;
```

```
    flush_copies();                    // LCM directive
  }
  reconcile_copies();                  // LCM directive
}
```

Each invocation writes to `A[#0][#1]`, which is also read by its four neighboring invocations. Compiler analysis easily detects this potential conflict, which the C** compiler rectifies with `mark_modification()` directives. The `flush_copies()` directive removes modified copies from a processor's cache before another invocation starts. Another directive, `reconcile_copies()`, causes the memory system to reconcile modified locations and update global state to a consistent value.

Because compiler analysis reveals that `stencil` accesses the entire array, the C** compiler could also preserve C** semantics by maintaining two copies of A—all reads come from the old copy of A and all writes go to the new copy of A. After each iteration, the code exchanges the two arrays with a pointer swap. This simple technique preserves the C** semantics with little overhead beyond the cost of twice the memory and cache usage.

8.5.4 Dynamic C** Programs

LCM offers greater benefits for programs with dynamic behavior that is difficult or impossible to analyze. These programs require extensive (and expensive) runtime operations to run in parallel [Saltz *et al.* 1991]. For example, consider an adaptive mesh version of `stencil`, which selectively subdivides some mesh points into finer detail. It is part of a program that computes electric potentials in a box. The program imposes a mesh over the box and computes the potential at each point by averaging its four neighbors. At points where the gradient is steep, finer detail is necessary and the program subdivides the cell into four child cells. This process iterates until the mesh relaxes. Initially, points on the mesh are represented in a two-dimensional matrix, but dynamically allocated quad-trees capture cell subdivision:

```
// Update my quad-tree in the mesh
double Mesh::update_mesh() parallel
{
    // What part of tree changed?
    *self = update_quad_tree(self, neighbors);

    // Return maximum of local values
    return %> local_epsilon;
}

// Main program - do the iterations
main()
{
    ...
    create_mesh();
    while (difference >= epsilon)
        difference = update_mesh();
    ...
}
```

In this program, the mesh changes dynamically so a compiler cannot determine which parts will be modified. Without an LCM system, a compiler must conservatively copy the entire mesh between iterations to ensure C**'s semantics. With LCM, the memory system detects modifications and copies only data that is modified.

8.6 Polygon Overlay Example

As in the other chapters in this book, we illustrate our language with a C** program that computes polygon overlays. This problem starts with two maps, A and B, each covering the same geographic area and each composed of a collection of non-overlapping polygons. This calculation computes the intersection of the two maps by computing the geometric intersection of polygons from each map. As described in Appendix C, we assume that polygons are non-empty rectangles and that the entire collection fits in memory.

This section outlines two implementations of the polygon overlay calculation in C**. The first is simple and inefficient (Section 8.6.1), but fits the data-parallel style well. However, as in life, style is no substitute for thought, and the second version uses an auxiliary data structure to greatly reduce the cost of computation (Section 8.6.2).

```
struct poly_s {                      // a polygon
    short xl, yl;                    // low corner
    short xh, yh;                    // high corner
};

struct polyVec (poly_s) []          // polygon Aggregate
{
    ···member functions omitted···
};

polyVec *leftVec, *rightVec;        // input vectors
```

Program 8.5
C** Declarations for Naïve Overlay Algorithm

8.6.1 Naïve C** Implementation

The naïve program directly applies data parallelism to the problem.
Each polygon in one map executes a data-parallel operation that computes its intersection with every polygon in the second map. The non-
empty intersections form the result of the computation. This method is
simple, but extremely inefficient, since most intersections are empty.

Program 8.5 shows the relevant C** declarations for this program.
Each polygon is represented by the coordinates of its lower left and
upper right corners. The Aggregate class, `polyVec`, holds polygons from
an input map.

The parallel C** function `polyVec::computeVecVecOverlay()` (in
Program 8.6) computes the intersection of polygon `self` (which, analogous to `this`, points to the polygon a invocation is responsible for)
with the second vector of polygons `vec`. Each non-empty intersection
is added to a local list `theList`, and independent local lists are combined with the user-defined reduction `merge()` in Program 8.6. The
data-parallel overlay operation is applied to the first vector of polygons
by the statement:

```
results = (leftVec->computeVecVecOverlay(rightVec)).head;
```

For efficiency reasons, the data-parallel operation in Program 8.6 returns a structure containing pointers to the head and tail of its list of
polygons. The `merge()` routine destructively concatenates two lists by
changing the tail of the first to point to the head of the second one.

```
polyList_s polyVec::computeVecVecOverlay(polyVec *vec) parallel
{
    polyList_s theList = {NULL, NULL};      // ptrs to head and tail

    for (int i=0; i<vec->cardinality(0); i++) {
        polyNode_p tmp = polyOverlay(self, &((*vec)[i]));
        if (tmp != NULL)
            theList.insert(tmp);
    }
    return %merge theList : nullList;       // user-defined reduction
}

void merge(polyList_s *result, polyList_s theList)
{
    if (result->head==NULL && result->tail==NULL) {
        *result = theList;                  // If result NULL
    } else if (!(theList.head==NULL && theList.tail==NULL)) {
        result->tail->next = theList.head;
        result->tail = theList.tail;
    }
}
```

Program 8.6
C** Code for Naïve Overlay

8.6.2   Grid Partitioning a Map

We greatly improved the performance of the computation by exploiting locality—both geographic, in the problem, and spatial and temporal, in the computer. Instead of comparing every polygon against every other polygon, the revised program compares a polygon against the far smaller collection of polygons that are spatially adjacent. This program *partitions* the space in the second polygon map into a rectilinear grid and uses this grid to reduce the number of polygons that must be examined. This change requires a new, two-dimensional, **partition** class (in Program 8.7) to maintain the decomposed polygon map. Each cell in the partition contains a list of polygons that are partially or entirely within the cell. The second list in a cell is used in the double partition approach (Section 8.6.2).

The partitioning approach requires a new overlay routine, shown in Program 8.8. It only needs to compare a polygon against polygons in

```
struct polyNode_s {              // polygon list cell
    poly_s        poly;          // the polygon
    polyNode_s *next;            // link to next
};
typedef polyNode_s *polyNode_p;

struct partition_s {
    polyNode_p  lists[2];        // pair of lists
};

struct partition(partition_s) [][]
{
    ···other member functions omitted···
};
```

Program 8.7
Declarations for Partition Algorithm

the partition cells that it overlaps. These cells can be quickly identified
from the two endpoints that define the polygon. A polygon overlaps
all partition cells between the partition that contains its lower left and
upper right corners.

With the naïve program, computing the overlay of two data sets containing approximately 60K polygons each resulted in over 3.6 billion
polygon comparisons. By contrast, the partitioning version, using a
partition of 45 by 45 cells, required only 3.6 million comparisons—an
improvement of three orders of magnitude.

Since a pair of polygons may overlap in several partitions, the code
must be careful to avoid recording duplicate intersections. The C** program, in the routine ownPoly(), records the intersection of two polygons
only when the lower corner of the overlap falls within the current partition cell.

The distribution of polygons in partition cells affects load balancing
and hence the program's performance. We use a simple heuristic to
partition the polygons. The program first calculates the number of cells
in each partition from the area of an input polygon map and the number
of polygons it contains. The program then computes the average polygon
area and sets the partition cell size to some multiple of the average

```
#define ownPoly(x,y,p)\
        ((findCell(p->poly.xl)==x) && (findCell(p->poly.yl)==y))

#define findCell(x)   ((int)(((x)-1) / (cellSize)))

polyList_s polyVec::computeVecPartOverlay(partition *p) parallel
{
  polyList_s theList = {NULL, NULL};

  int xStart = findCell(self->xl);      // find appropriate cells
  int xStop  = findCell(self->xh);
  int yStart = findCell(self->yl);
  int yStop  = findCell(self->yh);

  for (int x=xStart; x<=xStop; x++)     // step through cells
    for (int y=yStart; y<=yStop; y++)
      for (polyNode_p ptr=((*p)[x][y].lists[0]);
           ptr!=NULL;
           ptr=ptr->next) {
        polyNode_p tmp = polyOverlay(self, &(ptr->poly));
        if ((tmp != NULL) && (ownPoly(x,y,tmp)))
theList.insert(tmp); // link in overlap
        else if (tmp != NULL)
delete tmp;              // not owned, delete
      }
  return %merge theList : nullList;
}
```

Program 8.8
Overlay Routine for Partition Algorithm

polygon area, called the *granularity*. More will be said about choices of granularity in Section 8.6.4.

The code in Program 8.9 partitions the Aggregate of polygons. The data parallel function invocation on a polygon copies the polygon into the appropriate partition cells. Since this process is many-to-many communication, with the potential for write conflicts, a user-defined reduction (insertPoly()) links polygons into a partition's cell list.

Note that the reduction assignment passes a polygon structure, not a pointer to a polygon. This is for efficiency. Passing a pointer as an argument to the user-defined reduction operation means that insertPoly()

```
void insertPoly(polyNode_p *result, poly_s thePoly)
{
  polyNode_p ptr = new polyNode_s;// allocate new node
  ptr->poly = thePoly;            // fill it in
  ptr->next = *result;            // link node into list
  *result = ptr;                  // return result
}

void polyVec::partitionVec(partition *p, int n) parallel
{
  int xStart = findCell(self->xl);   // find dest cells
  int xStop  = findCell(self->xh);
  int yStart = findCell(self->yl);
  int yStop  = findCell(self->yh);

  for (int x=xStart; x<=xStop; x++) // do combining writes
    for (int y=yStart; y<=yStop; y++)
      &((*p)[x][y].lists[n]) =%insertPoly *self;
}
```

Program 8.9
Code to Partition a Polygon Vector

must dereference the pointer to obtain a copy of the polygon to link into
the list. This dereference requires communication if the reduction occurs
on a processor other than the one that allocated the polygon. Passing
polygons, instead of pointers, causes the polygon data to be sent directly
to the processor that performs the reduction and eliminates a potential
extra round of communication.

The same reasoning, in reverse, applies to the overlay routine in Program 8.6. The solution is formed by a reduction that references pointers
to the head and tail of each invocation's polygons list. Thus, only a pair
of pointers are passed between processors. If the code used a combining
assignment, similar to the one in Program 8.9, it would transmit all polygons in the list, instead of just the list's head and tail. Of course, sending
the polygons might be more efficient if the processor that invoked the
data-parallel operation later read the entire result.

Partitioning Both Maps A natural extension of the partitioning
approach is to partition *both* polygon vectors and overlay the partitions

```
polyList_s partition::computePartPartOverlay() parallel
{
  polyList_s theList = {NULL, NULL};

  for (polyNode_p p1=self->lists[0]; p1!=NULL; p1=p1->next) {
    for (polyNode_p p2=self->lists[1]; p2!=NULL; p2=p2->next) {
      polyNode_p tmp = polyOverlay(&(p1->poly), &(p2->poly));
      if ((tmp != NULL) && (ownPoly(#0,#1,tmp)))
        theList.insert(tmp);
      else if (tmp != NULL)
        delete tmp;
    }
  }
  return %merge theList : nullList;
}
```

Program 8.10
Overlay Routine for Double Partition Version

cell by cell. Although this double partitioning approach performs the same number of comparisons as the single partition version, it exploits memory locality more effectively. Each grid cell now contains two lists of polygons, one list for each map. Since both of a cell's polygon lists are allocated on the same processor, the polygon comparison phase requires no communication. Program 8.10 lists the parallel overlay function.

Although the extra partitioning step increases execution time for small numbers of processors, the double partition code has better locality, and therefore incurs fewer misses, which increases scalability. For example, a run with 60K polygon data sets on 32 processors resulted in 2151 coherence misses during the overlay phase of the single partition code. The double partition overlay phase incurred only 46 misses. Section 8.6.4 shows that this change results in more nearly linear scaled speedups for the double partition version.

8.6.3 Performance Tuning

The initial version of the partitioned code ran reasonably well, but several changes improved both the speed of the C** code and its scalability. Although C** is a high-level language, we were able to perform these optimizations within the language.

Memory Management   The program creates and destroys many list nodes during the partitioning and overlay phases. Measurements showed that it spent considerable time in calls to `malloc()` and `free()`. Furthermore, malloc's 8-byte memory overhead for each allocation greatly increased the total memory requirement. We therefore implemented our own list of free polygon list nodes on each processor. When the list is exhausted, the program requests four pages of memory (16 kbyte) and carves it into pieces of the appropriate size.

Communication Reduction   In order to obtain good speedups on a distributed shared memory machine such as the CM-5, it is important to reduce communication when possible. This section describes three optimizations that decrease communication.

The first improvement changed polygon coordinates to `shorts`, instead of `ints`. This cut both the memory and communication requirements in half. Also, padding the partition cells to 32 bytes reduced false sharing.

Since polygon maps are accessed sequentially, our second optimization uses a large unit of coherence to exploit temporal locality. Our memory coherence protocol, implemented in software, allows us to maintain coherence on larger 1024-byte blocks, rather than the default 32-byte blocks [Reinhardt *et al.* 1994]. This change reduced the number of cache faults on shared data significantly. For example, on data sets containing approximately 60K polygons each, and running on 32 processors, the number of cache misses dropped from 60,876 to 4,962.

The final optimization further reduced communication in the double partition code by distributing the grid data and grid computation identically. The shared-memory substrate distributes global data using round-robin page placement, while C**'s runtime system divides invocations in equal blocks. By adjusting the number of partition cells to occupy a power-of-two number of pages, this optimization ensures that a processor accesses exactly those grid cells that are allocated to it. Thus, the entire overlay computation requires no communication other than the reduction to combine pieces of the solution.

Area Optimizations   Both the single and double partitioning approaches can benefit from an area-based optimization. Once a polygon's entire area has overlapped other polygons, it can be removed from consideration. Discarding polygons reduces the number of comparisons and therefore the cost of calculating the intersection.

For the single partition version, each polygon from the first map records its unused area. When the area is consumed, the polygon is discarded. A more aggressive approach could record unused areas of polygons in the second map as well. The second optimization is inappropriate for the single-partition version since it requires changes from one invocation to be visible to all others. The results in the next section only use the simple optimization for the single-partition code.

The double-partition approach requires more complex analysis since a polygon in the first map cannot be discarded unless it is completely enclosed in a partition cell. However, a slightly more complex area calculation, which starts with the portion of a polygon enclosed by a cell, works well. Furthermore, the double-partition version can exploit the second optimization because both lists of polygons within a cell are accessed by the same parallel function invocation. Unfortunately, measurements showed that the cost of building and maintaining a second data structure to record polygon areas outweighed the benefits of the more aggressive optimization. As the granularity of a partition increases, the optimization becomes more attractive. However, our measurements showed that it was better to use smaller granularities and the first area optimization than larger granularities and both optimizations. Thus, the results for the double-partition code use only the first area optimization.

8.6.4   Results

All measurements were run on a 32-processor partition of a Thinking Machines CM-5. Our timings do not include the time to read the data from disk. On the CM-5, the time to read the input files is larger than the time to actually perform the computation. For example, on the 60K polygon data sets and 32 processors, it takes more than 20 times longer to read the data than to compute the overlay. Since the CM-5 does not support parallel I/O, the input files are read by a front-end process and sent to a single CM-5 processor, which creates a serial bottleneck that would artificially limit the program's speedup.

For the same reason, we also did not include the time to distribute the input data across the processors. Since all data initially resides on the processor that read the file, distributing the data takes a large amount of time and forms a bottleneck. On 32 processors, the data distribution time is roughly equal to the time for two partitioning steps and the overlay computation. For reference, the graph in Figure 8.7 shows how including the distribution time would reduce the application's speedup. This bottleneck is clearly an area for future work.

Granularity   Selecting a granularity for partition cells (Section 8.6.2), as typical, requires tradeoffs. At first glance, small granularities appear best since they require fewer comparisons during the overlay phase. However, as the granularity decreases, polygons span partition cells more frequently. This increases memory requirements, since each of these polygons is duplicated. Partitioning with a granularity of 5 doubles the number of polygons that must be represented. Even with a granularity of 20, approximately 50% more polygons must be represented.

The granularity also affects the program's speedup. The partitioning phase runs best with large granularities, since few cell-spanning polygons require less communication. However, the overlay computation performs less work with small granularities. The best granularity is therefore a balance between the partition and overlay phases' needs. This balance is different for the single and double partition approaches, since the double partition code spends more time partitioning.

As was mentioned in Section 8.6.3, we adjusted the number of cells in the partition to ensure that the memory underlying a partition is a power-of-two number of pages. This limits the choice of granularity, but some latitude still remains. In the experiments below, we used a granularity of 30 for the smallest data set and a granularity of 36 for the other two data sets. These values were compromises that produced consistently high performance for varying numbers of processors.

The k100 data set   The k100 series of polygon maps were the largest ones provided. Each contains approximately 60,000 polygons. Figure 8.2 shows the execution times to compute the overlay for the first two data sets of this series. The runtime of the naïve program is not shown, since it is far larger than the partitioning versions. For example, on one processor, it requires more than 4500 seconds for the naïve computation, versus roughly 10 seconds for the partitioned program. Figure 8.3 shows the scaled speedups (speedups with respect to one-processor runs) for all three versions.

The naïve code has the best scaled speedup: 25.8 on 32 processors (an efficiency of 80.6%). The partitioning versions have scaled speedups of 16.0 and 20.7, for efficiencies of 52.0% and 64.7%. Detailed analysis of the partitioning versions showed that load imbalances reduced the

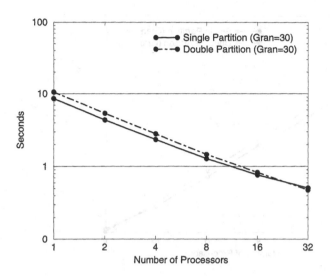

Figure 8.2
Execution Times for Overlay Phase for k100 Data Set (partition granularity 30)

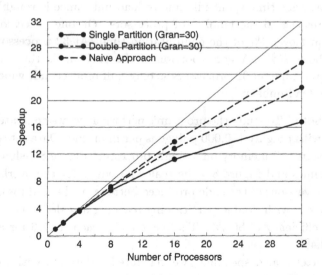

Figure 8.3
Scaled Speedups for Overlay Phase for k100 Data Set (partition granularity 30)

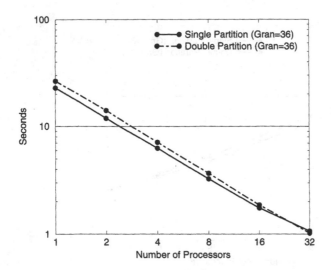

Figure 8.4
Execution Times for Overlay Phase for 150k Data Set (partition granularity 36)

speedup. The average time spent idle due to load imbalance is roughly constant with respect to the number of processors. On one processor, it amounts to just over 1% of the computation time. At 32 processors it makes up about 25%. A good portion of the problem is that the total computation time on 32 processors is only half of a second, which exacerbates the load imbalance.

Larger Data Sets To study the program's performance, we generated a new data set with roughly 150,000 polygons per input file. Data sets of this size used nearly all memory on a single processor. Figure 8.4 shows the execution times and Figure 8.5 the scaled speedups for the overlay phase. All three versions of the code produced better scaled speedups on the larger data set, with double partitioning reaching a scaled speedup of 25.7, for an efficiency of 80.4%. The naïve code reached 28.6 for an efficiency of 89.4%.

To obtain better scaled speedups, we generated a data set with approximately 300,000 polygons per input file. This problem could not run on one processor due to memory limitations, so we measured performance on 2–32 processors. Figure 8.6 shows the execution times and

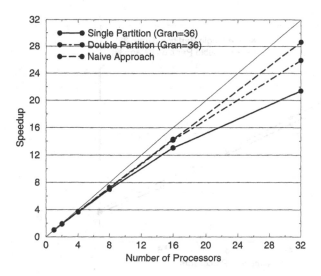

Figure 8.5
Scaled Speedups for Overlay Phase for 150k Data Set (partition granularity 36)

Figure 8.7 the scaled speedups. The double partition code achieved a scaled speedup of 13.6, for an efficiency of 85.0%. We could not measure the performance of the naïve code for this data set because it took too long to run (over 20 hours on 2 processors). Figure 8.7 also shows scaled speedups for the partition and overlay phases.

8.7 Conclusion

Designing a new programming language is in many ways like writing the Great American Novel—except that the rewards, both on the average and at the margin, are more lucrative for authors than language designers. Both occupations require overwhelming confidence that your wonderful new idea will succeed and prosper where the vast majority of your predecessors sank into oblivion.

C**'s conceit was that a parallel language could offer some benefits of SIMD programming, without some of its disadvantages, by restricting parallel execution semantics. C** research has focused on techniques for efficiently implementing these semantics and language extensions for

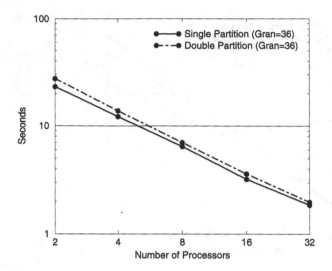

Figure 8.6
Execution Times for 300k Data Set (partition granularity 36)

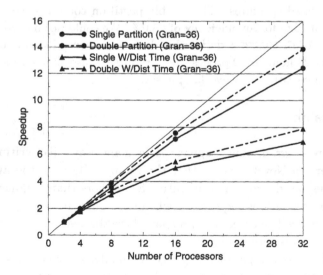

Figure 8.7
Scaled Speedups for 300k Data Set (partition granularity 36)

increasing the semantics' generality. In both respects, the research is successful. By exploiting Tempest user-level shared memory, the C** compiler and system implement a large-grain data-parallel language with a simple, clear semantics and little unnecessary overhead. Although the many polygon overlay examples are difficult to compare because of algorithm and processor differences, C**'s speedup curves are close to linear. In addition, our experience with C** demonstrates that user-level reductions are a powerful language feature that permits concise, efficient implementation of many parallel algorithms, even within the constraints of large-grain data parallelism.

The course that we followed is, unfortunately, unlikely to lead to wide popularity and use of C**. The recent languages on the best seller lists— C, C++, Perl, Tcl—are an amalgamation of ideas from earlier research languages and all began with a low-cost, widely-available implementation. pC++ (Chapter 13) is consciously following this model. It is unclear, however, if this model will succeed for high-performance computing since portability is often the enemy of performance. Seeing little hope of writing a best seller, our efforts followed a different approach and concentrated on implementing, developing, and demonstrating a few ideas.

During this research, several more general observations have become clear. First, the programming language community is too introspective. In recent years, it has begun a dialog with the applications community. However, it still does not interact with computer architects, to understand and influence future machines. Machines are still designed and built to fit perceived needs of users, without much consideration to the requirements of languages or compilers [Arpaci et al. 1995]. In the end, the users, compiler writers, and architects all suffer.

The C** research has been conducted as part of the Wisconsin Wind Tunnel Project [Hill et al. 1994], which is studying the hardware/software tradeoffs in parallel shared-memory machines. A key design tenet of the Wind Tunnel research is that hardware should provide mechanisms and software should implement policy. C** has exploited this approach by using the Tempest mechanisms to implement its language semantics in the memory system. Hardware provides low-cost tests that detect exceptional conditions without slowing normal execution.

Second, following a moving target is hard. Four years ago, we introduced parallelism into C** by extending the class mechanism. Today, we would likely specify Aggregates with templates (like the Amelia Vector Template Library of Chapter 2). When we started, templates were a new language feature that compilers partially and poorly implemented. Today, templates are a widely used and important language feature that most compilers still implement poorly.

Our primary problem was that C++ is a very complex language and the continual standardization process increased the number and complexity of its features. As a consequence, C++ compilers are complex, poorly written, and constantly changing. Adding our minor changes to C++ required considerable time and effort better spent on research. Templates, when properly implemented, may permit language extension without language modification.

Finally: too many languages, not enough evaluation; or, what makes a good language? In the absence of objective criteria, everyone will continue using and teaching familiar languages whose compilers are at hand. Without quantitative comparisons against alternative languages and implementations, it will remain impossible to write a programming languages paper that excites more than a small handful of readers. In a better world, new language features (and implementations) would be compared by measures that matter, such as performance, conciseness, and readability.

This book takes a first step in that direction. By comparing the many implementations of the polygon overlay code, a reader can begin to evaluate the many parallel C++ languages. Of course, all of the usual disclaimers ("it's only one program running on an experimental implementation on a slow, old machine") apply if our C** code does not fare well.

Acknowledgments

This work is supported in part by Wright Laboratory Avionics Directorate, Air Force Material Command, USAF, under grant #F33615-94-1-1525 and ARPA order #B550, an NSF NYI Award CCR-9357779, NSF Grants CCR-9101035 and MIP-9225097, DOE Grant DE-FG02-93ER25176, and donations from Digital Equipment Corporation and Sun Microsystems. The U.S. Government is authorized to reproduce and distribute reprints for Governmental purposes notwithstanding any

9 ICC++

Andrew A. Chien and Julian T. Dolby

9.1 Introduction

Illinois Concert C++ (ICC++) is designed to bring object orientation
to bear on managing the complexity of concurrency and distribution in
parallel programs. By integrating concurrency and the object model,
ICC++ facilitates the construction of programs which exploit irregular and adaptive computational methods and intricate distributed data
structures. The design of ICC++ was driven by two goals: providing a
clean object model in a concurrent context and permitting the expression of concurrency with minimal disruption to the structure of C++.
Furthermore, ICC++ is structured to permit the application of modern
compiler optimization techniques, especially aggressive interprocedural
analyses and transformations. This design enables ICC++ to support:

1. construction of *concurrent data abstractions*;

2. convenient expression of *irregular and fine-grained concurrency*;

3. high *sequential and parallel performance*; and

4. *single source code* for sequential and parallel program versions.

We believe that these elements are necessary for the widespread acceptance of concurrent object-oriented programming. First, data abstraction is the key feature of object-oriented programming; it must be
possible to build abstractions and ensure their correctness in the face of
concurrent operations upon them. Second, object-oriented programs are
by their nature fine-grained, with many objects and small procedures;
the natural expression of concurrency is often in these units. To preserve a natural object-oriented programming style, concurrency must be
expressed within this structure.

Third, performance is a major justification for parallelism, so high
performance is essential. Because many parallel programs are also executed on sequential platforms, parallelizing a program must not preclude
its efficient execution on one or a small number of processors. Finally,
single source code is important because the vast majority of software is
developed for uniprocessors. Having a single source code dramatically

increases the accessibility of concurrency by allowing programs to be parallelized without radical rewriting.

To support the four requirements detailed above, ICC++ provides three key features:

Extensional concurrency constructs: ICC++ provides constructs for specifying *potential concurrency*, i.e., for specifying a partial order of execution. This allows an implementation to serialize execution as necessary for efficiency. These constructs add concurrency incrementally, thus allowing it to be introduced without disturbing program structure.

An object consistency model: ICC++ specifies an object consistency model which allows programmers to reason about a data abstraction's correctness. Furthermore, ICC++ also provides concurrency guarantees for objects that enable programmers to reason about progress. Because it may be preferable to implement a data abstraction with several objects, the consistency model can be extended across multiple objects.

Integrated arrays and objects: ICC++ integrates objects and arrays in object collections, which are arrays with an extensible object interface. Collections can have member functions, and can be used to build concurrent abstractions.

These three key features are explained in Sections 9.2 to 9.4. Section 9.5 discusses the unstructured concurrency primitives of ICC++. The implementation and performance of the polygon overlay program are described in Sections 9.6 and 9.7 respectively. Section 9.8 discusses related work and issues and Section 9.9 closes by summarizing the chapter.

9.2   Concurrency

ICC++'s concurrency constructs are designed to support convenient expression of concurrency, single source code for sequential and parallel program versions, and efficient sequential and parallel language implementations. Together, these three goals imply that concurrency should be introduced as an extension to existing language structures, and that the concurrent constructs should leave compilers as much implementation flexibility as possible. ICC++ provides two primary concurrency constructs: conc blocks and conc loops. Both are extensions to standard C++ syntax and are designed to enable incremental parallelization of existing code. Furthermore, both introduce *potential concurrency*, not guaranteed concurrency, and thus provide the implementation the freedom to serialize where appropriate for efficiency.[1]

9.2.1 conc Blocks

The primary construct for introducing potential concurrency in ICC++ is the conc block, an extension of blocks in C++. A conc block specifies that the contained statements are only partially ordered based upon local data dependences. conc blocks are defined use the new keyword conc:

$$\text{conc } \{ \ S_1; \ \cdots; \ S_n; \ \}$$

A conc block is a compound statement which defines the following partial order $\prec$ on its constituents:

$$S_i \prec S_j \iff i < j \text{ and } S_i \Rightarrow S_j$$

where $S_i \Rightarrow S_j$ indicates that statement S_j depends upon S_i. Statements in a conc block are executed such that if $S_i \prec S_j$, then S_i will be executed completely before S_j is begun.

S_j depends upon S_i if any identifier which appears in both S_i and S_j is assigned in one of them, or if S_i contains a jump statement (i.e., a break, continue, or goto). The first rule allows concurrent operations upon objects via pointers, while preserving sequential semantics for local variables, including the pointers themselves. Thus:

```
conc { a->b(); a->c();}
```

would be concurrent but:

```
conc { a = new Foo(); a->b(); }
```

would be sequential. The second rule gives jump statements a natural semantics by serializing the conc block around them. A conc block is finished when all statements within it have completed. For concurrency

---

[1]ICC++ also includes primitives which guarantee concurrency for situations where such guarantees are required (Section 9.5). However, as these primitives dictate an implementation to the system, they are expensive, and should be used with care.

control purposes, nested blocks are treated as single statements within the block in which they are nested.

These rules are designed to expose concurrency while preserving sequential semantics where it is essential. Serializing state changes for local variables allows existing compound statements that declare and use local variables to be transformed into conc blocks, exposing concurrency for object invocations within them. This exploits the distinction between built-in types (e.g., int and float) and user-defined objects in C++. Built-in types cannot provide concurrency control, so their uses are serializing, but user-defined objects all have concurrency control in ICC++, so operations on objects are allowed to execute concurrently. Similarly, providing natural semantics for jump statements allows conc to be applied to existing code where unstructured control is used.

By specifying *potential* concurrency rather than *guaranteed* concurrency, the conc block provides implementation flexibility. Statements in a block need not be scheduled fairly, enabling a compiler to serialize sections and inline procedure calls where appropriate for efficiency. In this manner, the implementation can choose appropriate grain sizes for efficient execution on a variety of machines.

9.2.2 conc Loops

Each of the C++ looping constructs can be modified by conc, just as with C++ blocks. C++ loop constructs have no distinguished loop variable, as do for in Pascal and do in Fortran. Thus, the semantics of the concurrent loop constructs must expose cross-iteration concurrency while retaining reasonable behavior for the local variables. Since all C++ loops allow control flow operations (i.e., break and continue), concurrent loops must support them as well. In ICC++ conc loops, loop-carried data dependences are respected for scalar variables, but other dependences, such as those through arrays or pointer structures, are not. Essentially, conc loops are dynamically unfolded conc blocks, with local variables renamed for each iteration. For example, the loop:

```
conc while (j > 10){
  a->foo(j);
  j -= 1;
}
```

is implicitly expanded to:

```
if (j > 10) conc {
  a->foo(j);
  j0 = j - 1;
  if (j0 > 10) conc {
    a->foo(j0);
    j1 = j0 - 1;
    ...
  }
}
```

The design of concurrent loops is similar to that of conc blocks. Respecting scalar variable dependences and permitting control flow operations within loops simplifies the addition of concurrency. As with conc blocks, the conc looping constructs express *potential* concurrency; no guarantees of actual concurrency are provided. This allows actual implementations considerable latitude in scheduling iterations; in particular, subsets can be run sequentially.

9.2.3 Examples

To make our discussion more concrete, we provide some examples of conc blocks and loops. Consider the following quicksort() routine, taken from the polygon overlay program:

```
void quicksort(poly_t vec[], int l, int r){
  if ((r-l)>THRESHOLD) {
    int i = partition(vec,l,r);
    quicksort(vec,l,i);
    quicksort(vec,i+1,r);
  } else {
    simple_sort(vec, l, r);
  }
}
```

A parallelized quicksort() requires only the addition of a single conc annotation, and is excerpted from Section 9.6:

```
void quicksort(poly_t vec[], int l, int r){
  if ((r-l)>THRESHOLD)
    conc {
      int i = partition(vec, l, r);
      quicksort(vec,l,i);
      quicksort(vec, i+1, r);
    }
```

```
    else {
      simple_sort(vec,l,r);
    }
  }
```

The `quicksort()` example illustrates how `conc` can often be added without requiring structural program changes. In this case, the `conc` block respects the local dependence for `i` while allowing the recursive `quicksort()` calls to execute concurrently.

The code below (also taken from polygon overlay) presents an example of how `conc` looping structures can be used. Again, the concurrency can be introduced with no disruption of the surrounding program.

```
conc for (il=0; il<leftlimit; il++){
  conc for (ir=0; ir<rightlimit; ir++){
    newLn = polyOverlayLn(left->vec[il], right->vec[ir]);
    if (newLn != NULL){
      newLn->link = outList;
      outList = newLn;
    }
  }
}
```

The loops above represent a naïve parallelization of the simplest polygon overlay algorithm. Because all of the `polyOverlayLn()` calls are independent, they could be executed in parallel if they were the only statements in the loop body. However, the `if` statement accumulates the new polygons into a list, serializing the innermost loop. To really generate concurrency, the code would have to accumulate the new polygons in parallel (see Section 9.6).

The two loops below illustrate the basic uses of `conc` looping constructs:

```
conc for (i=0; i<SIZE; i++){          // loop 1
  elements[i].doit(partners[i]);
}
conc while (i != NULL){               // loop 2
  i->element_update();
  i = i->next;
}
```

Loop 1 is parallel across all members of `elements[i]` and `partners[i]`. In effect, the semantics are identical to Fortran-90's `doall`: all loop iterations are executed in parallel. Loop 2 runs down a list, triggering calls to `element_update()` for each element. The semantics of this loop are similar to `doacross` in Fortran-90: loop iterations are partially overlapped, subject to the data dependences. In this case, the calls to `element_update()` will be concurrent, but will be launched one at a time as loop progresses down the list. This shows the utility of enforcing scalar dependences, but with renaming semantics to expose concurrency. In both cases, the loops terminate when all of their iterations have completed.

9.3 Objects, Abstractions, and Concurrency

The core of object-oriented programming is building data abstractions which can be modified with a well-defined set of operations [Liskov 1988a, Wirth & Gutknecht 1992, Wirth & Gutknecht 1992]. These operations (i.e., member functions in C++) transform the data abstraction from one consistent state to another. In a concurrent program, such member functions might be interleaved, exposing inconsistent states, and thereby destroying the encapsulation (and perhaps also the correctness) of the data abstraction. To avoid such problems, concurrent object models generally must prevent the interleaving of members which can violate encapsulation [Agha 1990, Yonezawa 1990, Chien & Dally 1990, Chien 1993, America 1987, Bal et al. 1992, Kalé & Krishnan 1993, Grimshaw 1993].

Concurrent object models must also be designed with programmability and single source maintenance in mind. For instance, a simple model which provides a single monitor for each object might prohibit recursive calls, breaking many sequential programs, and requiring programmers to program around the language. Our extensive experience with Concurrent Aggregates explored such a model, but programmers generally found it burdensome and a fruitful source of program deadlock. In addition, because of the complex lock dependence structures that could be built with such a model, it prevented numerous optimizing code transformations.

The ICC++ object concurrency model constrains concurrency enough to maintain the logical atomicity of operations, but it permits much more concurrency than models based on a single monitor. The model has

three elements: an object consistency model, a mechanism for extending
that model to multiple objects, and a model for constructing atomic
operations over multiple abstractions.

9.3.1   Object Data Abstractions

ICC++ defines an *object consistency model* and *object concurrency guarantees* to allow a programmer to reason about program correctness and
progress. The consistency model ensures local serializability of operations by ensuring that method calls do not disrupt each other. Concurrency guarantees define which member calls must run concurrently,
allowing programmers to reason about program progress.

Object Consistency Model   In ICC++, concurrent method invocations on an object are constrained so that intermediate object states
created within a member function are not visible. In essence, this means
that the operations are locally serializable; the effect on member variables is as if the member functions operated one after another. This
preserves the same notion of consistency provided in a sequential object
model: each member call leaves the object in a consistent state for subsequent calls. For concurrency control purposes, a member function call
is considered to include nested calls on `this`. Object state modifications
during the execution of such nested calls are therefore not visible. Finally, direct access to object state from outside member functions (e.g.,
`a->field_name`) are subject to the same consistency model by requiring
use of implicitly-defined accessor members.

Object Concurrency Guarantees   Concurrency guarantees enable
a programmer to reason about progress in a concurrent program. For
each object locally, ICC++ guarantees that member function calls whose
effect on object state is explicitly independent will execute concurrently.
Explicit independence is determined by forming may-read and may-write
sets as a conservative approximation of member effects. For example,
concurrency is guaranteed for two methods which share no member variables and those that employ read-only sharing of member variables. The
notion of explicit independence is transitive: the may-read and may-
write sets include accesses within nested calls on `this`. This simple concurrency guarantee allows many programs that partition object state

into independent read and write sets to be written without additional synchronization, and without fear of deadlock.

As an example, consider a semaphore object:

```
class Semaphore {
private :
  int i;
public :
 Semaphore(int ii = 0){
    i = ii;
  }
  int p(void){
    if (i==0) return ++i;
    return 0;
  }
  int v(void){
    if (i==1) return i--;
    return 0;
  }
};
```

Because the semaphore's p() and v() operations both potentially read and write the instance variable i, no concurrency is allowed—much less guaranteed—between them.

A similar example is the following simple barrier object:

```
class barrier {
private :
  int countto, arrived, flag;
public :
  barrier(void){
    countto = arrived = flag = 0;
  }

  void begin_barrier(int expected){
    arrived = flag = 0;
    countto = expected;
  }

  int enter_barrier(void){
    arrived++;
    if (arrived == countto) return 1;
    return 0;
  }
```

```
    void post_flag(void){ flag = 1; }

    int test_barrier(void){ return flag; }
};
```

The **barrier** class is called once with **begin_barrier()** to initialize its consensus count. Threads then call **enter_barrier()** to signal their arrival, and check **test_barrier()** to see when the barrier has completed. If the value returned by **test_barrier()** is 1, the barrier is complete, so the thread calls **post_flag()**. A distinct **flag** variable allows calls to **enter_barrier()** and **test_barrier()** to execute concurrently, ensuring that the barrier can complete. Without the concurrency guarantees, a programmer might be forced to split the **flag** state into another object in order to ensure concurrent progress of both **test_barrier()** and **enter_barrier()**.

9.3.2   Concurrency Control Across Multiple Objects

Data abstractions are often conveniently implemented as ensembles of objects, shallow hierarchies, trees, networks, and other pointer-based structures. For example, C++ objects sometimes have fields that point to arrays, allowing the arrays to vary in size. The ICC++ concurrency control model allows consistency guarantees to be extended over several objects by using the **integral** declaration specifier. **integral** is a new type specifier that can be applied only to member variables and extends object consistency to include all references to that member variable. That is, all references to an **integral** member variable are considered read/write operations on it, providing local serialization. Note that this does not ensure global serialization, since the object whose reference is declared **integral** could be shared. However, this model handles the common case in which the **integral** variable points to private state, and can be implemented efficiently with only local operations.

The code in Program 9.1 illustrates the use of **integral**. For example, the **buckets** member in Program 9.1 is declared **integral** to incorporate it into the hash table's concurrency control. The **integral** specifier is needed to guarantee that calls to **HashTable::add()** and **HashTable::find()** are mutually exclusive; **HashTable::add()** does not affect the immediate state of the **HashTable** itself, so multiple calls to it could otherwise interleave. Such interleaved calls would, in turn, in-

```
class Bucket;
class HashTable{
  integral Bucket buckets[];     // collection of buckets
  int n_buckets;                 // number of buckets

  // locate the bucket in which a given key would be found
  Bucket& find_bucket(Key k) {
    return buckets[k.hash % n_buckets];
  }
 public :
  // Bucket::find returns an element based upon a given key
  Element find(Key k) {
    return find_bucket(k).find(k);
  }
  // Bucket::has returns TRUE if the bucket has the key
  // Bucket::add puts a given element in the bucket
  Element add(Element e) {
    Bucket& b = find_bucket(e.key);
    if (! b.has(e.key)) b.add(e);
    return e;
  }
friend bool operator >=(HashTable&, HashTable&);
};
```

Program 9.1
Extending Concurrency Control to Contained Objects Using integral

terleave calls to Bucket::has() and Bucket::add(). This could cause the same element to be inserted multiple times. However, since the state of buckets is read by HashTable::add(), declaring buckets to be integral prevents this interleaving.

While integral supports coherence for a single abstraction, some operations require consistency across multiple abstractions. For instance, a set difference operation on mathematical sets could need to prevent changes to both set arguments so as to remain consistent. And in general, coordinating concurrent activities requires coordinated updates across several distinct abstractions [Gray & Reuter 1993, Liskov 1988b].

friend functions may be part of the interfaces of multiple classes, making them a natural basis for coordinating updates across multiple objects. They provide the same guarantees as members for *all* their friendly arguments; that is, friends ensure that intermediate states

of *all* friendly arguments are invisible. This means the execution of
a `friend` function is locally serializable with respect to *each* friendly
argument.

```
bool operator >=(HashTable &left, HashTable &right) {
  for(int i = 0; i < right.n_buckets; i++) {
    Bucket &b = right.buckets[i];
    for(int j = 0; j < b.n_elements; b++) {
      if (!left.find(b[j])) return false;
    }
  }

  return true;
}
```

Above is the code for `operator >=`, which was declared `friend` in
`HashTable`; it checks whether `left` is a superset of `right`. There is a potential for wrong answers if *either* `left` *or* `right` are modified. Declaring
this function a `friend` prevents this from happening, as `friend` ensures
that it will be consistent with respect to both `left` and `right`.

9.3.3   Discussion

Our experience with monitor-based concurrency control models in Concurrent Aggregates highlighted the problems of their use (e.g., a pen-
chant for deadlock) and optimization (e.g., limited code transformations), and thus motivated ICC++'s concurrent object model. A language's concurrency control model can affect execution efficiency. Our
concurrency control model is defined in terms of visible state changes,
rather than locking or exclusivity, to allow the compiler to optimize
concurrency control. Declaring intermediate states to be invisible gives
objects thread-safe semantics, and also allow object state to be safely
cached in registers under compiler control. Concurrency control also interacts with derivation, and our concurrency model has been designed
with this *inheritance anomaly* in mind, as discussed in Section 9.8.

While transactions and nested transactions provide an elegant, flexible model for composing objects into larger abstractions, they are far
too expensive for object-level concurrency. To exploit concurrency at
this level, overheads of at most a few instructions can be tolerated. The
`integral` mechanism meets this cost constraint because its local definition of consistency allows it to be implemented with local bit-mask

operations. The **friend** mechanism provides a truly consistent view of two objects, and thus is more expensive, potentially requiring remote locking. ICC++ includes **friend** as a building block when such expensive structures are really essential.

9.4 Arrays, Objects, and Collections

ICC++ provides *collections*, which extend C++ arrays and integrate them into the object model. This allows array-level functionality to be expressed using member functions of an array class. Our collection classes support a wide variety of concurrency patterns, from a data-parallel array model to more complex concurrent abstractions. They are related to collections in pC++ (Chapter 13) when used for data parallelism, but each element has access to the entire collection, which allows them to implement more complex composite behavior as well. Finally, collections allow distributions to be explicitly specified [ICC 1995].

9.4.1 Defining Object Collections

Collections are defined by adding "[]" to the type name in a standard class declaration. This declaration creates two distinct classes: one for the elements, called **type**, and the other for the collection itself, called **type[]**; declared members can pertain either to the element or to the collection class. To prevent ambiguity, declarations for the entire collection need explicit type qualification. Each instance of a collection class has the collection members, and a linearly-addressable set of elements, each of which have the element members. Nested collections are defined using multiple sets of [], and intermediate levels of them are both collections themselves and elements of the enclosing level. A simple collection definition is:

```
// a collection definition
class Counter[] {
    int elt_total;              // an element member variable
    int Counter[]::total;       // a collection member variable
  public:
    Counter(void);              // an element constructor
    Counter[](void);            // a collection constructor
```

```
    int count(int);              // element member functions
    int elt_sum(int);
    int Counter[]::sum(void);    // a collection member function
};
```

This declaration creates two classes: the `Counter[]` collection type and the `Counter` element type. The `Counter` element has just one field: `elt_total`. The `Counter[]` collection consists of a linearly address-able set of `Counter` objects and one field of collection state: `total`. `Counter[]` has the member function `sum()`, and `Counter` has the member functions `count()` and `elt_sum()`. Notice that the collection decla-rations are qualified and the element declarations are not; all unqualified declarations in a collection definition belong to the element type, and declarations for the whole collection must be qualified with the collection type name.

Since collections are classes, derivation is supported for them. It works class-wise so that `derived` inherits from `base` and `derived[]` inherits from `base[]`. For nested collections, each level inherits class-wise from the corresponding level in the base collection class.

9.4.2   Using Collections

Collections are declared and used just as arrays are, using identical `[]` syntax for both declaration and indexing. Additionally, collection mem-bers, both variables and functions, are used just like those of any other object, as in:

```
Counter Foo[15];
conc for(int i = 0; i < 15; i++)
  Foo[i].count(i);
cout << Foo.sum();
```

Note that since there are no syntactic dependencies between the itera-tions of the `conc for` loop, the `count()` calls can proceed in parallel. In addition, because the execution of iterations is not specified, the com-piler is free to reorganize them for higher efficiency, as parallel compilers traditionally do.

This example illustrates the simplest use of collections: to express data parallelism by simply applying the same method to every element of a collection. As in pC++, this construes data parallelism as object parallelism, a generalization of the data-parallel vector operations in languages such as Fortran-90.

9.4.3 Concurrent Abstractions

Collections are a convenient way of expressing distributed abstractions which present a concurrent interface. Collections have predefined members which give elements access to the entire collection. Among these are index(), which yields an element's position in the collection, and <collection-type>::this, which refers to the collection object itself. The collection itself has predefined members besides operator [], including size(void), which returns the number of elements in the collection. Other predefined collection members are documented in [ICC 1995].

Consider the following example template definition:

```
template<class Constituent>
class MultiSet[]{
 private :
  Constituent elts[];
  int elt_count;
 public :
  // constructors omitted
  Constituent add_elt(Constituent elt){
    return elts[elt_count++] = elt;
  }
  int find_elt(Constituent elt){
    return MultiSet[]::this->find_elt(elt);
  }
  int find_elt_internal(Constituent elt){
    int count = 0;
    for (int i=0; i<elt_count; i++)
     if (elts[i] == elt) count++;
     return count;
  }
  int MultiSet[]::find_elt(Constituent elt){
    int count = 0;
    conc for(int i = 0; i < size(); i++)
      count += (*this)[i].find_elt_internal(elt);
  }
};
```

The MultiSet abstraction is a distributed multiset in which different constituents are stored in each collection element. Constituents are inserted into specific elements; looking up an element therefore involves looking across the entire collection. The ability of elements to access the entire collection allows the `MultiSet` elements to cooperatively implement a concurrent interface to the abstraction. Multiple calls to `add_elt()` can proceed simultaneously when called upon different elements of the collection, as in:

```
MultiSet<int> set[17];
int stuff[100];

conc for(int i=0; i<100; i++)
  set[i%17].add_elt(stuff[i]);
```

Note that the use of templates and collections allows `MultiSet` to be a re-usable abstraction that presents a concurrent interface. This combination makes libraries of concurrent abstractions possible.

9.4.4   Discussion

Collections in ICC++ represent a unification of collections as distributed arrays of objects [Lee & Gannon 1991, Sheffler & Chatterjee 1995] and the aggregate approach [Chien & Dally 1990]. The array approach is more compatible with the preexisting C++ notion of arrays, in part because it has distinct collection and element types. A drawback to the independence of the types is that the element members have no primitive mechanism to refer to the whole collection, making it harder to implement concurrent abstractions like the `MultiSet` above. The aggregate approach supports cooperation among the constituents by allowing them to name each other, but combining the array and constituent types complicates derivation of collection definitions from object definitions. By creating two *distinct* but *related* types, ICC++ collections combine the advantages of both approaches.

This approach to collections, which integrates arrays into the object model, also divorces arrays and pointers. C++ vitiates pointers, allowing arithmetic only within C++ *aggregates* (i.e., objects and arrays).[2] ICC++ forbids using pointers as arrays, replacing them with array-typed references. This choice not only allows more precise program analysis, it also provides uniform typing for multidimensional arrays.

---

[2]In this case, "aggregate" follows the C++ usage of the term.

In addition, it allows the implementation to distribute collections without complex implementations of pointer arithmetic, but it necessitates some changes to C++ syntax. `type []` must be used instead of `type * ` wherever an array variable is declared or defined. Two-dimensional arrays must be declared using `type [] []`, and analogously for higher dimensionalities.

9.5 Unstructured Concurrency

Concurrent blocks and loops provide a structured mechanism for expressing concurrency using traditional C++ control structures. However, a less-structured mechanism is sometimes required to express complex concurrency. ICC++ provides `spawn` and `reply` to support such unstructured concurrency. The `spawn` statement generates parallelism, while the `reply` object gives the user precise control of caller/callee synchronization.

9.5.1 Spawn

The statement:

```
spawn s;
```

creates a new thread to execute the statement `s`, which can be an arbitrary (possibly compound) statement. All local variables in scope at the `spawn` statement become read-only constants in the spawned thread. This prevents unsynchronized access to them by the spawning and spawned threads.

The spawned and spawning threads are guaranteed to run concurrently. This contrasts with `conc`, which is an annotation. This guarantee provides the programmer with more direct control over concurrency, but can be expensive to enforce, and should be used only when absolutely vital. In this context, "concurrently" means only that neither *must* wait for the other. The execution of spawner and spawnee *will* be interleaved if that is required. This is formally known as *weak fairness*.

9.5.2 Reply

The `reply` object may be used to differentiate a function that is returning a value from a function that is exiting. Conceptually, every function has a logical object called `reply`, which accepts `operator` $()(\tau)$, where τ is the function's return type. The `reply` object is of the ICC++ built-in type `reply_t`. Calling `reply` returns a value to the function's caller without terminating the function, allowing caller and callee to continue concurrently.

```
void main(void) {
  Worker worker;
  ...
  int total = compute_total(worker);
  ...
}

int compute_total(Worker &worker) {
  reply(worker.total());
  worker.clear_caches();
}
```

In the above example, `compute_total()` is ready to return an answer before it has finished executing. The `reply` idiom allows `compute_total()` and `main()` to continue concurrently.

9.5.3   Unstructured Idioms

`spawn` and `reply` can be used to implement customized communication and synchronization structures. For example, tail forwarding [Howard et al. 1989] can accomplished with `spawn reply(e)`:

```
int factorial(int i) {
  if (i < 1)
    return 1;
  else
    spawn reply(i*factorial(i-1));
}
```

The expression `e` will be spawned and the spawned thread will return the result to the caller of the spawning function.

The `reply` object can also be passed out of a function, effectively delegating the job of returning a value to some other function. This can be used to create synchronization structures, such as the following barrier:

```
class Barrier {
  int limit;
  int count;
  reply_t replies[];
public:
  Barrier(int ilimit) {
    count = 0;
    limit = ilimit;
    replies = new reply_t[ilimit];
  }
  void wait(void) {
    replies[count++] = reply;
    if (count == limit)
      for(int i = 0; i < limit; i++)
        replies[i]();
  }
};
```

With the Barrier() given above, functions can synchronize by all calling wait(), where the reply objects are stored in an array. When they have all arrived, the barrier will return values to all of them simultaneously:

```
Barrier b(10);

void Worker::work(void) {
  // computation here
  b.wait();
  // communication here
  b.wait();
  ...
}
```

9.6 Polygon Overlay

This section discusses how we parallelized the polygon overlay problem in ICC++. We focus on the changes needed to the code and how data locality was managed. Performance results are given in Section 9.7

9.6.1 Porting to ICC++

We developed our polygon overlay program using the sequential ANSI C implementation as a starting point. While this program was essentially acceptable to our ICC++ compiler, several minor changes were required.

For completeness, and to give the reader an idea what program porting effort would be required, we list these changes exhaustively. Note that the first two points are artifacts of our current preliminary implementation.

1. Because the data representation used by the ICC++ runtime is not identical to the standard C++ representation, we were unable to use the qsort library, so we wrote a new quicksort routine. This would have been necessary for parallelization in any event.

2. The differences between the ICC++ runtime system and C++ regarding object layout also made it impossible to use functions like fopen() directly. We wrote a library of wrapper functions that manipulated files using fopen(), fscanf() and the like, and communicated only ints to the ICC++ program. This will be unnecessary when we complete a simple interface to the stdio library.

3. The original code made heavy use of pointers to create polygon arrays. Because ICC++ does not allow pointers to be used as arrays, we rewrote the array allocation statements (a few lines), and all type declarations which described the "arrays" (converted to collections). In most cases this simply involved changing a declaration like poly_t* polygons to poly_t[] polygons.

We use the overlay() function as example to illustrate the changes (and shared code). The original program exploits the equivalence between pointers and arrays. Array indexing is done implicitly using two points, pl and pr, and pointer arithmetic is used to sequence the arrays. ICC++ requires that arrays and collections be explicitly declared using the [] syntax, which produces the code shown in Program 9.2. Note the only difference is in the call to polyOverlayLn(), where array accessing is explicit.

The ICC++ version uses explicit array indexing and passes pointers to elements of the arrays, thus preserving the interface to functions such as polyOverlayLn(). In this case, using explicit array indexing produces code of equal efficiency and may even make the code structure more lucid.

```
polyVec_p overlay(
    polyVec_p       left,                    // left input vector
    polyVec_p       right                    // right input vector
){
    int             il, ir;                  // loop indices
    polyLn_p        outList = NULL;          // output list
    polyLn_p        newLn = NULL;            // newly-created polygon link

    for (il=0; il<left->len; il++){
      for (ir=0; ir<right->len; ir++){
        newLn = polyOverlayLn(&(left->vec[il]), &(right->vec[ir]));
        if (newLn != NULL){
          newLn->link = outList;
          outList = newLn;
        }
      }
    }
    return polyLn2Vec(outList);              // convert on the way out
}
```

Program 9.2
ICC++ Code for Naïve Algorithm

9.6.2 Parallelization

We parallelized two polygon overlay algorithms: the naïve algorithm and the area-linked algorithm. These two were chosen because they exemplified the two major data structure interactions (i.e., array-array and array-list) present in the polygon overlay program. In addition, the majority of algorithmic speedup was achieved with the area-linked algorithm for polygon overlay.

The first stage of parallelizing these algorithms was to add conc annotations to the main loops, as shown in Programs 9.3 and 9.4. With these small changes, both algorithms are concurrent, and the basic object consistency model is sufficient to ensure correct output. However, the loops are still serialized by the accumulation of new polygons into the output list. Note that the code sequences in Programs 9.3 and 9.4 are essentially what was run to produce the sequential performance figures in Section 9.7.

```
conc for (il=0; il<leftlimit; il++){
  conc for (ir=0; ir<rightlimit; ir++){
    newLn = polyOverlayLn(&(left->vec[il]), &(right->vec[ir]));
    if (newLn != NULL){
      newLn->link = outList;
      outList = newLn;
    }
  }
}
```

Program 9.3
Parallelized Kernel of overlay() Function

```
// declarations as in sequential program
rightList = polyVec2AreaLn(right, TRUE);
conc for (il=0, pl=left->vec; il<left->len; il++, pl++){
  leftArea = polyArea(pl);
  rightPre = rightList;
  conc while ((leftArea > 0) &&
              ((rightCurr = rightPre->link) != NULL)){
    if ((newLn = polyOverlayLn(pl, rightCurr->poly)) != NULL){
      add new polygon as in sequential program
    }
    if (rightCurr->area == 0){
      rightPre->link = rightCurr->link;
    } else{
      rightPre = rightCurr;
    }
  }
}
```

Program 9.4
Parallelized Kernel of overlayAreaLinked() Function

To achieve scalable parallel performance, it is necessary to change the sequential accumulation structure from a list to a parallel accumulation structure. We chose the natural extension of a single global list into per-processor lists. This change, in conjunction with locality optimizations, is described below.

9.6.3   Distributing `PolyOver`

Because data locality is critical to achieving high performance, it is necessary to reorganize the computation to increase the node-level re-use of data. For both the naïve algorithm and area linked algorithms (i.e., the `overlay()` and `overlayAreaLinked()` functions), the basic idea of the new structure is to distribute the right vector, `right->vec`, across the nodes, so each node has a local portion. Then, for each element of the left vector, `left->vec`, each nodes does the overlay with its local portion of `right->vec`. Thus, `right->vec` is partitioned across the nodes, but `left->vec` remains a global data structure, which is neither replicated nor explicitly partitioned. Note that this data decomposition preserves the list structure (for the area-linked algorithm) and therefore is of similar efficiency to the sequential program. Some of the changes required to implement this were as follows:

- A distributed list class, `polyLn_array[]`, was defined to accumulate generated polygons on each node. The distributed list has NUM_PROCS elements, where NUM_PROCS is the number of nodes.

- The inner loop was made a member of the `polyLn_array` distributed list element, to simplify local accumulation of the results.

- An outermost loop was added to express, in a single iteration, the polygon overlays for one processor.

As shown in Program 9.5, the `accum[]` collection implements the parallel list, with operations `local_overlay()`, `push()`, and `last_one()` for building the output polygons, accumulating them, and stringing the lists together to interface to the existing output routines. `local_overlay()` overlays the polygon passed in against all of the polygons on that processor, thus providing a tight inner loop of purely local computation. Similarly, the `last_one()` method code shown below runs down the local list to find its end:

```
polyLn_p polyLn_array[]::last_one(){
  polyLn_p current, previous;
  current = link;          // start with my pointer
  while (current != NULL){
    previous = current;
    current = current->link;
  }
  return previous;
}
```

Tuning the locality for the area-linked polygon overlay algorithm was a bit more involved, but was achieved with essentially the same strategy. The same parallel list structure, `accum[]`, is used to collect the new polygons. However, because the area-linked algorithm prunes both lists based on the area remaining, it maintains a linked list for `right->vec`. This linked list forms a sequential bottleneck, so to parallelize the program effectively, we again changed the sequential list structure to a parallel list data structure. This is shown in Program 9.6. Note that our data decomposition partitions `right->vec`, but because it does not partition `left->vec` it is of similar efficiency to the sequential program.

Empirical comparisons confirm that our parallel area-linked implementation performs a similar number of polygon compares as the sequential implementation, although it does more work as the degree of parallelism increases.

The parallel list data structure effectively enables parallelism, and also achieves high data locality for each processor. As with the accumulation list, this parallel list structure supports `push()` and `next()` operations; the object concurrency model provides all of the necessary synchronization to ensure correct results. Note that the area-linked algorithm uses a linked list and polygon deletion to reduce the number of polygon-polygon comparisons. Our parallel area-linked algorithm preserves the efficiency of the sequential version; as a result, there is not enough work to generate much parallelism.

A naïve partitioning that distributed both vectors (or replicated one of them) across the nodes would effectively destroy the performance of the area-linked approach because the total area that overlays a given polygon might be distributed across the nodes. In this case, no single node would be able to delete it from its work list. By retaining the left vector as a global structure, we avoid this problem by accumulating areas

```
void polyLn_array::local_overlay(int proc, int limit, int stride,
                                 int xl, int yl, int xh, int yh,
                                 poly_t (*vec)[]){
  for (int i=0; i<limit; i+=stride){
    if (polyLn_p newLn = (*vec)[i].OverlayLn(xl, yl, xh, yh))
      push(newLn);
  }
}
void overlay(polyVec_p left, polyVec_p right){
  int stride = NUM_PROCS;
  poly_t (*leftvec)[],(*rightvec)[];
  polyLn_array (*accum)[] = new polyLn_array[NUM_PROCS];

  conc for (proc = 0; proc < NUM_PROCS; proc++){
    int upper_limit = right->len+proc;
    conc for (il=0; il<left->len; il++){
      poly_p left_el = &(*left->vec)[il];
      (*accum)[proc].local_overlay(proc, upper_limit, stride,
                                   left_el->xl, left_el->yl,
                                   left_el->xh, left_el->yh,
                                   right->vec);
    }
  }
  conc for (proc = 0; proc < (NUM_PROCS-1); proc++){
    polyLn_p last_one = (*accum)[proc].last_one();
    last_one->link = (*accum)[proc+1].link;
  }
}
```

Program 9.5
Locality-Tuned Naïve Polygon Overlay Algorithm

```
int polyLn_array::local_OverlayAreaLn( int running_area,
    int l_xl, int l_yl, int l_xh, int l_yh, polyAreaLn_p list)
{ polyLn_p newLn;
  polyAreaLn_p current = list, prev = NULL;
  int leftArea = running_area, newArea = 0;
  while ((current != NULL)&&(leftArea>0)){
    newLn = current->poly->local_OverlayLn(l_xl,l_yl,l_xh,l_yh);
    if (newLn != NULL){
      push(newLn);
      newArea = newLn->poly.area();
      leftArea -= newArea;
      current->area -= newArea;
      if (current->area == 0){
        if (prev != NULL) prev->snap();
        current = current->link;
      } else { prev = current; current = current->link; }
    } else { prev = current; current = current->link; }
  }
  return leftArea;
}
void poly_s::local_OverlayAreaLn(polyLn_array (*accum)[],
                                 polyAreaLn_array (*input)[])
{ int leftArea = area(), proc = 0;
  while ((leftArea>0)&&(proc < NUM_PROCS)){
    leftArea = (*accum)[proc].local_OverlayAreaLn(
                 leftArea, xl, yl, xh, yh, (*input)[proc].link);
    proc++;
  }
}
// calling loop
polyLn_array (*accum)[] = new polyLn_array[NUM_PROCS];
polyAreaLn_array (*input)[] = new polyAreaLn_array[NUM_PROCS];
polyVec2AreaLn(right, input);
leftvec = left->vec;
conc for (il=0; il<leftlimit; il++)
  (*leftvec)[il].local_OverlayAreaLn(accum,input);
```

Program 9.6
Parallel Version of Area-Linked Polygon Overlay Algorithm

for the left vector globally. Hence, while parallel execution will cause this approach to perform somewhat more comparisons, the area-linked approach should not degrade into the naïve case.

9.7 Performance

The Illinois Concert C++ compiler exploits the Concert project's optimization technology for concurrent object-oriented programs, including static type inference [Plevyak & Chien 1994], an aggressive application of cloning [Plevyak & Chien 1995] and inlining [Plevyak *et al.* 1995a]. It has been demonstrated to yield concurrent object-oriented programs with high sequential efficiency and to efficiently support fine-grained object-oriented programs. This base, originally developed for the Concurrent Aggregates [Chien 1993] programming language, has been adapted to also support ICC++.[3] The adaptation of this compiler is continuing, so the performance figures we quote are for a preliminary implementation. All execution times are reported in seconds.

9.7.1 Sequential Performance

The sequential performance of the ICC++ polygon overlay program was measured by running it on a multiprocessor simulator. This simulator has significant performance disadvantages compared to a sequential C++ program: it uses threads to provide runtime services (incurring context-switching overhead), executes "parallel ready" code that can deal with distributed data, and provides fully automatic storage management. The simulator is used because the runtime system requires multithreading. For the sequential performance numbers presented, locality and concurrency control annotations were added to the computational kernels. These annotations, which enable the compiler to eliminate locality checks and locking operations, are applied to call sites (i.e., places in the code where function calls appear). However, because we consider the current form of annotations to be rather primitive, they are not presented in detail. Table 9.1 shows the performance of our

---

[3]Since this compiler technology was developed for a language with dynamic typing, it is flexible enough to support extensions of C++ which relax the static type system.

Inputs	Algorithm	C++ (sec)	ICC++ (sec)	Ratio (ICC++/C)
k100.00 k100.01	naïve	2767	5242	1.89
	area-linked	41	61	1.49
k100.10 k100.11	naïve	2850	5503	1.93
	area-linked	38	64	1.68
k100.18 k100.19	naïve	2863	5713	2.00
	area-linked	37	62	1.68

Table 9.1
Sequential Performance of Polygon Overlay on SS20/51

program.[4] These figures show that ICC++ can come within a factor of 2 of sequential performance.

Six data sets containing approximately 60,000 polygons each were used for these tests; no large data-dependent differences in execution time were noted. These performance numbers provide a baseline for evaluating the performance of ICC++. The sequential performance of the ICC++ program is generally one-half to two-thirds of that of the C++ program. Note, however, that the C++ program does not use any C++ object-oriented mechanisms. The majority of the performance difference is due to additional storage management overhead (i.e., automatic garbage collection) and to concurrency control overheads which are unnecessary in a sequential program.

9.7.2   Parallel Performance

The naïve and area-linked algorithms are parallelized and tuned for locality. In addition to the code changes described in the previous section, annotations added in the computational kernels allow the compiler to eliminate locality checks and locking operations. They also provide explicit control over inlining decisions. As before, these are call-site annotations, but because we consider the current form of annotations to be rather primitive, they are not presented in detail. This enables the compiler to generate efficient sequential kernels. The overall execution times for both algorithms, and for their respective C++ equivalents on

---

[4]All of these measurements were taken on a SPARCStation SS20/51. Both the code generated by ICC++ and the original C++ program were compiled using **g++** **v2.6.3** with **-02** optimization.

PEs	sequential	1	2	4	8	16	32	64	128
input		4	6	6	7	9	19	54	182
overlay		333	171	133	64	33	18	10	8
output		4	3	2	2	3	3	6	6
overall	158	358	189	149	77	47	41	82	211

Table 9.2
Naïve Algorithm, 12K-polygon Data Sets on the T3D (all times in seconds)

PEs	sequential	1	2	4	8	16	32
input		3	6	6	7	9	20
listify		0.2	0.2	0.1	0	0	0
overlay		173	171	82	42	23	13
output		4	3	2	2	2	3
overall	110	190	189	95	55	35	38

Table 9.3
Area-Linked Algorithm, 12K-polygon Data Sets on the T3D (all times in seconds)

one node, are shown in Tables 9.2 to 9.5. These numbers were all taken on a Cray T3D, with the sequential times determined by running the original C code on one node.[5] We show performance on both small data sets, containing approximately 12,000 polygons each, and on data sets containing approximately 60,000 polygons each. The larger sets are included to allow comparisons with other systems; the small set is shown since our system cannot run the large ones on less than four T3D nodes.

Our results for 12K-polygon data sets illustrate the performance our preliminary ICC++ compiler can achieve on the Cray T3D: the sequential time on one node is roughly half that of the sequential C++ code. The parallel speedup for the naïve polygon overlay phase alone (Table 9.2 and Figure 9.1) is about one quarter of the ideal until 64 nodes (where it is 16), but only rises to 20 when the number of nodes is doubled to 128. When speedup is computed against the one-node performance of the ICC++ code, the speedup is roughly half ideal until 64 nodes. The results achieved using the area-linked algorithm are slightly better (Table 9.3 and Figure 9.2), with the speedup being slightly better than

---

[5]The ICC++-generated code and the original C++ program were compiled with the Cray CC compiler without optimization, as optimization generally provides no benefit with this compiler.

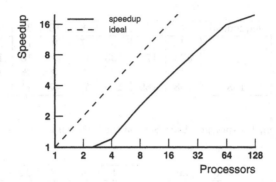

Figure 9.1
ICC++ Speedups (Naïve Algorithm, 12K-polygon Data Sets)

PEs	sequential	4	8	16	32	64	128
input		35	41	44	81	270	708
overlay		3283	1475	739	371	188	99
output		9	11	12	11	12	12
overall	3500	3359	1603	835	487	494	818

Table 9.4
Naïve Algorithm, 60K-polygon Data Sets on the T3D (all times in seconds)

one-fourth ideal (5 on 16 nodes and 9 on 32 nodes). When calculated
with respect to ICC++ single-node performance, though, speedup is
roughly one-third ideal. Speedup of the smart algorithm is similar to
that of the naïve one, since our parallelization of the smart algorithm
preserves the optimizations of the sequential code.

Full-Size Sets Due to the storage overhead for objects in our runtime
system, the full-sized data sets are too large for the ICC++ program
to run on one or two nodes, so performance numbers are shown for 4
and up. Direct comparison with sequential performance is impossible,
but we would expect the same slowdown of approximately two that was
seen for the small sets. As Table 9.4 and Figure 9.3 show, the speedup
for the naïve algorithm is slightly superlinear starting from 4 nodes, and
better than one-fourth ideal when calculated from the sequential code's
running time.

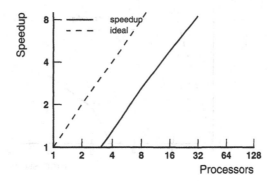

Figure 9.2
ICC++ Speedups (Area-Linked Algorithm, 12K-polygon Data Sets). Note that our
implementation preserve the sequential algorithms' efficiency so there is little
computation.

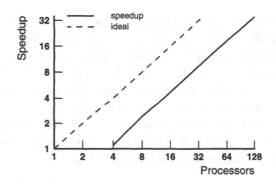

Figure 9.3
ICC++ Speedups: Naïve Algorithm, 60K-Polygon Data Set on the T3D

PEs	sequential	4	8	16	32
input		31	36	43	70
listify		0.4	0.2	0.1	0.1
overlay		68	49	42	39
output		11	12	10	13
overall	57	117	103	100	127

Table 9.5
Area-Linked Algorithm, 60K-polygon Data Sets on the T3D (all times in seconds).
Note that our algorithm preserves sequential optimization.

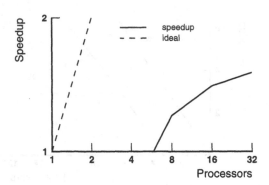

Figure 9.4
ICC++ Speedups: Area-Linked Algorithm, 60K-Polygon Data Set on the T3D
(Note that our implementation preserves the sequential algorithms' efficiency so
there is little computation.)

The speedup for the area-linked algorithm (see Table 9.5 and Figure 9.4), on the other hand, is very poor: going from 4 to 32 nodes
yields a speedup of only 1.7. This is much worse than for the small
data set, simply because the large data set is sorted. The area-linked
algorithm is heavily dependent upon input file ordering for high performance, and there is very little work when the file is sorted. Note that
our parallel implementation preserves the efficiency of the area-linked
algorithm as described in Section 9.6.3. Also, the amount of work per
polygon varies, making load balancing difficult.

Discussion   As can be seen, the majority of the time spent in the
naïve algorithm is spent in the polygon overlay computation, until I/O
time takes over for large numbers of nodes. However, for the area-
linked algorithm, a significant fraction of the time is spent preparing for
I/O, which performs badly enough to make the parallel code actually
slower than the sequential C++ for the large, sorted data sets. For
realistic algorithms, parallelizing the I/O phases is clearly necessary to
achieve good performance. Thus, a high-performance implementation
would have to parallelize the I/O sections of the program, for example
by using mapped files. There are no significant obstacles to doing this
in ICC++, but we did not have the time to complete the parallelization.

Instead, we chose to isolate the I/O times from the basic polygon overlay functionality.

9.8 Discussion and Related Work

9.8.1 C++ Compatibility

Our intention in designing ICC++ was to avoid gratuitous incompatibilities with sequential C++ programs. As a result, large sections of C++ programs can be incorporated into ICC++ programs with purely mechanical changes. However, there are two important differences between C++ and ICC++. First, ICC++ eliminates pointer arithmetic, requiring explicit array type declarations for collections (encapsulated arrays). This change ensures that pointers are not used to point into arbitrary locations, which would reduce the effectiveness of aggressive compiler analysis techniques. Second, ICC++ objects have well-defined concurrency control semantics. These semantics can result in deadlock for indirect recursive calls, which is clearly a departure from sequential C++ semantics. External C++ functions can be called easily from ICC++, and seamless interoperability will be achieved with the proposed CORBA IDL binding of C++. In summary, we believe ICC++ will allow many programs to be migrated from C++ with moderate effort, and the resulting ICC++ programs can serve as a single source for both sequential and parallel code versions. To do this, we are building a simple ICC++ to C++ translator which will support all but the guaranteed concurrency features.

9.8.2 Derivation and Concurrency

The *inheritance anomaly*, which arises from the interaction of object state changes and the explicit expression synchronization in program code structures, is a well-known problem in the concurrent object community [Matsuoka & Yonezawa 1993]. Because concurrent programs often include explicit synchronization, the anomaly makes re-use of class definitions and method code through derivation problematic. In general, subclass designers must examine the implementations of the base classes and perhaps redesign them before extending them with instance variables or member functions. To illustrate the problem, Program 9.7

```
class elt;

class BoundedQueue : public Pabc {
  int in, out;
  static int QUEUE_BOUND;
  elt buf[QUEUE_BOUND];
 public:
  void put(elt &i) {
    buf[in++] = i;
    if (in == QUEUE_BOUND) in = 0;
  }
  elt get(void) {
    elt& i = buf[out++];
    if (out == QUEUE_BOUND) out = 0;
  }
  void main(void) {
    in = out = 0;
    if (in == out)
      Paccept(put);
    else if (out == (in + 1) % QUEUE_BOUND)
      Paccept(get);
    else
      Paccept(put,get);
  }
};
```

Program 9.7
Concurrent Base Class

uses ABC++ syntax (Chapter 1). Derivation from the BoundedQueue class is limited by problems with the inheritance anomaly.

In order for a subclass to add new methods, the main() function must be rewritten. Preserving correctness while doing this requires understanding all of the methods defined for the queue. As illustrated in Program 9.8; the addition of BoundedQueued2::put2() requires the redefinition of BoundedQueue2::main(), and clearly the implementor of BoundedQueue2 must know about all of BoundedQueue's methods to write the new main().

Adding new instance variables cause similar problems; in general all of the methods must be considered to ensure consistency. In many cases, a significant fraction of the methods may have to be rewritten, dramat-

```
class BoundedQueue2 : public BoundedQueue {
  void put2(elt &i, elt &j) {
    buf[in++] = i;
    if (in == QUEUE_BOUND) in = 0;
    buf[in++] = j;
    if (in == QUEUE_BOUND) in = 0;
  }
  void main(void) {
    in = out = 0;
    if (in == out)
      Paccept(put,put2);
    else if (out == (in + 1) % QUEUE_BOUND)
      Paccept(get);
    else if (out != (in + 2) % QUEUE_BOUND)
      Paccept(put,put2,get);
    else
      Paccept(put,get);
  }
};
```

Program 9.8
Concurrent Derived Class

ically reducing the benefits of re-use. Finally, if a concurrent object-oriented language uses method-oriented specification of synchronization (no `main()` function), this merely distributes the concurrency control structure and does not eliminate the problem.

ICC++'s object consistency model addresses the inheritance anomaly by defining the synchronization required between methods solely in terms of local sequentializability. The code needed for synchronization among methods is determined by the system independently for each class, regardless of inheritance. Therefore, derivation which adds methods, overrides methods, or adds instance variables just results in further synchronization constraints for the derived class. This allows classes to be extended and re-used, but focusing only on local sequentializability provides a weaker consistency model than traditional Actors.

9.8.3   Parallel C++ Efforts

The wide variety of parallel C++ efforts can be divided into two general categories: data-parallel and task-parallel extensions. Data-parallel extensions of C++, such as pC++ (Chapter 13) and C** (Chapter 8) employ collections or aggregates [Chien & Dally 1990, Chien 1993, Sabot 1988] to describe parallelism, using objects to increase the flexibility of the data-parallel model. However, data-parallel languages cannot easily express more irregular and client-server forms of concurrency, which limits the domain of applications in which they can be used. Rewriting sequential programs as efficient data-parallel programs often requires significant reorganization, as aligning data structures to create efficient parallel collections can cause major program structure disruptions.

The diversity of task-parallel extensions of C++ is much greater; these can be loosely categorized based on their treatment of objects and concurrency. First, there are languages (or libraries) that introduce concurrency without changing the object model, such as PRESTO [Bershad et al. 1988], COOL (Chapter 6), CHARM++ (Chapter 5), and ES-Kit++ [Smith & Chatterjee 1990]. These languages require the programmer to build concurrency control by convention, providing no language support for object consistency or building abstractions from larger collections of objects. Second, many languages (or libraries) use objects to encapsulate concurrency, exploiting objects to represent data parallel collections or coarse-grained tasks, including DOME [Beguelin et al. 1994] and Mentat (Chapter 10). In these languages, concurrency control may be expressed explicitly in a library or implicitly via dataflow dependences. The encapsulation of concurrency in these models is generally expensive and is used only sparingly for coarse-grained abstractions. CC++ (Chapter 3) provides **atomic** functions, but as these are not allowed to access other objects, they can only be used to build single-object data abstractions. Finally, the meta-architecture of MPC++ (Chapter 11) provides a programmable language syntax and semantics capable of supporting both data parallelism, control parallelism, and complex synchronization structures (as in Concurrent Aggregates, ABCL/1, or other Actors-based languages). However, because of its very flexibility, it is difficult to make specific comparisons to MPC++, and the impact of the meta-architecture of implementation efficiency is as yet undetermined [Ishikawa *et al.* 1995]. In contrast to these systems, ICC++ provides an object model that integrates both concurrency control and concurrency guarantees, and is extensible, supporting concurrent data abstractions built with several objects.

Another important distinction among parallel dialects of C++ is the scheduling or concurrency guarantees provided by the language. Data-parallel languages have sequential semantics, so data-parallel C++ dialects provide no concurrency guarantees. Of the task-parallel C++ dialects, CHARM++ provides explicit control over scheduling [Kalé & Krishnan 1993], and CC++ [Chandy & Kesselman 1993] provides guaranteed fair thread scheduling for all **par** constructs. In contrast, ICC++ emphasizes *potential concurrency*, and gives concurrency guarantees in a data-oriented form. This gives the implementation freedom to select an execution granularity (thread sizes) for efficiency, facilitating efficient sequential execution. If necessary, ICC++ provides a **spawn** statement (explicit thread creation) which can be used to guarantee concurrency [ICC 1995].

9.8.4 Other Concurrent Object-Oriented Languages

Though there are a wide variety of non-C++ concurrent object-oriented languages [Yonezawa 1990, Chien & Dally 1990, America 1990, Murer *et al.* 1993, Konaka 1993, Andersen 1994], we focus on Actor-based languages [Agha 1986] because they closely integrate object-oriented message passing and concurrency. This allows programmers to reason at the level of object operations and not memory references. However, the actor model provides neither a clear basis for building data abstractions from collections of objects, nor concurrency guarantees. In contrast, ICC++ includes both concurrency guarantees and language support for building abstractions from ensembles (structures or collections) of objects. In addition, most of the Actor-based languages to date have been inefficient in their implementation. Recent work in our group [Plevyak & Chien 1994, Plevyak et al. 1995a, Plevyak et al. 1995b] and others [Taura et al. 1993] demonstrates that this need not be the case.

9.8.5   Illinois Concert Project

ICC++ is the second language supported by the Concert project, the first having been Concurrent Aggregates [Chien 1993, Chien & Dally 1990]. ICC++ is fully described in [Chien & Reddy 1995, ICC 1995]. For the past five years, our group has investigated the design of concurrent object-oriented programs [Chien et al. 1994, Chien 1993, Chien 1990], and has built application programs totaling over 40,000 lines. In addition, we have studied the design of concurrent object-oriented languages and their implementation exploring a variety of aggressive compiler and runtime techniques. The design of ICC++ was based on this experience, and an extensive survey of parallel object-oriented approaches.

The Illinois Concert system is a complete development environment for irregular parallel applications [Chien & Dolby 1994]. The Concert system supports a concurrent object-oriented programming model, and includes a globally optimizing compiler, efficient runtime system, symbolic debugger, and an emulator for program development. This system employs novel compiler techniques [Plevyak & Chien 1994, Plevyak et al. 1995a, Plevyak et al. 1995b] and runtime techniques [Plevyak et al. 1995b, Karamcheti & Chien 1993] to achieve efficient execution of fine-grained programs on both sequential and parallel platforms. The Concert system has demonstrated sequential performance matching C and surpassing C++ on demanding numerical benchmarks such as the Livermore Kernels [Plevyak et al. 1995a], and superior speedups and absolute performance on a parallel molecular dynamics application called CEDAR [Carson 1985] on the Cray T3D [CRI 1993, Numrich 1994] and Thinking Machines CM-5 [TMC 1991]. Our ICC++ compiler exploits the same aggressive compiler analysis and code optimization.

9.9 Summary

ICC++ is a new C++ dialect designed to support both efficient sequential and parallel execution. By allowing concurrency to be introduced incrementally, ICC++ allows sequential and parallel program versions to be maintained with a single source and permits convenient expression of irregular and fine-grained concurrency. By defining a simple object consistency model and a flexible set of extensions, ICC++ supports the construction of concurrent data abstractions. Distributed data abstractions are further supported with a compatible extension of arrays called collections. Finally, by focusing on programmer annotation for *potential* concurrency, not actual concurrency, ICC++ allow the system to optimize execution granularity to match the underlying machine, providing both high performance sequential and parallel execution on both shared- and distributed-memory systems.

9.10 Future Work

We anticipate releasing an implementation of ICC++ in late 1995. Our current implementation of ICC++ is operational on uniprocessors, the Thinking Machines CM-5, and the Cray T3D machines with the performance described in this chapter. However, because the implementation has only been operational for a few months, we are still implementing a number of C++ specific optimizations which were not previously required in the Concert system. Future efforts will include novel optimizations for efficient parallel code generation, concerted optimization across the compiler and runtime, working and optimized versions of the ICC++ system for distributed shared memory machines and clustered symmetric multiprocessor machines, and extensive application studies. These last are already well underway; one large application and numerous kernels are currently being ported to ICC++.

Acknowledgments

The authors gratefully acknowledge the help of all of the Concert project team, specifically Vijay Karamcheti, John Plevyak and Xingbin Zhang, who worked on the Concert compiler and runtime system, and partici-

pated in the design of ICC++. A great many other people have been
involved in the language design process as well; they include Professors
Uday Reddy, Sam Kamin, Sanjay Kalé and Prith Banerjee. In addition,
Rob Hasker, Howard Huang, Steven Parkes and T. K. Lakshman have
contributed to the design effort.

The research described in this paper was supported in part by NSF
grants CCR-9209336 and MIP-92-23732, ONR grants N00014-92-J-1961
and N00014-93-1-1086 and NASA grant NAG 1-613. Andrew Chien is
supported in part by NSF Young Investigator Award CCR-94-57809.
Parallel machine runs used the Cray T3D machines at the Pittsburgh
Supercomputing Center and the NASA Jet Propulsion Laboratory.

10 Mentat

Andrew S. Grimshaw, Adam Ferrari, and Emily A. West

10.1 Introduction

Some material in this section is revised from [Grimshaw 1993], and appears with the permission of the IEEE.

Mentat is an object-oriented, control-parallel programming system designed to address three problems: the difficulty of writing parallel programs, the difficulty of achieving portability of those programs, and the difficulty of exploiting contemporary heterogeneous environments. The original design objectives of Mentat were to provide:

- easy-to-use parallelism;
- high performance via parallel execution;
- system scalability from tens to hundreds of processors; and
- portability across a wide range of platforms.

The premise underlying Mentat is that writing programs for parallel machines does not have to be hard. Instead, it is the lack of appropriate abstractions that has made parallel architectures difficult to program, and hence inaccessible to mainstream programmers.

10.1.1 The Mentat Philosophy

Mentat's design is guided by two observations. The first is that programmers understand their application domains, and can therefore often make better data and computation decomposition decisions than can compilers. Evidence for this is the fact that most successful applications have been hand-coded using low-level primitives. The second observation is that management of tens to thousands of asynchronous tasks, where timing-dependent errors are easy to make, is beyond the capacity of most programmers. Compilers, on the other hand, are very good at ensuring that events happen in the right order, and can more readily and correctly manage communication and synchronization than programmers. The design of Mentat is therefore driven by the observation that there are some things people do better than compilers, and that there are some things that compilers do better than people. Rather than

asking either do the whole job, we exploit the comparative advantages
of each.

Mentat has also been heavily influenced by work in object-based operating systems [Jones 1979, Wulf 1974] and by object-oriented software development [Wegner 1987]. The object-oriented paradigm has
proven to be a powerful framework for sequential software engineering.
Programming-in-the-large, encapsulation, polymorphism, fault contain-
ment, and software re-use have all made the task of constructing complex
sequential software more tractable. The belief that these same things
could help manage the complexity of parallel software led to an early
decision to adopt an object-oriented approach to parallel processing.

10.1.2   Parallelism Encapsulation

Mentat has two primary components: the Mentat Programming Language (MPL) [Mentat 1994] and the Mentat runtime system [Grimshaw
et al. unpub.]. MPL is an object-oriented programming language based
on C++. The basic idea in MPL is to allow the programmer to specify those C++ classes that are of sufficient computational complexity
to warrant parallel execution. This is accomplished using the `mentat`
keyword in the class definition. Instances of Mentat classes are called
Mentat objects; each constitutes a separate address space. Programmers use instances of Mentat classes much as they would any other
C++ class instance. The compiler generates code to construct and execute data-dependency graphs in which the nodes are Mentat object
member function invocations, and the arcs are the data dependencies
found in the program. The Mentat runtime system constructs coarse-
grain data-dependence (i.e., dataflow) graphs at runtime by observing
where, when, and how certain variables identified by the compiler are
used. It then manages the execution of the dependence graphs to ensure
that the dependencies in the program are enforced.

The encapsulation of computation within Mentat objects and the
use of data-dependence graphs allows Mentat to extend the concepts
of object implementation and data encapsulation to include parallelism
encapsulation. Parallelism encapsulation takes two forms that we call
intra-object and *inter-object*. Intra-object encapsulation of parallelism
means that callers of a Mentat object member function are unaware of
whether the implementation of a member function is sequential or parallel. For example, consider an instance `matrix_op` of a `matrix_operator`

Mentat class. This class has a member function mpy() that multiplies
two matrices and returns their product. When a user invokes mpy() in:

```
X = matrix_op.mpy(B,C);
```

it is irrelevant whether mpy() is implemented sequentially or in parallel;
all that matters is whether the correct answer is computed.

Inter-object encapsulation exploits parallelism between Mentat object
member function invocations. Opportunities for this type of parallel
execution are reflected in the data-dependence graph, which the runtime
system automatically constructs as the program executes. Using this
graph, the data and control dependencies between Mentat class instances
engaged in invocation, communication, and synchronization are detected
and managed without programmer intervention.

Intra-object parallelism encapsulation and inter-object parallelism encapsulation can be combined. Indeed, inter-object parallelism encapsulation, within the implementation of a member function, is intra-object
parallelism encapsulation as far as the caller of that member function is
concerned. Thus, multiple levels of parallelism encapsulation are possible, with each level hidden from the level above.

To illustrate parallelism encapsulation, suppose X, A, B, C, D and E are
all matrix pointers in:

```
X = matrix_op.mpy(B,C);
A = matrix_op.mpy(X,matrix_op.mpy(D,E));
```

A sequential machine would first multiply the matrices B and C, storing
the result in X. It would then multiply D and E, and finally create the
product of X and the result of D*E. If we assume that each multiplication
takes one time unit, then three time units are required to complete the
computation.

In Mentat, the compiler and runtime system detect that the first two
multiplications, B*C and D*E, are not data dependent on one another
and can safely be executed in parallel. When this is done, the results
are automatically forwarded to the final multiplication. That result is
then forwarded to the caller, and assigned to A. Figure 10.1a graphically illustrates inter-object parallelism encapsulation by showing the
execution graph for this sequence of operations.

The difference between the programmer's sequential model and the
parallel execution of the two multiplications afforded by Mentat is an

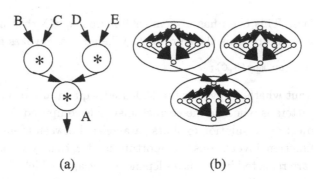

Figure 10.1
Parallel Execution of Matrix Multiply Operations

example of inter-object parallelism encapsulation. In the absence of other parallelism, or overhead, the speedup for this example is a modest 1.5.

However, that is not the end of the story. Additional, intra-object, parallelism may be realized within each matrix multiplication as shown in Figure 10.1b. The compiler and runtime system will transparently expand a member function invocation into a parallel subgraph if it has a parallel implementation. Suppose each matrix multiply is executed in eight pieces. As the multiplication is implemented using more pieces, even larger speedups will result. The key point is that the programmer need not be concerned with data-dependence detection, communication, synchronization, or scheduling; the compiler does it.

10.1.3   The Mentat Environment

Mentat has been ported to a variety of platforms that span the latency and bandwidth spectrum from heterogeneous workstation networks to massively-parallel processors (MPPs) and shared-memory multiprocessors. Workstation platforms include Sun SPARCStation, IBM RS6000, Hewlett-Packard, and Silicon Graphics. Parallel computers have included the BBN Butterfly, the Intel iPSC/2, iPSC/860, and Paragon, the Convex Exemplar, the SGI PowerChallenge, and the IBM SP-1 and SP-2. With the exception of the iPSC/860, we have achieved full source code portability across all of these platforms.

Between 1990 and late 1992, Mentat consisted of a compiler and runtime system, and was used exclusively in homogeneous systems. Since then, Mentat has grown into a complete parallel processing system that is targeted primarily, though not exclusively, at mixed workstation and MPP environments. A typical Mentat configuration is heterogeneous containing different types of workstations (often with different speeds within a type), and possibly an MPP. All system components, particularly the schedulers and accounting tools, reflect this new environment.

Among the services and utilities included in the current distribution of Mentat are system fault tolerance and automatic reconfiguration, load monitors, configuration management tools, resource management tools, a full post mortem debugger, a virtual file system with associated I/O support, automatic binary replication across file systems, a class description database that keeps track of binary versions and manages binary invalidation, support for PVM [Geist *et al.* 1994], mechanisms to allow the same source to be compiled to parallel and sequential applications, and resource usage accounting tools. Information on all of these tools and features is available in the on-line users' manual.

10.1.4 Roadmap

The objective of this chapter is to provide the reader with an introduction to Mentat and to provide intuition as to the performance that can be expected from Mentat applications. We begin by examining the basics of the Mentat programming language and its runtime model. We then discuss the performance of applications, including the polygon overlay problem. For each application, we ask:

1. what is the shape of the Mentat solution? and

2. how did the implementation perform?

For more information please see [Grimshaw 1993, Grimshaw *et al.* 1993a, Grimshaw *et al.* 1993b, Grimshaw *et al.* unpub.] or visit our WWW page:

http://www.cs.virginia.edu/~mentat/

10.2 The Mentat Programming Language

Some material in this section is revised from [Mentat 1994], and appears with the permission of the University of Virgnia.

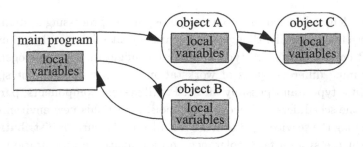

Figure 10.2
The Mentat Object Model

Rather than being a new language for writing parallel programs, MPL extends C++ in three ways: Mentat classes, return-to-future (`rtf()`), and `mselect`/`maccept`. Mentat's object model, shown in Figure 10.2, distinguishes between two types of objects: *contained* objects and *independent* objects. Contained objects are objects contained in another object's address space. Instances of C++ classes, integers, structures, and so on are contained objects. Independent objects possess a distinct address space, a system-wide unique name, and a thread of control. Communication between independent objects is accomplished via member function invocation and return. Independent objects are analogous to Unix processes.

Mentat objects are instances of Mentat classes and are independent objects. Both the main program and Mentat objects may contain local variables.

10.2.1   Mentat Classes

In C++, objects are defined by their class. Each class has an interface section in which member variables and member functions are defined. Mentat classes are expressed similarly. The programmer defines a Mentat class by using the keyword **mentat** in the class definition. The programmer may further specify whether the class is **regular**, **persistent**, or **sequential**. For example, the interface below defines the **regular** Mentat class **integer_ops** with three functions:

```
regular mentat class integer_ops{
 public:
  int add(const int arg1,const int arg2);
  int mpy(const int arg1,const int arg2);
  int sqrt(cont int arg1);
};
```

Regular Mentat class instances (**regular** objects) are stateless; their member functions are pure, side-effect free functions. A consequence of this is that all instances of a particular **regular** class are equivalent. The system is therefore free to re-use an existing instance or instantiate a new instance to service each member function invocation. Also, because the methods of **regular** classes do not depend on any persistent state, the system may schedule invocations of those functions on any processor in the system.

Persistent and **sequential** Mentat class instances may maintain state information between method invocations. Each **persistent** or **sequential** object is therefore unique. Because the address spaces of Mentat objects are disjoint, we do not allow **persistent** and **sequential** class definitions to include public member variables. The only way to observe or manipulate the state of a **persistent** or **sequential** object is through member function invocation. Further, because each Mentat object has a single thread of control, each is in essence a monitor [Hoare 1974]. This is not an implementation artifact; rather, we felt that by permitting only a single thread of control we would eliminate both race conditions on member variables and the need to provide a mechanism to control such races.

Persistent Mentat object member function invocations begin execution as soon as all of their arguments are available, irrespective of potential causal relationships. For example, the order in which a single caller issues invocations on a persistent Mentat object may not be the order in which those invocations are executed. Sequential Mentat classes differ from **persistent** classes in that the order of member function execution on a **sequential** object is guaranteed to be the same as the invocation order in the caller. Sequential classes may therefore be viewed as a special case of **persistent** classes. Note, however, that the keyword **sequential** does not refer to the internal implementation of the class; the implementation of **sequential** class member functions can be either parallel or serial.

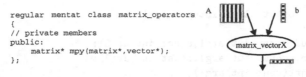

```
regular mentat class matrix_operators
{
// private members
public:
    matrix* mpy(matrix*,vector*);
};
```

(a) regular mentat class definition

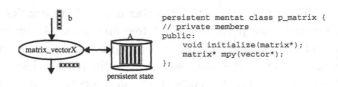

```
persistent mentat class p_matrix {
// private members
public:
    void initialize(matrix*);
    matrix* mpy(vector*);
};
```

(b) persistent mentat class definition

Figure 10.3
Matrix-Vector Product (a) Using **regular** Objects (b) Using a **persistent** Object

To illustrate the difference between **regular** and **persistent** Mentat classes, suppose we wish to perform a matrix-vector product, in parallel. Each element of the result will be computed by performing a dot product between a row of the matrix and the vector.

Because matrix-vector product is a pure function, we could choose to define a **regular** Mentat class **matrix_operators** as in Figure 10.3a. In this case, every time we invoke mpy(), the system will logically create a new Mentat object to perform the multiplication—logically, because the system may choose an existing instance of the **regular** Mentat class rather than pay the cost of instantiating a new object. Once this object is known to exist, both arguments will be transported to it.

Alternatively, we could choose to define a **persistent** Mentat class p_matrix as in Figure 10.3b. To use a **p_matrix**, an instance must first be created and initialized. Matrix-vector multiplication can then be accomplished by calling mpy(). When mpy() is used, only the argument vector is transported to the **persistent** object; successive calls result in argument vectors being transported to the same object. The matrix A is the state of the object and does not need to be transported. If A is a 1024×1024 floating point matrix, the difference in communication volume is 4 Mbyte. In both the **persistent** and **regular** case, the implementation of the class may hierarchically decompose the object into sub-objects, and operations into parallel sub-operations.

The following example is taken from [Grimshaw 1993], and appears with the permission of the IEEE.

To illustrate the power of **regular** Mentat classes, we show how they can be used to construct a simple pipeline (Figure 10.1). We begin by defining the **regular** Mentat class **data_processor**, whose member functions **filter_one()** and **filter_two()** process blocks of data. After some initialization, which creates and opens input and output files, the loop in the code fragment sequentially reads **MAX_BLOCKS** data blocks from the file **input_file**, processes them using the two filters, and writes the results to **output_file**. Since Mentat method invocations are non-blocking, the loop is automatically unrolled at runtime and a pipeline is formed. Note that the variable **res** is used as a temporary variable and as a conduit for information passing between the filters.

Each pipe stage takes 10 time units, a single communication is 5 time units. Thus the time for a single iteration is four times the communication time (i.e., 20 time units) plus four times the execution time (i.e., 40 time units) for a total of 60 time units. The average time per iteration for the Mentat version is just over 10 time units. The first result will be available at time 60 and once the pipe is filled, results will be produced every 10 time units. Note that there are only four communications as opposed to 8 because intermediate results are not returned to the caller, rather they are passed directly where needed.

Consider the effect of quadrupling the time to execute **filter_one()** from 10 to 40 time units, thus creating a single heavy stage. Using the standard pipe equation the first result is available at time 90, and successive values every 30 time units. However, results from the Mentat implementation will still be available every 10 time units.

The standard pipe equation assumes that there is just one functional unit for each stage. This assumption is invalid for a pipeline implemented using **regular** Mentat objects. Because the **data_processor** class is a **regular** Mentat class, the system may instantiate new instances at will to meet demand. A new instance of **data_processor** to service **filter_one()** requests is created whenever a result is generated by the read stage. For the Mentat implementation, there would be five instances of the **data_processor** class active at a time, four performing filter one, and one performing filter two. Thus, the time per iteration

```
regular mentat class data_processor{
 public:
  data_block* filter_one(data_block*);
  data_block* filter_two(data_block*);
};
main() {
    m_file in_file,out_file;
    data_processor dp;
    int i,x;
    data_block *res;

    in_file.create();
    out_file.create();

    x = in_file.open((string*)"input_file",1);
    x = out_file.open((string*)"output_file",3);

    for (i=0;i<MAX_BLOCKS;i++){
      res = in_file.read_block(i);
      res = dp.filter_one(res);
      res = dp.filter_two(res);
      out_file.write_block(i*BLK_SIZE,res);
    }
}
```

Program 10.1
A Pipelined Data Processor

for the Mentat version remains unchanged at 10 time units, if there are
sufficient computational resources.

10.2.2   Using Mentat Objects

Member function invocation on Mentat objects is syntactically the same
as on C++ objects. Semantically, however, there are important differences. First, Mentat member function invocations are non-blocking,
providing for the parallel execution of member functions when data dependencies permit. Second, each invocation of a **regular mentat** object
member function may cause the instantiation of a new object to service the request. This, combined with non-blocking invocation, means
that many instances of a **regular** class member function can be executing concurrently. Finally, Mentat member functions are always call-by-

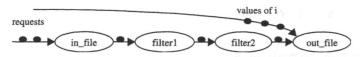

Figure 10.4
Program Execution for a Pipelined Data Processor

value, because our model does not provide shared memory. All parameters are physically copied to the destination object. Similarly, return values are by-value. Pointers and references may be used as formal parameters and as results; the effect is that the single object to which the pointer refers is copied.

Variable-size arguments are supported as well, as they facilitate the writing of library classes such as matrix algebra classes. Variable sized objects used as parameters or return values must be memory contiguous and support a `size_of()` method which returns the size of the object in bytes. The Mentat library provides a number of convenience classes (e.g., matrices, arrays, lists) to make common cases easy, as well as a "transportable_block" base class to make deriving new transportable variable-sized classes straight forward. Descriptions of a number of classes provided to support common variable sized argument types (e.g., matrices, vectors, lists) and the mechanisms for creating new variable-size transportable classes are provided in the Mentat reference manual [Mentat 1994]

Instances of Mentat classes (i.e., Mentat objects) are used like C++ objects. In general the execution of a code fragment proceeds normally (i.e., sequentially) until a statement is reached which contains a Mentat expression. At this point, all arguments are marshalled and a program graph node is generated which contains the name of the object and the member function invoked. Program execution is driven by the arrival of data on arcs (Section 10.3.1). Execution proceeds without blocking until either a value is needed or a value is returned using `rtf()`. At that point the program graph is executed in parallel, and return values are sent where they are needed to satisfy data dependencies. Note that program graph construction, argument marshalling, and graph execution are the responsibility of the MPL compiler and the Mentat runtime system. Programmers never see the program graphs, much as most programmers never see the assembly code generated for sequential programs.

As an example, consider:

```
{ // Sum the first N squares
   integer_accumulator A;
   integer_ops B;
   A.create(0);                    // create accumulator with value 0
   for (int i=0; i<N; i++)
      A.add(B.mpy(i,i));           // does not block
   cout << A.current_value();      // strict expression
}
```

The loop above executes without blocking; up to N instances of the
integer_ops class may run in parallel. Note that parallel execution of
the B.mpy() operation is achieved simply by using the member function.
All of the A.add() operations are executed on the same object instance
which is created and initialized with the A.create(0) statement.

Of course, if we compiled and executed the above code fragment in
Mentat, the parallel version of the program would execute far slower
than an equivalent sequential program. The reason is that integer operations are too fine-grained for Mentat to exploit usefully. Larger-grain
operations are usually required for good performance.

10.2.3   Choosing Mentat Classes

As the previous example illustrates, not all classes should be Mentat classes. In particular, objects that do not have a sufficiently high
computation-to-communication ratio should not be Mentat objects. Exactly what is "sufficiently high" is architecture-dependent; in general,
we have found that several hundred instructions is a minimum. At
smaller grain sizes, communication and runtime overheads take longer
than member function execution, and programs slow down rather than
speed up.

Experience shows that a class should be a Mentat class if any one of
the following conditions is true:

- its member functions are computationally expensive;

- its member functions exhibit high latency (e.g., perform I/O);

- it encapsulates shared state information (e.g., a shared queue); or

- it performs a coordination role.

Classes whose member functions have a high computational cost or high latency should be Mentat classes so that their computation may be overlapped with the computation of other functions and latencies. Examples of computationally expensive operations include the multiplication of large matrices, finding objects in an image, or computing the configuration of a molecule.

I/O classes that support operations such as reading an image or searching a database are also good candidates for Mentat classes because the I/O can be executed in parallel with other operations. For example, we could read in a sequence of images from an image database and pipeline the subsequent computations.

Shared state objects should be Mentat classes because there is no shared memory in our model—shared state can only be realized using Mentat objects.

Finally, a class is sometimes made a Mentat class so that it can perform a coordination role for other Mentat objects. In the sum of squares code shown earlier, for example, the accumulator performs a coordination role of sorts. The summation could have been performed in the `for` loop itself, as in:

```
for (int i=0; i<N; i++)
   j = j + B.mpy(i,i);
```

but this implementation would result in serial execution, because the Mentat compiler generates code to block execution whenever the result of a Mentat operation (such as `B.mpy(i,i)`) is used in a strict expression (such as addition). Thus, the program would block on every loop iteration, sequentializing execution. By using the accumulator Mentat object as a coordinator we eliminate the need for this synchronization. Another example of a coordination role arises when a Mentat object contains other Mentat objects. For example, an image class may be composed of multiple sub-images. A member function to convolve the image would convolve each of the sub-images in turn.

10.2.4   Instantiation and Binding of Mentat Objects

Instantiation of a Mentat object is slightly different from the standard C++ object instantiation semantics. First, consider the C++ fragment:

```
{ // open new scope
  int X;
  p_matrix mat1;
  matrix_operators m_ops;
} // end scope
```

In C++, when execution enters the scope in which X is declared, a new integer is created on the stack. In MPL, because p_matrix is a Mentat class, mat1 is the name of a Mentat object of type p_matrix; it is not the instance itself. Thus, mat1 is analogous to a pointer. Such names are also called Mentat variables.

Mentat variables (e.g., mat1) can be either *bound* or *unbound*. When a Mentat variable comes into scope or is allocated on the heap, it is initially an unbound name: it does not refer to any particular instance of the class. Thus, a new p_matrix is not instantiated when mat1 comes into scope. A bound name refers to a specific instance of a Mentat class.

Mentat variables whose class is a **regular** Mentat class are never bound by the programmer. Instead the programmer simply uses the variables. The Mentat runtime system logically creates a new instance for each member function invocation. An example is Program 10.1, in which up to N instances of the **integer_ops** class could be created, one to service each invocation of the **mpy()** member function.

A Mentat variable of a **persistent** or **sequential** Mentat class may become bound in one of three ways: it may be explicitly created using **create()**, it may be bound by the system to an existing instance using **bind()**, or the name may be given the value of a bound name by an assignment.

By using the **create()** call, the user tells the system to instantiate a new instance of the appropriate class. The user may allow the system to schedule the instance, indicate a specific host location for the new object, or indirectly specify a host by identifying an existing Mentat object with which the new object should be co-located.

10.2.5　Return-to-Future rtf()

The return-to-future function (**rtf()**) is the Mentat analog of the **return** of C++. It provides the mechanism by which Mentat member functions return a computed value to successor nodes in the macro-dataflow graph, but does not cause termination of the invoking sub-program (the normal C++ **return** mechanism still serves this purpose). The returned value is forwarded to all member function invocations that are data-dependent on it, and to the caller if necessary. In general, copies may be sent to several recipients (for example, the return value may be required as a parameter to a number of other member functions of Mentat classes). The implementation of the `integer_ops::add()` member function illustrates the basic case:

```
integer_ops::add(const int arg1, const int arg2){
  rtf(arg1+arg2);    // Use rtf() to return computed value
  return arg1+arg2; // Use return to signify function end
}
```

`rtf()` differs from **return** in three significant ways. First, before a function can return a value in C++, the value must be available. This is not the case with `rtf()`. Recall that when a Mentat object member function is invoked, the caller does not block. Rather we ensure that the results are forwarded wherever they are needed. Thus, a member function may `rtf()` a "value" that is the result of another Mentat object member function that has not yet been completed or perhaps even begun execution. Indeed, the result may be computed by a parallel subgraph obtained by detecting inter-object parallelism. In this case, an arc is constructed to the member function invocation which is using the result value.

Second, a C++ **return** signifies the end of the computation in a function while an `rtf()` does not. An `rtf()` only indicates that the result value is available (note, a result value is as defined above—it may be an actual value, or just the "promise" of a value computed by some future Mentat method invocation). Since each Mentat object has its own thread of control, additional computation may be performed after the `rtf()` (e.g., to update state information or to communicate with other objects). In the message passing community this is often called send-ahead. By making the result available as soon as possible, we permit data-dependent computations to proceed concurrently with the local computation that follows the `rtf()`. However, a single member function should only execute one `rtf()` (i.e., data dependencies should only be satisfied once)—subsequent calls to `rtf()` result in a runtime error.

Third, a **return** returns data to the caller. Depending on the data dependencies of the program, an `rtf()` may or may not return data to

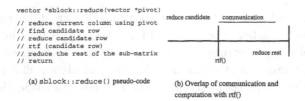

```
vector *sblock::reduce(vector *pivot)

// reduce current column using pivot
// find candidate row
// reduce candidate row
// rtf (candidate row)
// reduce the rest of the sub-matrix
// return
```

(a) sblock::reduce() pseudo-code

(b) Overlap of communication and computation with rtf()

Figure 10.5
Gaussian Elimination with Partial Pivoting Illustrating the Use of **rtf()**

```
TM::read(int transaction_id, int record_number) {
    check_if_ok(transaction_id, READ, record_number);
    // Assume that check_if_ok handles errors
    rtf(DM.read(record)); // Note tail-recursive call
}
```

(a) Code fragment for Transaction Manager,
read() member function

Client → TM:read → DM.read

(b) Call graph illustrating communication
for TM::read()

Figure 10.6
Tail Recursion

the caller. If the caller does not use the result locally, then the caller does not receive a copy. This saves on communication overhead.

Consider a **persistent** Mentat class **sblock** used in Gaussian elimination with partial pivoting. In this problem, illustrated in Figure 10.5, we are trying to solve for x in $Ax = b$. The **sblocks** contain portions of the total system to be solved. The **sblock** member function:

vector* sblock::reduce(vector*);

performs row reduction operations on a submatrix and returns a candidate row. Pseudo-code for the reduce operation is given in Figure 10.5a. The return value can be quickly computed and returned via **rtf()**. The remaining updates to the **sblock** then can occur in parallel with the communication of the result (Figure 10.5b). In general, the best performance is realized when methods invoke **rtf()** as soon as possible.

As another example, consider a transaction manager (TM) that receives requests for reads and writes and checks to see if the operation is permitted. When an operation is permitted, the TM performs the operation via the data manager (DM) and returns the result. Figure 10.6a illustrates how the read operation might be implemented. In an RPC system, the record read would first be returned to the TM and then to the user. In MPL the result is returned directly to the user, bypassing the TM (Figure 10.6b). Further, the TM may immediately begin servicing the next request instead of waiting for the result. This can be viewed as a form of distributed tail recursion or simple continuation passing. In general, the "returned" graph may be arbitrarily complex, as in the matrix multiplication example.

10.2.6 mselect/maccept

The **mselect/maccept** construct of MPL is modeled after Ada's select/accept [DoD 1982]. It is used to conditionally accept a subset of the member functions of the class. It can also be used to accept a member function call before the execution of the current member function is complete. When used in the context of an **mselect/maccept**, member functions are referred to as entry points or entries.

Each entry in an **mselect/maccept** may be controlled using a guard. The guards are Boolean expressions based on local variables and constants. A guard may be assigned to each possible entry point (the default when no guard is specified is the constant "true"). If a guard evaluates to true, its corresponding entry point is a candidate for execution. If more than one guard evaluates to true, the member function is chosen non-deterministically.

An example of **mselect** is shown in Program 10.2. The availability of the **func2()** entry is controlled using a guard; other entries have the default "true" guard. Each of the guards is evaluated in some non-deterministic order until one of the guards evaluates to true and there is a pending invocation on that function. The corresponding member function for that guard is then executed. Once that function has been executed, control passes to the next statement beyond the select.

```
mselect{
              : maccept int func1(int arg1);
                break;
   [delay>0] : maccept int func2();
                break;
              : maccept int func3();
                break;
}
```

Program 10.2
Example of mselect Statement

10.2.7   Compilation

Programs written in MPL are compiled by the Mentat Programming
Language compiler mplc. Each Mentat class definition must be contained in a separate file and each Mentat class must be compiled separately. mplc manages a series of parsing and code generation passes.
First the MPL code is passed through the C++ preprocessor to remove
all #includes and #defines. The preprocessed code is then passed into
the MPL front end, called mplfront. mplfront then parses the MPL
code, removing the Mentat keywords and producing C++ code with
appropriate calls to the runtime system. The result is a translation file
whose name has the suffix .trans.c. Compilation is completed when
mplc invokes a C++ compiler on the translation file. The options to
mplc are a superset of the C++ compiler options. All compile options
specific to the C++ compiler are ignored by mplc and passed on.

A number of library classes facilitate application development in Mentat, including a Mentat stream facility, array and vector classes, a file
interface for array and vector classes, and a sparse vector class.

A useful facility provided by Mentat is the "-DSERIAL" compilation
flag, which can be specified to build sequential versions of many Mentat applications (some Mentat applications, such as those utilizing the
non-deterministic **mselect** language feature, have no serial equivalent).
When used in concert with a number of macros defined by the Mentat
library, this option can allow the programmer to maintain a single set
of sources for both parallel and sequential versions of an application.
This is convenient for users who wish to run applications in both parallel and sequential environments, as they need not be burdened with

keeping multiple versions of their source code consistent. It also allows sequential debugging techniques to be used for Mentat applications in many cases.

10.3 The Runtime System

10.3.1 Runtime Dataflow Detection

The objective of runtime dataflow detection is to dynamically detect and manage data dependencies between Mentat object invocations, and to map the resulting dependence graph onto a macro-dataflow (MDF) program graph [Grimshaw 1993]. Mentat object function invocations correspond to nodes in the MDF program graph, while the data dependencies between Mentat object function invocations correspond to arcs. The dataflow detection library routines monitor the use of Mentat objects and certain variables (called result variables) at runtime to produce data dependence graphs.

Let A be an instance of a Mentat class with a member function:

```
int A::operation1(int,int)
```

A *Mentat expression* is one in which the outermost function invocation is an invocation of a Mentat member function. For example:

```
A.operation1(4,5);
```

A Mentat expression may be nested inside of another Mentat expression, as in:

```
A.operation1(5,A.operation1(4,4));.
```

A *Mentat assignment* statement is formed by assigning the result of a mentat expression to a variable, e.g.,:

```
x = A.operation1(4,5);.
```

A *result variable* (RV) is a variable that occurs on the left-hand side of a Mentat assignment statement at some point in a program, e.g., w in Figure 10.7. Each RV is in one of two states: *delayed* or *actual* depending on whether the variable has a valid value. If the state is actual, then the variable's value is current and may be used. A variable becomes delayed at runtime when it is used on the left hand side of a Mentat assignment. Recall that we do not block when we invoke a Mentat object member function. If the RV is delayed, a computation instance is used to compute the value when it is needed. A computation instance stores invocation-specific information, such as the name of the invoked object, the function invoked, the actual parameter list, and a list of objects that need a copy of the result of the member function.

We define the *potential result variable set* (PRVS) to be the set of all result variables. Membership in the PRVS is determined at compile time. We define the *result variable set* (RVS) to be the set of all result variables that have a delayed value. Membership in the RVS varies during the course of object execution. A variable may be a member of the PRVS and never be a member of the RVS.

The runtime system performs dynamic dataflow detection by monitoring the members of the RVS. The system maintains a table containing the addresses of result variables and pointers to corresponding computation instances. Computation instances in the table correspond to the most recent Mentat assignment to the result variables. Each time the actual computed value contained in a result value variable is used by the program (e.g., it appears on the right-hand side of an assignment statement), the system satisfies the data dependency by tracking the progress of the associated computation instance.

A result variable is added to the RVS when it occurs on the left hand side of a Mentat assignment statement. Adding a result variable to the RVS involves storing the address and corresponding computation instance pointer in a system table. If an entry already exists for the result variable address then the computation instance pointer is overwritten. This mechanism implements the single assignment rule for result variables by resolving any false dependencies. A result variable is removed from the RVS only when the result will never again be used on the right-hand side of an expression.

Whether an expression using a result variable blocks the thread of control depends upon whether the expression is a Mentat expression (Figure 10.7a) or a strict expression (Figure 10.7b). If it is a Mentat expression (i.e., has a corresponding computation instance) the system does not wait for a return of the result variable argument. Rather, the result is forwarded by the object named in the first computation instance directly to the object named in the second. If the result variable

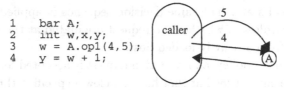

```
1     bar A,B,C;
2     int w,x,y;
3     w = A.op1(4,5);
4     x = B.op1(6,7);
5     y = C.op1(w,x);
6     rtf(y);
```

(a) Marshall the arguments 4, 5, 6, 7 and

draw an arc from A.op1() and B.op1()

to C.op1(). Execution never blocks.

```
1     bar A;
2     int w,x,y;
3     w = A.op1(4,5);
4     y = w + 1;
```

(b) w is used in a strict expression (+),
block and wait for the value.

Figure 10.7
Two Uses of Result Variables. In this example, **bar** is a **regular** Mentat class

argument is never used in a strict expression then it is never returned
to the caller by its computation instance. Until an RV is used in a strict
expression, the evaluation of a computation instance does not block the
caller.

In the case of a strict expression where the program requires a value
in order to proceed, the caller begins evaluation of the result variable
and blocks until the result is available. At that point it is placed in the
appropriate location in memory.

10.3.2   Scheduling

In general, optimally scheduling a set of tasks across a set of resources
in order to minimize or maximize a particular function is NP-Hard.
However, it has been shown that acceptable scheduling decisions can be
made using heuristics. There is a rich literature on heuristic scheduling
in distributed systems; using the classification scheme given in [Casavant
& Kuhl 1988], our FALCON (Fully Automatic Load COordinator for
Networks) scheduler employs a distributed, sender-initiated, adaptive

scheduling algorithm to achieve load sharing, and is based on the job-based queuing model presented in [Eager *et al.* 1986]. In this model, the current system state is used to describe the distribution of load among system components.

The function of the FALCON scheduler is to assign Mentat objects to processors in order to minimize the total execution time of the application. The scheduling function is a distributed algorithm employed by a set of instantiation manager daemons, one on each host in the system. This function decides whether to process a task locally or remotely (i.e., the transfer policy), and where to send a task selected for transfer (i.e., the location policy). Each instantiation manager makes decisions based on local state. The same decision sequence is applied to all task requests regardless of whether the request originated at the host or was transferred from a heavily-loaded host.

In our transfer policy, an invocation request is accepted for scheduling locally if the current load at that host is below a specified threshold or if the request has reached a specified transfer limit. Otherwise, the request is forwarded to another host. Once a task is accepted at a host it remains until completion—tasks do not migrate in our system.

The location policy is applied to requests which have been designated for remote scheduling by the transfer policy. The location policy determines which remote host will receive the transferred invocation request. The user selects one of three location policies at system start-up: random, round-robin, or a "best-most-recently" policy which selects the least loaded host from which a scheduling request was most recently transferred.

We found that this basic scheduling mechanism does not work well in highly parallel environments. In retrospect, the reasons are clear. The assumptions of the queueing model we used were independent jobs, Poisson arrivals, and Poisson service times; the performance metric was average completion time. However, the reality of parallel processing environments is rather different from that of distributed systems. In a parallel processing environment, one is faced with a task scheduling problem, in which a dependence graph must be scheduled, rather than a job scheduling problem. Tasks often arrive together and have equal service times (e.g., are components of a data-parallel set of tasks), and thus violate the Poisson assumptions. Because data-parallel components often dominate application performance, task set completion is determined by the completion time of the slowest of the data-parallel tasks. Thus, the effect of placing two tasks on the same processor is to double the execution time of the application. As the load increases, the probability that two tasks will be placed on the same processor becomes very large. This brings us to the final difference in the two environments: users of parallel processors want to run the machine near 100% utilization, yet that is exactly where the queuing theory suggests that schedulers based upon simple policies will fail.

We have attacked this problem by constructing scheduling agents that are specifically targeted at data-parallel computations, and by dynamically switching from sender-initiated to receiver-initiated policies for `regular` objects. The first of these mechanisms is complete and has had a significant impact on performance.

Weissman has constructed a framework for automating partitioning and placement decisions for data-parallel computations across a system whose resources exhibit a diverse set of computational power and communication capabilities [Weissman & Grimshaw 1995, Weissman 1995]. The framework uses a combination of information about the computation and communication structure of the data-parallel program and the computation and communication capacities of current system resources to partition and place data-parallel computations.

10.4   Application Experience

> Some material in this section is revised from [Grimshaw 1995], and appears with the permission of Elsevier Science.

The bottom line for parallel processing systems is performance on real applications. If a parallel language is prohibitively difficult to use, the benefits of high-performance are diminished, thus our goals include both performance and ease-of-use. Over the past four years we have tried to answer three questions about Mentat and our approach to object-oriented parallel processing:

- Is MPL easy to use?

- Is the performance acceptable to users?

- What is the performance penalty with respect to hand-coded implementations?

To answer these questions we implemented both real and synthetic applications. Our selection criteria were that each application had to be representative of a distinct class of applications, and that each had to be of genuine interest to identifiable users. Further, we wanted variety in our applications and not just linear algebra codes. In all cases our implementations have been developed in collaboration with domain scientists who had an interest in the codes. For some of the applications, a hand-coded parallel C or Fortran implementation already existed, against which we could compare the performance of our Mentat implementation.

The set of Mentat applications is very diverse and includes matrix algebra libraries for dense linear systems, DNA and protein sequence comparison (biochemistry), automatic test pattern generation (electrical engineering), genetic algorithms (searching a combinatorial space), image processing (both libraries and for target recognition), and parallel databases (computer science) to name a few. Only a few of these were implemented by our research group at the University of Virginia. Below, we present results for three of those applications: DNA and protein sequence comparison, the stencil libraries, and the polygon overlay problem. Other applications are reported in the literature, including dense linear algebra libraries [MacCallum & Grimshaw 1994], finite element analysis [Weissman et al. 1994], automatic test pattern generation [Srinivasan 1994], and the NAS benchmarks [Ferrari 1995].

10.4.1   DNA and Protein Sequence Comparison

Some material in this section is revised from [Grimshaw et al. 1993b], and appears with the permission of the IEEE.

Our first application is DNA and protein sequence comparison. Biologists today can determine the sequence of amino acids making up a protein more easily than they can determine its three-dimensional structure, and hence its function. The current technique used for determining the structure of new proteins is to compare their sequences with those of known proteins. This task involves comparing a single query sequence against a library of sequences, each of which can be represented as strings of characters. Any two sequences can be compared using one of several algorithms to generate a score that reflects their commonality. Three popular algorithms are Smith-Waterman [Smith &

```
regular mentat class sw_worker{
  ···private member data and functions···
 public:
  result_list *compare(sequence, libstruct, paramstruct);
  // Compares sequence against a subset of the library. Returns
  // a list of results (sequence id, score).
}
```

Program 10.3
Regular Mentat Class Definition for scanlib Worker

Waterman 1981], FASTA [Pearson & Lipman 1988], and Blast [Altschul
et al. 1990]. Smith-Waterman is the benchmark algorithm; it generates
the most reliable scores, but requires considerable execution time. The
other two algorithms are heuristics which give a score of lower quality
in much less time. For example, FASTA is less accurate, but twenty to
fifty times faster, than Smith-Waterman.

A common operation is to compare a single sequence against an entire
database of sequences. This is known as the scanlib problem. A sorted
list of scores is generated, and the sequence names of the top N (usually
20) sequences and a score histogram are generated for the user.

A second common operation is to compare two sequence libraries, i.e.,
to compare every sequence in a source library against every sequence in
the target library. For each sequence in the source library, statistics are
generated on how the sequence compares to the target library as a whole.
This is known as the complib problem. An important attribute of both
types of comparison is that individual comparisons are independent of
one another, and can thus be parallelized with relatively little overhead.

The Mentat implementation of scanlib uses regular Mentat class
workers to perform the comparisons. A skeletal class definition for the
Smith-Waterman worker is given in Program 10.3. Note that it is a
regular class, which indicates that compare() is a pure function, and
that the system may instantiate new instances as needed. Private member variables have been omitted for clarity. The single member function, compare(), takes three parameters: a sequence structure containing the source sequence to compare; a libstruct structure which
contains information defining a subrange of the target library; and a
paramstruct structure which contains algorithm-specific initialization

···get the number of workers···
···divide the library into a partition for each worker···

```
sw_worker worker;
// invoke the comparison for each partition of the library
for (i = 0; i < num_workers; i++){
    // compute library parcel boundaries
    results[i] = worker.compare(the_seq, libparcelinfo, param_rec);
}
// for each partition's result, and for each comparison
// within the partition, compute statistics
for (i = 0; i < num_workers; i++){
    for (j = 0; j < results[i]->get_count(); j++){
        // record mean, stdev, and histogram information for each result
    }
}
```

Program 10.4
Main Program Structure of scanlib

information. compare() compares the source sequence against every sequence in its library subrange and returns a list of result structures. Each
result structure has a score and the library offset of the corresponding
sequence.

The important features of the main comparison program are shown
in Program 10.4. Note that we only had to declare one worker, and
that the code looks as though the single worker is being forced to do its
work sequentially. Recall, however, that since the worker is of a **regular**
Mentat class, each invocation instantiates a separate logical copy of the
worker object, so each copy may perform the comparisons in parallel.

Performance on the iPSC/2 is given in Table 10.1 for both the Mentat implementation and for a hand-coded message-passing C implementation. A 3.8 Mbyte target library containing 9633 sequences was
used. LCBO and RNBY3L are two different source sequences which
are 229 and 1490 bytes long respectively. Execution times for both the
Smith-Waterman and the much faster FASTA are given. Performance
on this application clearly demonstrates that for naturally parallel applications with no inter-worker communication and little worker-master
communication, neither the object-oriented paradigm nor dynamic management of parallelism seriously affect performance. Indeed, the perfor-

Workers		1		3	
Sequence	Algorithm	M	N	M	N
LCBO	FASTA	167	162	59	57
LCBO	SW	-	-	5749	5719
RNBY3L	FASTA	439	416	150	153

Workers		7		15	
Sequence	Algorithm	M	N	M	N
LCBO	FASTA	28	26	17	16
LCBO	SW	2472	2460	1162	1154
RNBY3L	FASTA	67	64	35	32

Table 10.1
iPSC/2 Execution Times for `scanlib` (sec). Mentat times labeled "M"; times for a version using native low-level programming interface labeled "N".

mance of the Mentat version is always within 10%, and usually within 5% of the lower level version.

The `complib` implementation is more complex, although the main program is still straightforward. The main program manipulates the source genome library, the target genome library, and a recorder object that performs the statistical analysis and saves the results [Grimshaw et al. 1993b]. The main program loop is shown in Figure 10.8. Its effect is to form a pipe, in which sequence extraction, sequence comparison, and statistics generation execute in a pipelined fashion. Each high-level sequence comparison is transparently expanded into a fan-out, fan-in program graph whose leaves are workers. The source sequence is transmitted from the root of the tree to the leaves. The internal nodes of the reduction tree are collator objects which sort and merge the results generated by the workers.

The main loop of the program is shown in (a). Three objects are manipulated, the source, the target, and the post-processor. The pipelined program graph is shown in (b). `target.compare()` has been expanded showing sixteen workers in (c). The fan-out tree distributes the source sequence to the workers, while the fan-in tree sorts the resulting comparison scores.

Table 10.2 presents results for five `complib` implementations on a network of 16 Sun IPC workstations. The execution times for four lower-

```
for(i=0;i<num_source_seq;i++) {
    //for each sequence
    s_val = source.get_next();
    //Compare against target library
    result = target.compare(s_val);
    //Do statistics
    post_process.do_stats(result,s_val);
}
```

(a)

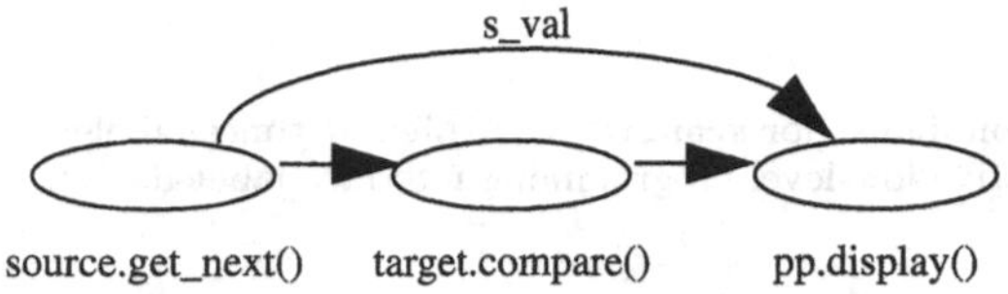

source.get_next()   target.compare()   pp.display()

(b)

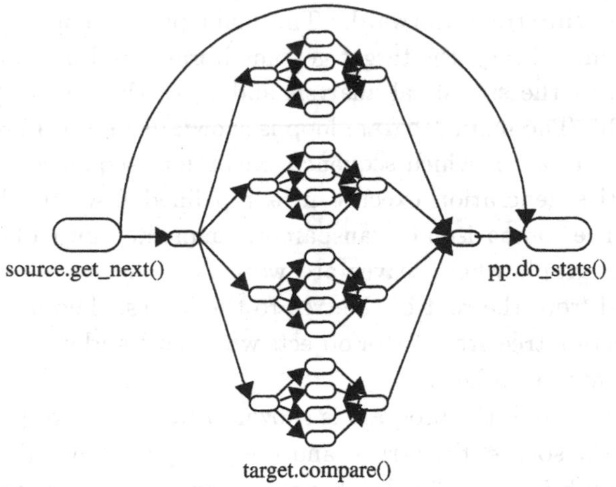

source.get_next()   pp.do_stats()

target.compare()

(c)

Figure 10.8
Mentat Implementation of `complib` (a) main loop (b) pipelined program graph (c)
expanded `target.compare()`

Workers	Express	Linda	Mentat (2.6)	P4 (1.3b)	PVM (3.2.6)
3	220	211	**202**	218	206
7	98	95	**91**	98	92
11	80	62	63	65	**60**
15	NA	50	**48**	49	49
Sequential Time: 583					

Table 10.2
Complib Performance on SUN IPC Workstations (sec)

level implementations are compared to the Mentat time. We note that
complib performs considerable communication—when fifteen workers
are used, over 14 Mbyte of data are moved through the pipeline shown
in Figure 10.8. We used the faster FASTA algorithm, a twenty sequence
source library and a 10,716 sequence target library. The same kernel C
code to actually perform the comparisons was used by all five implementations.

10.4.2   Stencil Libraries

Some material in this section is revised from [Karpovich *et al.*
1993], and appears with the permission of the IEEE.

Stencil algorithms are used in a wide range of scientific applications,
such as image convolution and numerical solution of partial differential
equations (PDEs). Stencil algorithms have several features in common:

- the input data set is an array of arbitrary dimension and size;
- there is a stencil that defines a local neighborhood around a data
  point;
- some function is applied to the neighborhood of points that are covered
  when the stencil is centered on a particular point; and
- this function is applied to all points in the data set to obtain a new
  data set.

Figure 10.9a shows a two-dimensional 3×3 stencil that indicates that
each output value will depend only on the north, east, west, and south
(called NEWS) neighboring points of the corresponding point in the
input array. The associated function is an example of a stencil function
that uses NEWS neighbors.

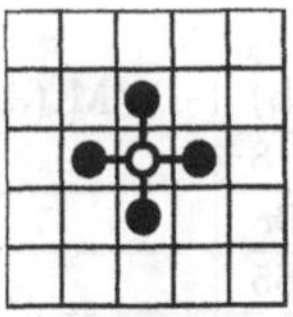

$$F_{i,j} = \frac{I_{i-1,j} + I_{i+1,j} + I_{i,j-1} + I_{i,j+1}}{4}$$

(a)

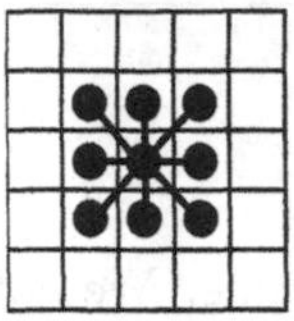

$$F_{i,j} = \sum_{k=0}^{2} \sum_{l=0}^{2} (I_{i+k-1,j+l-1} \times M_{k,l})$$

(b)

Figure 10.9
Typical 2-Dimensional Stencils. *F: final matrix, I: input matrix, M: convolution mask.*

We have defined a base stencil class, `Stenciler`, to manage those issues that are common to all stencil algorithms and provide a framework for the creation of classes tailored to specific applications [Karpovich *et al.* 1993]. The base class contains built-in member functions to perform common tasks, such as managing data communication between pieces. The base class also contains stubs for member functions that the user must define, such as the stencil function. This approach minimizes the effort needed to create new stencil applications through re-use of common code while supporting flexibility in creating parallel stencil applications.

An instance of a `Stenciler` or derived class is designed to handle one piece of the total array. Each `Stenciler` instance can create additional workers to split the workload into smaller pieces. These pieces, in turn, may be further divided, creating a tree of pieces as shown in Figure 10.11. Each new level of the tree has a "contained-in" relationship to the previous higher level. The leaves of this tree structure are the workers that perform the stencil function. The interior instances are managers for the workers below them; the managers distribute and synchronize the work of their sub-piece and collect the results. This hierarchical structure is a powerful and flexible tool for decomposing a stencil problem, especially when running on different hardware platforms.

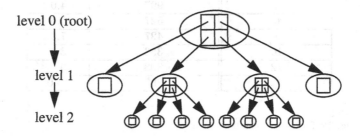

level 0 (root)

level 1

level 2

Figure 10.10
Tree of **Stenciler** Instances

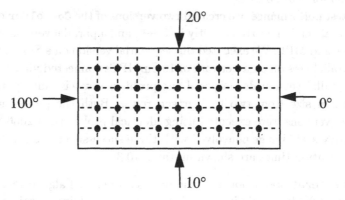

Figure 10.11
Canonical Grid Approximation of Heated Plate used in PDE Example

Number of Pieces	Best Execution Time	Speedup
1	2973	N/A
2	1473	2.0
4	997	4.0
6	527	5.6
8	427	7.0
10	353	8.4
12	308	9.7
14	297	10.0

Table 10.3
Convolver Performance Results (sec)

Image Convolution   To illustrate the use of the stencil framework, we implemented an image convolver. Image convolution is a common application in digital image processing. In two-dimensional image convolution, a small two-dimensional stencil called a filter or mask defines a region surrounding each pixel whose values will be used in calculating the corresponding point in the convolved image. Each element of the filter is multiplied by the corresponding neighbor of the current pixel, and the results are summed and normalized. Figure 10.9b shows a stencil function for a 3×3 mask.

To test performance, we created two versions of the Convolver class, a sequential version written strictly in C++, and a parallel version written in C++ and MPL. We executed the sequential version on a Sun IPC, and the parallel version on a network of 16 Sun IPCs connected via Ethernet. The parallel version decomposed the problem row-wise into partitions ranging in size from two to fourteen rows. Both the sequential and parallel versions were executed using identical problems: a 2000×2000 8-bit grey scale image convolved with three successive 9×9 filters. The best execution times are shown in Table 10.3.

Jacobi Iteration   Another common class of stencil algorithms are iterative methods. Jacobi iteration is a method for solving certain systems of equations of the form $Ax = b$, where A is a matrix of coefficients, x is a vector of variables, and b is a vector of constants. The general procedure for using Jacobi iteration is to first guess a solution for all variables, and then to iteratively refine the solution until the difference between successive answers is below some pre-determined threshold.

Number of Pieces	Best Execution Time	Speedup
1	2619	N/A
2	1381	1.9
4	697	3.8
6	473	5.5
8	428	6.1
10	407	6.4
12	383	6.8
14	370	7.1

Table 10.4
PDE_Solver Performance Results (sec)

We used Jacobi iteration to find the steady-state temperature in the interior of a plate that has a constant temperature applied around its boundaries (Figure 10.11). The temperature in the interior region is approximated by dividing the plate into a regular two-dimensional grid pattern and solving for each of the grid points. The values at each point are approximated by the average of the values in the NEWS neighboring points. This transforms the problem into a system of linear equations which can be solved using Jacobi iteration. The form of the stencil for Jacobi iteration is shown in Figure 10.9a.

We evaluated the performance of our PDE solver application in the same manner used for the image convolution example. A sequential version in C++ and a parallel Mentat version were run on the hardware described for the image convolution example. The problem size used consisted of a 1024 × 1024 grid of floating point numbers. Table 10.4 shows the best execution times.

10.4.3   Polygon Overlay

The final application we will describe is the polygon overlay problem. We designed and implemented two data-parallel algorithms for this problem which are conceptually similar but differ in their scheduling disciplines and use of Mentat class types. The first, a pure dataflow version, uses **regular** objects and relies on the Mentat runtime system scheduler. The second is based on **persistent** objects, and employs a static scheduling scheme implemented in the user code.

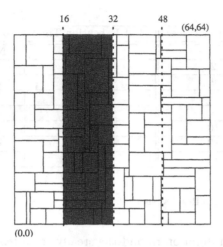

Figure 10.12
Polygon Map Partition

A **sequential** Mentat class, **mpo_polylist**, is used for input and
output of polygon maps in both Mentat versions of the application.
The **mpo_polylist** class interface defines methods which read a polygon
set from disk, partition a polygon set given a range of x coordinates,
append polygons to an existing polygon set, and write a polygon set to
disk (the **append()** method is used in result collection). Instances of this
class contain the entire polygon set for a single map. An example of a
polygon set partition is shown in Figure 10.12. In this example, all of the
polygons, fully or partially covered by the shaded region, correspond to
a single partition, assuming the map is partitioned into four equal pieces.

The dataflow version of the application employs **regular** Mentat objects. The computation of the overlay is performed by a single, pure function method, **compute_overlay()**, which is a member of the **regular**
Mentat class **mpo_comparator**. The method implementation is sequential and is algorithmically similar to the kernel of the original sequential
version.

The overlay algorithm is orchestrated by a main program which creates three **sequential mpo_polymap** Mentat objects, one for each of the
input maps and a third for the output map. Each of the input objects
reads a polygon map from disk. The maps are divided into equal partitions across the x axis, and the **compute_overlay()** method is invoked

once for each pair of corresponding partitions. Each invocation uses a
separate instance of the class; the actual partitions are communicated
by the input objects to the worker objects as arguments. The results of
each worker are passed to the output object which writes them to a file
once all workers have completed. The central loop is:

```
for (i=x_min; i<x_max; i+=partition_width)
  output.append_polygons (
    comparator.compute_overlay (
      input1.get_x_range(i,i+partition_width),
      input2.get_x_range(i,i+partition_width)
    )
  );
```

There are two important points to note regarding this code fragment.
First, the overlay methods are not executed sequentially. The Mentat compiler detects the lack of data dependencies across iterations and
allows invocations of the `compute_overlay()` operation to proceed in
parallel. The Mentat system logically creates a separate worker object
for each of these invocations. The communications required to forward
the arguments to future `compute_overlay()` methods are overlapped
with currently running compute-intensive overlay operations. Second,
because results are not returned to the caller unless they are used, this
code fragment will not result in wasted communication. Instead, results
are forwarded directly to the objects that require them. The basic communication graph for the **regular** object version of the application is
depicted in Figure 10.13.

Our second implementation of polygon overlay differs from the first in
that **persistent** objects are used as workers. The **persistent** worker
objects are each initialized with a partition of a polygon map. A method
called `compute_overlay()` is defined in the **persistent** Mentat class
interface which takes a partition of a second polygon map as its only
argument. The method computation involves overlaying the local partition and the argument partition. As in the **regular** object version, the
input and output of the polygon maps is handled by three **sequential**
objects. Two objects are responsible for partitioning each of the input
maps and the third object collects and writes the resulting map to disk.
In this version, the number of partitions per input map are not necessarily equal—using more than one `compute_overlay()` method per worker

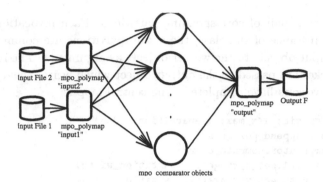

Figure 10.13
Communication Graph for Pure Dataflow Version of Polygon Overlay Using
Regular Objects

allows computation to be overlapped with communication of input parameters and results. A simple, equal-width partition version is:

```
partition_width1 = (x_max - x_min) / n_workers;
for (i = 0; i<n_workers; i++){
  x = x_min + (i * partition_width1);
  workers[i].set_reference_map
            (input1.get_x_range(x,x+partition_width1));
}

partition_width2 = partition_width1 / methods_per_worker;
for (i = 0; i<n_workers; i++){
  x = x_min + (i * partition_width2);
  output.append_polygons (
    workers[i].compute_overlay(
      input2.get_x_range(x,x+partition_width2)
    )
  );
}
```

Again, while the invocations of the **persistent** worker objects' methods appear to be sequential, the lack of data dependencies will be detected by the Mentat runtime system and the overlay operations will
proceed in parallel. We avoid unnecessary communication by not passing the polygon map partitions back to the main program. The basic
application communication graph is depicted in Figure 10.14.

Performance tests of the polygon overlay application were run on a
dedicated cluster of eight SPARCStation 1+ hosts connected by thin

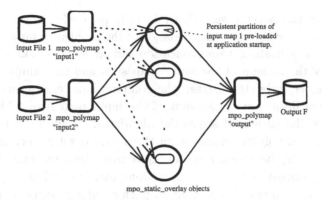

Figure 10.14
Communication Graph for Polygon Overlay Using Persistent Mentat Objects

Problem Size	Sequential	Regular Objects	Persistent Objects
60,000	72	33	42
300,000	964	303	236

Table 10.5
Execution Times (sec) for Polygon Overlay Using Mentat on 8 SS 1+ Nodes

Ethernet. The workstations were each configured with 32 Mbyte, and ran SunOS 4.1.1. We compare our results to the best sequential version of the polygon overlay problem running on a single host of the type described above.

The sequential version was compiled with CenterLine's `clcc` version 2.0.2 C compiler. The Mentat versions were compiled using the Mentat compiler, `mplc`, which employs CenterLine's `CC_CenterLine` version 2.0.2 as a C++ back end. In all cases, the "-O2" level optimization flag was specified.

We ran two problem sizes, using the maps containing 60K polygons each that were provided with the initial sequential implementation, and maps containing approximately 300K polygons each which we generated using the `mapgen` utility. The results of our performance tests are given in Table 10.5. The best times for each case are reported.

The overall observation is that while speedup over the sequential version is achieved, it is not as great as expected; 2.2 in the small case, and 4.1 in the larger case. This relatively poor efficiency is a symptom of the low computational demands of the problem compared to the costs of parallelization. Communication and process creation costs grow linearly with the sum of the input map sizes and the number of partitions respectively. In contrast, the computational cost grows slightly worse than linearly with the sum of the input map sizes. This is an artifact of the optimized sequential algorithm. While both the naïve and optimized polygon overlay algorithms have worst case complexities which grow as the product of the input map sizes, the expected case for the optimized algorithm (i.e., random, evenly distributed polygons over the input maps) is observed to perform significantly better than its quadratic worst case. The overhead of distributing the work thus significantly limits the benefits of parallelization for this code.

A second observation is related to the relative performance of the **regular** and **persistent** object versions of the application. In the small case, the **regular** object version outperforms the **persistent** object version, while the opposite is true for larger inputs. This is caused by two competing factors: initialization overheads and scheduling decisions. The **regular** objects version generates less initialization overhead because worker creation (which is performed by the system) proceeds in parallel with partition distribution. The **persistent** objects case is likely to see better load balance on this homogeneous system, as the scheduling and partitioning is performed manually. For the smaller problem size, the added initialization costs in the **persistent** objects version outweigh the benefits of good load balance and low scheduling overhead—the computation is simply not costly enough to make up the introduced overheads. For the larger problem size, on the other hand, the added initialization costs are made up for by the more even distribution of a more costly workload.

10.5   Lessons Learned

Mentat is now a mature project. Along the way we made some mistakes and discovered elements of the system that could be improved. Many of these relate to the language design and implementation. Below are some of the things we believe we got wrong, and how they could be fixed.

10.5.1 Pure Functions

Regular Mentat class member functions are pure functions. The different member functions within a class have no shared state, and no relation to one another other than they are in the same class and their implementations are in the same binary file.

When the decision was made to have **regular** classes, it was thought that the elegance of having a single mechanism for parallelism—Mentat classes—would outweigh the strangeness of stateless objects. That has not been the case. It is difficult to explain to users why it is necessary to declare a class instance just to call a function.

We now believe that it is more important to support users' intuitions and to leverage their experience base than it is to tightly constrain the number of new mechanisms introduced into C++ by Mentat. A better design would be to have **persistent** and **sequential** Mentat classes, and *Mentat functions*, where Mentat functions would replace **regular** objects. The key word **mentat** could then be used as in:

```
mentat int foo(int x, int y);
z = foo(5,foo(10,5));
```

10.5.2 Data-Parallel Computations

Many data-parallel applications operate on large data sets; the amount of computation performed is strongly correlated with the size and access patterns of the data set. Achieving good performance for these applications is dependent on properly allocating the data (and thus the computation) among processors in order to balance the computational load. A number of common allocation patterns for regular data structures have been documented in the literature, and the steps required to perform these allocations are well known [Bodin 1993a, Fox 1993, Hatcher *et al.* 1991, Loveman 1993]. Typically, the steps are very tedious to do by hand. Compiler support makes their implementation much simpler and less error-prone.

MPL consists of a small number of extensions to C++ and supports task parallelism. This paradigm is flexible and can be used to implement a wide range of applications, including data-parallel applications. Indeed, we have seen good performance for data-parallel applications which have been developed using Mentat. However, the programmer must perform the allocation and management of the data set by hand.

This situation can quickly lead to unnecessary complexity in the implementation and is a shortcoming in the current version of the language. At the expense of a larger language, compiler support can be provided which simplifies the implementation of data-parallel applications. We are currently designing additional language mechanisms to support the data-parallel paradigm, to integrate the data-parallel and task-parallel paradigms, and to support nested data parallelism [West & Grimshaw 1995, West 1994b].

10.5.3 Shallow Copying

Parameter passing in MPL is call-by-value. If a parameter is a pointer, MPL currently performs a shallow copy of the pointed to object. In many circumstances the user would like to pass more complex data structures that include pointers to other objects. The difficulty with this is the need to marshal the parameters sent to remote calls, and the structures returned, into messages for transport.

Automatically generating code to marshal data structures containing pointers is hard in C++. For example, data structures may include unions, which would require the compiler or runtime system to guess the nature of structures. In addition, cycles can be present in the graph formed by the pointers in a data structure; these must be detected and managed.

Because of these difficulties, we have not yet generated automatic marshalling functions. We have, however, considered two possible solutions, some combination of which will appear in a later version of the language. First, the compiler could generate marshalling functions and produce warning messages when potentially dangerous situations are encountered (e.g., unions). Second, the user could be permitted to provide class-specific marshalling and unmarshalling functions which would be called automatically at runtime as needed. Such a mechanism is implemented in the "mobile object" facility of CHAOS, where transportable objects are derived off of a virtual base class whose interface includes pack() and unpack() methods.

10.5.4 Virtual Functions

Many C++ compilers implement virtual functions by embedding a pointer to a class-specific virtual function table just before the data members of the class instance. At runtime, this pointer is dereferenced and a function is looked up in the table using its function number.

When an object is used as a parameter in an invocation of a Mentat object member function, it is copied from the address space of the caller to the address space of the callee. The virtual function table pointer is copied as well. The problem is that the virtual function table may not exist at the same address in the callee as the caller. In fact, because Mentat objects are separately compiled from the programs and objects that use them, the parameter's class may not have existed when the callee was compiled and could thus be unknown to the callee. The result is that if a virtual function is used on the actual parameter in the callee the result is undefined, it will cause a memory fault unless the virtual function table for the class happens to be at the same address.

To solve this problem we could send the type information with the parameter, look the type up at the receiving end, and re-adjust the virtual function pointers as required. However, to be thorough, we would need to adjust the pointers for all of the data members of the parameter as well, and all of their members, and so on. While this can be complex, since the complete class structure is known at compile time, we could generate code to do the necessary adjustments. Once again though, the actual class of the parameter may be unknown to the callee.

We have chosen to ignore this problem because we do not know how to handle the case where the class is unknown to the callee. For example, sending the class of each actual parameter would significantly increase the communication overhead associated with method invocation. While not supporting parameters with virtual functions leads to an artificial language restriction, our user base has not asked that this be fixed.

10.5.5 Non-Preemptable Member Functions

Mentat objects are monitor-like: a single thread is associated with each object and while a member function is executing, it will not be preempted. Disallowing preemption simplifies the programmer's task by eliminating the need to be concerned about race conditions on member variables. However, our users have indicated that there are situations under which they really need pre-emption. Usually this takes the form of updating objects with some state which is global to the program, such as the current lowest-cost path in a traveling salesperson problem.

Users have programmed around the lack of pre-emption by explicitly polling with `mselect`/`maccept` at selected points in their code. We feel that the need to poll reflects a design flaw in the language. To address this problem, we plan to introduce a function modifier for Mentat class member functions that indicates that the function should be executed in a preemptive fashion whenever it is invoked:

```
persistent mentat class foo{
  public:
    int f();                  // standard member function
    immediate int g(int x);   // invoked on arrival
};
```

This begs the question of whether these "interrupts" should be maskable, or what should happen when an interrupt arrives as another interrupt is running. An elegant solution to these issues would be to use the path technique of Path Pascal [Campbell & Kolstad 1980] to control internal concurrency and order accesses to the object. In the current implementation, we kept the mechanism very simple: only one interrupt is handled at a time, and interrupts cannot be masked.

10.5.6 Object Instantiation and Scheduling

Recall that when a Mentat object comes into scope, a new instance is not created. Instead a new unbound object name is created. This is inconsistent with C++ instantiation rules and has caused our users some difficulty. The reasoning behind the difference was that we wanted a variable name that could be bound at the user's discretion, including creating a new instance.

In retrospect this was a mistake—it was inconsistent with users' expectations, and did not provide sufficient binding flexibility to justify the schism with C++ semantics. The language will therefore be changed to so that when a new instance comes into scope a new Mentat object will be created. At the same time we will provide an `operator=` for each class so that assignment of one object to another will have the expected default effect of copying one object's state onto another's.

To provide and enhance the instantiation flexibility of the old method, we will introduce a new base type, `mentat_address`. A `mentat_address` will be similar to a reference, i.e., it will point to an object. We will overload the `new()` operator for Mentat classes, providing several different versions taking parameters specifying scheduling hints to the runtime system. In particular, the **new()** operator will have versions for creating parallel sets of Mentat objects with various topologies, such as one- and two-dimensional arrays, trees, and so on. The implementation will ensure that no two objects created in this way are placed on the same processor.

10.5.7   rtf()

The return-to-future (**rtf()**) construct has been confusing to many users, as the concept of sending ahead a result is not always intuitive. In fact, most users **rtf()** a value and then immediately return, which provides no benefit.

One suggestion for remedying this, proposed by Steve Sayre of the Science Applications International Corporation, is to use a Pascal-like syntax for function return, as in:

```
int foo::g(int x){
  ···some computation···
  g = some value;   // the value is sent ahead as with the
                    // current rtf mechanism
  ···then some more computation···
  return;
}
```

This syntax decouples expressing the return value of a function and marking sub-program termination. At the same time, it has a semantics similar to many who are familiar with Pascal.

10.6   The Future

> Some material in this section is revised from [Grimshaw 1995], and appears with the permission of Elsevier Science.

In the four years that Mentat has been operational, we have developed several applications and learned much about the Mentat approach. Like all other parallel processing systems, Mentat performs well on some applications and less well on others. The primary factors that influence performance are application granularity and application load balance. Not surprisingly, Mentat performs poorly when application granularity is small or when the application has load imbalances that Mentat cannot correct. There is not much that can be done about the granularity restrictions—there are inherent limits on the degree to which overheads (e.g., communication costs) can be lowered. The underlying communication systems of MPPs favor large-grain computations, a fact which is unlikely to change. With respect to load imbalance, there is room for significant improvement in the areas of dynamic scheduling of objects, and dynamic re-distribution of data-parallel objects; we are presently working on both.

Meanwhile, we have learned that combining the object-oriented paradigm with compiler-based detection and management of parallelism can yield performance competitive with that of hand-coded message-passing implementations. We believe that the future of parallel programming will therefore not be limited to message-passing, and that the benefits of the object-oriented paradigm can be realized in high-performance parallel environments.

Now that we have demonstrated the efficacy of the Mentat approach in a largely homogeneous parallel processing environment, our next challenge is to tackle first campus-wide, and then nation-wide, wide-area heterogeneous parallel processing. The Legion project at the University of Virginia is working toward providing system services that provide the illusion of a single virtual machine to users, one that provides both improved response time and greater throughput [Grimshaw 1994]. Legion is targeted towards nation-wide computing. Rather than construct a complete system from scratch we have chosen to construct a campus-wide testbed, the campus-wide virtual computer (CWVC), by extending Mentat. Even though the CWVC is smaller, and the components closer together, than in a full scale nation-wide system, it presents many of the same challenges. The processors are heterogeneous, the interconnection network is irregular, there are enormous differences in bandwidth and latency, and the machines are currently in use for on-site applications that must not be negatively impacted. Further, each department operates essentially as an island of service, with its own file system.

The CWVC is both a working prototype and a demonstration project. Its objectives are to demonstrate the usefulness of network-based, heterogeneous parallel processing to computational science problems; to provide a shared high-performance resource for university researchers; to provide a given level of service (as measured by turnaround time) at reduced cost; and to act as a testbed for the large-scale Legion. The prototype is now operational; it contains an IBM SP-2 and over eighty workstations from four different manufacturers in five different buildings.

Acknowledgments

No project of the scope of Mentat is the product of a single individual. We would like to thank collaborators James Aylor, Robert Ferraro, William Pearson, and Tim Strayer, and all of the students over the last six years who have made Mentat possible by implementing components of the system and by working on all save one of the above applications: Gorrell Cheek, Adam Ferrari, Mike Lewis, Ed Loyot, John Karpovich, Laurie MacCallum, Dave Mack, Mark Morgan, Padmini Narayan, Ahn Nguyen-Tuong, David Shiflet, Sherry Smoot, Virgil Vivas, Emily A. West, and Jon Weissman. This work has been partially funded by grants NSF ASC-9201822 and CDA-8922545-01, NASA NGT-50970, NLM LM04969.

11 MPC++

Yutaka Ishikawa, Atsushi Hori, Hiroshi Tezuka,
Motohiko Matsuda, Hiroki Konaka,
Munenori Maeda, Takashi Tomokiyo,
Jörg Nolte, and Mitsuhisa Sato

11.1 Introduction

Japan's Real World Computing Program is developing a new type of flexible information processing incorporating speech and motion recognition, robot control, and other real world applications. Our aim is to provide researchers in these application areas with a high-performance computing environment. An extended C++ language, called MPC++ [Ishikawa *et al.* 1994, Ishikawa 1994, Ishikawa 1995], has been designed to run on a massively parallel machine called RWC-1 [Sakai *et al.* 1994] that is being developed in our program. Information on the Real World Computing Program can be found at:

> http://www.rwcp.or.jp/

and on MPC++ at:

> http://www.rwcp.or.jp/people/mpslab/mpc++/mpc++.html

MPC++ supports control-parallel programming through primitives and other parallel abstractions through meta-level programming. The MPC++ meta-level programming facility enables a language or library designer, or a compiler writer, to extend or modify C++ language features. For example, a data-parallel language facility will be introduced using this meta-level facility.

Besides the RWC-1, MPC++ will also be used in distributed environments. Currently, MPC++ is operational on a workstation cluster consisting of nine[1] Sun SPARCStation 20 workstations using the Myricom Myrinet network [Boden *et al.* 1995].

This chapter begins by presenting the design philosophy of MPC++, and comparing it with other approaches to high-performance computing.

---

[1]This system will consist of 36 workstations by February 1996.

An overview of MPC++, with some programming examples, is then given in Section 11.3. Section 11.4 shows how to realize a class library for synchronization and demonstrates how a new statement for that library can be implemented in MPC++. The performance of MPC++ on the workstation cluster is shown in Section 11.6; that implementation is briefly described in Section 11.5. Our implementation of polygon overlay is shown in Section 11.7. Finally, we conclude this chapter in Section 11.8.

11.2   The MPC++ Approach to High Performance Computing

Researchers have developed high-performance parallel programming systems in several ways. For example, some systems are implemented using communication libraries such as PVM [Beguelin *et al.* 1991] and MPI [MPI 1994]. Since versions of these libraries exist for most parallel systems, programs using such systems are highly portable. However, if users cannot adapt their algorithms to these systems, they must write the program using the communication library, such as PVM and MPI, directly. It may take considerable time to do this efficiently.

HPF [Koelbel *et al.* 1994] introduces compiler directives which give the compiler hints for task and data distribution. To obtain a good parallelization, the user must specify a data distribution which maximizes locality and minimizes computation.

The various language extensions presented in other chapters of this book provide good abstractions for obtaining good performance and also for making programming easier in some application fields. However, unlike the library approach, if users write programs using language extensions, their programs can only be compiled where compiler developers have implemented those extensions.

The MPC++ approach to high-performance parallel programming differs from all of the above. MPC++ incorporates both a small set of parallel description primitives and an extendable/modifiable programming language facility. Higher parallel constructs, such as data-parallel statements and active objects, are then implemented by using the extendable/modifiable programming language facility.

The parallel description primitives are designed to support multi-threading and message-driven execution. These primitives are a *function instance*, which is an abstraction of thread invocation by message passing, and *message entry* and *token* constructs, which are abstractions of communication between threads.

We designed a meta-level architecture for C++ to realize the extendable/modifiable programming language. By a meta-level architecture, we mean that the semantics of the language are defined in the language itself. The MPC++ meta-level architecture [Ishikawa 1995] defines an abstract compiler described in C++, and a modification facility called the MPC++ meta-object protocol (MOP). Using the MPC++ MOP, programmers can easily introduce new syntactic constructs and redefine default code generation to implement new parallel programming constructs. Moreover, language system developers can optimize code and port the system to new machines efficiently.

Abstractions introduced by designers may be supplied in MPC++ source files, where they are specified using the MPC++ meta-level programming facility. The users can use the abstractions they need by including such files in their own source files. For example, let us suppose that the file foo.h specifies a data-parallel computation abstraction, while the file bar.h specifies a control-parallel abstraction. If a user wants to use both abstractions, she/he just writes:

```
#include "foo.h"
#include "bar.h"
···data parallel and task parallel program···
```

Of course, those specifications must not interfere with each other.

As shown in Figure 11.1, synchronization structures and communication libraries can be implemented in user-level classes. A detailed description will be given in Section 11.4.

11.3 Language Overview

11.3.1 Control Parallelism Facility

The MPC++ programming model assumes a distributed-memory parallel system. However, users may access the local memory on any remote physical processor via a communication primitive. Program code is distributed to, and run on, all physical processors. Each process has several

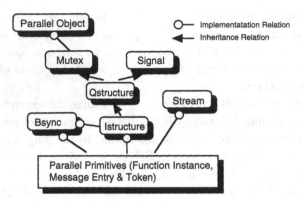

Figure 11.1
Example MPC++ Classes

threads of control. These are not preemptable (i.e., a thread continues to execute until it waits for a message or exits).

A program may locally or remotely invoke a *function instance* which has a thread of control. Specifically, invoking a function instance creates a new thread, executes the function, and then deletes the thread. The program invoking the function instance may block until the end of the invoked function instance execution, or it may execute the subsequent statements and synchronize with the invoked function instance later.

Communication channels are specified by *message entries*, each of which is an entry point at which a message may be received. To send a message to an entry point, the sender must have the *token* of that entry point. In other words, the token gives the holder the capability to send a message to the entry point that it specifies. A token is obtained by referring to the message entry variable. A detailed description will be given later.

All variables are local to processors. If the scope of a variable is a source file (i.e., file scope), storage for it is allocated on each processor. When such a variable is referred to on a processor, the local memory is accessed. The address of a file-scope variable is the same on all processors.

Function Instance   Consider a function instance invocation expression which invokes the `foo()` function instance on processor 2:

```
i = foo() @ [2];
```

The value of the expression enclosed in [] after @ specifies the processor where the function instance is created. The thread invoking the foo() function instance is blocked until the return value arrives, at which point the value is assigned to variable i. In other words, the function instance invocation realizes remote procedure call (RPC). If no value is specified in the processor number field, as in:

```
i = foo() @ [];
```

the function instance is created on the processor on which the expression is executed.

In the example above, the thread of the function instance is added to the ready queue of the processor and the thread making the call is blocked. This function instance invocation expression therefore involves thread scheduling. Note that regular function calls are executed without thread scheduling.

As another example, consider:

```
foo() @ () [2];
```

In this program fragment, "()" is inserted between "@" and "[]". This expression realizes *fork* semantics: the foo() function instance is invoked, but the invoking thread continues to execute. Such an expression is called an *asynchronous function instance invocation*. For example, if the following two asynchronous foo() function instance invocations are executed, two threads execute the function foo() on processor 2:

```
foo() @ () [2];
foo() @ () [2];
```

Parameters of Function Instances A pointer to any type in local memory may not be passed to a function instance created on a remote processor. Also, a structure containing a pointer to any type in local memory may not be passed to a function instance created on a remote processor. Thus, swap(ia)@[10], in the following example, is an illegal statement because the swap() function is invoked with a pointer variable to local storage; swap(ia)@[] is a legal statement because the function instance is locally invoked.

```
swap(int *ip)
{
  int i = *ip;
  *ip = *(ip + 1); *(ip + 1) = i;
}
main()
{
  int ia[2];
  ...
  swap(ia) @ [10];      // error
  swap(ia) @ [];        // OK
  swap(ia);             // OK
}
```

In order to pass a local address to another processor, a global pointer such as those used in CC++ (Chapter 3), EM-C [Sato *et al.* 1994a], and Split-C [Culler *et al.* 1993] may be implemented using the MPC++ meta-level facility. For example:

```
swap(int * global ip)
{
  int i = *ip;
  *ip = *(ip + 1); *(ip + 1) = i;
}
main()
{
  int ia[2];
  swap((int *global) ia) @ [10];     // OK
  swap((int *global) ia) @ [];       // OK
  swap((int *global) ia);            // OK
}
```

All statements are legal here because the parameter of the swap() function is a global pointer to the integer. The cast (int *global) is responsible for changing the representation from a C pointer to a global pointer.

Message Entry and Token A message entry is a construct that is able to receive a message. Each message entry has a token which provides the capability of sending a message to that entry. The message entry has one token at initialization time. The token may be passed to another function instance so that the instance may send a message to the message entry. When the token for a message entry has been passed,

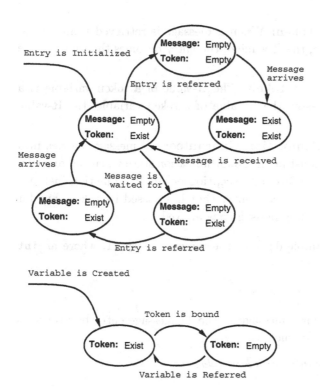

Figure 11.2
State Transition of Entry and Token

no more message entry tokens are allowed to pass. When the message is received at the message entry, the message entry generates a new token since a token can only be used once. These properties are called the single message passing semantics of the message entry and token.

State transitions of an entry and token are shown in Figure 11.2. An entry has two state variables, called **Message** and **Token**, that indicate whether or not a message has arrived and whether a token exists, respectively. The following properties guarantee the single message passing semantics of the message entry and token:

Single Reference of a Message Entry Variable: The message entry has one token at initialization time. The R-value (reference value) of a message entry variable is a token. After accessing the R-value of a message entry variable, the R-value becomes undefined (**UNDEF**).

Re-Usability of a Token: When a message is retrieved from a message entry variable, the R-value of the entry becomes the token of the entry.

Single Reference of a Token: The R-value of a token variable is a token. After accessing the R-value of a token variable, the R-value becomes `UNDEF`.

Communication Completion Guarantee: All message entries in a function instance must be in the initialization state when the function instance exits. Therefore, an exception occurs if a function instance exits while it has a message entry that has passed its token, but for which no corresponding message has arrived.

The following example declares the message entry `11`, where an `int` value is received:

```
entry(int) 11;
```

The program waits for a message at the `11` message entry by programming a *wait* statement, such as:

```
11(i):   // wait statement; receive value
```

A token variable which can keep the token of the above message entry is declared as follows:

```
token(int) t1;
```

The operator `<-`, called the *send operator*, is used to send a message to the message entry associated with a token. For example, sending the value `10` via the token `t1` is coded as:

```
t1 <- [ 10 ];
```

Program 11.1 uses message entries and tokens. The function `myval()` takes a token variable as its argument, which gives `myval()` the capability of sending an integer value. After the function sends the value `mypenum`, representing the processor number, it continues to execute any subsequent statements. The `foo()` function invokes the `myval()` function instance asynchronously.

After invoking the `myval()` function instance, the R-value of `11` becomes `UNDEF` since the token of `11` is passed to the function. Execution

```
void myval(token(int) t1)
{
  t1 <- [ mypenum ];
  ...
}

foo()
{
  int i, k = 0;
  entry(int) l1;
  for (i = 0; i < 10; i++){
    myval(l1) @ ()[i];
    ...
    l1(i):  // receive
    k += i;
  }
}
```

Program 11.1
Message Entry and Token

is blocked at the l1 message wait statement. Execution resumes after a message is received at the statement, and the R-value of the l1 message entry again becomes the token of the entry.

Message Entry as a Continuation The value returned from a function instance is passed to the caller by a token called a *return token*. The expression:

```
i = foo(1) @ [];
```

is equivalent to the following statements:

```
entry (int) l1;
foo(1) @ (l1) [];
l1(i):
```

Here, enclosed in () after the @, a return token is given. The token l1 is passed to the function instance as the return token. When the return statement is executed in the foo() function instance, the value returned is sent to the l1 entry via the return token. The return value is then bound to the variable i.

If a return token is not specified as shown in:

```
foo() @ () [2];
```

the *null token* is passed as the return token. The value of the return statement in the foo() function instance is then thrown away, since a message via the null token is thrown away.

Multiple Wait   The wait statement is used to wait for multiple message entries. The example below waits for messages arriving at entries l1 and l2. When one of them arrives, the corresponding statements are executed, (i.e., when the message for l1 arrives, the statements denoted by S1 are executed). Since the function instance has a single thread of control, if the other message arrives during execution, it is enqueued. When execution reaches the **break** statement, subsequent statements of the **wait** statement are executed.

```
extern int  p1();
extern int  p2();
bar()
{
  entry(int) l1;
  entry(int) l2;
  int i;

  p1() @ (l1)[1];
  p2() @ (l2)[2];

  wait {
    l1(i):
      S1;
      break;
    l2(i):
      S2;
      break;
  }
}
```

11.3.2   Discussion of Control Parallelism Features

Non-preemptive Threading   Several issues influenced our choice of a non-preemptive model for threading:

Reducing race conditions: If we assumed preemptive thread execution, all shared variables would have to be handled carefully in each thread, including both those in file scope and the data members of objects. In short, we would have to allow for, or prevent, race conditions. The non-preemptive MPC++ execution model reduces these concerns.

Efficient implementation: If we assume preemptive thread execution, the threads would have to be scheduled by the operating system kernel to ensure fairness. A non-preemptive model, implemented with a user-level thread library, is more efficient.

Because our thread system is non-preemptive, threads may not call kernel primitives that would block their execution. In the future, those primitives will be implemented by an MPC++ library and an auxiliary process. The library communicates with the auxiliary process, which actually implements the primitives, so that the original thread does not have to block in the kernel.

Drawbacks on shared-memory parallel machines: One drawback of the multithreaded, but non-preemptive, model is that it is not well-suited to shared-memory platforms. Specifically, we cannot allow several processors in a shared-memory machine to execute threads concurrently, because the non-preemptive model assumes that the threads in a process are not running simultaneously.

Message Entry and Token A message must be received on the thread that declares the message entry; in other words, the message entry or its pointer cannot be passed to another thread. If users want to pass a message entry to a function instance so that the instance can receive a value, a synchronization structure class shown in Section 11.4 should be used.

The following questions might arise in the design of message entries and tokens:

1. **Why was a synchronization structure, such as the I-structure [Nikhil & Pingali 1989], not provided as a class instead of introducing a new language construct?** Providing a synchronization structure as a class might seem better than the MPC++ approach because it would not require any language extensions. However, it is difficult to program multiple waits for arriving messages without introducing a new language construct.

Function Name	Description
objBind()	register a syntax tree class and a lexical token
gensym()	generate a symbol
printf()	same as in the C printf() routine
warningMessage()	produce a warning message
errorMessage()	produce an error message

Table 11.1
Some MPC++ Meta-level Primitive Functions

2. **Why was a synchronization structure, such as the I-structure, not introduced as a basic type instead of introducing a new concept?** We believe that the message entry and token mechanism is more primitive than a synchronization structure such as the I-structure. In particular, message entries and tokens are directly translated to the parallel machine code of the RWC-1 in some cases [Ishikawa *et al.* 1994].

3. **Why do the declarations of token and entry not use the syntax of C++ templates?** C++ templates do not allow us to define token and entry template classes whose template elements are of variable length.

11.3.3 Meta-level Architecture

As shown in Figure 11.3, the meta-level architecture defines a meta-system in which the lexical analyzer, parser, code generator, and name table objects form an abstract compiler, and syntax tree objects represent the parse tree of a program. A meta-system modification facility, the MPC++ meta-object protocol (MOP), supports easy meta-level programming.

The lexical analyzer object has a keyword table where new keywords and their lexical token values and syntax tree classes are registered by the base-level program. The object takes a C++ program and produces a sequence of tokens. In the example of Figure 11.3, a 3-tuple of a new keyword mutex, token value Stmt1-id, and a syntax tree class called MutexStmt, has been registered in the keyword table. When the lexical analyzer object processes the program shown in the figure, it can produce sequences such as:

```
Stmt1-id, '(', Identifier, ...
```

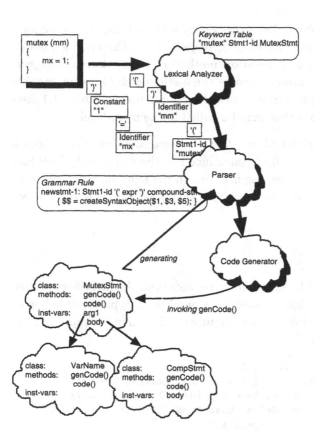

Figure 11.3
MPC++ Meta-level Architecture

When the Stmt1-id token is produced for the mutex keyword, an instance of MutexStmt is also created.

The parser object contains the grammar for both basic C++ and the extension patterns introduced by the user. This object receives tokens from the lexical analyzer object and creates syntax tree objects based on these grammars. When the parser object receives the token sequence shown in Figure 11.3, the grammar of an extension pattern:

```
"Stmt1-id '(' expr ')' compound-stmt"
```

is applied. Then, the syntax tree object shown in Figure 11.3 is created.

The syntax tree object has methods `type()` and `code()` for reporting data type and generating code, respectively. The code generator object invokes the code generation method of the syntax tree object, `genCode()`, which eventually invokes the method `code()`. A name table object maintains type, variable, and function names. Table 11.1 lists the primitive functions that may be called in the meta-level.

Meta-level C++ Extension   A syntax tree constant that defines a syntax tree object statically is introduced in the meta-level C++ language system. For example, the first line in the following example is an *expression syntax tree constant*, while the next line is a *statement syntax tree constant*:

```
'( 1 + 2 + 3 )
'{ int i; i = 10; }
```

A user may use variables in a syntax tree constant. An identifier variable begins with a dollar sign followed by a number. A type variable begins with two dollar signs followed by a number. These number represent the parameter's position:

```
'($1 + $2).genCode(os, 10, 20);
'{ struct $1 { int i; }; }.genCode(os, gensym("foo"));
'{ $$1 $2; }.genCode(os, base_typeid(int), gensym("a"));
'{ $$1 $2[$3]; }.genCode(os, base_typeid(float),
                         gensym("f"), 10);
```

A syntax tree constant has a method `genCode()` which takes as arguments an output stream and values for variables in the syntax tree constant. Invoking the method `genCode()` on the previous examples generates the following code:

```
10 + 20;
struct foo { int i; };
int a;
float f[10];
```

MPC++ Meta-Object Protocol   The keyword `$meta` is introduced to tell the compiler to shift to the meta-level. For example, the following example declares the global integer variable `g1` and the global `SynObj` pointer variable `sobj` so that type `SynObj` is a predefined type in the meta-level:

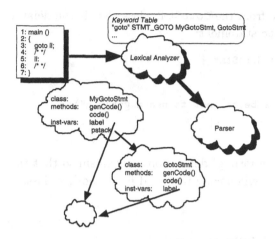

Figure 11.4
Syntax Tree Object 1

```
$meta int     g1;
$meta SynObj *sobj;
```

The following meta-level compound statement is evaluated when the compiler parses it:

```
$meta {
  printf("hello metaworld.\n");
}
```

That is, the following message will appear at the compile time, since the primitive function `printf()` will be executed by the meta-level:

```
hello metaworld.
```

Users can introduce new syntax and modify the semantics of C++ using a special interface. Three extension patterns are predefined: a new modifier for a specifier or for a declarator, a new expression, and a new statement. To allow the user to introduce this new syntax, functions that register new keywords and create new syntax tree classes are provided. The user can program syntax tree methods that transform sources and generate code to define new syntax or to modify the semantics of C++.

To show how the semantics of C++ can be modified in MPC++, we modify the compilation of the `goto` statement. The following program derives a class `MyGotoStmt` from the `GotoStmt` class that is the default syntax tree class of the `goto` statement:

```
$synobjdef MyGotoStmt : GotoStmt {
  public:
    code(OStream) {
      warningMessage("It's better not to use a goto.\n");
    }
};
```

A syntax tree object has a form of delegation mechanism so that the code generation strategy is dynamically inherited from another class.

The program:

```
$meta {
  objBind(STMT_GOTO, typeid(MyGotoStmt));
}
```

invokes the `objBind()` primitive function, whose arguments are a lexical token and the type identifier of a class. The call to `objBind()` tells the lexical analyzer object that an instance of class `MyGotoStmt` should be created when it encounters the `goto` keyword. The instance of `MyGotoStmt` has a pointer, called the *protocol stack pointer*, to an instance of the default class `GotoStmt` (Figure 11.4). When the `genCode()` method of the `MyGotoStmt` instance is invoked by the parser object, it calls the `code()` method. If the return value is `GEN_CONT`, the `genCode()` method calls the `genCode()` method of an object pointed by the protocol stack pointer which will call the `code()` method of that object. In the example, the `code()` method of `MyGotoStmt` is evaluated and then the `GotoStmt`'s `code()` method is called.

After parsing the following program, a 3-tuple of keyword `goto`, token value `STMT_GOTO`, and class `DisplayGotoStmt`, is registered in the keyword table. Then, the lexical analyzer object creates an instance of class `DisplayGotoStmt` (shown in Figure 11.5) when it encounters the `goto` keyword:

```
$synobjdef DisplayGotoStmt : GotoStmt {
  public:
    code(OStream os) {
      '{ printf("a goto statement is executed.\n"); }.genCode(os);
      return GEN_CONT;
    }
```

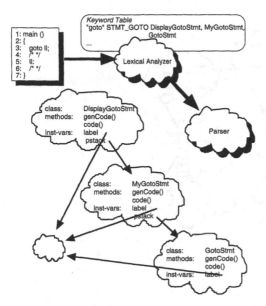

Figure 11.5
Syntax Tree Object 2

```
};
$meta {
    objBind(STMT_GOTO, typeid(DisplayGotoStmt));
}
```

The **code** methods of **DisplayGotoStmt**, **MyGotoStmt**, and **GotoStmt**
are evaluated in that order. The user will see the following message
during compilation:

test.cc, line 3 warning It's better not to use goto statement.

The following message will be produced at runtime because the **code()**
method of **DisplayGotoStmt** generates the **printf()** routine call:

a goto statement is executed.

Since code generation methods are stacked in this way, we call it a code
generation *protocol stack*.

The types of new statements allowed in the MPC++ meta-level architecture are a keyword followed by a compound statement, a keyword with some arguments followed by a compound statement, or a

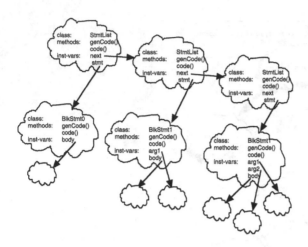

Figure 11.6
New Statements

new label statement followed by arguments. The meta-level declarator
$syntaxdef $statement registers the keyword and its statement type
in the lexical analyzer. For example, the code:

```
$syntaxdef $statement "blkstm0" BlkStm0 : public Stmt0 {
  public:
    code(OStream);
};
$syntaxdef $statement "blkstm1" BlkStm1 : public Stmt1 {
  public:
    code(OStream);
};
$syntaxdef $statement "blkstm2" BlkStm2 : public Stmt2 {
  public:
    code(OStream);
};
```

introduces three new statements: blkstmt0, blkstmt1, and blkstmt2.
The classes Stmt0, Stmt1, and Stmt2 are primitives representing zero-,
one-, and two-argument statements respectively. The classes BlkStmt0,
BlkStmt1, and BlkStmt2, which are derived from Stmt0, Stmt1, and
Stmt2 respectively, are responsible for generating statements blkstmt0,
blkstmt1, and blkstmt2. The user is required to program the code()
method to describe code generation. After the above example and

`code()` method declarations have been processed, the following program can be compiled:

```
blkstm0 { /* statement */ }
blkstm1 (/*expr*/) { /* statement */ }
blkstm2 (/*expr*/; /*expr*/) { /* statement */ }
```

The syntax tree objects created are shown in Figure 11.6.

The following example shows the introduction of a declarator modifier `global` which realizes a global pointer:

```
$syntaxdef $modifier $decl global GlobalModifier :
  SpecModifier
{
 public:
  int code(OStream, SpecDecl *);
  int type() { return base_typeid(globalAddress); }
};
$meta GlobalModifier::code(OStream os, SpecDecl *)
{
  '[ struct globalAddress ].genCode(os);
  return GEN_END;
}
```

The `code()` method is responsible for generating the implementation for a global pointer variable. "`'[...]`" is a *type syntax tree constant* which generates a type when the `genCode()` method is called.

The declaration `int * global p;` is legal after the above meta-level declaration has been evaluated and leads to the following code being generated:

```
struct globalAddress p;
```

The type of the variable `p` is represented as shown in Figure 11.7. The program below shows the class `GlobalPtrRefExpr` derived from `PtrRefExpr` to handle the pointer dereference for the global pointer:

```
$synobjdef GlobalPtrRefExpr : PtrRefExpr {
 public:
   code(OStream os) {
      SpecDecl   *type;
      SpecDecl   *nexttype;
```

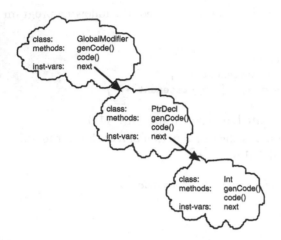

Figure 11.7
Global Pointer

```
        type = next->getType();
        if (typeid(type) == base_typeid(globalAddress)) {
            nexttype = type->getNext();
            if (typeid(nexttype) == typeid(PtrDecl)) {
                nexttype = nexttype->getNext();
                '( _mpcRemoteMemRead($2.pe, $2.laddr,
                        sizeof($$1)), *(($$1 *) $2.laddr) )
                                    .genCode(os, nexttype, next);
                return GEN_END;
            }
        }
        return GEN_CONT;
    }
};
$meta {
    objBind(EXPR_PTRREF, typeid(GlobalPtrRefExpr));
}
```

The `GlobalPtrRefExpr` object has variable `next` which holds the next
expression of the pointer dereference. For example, the `next` value of
the expression "`*p`" is the representation of "`p`".

Executing the above program, the expression "`*p`" is transformed into
the following library call:

```
_mpcRemoteMemRead(p.pe, (char*) &p.laddr, sizeof(int),
                  *((int*)p.laddr))
```

11.4   Class Library and Language Extension

In order to show how a library designer can create classes to extend the MPC++ language, we will build the **Mutex** class shown in Figure 11.1,

The class **Istructure** shown below realizes the modified version of the synchronization structure I-structure described in [Nikhil & Pingali 1989]. Unlike the I-structure, **Istructure::read()** removes the data from the structure.

```
class Istructure {
 private:
  entry(void * global p) ee;
 public:
  Istructure();
  void * global read()
  {
    void * global p;
    ee(p):
    return p;
  }
  void write(void * global p)
  { ee <- [ p ]; }
};
```

The class **Istructure** has one data member called **ee**, and two member functions, **write()** and **read()**. The member function **write()** sends its argument to the entry **ee**. Note that when **ee** appears on the left of the send operator, it is actually the token of the entry, since it is a reference (R-value) of the entry. The member function **read()** receives a message at entry **ee**. According to the state transition of an entry shown in Figure 11.2, it does not matter whether the **read()** or **write()** function instance is invoked first.

The Q structure [Sato *et al.* 1994b], which enables multiple reads and writes, can be defined by introducing a class **IstructureList** (code not shown) to store suspended read/write operations. The **Qstructure** class is implemented using **IstructureList** (Program 11.2).

The **Mutex** class, with methods **enter()** and **leave()**, may be realized using the **Qstructure** class as shown below:

```
class Qstructure {
 private:
  IstructureList *top, *end;
  int state;
 public:
  Qstructure() { top = end = NIL; }

  void write(Object *ov)
  {
    if (top == NIL){
      top = end = new IstructureList;
      top->write(ov); state = WROTE;
    } else if (state == WAITING_W){
      top->write(ov); top = top->next;
      if (top == NIL) end = NIL;
    } else {
      end->next = new IstructureList; end = end->next;
      end->write(ov);
    }
  }

  Object * read()
  {
    Object *ov;
    IstructureList *il;

    if (top == NIL){
      il = top = end = new Istructurelist;
      state = WAITING_W;
    } else if (state == WROTE){
      il = top; top = top->next;
      if (top == NIL) end = NIL;
    } else {
      end->next = new IstructureList;
      il = end = end->next;
    }
    ov = il->read(); delete il; return ov;
  }
};
```

Program 11.2
The Q-Structure

```
class Mutex {
 private:
  Qstructure qq;
 public:
  Mutex()       { qq.write(0); }
  Mutex *enter() { qq.read(); return this; }
  void  leave() { qq.write(0); }
};
```

The critical section is programmed in such a way that the method
enter() must be invoked before the critical section is entered, and the
method **leave()** must be invoked on exiting the critical section. An
example is:

```
Mutex mm;
sub()
{
  mm.enter();
  critical section
  mm.leave();
}
```

One risk of the programming style shown here is that the critical section would remain unfinished if the programmer forgot to invoke method
leave(). Thus, the library designer would want to provide a new statement **mutex** to support a structured programming style:

```
Mutex mm;
void sub()
{
  mutex(mm){
    critical section
  }
}
```

In this chapter, we cannot show the full-featured implementation of
the **mutex** statement, but instead show a simplified implementation.

The following code realizes a simple **mutex** statement.[2] The **code()**
method of **MutexStmt** is responsible for generating code for the statement:

---

[2]The paper [Ishikawa 1995] shows the full implementation that allows the user to
program a **break** or **return** statement inside the **mutex** statement.

```
$syntaxdef $statement "mutex" MutexStmt : public Stmt1 {
  int code(OStream);
};
$meta MutexStmt::code(OStream os)
{
  SynObj *mutexp;
  mutexp = gensym();
  exitLabel = gensym();
  if (expr1->getType() == base_typeid(Mutex)) {
    '{ Mutex *$1;
        $1 = ($2).enter();
     }.genCode(os, mutexp, expr1);
    body->genCode();
    '{ $1->leave(); }.genCode(os, mutexp);
  } else if (expr1->getType() == base_typeid(Mutex*)) {
    '{ Mutex *$1;
        $1 = ($2)->enter();
     }.genCode(os, mutexp, expr1);
    body->genCode();
    '{ $1->leave(); }.genCode(os, mutexp);
  } else {
    errorMessage("illegal mutex operand");
  }
  return GEN_END;
}
```

The MutexStmt object has expr1 and body member variables, which
denote the mutex argument and body statement respectively. Since the
mutex statement may take either a Mutex object or a pointer to such
an object as an argument, the code generation method deals with those
cases.

11.5   Implementation

Figure 11.8 shows the organization of the current MPC++ compiler.
The front end processor generates either an intermediate code called
EXC, or C++ source code with stub routines from the original MPC++
source program. The front end processor also handles the meta-level
processing.

The back-end processor for RWC-1, which includes the optimizer, generates native code from the intermediate code. The GNU g++ compiler

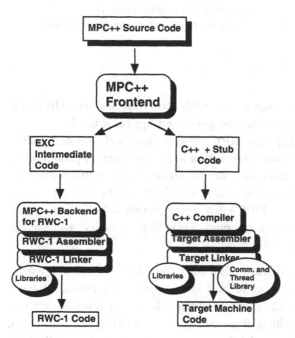

Figure 11.8
MPC++ Compiler

Function Name	Description
_mpcSelfPE()	get the processor number
_mpcNumPE()	get the number of processors
_mpcInitEntry()	initialize an entry variable
_mpcSelfAsyncInvoke()	invoke a function instance locally
_mpcRemoteAsyncInvoke()	invoke a function instance on a remote PE
_mpcWait()	wait a message at an entry
_mpcSendToToken()	send a message via an token
_mpcRemoteMemRead()	read data from remote memory
_mpcRemoteMemWrite()	write data to remote memory
_mpcThreadTerminate()	terminate the current executing thread

Table 11.2
Part of the MPC++ Runtime Library

is used to compile C++ source code with stub routines. For the workstation cluster implementation, the g++-based option is used.

We have been developing the MPC++ system on a cluster of SPARC-Station 20 workstations connected with a Myricom Myrinet [Boden *et al.* 1995]. An application program runs as processes distributed over the workstations. Each process contains several MPC++ function instances (threads). Therefore, the MPC++ runtime requires both fast thread invocation and a low-latency communication library, which we have implemented as follows:

Fast thread runtime library: Because the MPC++ thread execution model is non-preemptive and kernel-supported threads have a higher execution cost than user-level threads, a user-level library was implemented. Using the option -mflat of the GNU g++ compiler on the SPARC architecture, registers are loaded/stored without flushing the register window during context switch.

Small message header size: Since message headers represent overhead in the network implementation, we designed as small a header as possible. The header includes the message type, message size, sender, function address, and return continuation; the last of these identifies the PE, message type, message size, and ID. Because we assume that the number of processors involved in a program and the message size are both less than 1024, those values are represented as 10-bit integers. The function address and return continuation ID are both one word. Thus, the message header size is 4 words.

Fast communication library: The Myrinet communication board's processor handles a datalink-level communication protocol. We have been implementing driver software directly on the board. Unlike the Myrinet API provided by Myricom, routing is fixed, so that processing in the board processor is minimized.

The runtime system on each processor repeatedly performs the following procedures:

Communication: A communication primitive is used to check if a message has arrived. If a message has arrived, the message is extracted. If a message is for a function instance invocation, a thread is created and placed in the thread ready queue. Note that the runtime system may not be blocked during message receipt.

Local thread: If a ready thread exists in the ready queue, it is extracted and executed. Execution continues unless a message receive statement is encountered or the thread exits.

11.6 Basic Performance

We measured the runtime costs of MPC++ on a cluster of 75 MHz Sun SPARCStation 20 workstations running SunOS 4.1.4 (Figure 11.9). Table 11.3 compares MPC++ function instance invocation against the pthread library [Mueller 1993] and the SunOS LWP (Light-Weight Processes) library [Sun 1990]. The program measured is shown in Program 11.3. In the pthread and SunOS LWP libraries, we implemented the same semantics as the MPC++ program, including thread creation, context switch to the created thread, execution of pingpong in the created thread, thread termination, and context switch in the function instance invocation.

The round trip communication latency in our communication library is shown in Figure 11.10. A 4-byte round trip takes 37.4 μsec. In Figure 11.11, the local/remote function invocation cost, (i.e., the time from invoking a function instance in a remote host to receiving the return value), is measured by increasing the number of integer arguments. This

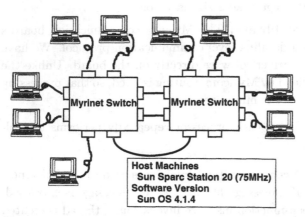

Figure 11.9
A Workstation Cluster

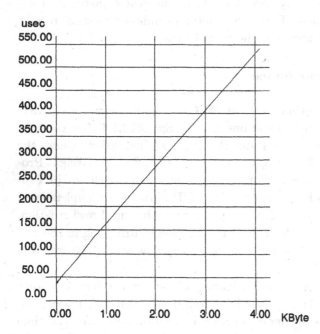

Figure 11.10
Round Trip Latency

System	Time (μsec)
MPC++	3.3
pthread	156.0
SunOS LWP	85.5

Table 11.3
Comparison of Ping-Pong Times

```
#define ITERATION 10000
#ifdef  LOCAL_PINGPONG
#define REMOTE
#else
#define REMOTE    2
int pingpong() { return 0; }
main()
{
  // start timer
  for (i=0; i<ITERATION; i++){
    pingpong() @ [REMOTE];
  }
  // end timer
}
```

Program 11.3
Ping-Pong Program

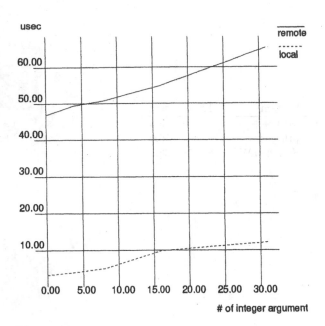

Figure 11.11
MPC++ Function Instance Invocation

processing involves thread creation on the remote PE. The cost of remote invocation with no arguments is 46.8 μsec.

11.7   Polygon Overlay

11.7.1   Implementation

Our approach to the polygon overlay problem is to use a straightforward partitioning of the input maps. The first map is partitioned into sub-maps and kept on the managing processor (PE 0), while the second map is broadcast to all processors at the beginning of the job. The sub-maps kept on PE 0 are delivered to processors on demand. Every processor performs the following procedures: take a sub-map from PE 0, find the overlay between the sub-map and the second map, and send the overlay back to PE 0. The first and last stages are implemented by invoking function instances.

The outline of our implementation is as follows:

```
struct poly { ... };
struct poly_vec { poly_vec *next; int count; poly v[50]; };

int get_region_no_from_pe0();
poly_vec take_poly_vec_from_pe0(int);
void append_poly_vec_on_pe0(poly_vec);

void overlay_and_collect()
{
  poly_vec *polyvec0, *polyvec1, *polyvecnew;

  for (;;) {
    int region = get_region_no_from_pe0()@[0];
    if ( region < 0 ) return;

    poly_vec dummy, *vec = &dummy;
    do {
      poly_vec *v = new poly_vec;
      *v = take_poly_vec_from_pe0(region)@[0];
      vec = vec->next = v;
    } while ( vec->next != 0 );
    polyvec1 = dummy->next;

    // sequential overlay calculation
    polyvecnew = overlay(polyvec0, polyvec1);

    for (poly_vec *v = polyvecnew; v; v = v->next)
      append_poly_vec_on_pe0(*v)@()[0];
  }
}
```

Program 11.4
Skeletal Code of Polygon Overlay

Partitioning: One of two maps is partitioned into a disjoint set of sub-maps $M_0 \ldots M_n$. The number of partitions is far larger than the number of processors in order to balance the divide-and-conquer algorithm. This step is performed sequentially on PE 0.

Broadcasting: The other map is simply broadcast to all processors. Let this map be called N.

Main Processing: The following steps are repeated by each processor until no more sub-maps are available on PE 0:

Taking a sub-map from PE 0: Each processor asks PE 0 for a submap, one at a time. If a sub-map is available, it receives one. If there are none, the processor is finished.

Filtering with a bounding box: For the given sub-map M_i, the processor calculates its bounding box and filters through map N with the bounding box. A rectangle in map N must intersect the bounding box to make an overlap.

Matching for overlaps: The processor works on the rectangles from the sub-map M_i and the ones which pass the bounding box filter, and makes a new map of overlapping rectangles. The matching of rectangles is done using the naïve sequential matching algorithm.

Collecting the created maps: The new map of overlapping polygons is sent back to PE 0, where it is appended to the result map. Finally, the processor frees temporary storage and then repeats these steps.

Using the k100 data set, whose maps consist of approximately 60,000 polygons, we partitioned the maps into 256 sub-maps. In order to maintain the geometric locality of the rectangles, we divided the whole area of the map into 16×16 subareas, and partitioned the rectangles according to their lower left corners.

The skeleton of the MPC++ code is shown in Program 11.4. Note that the rectangles in a map are communicated as a list of poly_vec structures, which are small sets of rectangles. The next field of poly_vec is a pointer, but since it is only used as an end of list mark (i.e., for a zero/non-zero check), this is legal.

Some minor tunings on sequential overlay calculation were applied before benchmarking, which include skipping overlap checks by using

Processors	Total cost	Broadcasting cost
1	3.55	0.10
2	2.66	0.23
3	2.11	0.34
4	1.70	0.34
5	1.64	0.47
6	1.55	0.47
7	1.47	0.47
8	1.44	0.47
9	1.50	0.60

Table 11.4
Polygon Overlay Performance (all times in seconds)

the fact that the rectangles in a map are sorted by their lower-left corner coordinates.

11.7.2 Performance

The polygon overlay program was benchmarked in our current MPC++ environment using the k100 data set. We tested two cases: (1) PE 0 is involved with main processing, in addition to servicing sub-map distribution, and (2) PE 0 just services sub-map distribution. The results are shown in Table 11.4 and Table 11.5. The total cost includes the initial map broadcasting and result collection, but not the time taken for file I/O on PE 0. The broadcasting cost shows the time taken to broadcast map N to all processors as part of the total time.

The results show that case one achieves good performance for up to three processors. However, case two achieves higher performance for four or more processors. The reason is that, in case one, PE 0 cannot respond to sub-map requests from others while the processor is performing the main processing. This increases idle time on the other processors.

Our results are also shown in Figure 11.12; the corresponding speedups are shown in Figure 11.13. The speedup figures include the cases in which the broadcasting cost is excluded.

The time taken to partition a map sequentially is around 0.15 sec in all cases. Since broadcasting is done through a tree of processors, the time taken increases as the logarithm of the number of processors.

As shown in Figure 11.13, reasonable scalability is achieved if we omit the broadcasting cost. In the total cost, however, lower speedup

Processors	Total cost	Broadcasting cost
2	3.86	0.21
3	2.27	0.34
4	1.70	0.35
5	1.54	0.47
6	1.39	0.47
7	1.29	0.47
8	1.24	0.47
9	1.35	0.60

Table 11.5
Polygon Overlay Performance (excluding PE 0 from calculation, all times in seconds)

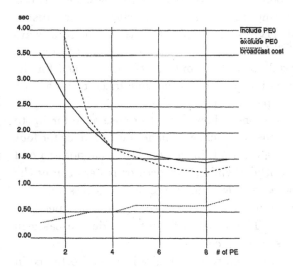

Figure 11.12
Polygon Overlay Result

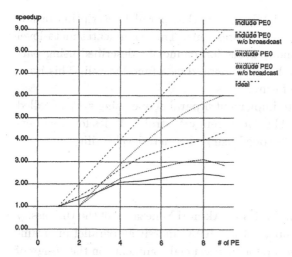

Figure 11.13
Polygon Overlay Speedup

is achieved because the cost of broadcasting map N to all processors
(which requires 960 kbyte of data to be transferred) is substantial. This
broadcast requires about 1000 function instance invocations, each with
about 960 bytes of arguments.

11.8   Concluding Remarks

We have shown an approach to constructing a high-performance computing environment by employing the notion of meta-level processing.
MPC++ defines a small set of parallel primitives that realize thread
invocation and message passing. Other parallel programming facilities,
such as global pointers, synchronization structures, and data-parallel
constructs are implemented in the meta-level facility. As examples,
we demonstrated implementations of **global pointer** and **mutex** statements.

The MPC++ meta-level capability is not needed for the polygon overlay programming example used in this book. Benchmark results show
that MPC++ function instance invocation, in the workstation cluster,
achieves reasonable cost for distributing computation, but not for broadcasting large amounts of data.

One current limitation of MPC++ is that parallel description primitives are statements instead of expressions. This complicates meta-level programming because a new expression cannot be described using parallel primitives, but must be implemented as a function call. This issue will be considered in the future.

MPC++ will be used to implement a parallel operating system called SCore [Hori *et al.* 1993]. The concurrency control facilities for the operating system kernel will be coded using the meta-level facility.

Acknowledgments

The authors wish to thank Professor Akinori Yonezawa, of the University of Tokyo, and other members of the RWC massively-parallel programming language working group for their crucial comments on the design of MPC++. The basic MPC++ parallel programming model is inspired by the RWC-1 massively parallel machine designed by Dr. Shuichi Sakai and his group at the RWC Tsukuba Research Center; the authors are grateful to the group, and to Francis O'Carroll and Toshiyuki Takahashi, who read the draft of this manuscript and gave us valuable comments. Finally, the authors wish to express their gratitude to Dr. Junichi Shimada, director of the RWC partnership.

This work is a part of the Real World Computing Program, a ten-year project that began in the autumn of 1992. The program is supported by Japan's Ministry of International Trade and Industry (MITI).

12 MPI++

Anthony Skjellum, Ziyang Lu,

Purushotham V. Bangalore, and Nathan Doss

As a de facto standard for multicomputers and networks of workstations, MPI is naturally of interest to C++ programmers who use such systems. MPI programming is currently done using the language bindings defined by the MPI Forum for C and Fortran-77 [MPI 1994]. While the MPI committee deferred the job of defining a C++ binding for MPI to MPI-2 [MPI2 1995], it is already possible to develop MPI-based programs in C++ using one of several support libraries [Bangalore *et al.* 1994, Coulaud & Dillon 1995, Hsieh & Sotelino 1994].

One such enabling system, MPI++, is the focus of this chapter. The system illustrates the value added by C++ to message-passing programming, and conversely the usefulness of MPI for parallel programming with C++. MPI++ is a performance-conscious way to exploit parallelism with C++ that does not require the development of a portable and mature compiler environment for distributed-memory environments. We have emphasized performance-portability—good performance and good portability at the same time. This emphasis constrained how eagerly we exploited certain features of C++ when creating our parallel environment on top of MPI.

12.1 MPI Overview

Message passing is a widely-used paradigm in parallel programming. During the development of massively parallel and cluster environments for parallel processing during the 1980s, there was neither real portability of codes nor an agreed upon notation for message-passing programs. Many portable libraries were developed to address these problems, such as P4 [Butler & Lusk 1992], Zipcode [Skjellum *et al.* 1994], Chameleon [Gropp & Smith 1993], PARMACS [Calkin *et al.* 1994], and PVM [Geist *et al.* 1993]. These systems differed in the kind, flexibility, semantics of, and quality of services they provided, depending on whether they emphasized tightly- or loosely-coupled machines. That meant that a standard could not be created merely by choosing one of the existing vendor-specific or portable systems available at that time.

However, by mid-1992 it was clearly time to define a standard for message-passing systems that would incorporate and improve upon the best features of existing systems and practice [Kennedy (ed.) 1992]. The result, MPI, was developed by a de facto working group called the MPI Forum, with input and participation from industry, national laboratories, and universities [MPI 1994]. The authors of the important pre-existing systems participated in defining the standard.

MPI provides many features that support writing portable, efficient, scalable parallel programs. Because of space limitations, the summary below foregoes many of the details of its syntax, semantics, and practical assumptions. Readers are referred to [Gropp *et al.* 1994], which is an accessible introduction to MPI, and to the formal standards document [MPI 1994], which is also available at:

    http://www.mcs.anl.gov/mpi/mpi-report/mpi-report.html

The source code of MPI++ is available from:

    http://www.erc.msstate.edu/mpi/mpi++/

along with our implementation of the polygon overlay example used in this chapter. MPICH, the model implementation of MPI developed by Argonne National Laboratory and Mississippi State University, is available by anonymous `ftp` from `info.mcs.anl.gov`. General information on MPI is available from:

    http://www.erc.msstate.edu/mpi/

There is also a newsgroup, `comp.parallel.mpi`, where all aspects of MPI are discussed.

In the sections below, we concentrate on some key concepts of MPI that are directly relevant to our design of MPI++, and to the scope of the parallel models achievable with it. In particular, we describe MPI's persistent objects, such as communicators and groups,, since these are clean, consistent, opaque objects that fit naturally into an object-oriented programming model. They further dictate that MPI implementations are all essentially object-based in many respects, which both simplifies and adds complexities to MPI++.

12.1.1 Summary of MPI Features

MPI supports both point-to-point and collective message passing among communicating sequential processes. The MPI standard defines the semantics of MPI, as well as C and Fortran-77 bindings. The following classes of operations are supported:

- Point-to-point transmission in various modes (blocking, non-blocking, synchronous, buffered, and combinations thereof).

- Collective communication between processes specified by groups (barrier, reductions, broadcasts, gathers, scatters, and scans).

- Constructors for formulating communication structures (defining subgroups, building new communicators, and duplicating existing communicators).

- Mechanisms for single group (data-parallel) and dual-group (dataflow or bipartite) communication structures.

- Virtual topologies that allow processes to be named and manipulated in schemes suited to application use.

In particular, the following major concepts are defined by MPI:

group: An ordered collection of processes. All communication has a group scope. Groups are mainly used within communicators.

rank: The name of a process relative to a group. Each process in a group has a unique rank, which is an integer in the range $0 \ldots N - 1$ for N processes. The most fundamental names of processes in MPI are ranks in the MPI_COMM_WORLD group.

context: An abstract mechanism by which processes in a group separate their communication from other communication in the system. Constructors for communication provide this context information in communicator structures.

communicator: The opaque object used to select the group and the context of communication. Communicators are used for both point-to-point communication (where group ranks become the names of senders and receivers), and collective communication (where group membership defines who participates). Intra-communicators work on a single group; inter-communicators work between two groups. In MPI-1, inter-communicators have no-data oriented collective operations and a limited set of constructors. MPI-2 will support additional functionality.

data type: An opaque object that describes the kind of information being transferred (such as integers). Predefined and user-defined data types allow MPI to encapsulate heterogeneous conversions without user intervention, while providing a higher-level interface for gathering and scattering non-contiguous data.

request object: Initiation of a non-blocking operation (such as non-blocking send or receive) gives the initiator an opaque handle for later inquiry about that operation. At completion of an operation (or in event of an error), such a request object can be transformed into a status object, which gives the user further information about the completed operation.

status object: A non-opaque object whose fields can be accessed to determine what happened when an MPI operation completed. One common use for status objects is in non-blocking operations.

Table 12.1 lists a usable subset of MPI calls. A total of 129 calls are provided by the standard, but most applications utilize only a few of these.

MPI provides an initial communicator called `MPI_COMM_WORLD` that contains all processes. MPI-2 [MPI2 1995] will extend this to support expandable "worlds". Using the constructors provided, programmers can create new communicators by splitting or merging existing communicators to form new communication spaces.

Finally, MPI defines a rule concerning progress requirements for all implementations. While this is a point of contention with implementors, it sets MPI apart from other systems in terms of the higher portability of MPI programs between diverse platforms.

12.1.2   Parallel Models Supported

Several computational models are supported by MPI, and hence by MPI++. These include the following:

data parallelism: Each MPI communicator supports collective, group-oriented, as well as unstructured, communication among group members. The data-parallel model is the simplest way to program using MPI. As noted in Figure 12.1, lexical scoping of messages for nested

Extremely basic subset:	
MPI_INIT	Initialize MPI
MPI_COMM_SIZE	Find out how many processes there are
MPI_COMM_RANK	Find out which process rank I am
MPI_SEND	Send a message (blocking)
MPI_RECV	Receive a message (blocking)
MPI_FINALIZE	Terminate MPI
Non-blocking, point-to-point and related:	
MPI_ISEND	Send a message (non-blocking)
MPI_IRECV	Receive a message (non-blocking)
MPI_WAIT	Wait on pending message
MPI_GETCOUNT	Get size of received message
Group-scoped collective communication:	
MPI_BCAST	One-to-all broadcast
MPI_REDUCE	All-to-one reduction operation
MPI_ALLREDUCE	All-to-all reduction operation
Communicator constructors/destructor:	
MPI_COMM_SPLIT	Make K new communicators from one
MPI_COMM_DUP	Duplicate a communicator
MPI_COMM_FREE	Delete a communicator
Some data-motion operations:	
MPI_GATHER	Gather data into one process
MPI_SCATTER	Scatter data across processes
Support for timing:	
MPI_WTIME	Timing routine (relative time)
MPI_WTICK	Timing routine (clock tick size)

Table 12.1
A Usable Subset of MPI Functions

parallel calls[1] is supported, principally via MPI_COMM_DUP. When data parallelism is used in concert with the task-parallel model mentioned next, a hierarchy of nested parallel computations can be achieved.

task parallelism: Using MPI_COMM_SPLIT, communicators can be split into K disjoint new communicators with a single call (where K is at most the number of processes in the original communicator). Successive calls to this function can be used to create hierarchical and/or overlapping communication spaces. Figure 12.2 demonstrates a simple instance of task parallel programming, based on splitting processes into disjoint groups, followed by independent computation, and concluded by communication and/or computation by the entire group.

medium-grain dataflow: Inter-communicators can be constructed to support full-duplex communication *between* two process groups. These can then support dataflow computations, as well as symmetric communication between two parallel groups (e.g., parallel client-server communication). Figure 12.3 shows a simple two-group dataflow computation, similar to the task-parallel computation of Figure 12.2, but incorporating inter-group communication and a dependency of one group ($G2$) on the computation of the other ($G1$).

While each of these models is individually straightforward, MPI does not limit their combination. This enables the construction of complex applications. Furthermore, because communicators provide safe communication spaces, decisions made about sending messages within one computation do not affect the correctness of other parts of an application, MPI++ inherits these desirable features from MPI.

One noteworthy limitation of MPI, to be relaxed in MPI-2, is the requirement that all processes be created at the outset of the computation. Relaxing this requirement will lead to multiple worlds. These will be connected by inter-communicators and/or intra-communicators, depending on the way new processes join the computation, and on the design choices made by the application programmer.

12.1.3 MPI++ Origins and Overview

As stated earlier, the official C++ language binding for MPI was deferred to MPI-2. However, we felt that programmers working on real

---

[1] A "parallel call" means that the same function is called in a set of processes, with loose synchronization.

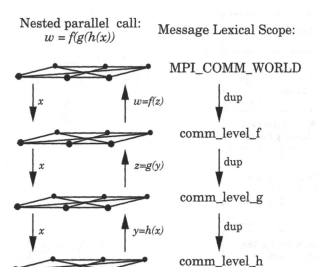

Nested parallel call:
$$w = f(g(h(x)))$$

Message Lexical Scope:

MPI_COMM_WORLD

x $w=f(z)$ dup

comm_level_f

x $z=g(y)$ dup

comm_level_g

x $y=h(x)$ dup

comm_level_h

Figure 12.1
Data-Parallel Programming Using Lexical Scoping of Messages

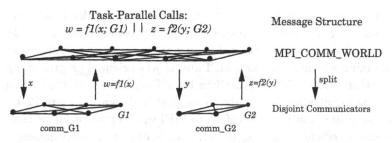

Task-Parallel Calls:
$$w = f1(x; G1) \ | \ | \ z = f2(y; G2)$$

Message Structure

MPI_COMM_WORLD

x $w=f1(x)$ y $z=f2(y)$ split

$G1$ $G2$ Disjoint Communicators

comm_G1   comm_G2

Figure 12.2
Task-Parallel Programming Using Multiple Communicators

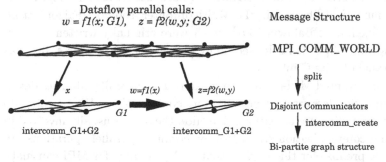

Dataflow parallel calls:
$$w = f1(x; G1), \quad z = f2(w,y; G2)$$

Message Structure

MPI_COMM_WORLD

split

x $w=f1(x)$ $z=f2(w,y)$ Disjoint Communicators

$G1$ $G2$ intercomm_create

intercomm_G1+G2   intercomm_G1+G2   Bi-partite graph structure

Figure 12.3
Dataflow Programming Using Inter-Communicators

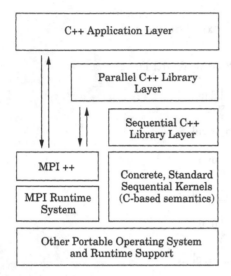

Figure 12.4
MPI++ Parallel Application Architecture

applications are generally willing to accept modest tradeoffs of peak performance for worthwhile software engineering benefits, and so would be interested in an object-oriented interface for message passing. The idea of taking advantage of both MPI and object-oriented programming led us to start work on MPI++ early in 1994 [Bangalore *et al.* 1994]. The application architecture we sought to support is shown in Figure 12.4.

Another goal of our C++ interface to MPI was to provide an extensible, portable, efficient, heterogeneous-capable object-oriented message-passing library that could be used to build scalable, object-oriented numerical libraries. Our motivation was a desire to convert the existing numerical libraries in the Multicomputer Toolbox [Falgout *et al.* 1992, Skjellum & Baldwin 1991] which were originally written in C using Zipcode. Zipcode itself used many object-oriented features, but was constrained by its C interface.

We also wanted MPI++ to help make to make parallel libraries development easier, less error prone, and more commonplace. We expect to do this by providing useful features that hide the details usually involved in building communication structures for common parallel operations. In fact, the premise for this work is that a class library for MPI can make an high performance and portable, parallel C++ environment, without specific compiler support for such parallelism. This can be shown constructively, as applications with and without specific compiler support are compared for performance and portability, over time.

MPI++ has evolved since we started work on it in 1994. It will continue to evolve as sequential C++ compilers become more mature (e.g., provide better support for templates). Furthermore, MPI itself is still expanding: work on defining MPI-2 is meant to continue at least to the end of 1996.

12.2   Design and Implementation of MPI++

The requirements that have guided our design and implementation in this project are:

- The MPI++ interface should be consistent with the MPI C interface.

- Performance-portability should be comparable to that of the C interface. That is, MPI++ features should be light-weight whenever the corresponding C functions are light-weight.

- MPI++ should exhibit a clean design that is prototypical of well-written object-orient programs.

The following subsections consider each of these requirements in turn, discussing the rationale behind them, and their influence on our design decisions.

12.2.1   The MPI++ Interface

Because of the standardization process, MPI's language-independent semantics are not subject to rapid change. It is thus attractive (as well as prudent) to follow the MPI standard carefully when we design and implement a C++ interface for it, even though this is not an official language binding. Moreover, since MPI has a C language binding, of which many potential users of MPI++ already have a working knowledge. Ideally, it should take little effort for such users to migrate from the C interface to MPI++. These considerations strongly suggest that the MPI++ interface be both syntactically and semantically consistent with the C interface. Semantic consistency requires that the counterparts in the two interfaces must perform the same function without unexpected side effects, including effects on performance. This prevents erroneous uses or unexpected performance penalties when one switches from one interface to the other.

The relationship between the standard C interface and the MPI++ interface is illustrated below with examples.

Example: SPMD "Hello, there" Program 12.1 shows the C version of an SPMD program adapted from the MPI document [MPI 1994]. As this program illustrates, every MPI program must initialize the MPI environment by calling `MPI_Init` before calling any other MPI functions.[2] A call `MPI_Finalize` is made at the end of the program to clean up the MPI environment. `MPI_Comm_size` is used to determine the number of processes in the communicator. `MPI_Comm_rank` is used to determine the position, or rank, of the calling process in the communicator. The process with rank zero sends a message to the highest-numbered process; all other processes simply terminate.

The MPI++ version of this program is given in Program 12.2 The first thing to note is that the statement `#include <mpi.h>` has been replaced by `#include <mpi++.h>`. Another change to notice is that the prefix `MPI_` has been changed to `MPIX_`. A prefix other than `MPI_` was needed in order to avoid name conflicts, since MPI++ was implemented on top of the C interface. (Through the use of the C preprocessor, we provide shortcuts that allow the use of the `MPI_` prefix. However, we prefer to use the `MPIX_` prefix because MPI++ is not a standard interface of MPI, and only standard bindings may use the `MPI_` prefix.)

The biggest difference between the two versions is that the communicator `MPIX_COMM_WORLD` is an object with methods in the C++ version. For example, the function calls in the C version:

```
MPI_Comm_rank(MPI_COMM_WORLD, &rank);
MPI_Comm_size(MPI_COMM_WORLD, &size);
```

appear in the MPI++ version as methods `MPIX_COMM_WORLD`:

```
MPIX_COMM_WORLD.Rank(&rank);
MPIX_COMM_WORLD.Size(&size);
```

Likewise, the send and receive calls that, in the C code, take the communicator `MPI_COMM_WORLD` as an argument:

---

[2]This code shows that the C and C++ language bindings must choose a capitalization convention. The language-neutral form of MPI puts all names in all upper case.

```
#include <mpi.h>
#define MAX_MESSAGE_SIZE  20
#define MESSAGE_TAG       99
main(int argc, char **argv)
{
  char        message[MAX_MESSAGE_SIZE];
  int         rank;
  MPI_Status status;

  MPI_Init (&argc, &argv);
  MPI_Comm_rank(MPI_COMM_WORLD, &rank);
  MPI_Comm_size(MPI_COMM_WORLD, &size);
  if (rank == 0) {
    strcpy(message, "Hello, there");
    MPI_Send(message, strlen(message)+1, MPI_CHAR, size-1,
             MESSAGE_TAG, MPI_COMM_WORLD);
  } else if (rank == (size-1)){
    MPI_Recv(message, MAX_MESSAGE_SIZE, MPI_CHAR, 0,
             MESSAGE_TAG, MPI_COMM_WORLD, &status);
    printf("received :%s:\n", message);
  }
  MPI_Finalize();
}
```

Program 12.1
MPI (C) version of a Simple Messaging Code

```
MPI_Send(message, strlen(message)+1, MPI_CHAR, size-1,
         MESSAGE_TAG, MPI_COMM_WORLD);
MPI_Recv(message, MAX_MESSAGE_SIZE, MPI_CHAR, 0,
         MESSAGE_TAG, MPI_COMM_WORLD, &status);
```

are also methods of MPIX_COMM_WORLD:

```
MPIX_COMM_WORLD.Send(message, strlen(message)+1,
                     MPIX_CHAR, size-1, MESSAGE_TAG);
MPIX_COMM_WORLD.Recv(message, MAX_MESSAGE_SIZE, MPIX_CHAR, 0,
                     MESSAGE_TAG, &status);
```

The other arguments remain the same. The two "book end" calls in the
C version:

```
MPI_Init(&argc, &argv);
MPI_Finalize();
```

```
#include <mpi++.h>
const int MAX_MESSAGE_SIZE = 20;
const int MESSAGE_TAG      = 99;
main(int argc, char **argv)
{
  char        message[MAX_MESSAGE_SIZE];
  int         rank;
  MPIX_Status status;

  MPIX_COMM_WORLD.Init(&argc, &argv);
  MPIX_COMM_WORLD.Rank(&rank);
  MPIX_COMM_WORLD.Size(&size);
  if (rank == 0){
    strcpy(message, "Hello, there");
    MPIX_COMM_WORLD.Send(message, strlen(message)+1, MPIX_CHAR,
                         size-1, MESSAGE_TAG);
  } else if (rank == (size-1)){
    MPIX_COMM_WORLD.Recv(message, MAX_MESSAGE_SIZE, MPIX_CHAR,
                         0, MESSAGE_TAG, &status);
    cout << "received" << message << endl;
  }
  MPIX_COMM_WORLD.Finalize();
}
```

Program 12.2
MPI++ Version of a Simple Messaging Code

are replaced by the corresponding methods MPIX_COMM_WORLD:

```
MPIX_COMM_WORLD.Init(&argc, &argv);
MPIX_COMM_WORLD.Finalize();
```

Most MPI functions are available as methods of a class in MPI++.
MPIX_COMM_WORLD is an instance of the MPIX_Comm_world class, whose
methods include many of the MPI functions that take a communicator
as an argument in C. One way to describe the relationship between the
C binding and MPI++ is to say that we have moved the communicator
argument to the front of the function call, making it the object to be
dereferenced. This has let us drop the prefix "MPI_" or "MPI_Comm"
from member function names. The class hierarchy described in the next
subsection, as well as the examples in Section 12.3, show the value and
power of this approach.

The above sample program also shows the choices we made to keep a consistent interface. For example, while it is usual to pass arguments by reference in C++, we decided to keep the C calling conventions, and to pass arguments by address.

```
MPIX_COMM_WORLD.Rank(rank);    // assumes reference semantics
MPIX_COMM_WORLD.Rank(&rank);   // pointer semantics
```

We made this choice in order to keep MPI++ as similar as possible to the C binding; this choice is discussed further in Section 12.5.

As another example, the code Program 12.3 shows how to partition communication into separate communicating groups.

12.2.2 Object-Oriented Design of MPI++

As discussed in Section 12.1, the MPI specification is object-based. It is therefore relatively easy to identify the major classes for MPI++. In general, class hierarchies can be either single-rooted or forests [Weinand et al. 1989]. Either approach could have been used in the design of MPI++. However, there are trade-offs between them. The single-rooted approach, in which all objects are ultimately derived from an abstract superclass, results in a more uniform and sophisticated system. Because the single-rooted approach requires further refinement of common properties of the classes, and introduces a fundamental connection between all classes, we wanted to be sure that this abstraction was correct, and justifiable. Hence, we decided that this style of design would be most suited for a second phase of object-oriented design, once we had greater experience with and comfort with the initial design. We were also convinced that, at this second stage, we might choose also to make a further departure from the C interface. On the other hand, the forest approach, in which a number of superclasses support the user-accessible objects, fits the MPI specification naturally. We believed that using it would result in a system that was more likely to be consistent with the C interface, and also initially easier to build.

The Communicator-based Classes The classes based on communicators are the backbone of the MPI++ architecture. Their hierarchy is illustrated in Figure 12.5. The base class MPIX_Comm contains all the functions common to both intra- and inter-communicators, such as point-to-point communication and accessor functions. Its interface is sketched out in Program 12.4.

```
#include <mpi++.h>
main(int argc, char **argv)
{
  char        message[MAX_MESSAGE_SIZE];
  int         rank;
  MPI_Status  status;
  MPI_Group   group;

  MPIX_COMM_WORLD.Init(&argc, &argv); // Collective
  MPIX_COMM_WORLD.Rank(&rank);        // Local
  MPIX_COMM_WORLD.Group(&group);      // Local

  // world1 and world2 are duplicates of MPI_COMM_WORLD:
  MPIX_Comm_intra world1(MPIX_COMM_WORLD);
  MPIX_Comm_intra world2;  MPIX_COMM_WORLD.Dup(&world2);

  // split_world1 and split_world2 will each contain 1 process
  // after the calls below:
  MPIX_Comm_intra split_world1(MPIX_COMM_WORLD, rank, 0);
  MPIX_Comm_intra split_world2;
  MPIX_COMM_WORLD.Split(rank,0,&split_world2);

  // group_world1 and group_world2 will be copies
  // of MPI_COMM_WORLD after these calls:
  MPIX_Comm_intra group_world1(MPIX_COMM_WORLD, group);
  MPIX_Comm_intra group_world2;
  MPIX_COMM_WORLD.Create(group,&group_world2);

  // End of the program
  MPIX_COMM_WORLD.Finalize();
}
```

Program 12.3
A Simple MPI++ Program Creating New Communicators

```
// Declarations
class MPIX_Comm {
 public:
  MPIX_Comm();                                // Constructor
  virtual ~MPIX_Comm();                       // Destructor
  virtual int Free();                         // Free
  virtual int Dup(MPIX_Comm*);                // Initializer
  // Environment
  virtual int Abort(int);
  virtual int Errhandler_set(MPI_Errhandler&);
  virtual int Errhandler_get(MPI_Errhandler*);
  // Accessors
  virtual int Size(int *);
  virtual int Rank(int *);
  ...
  // Sends
  virtual int Send(void *,int,MPI_Datatype,int,int tag=0);
  ...
  // Receives
  virtual int Recv(void*,int,MPI_Datatype,int,int,MPIX_Status*);
  ...
  // Pack and Unpack operations
  virtual int Pack(void*, int, MPI_Datatype, void *, int, int*);
  virtual int Unpack(void*, int, int*, void*,int, MPI_Datatype);
  ...
  // Overloaded operators (= does copying, not parallel duplication)
  virtual MPIX_Comm& operator=(const MPIX_Comm& old_comm);
  virtual int operator==(const MPIX_Comm&);
  virtual int operator!=(const MPIX_Comm&);
 private:
  ...
}
extern MPIX_Comm          MPIX_COMM_NULL;
extern MPIX_Comm_world    MPIX_COMM_WORLD;
```

Program 12.4
Interface of the MPIX_Comm Class

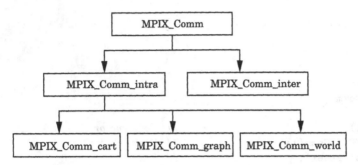

Figure 12.5
Hierarchy of Communicator-Based Classes

The `MPIX_Comm_intra` (intra-communicators) class, which is derived from `MPIX_Comm`, contains collective communication functions, topology functions, and miscellaneous functions that do not apply to inter-communicators. A sketch of its interface is given in Program 12.5.

The `MPIX_Comm_inter` (inter-communicators) class is also derived from the `MPIX_Comm` class. It contains only those functions peculiar to itself. Program 12.6 gives a sketch of its interface.

While most of these methods are straightforward to use, users must note several points. First, the destructor for the `MPIX_Comm` class does not free the communication resources associated with the communicator. All instances of `MPIX_Comm` must therefore be freed explicitly, as in C, using `MPIX_Comm::Free()`.[3]

Second, users must distinguish between using the overloaded "=" operator for communicators and instantiation via the communicator's copy constructor. For example, during copy construction, a call made by all processes of the group is illustrated. This call causes a deep copy of the communicator to occur, which involves synchronization across the processes that made the call:

```
// communicator instantiation calls
// MPIX_Comm_intra::MPIX_Comm_intra(const MPIX_Comm&)
MPIX_Comm_intra c1 = comm1; // parallel call, deep copy occurs
```

---

[3]We have thus retained the semantics of the C binding. This notionally follows the restrictive approach we applied when defining **operator=** as a shallow copy: we have chosen not to introduce implicit synchronization across process groups, except when communicators are copied.

```
class MPIX_Comm_intra : public MPIX_Comm {
public:
  // Constructors
  MPIX_Comm_intra(void);
  MPIX_Comm_intra(const MPIX_Comm_intra&);
  MPIX_Comm_intra(const MPIX_Comm_intra&, const MPIX_Group&);
  MPIX_Comm_intra(MPIX_Comm_intra&, int, int);
  // Initializers
  virtual int Create(const MPIX_Group&, MPIX_Comm_intra*);
  virtual int Split(int, int, MPIX_Comm_intra *);
  // Collective operations
  virtual int Barrier(void);
  ...
  // Topology functions
  virtual int Cart_create(int, int dims[], int periods[], int,
                          MPIX_Comm_intra*);
  ...
};
```

Program 12.5
Interface of the MPIX_Comm_intra Class

```
class MPIX_Comm_inter : public MPIX_Comm {
 public:
  // Constructors
  MPIX_Comm_inter(void);
  MPIX_Comm_inter(const MPIX_Comm_inter&);
  // Accessors
  virtual int Remote_size(int*);
  virtual int Remote_group(MPIX_Group*);
  // Intra-communicator constructor
  virtual int Merge(int, MPIX_Comm_intra*);
};
```

Program 12.6
Interface of the MPIX_Comm_inter Class

By way of contrast, `operator=` is a local call: when pre-existing objects are assigned to, no parallel operations are done. We note that this is a shallow copy of the communicator.

```
// overloaded MPI_Comm::operator=(const MPI_Comm&) which
// does not create a duplicate of comm1
MPIX_Comm_intra c2; // initialized to be MPI_COMM_NULL
c2 = comm1;          // local call
```

In short, setting one `MPIX_Comm_intra` instance equal to another does not create a new communicator. Thus, only one of the two communicator instances above should call `MPIX_Comm_intra::Free()`. The user must decide how to manage this freeing operation themselves.[4] This follows the logic that C operators, extended to C++ objects, should not have unexpected side effects. In practice, the above property can be avoided by using techniques such as reference counting [Coplien 1992], but the real issue is the potential for deadlock. If `operator=` required loosely-synchronous invocation over the entire group involved in the communication, subtle bugs involving synchronization could arise from seemingly local operations.

Figure 12.5 shows three subclasses that are derived from `MPIX_Comm_intra`: `MPIX_Comm_world`, `MPIX_Comm_cart`, and `MPIX_Comm_graph`. The first of these is special, in that there is exactly one instance of it in any MPI program. This instance is called `MPI_COMM_WORLD`. To prevent users from creating additional instances of this class, `MPIX_Comm_world` is designed and implemented as a singleton [Gamma *et al.* 1995]. This class adds two methods to `MPIX_Comm_intra`, which are used to manipulate the MPI environment:

```
int Init(int *argc, char*** argv)
int Finalize()
```

The other two subclasses derived from `MPIX_Comm_intra` provide support for virtual topologies. A virtual topology is a machine-independent naming abstraction used to describe communication operations. in terms that are natural to an application. `MPIX_Comm_cart` supports Cartesian topologies, i.e., topologies based on rectangular coordinates. `MPIX_Comm_graph` supports general graph topologies, in which processes are nodes of an arbitrary graph.

---

[4] The next release of MPI++ will use reference counting to simplify this issue for users.

The Group Class   Program 12.7 sketches the interface of the MPIX-Group class, most of whose are straightforward. MPIX_Group objects are not explicitly used in communication; their only use in MPI is for describing group members when building new communicators using MPIX_Comm::Create(). They are therefore not as important as the communicator classes in most MPI++ programs. However, we expect them to be more important in MPI-2, which will have a dynamic process model using groups as well as communicators.

The Data Type Class   In addition to the basic data types such as int, float, and char, MPI provides functions for building derived data types, including vector, indexed, and structured types. New data types are built recursively from previously-defined data types. Figure 12.6 shows the hierarchy of data type classes for MPI++.

As can be seen, the data types used in the MPI C binding fit into the object-oriented programming model without further abstraction. In our current implementation, we have chosen not to make C++ wrappers for them.

The Handler Classes   The four remaining classes in the MPI++ class hierarchy are used during non-blocking communications. They are MPIX_Request, MPIX_Status, MPIX_Request_collection, and MPIX-Status_collection. Their methods correspond to the appropriate MPI C functions that act on them. For example, the C function:

```
MPI_Wait(MPI_Request *request, MPI_Status *status);
```

becomes:

```
MPIX_Request request;
request.Wait(MPIX_Status *status)
```

Program 12.8 shows a sketch of the interface for MPIX_Request; the interface for MPIX_Status is illustrated in Program 12.9. The interfaces for MPIX_Request_collection and MPIX_Status_collection are similar. The methods for MPIX_Request_collection correspond to MPI C functions that apply to an array of type MPI_Request.

Comments on Design   From the above discussion, one can see that MPI++ offers most of the major functionality of MPI's C interface. The

```
class MPIX_Group {
public:
  // Constructor
  MPIX_Group(void);                          // create an empty group
  MPIX_Group(const MPIX_Group& old_group);   // copy a group
  virtual ~MPIX_Group(void);                 // Destructor
  virtual int Free(void);                    // Free a group
  virtual MPIX_Group& operator= (const MPIX_Group&);
  // Group accessors
  virtual int Size(int *);
  ...
  // Group manipulation
  virtual int Union(const MPIX_Group&, MPIX_Group*);
  ...
  // Overloaded set operators
  virtual MPIX_Group operator- (const MPIX_Group&);
  virtual MPIX_Group operator+ (const MPIX_Group&);
  ...
  // Overloaded self-modifying operators
  virtual MPIX_Group& operator-= (const MPIX_Group&);
  virtual MPIX_Group& operator+= (const MPIX_Group&);
  ...
  // Shift members off the ends of a group
  virtual MPIX_Group          operator<< (const int);
  virtual inline MPIX_Group   operator>> (const int);
  ...
  // Compare the members of groups
  virtual int operator== (const MPIX_Group&);
  virtual int operator!= (const MPIX_Group&);
private:
  MPI_Group group;
  ...
};
extern MPIX_Group MPIX_GROUP_EMPTY;
extern MPIX_Group MPIX_GROUP_NULL;
```

Program 12.7
Interface of the MPIX_Group Class

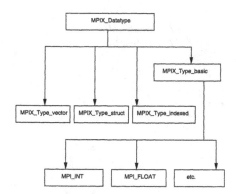

Figure 12.6
Hierarchy of Data Type-Based Classes

```
class MPIX_Request {
public:
  // Constructor
  MPIX_Request();
  // Destructor
  virtual ~MPIX_Request();
  // Request destructor
  virtual int Free();
  // Request operations
  virtual int Wait(MPIX_Status *);
  virtual int Test(int*, MPIX_Status*);
  ...
  // Overloaded operations
  MPIX_Request& operator=(const MPIX_Request&)
private:
  MPI_Request request;
  ...
};
```

Program 12.8
Interface of the MPIX_Request Class

```
class MPIX_Status {
 public:
  MPIX_Status();                    // Constructor
  virtual ~MPIX_Status();           // Destructor
  // Status accessors
  virtual int MPI_TAG();
  virtual int MPI_SOURCE();
  virtual int Test_cancelled(int *);
  ...
 private:
  MPI_Status status;
  ...
};
```

Program 12.9
Interface of the MPIX_Status Class

features currently missing, such as profiling and environmental inquiry functions, are mostly of an auxiliary nature, and could be added easily.

MPI++ employs several standard object-oriented concepts. First, it uses inheritance (white box re-use). In particular, the communicator-based class hierarchy gives flexibility to, and promotes re-usability and extensibility in, the design of parallel libraries. For example, if a particular application requires a two-dimensional Cartesian topology of dimension $P \times Q$, then the user can create one with minimal effort using inheritance and customize. A sample interface might look like:

```
class MPIX_Grid2d : public MPIX_Comm_intra {
public:
  MPIX_Comm_intra Row, Column;      // Row/col communicators
  MPIX_Grid2d(void);                // Constructor
  ~MPIX_Grid2d(void);               // Destructor
  int Free(void);                   // Free grid
  int Dup(MPIX_Grid& grid_out);     // Duplicate grid
  // Initialize grid
  int Init(MPIX_Comm_intra& comm_in, int P, int Q);
  // Overloaded point-to-point operations
  int Send(void*, int, MPIX_Datatype, int P, int Q, int tag);
  int Recv(void*, int, MPIX_Datatype, int P, int Q, int tag,
           MPIX_Status&);
  ...
  // Overloaded collective operations
```

```
    int Bcast(void*, int, MPIX_Datatype, int P, int Q);
    int Reduce(void*, void*, int, MPIX_Datatype, MPI_Op,
              int P, int Q);
    ...
    // Grid accessors
    int P(void);
    int Q(void);
    int p(void);
    int q(void);
  private:
    int P_, Q_; // dimensions of grid
    int p_, q_; // local process's position in grid
};
```

The row communicator would contain all the processes in the same logical row of the grid, and would be used for communication local to the row. The column communicator would contain the processes sharing in the same logical column, and would be used analogously. Point-to-point functionality is overloaded to accept grid-specific process names, such as coordinate (5,3), instead of process ranks. Such functionality had to be hard-wired into our previous system, Zipcode. This is because our design takes advantage of the underlying object-based design of MPI. The resulting MPI++ design, looked at as a class hierarchy, is thus relatively shallow and wide in terms of the C++ objects, and little overhead is consequently introduced. Polymorphism is a third key feature of object-oriented design. Methods in MPI++ classes are declared **virtual** in conformance with the Inheritance Canonical Form, in order to support re-use by users of the classes. Thus, MPI++ was designed for simple inheritance by users, though the implementation of MPI++ itself does not currently support virtual inheritance. We expect, in future, to exploit inheritance within the implementation to support a better design for MPI data types.

Finally, MPI++ uses operator overloading and default arguments to provide simpler and more intuitive member functions. For example, MPI++ overloads the - operator to have the same effect as the MPIX_Group::Difference member function. Other examples include the | and & operators for MPI_Group::Union and MPIX_Group::Intersection respectively, and the use of << and >> to shift a specified number of group members off the front or end of a group.

Furthermore, the `tag` argument in communication calls is usually an optional argument, which MPI++ sets to 0 by default. This simplifies programs that do not use tags, as the following extract from the example in Section 12.2.1 shows:

```
if (rank == 0){
  strcpy(message, "Hello, there");
  // this form of send omits a tag, and is supported by overloading
  MPIX_COMM_WORLD.Send(message, strlen(message)+1, MPI_CHAR,
                       size-1);
} else if (rank == (size-1)){
  // this form of receive omits a tag, and is supported by overloading
  MPIX_COMM_WORLD.Recv(message, MAX_MESSAGE_SIZE, MPI_CHAR,
                       0, &status);
  cout << "received" << message << endl;
}
```

12.2.3   Implementation Issues

Because the implementation of MPI++ builds on the C interface, and because we have maintained a close link between the semantics of MPI and MPI++, the overhead of MPI++ is small. Specifically, the use of inline member functions ensures that MPI++ uses no more function calls than its underlying MPI implementation, except in rare instances. This strategy assumes use of a modern C++ compiler, capable of inlining such calls.

If one is using MPI++ with MPICH (a reference implementation of standard MPI) the MPI++ library and header files should be installed in the same locations as their MPI equivalents. Compilation will then be done using:

```
CC -I/usr/local/mpi/include -c prog.C
CC -o prog  prog.o -L/usr/local/mpi/lib -lmpi++ -lmpi
```

At the time of this writing, MPI++ has been tested using the GNU C++ compiler g++, the SunSPARCworks CC, and IBM's xlC. The resulting MPI++ executables have been tested on Sun workstations and the IBM SP-2. Since MPI++ uses standard C++, it is expected that it will work on other platforms too.

12.3   Example: Polygon Overlay

In this section, we use the polygon overlay problem to illustrate more features of MPI++. In particular, we shall show how encapsulation and inheritance help to manage complexity.

12.3.1   Solution #1

This solution uses a master-slave model [MPI 1994]. The master process reads in the polygons from the first map and distributes them evenly to all the slave processes. Polygons from the second map are then read in one by one, and broadcast one to each of the slaves. The intersection of each polygon from the second map with each polygon in the first map is computed in parallel. The results are sent back to the master process, and written to a file.

Programs 12.10 and 12.11 shows a C-like version of this approach using MPI++. As one can see, as problems get more complicated, the if-else structure used in Program 12.2 becomes harder to construct and read.

The next version, shown in Program 12.12, uses classes to manage processes. Conceptually, all the processes are similar. Each process has a set-up phase, a work phase, and a completion phase. Their differences are encapsulated in separate methods; virtual constructors [Coplien 1992] are used to create appropriate instance of each process. The header file for this example is shown in Programs 12.13 and 12.14.

For a simple problem such as polygon overlay, this auxiliary class structure may not seem to gain us much. However, it does make the application more manageable and maintainable, and abstracts common behavior using inheritance. When dealing with more complicated applications, this approach is an important tool for making the parallel program manageable and readable.

12.3.2   Solution #2

The previous solution used only MPI_COMM_WORLD (the default communicator). This is acceptable for simple codes, but in more complex systems, where only part of the code is defined by any single programmer, it is usually not a good idea. Programmers should exploit the safety afforded by MPI by isolating messages in each layer of the code. It is also a good

```
#include "mpi++.h"
#include <iostream.h>
const int COORD = 4;
main(int argc, char **argv)
{
  MPI_COMM_WORLD.Init(&argc,&argv);
  int rank,size;
  MPI_COMM_WORLD.Rank(&rank);
  MPI_COMM_WORLD.Size(&size);
  // The master process
  if (rank == 0){
    // Open files, read #polygons in first map, allocate memory, etc.
    ...
    // Broadcast #polygons in first map
    MPI_COMM_WORLD.Bcast(&count, 1, MPI_INT, 0);
    // Declarations for non-blocking send
    MPI_Request_collection request(size-1);
    MPIX_Status_collection status_coll(size-1);
    // read polygons & send each processor its share
    ...
    MPI_COMM_WORLD.Isend(vect, its_share*COORD, MPI_INT, i,
                         &request[i-1]);
    // Close first map file & wait for completion of sends
    ...
    request.Waitall(&status_coll);
    // Broadcast polygons from second map one at a time
    ...
    MPI_COMM_WORLD.Bcast(buffer, COORD, MPI_INT, 0);
    // Gather results & write to file (#intersections in status.Get_count)
    while (number_done < size-1){
      MPI_COMM_WORLD.Recv(vect, count, MPI_INT, MPI_ANY_SOURCE,
                          &status);
      status.Get_count(MPI_INT, &number_of_intersection) ;
      ...
    }
    // Close files and terminate slaves
    buffer[0] = -1;
    MPI_COMM_WORLD.Bcast(buffer, COORD, MPI_INT, 0);
  }
```

Program 12.10
Naive Approach to Utilizing MPI++ (continues over page)

```
    // slave process
    else {
        // Wait for #polygons in first map, compute own share of
        // polygons, allocate memory, and receive polygons
        MPI_COMM_WORLD.Bcast(&count, 1, MPI_INT, 0);
        ...
        MPI_COMM_WORLD.Recv(vect, its_share*COORD, MPI_INT, 0,
                            &status);
        // accept second-map polygons, do comparison,
        // and send result back to master
        do {
            inter_count = 0;
            MPI_COMM_WORLD.Bcast(buffer, COORD, MPI_INT, 0);
            ...
            MPI_COMM_WORLD.Send(result_vect, inter_count*COORD,
                                MPI_Int, 0);
        } while(buffer[0]>0);
    }
    MPI_COMM_WORLD.Finalize();
    return(0);
}
```

Program 12.11
Naive Approach to Utilizing MPI++ (continued from previous page)

```
// main program
#include "polygon.h"
main (int argc, char** argv)
{
    MPI_COMM_WORLD.Init(&argc, &argv);
    int myrank;
    MPI_COMM_WORLD.Rank(&myrank);
    General_process process(myrank, argc, argv);
    process.SetUp();
    process.SendData_work();
    process.SendRecvData_work();
    process.Finish();
    MPI_COMM_WORLD.Finalize();
    return(0);
}
```

Program 12.12
Main Program of Class-Oriented Polygon Overlay Program

```
// Abstract class
class Process {
 public:
  Process() { }                        // Constructor
  virtual ~Process() { }               // Destructor
  virtual void SetUp() = 0;            // make superclass abstract
  virtual void SendData_work() { }
  virtual void SendRecvData_work() { }
  virtual void Finish() { }
 protected:
  int size, rank, total_count, share_count, extra_count, *vect;
  MPI_Status status;
  int argc;
  char** argv;
};

class Master_process : public Process {
 public:
  Master_process(int r, int c, char** v)
  {rank = r; argc = c; argv = v;}
  ~Master_process () { }
  void SetUp();
  void SendData_work();
  void SendRecvData_work();
  void Finish();
 private:
  int length;
  ifstream infile, infile2;
};
```

Program 12.13
Definitions for Class-Based Polygon Overlay Program (continues over page)

```
class Slave_process : public Process {
 public:
  Slave_process(int r, int c, char** v)
  { rank = r; argc=c; argv=v;}
  ~Slave_process () { }
  void SetUp();
  void SendRecvData_work();
  // SendData_work() and Finish() not overwritten for slaves
 private:
  int my_count, *result_vect;
};

class General_process : public Process {
 public:
  General_process(int r, int c, char** v){
    if (r == 0) repProcess = new Master_process(r, c, v);
    else        repProcess = new Slave_process(r, c, v);
  }
  ~General_process(){ delete repProcess; }
  void SetUp(){ repProcess->SetUp(); }
  void SendData_work() {repProcess->SendData_work();}
  void SendRecvData_work() {repProcess->SendRecvData_work();}
  void Finish() {repProcess->Finish();}
 private:
  Process *repProcess;
};
```

Program 12.14
Definitions for Class-Based Polygon Overlay Program (continued from previous page)

idea for the main program to work with a duplicate of MPI_COMM_WORLD, to be sure it is isolated from messages started by other parts of the code.

To illustrate these ideas, as well as the use of inheritance with MPI++, we provide a pipelined control-parallel solution to the polygon overlay problem. Two controllers distribute data: the first one reads in the polygons from the first map and distributes them to the pipeline workers, while the second sends polygons from the second map to the first pipeline worker. From there, those polygons stream through the pipeline. The results are stored locally until a buffer is filled, and then sent back to the first controller for output.

In our implementation, we first duplicate the input communicator MPI_COMM_WORLD to get a new communicator NewWorld, to which all the processes continue to belong. This communicator is then split into a controller communicator, which contains all the controller processes, and a worker communicator which contains all the pipeline worker processes. An inter-communicator inter is also created, which is used to communicate between controllers and workers. Programs 12.15 to 12.18 sketch our implementation of the pipelined version. For the sake of brevity, only the main ideas are presented.

A sample main program is sketched in Programs 12.17 and 12.18. The emphasis is on the use of different communicators.

In the main program of the pipelined implementation, a process selects an appropriate communicator, according to which type of communication is to be accomplished. For example, the controller responsible for distributing the polygons of the first map only needs to send the polygons in that map to all the workers. It does not need to do a global broadcast to every process; we avoid such unnecessary communication and synchronization by structuring the communicators with appropriate subsets of processes. Similarly, the controller uses the inter-communicator to send a message to one of the workers. That worker then broadcasts the message to all workers using the communicator local to the workers.[5] In fact, since each process belongs to a local communicator and an inter-communicator, it knows how to communicate with others, so each can be developed, compiled, and executed as individual program.

This approach of arranging processes into groups associated with different communicators is one way of taking advantage of MPI++'s class

---

[5]In MPI-2, inter-communicators will support cross-group broadcasts.

```
const int numOfController = 2;
const int local_leader = 0;
class NewWorld {
 public:
  NewWorld(MPIX_Comm_intra& communicate)
  { communicate.Dup(&world); }
  ~NewWorld(void){ world.Free(); }
  // Customized accessors
  MPIX_Comm_intra& World() { return world; }
  int Rank(){ int rank; world.Rank(&rank); return rank; }
  int Size(){ int size; world.Size(&size); return size; }
 private:
  MPIX_Comm_intra world;  // Contains all processes.
};

class Controller : public NewWorld {
 public:
  Controller(MPIX_Comm_intra& comm, int color) :
    NewWorld(comm)
  {
    World().Split(color,  Rank(), &local);
    int remote_leader = numOfController;
    local.Intercomm_create(local_leader, World(),
                           remote_leader, 0, &inter);
  }
  ~Controller()
  // Accessors
  MPIX_Comm_intra& Local() { return local; }
  MPIX_Comm_inter& Inter() { return inter; }
  int Local_Rank()
  {
    int rank;
    Local().Rank(&rank);
    return rank;
  }
 private:
  MPIX_Comm_intra local;  // all controllers
  MPIX_Comm_inter inter;  // inter-communicator communication
                          // with workers
};
```

Program 12.15
Definitions for Pipelined Polygon Overlay Program Using Multiple Communicators
(continues over page)

```
class Worker : public NewWorld {
 public:
  Worker(MPIX_Comm_intra& comm, int color) : NewWorld(comm){
    World().Split(color, Rank(), &local);
    int remote_leader = 0;
    local.Intercomm_create(local_leader, World(),
                           remote_leader, 0 , &inter);
  }
  ~Worker()
  // Accessors
  MPIX_Comm_intra& Local() { return local; }
  MPIX_Comm_inter& Inter() { return inter; }
  int Local_Rank() {int rank; Local().Rank(&rank); return rank; }
  // Finding polygon intersections
  int compute(int, int, int*, int*, int*);
 private:
  MPIX_Comm_intra local;    // all workers
  MPIX_Comm_inter inter;    // inter-communicator for
                            // worker-controller communication
};
```

Program 12.16
Definitions for Pipelined Polygon Overlay Program Using Multiple Communicators
(continued from previous page)

hierarchy. For more complex problems, it proves even more valuable. Moreover, it supports clean and readable parallel codes. For example, in the code above, we defined an accessor method in the base class NewWorld that gave the global process rank:

```
int NewWorld::Rank();
```

We also defined an accessor in the derived classes to give the process rank within its local communicator:

```
int controller::Local_rank();
int worker::Local_rank();
```

While we could use the accessor methods provided by MPI++ to achieve the same effect, these user-defined methods are easier to use, and more meaningful in particular applications. User can also provide member functions appropriate to specific application. For example, in

```
#include "mpi++.h"
#include "pipeline.h"
const int COORD = 4;
main(int argc, char **argv)
{
  MPI_COMM_WORLD.Init(&argc,&argv);
  int rank,size;
  MPI_COMM_WORLD.Rank(&rank);
  MPI_COMM_WORLD.Size(&size);
  // The controller processes
  int color = (rank < numOfController);
  if (rank < numOfController){
      Controller process(MPI_COMM_WORLD, color);
      if (rank==0) { // The first controller
          ...
          // Use inter-communicator to send # polygons of
          // first map to first worker
          process.Inter().Send(&count, 1, MPI_INT, 0);
          // Use inter-communicator to send each processor
          // its share of polygons
          ...
          process.Inter().Send(vect, its_share*COORD,
                               MPI_INT, i);
          // Use inter-communicator to gather results from
          // each worker & write to file
          ...
          process.Inter().Recv(vect, count*COORD, MPI_INT,
                               MPI_ANY_SOURCE, MPI_ANY_TAG,
                               &status);
          ...
      }
      else if (rank==numOfController-1){ // last controller
          // Use inter-communicator to send one polygon of
          // second map each time to first worker until end
          process.Inter().Send(buffer,COORD, MPI_INT, 0);
          ...
      }
  }
}
```

Program 12.17
Main Program of the Pipelined Polygon Overlay Program Using Multiple
Communicators (continues over page)

```
// The worker processes
else {
  Worker process(MPI_COMM_WORLD, color);
  if (rank==numOfController){ // first worker
    // Use inter-communicator to receive # polygons
    // of the first map
    process.Inter().Recv(&count, 1, MPI_INT, 0,
                         &status);
  }
  // Use intra-communicator to broadcast to all workers
  process.Local().Bcast(&count, 1, MPI_INT, 0);
  ...
  // Use inter-communicator to receive own share of
  // first-map polygons
  process.Inter().Recv(vect, its_share*COORD, MPI_INT,
                       0, &status);
  ...
  // Except for first worker, the polygons of second map
  // stream through the workers using intra-communicator
  do {
    if (rank==numOfController)
      process.Inter().Recv(buffer, COORD, MPI_INT,
                           numOfControlle-1, &status);
    else
      process.Local().Recv(buffer, COORD, MPI_INT,
                           process.Local_Rank()-1,
                           &status);
    // Do comparison
    ...
    if (rank != size-1)
      process.Local().Send(buffer, COORD, MPI_INT,
                           process.Local_Rank()+1);
  } while(buffer[0]>0);
}
MPI_COMM_WORLD.Finalize();
return(0);
}
```

Program 12.18
Main Program of the Pipelined Polygon Overlay Program Using Multiple
Communicators (continued from previous page)

the above **worker** subclass, member functions can be created for receiving data from the previous worker in the pipeline, or sending data to the next worker in the pipeline. Member functions could also be defined for returning results to the controller process that is collecting data.

12.4 Performance Tests

The two programs described in the preceding section were compiled using **mpCC** with the **-g** option, and run on an IBM SP-2. The model implementation of MPI, MPICH [Doss *et al.* 1993], was used with MPI++.

Two maps were randomly generated on 4000 × 4000 grids, one containing 203,483 polygons and the other containing 203,456 polygons. For the purpose of illustration, these maps were not sorted; the two programs simply compared each pair of polygons from the two maps to find all the overlaps. The same strategy was also used in the sequential program.

On the IBM SP-2, the IP (Internet Protocol) mode for communication was used. Two runs were conducted for each program and each number of nodes. Due to node switch contention, slightly different timing results were obtained. Table 12.2 lists the average timings and standard deviations obtained.

The data in the table do not include any I/O time. In the master-slave implementation, one process was solely for distributing data, so the number of processes actually computing was one less than the total number of processes. In the pipeline implementation, two processes were used only for data distribution, so the number of processes actually computing was two less than the total number of processes. A buffer of 1000 polygons was used locally for each pipeline worker process in our sample program.

The timing results are plotted in Figure 12.7. It shows that for small number of processors, the master-slave implementation used less processing time than the pipeline implementation, while the reverse was true for larger number of processors. When the number of processors used is small, the overall overhead of communication is low. In this case, the master-slave implementation runs faster, as it uses one more processor for computing than the pipeline. As more processors are used, the overhead of communication becomes relatively more significant, so the

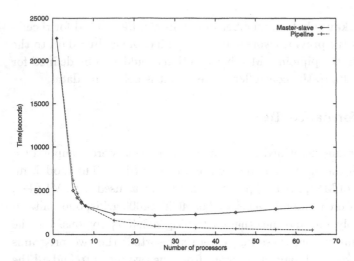

Figure 12.7
Execution Time vs. Number of Processors

lower communication overhead of the pipeline implementation delivers higher performance.

12.5   Summary, Conclusions, and Future Work

This chapter has introduced MPI++ at several levels. Unlike some of the other systems described in this book, MPI++ does not require direct compiler support. It is therefore exceptionally portable, as it can function wherever MPI runs. As MPI implementations are rapidly improving, the performance of MPI++ applications should be competitive with other explicit, and parallel-compiler-supported solutions for parallel programming.

In this section, we consider some criticisms of the current version of MPI++. We also comment on the ongoing effort to define MPI-2, as this impacts MPI++ in two ways: new functionality in MPI will have to be supported in a future release of MPI++, and a C++ language binding is being considered for MPI-2.

One possible future path for MPI++ is that part or all of it becomes standardized in MPI-2's C++ language binding. In that case, the MPI++ project and its related effort, MPICH, would effectively merge. Alternatively, a different C++ language binding might emerge,

Processors used (computing)	Algorithm Used	Average time (sec)	Standard Deviation
1 (1)	Sequential	22643.4	11.0
5 (4)	Master-Slave	5007.3	8.5
5 (3)	Pipeline	6201.2	8.0
6 (5)	Master-Slave	4184.6	15.5
6 (4)	Pipeline	4699.5	7.5
7 (6)	Master-Slave	3618.4	44.5
7 (5)	Pipeline	3786.1	4.0
8 (7)	Master-Slave	3260.8	111.5
8 (6)	Pipeline	3227.2	49.0
15 (14)	Master-Slave	2331.9	28.0
15 (13)	Pipeline	1609.2	1.0
25 (24)	Master-Slave	2172.0	41.5
25 (23)	Pipeline	943.1	68.0
35 (34)	Master-Slave	2289.8	103.5
35 (33)	Pipeline	779.1	6.5
45 (44)	Master-Slave	2513.8	25.5
45 (43)	Pipeline	651.4	5.5
55 (54)	Master-Slave	2899.1	44.0
55 (53)	Pipeline	579.1	2.0
64 (62)	Master-Slave	3145.9	108.5
64 (63)	Pipeline	537.6	0.01

Table 12.2
Polygon Overlay Timings

which could lead to us either discontinuing MPI++ or providing it as an alternative to the official MPI-2 language binding. Our decision would depend on the functionality that is chosen for the MPI-2 binding. Finally, the MPI Forum might choose to drop its C++ language binding effort, thereby leaving the C binding as the base software for C++ development.

12.5.1 Current MPI++

Design Rather conservative choices were made in the current design of MPI++ about the use of C++ features. Specifically, in our effort to retain a large measure of compatibility with the C interface, certain interfaces remain quite C-like in nature. However, the class structure of C++ was exploited in some cases.

What is missing from this, largely because MPI objects are already reference-counted, is discussion of nested classes, inheritance, and the handle/body (or envelope/letter) idioms discussed by Coplien [Coplien 1992]. The MPI++ objects that implement opaque MPI objects are relatively simple because the C objects they encapsulate are already quite easy to manage. However, because the C binding has neither hooks for inheritance, nor an external interface to support tight binding of the C++ interface, certain concessions were inevitable.

For example, it is not possible to layer certain calls involving arrays of request objects on top of the equivalent MPI calls (e.g., MPI_Wait and MPI_Waitall). Specifically, one cannot pass an array of C++ requests to the C routine, because the objects differ in content and format. For this reason, it is tempting not to use some of the built-in MPI functionality that works on arrays of C objects, but rather to use more primitive MPI functions, and do the array versions in the MPI++ implementation. However, this could dramatically affect the performance and/or deadlock properties of the C++ version. Our design requirements forbid so large a deviation from the original underlying implementation.

A workable solution to this problem is to consider a ground-up implementation of MPI in C++, basing the system on a small abstract device, as is currently done in the C version. Considerable improvements would potentially result if the entire system were C++, rather than just the uppermost layers, and some of these could lead to improved functionality as well as higher performance. Such an implementation is an ideal next step for the MPI++ project. If this occurs, our current work would be the basis for the C++ language binding of that implementation. We would choose to layer C and Fortran-77 bindings on top of the C++ code, unlike the current layering schemes, which typically place the C code below other language bindings.

General Parallel Application Architecture   The current MPI++ system does not, by itself, support the full parallel application architecture shown in Figure 12.8. We are convinced that this is needed for practical applications, and that it is attainable given current technology. However, significant infrastructure must first be created in order to provide the critical mass needed to enable real applications in this environment.

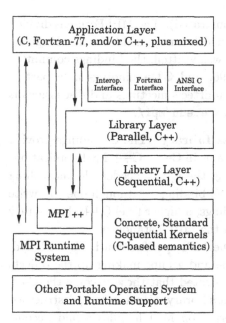

Figure 12.8
Future MPI++ Parallel Application Architecture

Application Experience   Relatively small amounts of code have been written in MPI++ as compared to MPI's C and Fortran-77 bindings. Hence, we lack the perspective that such experience would provide about the efficacy of features we have provided, and the usefulness of the extensibility of the classes we have defined. For example, we have not explicitly provided for multiple inheritance based on our classes, although we have followed Coplien's Inheritance Canonical Form for simple inheritance [Coplien 1992]. We expect to get additional feedback from application programmers, which could lead to significant additions or changes in functionality. Furthermore, other approaches to C++-based message passing are likely to give us impetus for change and improvement.

12.5.2   MPI-2

The MPI Forum reconvened in March of 1995 to begin discussions about extending the MPI Standard. One of the guiding principles for MPI-2 meetings is to extend the MPI-1 Standard rather than changing it (unless grave errors in MPI should be demonstrated). The MPI Forum is divided into several subcommittees, one of which is responsible for new language bindings. At the time this chapter was written, the bindings committee was considering Ada-95, Fortran-90, and C++ bindings as a part of MPI-2. Information about the committee's meetings and discussions is available at `http://www.erc.msstate.edu/mpi/`.

C++ Bindings and C++ Class Library The C bindings provide one interface for writing MPI programs in C++. C++ MPI applications may be written by simply including the `mpi.h` header file and calling MPI functions as described by the C bindings. Although one can write C++ applications using the C bindings, a higher level C++ class library is being considered for inclusion in the MPI-2 standard.

As we have already observed, the MPI specification is object-based, with MPI requests, communicators, and groups making up the objects in the system. Early proposals advocated that these become the C++ classes making up the MPI C++ class library. Constructors, destructors, accessors, and functions that operate on MPI handles would become methods of these classes. Concepts not explicitly present in the MPI standard are not likely to be included in an MPI-2 class library.

Should the MPI-2 Standard Contain a C++ Class Library? The MPI Forum has not yet voted on whether or not a C++ class library will be included in the MPI-2 Standard. Some arguments in favor of this are:

1. A standardized class library would have a better chance of promoting the use of MPI among people coming from an object-oriented background and broadening the scope for parallel programming in object-oriented languages based on MPI.

2. Lack of a standardized class library would not satisfy the object-oriented community's expectations and would leave them with three alternatives: not using MPI, inventing their own (idiosyncratic) higher level abstractions, or forming a group to define a common, higher level binding. The MPI Forum is probably the best community to sponsor the third alternative, thus saving others from the negative impacts of the second alternative.

3. If we do not provide a C++ class library as part of the standard, there will be many non-standard MPI C++ class libraries.

Arguments against an MPI C++ class library are:

1. A C++ class library for MPI is something more than bindings. Although a class library is an important effort, it is beyond the scope of simply language bindings for MPI. The general specification of MPI is (intentionally) language- and implementation-independent. The bindings provide the interface between the MPI functionality and a real language that wants to use that functionality. As such, MPI bindings should only provide the interface between a C++ class library and MPI.

2. A class library specification will involve a significant amount of implementation detail, unlike any other part of the MPI specification thus far.

3. One of MPI's main goals was to support the development of portable libraries. Standardizing a library that can be easily built on top of MPI is unnecessary and should be considered syntactic sugar.

4. It is beneficial that there be many MPI C++ class libraries. A likely outcome would be many portable MPI C++ class libraries, each of which provides a different useful set of abstractions.

12.5.3 Conclusions

At the outset of this work, we felt that a class library based on MPI could provide a useful parallel C++ environment. What remains to be studied is whether an inherently parallel compiler-based environment, with commands to support and manage parallelism, can provide things that C++, as extensible as it is, cannot. We look forward to such a comprehensive study, as we believe this will help drive further research into the most fruitful directions for parallel C++ systems. Furthermore, we look to significant application experience as a guide toward what MPI++ should and should not provide to support libraries and applications.

For the present, we will continue with our library-based approach, working to improve its functionality while retaining its performance-portability. We further plan to investigate a fully C++ implementation of MPI.

Acknowledgments

Support has been provided by the U.S. Department of Energy under contract DE-FC04-94AL9892. Additional funding for this work is acknowledged under ARPA Order D350, Contract through Rome Laboratories, 1995. This research has also been supported in part by the NSF Engineering Research Center for Computational Field Simulation at Mississippi State University. We also would like to thank the Maui High Performance Computing Center, where all the performance tests for the polygon overlay application were conducted.

13 pC++

Shelby X. Yang, Dennis Gannon, Peter Beckman,
Jacob Gotwals, and Neelakantan Sundaresan

pC++ is a data-parallel extension to C++ that is based on the concept of *collections* and *concurrent aggregates*. It is similar in many ways to newer languages like ICC++ (Chapter 9), Amelia (Chapter 2) and C** (Chapter 8) in that it is based on the application of functions to sets of objects. However, it also allows functions to be invoked on each processor to support SPMD-style libraries and it is designed to link with HPF programs. pC++ currently runs on almost all commercial massively-parallel computers, and is being used by the NSF Computational Grand Challenge Cosmology Consortium to support simulations of the evolution of the universe. In this chapter we describe the language and its performance on a variety of problems.

13.1 Introduction

The goal of the pC++ project was to design a simple extension to C++ for parallel programming that provides:

- a platform for parallel object-oriented software capable of running without modification on all commercial MIMD systems;

- an interface to SPMD libraries such as SCALAPACK++ [Choi *et al.* 1994], A++ [Lemke & Quinlan 1993] and POOMA (Chapter 14);

- an interface to High Performance Fortran (HPF) [Koelbel *et al.* 1994];

- an interface to control-parallel C++-based languages such as CC++ [Chandy & Kesselman 1993] (Chapter 3);

- a way to exploit parallel I/O systems and persistent object databases; and

- a complete programming environment including all the tools that users of conventional C++ systems expect, as well as tools for parallel performance analysis and debugging.

We do not think that pC++, or other object-oriented parallel programming languages, should be viewed as replacements for Fortran-90 or HPF. Rather, object-oriented parallelism should be used to express those types of parallelism that cannot easily be expressed in these languages. To accomplish this, pC++ exploits the two defining characteristics of object-oriented design: encapsulation and inheritance (Appendix A).

pC++ is based on a *concurrent aggregate* model of data parallelism. This means that a pC++ program consists of a single main thread of control from which parallel operations are applied to *collections* of objects. Each object in a collection is an instance of an *element* class. pC++ has two basic extensions to the C++ language: a mechanism to describe how operations can be invoked over a set of objects in parallel, and a mechanism to refer to individual objects and subsets of objects in a collection.

pC++ has been implemented on a wide range of commercially available parallel systems; we describe its performance on such platforms later in this chapter. Other examples of pC++ programs and performance can be found in [Gannon & Lee 1991, Gannon & Lee 1992, Gannon 1993, Bodin 1993a, Gannon *et al.* 1994c]. Our primary experience with testing the pC++ ideas on large scale problems has come from our involvement with the NSF Grand Challenge Cosmology Consortium GC^3. This chapter describes some of these applications. We also discuss two libraries that support parallel I/O and persistent objects in pC++ programs.

One of the most interesting by-products of the pC++ project has been a language preprocessor toolkit called Sage++ [Gannon *et al.* 1994a]. This toolkit has been extended in a variety of ways and is used for a large number of applications, including the TAU programming environment described in Chapter 15.

13.2   History

In 1984, the parallel programming research group at Indiana University, working with the Center for Supercomputing Research and Development (CSRD) at the University of Illinois, developed an extension to the C programming language called Vector Parallel C (VPC) [Gannon *et al.* 1989]. VPC used parallel loops for spawning new threads of control, a vector notation similar to Fortran-90 for data-parallel operations, and assumed a shared-memory model of execution.

By 1986, we had become interested in distributed-memory multicomputers, and decided to build a new system based on object-oriented design ideas. Our goal was to implement parallel control mechanisms by applying member functions to sets of objects. The first problem to be solved was how to describe a generic set of objects in C++. At the time, the C++ template mechanism was not yet a complete proposal to the C++ standards committee, although early public documents such as [Stroustrup 1988] guided our thinking.

Even had they existed, templates would not have solved all of our problems. To see why, consider the following definition of a set of objects of type T derived from a templatized container class Set:

```
Set<T> S;
```

Suppose that the set element type T takes the form:

```
class T {
public:
  void foo();
};
```

Our desire was to be able to apply the member foo() to the entire set S in parallel with the expression S.foo(). Unfortunately, this could not be done using the standard overloading and inheritance mechanisms of C++. Furthermore, because there were no implementations of templates in C++ at that time, we decided to add an extension to pC++ to represent a type of class called a *collection*. Each collection had one built-in "template" parameter called **ElementType**. To simplify the compiler, we put the mechanisms for managing a distributed set of elements into a library called the **SuperKernel** collection. The way in which these collection classes are used is described in detail in the next section.

About the time that our first implementation of pC++ for shared-memory multiprocessors was complete, the HPF Forum was being established. Because HPF was also a data-parallel programming language, we were convinced that we needed to base the allocation and data distribution mechanisms for collections on distributed-memory systems on the HPF model. Such a design would help make it possible to share distributed data structures with HPF implementations (although this idea has never been tested). In retrospect, we have realized that, for most users, a standard interface to single-node Fortran-90 is more important than compatibility with HPF. This is because the majority of large pC++ applications that are in production use are written with Fortran subroutines that have been scavenged from older sequential and vector versions of the application.

In 1992, ARPA provided the support for a complete redesign of pC++ and a public release. The final version of pC++ (version 2.0) will be released in early 1996. This chapter describes this new version of the language.

13.3   Overview of pC++ Version 2.0

pC++ was designed to work on both multiprocessors and multicomputers. We use the HPF model to describe the way in which an array-like data structure can be distributed over the memory hierarchy of a parallel computer. To build a collection of objects from some class type T, which is called an *element* class[1] in pC++, one needs a distribution and an alignment object. The distribution object defines a grid and a mapping from the grid to the physical processors on a parallel machine. The alignment object specifies the shape, size, and the mapping of the element objects to the grid points. In addition, a processor object of type **Processors** is needed to represent the set of processors available to use. For example:

```
Processors P;
Distribution D(100, &P, BLOCK);
Align A(20, "[ALIGN(X[i], D[i+10])]");
```

creates an one-dimensional grid of a size of 100 which is mapped to the processors of the machine by blocks. If there are 20 processors, grid positions 0 through 4 are mapped to processor 0, positions 5 through 9 are mapped to processor 1, etc. The alignment object aligns the logical vector X[0:19] with the grid positions D[10:29].

Given a distribution, an alignment and the class type of the element objects, it is easy to build a collection. The starting point is the **SuperKernel** collection provided by the pC++ collection library. This

---

[1]In its current implementation, elements of a collection must be of the same type.

collection is the base type for all other collections. It builds arrays of element objects and provides a global name space for the element objects. Thus, the declaration:

```
SuperKernel<T> MyCollection(&D, &A);
```

creates a collection called `MyCollection`, consisting of a set of 100 objects of type T distributed in the manner described above.

The most important feature of a collection is the ability to apply a function in parallel across all the element objects. For example, if T is defined as:

```
class T {
  ...
 public:
  void foo();
  int x, y, z;
  float bar(T &);
  ...
};
```

a parallel application of `foo()` to all elements of `MyCollection` would take the form:

```
MyCollection.foo();
```

In the case above, `foo()` has a void result, so `MyCollection.foo()` has a void result as well. However, pC++ extends the type system so that, for example, if `x` is a type `int` data member of the element class, then `MyCollection.x` is an object of type `SuperKernel<Int>`, where `Int` is a library class with one integer value. The expression:

```
MyCollection.x = 2*MyCollection.y + MyCollection.z;
```

is therefore a parallel computation involving element-wise multiplication, addition and assignment on the members of each element of the collection.

Similarly, if `t` is of type T the expression `MyCollection.bar(t)` applies `bar(t)` to each element of the collection. The result is of type `SuperKernel<Float>`. Also, if C is another collection whose size is the same as `MyCollection` and whose element type is T, the expression

```
MyCollection.bar(C)
```

will apply `bar()` to the ith element of `MyCollection` using the ith element of `C` as an argument.

An operation must often be applied to a subset of the elements of a collection. pC++ extends the Fortran-90 vector notation so that descriptors of the form `base:end:stride` can be used to select elements from a collection. For example:

```
MyCollection[0:50:2].foo()
```

will apply `foo()` to the first 25 even numbered elements of the collection.

To access an individual member of a collection, one can use the overloaded operator () which returns a *global* pointer to an element, i.e., a pointer that can span the entire address space of a distributed-memory machine. For example:

```
MyCollection(i)
```

returns a global pointer to the ith element in the collection. In this way, any object can have a global address. The function call:

```
MyCollection(i)->foo();
```

is a remote invocation. It sends a message to the processor that contains the ith element of `MyCollection`, and a thread on that processor executes the function.[2]

Programmers often need to create specialized collections with properties appropriate for their particular applications. The task of building a new derived collection is almost the same as building a derived class in C++. The definition of a collection derived from **SuperKernel** takes the form:

```
Collection MyCollectionType: SuperKernel {
public:
   // Public data members duplicated on each processor
   // Public member functions executed in parallel on all processors
MethodOfElement:
   // Data members and member functions here are added to
   // the element class
};
```

_____

[2]Remote invocation of this kind is part of pC++ 2.0, and is not part supported by the current pC++ 1.0 distribution.

There are two types of data and member functions in a collection definition. Data and functions labeled as `MethodOfElement` represent new data members and functions that are to be added to each element class. Such member functions are invoked and executed in the same way that ordinary element class member functions are invoked and executed. Data members not labelled as `MethodOfElement` are defined once on each processor; functions not labeled `MethodOfElement` are invoked in SPMD mode. This is similar to the extrinsic function execution model in HPF. More precisely, pC++ has a single sequential thread of control for all operations other than collection member function calls. Collections are data aggregates that may be distributed over multiple address spaces. Invoking a collection member function that is not a `MethodOfElement` member causes a thread of control in each address space to execute the function. These new threads of execution are independent and run in parallel. The programmer is free to embed explicit communication and synchronization in these functions. The functions are barrier synchronized before control is returned to the single sequential main thread. On distributed-memory systems, where there is one processor per address space, the number of threads that are running concurrently in a non-`MethodOfElement` call is one per processor. For `MethodOfElement` function calls there is one function invocation per element in the collection.

13.3.1 pC++ Runtime System

pC++ is extremely portable. It currently runs on the Cray T3D, IBM SP-2, Intel Paragon, Meiko CS-2, SGI PowerChallenge, Thinking Machines CM-5, Convex Exemplar, and networks of workstations. The key to this portability is the simple execution model and layered runtime system. The first runtime layer is machine independent and is defined by the pC++ compiler (source-to-source translator). The compiler generates calls to the C++ class library whose interface is defined in `kernel.h`. There are two versions of this class library layer: one for SPMD execution and one for fork/join thread-based execution.

For distributed-memory machines, SPMD execution is used, and the pC++ compiler converts parallel invocations such as:

```
MyColl.foo();
```

into loops over the local collection elements using the "owner computes" rule as shown below. First the data type

```
MyCollection<T> MyColl(...);
```

is converted by the compiler to an explicit C++ class

```
MyCollection_T MyColl(...);
```

and the function invocation is converted into the loop

```
for (i= MyColl->FirstLocal(); i >= 0; i = MyColl->NextLocal(i))
  MyColl(i)->foo();
pcxx_Barrier();
```

The generated loop uses the overloaded () operator, provided by the pC++ class library, to find the ith collection element. After each processor has applied foo() to its local elements, a barrier synchronization between processors in initiated.

Shared-memory machines can use the SPMD model shown above, or the pC++ compiler can generate a special thread-based runtime interface. More specifically, the loop above now takes the following abstract form. Let us assume that there are k processors available

```
fork_threads(k); // create or allocate k threads of execution
// each thread executes the following
int s = MyColl->size(), me = my_thread_id();
for(int i = (s/k)*me; i < min(s, (s/k)*(me+1)); i++)
  MyColl(i)->foo();
join_threads(k); // wait for all thread to reach this point
                 // and terminate or suspend all but one
```

The abstraction of work is sufficiently general to permit many different thread packages. An implementation could create a new thread for each element, i.e., let $k = s$, or use a set of k persistent threads.

13.3.2   Tulip

The next portion of the runtime system is the machine-dependent layer, called Tulip. Tulip describes an abstract machine, and defines standard interfaces for basic machine services such as clocks, timers, remote service requests, and data movement. Tulip has a C interface, and has no knowledge of pC++ or the class library, which are built on top of Tulip. Therefore, wherever Tulip can be ported, pC++ can run.

Tulip has several basic abstractions:

context: An address space. A Unix process on a symmetric multiprocessor would be a single context. Light-weight threads share a context. A machine such as the SP-2 can support several contexts per node.

local pointer: A simple, untyped, memory address. A local pointer is valid only in the context in which it was created.

global pointer: The tuple (context, local pointer). A global pointer uniquely identifies any memory address in the computational hardware.

Those abstractions are used in the following basic functions:

```
tulip_Put(tulip_GlobalPointer_t destination, char *source,
          int length, tulip_ACK_t *handle);

tulip_Get(char *destination, tulip_GlobalPointer_t source,
          int length, tulip_ACK_t *handle);

tulip_RemoteServiceRequest(int context, char *buffer,
                           int length, tulip_ACK_t *handle);
```

Put() and Get() simply move data between contexts. They are very similar to memcpy(), except destination and source are global pointers respectively. Furthermore, an acknowledge handle is provided so the status of the data transfer can be monitored. If the handle is NULL when the function is called, no acknowledgment is done. The functions are non-blocking, so that they can be easily integrated with user-level thread packages.

The remove service request mechanism provides asynchronous communication between contexts. It is particularly useful for bootstrapping, building remote procedure execution for pC++ (see Section 13.3), and transmitting short control messages to other contexts.

The basic abstractions and functions are supported on three architectural models: shared memory, message passing, and network DMA. The SGI PowerChallenge and Convex Exemplar are examples of shared-memory machines. The hardware maintains cache and memory consistency, and communication is done by simply sharing pointers. In this case, Put() and Get() need not be used, because those functions move data between contexts. On a shared-memory machine, there is usually only one context. However, if Put() or Get() are used, they are simply a call to memcpy() followed by the TRUE acknowledge handle.

Two examples of message-passing machines are the Intel Paragon and IBM SP-2. Since Put() and Get() are one-sided communication primitives, and do not require synchronization, either active messages or polling loops must be used to detect when a data movement request arrives. For each Get(), a recv() is posted for the anticipated data, then a data request message is sent to the remote context (i.e., node). When the sender detects the data request message during a message poll, the data is sent to the awaiting recv() without a buffer copy. Put() uses a similar mechanism, but requires an extra round trip to avoid any buffer copies. If the message is sent to the remote context "eagerly", the extra round trip latency is not incurred, but the messaging system must copy and buffer the data.

The Meiko CS-2 and Cray T3D are network DMA machines. They are not, from the programmers perspective, truly shared memory, since transfers to "remote" memory must be done through special system calls. On the other hand, there is no synchronization or polling required to move data. Consequently Get() and Put() can be written as calls to these underlying vendor-supplied transport functions.

For all machines, a polling loop or interrupt must be used to detect a remote service request. Currently, Tulip uses a polling loop to detect requests. However, as active message layers for machines such as the SP-2 become available, Tulip will be rewritten to take advantage of fast handlers and eliminate the need for polling.

13.3.3   I/O

pC++/streams is a library which supports a simple set of high level I/O primitives on pC++ collections [Gotwals *et al.* 1995]. To illustrate its capabilities, we describe how pC++/streams can be used to checkpoint a collection having variable-sized elements.

Assume our application simulates the behavior of particles in three-dimensional space. We can model the particles with a one-dimensional distributed array of variable-length particle lists, each of which keeps track of the particles in the region of the three-dimensional array local to that processor.

```
class Position {
  double x, y, z;
};
```

```
class ParticleList {
  int numberOfParticles;
  double * mass;          // variable sized
  Position * position;    // arrays
};

Collection DistributedArray {
  updateParticles();
};

Processors P;
Align a(12,"[ALIGN(collection[i], template[i])]");
Distribution d(12, &P, CYCLIC);

DistributedArray<ParticleList> particleArray(&d,&a);
```

The programmer can write a function to checkpoint the `particleArray` collection as follows:

```
#include "pc++streams.h"
void saveParticleArray() {
  oStream stream(&d, &a, "myFileOne");
  stream << particleArray;
  stream.write();
}
```

The first line of `saveParticleArray()` defines an output pC++/stream called `stream`, connected to the file `myFileOne`. The second line inserts the entire `particleArray` collection into the buffers of the stream. The third line causes those buffers to be written to the file, using parallel I/O. The file associated with the stream is closed automatically when the program block in which the stream was declared is exited. The programmer would write a function to restore the checkpointed `particleArray` as:

```
void loadParticleArray() {
  iStream stream(&d, &a, "myFileOne");
  stream.read();
  stream >> particleArray;
}
```

pC++/streams also allows selective I/O on individual fields of collection elements:

```
stream << particleArray.numberOfParticles;
```

pC++/streams supports I/O on collections with complex elements (e.g., variable-sized elements, tree-structured elements, etc) by giving the programmer a straightforward mechanism for defining how these data structures are to be read and written: stream insertion and extraction functions. A pC++/stream is actually a collection of element-streams, one per element of the collection to be written from or read into. An insertion or extraction function allows the programmer to indicate exactly how data is to be exchanged between a given element-stream and its corresponding element. In our example, the programmer would define an insertion function for **ParticleLists** as:

```
declareStreamInserter(ParticleList &p) {
   eltBuf << p.numberOfParticles;
   eltBuf << array(p.mass, p.numberOfParticles);
   eltBuf << array(p.position, p.numberOfParticles);
}
```

declareStreamInserter() is a macro that defines **eltBuf**, a reference to the element-stream. The **array()** macro tells pC++/streams that **mass** and **position** are dynamically-allocated arrays, both of size **numberOfParticles**; extraction functions are defined similarly.

13.3.4   Persistence

pC++/persistence is an I/O library supporting persistence for pC++ collections. This library is currently implemented using the SHORE persistent object system from the University of Wisconsin-Madison [Carey *et al.* 1994].

Normally, elements of pC++ collections are transitory, i.e., their data disappears when the program terminates. In order to preserve transitory data, the programmer must output that data to a file before the program terminates, using either an I/O mechanism supported by the operating system or a higher-level library such as pC++/streams.

pC++/persistence allows programmers to define persistent collections whose elements can contain persistent data in addition to ordinary transitory data. The persistent section of each element is automatically preserved across program executions; no application I/O code is required to save or load this data. A transaction mechanism is supported, allowing programmers to checkpoint persistent data with a single line of code that commits a transaction. In addition, the persistent part of a collection is concurrently accessible by multiple pC++ programs, with no explicit code for communication required. Concurrent access to persistent data can allow simplified programming of concurrent computation and visualization, computational steering, and modular multi-disciplinary simulations, since no application code needs to be devoted to I/O or communication of the persistent data.

As an example, we first we define the per-element persistent data using SDL (SHORE Data Language). For simplicity, our persistent data consists of just a single long integer per element, call myPersistentLong:

```
module MyElement {
  interface PersistentElementData {
    public:
      attribute long myPersistentLong;
  };
}
```

This SDL specification is processed by the SHORE SDL type compiler, informing SHORE of the structure of the persistent part of our elements.

We next define an element class MyElement in ordinary pC++. We derive it from the class PersistentElement, and define an ordinary transient data member (myTransientLong) in the usual way:

```
#include "PersistentElement.h"

class MyElement : public PersistentElement{
 public:
  long myTransientLong;
  void P_initialize();
  void hello();
};
```

The class PersistentElement contains a member P through which the persistent part of each element is accessed:

```
void MyElement::hello() {
  printf(" Hello world: %ld %ld",
         myTransientLong, P->myPersistentLong);
}
```

The function P_initialize(), defined within MyElement, gives the application programmer a mechanism for initializing the persistent part of each element. P_initialize() is called immediately after the persistent part of each element is first created.

```
void MyElement::P_initialize() {
  P.update()->myPersistentLong = 1234;
}
```

The call to `P.update()` above informs pC++/persistence that the persistent part of the element is to be modified, rather than just accessed.

A persistent collection is defined just like an ordinary collection, except that it is derived from `PersistentCollection`:

```
#include "PersistentCollection.h"

Collection MyCollection: public PersistentCollection {
 public:
  MyCollection(Distribution *T, Align *A,
               char *persistentCollectionName);
 MethodOfElement:
  virtual void hello();
};

MyCollection::MyCollection(Distribution *T, Align *A,
                           char *persistentCollectionName)
  : PersistentCollection(T, A, persistentCollectionName) {}
```

When the programmer instantiates the collection X below, the string `myPersistentCollectionName` is passed into the collection constructor, and then to `PersistentCollection`. This string identifies a particular database of persistent elements to be associated with the collection.

```
void Processor_Main(int argc, char **argv){
  Processors P;
  Distribution T(SIZE, &P, BLOCK);
  Align A(SIZE,"[ALIGN(V[i], T[i])]");
  MyCollection<MyElement>
    X(&T, &A, "/myPersistentCollectionName");

  beginTransaction();
  X.hello();
  commitTransaction();
}
```

Changes to the persistent part of a collection must be made within a transaction, initiated by `beginTransaction()`. These changes do not become permanent and are not visible to other applications until the transaction is committed with a call to `commitTransaction()`. So to checkpoint the persistent part of a collection, all that is required is a call to `commitTransaction()`.

pC++/persistence is still under development at the time of the writing of this text; some details may change and some functionality may be added before the implementation is complete.

13.4   An Example: Parallel Sorting

To see how pC++ is used, consider the problem of sorting a large vector of data using a parallel bitonic sort algorithm. A bitonic sequence consists of two monotonic sequences that have been concatenated together where a wrap-around of one sequence is allowed. That is, it is a sequence:

$$a_0, a_1, a_2, \ldots, a_m$$

where $m = 2^n - 1$ for some n, and for index positions i and j, with $i < j$, $a_i, a_{i+1}, \ldots, a_j$ is monotonic and the remaining sequence starting at $a_{(j+1)\bmod n}$, where a_0 follows a_n, is monotonic in the reverse direction.

Merging a bitonic sequence of length k involves a sequence of data exchanges between elements that are $k/2$ apart, followed by data exchanges between elements that are $k/4$ apart, etc. The full sort is nothing more than a sequence of bitonic merges. We start by observing that a set of two items is always bitonic. Hence for each even i, the subsequence a_i and a_{i+1} is always bitonic. If we merge these length two bitonic sequences into sorted sequences of length two and if we alternate the sort direction, we then have bitonic sequences of length four. Merging two of these bitonic sequences (of alternating direction) of length 4 we have sorted sequences of length 8. The sequence of data exchanges is illustrated in Figure 13.1.

In pC++, a pure data-parallel version of this algorithm can be built from a collection `List` of objects of type `Item` as shown below. Each item contains an object of type `E` which is assumed to be the base type of the list we want to sort:

```
struct E {
public:
  int key;
};
```

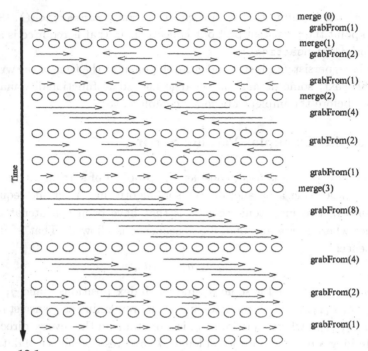

Figure 13.1
Data Exchanges in Bitonic Sort

```
class Item {
 public:
  E a;
};
```

The `List` collection contains one public function `sort()` and a number of fields and members that are defined in the `MethodOfElement` section. Because the parallel algorithms require parallel data exchanges, we must have a temporary `tmp` to hold a copy of the data to be exchanged for each element. In addition, there are two flags, `exchangeDirection` and `sortDirection` which are used to store the current exchange direction and the current sort order respectively. As can be seen in Figure 13.1, the value of these flags depends on the location of the element in the list as well as the point in time when an exchange is made.

The pC++ definition of the `List` collection can be summarized as follows:

```
Collection List : SuperKernel {
 public:
  void sort();
  int N;  // number of elements
 MethodOfElement:
  E tmp;
  virtual E a;
  int sortDirection, exchangeDirection;
  void set_sort_direction (int k) {
    sortDirection = (index1/k)%2;
  }
  void set_exchange_direction(int k) {
    exchangeDirection = (index1/k)%2;
  }
  void merge(){
    if (((sortDirection == exchangeDirection) &&
         (this->a.key > tmp.key)) ||
        ((sortDirection != exchangeDirection) &&
         (this->a.key <= tmp.key))){
      this->a = tmp;
    }
  }
  void grabFrom(j){
    if(exchangeDirection == 1)
      tmp = (*thisCollection)(index1+j)->a;
    else
      tmp = (*thisCollection)(index1-j)->a;
  }
};
```

In general, **MethodOfElement** functions are those element-wise operations in an algorithm that depend on the relation of one element to the whole collection or to other elements in the collection. For example, the function **grabFrom(int j)** is a method that, when applied to one element at position k, will access the data in the element at position j+k.

The **SuperKernel** class has two other members, **thisCollection** and **index1**. These are a pointer to the containing collection and the position of the element in the collection, respectively. The function **merge()** uses the current state variables **sortDirection** and **exchangeDirection** to determine which element of the data to keep after the exchange step.

The `sort()` function is then a sequence of merge steps, each of which contains a sequence of exchanges as shown below. The main program allocates a list of items and then calls the sort function.

```
List::sort(){
  int k = 1;
  for (int i = 1; i < log2(N); i++){  // merge(i) step
    k = 2*k;
    this->set_sort_direction(k);
    for (int j = k/2; j > 0; j = j/2){ // exchange(j) step
      this->set_exchange_direction(j);
      this->grabFrom(j);
      this->merge();
    }
  }
}

Processor_main(){
  Processors P;
  int N = read_problem_size();

  Distribution D(N,&P,BLOCK);
  Align A(N,"[ALIGN(X[i],D[i])]");
  List< Item >  L(&D, &A);
  ...
  L.sort();
}
```

This version of the program works, but has a serious flaw. If the size of the list to be sorted is N and there are only $P \ll N$ processors in the system, the bitonic sort has parallel complexity $O(\frac{N}{P} \log^2 N)$, which is far from optimal. To improve the efficiency, we can build a hybrid algorithm as follows. Let us break the list of N into P segments of length $K = \frac{N}{P}$. We begin the sort by applying a quicksort to each segment, but sorting them in alternating directions. Now each pair of adjacent sorted segments forms a bitonic sequence and we can apply the bitonic merge as before. However, at the end of each merge step, the list in each segment is only a bitonic sequence, not a sorted sequence. We must then apply a local bitonic merge to sort it. If we rewrite the algorithm above with a **Segment** class replacing the **Item** class and expanding the tmp variable to an array we only need to make a few modifications to the program. These changes, shown below, consist of inserting the calls

to the local quicksort and local bitonic merge in the sort function. The
grabFrom() and merge() functions also need to be replaced by ones
that can accommodate an array.

```
// P is the number of elements (processors)
// N is the total number of elements to sort
// K = N/P is the size of each segment

class Segment{
 public:
 E a[K]
   quickSort(); // O(K log(K))
   localBitonicMerge(int direction); // O(K)
};

List::sort(){
   int k = 1;
   this->quickSort();
   for (int i = 1; i < log2(P); i++){  // merge(i) step
     k = 2*k;
     this->set_sort_direction(k);
     for (int j = k/2; j > 0; j = j/2){ // exchange(j) step
       this->set_exchange_direction(j);
       this->grabFrom(j);
       this->merge();
     }
     this->localBitonicMerge(d);
   }
}

void SortedList::grabFrom(int dist){
  E *T;
  int offset = (d2)? -dist: dist;
  T = &((*ThisCollection)(index1+offset)->a[0]);
  for(int i = 0; i < K; i++) tmp[i] = T[i];
}
void SortedList::merge(){
  for (i = 0; i < K; i++)
    if(((d == d2) && (a[i].key > tmp[i].key)) ||
       ((d != d2) && (a[i].key <=tmp[i].key))){
      a[i] = tmp[i];
    }
  }
};
```

Assume that the quicksort computation runs with an average execution time of $DK \log K$ for some constant D, that we can ignore the cost of the barrier synchronization, that there are $P = 2^n$ processors available, and that the size of the list to be sorted is N. The time to sort is then roughly:

$$T(N) = \frac{N}{P}C \log^2 P + D\frac{N}{P} \log \frac{N}{P} + \log P$$

where C is a constant that depends upon communication speed. Given a sequential complexity of $DN \log N$ we see that the parallel speed-up is of the form:

$$Speedup(N, P) = \frac{P}{1 + \frac{C \log^2 P}{D \log N}}$$

which, for large N, approaches P.

This algorithm has been tested on a variety of machines and it is both portable and fast. Sorting one million items takes 3.56 seconds on a 64-node Paragon and 1.68 seconds on an 8-node SGI PowerChallenge. However, comparing this to the standard system routine `qsort` reveals that the speedup is not great. On the same data set with one node of the SGI PowerChallenge, `qsort` requires 10.21 seconds. Hence the speed-up of our algorithm is 6.08 on 8 processors. This value matches the formula above when $C = D$.

13.5   The Polygon Overlay Program

The following algorithm is used to implement the polygon overlay code in pC++. Given two maps A and B as input, map A is divided into smaller maps A_s. These smaller maps are then distributed over the elements of a pC++ collection. If there are N polygons in map A to be divided and P collection elements, then each element gets N/P polygons, except element zero, which gets $N/P + N \bmod P$ polygons (Figure 13.2).

Map B is duplicated in each element. During a parallel computation, each element finds the overlay of map A_s and map B. In the output stage, the resulting overlay map in each element is combined with the maps in the other elements to form the final overlay map. No inter-element communication is required during the parallel computation and thus the computation is carried out in the embarrassingly parallel fashion. In this algorithm, map B is not divided and distributed; if it were,

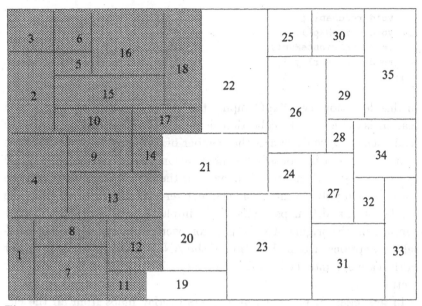

Figure 13.2
Polygon Map Distribution Scheme ($N = 35$ polygons, $P = 2$ collection elements)

it would be difficult for an A_s map to know whether it overlaps with a B_s map which is in another element. A more elaborate parallel algorithm would be required, and inter-element communication would be unavoidable. We discuss this further later in this section.

The pC++ element class is defined as follows:

```
class Patch {
 public:
  polyVec_p leftVec, rightVec, outVec;
  Patch() {}
};
```

where `leftVec`, `rightVec`, and `outVec` are, respectively, pointers to map A_s, map B, and their resulting overlay. The pC++ collection is defined as follows:

```
Collection Overlay : public SuperKernel {
 public:
  Overlay(Distribution *D, Align *A);
 MethodOfElement:
  virtual polyVec_p leftVec, rightVec, outVec;
```

```
        void readMap();
        void writeMap();
        void distributeMap();
        void findOverlay();
    };
```

In this definition, readMap() inputs the two polygon maps. The actual reading is carried out by collection element zero. After the two maps are read, element zero calculates the number of polygons all other elements should have and broadcasts the information. In distributeMap(), all other processors then fetch their piece of the first polygon map and the entire second polygon map from element zero. findOverlay() finds the overlay of A_s and B maps. In its pC++ implementation, findOverlay() simply calls the original ANSI C polygon overlay functions based on user-selected options. No modification of the ANSI C code is needed, except in the case of a modified list-deletion algorithm described in later in this section.

In writeMap(), element zero gathers overlay maps from all the elements. It calls a sorting routine to sort the polygons in a special order and writes the entire overlay map out. The sorting could have been done in parallel using the modified bitonic merge sort described in Section 13.4. However, since our focus was on the parallelization of the polygon overlay algorithm itself, we did not parallelize the sorting routine. The actual implementation of function findOverlay() is given in the following piece of code.

```
    void Overlay::findOverlay()
    {
      double time;
      pcxx_UserTimerClear(index1);
      pcxx_UserTimerStart(index1);
      if (useLnArea && useOrder){
        /* sorted-ordered list-deletion overlay */
        outVec = overlayAreaLinkedOrder(leftVec, rightVec);
      } else ···{
        ···as in sequential code···
      }
      pcxx_UserTimerStop(index1);
      time = pcxx_UserTimerElapsed(index1);
      printf("Time for element %d : %lf", index1, time);
    }
```

where `pcxx_UserTimer` functions clear, start, and stop a timer numbered by the element's index. `pcxx_UserTimerElapsed` reports the elapsed time. The main program is:

```
void Processor_Main() {
    int elem_count = pcxx_TotalNodes();
    Processors P;
    Distribution D(elem_count,&P,BLOCK);
    Align A(elem_count,"[ALIGN(X[i],D[i])]");
    Overlay<Patch> X(&D,&A);
    X.readMap();
    X.distributeMap();
    X.findOverlay();
    X.writeMap();
}
```

where `pcxx_TotalNodes` returns the number of processors used for the computation.

The pC++ code was tested on a variety of platforms including a Cray T3D, an IBM SP-2, a SGI PowerChallenge, an Intel Paragon, and a Sun SPARC 10. Two maps each containing about 60,000 polygons were used as input. Three sets of tests were conducted using the naïve overlay algorithm, the list-deletion overlay algorithm, and a modified list-deletion overlay algorithm.

The modified list-deletion algorithm can be described as follows. As illustrated in Figure 13.3, we are given two maps A and B. A is indicated by shaded area. Polygons in map A are separated by solid lines. Polygons in B are separated by dashed lines. Assume the polygons are sorted according to the x coordinates of their upper right corner, the ordering scheme used in the ANSI C code, so that comparison of the two maps would begin with the polygons in the lower left corners of both maps. In both the modified and the original list-deletion algorithms, when the lower left corners of maps A and B coincide, the loop which compares polygons in B with polygon I in A begins with the polygon pointed by arrow 1. The subsequent comparisons of polygons in B with polygon II in A begin with the polygon pointed arrow 2, because the polygon pointed by arrow 1 has been eliminated in earlier comparisons. Similarly, subsequent comparisons of polygons in B with polygon III in A begin with the polygon pointed arrow 3. In list-deletion algorithm, when the lower left corners of the maps do not coincide, all comparisons

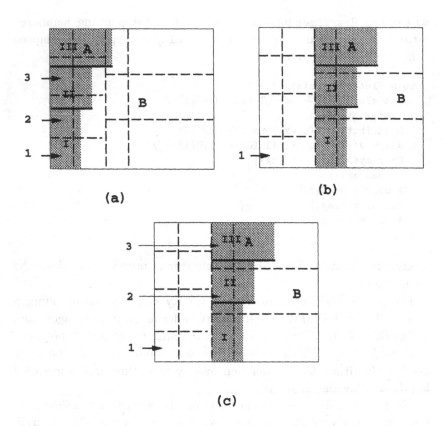

Figure 13.3
Comparing List-Deletion and Modified List-Deletion Algorithms

of polygons in B with polygons I, II, III in A begin with the polygon
pointed by arrow 1. This is because polygons to the left of map A are
never eliminated in the comparison process. In the modified list-deletion
algorithm, when the lower left corners of the maps do not coincide, only
comparisons involving polygon I begin with the polygon pointed by arrow 1. Subsequent comparisons involving II and III begin with the
polygons pointed by arrow 2 and 3 respectively.

Our experiments with the list deletion algorithm revealed that it does
not scale well. The extra work required to compare polygons in map A
with polygons in map B where no overlay occurs can degrade the algorithms performance to well below that of the naïve algorithm. Because

Platform	Number of Processors						
	1	2	4	8	16	32	64
Intel	3782.4	1942.4	983.4	494.9	248.1	124.2	
Paragon	28.5	1414.8	1048.7	612.7	327.6	168.8	85.6
	29.1	14.5	7.6	4.3	2.9	2.0	1.66
Cray	2135.7	1143.2	590.2	299.8	151.1	75.8	
T3D	19.9	990.5	735.7	429.6	229.6	118.2	
	19.5	10.6	5.7	3.2	2.1	1.5	
IBM	1587.7	812.1	410.4	205.7	103.3		
SP-2	10.2	554.4	430.1	238.8	127.6		
	10.6	5.4	2.9	1.7	1.0		
SGI	1409.8	724.8	367.6	185.1			
Power	11.7	547.1	405.4	236.2			
Challenge	11.7	6.6	4.0	2.5			
Sun	1562.3						
SPARC 10	14.0						
	13.4						

Table 13.1
Time Spent in `findOverlay()` (sec) for K100.00 and K100.01 Data Sets (60K
polygons each). For each platform, results are shown for the naïve, list-deletion,
and modified list-deletion algorithms in order.

the polygons in all the maps we used for our tests were already sorted,
the modified the list-deletion overlay algorithm could be applied. The
resulting improvement in performance was dramatic. The benchmark
results of the three sets of experiments are shown in Table 13.1 and
Figure 13.4.

As can be seen in Table 13.1 and Figure 13.4, on all the machines we
were able to obtain nearly linear speedups for the naïve and the modified
list-deletion algorithm. The speedup curves decreased slightly for the
modified list-deletion algorithm as the number of processors increased.
This was due to the fact that as workload on each processor decreased,
the overhead became more prominent. The results show that the parallel
algorithm we adopted worked very well for the naïve and the modified
list-deletion algorithm. The original list-deletion algorithm is not well-
suited for parallel execution, causing the parallelized code to perform
poorly.

Another way to parallelize the list-deletion algorithm without modifying the sequential list-deletion algorithm is to divide B into B_s and

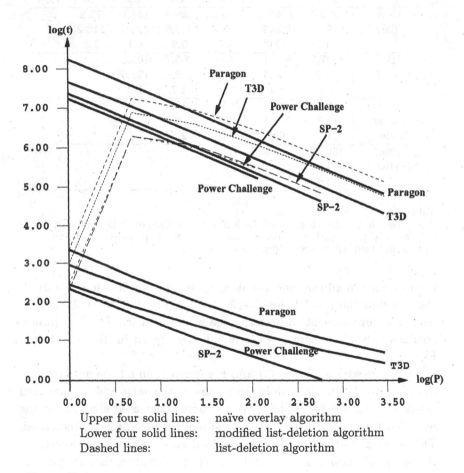

Upper four solid lines: naïve overlay algorithm
Lower four solid lines: modified list-deletion algorithm
Dashed lines: list-deletion algorithm

Figure 13.4
Execution Times vs. Number of Processors

distribute B_s as we did with A_s. Assuming, after the division and distribution, A_s and B_s roughly cover the same area, finding the overlay of them will be straight forward. Once the overlay of A_s and B_s is found, the collection elements exchange the part of B_s where no overly is found, and a second phase of parallel operation can be carried out. This parallel algorithm requires N phases of parallel operation where N is the number of collection elements (usually chosen to be equal to the number of processors). This algorithm also requires that the input polygons be sorted.

However, it should be noted that the result of the modified list-deletion algorithm is a distributed list of polygons which are locally sorted but not globally sorted. However globally sorting the polygons is a very simple task. The sorting algorithm described in Section 13.4 has been applied to a data set of this size and the time to sort it was 0.35 seconds on an 8-processor SGI PowerChallenge. Hence the execution times in the table above should have about one third of a second added to account for the final sort.

A large fraction of the code in many parallel applications is devoted to I/O. For example, in an early version of the polygon overlay program using ordinary Unix file I/O, 200 lines of code (approximately 10% of the total), was devoted to I/O. In addition to programming time overhead for file I/O, there is run time overhead as well; I/O is increasingly being identified as a bottleneck in parallel applications.

pC++/streams (Section 13.3.3) can reduce the programming time and runtime overhead associated with file I/O in pC++ applications. Rewriting the original Unix I/O in the polygon overlay program using streams reduced I/O code from 200 lines to 70 lines.

13.6 The Self-Consistent Field Code

Here and in Section 13.7 we describe our work with the Grand Challenge Cosmology Consortium (GC^3). This work is abstracted from two longer papers: [Yang et al. 1994] and [Gannon et al. 1994b].

One of the N-body codes developed by the GC^3 researchers is the Self-Consistent Field (SCF) code, which is used to simulate the evolution of galaxies. It solves the coupled Vlasov and Poisson equation for collisionless stellar systems using the N-body approximation approach.

To solve Poisson's equation for gravitational potential:

$$\nabla^2 \Phi(\vec{r}) = 4\pi \rho(\vec{r}),$$

the density ρ and potential Φ are expanded in a set of basis functions. The basis set is constructed so that the lowest order members well-approximate a galaxy obeying the de Vaucouleurs $R^{1/4}$ projected density profile law. The algorithm used is described in detail in [Hernquist & Ostriker 1992].

The original SCF code was written in Fortran-77 by Lars Hernquist in 1991. In 1993, the code was converted to Thinking Machines CM Fortran by Greg Bryan. Experiments conducted on the 512-node CM-5 at the National Center for Supercomputing Applications (NCSA) indicate that with 10 million particles the CM Fortran code can achieve 14.4 GFLOPS on 512 nodes of the CM-5 [Hernquist *et al.* 1995].

The expansions of the density and potential take the following forms:

$$\rho(\vec{r}) = \sum_{nlm} A_{nlm} \rho_{nlm}(\vec{r})$$

$$\Phi(\vec{r}) = \sum_{nlm} A_{nlm} \Phi_{nlm}(\vec{r})$$

where n is the radial quantum number and l and m are quantum numbers for the angular variables. Generally, the two sums will involve different expansion coefficients. But the assumption of bi-orthogonality ensures a one-to-one relationship between terms in the expansions for the density and potential. The basis sets ρ_{nlm} and Φ_{nlm} also satisfy Poisson's equation:

$$\nabla^2 \Phi_{nlm}(\vec{r}) = 4\pi \rho_{nlm}(\vec{r})$$

and are given by:

$$\rho_{nlm}(\vec{r}) = \frac{K_{nl}}{2\pi} \frac{r^l}{r(1+r)^{2l+3}} C_n^{2l+3/2}(\xi)\sqrt{4\pi} Y_{lm}(\theta, \phi)$$

$$\Phi_{nlm}(\vec{r}) = -\frac{r^l}{(1+r)^{2l+1}} C_n^{2l+3/2}(\xi)\sqrt{4\pi} Y_{lm}(\theta, \phi)$$

$$\xi = \frac{r-1}{r+1}$$

where K_{nl} is a number related only to n and l, and $C_n^{2l+3/2}(\xi)$ and $Y_{lm}(\theta, \phi)$ are ultraspherical polynomials and spherical harmonics, respectively. After some algebra, the expansion coefficients become

$$A_{nlm} = \frac{1}{I_{nl}} \sum_k m_k [\Phi_{nlm}(r_k, \theta_k, \phi_k)]^*$$

where I_{nl} is a number and m_k is the mass of the kth particle. Once the gravitational potential is found, the gravitational force per unit mass can be obtained by taking the gradient of the potential and the particles can be accelerated accordingly.

13.6.1   The pC++ Version of the SCF Code

We design a C++ class called **Segment** to represent a subgroup of the N particles used in the simulation. As we have discussed earlier, the major procedure in the SCF code is to compute the sums for the expansion coefficients A_{nlm}. Our approach is to first compute local sums within each **Segment** object. After this, global sums are formed by a global reduction. The global sums are then broadcast back to each **Segment** object where the particles are accelerated by the gravitational force. Fortran subroutines in the original Fortran code can be used as member functions of the **Segment** class, although subroutines involving interelement communication and I/O need to be modified.

The Fortran subroutines are called by pC++ through a specially designed Fortran interface [Yang *et al.* 1994]. The **Segment** class is declared (with many unimportant variables and member functions omitted) as follows:

```
class Segment {
public:
  FArrayDouble x, y, z, vx, vy, vz, ax, ay, az, mass,
               plm, clm, dlm, elm, flm, dplm;
  double sinsum[lmax+1][lmax+1][nmax+1],
         cossum[lmax+1][lmax+1][nmax+1];
  Segment();
  void compute_polynomial();
  void compute_acceleration();
  void update_position();
  void update_velocity();
};
```

The data type **FArrayDouble** is defined in the Fortran library; it serves as an interface to Fortran double precision arrays. The **FArrayDobule** variables defined above are one-dimensional arrays that contain the positions, the velocities, the accelerations, and the masses of particles belonging to a **Segment** object, and the expansion coefficients and values of the polynomial. **sinsum** and **cossum** contain the local sums and eventually the global sums of the expansion coefficients. The class member functions call Fortran subroutines: **compute_polynomial()** computes the polynomials and local sums, **compute_acceleration()** computes the acceleration for each particle, and **update_position()** and **update_velocity()** update the positions and velocities of particles.

The collection that distributes the elements, allocates memory, and manages inter-element communication is declared as below. Again, many less important member functions are omitted for brevity:

```
Collection SelfConsistField : public Fortran {
 public:
   SelfConsistField(Distribution *D, Align *A);
   void InParticles();
   void InParameters();
   void OutParticles(int nsnap);
 MethodOfElement:
   virtual void compute_polynomial();
   virtual void compute_acceleration();
   virtual void update_position();
   virtual void update_velocity();
   void read_segment();
   void write_segment();
};
```

The functions declared here are pC++ functions. Their main purpose is to handle I/O. **InParticles()**, **InParameters()**, and **OutParticles()** read input files and write to output files, while **read_segment()** and **write_segment()** are called by **InParticles()** and **OutParticles()** to perform parallel I/O. Functions that are already defined in element class **Segment** are declared as virtual functions in this collection declaration. The inherited **Fortran** collection is a parent collection which handles inter-element communication. **Fortran** itself is derived from the **SuperKernel** collection.

The main program is:

```
void Processor_Main() {
  elem_count = pcxx_TotalNodes();
  Processors P;
  Distribution D(elem_count, &P, BLOCK);
  Align A(elem_count, "[ALIGN(X[i], D[i])]");
  SelfConsistField<Segment> X(&D, &A);
  // read initial model
  X.InParameters();
  X.InParticles();
  X.compute_polynomial();
  X.ReduceDoubleAdd(offset,variable_count);
  X.compute_acceleration();
  // main loop
  for (n = 1; n <= nsteps; n++) {
    X.update_position();
    X.compute_polynomial();
    X.ReduceDoubleAdd(offset, variable_count);
    X.compute_acceleration();
    X.update_velocity();
    X.OutParticles(n);
  }
}
```

The ReduceDoubleAdd reduction function is inherited from SuperKernel. offset is measured from the beginning of the class Segment to the beginning of the field sinsum, and variable_count is the total number of array elements in sinsum and cossum. A leapfrog integration scheme is used to advance particles.

13.6.2 Benchmark Results

Our experiments with the pC++ SCF code were conducted on a Thinking Machines CM-5, an Intel Paragon, an SGI PowerChallenge, an IBM SP-2, and a Cray T3D. For comparison, we also ran the CM Fortran SCF code on the CM-5. 51,200 particles were used for the simulation. The system was allowed to evolve for 100 time steps. The results of these experiments are listed in Table 13.2

As can be seen, the SCF code scales up very well on the parallel machines. On the CM-5 the pC++ version is about 1.1 times faster than the CM Fortran code. This is mainly because the pC++ code used a faster vector reduction routine, while the CM Fortran code used a scalar

| | Number of Processors | | | |
Platform	8	16	32	64
Cray T3D		223.0	115.3	
Intel Paragon		667.3	332.5	168.5
IBM SP-2		186.9	103.5	
SGI PowerChallenge	116.9	58.6		
TMC CM-5 (pC++)			45.8	
TMC CM-5 (CM Fortran)			50.3	

Table 13.2
SCF Execution Time (sec) for Evolving 51,200-Particle Stellar System for 100 Time
Steps. Expansions were truncated at $nmax = 6$, $lmax = 4$.

reduction routine. The code achieved highest speed—approximately
50 MFLOPS per processor—on the SGI PowerChallenge.[3]

13.7   The Particle Mesh Code

Another N-body code in the dossier of the GC^3 group is the Particle
Mesh (PM) code [Ferrell & Bertschinger 1993]. Originally implemented
in Fortran-77 and CM Fortran, the particle-mesh method used in the
PM code computes long-range gravitational forces in a galaxy or galaxy
cluster system by solving the gravitational potential on a mesh. The
three-dimensional space is discretize by a three-dimensional grid. An
average density for each grid point is then computed using a Nearest
Grid Point scheme, in which the density value at a grid point is the sum
of all masses of the particles nearest to that grid point. Once the density
values at the grid points are known, Fourier transforms are performed to
compute the potential values at those points. The potential values at the
grid points are finally interpolated back to the particles, and the particle
positions and velocities are updated. The natural data structures for this
are an one-dimensional particle list and a three-dimensional mesh.

---

[3]The pC++ version of the SCF code described here was used recently in an
experiment involving a simulation of 16 million particles, one of the largest such
simulations to date. The computation was distributed over two MPPs, the 512-node
CM-5 at NCSA and the 512-node T3D at PSC, and run in parallel. Communication
between the two codes was done using MPICH over the Internet.

13.7.1 The Particle List Collection

The particles in the simulation are first sorted according to their affinity to mesh points; particles closest to a given mesh point are neighbors in the sorted list. The sorted list is then divided into segments and each segment forms an element of a particle list collection.

There are two approaches that we can follow when dividing the sorted list. There is a tradeoff between data locality and load balance associated with the two approaches. In the first approach, the sorted list is evenly divided so that the segments have the same length. In the second, particles belonging to the same mesh points are grouped into the same segment and segments will have different lengths.

In the first approach, load balancing is ensured because each processor has the same number of particles. However, this approach may cause particles belonging to the same mesh point to be distributed among different elements, thus requiring more inter-element communication and remote updates. The second approach allows a greater exploitation of data locality, but there is a potential load balancing problem. As the system evolves, particles (stars or galaxies) tend to group together into clumps. Consequently, some mesh points may have 1000 times more particles than other mesh points, and segments that have these mesh points will have much longer lengths. Since we usually distribute the collection elements (in this case segments) evenly across the processors in a parallel machine, the processors that have those long segments will do more work. We therefore decided to follow the first approach.

The Segment class is defined as:

```
class Segment {
 public:
  int particle_count;
  FArrayDouble x, mass, g, v;
  Segment();
};
```

where x, mass, g, and v represent the position, the mass, the acceleration induced by gravity, and the velocity of a particle, respectively.

The ParticleList collection is defined as:

```
Collection ParticleList : public Fortran {
 public:
   ParticleList(Distribution *D, Align *A);
   void SortParticles();
 MethodOfElement:
   void pushParticles(Mesh<MeshElement> &G);
   void updateGridMass(Mesh<MeshElement> &G);
   ...
};
```

The function `SortParticles()` sorts particles in lexicographic order
according to their positions. The particles within each segment are first
sorted using the standard C library quicksort function `qsort()`. A global
parallel sort is then performed using the bitonic sort of Section 13.4.

`pushParticles()` uses the gravitational force to update the positions
and velocities of the particles. The argument passed to `pushParticles()`
is a collection designed for the mesh data structure (Section 13.7.2). The
mesh collection is passed to `pushParticles()` so that potential values
at the grid points can be accessed by particles in the `Segment` element
and used to update the particles' velocities and positions. The function
`updateGridMass()` is used to add the mass of a particle to the total
mass of the mesh point to which it is closest. This function first loops
through the particles local to a segment and accumulates a local total
mass for each mesh point. It then adds the local total mass to the mesh
point's total mass by a remote update operation on the appropriate mesh
point. Because remote updates are expensive, the particles are sorted
to minimize the number of remote updates.

13.7.2   The Mesh Collection

The mesh is logically a three dimensional array of mesh points, each
containing values for density and position. Because an FFT is used to
solve the gravitational potential equation, the data structure is designed
as an one-dimensional collection, each element of which contains a slice
of the three-dimensional mesh:

```
class MeshElement {
 public:
   double density[x_dim_size][y_dim_size];
   MeshElement();
   void add_density(double density, int x_zone, int y_zone);
};
```

`add_density()` is remotely invoked by `Segment` elements to deposit mass on grid points.

The collection `Mesh` is defined as:

```
Collection Mesh : Fortran {
 public:
  Mesh(Distribution *T, Align *A);
  void computePotential();
 MethodOfElement:
  void xyFFT_forward();
  void zFFT_forward();
  void zFFT_backward();
  void xyFFT_backward();
  void transpose_xy_to_xz();
  void transpose_xz_to_xy();
};
```

The function `computePotential()` computes the gravitational potential using the total mass at each mesh point. It calls the FFT routines listed under `MethodOfElement`. The density distribution is first transformed into the wavenumber domain by a FFT along the x, y, and z directions. After solving the Poisson's equation for the gravitational potential in the wavenumber domain, the potential (or force components) is transformed back into the spatial domain.

The FFT transform in the x, y, and z directions is performed by the `Mesh` collection. The FFT in the x and y directions is straightforward, since each `MeshElement` contains an entire array of mesh points. To perform an FFT in the z-direction, data are transformed using the functions `transpose_xy_to_xz` and `transpose_xy_to_xy`.

13.7.3 The Main Simulation Loop

Given these collections, the main body of the simulation can be implemented as follows:

```
main(){
 int num_of_segments = pcxx_TotalNodes();
 int mesh_dim_z = 64;
 Processors P;

 Distribution Dist_PartList(num_of_segments, &P, BLOCK);
 Align Align_PartList(num_of_segments, "[ALIGN(G[i], T[i])]");
 ParticleList<Segment> part(&Dist_PartList, &Align_PartList);
```

```
Distribution Dist_Mesh(mesh_dim_z, &P, BLOCK);
Align Align_Mesh(mesh_dim_z, "[ALIGN(G[i], T[i])]");
Mesh<MeshPlane> mesh(&Dist_Mesh, &Align_Mesh);

// initialize particle list
...
// main loop
for (int i = 0; i < number_of_steps; i++){
  mesh.computePotential();
  particlelist.pushParticles(mesh);
  particlelist.sortParticles();
  particlelist.updateGridMass(mesh);
}
...
}
```

The main loop does computation on both the Mesh and ParticleList collections. First, the potential is computed in parallel on the grid. Second, the particle velocities and positions are updated. If particles have moved to new grid points, the appropriate data structures are then updated. The particles are then sorted, after which the particle masses are accumulated in their corresponding points for the next iteration step.

13.7.4 Benchmark Results

Our experiments with the pC++ PM code were conducted on a Thinking Machines CM-5, an Intel Paragon, an SGI PowerChallenge, an IBM SP-2, and a Cray T3D. For comparison, we also ran the CM Fortran PM code on the CM-5. 32,768 particles were used for the simulation. The system was allowed to evolve for 10 time steps. The results of these experiments are listed in Table 13.3.

As can be seen in the table, the code scales up relatively well on the T3D and PowerChallenge. On the CM-5, the pC++ code is considerably slower than the CM Fortran code. This is because the CM Fortran code can make use of transpose routines embedded in an FFT developed by Thinking Machines' engineers. The pC++ code has complicated data structures and cannot use those transpose routines. Again, the best performance was obtained on the PowerChallenge, although this architecture is limited to a small number of processors.

Platform	Number of Processors			
	8	16	32	64
Cray T3D		33.4	23.1	
IBM SP-2			81.0	
SGI PowerChallenge	30.4	16.1		
TMC CM-5 (pC++)			134.6	
TMC CM-5 (CM Fortran)			20.4	

Table 13.3
PM Execution Time (sec) for Evolving a 32,768-Particle Stellar System for 10 Time Steps. A 64 × 64 × 64 grid was used.

13.8 Conclusion and Project Evaluation

pC++ offers a simple data-parallel programming model which makes use of the object-oriented features of C++. Most scientific parallel computations have proven to be well-suited to this model of computation. However, we have discovered a number of serious limitations in our system. Some of these can easily be overcome, but others have led our research in new directions.

The current pC++ compiler is not well suited to support nested data parallelism. Computations for which the available concurrency is nested or "multi-level" are among the most interesting. Many of the important problems that confront the GC^3 effort involve dynamic and adaptive data structures. More specifically, multi-level, adaptive grid techniques, which are becoming standard in the simulation world, are not easy to express without support for dynamic, nested parallelism.

As a simple example, consider the problem of supporting collections of collections in the runtime environment. Because the current pC++ preprocessor translates the single threaded data-parallel style into direct SPMD emulation of data parallelism, it is difficult to allow nested parallel operations. Our thinking here has been greatly influenced by the NESL project at Carnegie-Mellon University [Blelloch 1993]. This research has demonstrated that a wide variety of nested parallel computations can be "flattened" by the compiler and runtime system to produce efficient code. However, most of the examples where this works are relatively static in structure; it is not clear how well this technique works for dynamic, adaptive computation.

C++ has been a moving target. The majority of parallel C++ efforts were constructed without thinking about the impact of the template system and the Standard Template Library (STL). Templates and the STL have introduced concepts into the C++ programming methodology that are different from the standard object-oriented concepts that most users understand. However, the template mechanism in C++ and the STL have taught us to think about libraries of "generic functions" that work in harmony with object-oriented design ideas. Our future work on parallel C++ will embrace these concepts.

C++ users are not willing to accept radical extensions to their programming language. While experimenting with parallel programming language ideas is exciting, extensions to C++ will have little impact unless there is consensus on a small set of changes to the language. Users require programming environments that are stable and that are supported by all vendors. For the future it may be important to design a meta-level control extension facility for C++ (similar to the Japanese RWCP MPC++ system [Ishikawa *et al.* 1995]) so that language extensions are not needed. With this approach, new parallel constructs could be added to the language by providing a library that would work with any C++ system.

It is a mistake to design a system that limits the parallel programming paradigms which can be used. One of the problems with pC++ is that it supports only one paradigm for writing parallel algorithms. While a data-parallel object-oriented style is good for some applications, it certainly does not cover all applications. For example, it is not easy to simulate the concurrency in an operating system with a data-parallel language. ICC++ (Chapter 9) and COOL (Chapter 6) are interesting because they mix general parallel control constructs with some special new object-oriented features. In general, it seems best to provide simple primitives on which users can implement a variety of different programming paradigms. We feel that CC++ (Chapter 3) does well in this respect.

Basic C++ optimization is still a major obstacle to performance on most systems. One of the most frustrating problems with high performance computing in any language is the low quality of code optimization compared to Fortran. This is one reason a clean interface to parallel Fortran is important. Very few of the high performance systems are able to optimize the more advanced programming constructs. As we learn to rely on template-based class libraries, good optimization techniques will become more complex and more important.

The evolution of C++ is driven by standards and ideas from many sources. In the distributed computing community, the Object Management Group (OMG) has established a standard for distributed object systems called the Common Object Request Broker Architecture (CORBA). The Object Data Base Group will soon describe a standard that may also have a major impact on parallel object-oriented computing. All of these activities represent technologies that must be considered when we think about parallel computation in object-oriented terms.

Acknowledgments

This research is supported by ARPA under Rome Labs contract AF 30602-92-C-0135, the National Science Foundation Office of Advanced Scientific Computing under grant ASC-9111616, and the National Science Foundation and ARPA Grand Challenge project, "The Formation of Galaxies and Large-scale Structure." and NSF CDA 93-03189. The authors also owe a special debt of thanks to François Bodin, who wrote the original pC++ compiler and to all of the users who sent bug reports.

14 POOMA

John V. W. Reynders, Paul J. Hinker,

Julian C. Cummings, Susan R. Atlas,

Subhankar Banerjee, William F. Humphrey,

Steve R. Karmesin, Katarzyna Keahey,

M. Srikant, and MaryDell Tholburn

14.1 Introduction

POOMA, the Parallel Object-Oriented Methods and Applications Frame-Work, is a C++ class library designed to provide a flexible environment for data-parallel programming of scientific applications. The FrameWork defines an interface in which the users—who need not be familiar with object-oriented programming—express the fundamental scientific content and/or numerical methods of their problem, and, optionally, give hints as to how to best decompose it across processors. Classes within the POOMA FrameWork perform the necessary data decomposition and communications.

The POOMA FrameWork is constructed in a layered fashion, in order to exploit the efficient implementations in the lower levels of the Frame-Work, while preserving an interface germane to the application problem domain at the highest level. Thus, it is possible to alter underlying implementations with no changes to the high-level interface. This is our approach to the encapsulation of parallelism within an object-oriented programming system. For the current status of the POOMA Frame-Work, we have provided a POOMA home page on the World Wide Web. Our URL is http://www.acl.lanl.gov/PoomaFramework.

14.2 History and Philosophy

The POOMA FrameWork was inspired by the Numerical Tokamak community's need to resolve the Parallel Platform Paradox, which states:

> The average time required to implement a moderate-sized application on a parallel computer architecture is equivalent to the half-life of the latest parallel supercomputer.

Although a strict definition of "half-life" could be argued, no computational physicist in the fusion community would dispute the fact that most of the time spent in implementing parallel simulations was focused on code maintenance, rather than on exploring new physics. Architectures, software environments, and parallel languages came and went, leaving the investment in a new physics code buried with the demise of the latest supercomputer. There had to be a way to preserve that investment.

The POOMA FrameWork grew out of the Object-Oriented Particle Simulation (OOPS) class library [Reynders *et al.* 1994, Reynders *et al.* 1995], which was developed at Los Alamos specifically for particle-in-cell (PIC) simulations [Birdsall & Langdon 1985] of fusion plasmas using gyrokinetic methods [Lee 1987]. Performing efficient PIC simulations is notoriously difficult on parallel architectures [Decyk 1995]. PIC codes written with classes from the OOPS library, however, allowed PIC simulations to move between parallel architectures with no change to the source code. Furthermore, the high-level, data-parallel representation of particle aggregates with OOPS classes provided several performance enhancements over previous object-oriented PIC simulations [Forslund *et al.* 1990].

The POOMA FrameWork extended the ideas of the OOPS classes to include a variety of high-level, parallel data types and greater functionality. The main goals of the POOMA FrameWork include:

1. Code portability across serial, distributed, and parallel architectures with no change to source code.

2. Development of re-usable, cross-problem-domain components to enable rapid application development.

3. Code efficiency for kernels and components relevant to scientific simulation.

4. FrameWork design and development driven, by applications from a diverse set of scientific problem domains.

5. Shorter time from problem inception to working parallel simulations.

14.2.1 Why Data-Parallel Programming?

When using explicit message passing, programmers must manage both the details of data layout across processor memories and the movement of data between them. In a data-parallel programming system [Hillis & Steele 1986], responsibility is delegated to a runtime system or a layer of classes responsible for parallel abstractions. Data-parallel systems encourage programmers to develop algorithms appropriate for the large data sets, which are the usual target of parallel scientific applications. Attempting to parallelize a serial code is much easier if the programmer considers a large number of processors at the outset.

Another strong argument for data-parallel programming is that encapsulation at the data level is typically equivalent to encapsulation at the mathematical level. Our experience is that data parallelism exposes the natural mathematical structure of a code, extracting it from layers of do loops. Operations on data-parallel objects can be encapsulated as parallel operators. Structuring a code in terms of data-parallel objects and operators dramatically increases code readability and correspondence with the original equations. It also facilitates identification of computational primitives suitable for optimization. The overhead incurred by use of an object-oriented framework to provide data parallelism can be offset by the efficiency gained in its ability to chain together mathematical operations.

14.2.2 Why a Framework?

A framework provides an integrated and layered system of classes. Each class in the framework is composed of or utilizes classes from lower layers. In the POOMA FrameWork, the upper layers contain distributed data classes that are abstractions of scientific problem domains (i.e., particles, fields, and matrices) and typical methods performed on these data types, such as binary operations, Fourier transforms, or Krylov solvers. Classes lower in the FrameWork capture the abstractions relevant to parallelism and efficient node-level simulation, including communication, domain decomposition, chained-expression optimization, and load balancing. The higher-level classes in the FrameWork are principally bookkeepers that delegate computational tasks to these lower layers.

This layered approach to object-oriented analysis and design provides a natural breakdown of responsibility in application development. Computer scientists and algorithm specialists can focus on the lower realms of the FrameWork, optimizing computational kernels and message-passing techniques without having to consider the application being constructed. Meanwhile, application scientists can construct numerical models from classes in the upper levels of the FrameWork, without knowing their implementation details. This clear separation of duties is made possible by the encapsulation of parallelism and application science in POOMA, which helps the programmer avoid interspersing message-passing commands and computational algorithms in the application code.

14.3 Implementation

14.3.1 Framework Layer Description

The POOMA FrameWork is composed of C++ classes. POOMA does not utilize language extensions; rather, parallelism is captured through a hierarchical layering of classes. Furthermore, no preprocessors or interpreters are invoked, which enables source-level debugging. The Frame-Work consists of the following five layers of classes:

- Application Layer
- Component Layer
- Global Layer
- Parallel Abstraction Layer
- Local Layer

As described earlier, the classes higher in the FrameWork represent abstractions directly relevant to application domains, whereas classes lower in the FrameWork represent the abstractions of parallelism and efficient computational kernels. The Global and Local Layers work together to define Global Data Types (GDTs) that perform matrix, field, and particle operations. The interactions between the Global and Local classes are mediated by objects from the Parallel Abstraction Layer (PAL), which is responsible for capturing key abstractions of parallelism, such as interprocessor communication, domain decomposition, and load balancing. The Component Layer, which is built upon the Global Layer, contains a rich set of algorithms directly relevant to scientific simulation (such as interpolations, Fast Fourier Transforms, and Krylov solvers). Classes in the Component Layer are generic and re-usable across problem domains, whereas members of the Application Layer represent a configuration of Component and Global objects interspersed with application-specific objects. These highest-level objects are complete physics simulations that serve as archetypes for the process of constructing applications with the POOMA FrameWork. Applications currently under investigation include Numerical Tokamak, Molecular Dynamics, high-speed multi-material CFD, and rheological flow simulations.

Code written with classes from within or above the Global Layer are capable of running with no source code changes on serial, distributed, and parallel architectures. We currently support most Unix workstations, Cray vector architectures, and MPI/PVM clusters of workstations (COWs). Parallel architectures supported include the IBM SP-2, the Cray T3D, the SGI PowerChallenge, and the Meiko CS-2. As discussed in Section 14.3.6, we are also researching the extension of our Parallel Abstraction Layer to enable portability to heterogeneous MPP clusters.

A principal feature of this layered framework approach is its extensibility. The PAL is designed for easy addition of new user-defined GDTs. If classes within the POOMA FrameWork contain functionality relevant to the target problem domain, a user may also exploit polymorphism to obtain the requisite behavior. The FrameWork provides further functionality by allowing penetration to any level. Thus, one may access and modify lower-level classes, including overloading their member functions with user-defined behavior. The FrameWork layers and their interaction are described in the sections that follow.

14.3.2   Global Data Types

The *Global Data Types* (GDTs) within the FrameWork provide the user with data-parallel representations for a variety of data types, including fields, matrices, and particles. The design of these high-level classes has been driven by applications, and hence they have matured with a rich set of member functions directly relevant to high-performance science and engineering simulation.

Because many scientific programmers are new to object-oriented programming, the interfaces to the FrameWork's GDT classes have been designed, where possible, to seem similar to a familiar procedural, data-parallel language syntax, such as that of Fortran-90. However, this does not preclude the use of inheritance and polymorphism to create new classes that map directly to problem domains of interest. With this in mind, the FrameWork has been designed and implemented with a shallow inheritance structure.

Each GDT object is an aggregate of several Local Data Type objects. These Global and Local objects interact to provide simple I/O and data visualization capabilities. At compile time, architecture-dependent I/O libraries may be linked in, as well as the Advanced Computing Laboratory's portable Generic Display Library (GDL), to extend these capabilities.

Although a lot of ground can be covered by using the GDTs that are already in place and specializing their behavior through inheritance, there are hooks within the FrameWork to enable further extensibility through the explicit installation of other user-defined GDTs. The process of taking a serial class library and parallelizing it is made easier through the re-use of classes from the FrameWork that encapsulate key parallel abstractions such as domain decomposition, load balancing, and communication.

Field Classes   The `Field` classes are N-dimensional arrays of floats, doubles, or integers. Data-parallel representation allows looped expressions, such as:

```
for (int i=0; i<Nx; i++) {
  for (int j=0; j<Ny; j++) {
    for (int k=0; k<Nz; k++) {
      A[i][j][k] = B[i][j][k] + C[i][j][k] + D[i][j][k];
    }
  }
}
```

to be replaced with the single line of code:

```
A[I][J][K] = B[I][J][K] + C[I][J][K] + D[I][J][K];
```

Here I, J, and K are `Index` objects that describe how the data-parallel array is traversed with ranges, strides, and offsets. In this simple case, with each `Field` utilizing the entire index range and a stride of one with no offset, the index notation is optional, since this is the default behavior. Both the `Field` and `Index` classes have overloaded operator member functions to enable expressions such as:

```
B[I][J][K] = A[I+1][J][K] + A[I-1][J][K] +
             A[I][J+1][K] + A[I][J-1][K] - 4.0 * A[I][J][K];
```

Here we assume that A and B are conforming Fields (their sizes in each dimension are identical) and that the Index objects I, J, and K traverse each Field entirely. Code written in this data-parallel fashion is compact, easy to debug, and provides a close computational analog to the mathematical expression under investigation.

A rich set of helper classes is available to the Field class. For example, a Boundary class helps Field objects resolve behavior at computational boundaries. Consider the Laplacian stencil defined above: if the Index objects span each Field entirely, what happens at a Field border when the Index has an offset such as I+1? In this case, the Boundary object contained in the Field object is invoked to determine the boundary condition at the border. The default behavior for all Field classes is periodic; however, a Field can have any combination of periodic, Dirichlet, Neumann, or mixed boundary conditions. This provides a much cleaner representation of boundary behavior than the elaborate combinations of cshift and eoshift operations required in other data-parallel languages such as CM Fortran.

The Field class is enabled by a comprehensive set of mathematical and data-parallel functions. These include both parallel versions of standard mathematical functions and data-parallel operations that reduce, spread, transpose, scatter, and gather data. There are also functions that allow data-parallel relational operators to select and de-select portions of the data within a Field object that will be subject to manipulations within a specified scope. This functionality is similar to the where construct or "masking" provided by HPF and other data-parallel languages.

The Field class is complementary in functionality to that of the A++/P++ serial and parallel array class libraries developed at Los Alamos National Laboratory [Lemke & Quinlan 1992]. We are currently working to merge these two classes into a single, highly-tuned array class library.

Banded Matrix and Vector Classes The Vector class provides optimized vector operations, such as binary operations, dot products, and norms. The NDiagMatrix class utilizes a striped, row-compressed data format to represent banded, structured matrices. It includes typical operations, such as transposing a matrix or multiplying two matrices. These classes interact to provide useful matrix-vector operations.

No single data-decomposition strategy can simultaneously be optimal for sparse, banded structured, and full matrices. Optimization of banded, structured matrix storage and operations was motivated by current POOMA applications (Numerical Tokamak, CFD, and rheological flow), which require banded-matrix operations for their elliptic and hyperbolic equation solvers. The necessary interoperability with other GDTs in the FrameWork is enabled by member functions within the NDiagMatrix and Vector classes that convert data to and from vector or banded, structured matrix format. Work is now underway to develop separate full and sparse matrix classes for future application areas.

The responsibilities of the Global and Local class member functions performing vector and matrix operations split clearly, with global operators handling communications and storage management, and local operators performing the actual computation. For example, element access, addition, and many other operations can be performed on the data in place; hence, the global member functions are simple. Furthermore, the global and local parts of an operator vary widely in the algorithms they utilize. For example, matrix-vector multiplication, squaring a matrix, and matrix transpose use different algorithms for the optimized global communication patterns and for the optimized local computations.

Particle Classes   In particle simulation programs, particles are free to move about a given domain while interacting with a fixed grid. However, if each particle is not continually repositioned upon the processor holding the grid cells nearest to its position, then the simulation will become dominated by interprocessor communication. The particle classes within the POOMA FrameWork provide the message-passing capability needed to address this problem, while maintaining an expressive data-parallel syntax for coding the numerical algorithms for particle motion and interaction.

A DPField (Double-Precision Particle Field) object represents a particle attribute such as a position, velocity, or electronic charge. A Particles object, which represents a distribution of particles, contains a set of DPField objects that describe the particles' attributes. Both the Particles and DPField objects point to the same data, but they provide the user with two different views.

A DPField object's overloaded operators and member functions allow the user to operate on separate attributes of the particles. For example, a particle position update of the DPField objects x0 (old position), x1 (new position), and v (velocity) with the double delta_t (time step) would be performed using:

```
x1 = x0 + delta_t * v;
```

The Particles class has a member function called swap() that is responsible for load balancing the particles as they move through the simulation domain. Given DPField objects containing the particle coordinates, and drawing upon data layout information provided by classes in the PAL, the swap() function performs the necessary particle swapping and memory management. Due to the expense and complexity of particle swapping, this operation has been made a high-level member function available to the user. This will aid in the understanding of program algorithms and will improve code performance.

Other member functions are provided in the Particles class to facilitate the calculation of forces on particles in a simulation. If one is computing forces or potentials on a grid (i.e., a particle-in-cell method), Gather and Scatter member functions are available to interpolate a field quantity to particle positions or accumulate a particle quantity onto the grid. These functions invoke an Interpolate class that is equipped with several common interpolation methods. This class can query the Field involved for critical information, such as whether the Field is cell-centered or vertex-centered. For particle-particle interaction forces, POOMA provides a member function called Interact() to accumulate forces on each particle due to neighboring particles within a given radius. This function circulates particles amongst the neighboring nodes in a predefined pattern, performing interprocessor communication as required and accumulating interparticle forces at each stop using a force function defined in the POOMA library or a user-defined one. By choosing the dimensions of the subdomain on each virtual node (Section 14.3.3) to be slightly larger than the cutoff radius for the interaction, the communications pattern can be restricted to nearest-neighbor nodes only, without any loss of generality. The data structures and communication pattern that Interact() implements correspond to the Cell Method [Beazley et al. 1995].

14.3.3   Parallel Abstraction Layer

Classes within the *Parallel Abstraction Layer* (PAL) are responsible for
encapsulating key features of parallel programming, such as interprocessor communication and domain decomposition, in order to support
GDTs composed of local (node-level) data objects. The global/local
programming paradigm extends the data-parallel programming model
by allowing a user to access the message-passing level from within an
active data-parallel program. This is accomplished through access to
runtime system information on GDT object data layouts and geome-
tries. Once the details of a data layout are known, it is possible to
establish the correspondence between individual pieces of data and the
processors in a runtime partition and to manipulate that data manually, whether on-node or as arguments of explicit sends and receives.
A data-parallel array descriptor provides the essential link between local and global array contents. A GDT object can thus be modified by
manipulating its individual pieces at the local level.

   This global/local paradigm precisely describes how POOMA implements its data-parallel interface. Using stored array-descriptor geometry
information, POOMA performs an explicit conversion of data-parallel
code to nodal C++ with message passing. The key abstractions of
global/local parallelism are encapsulated into three groups of classes
within the PAL: Global/Local Interaction classes (those managing the
interactions of GDT objects with their local constituents), `DataLayout`
classes (those responsible for data layout and processor geometry), and
`Communicate` classes (those responsible for moving data between nodes).

Global/Local Interaction Classes   Every GDT within the Frame-
Work consists of a mirrored pair of global and local classes. For each
instantiation of a GDT object, the Global/Local Interaction classes help
to instantiate an appropriate number of type-corresponding local objects
on each of the available processors. In an application code, the user
calculates only with GDT objects. In turn, each member function of
a global object works with PAL classes to locate the constituent local
objects and invoke the corresponding local member function. Thus,
the primary role of a GDT object is to act as a bookkeeper, while the
calculations actually are performed by the constituent local objects.

   Every Global and Local class in POOMA uses the letter/envelope
paradigm [Coplien 1992] and inherits from an abstract base class, which

is responsible for registering and interacting with classes in the PAL. Furthermore, a virtual constructor technique [Gamma *et al.* 1995] is employed to enable other classes within the FrameWork (such as the Chained Expression Object described in Section 14.3.4) to perform high-level operations on GDT objects without having to distinguish their types.

A key abstraction within the FrameWork is that of the "virtual" node. There can be several virtual nodes on a physical processor; a map of the virtual node IDs and corresponding physical node IDs is maintained by a PAL class called the **VnodeManager**. When a global object is instantiated, it actually spreads its constituent local objects across virtual nodes rather than physical nodes. Thus, the global and local objects know nothing about the actual number of physical processors available.

This abstraction allows us to move entire virtual nodes between physical nodes without changing properties of the global or local objects contained in a virtual node. The data configuration is made consistent by simply updating the virtual-to-physical node map. Thus, we exploit two levels of load balancing: balancing local data between virtual nodes and balancing virtual nodes between physical nodes. Modifying the virtual-to-physical node ratio allows the user to match data set sizes with the cache sizes of specific machines. This is important because code efficiency on many of the architectures on which the FrameWork runs is a highly sensitive function of data alignment in the cache.

Another advantage to storing data in a virtual node form is that it simplifies parallel I/O. Most parallel computer vendors do not have tools for saving data from a given system partition and then reading the same data back into a system partition of a different size. By maintaining data in a virtual node form (where a number of virtual nodes greater than the maximum partition size is used), the FrameWork need only update the virtual-to-physical node map as the data is read back in.

Data Layout Classes The **DataLayout** classes are responsible for defining the geometry of the GDTs and the interconnection of their constituent local objects. An abstract base class provides the necessary hooks into the PAL, while inherited classes provide information and functionality pertinent to each GDT in the FrameWork (i.e., there is a **FieldLayout** for **Field** objects, a **NDiagLayout** for **NDiagMatrix** objects, etc.). Thus, each GDT has a layout class tuned to its needs.

DataLayout objects are composed of smaller POOMA objects such as Neighbors, Offsets, and Sizes. This encapsulation of data layout abstractions enables code re-use when DataLayout classes for other data types are required for new GDTs integrated into the FrameWork.

The DataLayout classes that accompany the POOMA GDTs provide a variety of archetypal layout strategies, as well as default behavior when no data layout is specified. For example, given an N-dimensional Field object, one is able to specify which of its dimensions are to be distributed and which are to remain on-node. Once the subset of parallel axes are known, one is then able to choose from several parallel domain decomposition archetypes (hypercubes, hyperplanes, pencils, etc.) to complete the formation of the data layout.

Over the course of a simulation, DataLayout objects are constructed as part of the construction of GDT objects. The DataLayout objects mediate GDT operations that require interprocessor communication, and they are used to determine when two GDT objects can be used together in an expression. In the cases where the data layouts are the same, the objects are considered fully conforming. In cases where the global sizes of the objects are similar, but the layout across the virtual nodes is different, the objects are considered partially conforming. In this case, the DataLayout class interacts with PAL classes to generate a temporary GDT object that is fully conforming, and the data is moved to this layout before the operation is performed. When the global sizes are not the same, the objects do not conform, and the operation cannot be performed.

Communication Classes A wide variety of parallel computer architectures are available today, as well as several different communication libraries for interprocessor communication and process control. To provide a portable, transparent mechanism for supporting message-passing communications on distributed, parallel, and clustered parallel architectures (discussed in Section 14.3.6), two classes have been implemented and used throughout the FrameWork: Communicate and Message.

The Message class is used to encapsulate data in a format that allows for easy construction and data retrieval. Each Message consists of some number of items, where each item is a scalar or vector of any defined data type. Routines are provided by the Message class to query for information on the number, size, type, and contents of the items in a

Message. In essence, the Message class provides an arbitrary runtime structure that is used to hold data to be sent to or received from another node. Message objects can be concatenated together, copied, forwarded to other nodes, and written to or read from a file.

The Communicate class is a generic interface to the specific parallel communication library to be used. It is responsible for making sure the necessary processes are running on the parallel processors, and it contains the code to send and receive data between these processes. Each process is assigned a unique integer ID, from 0 to N-1 (where N is the total number of parallel processes), and there may be any number of processes on each physical processor. To use the Communicate class to send data to another process, a Message object is created, filled with the data to be sent, and then given to a Communicate object for delivery. Communicate provides routines for sending Message objects to a destination process, and for receiving Message objects from a sending process. Each Message is sent with a user-specified identification code (tag). Message objects may be received in any order, and options are provided to search for pending data from a specific process or pending data with a specific tag. Message objects that have the same source and destination node are passed to a message queue and are never introduced to the network. This approach also makes it possible to simulate some aspects of message-passing algorithms on serial architectures through reads and writes to local memory.

Through the use of this parallel communication abstraction, the work required to port an application to a new parallel communication library is greatly reduced. Development of a new version of the Communicate class (for a new base communications library or a new architecture-specific system) requires only four routines to be rewritten: initialization and termination of the parallel communication environment, and sending and receiving routines for the Message objects. At present, versions of Communicate have been developed for use with PVM and MPI clusters of Unix-based workstations, SMP architectures, and the Cray T3D, IBM SP-2, and Meiko CS-2 parallel supercomputers.

14.3.4   Chained Expression Object

One of the most powerful features of C++ is its ability to overload operators for user-defined types. Unfortunately, this feature is also one of the major reasons that the performance of C++ code does not compare well to that of C or Fortran.

A simple statement that demonstrates the problem is:

```
D = A + B + C;
```

Here A, B, C, and D are user-defined objects that have a large amount of data associated with them (such as vectors or arrays). The act of performing the binary operation + or = on two objects involves a call to an overloaded, binary-operator function. Thus, the above expression involves three separate calls that are "chained" together. In our example, A + B is evaluated, and the result is added to C. The result of that is then assigned to D. The POOMA FrameWork views expressions like these as "chained expressions", in which a series of overloaded function calls are chained together to arrive at the answer.

In the case of elemental types (int, float, double, etc.), it has become possible for compilers to optimize chained expressions. Overloaded binary operations inhibit such optimizations in C++ by breaking chained expressions into their binary elements. For large data sets, this can severely reduce overall performance.

Another source of performance degradation comes from the creation of temporary variables during expression evaluation. If users do not take steps to optimize default usage of copy constructors through reference-counting methods and shallow copies [Coplien 1992], a temporary object is created for each binary operation performed. This is not only time-consuming, but, for large user-defined types, can cause the code to run out of physical memory (due to the creation of temporaries) and can lead to virtual memory swapping.

These performance penalties prompted creation of the *Chained Expression Object* (CEO) in the POOMA FrameWork. The main goal of the CEO is to recognize complex expressions and bypass multiple function calls normally required in the implementation of overloaded operators. This is accomplished by modifying the way overloaded operators are used. Instead of performing the operation specified by a given function, the code updates the CEO with information concerning objects involved in the operation, and the CEO builds an expression stack for the statement at run time. When the assignment statement is finally encountered, the CEO matches the expression stack with a library of tuned expression kernels. If a match is found, the expression can be evaluated directly. If

not, the CEO "deconstructs" the expression stack into the largest possible
registered kernels to complete the evaluation.

For example, consider the following code:

```
// constructs a vector with 100 items
Vector A(100), B(100), C(100), D(100);
A = 1.0;          // assign value to every vector element
B = 2.0;
C = 3.0;
D = A + B + C;    // perform two + ops and the = op
```

A naïve implementation would perform the following operations:

```
Vector::Vector:Constructing vector 'A' with length of 100
Vector::Vector:Constructing vector 'B' with length of 100
Vector::Vector:Constructing vector 'C' with length of 100
Vector::Vector:Constructing vector 'D' with length of 100
Performing A = 1.000000
Performing B = 2.000000
Performing C = 3.000000
Vector::Vector:Constructing vector 'TMP1' with length of 100
Performing TMP1 = A + B
Vector::Vector:Constructing vector 'TMP2' with length of 100
Performing TMP2 = TMP1 + C
Performing D = TMP2
Destructing TMP2
Destructing TMP1
Destructing D
Destructing C
Destructing B
Destructing A
```

In contrast, by using the CEO, the POOMA FrameWork would execute
the same code in a more efficient manner:

```
Vector::Vector:Constructing vector 'A' with length of 100
CEO::registering expression kernel FLDFLDadd
CEO::registering expression kernel FLDFLDaddFLDadd
Vector::Vector:Constructing vector 'B' with length of 100
Vector::Vector:Constructing vector 'C' with length of 100
Vector::Vector:Constructing vector 'D' with length of 100
Performing A = 1.000000
Performing B = 2.000000
Performing C = 3.000000
```

```
Placing token FLD on expression stack
Placing token FLD on expression stack
Placing token add on expression stack
Placing token FLD on expression stack
Placing token add on expression stack
Performing D = FLDFLDaddFLDadd
Destructing D
Destructing C
Destructing B
Destructing A
```

Each operation registers itself with the CEO. When FLDFLDaddFLDadd is found during the execution of the assignment, the Vector pointers are passed in, and all the operations are executed inside a single function call. This allows the registered functions to place several operations on a single line in a for loop and reap the added performance over repeated binary operations. Furthermore, no temporaries are constructed, and no extra copies are performed. If an object on the right-hand side of the expression also were to appear on the left-hand side, a temporary would be created to store the intermediate value before assignment.

CEO in Parallel Scientific Simulation   The CEO provides a powerful expression-by-expression optimization capability. The gains in cache performance, CPU speedup, and reduced memory utilization are significant, while the expressive features of the GDTs are preserved. We have extended previous work on expression grouping [Parson & Quinlan 1994] to explore parallelism and chained-expression operations between heterogeneous data types. The FrameWork's use of virtual constructor techniques for its GDTs (described in Section 14.3.3) enables optimization of inter-type operations, providing efficient implementations of expressions such as particle gather/scatter operations on fields and stencil/field interactions.

The CEO plays a further role in parallel architectures by coordinating interprocessor communications and managing temporary border information, as is shown in a two-dimensional (2D) diffusion example in Section 14.4.1. The CEO defers all message passing to the = operator, at which time it determines which Field objects in the expression stack require updated border information. Current research is exploring inter-expression border re-use techniques to reduce the overall message-passing requirement.

An important insight gained from parallel application development efforts is the recurrence of stencil patterns (e.g., elliptic and hyperbolic stencil operations) in a variety of problem domains. This eases the effort in maintaining a comprehensive, tuned kernel library targeted to the application domain. If exact stencil matches are not found, the expression is deconstructed into the largest possible sub-expressions contained in the expression kernel library. Even in the pathological case where the largest pattern match reduces to a set of binary operations, a substantial savings is still gained through the avoidance of unnecessary temporary creation.

This structure allows developers to "freeze" a working, high-level description of the numerical algorithms they are using, and then extensively tune the performance by writing optimized kernels for critical sections of the code. The process of adding new kernels is simple, due to the straightforward structure of the expression kernels and their interaction with the FrameWork. The CEO and its supporting cast of optimized kernels are the key to how POOMA efficiently evaluates general data-parallel statements.

Currently, we are exploiting the design of the CEO to implement a runtime, code-generation capability for the POOMA FrameWork. In this manner, a simulation can be run in a "debug, code-generation" mode, in which expression stubs for non-matching kernels are interpreted into code modules. Thus, after a recompilation of the target class, the code can run in an optimized mode with no expression deconstructions or intermediate temporaries.

14.3.5 Component Layer

One of the most time-consuming aspects of scientific code development on parallel architectures is the process of rewriting code to match native scientific libraries as one moves to a new parallel architecture. The changes can be small (a different ordering of parameters), medium (communications are required to fit the requisite parallel data layout), or large (the routine your code depended upon on architecture A does not exist on architecture B, thus requiring you to write your own).

Classes from the Component Layer encapsulate many useful routines typically found in scientific libraries and some that provide functionality unique to the FrameWork. These classes are built upon GDT classes;

thus, they run with no changes on serial, distributed, and parallel architectures.

FFT POOMA provides an FFT class for Fast Fourier Transform analysis of a `Field` of any dimension. The library currently includes Radix-2 Complex-to-Complex, Real-to-Complex, and Complex-to-Real FFT components. An object of this class accepts `Field` data, moves the data into "pencils" (1D arrays of data contained on a single processor) aligned along the `Field` dimension that is to be transformed, performs the FFT, and returns the data to its original layout. The data layout is altered prior to the FFT in order to minimize interprocessor communication and increase efficiency. In order to perform an FFT on a `Field` object, an FFT object must be instantiated for that `Field`. This FFT object will know the lengths of the `Field` in each dimension and its data layout across the parallel processors, and it will pre-allocate pencils of memory for FFTs in each dimension of the `Field`. Any `Field` object that fully conforms with this `Field` (has the same dimensions, sizes, and data layout) can be Fourier transformed with the same FFT object.

When an FFT is requested, the user provides `Field` objects with real and imaginary components of the data, asks for a forward or inverse Fourier transform along a particular dimension of the field, and can provide a factor by which to scale the result (in order to renormalize the resulting field data). After the data is transposed into a layout of pencils, each processor will perform 1D FFTs on all its pencils. A subroutine written in C is provided to perform these FFTs, but one may substitute other optimized routines if desired.

The code below instantiates two `Field` objects and constructs an FFT object. Note that we need a `Field` object to construct the FFT object, as this construction sets up work arrays for use in FFTs.

```
Index I(64), J(64);
Field real(I,J);
Field imag(I,J);
FFT fftObject(real); // instantiate with a Field
fftObject.FFT_CC(real, imag, 1, 1, 1.0/sqrt(64)); // X-dim FFT
fftObject.FFT_CC(real, imag, 2, 1, 1.0/sqrt(64)); // Y-dim FFT
```

Table 14.1 shows performance results for 25 iterations of a 2D Complex-to-Complex FFT and inverse FFT on a 256×256 grid running on the Cray T3D.

Nodes	Seconds	MFlops	MFlops/Node
2	41.40	12.66	6.33
4	21.43	24.46	6.12
8	14.62	35.86	4.48
16	6.51	80.54	5.03

Table 14.1
FFT Performance

Krylov Solvers POOMA has a collection of scalable, preconditioned conjugate-gradient (PCG) solvers and provides user-friendly facilities for selection of solution methods and algorithms. The iterative Krylov **Solver** class is based on a conceptual decomposition of the general task sequence to be performed in PCG algorithms. The basic idea is to separate the initialization phase from the main-loop phase. The initialization phase includes the preconditioned factorization, if there is one. In the main-loop phase, the optional preconditioner solve is isolated from the rest of the computations. The FrameWork allows us to plug in different preconditioners with a conjugate-gradient algorithm without repeating any CG code.

POOMA provides a collection of CG algorithms (CG, BiCG, CGS, and BiCGStab) and preconditioners (Diagonal, Incomplete Cholesky, and Incomplete LU). A CG algorithm or a combination of a CG algorithm with a preconditioner is considered a specific solver "strategy" [Gamma *et al.* 1995]. All these strategies share a common structure for the **Solver** member function **Solve** (initialization followed by solve), and this is defined in an abstract class called **LSStrategy**. In a PCG solve, a strategy subclass is responsible for the factorization, as well as the initialization. Efficiency is gained since various factorization schemes are kernel operators of the **NDiagMatrix** and **Vector** classes. We employ a certain set of PCGs [Gupta *et al.* 1995, Kumar *et al.* 1993] that substitute the preconditioner solve within a PCG loop by a sequence of matrix-vector multiplications, thereby enhancing scalability. After the initialization (and factorization), the strategy class interacts with the specific CG class to perform the solve.

The **Solver** class provides a user-friendly interface for setting up a solver context (i.e., selecting a CG solve and preconditioner). This context then interacts with the specific strategy class for the chosen CG solve. The code below shows an example of using the `Solver` class for an ICCG solve.

```
int vnodes=16;
int rank=256;
// Fill up the matrix A using the Discretizer class (Section 14.3.5)
...
// Fill up the source vector b with appropriate values
Vector b(rank, vnodes);
...
// Allocate solution vector x
Vector x(rank, vnodes);
Solver L;
L.SetPrecond(IC);      // Choose preconditioner
L.SetCG(CG);           // Choose CG solver
x = L.Solve(A, b);     // Get solution vector x
```

Elliptic Discretization   Finite-difference solution of elliptic, partial differential equations involves two steps. First, the continuous system is discretized over a finite-difference grid, resulting in a linear matrix system. Then, this linear matrix system is solved using matrix computations. The POOMA `Discretizer` class discretizes general, second-order, elliptic, partial differential equations on a finite-difference grid in 1D, 2D, and 3D. It can handle equations with constant coefficients (e.g., the Poisson equation on a physically rectangular grid in Cartesian coordinates) or variable coefficients (e.g., the Poisson equation in a non-Cartesian coordinate system, and other general, second-order equations). Both cell-centered and vertex-centered grid discretizations are provided. Using a `Boundary` object, various boundary conditions (Dirichlet, Neumann, periodic, etc.) can be specified at different edges or faces.

A `Discretizer` object has both global and local components. The global component is used to specify the grid (dimension, number of points in each dimension, and the geometry of the grid), discretization stencil (e.g., five-point, seven-point, etc.), and coefficients of the equation (e.g., constant coefficients and/or variable coefficients). Once the grid, the stencil, and the coefficients are specified, the global component delegates the computing job to the local components. Local components are responsible for computing the stencil weights at each grid point. The `Discretizer` generates a block N-diagonal matrix as the output. Generating the matrix requires transformation of data from one `DataLayout`

(`FieldLayout`) to another (`MatrixLayout`). This transformation of data
from one layout to another is done utilizing the PAL `Communicate` class.
Such patterns of communication to transform objects from one data layout to another are very useful during a simulation (e.g., to transform a
`Field` object to a `Vector` object and vice versa, for an elliptic field
solver).

The code below is an example of using the `Discretizer` class to discretize the Poisson equation on a square grid in 2D. The `Discretizer`
generates a block N-diagonal matrix. Note that after this is done, the
`Solver` described in Section 14.3.5 might then be used to solve this
system.

```
int vnodes = 64;
int stencilPoints = 5;
FIndex I(256), J(256);
ArchType gridGeometry = Squares2D;
Discretizer D(I, J, gridGeometry, vnodes, stencilPoints);
Boundary *BC;
// Set proper boundary conditions on each side here
D.set_boundary(BC);
// Give coefficients of terms in partial differential equation here
D.set_coefficients(1.0, 1.0);
NDiagMatrix A(D.discretize());
```

Stencil Objects   The `Stencil` class provides the user with a short-
hand for long expressions with a fixed set of index offsets into an array.
For example, in our `Field` and `Index` notation, a 3D Laplacian operation
may be represented as shown below:

```
B[I][J][K] = A[I+1][J][K] + A[I-1][J][K] +
             A[I][J+1][K] + A[I][J-1][K] +
             A[I][J][K+1] + A[I][J][K-1] - 6.0 * A[I][J][K];
```

If this operation occurs several times throughout a simulation, however, the application code becomes obscured by the long expression and
there is an increased chance of coding error. Furthermore, in an N-
dimensional simulation on a non-orthogonal mesh, the number of stencil
points required for a second-order expression is 3^N—a potentially huge
expression. The `Stencil` class alleviates these concerns by storing the
coefficient and offset information in a single object.

Thus, expressions such as the one above may be written in the following compact notation:

```
B[I][J][K] = Laplacian(A[I][J][K]);
```

where `Laplacian` is our 3D Laplacian `Stencil` object. This object can be re-used throughout the simulation on any `Field` and is integrated with the `CEO` to optimize the inner-loop calculation and determine the appropriate interprocessor communications based on the `Stencil` offsets.

The construction of the `Stencil` is generalized, so that no changes to the source code are required when changing the dimensionality of a simulation. Thus, a scientist is able to simulate behavior in 1D on a workstation, and then move the code to a parallel architecture to explore behavior in full 3D with no changes to the structure of the source code.

The `Stencil` class includes overloaded operations that enable the construction of complex `Stencil` objects from simpler constituent `Stencil` objects. Given the differentiation `Stencil` objects `DX`, `DY`, and `DZ`, and the identity `Stencil` `I`, one can construct a `Stencil` for the Helmholtz operator and perform the operation on a `Field` with the following two lines of code:

```
Helmholtz = (DX*DX + DY*DY + DZ*DZ) + I;
Result[I][J][K]  =  Helmholtz(Source[I][J][K]);
```

As these examples show, the `Stencil` class provides a powerful mechanism for direct representation of mathematical abstraction in source code.

14.3.6   POOMA on Clustered Parallel Architectures

The POOMA team has been investigating the possibility of developing a programming environment for distributed parallel architectures that would enable spreading computation over many parallel resources at the same time and integrating parallel applications written using different tools or platforms. It is our hope that such an environment also would enable more re-use of parallel code and facilitate the implementation of distributed parallel code. Similar systems, such as the Common Object Request Broker Architecture (CORBA) [OMG 1993], have already been proposed and developed in the distributed systems community. Unfortunately, these systems do not provide a sufficient means of describing and implementing parallel objects or data sharing between different objects, and they do not address issues important to parallel processing, such as load balancing. Our first experiment leading to the development of a system adequate for clustered parallel architectures was undertaken in the summer of 1995. This initial design was meant to be a preliminary proof of the feasibility of such systems.

In order to enable communication between many MPPs, the POOMA FrameWork has been extended to include a hierarchical communication model. The original `Communicate` class has been replaced with a "virtual communication" class that determines the location of the receiving virtual node with respect to the sending virtual node. It then invokes either the communication services provided by the architecture or a combination of these services and network transport to deliver a message to its destination. The virtual nodes themselves are not aware of each other's location; the assignment of virtual nodes to particular machines has been left to the programmer, who configures the virtual machine over which computation is spread. A virtual machine is composed of clusters of virtual nodes, where every physical machine corresponds to the notion of a cluster of virtual nodes.

The system interfaces with CORBA in such a way that, given servers realizing any particular application, the clients can spread their computation over the chosen set of machines, specify what resources of any particular machine they want to use (e.g., the partition size), how they want to balance their load (e.g., how many virtual nodes they want to put on that particular machine), and other initialization information. The client then uses the CORBA Interface Definition Language's one-way functions to initiate the computation on all of these servers simultaneously. It is also possible to initialize computation without using CORBA, through an initialization object that reads in the necessary data from a file or obtains it in some other way, previously agreed upon.

Reliance on CORBA services to implement communication between clusters makes this initial system inefficient, and limits the set of platforms programmers can use. The use of the network transport will soon be replaced by a more efficient method, which will enable us to gather performance data, help identify useful scenarios, highlight problems, and offer a better understanding of the conditions and mechanisms necessary to couple distributed and parallel computing effectively. In addition to the current reliance on CORBA, the initial design rests on the assumption that all its pieces are implemented using the POOMA library. Providing full interoperability means designing an interface through which other libraries and parallel-language compilers could become parts of a distributed system. Therefore, our further plans include formulating a Parallel Interface Definition Language, which would make it feasible to integrate classes written in parallel languages into the system. We also intend to address the issues of reliable security mechanisms and efficient parallel processing in the final version of the system.

14.4 POOMA Appearance

In this section, we demonstrate how programs are written with classes from the POOMA FrameWork by discussing two codes in detail. The first example is a simple 2D diffusion code that illustrates some key features of the `Field` classes. The second code is a 2D electrostatic gyrokinetic particle simulation that utilizes many built-in functions of the `Particles` class.

14.4.1 2D Diffusion Code

The diffusion code in Programs 14.1 and 14.2 demonstrates some of the capabilities of the `Field`, `CEO`, and `Timer` classes provided in the POOMA FrameWork. The command-line input is assumed to contain the system size and the number of iterations to be performed. The problem the code solves is quite simple: starting with a 2D field of double-precision values, it deposits a non-zero value near the center of this field (simulating an initial density), and then for a number of iterations, has each element update its value with the average of itself and its eight neighbors. This operation (depicted in Figure 14.1) is referred to as a nine-point stencil.

Lines 1–11 are straightforward inclusions and declarations. Line 12 constructs a `PoomaInfo` object, which in turn constructs a `Communicate` object and a `VnodeManager` object. The `Communicate` object is responsible for interprocessor communication, whereas the `VnodeManager` is responsible for determining upon which physical node each virtual node resides. The `PoomaInfo` object has pointers to these two important objects, giving the user the capability to obtain information about the virtual node setup within the application code.

Line 13 constructs a `Timer` object to measure CPU time used by the code. This `Timer` object is an extension of a utility developed at

```
1   // Simple 2D Diffusion Simulation
2   #include <stream.h>
3   #include <unistd.h>
4   #include "POOMA.h"   // collection of header files for POOMA
5
6   #define MILLION 1000000.0
7
8   main(int argc, char *argv[])
9   {
10    double mFlops, startVal, endVal, seconds, relativeError;
11    int i, n, iter;
12    PoomaInfo* myinfo = new PoomaInfo(argc,argv);
13    Timer cpuTime;
14
15    sscanf(argv[1], "%d", &n);
16    sscanf(argv[2], "%d", &iter);
17    int centern = n/2;
18    long ops = 9 * n * n * iter;
19    Index I(n), J(n);
20    Field a(I,J);
21
22    startVal = 1000.0;
23    cpuTime.clear();
24    cpuTime.start();                              // start timer
25    a.atom_set(startVal, centern, centern); // put value in center
26    // loop on stencil operation
27    for (i=0; i<iter; i++) {
28      a = (a[I-1][J-1] + a[I-1][J] + a[I-1][J+1] +
29           a[I][J-1] + a[I][J] + a[I][J+1] +
30           a[I+1][J-1] + a[I+1][J] + a[I+1][J+1]) / 9.0;
31    }
32    cpuTime.stop();                               // stop timer
33    seconds = cpuTime.cpu_time();                 // get time
34    endVal = a.sum();                             // get sum
35    // compare final sum to original
36    relativeError = ABS(startVal - endVal) / ABS(startVal);
```

Program 14.1
2D POOMA Diffusion Code (continues over page)

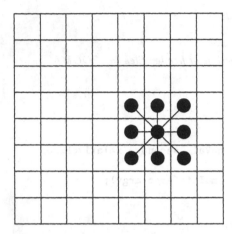

Figure 14.1
2D Nine-Point Diffusion Stencil

```
38    if ((myinfo->get_comm()->this_node())==0)
39    {
40      mFlops = ops / (seconds * MILLION);
41      cout << "Total floating point ops = " << ops << endl;
42      cout << "Total cpu time = " << seconds << endl;
43      cout << "Performance in mFlops = " << mFlops << endl;
44      cout << "Relative Error = " << relativeError<<endl;
45    }
46  }
```

Program 14.2
2D POOMA Diffusion Code (continued from previous page)

the University of Illinois to perform on a variety of serial, distributed, and parallel architectures. Lines 15–16 initialize the size of the field and the number of iterations using command-line arguments. Line 17 approximates the center of the field and assigns this value to centern, while line 18 calculates the number of operations that will be performed by the diffusion code.

Line 19 constructs two Index objects of length n. The Index objects control the pattern by which data is accessed within a Field object. Length, offset, and stride are all configurable. Line 20 constructs a 2D Field of doubles. The default layout assumes a domain decomposition that minimizes the surface-to-area ratio of the rectilinear sub-domains on each virtual node, although other layouts can be specified. Since this is the first Field object instantiated in this simulation, the Field also registers itself and all its expression kernels with a CEO.

Line 22 assigns the initial value to be deposited near the center of the field. Lines 23–24 clear and start the Timer object. Line 25 assigns the value startVal to the element in Field a at coordinates (centern, centern). The main loop begins at line 27; lines 28–30 perform the nine-point diffusion stencil. Once the loop is completed, lines 32–33 stop the timer and get the amount of CPU time spent executing the loop.

Line 34 uses the Field::sum() member function to do a global sum on the elements of the field to verify the conservation of mass. Line 36 calculates the relative error between the starting and ending values. Line 38 uses the PoomaInfo object (via Communicate) to obtain the physical node number. Node 0 then prints out the results in lines 40–44. Finally, in lines 45–46, destructors for the Field, Timer, Index, and PoomaInfo objects are called, since they are now out of scope. This also causes the call of destructors for Communicate, CEO, and VnodeManager.

For the diffusion example, a kernel performing a nine-point stencil operation is registered with the CEO. Thus, the CEO makes a single function call that performs the entire nine-point stencil. Before the kernel is called, however, the CEO checks to see if any of the Field references are "off-node". Field objects are constructed either with or without "guard" cells (sometimes also called "boundary" or "ghost" cells). If a Field has guard cells and the expression references an off-node element of that Field, then the CEO updates these guard cells by using the Communicate class (Figure 14.2).

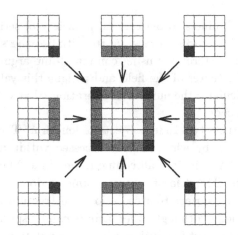

Figure 14.2
Communication Pattern for Border Update During 2D Nine-Point Diffusion Stencil

If the `Field` was constructed without guard cells, then a temporary
`Field` is constructed with the appropriate number of guard cells, and
those guard cells are updated using `Communicate`. The `CEO` maintains a
list of the temporaries created during an expression and deletes them at
the conclusion of the `Field::operator=` call. Thus, if one knows that
such off-node references will occur often in an application, one should
construct `Field` objects with the necessary borders at the outset.

Table 14.2 and Table 14.3 present breakdowns of time spent in two
slightly different versions of the diffusion code. In the first case, the
result of the stencil operation is put into a second `Field` object called
`b` and then explicitly copied back to `a` on a separate line of code. The
second case is that shown in Programs 14.1 and 14.2, where the `CEO`
handles the data dependency as explained in Section 14.3.4. All cases
were run on a single processor.

As can be seen in both tables, there is very little overhead incurred
by employing the `CEO`. Most of the time is spent in the inner `for` loops
of the nine-point stencil kernel operator. Furthermore, allowing the `CEO`
to handle data dependency, rather than performing an explicit copy,
avoids an expensive `memcpy()` call and makes the computation even
more efficient.

Registered kernels such as the one in our 2D diffusion code example are pieces of highly-tuned assembly, Fortran, C or C++ code that

```
double *out, *f[8];
out = A.data_address();
for (int i=0; i<8; i++)
  f[i] = F[i].data_address();
for (int y=0; y<ay; y++)
  for (int x=0; x<ax; x++)
    *out++ = (*f[0]++ + *f[1]++ + *f[2]++ +
              *f[3]++ + *f[4]++ + *f[5]++ +
              *f[6]++ + *f[7]++ + *f[8]++) / constant;
```

Program 14.3
Kernel for Nine-Point Stencil Operation

Routine	SGI Crimson	Sun HyperSPARC	IBM RS6000
stencil	74.0	72.2	83.5
memcpy	23.7	25.6	13.7
allocate memory	0.9	0.7	1.2
get_data	0.4	0.3	0.2
set_data	0.4	0.3	0.6
sum	0.2	0.2	0.3
other	0.4	0.7	0.5

Table 14.2
Breakdown of the Percentage of Time Spent in Each Routine on Various
Architectures (with Explicit Copying)

perform a specific task. When the kernel is called, it is passed all the
information required to describe the objects and operations involved in
the expression. This includes getting pointers to the actual field data,
and getting offset and axis length information. Once this information is
obtained, the expression is evaluated as a whole. Program 14.3 shows
an example of such a kernel.

The performance of the 2D diffusion code on the Cray T3D and the
IBM SP-2 are presented in Tables 14.4 and 14.5.

14.4.2 Gyrokinetic Simulation

Our gyrokinetic (GK) code performs a simple 2D, electrostatic, gyrokinetic particle simulation of a fusion plasma. It is comprised of a single
source file and header files that declare the constants and subroutines
used in the main code. The program reads an input file to obtain ba-

Routine	SGI Crimson	Sun HyperSPARC	IBM RS6000
stencil	97.1	97.2	96.4
allocate memory	1.1	0.9	1.4
get_data	0.6	0.4	0.3
set_data	0.4	0.3	0.5
sum	0.3	0.3	0.2
other	0.5	0.9	0.3

Table 14.3
Breakdown of the Percentage of Time Spent in Each Routine on Various
Architectures (Without Explicit Copying)

Nodes	Problem Size	MFlops	MFlops/Node
2	1024 × 1024	26.71	13.36
4	1024 × 1024	48.87	12.22
8	1024 × 1024	101.44	12.68
16	1024 × 1024	178.83	11.18
32	2048 × 2048	396.58	12.39
64	2048 × 2048	633.03	9.89
64	4096 × 4096	758.14	11.85

Table 14.4
Performance of 2D Diffusion Code on Cray T3D (with readahead on)

Nodes	Problem Size	MFlops	MFlops/Node
1	1024 × 1024	27.35	27.35
2	1024 × 1024	47.24	23.62
4	1024 × 1024	83.97	20.99
8	1024 × 1024	136.65	17.08
16	1024 × 1024	176.28	11.02
16	2048 × 2048	209.10	13.07
16	4096 × 4096	262.82	16.43

Table 14.5
Performance of 2D Diffusion Code on IBM SP-2

```
//  construct particle coordinate and data field objects
//  Max = maximum # of particles per virtual node
DPField xe1(Max), xe2(Max);     // old, new x position
DPField ye1(Max), ye2(Max);     // old, new y position
DPField ve1(Max), ve2(Max);     // old, new v_parallel
DPField we1(Max), we2(Max);     // old, new particle weights
DPField pex1(Max), pex2(Max);   // old, new particle E_x
DPField pey1(Max), pey2(Max);   // old, new particle E_y
DPField w(Max);                 // normalized weight
```

Program 14.4
Code for Construction of Particle Attributes

sic parameters describing the desired simulation, such as the number of particles, number of grid cells along each axis of the simulation domain, number and size of time steps, mass and charge of the plasma constituents, and the scale lengths of the equilibrium density and temperature profiles of the plasma. This code can be used to examine low-frequency, long-wavelength plasma instabilities, such as electron drift waves and ion-temperature-gradient modes [Connor 1986], in a simplified geometry. To begin this particle simulation, a Particles object is set up for each different particle species in the plasma, as shown in Program 14.4.

A DPField is constructed for each particle coordinate and for the other desired particle attributes, which in this case include a velocity, electric field values at the particle's position, and a "weight" to represent this particle's contribution to the deviation from plasma equilibrium. The weight is needed because a "δf" scheme [Parker & Lee 1992] is being employed in this code for improved signal-to-noise properties. POOMA offers the user various easy-to-use tools for initializing DPField data, including setting all DPField values to a constant, inserting random values, using pseudo-random, bit-reversed numbers [Halton 1960], and fitting a probability distribution (e.g., a Maxwellian distribution). Other initialization techniques can be added to the DPField class easily. Once the Particles object is instantiated, the DPField objects are hooked into the Particles object (Program 14.5) and initialized. After the Particles object is initialized and Field objects have been constructed to hold the charge density, the electrostatic potential, the electric field components, etc., we can begin the time step loop.

```
int TimeLevels = 2; // predictor-corrector needs two copies of position
int nDPFields = 9;  // number of dbl prec.fields attached to each particle
// construct Particles object to represent electron distribution
// ncx and ncy are input system box size
Particles electrons(TimeLevels, ncx, ncy, nDPFields);
// attach DPField objects to Particles object
electrons.set_coord(xe1, 0, 0).set_coord(xe2, 0, 1);
electrons.set_coord(ye1, 1, 0).set_coord(ye2, 1, 1);
electrons.set_dpfield(ve1, 0).set_dpfield(ve2, 1);
electrons.set_dpfield(we1, 2).set_dpfield(we2, 3);
electrons.set_dpfield(pex1, 4).set_dpfield(pex2, 5);
electrons.set_dpfield(pey1, 6).set_dpfield(pey2, 7);
electrons.set_dpfield(w, 8);
```

Program 14.5
Code for Attachment of Particle Attributes to Particles Object

We use a two-step, predictor-corrector scheme to advance in time. In each time step, we start with "old" (from the last time step) and "current" (from this time step) values for the particle positions and velocities. In the predictor step, we use the current velocities and electric field to advance the old positions and velocities to the "new" time level. Then, in the corrector step, we average the current and new values of the velocities and electric field, and use these averages to advance the current positions and velocities to the new time level. Both steps are performed in a time-centered manner.

Each step requires us to scatter the particles' charge density to the simulation grid, solve Poisson's equation to get the electrostatic potential, take finite differences to get the components of the electric field, gather this electric field to the particles' positions, and advance the particle positions, velocities, and weights. Code for the predictor step is shown in Program 14.6.

The `GatherNGP` and `ScatterNGP` procedures are gather and scatter functions that utilize a nearest-grid-point (NGP) `Interpolate` object to perform the interpolation between particle positions and grid points. Border-cell information is automatically updated on each `LocalField` object, so that particles have access to the grid cells they need. The GK code has a 2D domain that is periodic in both directions, so solving the Poisson equation is handled using FFTs and the application of form fac-

```
// accumulate electron charge density onto grid using positions (xe2,ye2)
gphi2 = 0.0; // clear grid
// scatter weights w onto gphi2
electrons.ScatterNGP(gphi2, w, xe2, ye2);
// FFT-based field solver
// Fourier transform charge density
fftob.FFT_CC(gphi, gphi_im, 1, 1, 1.0/sqrt(ancx));
fftob.FFT_CC(gphi, gphi_im, 2, 1, 1.0/sqrt(ancy));
// apply form factors (CEO recognizes/optimizes these operations)
gphi    = gphi*fmpo;
gphi_im = gphi_im*fmpo;
gphi    = gphi*fmax;
gphi_im = gphi_im*fmax;
// inverse transform on potential with scale factor for normalization
fftob.FFT_CC(gphi, gphi_im, 2, -1, 1.0/sqrt(ancy));
fftob.FFT_CC(gphi, gphi_im, 1, -1, 1.0/sqrt(ancx));
// compute finite-difference Ex and Ey electric field components
// (CEO recognizes these operations, updates border info, and optimizes)
ex2 = 0.5 * rhos * (gphi2[I+1,J] - gphi2[I-1,J]);
ey2 = 0.5 * rhos * (gphi2[I,J+1] - gphi2[I,J-1]);
// gather electric fields onto particle positions (xe2,ye2)
electrons.GatherNGP(ex2, pex2, xe2, ye2);
electrons.GatherNGP(ey2, pey2, xe2, ye2);
// advance particle positions, velocities, and weights using velocity and E field
// (CEO recognizes these operations and optimizes)
xe1 = xe1 - 2.0*dt*rhos*pey2;
ye1 = ye1 + 2.0*dt*rhos * (theta*ve2 + pex2);
we1 = we1 - 2.0*dt*rhos*swh*theta*pey2*ve2 / (vtxe*vtxe);
ve1 = ve1 - 2.0*dt*rhos*swh*theta*pey2 / vtxe;
// using predicted coords, swap particles
// to be on same processor as local grid data
electrons.swap(xe1, ye1);
```

Program 14.6
Time Step of Gyrokinetic Particle Code

tors in Fourier space. The finite differencing of the electrostatic potential to obtain the electric field is done by applying an optimized stencil operation to the `Field` containing the potential. Overloaded operators in the `DPField` objects allow the advance of particle positions, velocities, and weights to proceed with data-parallel array syntax. The `Particles` member function `swap()` is passed a set of particle coordinates to use in checking which particles have moved out of the local subdomain and need to be passed to a neighboring processor.

The GK code includes a simple diagnostic routine to compute the total kinetic energy of the particles and the field energy of the potential, in order to check energy conservation and monitor instabilities. In addition, GK has been equipped with calls to the Generic Display Library (GDL), a portable graphics package written at the Advanced Computing Laboratory. GDL provides simple function calls that take a 2D array of data and convert it into a pixel map, which graphically represents a color contour of the data set. The color contour plot is displayed on the terminal screen in real time during the simulation, and it can be updated at any time. This allows one to monitor the electrostatic potential, for example, as a plasma instability develops and is nonlinearly saturated. It is a powerful tool for both debugging and analysis of production runs. Program 14.7 illustrates just how easy it is to utilize GDL within the POOMA FrameWork.

The code shown in Program 14.7 is designed for debugging moderate-sized 2D simulations. Current research is focused on embedding GDL into a Graphical User Interface with Tcl/Tk [Ousterhout 1994] and merging classes in the POOMA FrameWork with parallel rendering techniques.

14.5   The Polygon Overlay Problem

The POOMA implementation of the polygon overlay problem is almost identical to the ANSI C base code, for a couple of reasons. First, one of the central themes in the design of the POOMA FrameWork is to ease migration from known programming environments (e.g., ANSI C) to the new programming environment of the FrameWork. In addition, it is more meaningful to compare performance numbers between the POOMA implementation and the ANSI C implementation if the same

```
// construct serial version of Field containing electrostatic field potential
// for graphical display
// all data resides in contiguous memory on node 0
SField iophi(gphi2);
// initialize X display for GDL (node 0 controls graphics display)
if (myNode==0) {
  int dummy = GDL_OpenDisplay(X11FB);   // open display in X11 mode
  GDL_SetColormap(RAINBOW_BLUE, NULL); // choose standard color map
}
...
// later... during time stepping loop
// output values of electrostatic potential
iophi.update();   // update values in Serial Field from parallel Field
// X display of SField using GDL
if (myNode==0)
  GDL_Display_double(iophi.get_data(), iophi.get_length(0),
                     iophi.get_length(1));
```

Program 14.7
Utilizing GDL in the Gyrokinetic Code

algorithm is used. Each of the sequential methods of polygon overlay were implemented and benchmarked on a Cray T3D, a PVM cluster of IBM RS6000 workstations, and an IBM SP-2.

14.5.1   POOMA Implementation Details

The POOMA polygon overlay program (Programs 14.5.1 and 14.5.1) required almost no change to the ANSI C source code. The I/O routines were modified so that the entire left vector was read into each processor, while the right vector was divided between the processors.

Two static, global, integer variables were added to hold the total number of processors and the number of this physical node (pnode). A PoomaInfo object was instantiated in main(), since data concerning the number of pnodes present is required before the instantiation of GDT objects. The PoomaInfo object checks to see if there is currently a Communicate object available. If not, PoomaInfo will create one. The Communicate object's tasks are to obtain the number of pnodes and to start running a copy of the executable on each pnode that is discovered. Next, the PoomaInfo object checks to see if a VnodeManager object has been instantiated. Once again, if not, it will create one. VnodeManager

```
#include "polyoverlay.h"
#include "Index.h"
#include "IField.h"
#include "PoomaInfo.h"

static int Nodes, MyNode;

int main(int argc, char_p argv[]) {
  ···definitions from sequential code···

  // Create PoomaInfo object and get pnode information
  PoomaInfo MyInfo(argc, argv);
  Nodes  = MyInfo.get_comm()->nodes();
  MyNode = MyInfo.get_comm()->this_node();

  ···handle arguments···
  ···read inputs···
  ···perform overlay···

  // Gather results from pnodes to pnode 0
  Index I(Nodes);
  IField Polys(I);
  int OutSecSize, TotalPolys, i, nodes;
  poly_p pp;
  // Get each node's number of polygons and sum
  Polys.atom_set(outVec->len, MyNode);
  OutSecSize = Polys.max();
  TotalPolys = Polys.sum();

  Index OP(OutSecSize * 4 * Nodes);
  IField OutVec(OP);                       // Create vector for result

  pp = outVec->vec;
  // Offset into result vector
  int ioffset = OutSecSize * 4 * MyNode;
```

Program 14.8
POOMA Polygon Overlay Code (continues over page)

```
// Each node writes polygon coordinates into result vector
// atom_set() is an atomic write
for (i = 0 ; i < outVec->len * 4 ; i += 4){
    OutVec.atom_set(pp->xl, ioffset + i     );
    OutVec.atom_set(pp->yl, ioffset + i + 1);
    OutVec.atom_set(pp->xh, ioffset + i + 2);
    OutVec.atom_set(pp->yh, ioffset + i + 3);
    pp++;
}

free(leftVec->vec);
free(rightVec->vec);
free(outVec->vec);

// Transfer result to outVec object for output
ALLOC(outVec->vec, Polys.sum(), poly_t);
pp = outVec->vec;
for (nodes = 0 ; nodes < Nodes ; nodes++){
ioffset = OutSecSize * 4 * nodes;
    // atom_get() is an atomic read
    for (i = 0; i < Polys.atom_get(nodes) * 4; i += 4){
        pp->xl = OutVec.atom_get(ioffset + i     );
        pp->yl = OutVec.atom_get(ioffset + i + 1);
        pp->xh = OutVec.atom_get(ioffset + i + 2);
        pp->yh = OutVec.atom_get(ioffset + i + 3);
        pp++;
    }
}
outVec->len = TotalPolys;

// Only Pnode 0 will do the sorting and output
if (MyNode==0) {
    ···sort using qsort···
    ···output···
}

// finish
return 0;
}
```

Program 14.9
POOMA Polygon Overlay Code (continued from previous page)

is responsible for keeping track of the virtual nodes (vnodes) on each physical node. The default behavior is to provide only one vnode per pnode, but a larger number may be requested. Once the `PoomaInfo` object is constructed, the variables `Nodes` and `MyNode` can be initialized.

Execution continues with the command-line processing being handled as in the serial code. The I/O source code (not shown) reads the first polygon file in serially. The second file is read by dividing the size of the file by the number of physical nodes present in the current machine. Each copy of the executable running then reads in only that portion of the second polygon file that it is responsible for.

When the input files have been read, each processor generates the polygon list for its input sets. Although an integer field (`IField`) is employed during the simulation, the embarrassingly-parallel nature of the polygon overlay problem does not exploit any of the communication-hiding features of the `Field` classes (like indexing operations). However, it does take advantage of the data-parallel `max()` and `sum()` operations.

When the output routines are called, the reverse of the input procedure takes place. The total number of polygons created is discovered by each processor setting an element in `Polys` to the number of polygons generated for its subset. The `IField` is summed to get the overall total. When the output routine is called, an `IField` variable large enough to hold the entire polygon list is constructed. Each processor fills its portion of this `IField` with generated polygons, and then pnode 0 writes out the entire solution set.

14.5.2 Performance Results

Some timings of the parallel POOMA versions of the various polygon overlay methods are shown in Table 14.6 and Table 14.7. A quick scan of the results indicates that the six strategies have very different scalings with the number of processors. Specifically, the List method is only one that did not benefit from applying additional processors. The reason this method does not scale linearly when the right vector is distributed amongst multiple processors has to do with the large number (roughly $M - M/N$, where M is the left vector size and N is the number of processors) of left vector polygons that get tested against all the right vector polygons without removing any polygons from the right vector linked list. The Area method also suffers from this flaw, and this causes the initial loss in efficiency for this strategy when scaling from one to

Arch	Opt	Nodes	Naïve	Ordered	Area-Ord
Cray T3D	-O2	1	1399.40	820.16	711.30
Cray T3D	-O2	2	728.07	558.60	703.78
Cray T3D	-O2	4	397.11	326.03	308.73
Cray T3D	-O2	8	200.53	174.42	166.31
Cray T3D	-O2	16	100.67	90.15	85.36
Cray T3D	-O2	32	50.48	45.91	42.82
IBM RS6000	-O3	1	844.28	659.37	335.36
IBM RS6000	-O3	2	426.94	583.17	297.76
IBM RS6000	-O3	4	210.87	337.77	170.66
IBM RS6000	-O3	8	104.83	129.31	71.73
IBM SP-2	-O3	1	951.22	726.86	419.43
IBM SP-2	-O3	2	478.06	539.02	316.84
IBM SP-2	-O3	4	238.39	312.93	179.16
IBM SP-2	-O3	8	120.73	165.50	96.73

Table 14.6
Polygon Overlay Code Timings (sec) on K100.00 and K100.01 Data Sets for the Naïve, Ordered, and Area-Ordered methods

Arch	Opt	Nodes	Area	List-Ord	List
Cray T3D	-O2	1	314.40	16.75	15.32
Cray T3D	-O2	2	703.78	8.44	805.53
Cray T3D	-O2	4	489.63	4.26	602.74
Cray T3D	-O2	8	278.65	2.17	351.92
Cray T3D	-O2	16	147.48	1.14	187.21
Cray T3D	-O2	32	75.79	0.61	95.16
IBM RS6000	-O3	1	226.58	8.22	8.09
IBM RS6000	-O3	2	350.83	4.02	353.63
IBM RS6000	-O3	4	185.84	2.03	223.35
IBM RS6000	-O3	8	124.98	1.05	125.24
IBM SP-2	-O3	1	246.26	9.21	8.47
IBM SP-2	-O3	2	390.35	4.67	407.75
IBM SP-2	-O3	4	261.63	2.35	300.03
IBM SP-2	-O3	8	147.37	1.25	174.74

Table 14.7
Polygon Overlay Code Timings (sec) on K100.00 and K100.01 Data Sets for the Area, List-Ordered, and List Methods

two processors. Both of these methods then improve as more processors are added.

The List-Ordered method is quite similar to the List method. However, it exhibits a roughly linear speedup with additional processors because it avoids wasting time comparing polygons that do not intersect by making use of the ordered arrangement of the polygons. This also explains the improved scaling of the Area-Ordered method versus the Area method. The Naïve approach also scales rather well in parallel. The Ordered method is clearly superior to the naïve approach on a single node (for the reason mentioned above), but it does not scale as well in parallel because the extra checks involved in the Ordered method do not pay off as the right vector becomes distributed over more and more processors.

14.6 Critique

Although there are many advantages to our approach to parallelism as described above, there are some limitations. Even though codes can move with no changes between parallel and serial environments, the motivation for this was to leverage serial environments for development against parallel environments for production. The POOMA FrameWork is tuned for solving large problems on parallel supercomputers efficiently. The techniques utilized to provide these performance gains on parallel architectures provide minimal gains on serial architectures.

The target users for the POOMA FrameWork are science and engineering application developers who, as a community, prefer programming in Fortran and other procedural languages. C++ is a powerful object-oriented language and the FrameWork exploits that power to mimic a procedural language, encapsulate parallelism, and chain expressions for efficient execution. However, there is still a perceivable lag in the capability of C++ compilers to optimize numerical codes, to compile code in a standard fashion, and to perform reliably. Thus, it will take some time before the scientific and engineering communities accept C++ as being as efficient a language as Fortran, and this will inhibit the transition to systems like POOMA.

In addition, because we have chosen to drive our system with scientific applications, the scope of POOMA is somewhat limited. This is not a general-purpose programming system; rather, it is specifically focused on facilitating the use of numerical tools common to scientific application codes on parallel computer architectures. This design decision will undoubtedly exclude other types of computer codes from utilizing tools in the POOMA FrameWork.

Finally, the FrameWork currently focuses on a SPMD approach to parallelism. Although a data-parallel approach captures a majority of scientific application domains and provides an intuitive casting of mathematical expressions directly into objects, there are those who argue that some algorithms are better cast in a task-parallel language. In the future, we hope to bridge this gap by combining classes from the POOMA FrameWork with task-parallel, runtime systems such as CHARM++ (Chapter 5).

Acknowledgments

This work has been supported primarily by the Department of Energy, Office of Scientific Computing. Results were obtained by utilizing resources at the Advanced Computing Laboratory in Los Alamos, the National Energy Research Supercomputer Center, and the Maui High Performance Computing Center. We would like to thank David Forslund, Dan Quinlan, Jeff Saltzman, and David Kilman for many helpful discussions during the development of the POOMA FrameWork.

15 TAU

Bernd Mohr, Allen D. Malony, and Janice E. Cuny

15.1 Introduction

Most users find parallel programming difficult for at least four reasons. First, parallel computing abstractions (e.g., data parallelism, control or task parallelism, producer/consumer parallelism) are diverse, differing mainly by the type of parallel behavior supported (or allowed) in a program's execution. In addition to learning the parallel programming languages and tools in a particular environment, a user must decide which parallel computing model provides the "best" execution for their problem. Deciding how to choose between models often requires a sophisticated understanding of the application, its underlying algorithms, the expressiveness of the language used, and effects of the system software and hardware architecture of the parallel machine. Unfortunately, this choice is complicated by the fact that not all parallel computing abstractions are equally well supported in existing programming systems. Second, most parallel programming systems do not insulate users fully from low-level hardware and system software concerns; those that do make it difficult for users to undertake performance debugging, and hence to realize the potential high performance of parallel systems. Third, program analysis tools for parallel programming are either not generally available, not particularly useful, or not integrated into a complete programming environment. Fourth, users' requirements for parallel computing are constantly changing: high performance is important, but so is the need to have parallel programs interoperate with graphics systems, networked resource servers, databases, and so on.

The most common way to address these issues at present is to develop languages which support specific parallel computing abstractions, such as HPF [Koelbel et al. 1994]. These languages invoke parallel operations via compiler transformations and calls to runtime system routines. Users gain programmability, since they specify parallelism abstractly and rely on the compiler to generate task and data mapping code, and portability, since the system can be re-targeted to new platforms. However, these gains often come at the expense of observability. Unless the programming system contains analysis tools that can relate a program's execution dynamics to its semantics, increased abstraction will make it difficult to debug or tune program performance. This suggests that tools should be designed specifically to meet the requirements of the language environment.

Since 1992, we have participated in building such an integrated tool set for pC++, a parallel C++-based language (Chapter 13). Our charter was to design and develop a program analysis tool system. The project was unique in that we decided early on to let the programming language requirements determine the tool specifications. This is in contrast to other projects to build program analysis tools, principally performance tools, where general measurement and analysis support is targeted, but this support may be deficient or cumbersome to use in specific language contexts. In addition, we leveraged the language system infrastructure to enhance the integration of compiler and analysis tools. The fact that our base language was C++ encouraged us to make our tools as flexible as possible, so that we could use encapsulation (for supporting data aggregation and parallel invocation) and inheritance (for building distributed data structures) in our implementations. Finally, since pC++ was designed to run on all parallel MIMD systems, our program analysis environment had to be portable as well.

The result of our efforts is called TAU, for Tuning and Analysis Utilities. In Section 15.2, we list the requirements that we felt TAU had to address. We discuss how TAU meets these requirements in its design, architecture, and implementation in Section 15.3. Each TAU tool is described in full in Section 15.4. Since the effectiveness of TAU can only be measured by its usefulness for the analysis of pC++ programs, Section 15.5 shows how TAU was used to analyze the pC++ implementation of polygon overlay, described in Section 13.5.

TAU is not without its shortcomings. A critique of its current state is given in Section 15.6. Section 15.7 discusses future development of TAU, particularly its extension to other parallel language environments and the incorporation of more sophisticated tools.

Also, for up-to-date information about TAU see:

http://www.cs.uoregon.edu/paracomp/tau

15.2   Design Requirements and Goals

Some material in this section is revised from [Mohr *et al.*
1994], and appears with the permission of Springer-Verlag.

TAU was designed to improve parallel programming productivity by
combining advances in parallel debugging, performance evaluation, and
program visualization tools. We feel the requirements that the design
and the tools had to address are common to next-generation parallel
programming environments, and include:

Give a user (program-level) view. Past tool development has been
   dominated by efforts directed at the execution level (e.g., efficient implementation of monitoring). Consequently, tool users are given little
   support for translating between program-level semantics and low-level
   execution measurements.

Support high-level parallel programming languages. The development of advanced parallel languages (e.g., HPF and pC++) sepa-
   rates users from execution-time reality. A successful tool must present
   information to users in the terms defined by the language they are using.

Integrate with compilers and runtime systems. Most debugging
   and performance analysis tools have been developed independent of
   parallel languages and runtime systems, resulting in poor re-use of
   base-level technology, incompatibilities in tool functionality, and interface inconsistencies in the user environment.

Enable portability, extensibility, and re-targetability. Users of
   portable languages need a consistent program development and analysis environment across multiple execution platforms. Tools should
   be extensible, so that they can accommodate new language or runtime system features, and re-targetable, so that the tool design can
   be re-used for different languages and environments.

Enhance usability. A high-level, portable, integrated tool is not automatically easy to use. In the past, too little emphasis has been put
   on interface design, which has led to tools being poorly used.

These requirements become even more significant as we develop parallel languages with highly optimized runtime systems. We believe that

the main problems are ones of tool design rather than functionality: existing tools implement a broad range of analysis techniques, but have not been successfully integrated into usable parallel programming environments. One way to improve integration is to base the design of tools on the particular performance and debugging requirements of the parallel language for which the tools will be used. In this manner, tools can specifically target program analysis support where tool application is well understood. However, this cannot be fully realized unless tools can leverage other programming system technologies (e.g., use the compiler to implement instrumentation).

15.3   TAU Overview

> Some material in Section 15.3 and Section 15.3.1 is revised
> from [Mohr *et al.* 1994], and appears with the permission of
> Springer-Verlag.

The TAU architecture defines how its components interoperate and fit in the pC++ language system. Below, we describe the TAU design and show how it addresses the programming productivity requirements of pC++. TAU is not a general solution to the problem of parallel program analysis. Instead, our goal was to demonstrate the potential benefits of a new development strategy for program analysis tools, one that promotes meeting specific analysis requirements over providing general-purpose functionality.

TAU was specifically designed to meet the requirements listed in the previous section:

Give a user (program-level) view. Elements of the TAU graphical interface represent objects of the pC++ programming paradigm: collections, classes, methods, and functions. These language-level objects appear in all TAU utilities.

Support high-level parallel programming languages. TAU is defined by the program analysis requirements of pC++, and was designed and implemented in concert with the pC++ language system. The most difficult challenges during the development of TAU were to determine what low-level instrumentation was needed to capture high-level execution abstractions, and how to translate performance data back to the application and language level.

Integrate with compilers and runtime systems. TAU uses the Sage++ toolkit [Gannon *et al.* 1994a] as an interface to the pC++ compiler for instrumentation and accessing properties of program objects. TAU is also integrated with the runtime system of pC++ for profiling, tracing, and debugging support.

Enable portability, extensibility, and re-targetability. We implemented TAU in C++ and C to ensure an efficient, portable, and reusable implementation. The same reasoning led us to use Tcl/Tk [Ousterhout 1994] for our graphical interface.

The TAU tools are implemented as graphical *hypertools*. While each is distinct, they act in concert like a single application. Each tool implements some defined tasks; if one tool needs a feature of another, the first sends a request to the second (e.g., "display the source code for a specific function"). This design allows easy extension. The Sage++ toolkit also supports Fortran-based languages, so TAU can be re-targeted to other programming environments.

Enhance usability. We tried to make the TAU tool set as user-friendly as possible. Many elements of the graphical user interface act like links in hypertext systems, in that clicking on them brings up windows which describe the element in more detail. This allows the user to explore properties of the application by interacting with the elements of most interest. The TAU tools also support *global features*. When a global feature is invoked in any tool, it is automatically executed in all TAU tools which are currently running. Examples of these global features are described later. TAU also includes a full hypertext help system.

15.3.1   TAU Architecture

Figure 15.1 shows an overview of the pC++ programming environment. The pC++ compiler front end takes a user program and pC++ class library definitions (providing predefined collection types) and parses them to create a program data base, or PDB. The PDB is accessed via the Sage++ library.

Through command line switches, the user can choose to compile a pC++ program for profiling or tracing. In either case, the instrumen-

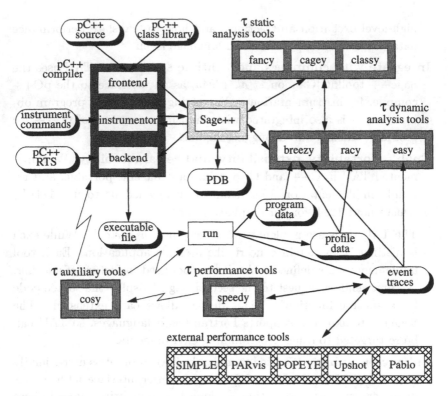

Figure 15.1
TAU Tools Architecture

tor is invoked to add the necessary instrumentation to the PDB (Section 15.4.2). The pC++ back end transforms the PDB into plain C++ with calls into the pC++ runtime system. This C++ source code is then compiled and linked by the C++ compiler on the target system.

The compilation and execution of pC++ programs can be controlled by Cosy (COmpile manager Status displaY). This tool provides a user-friendly and convenient way of compiling and linking pC++ programs (Figure 15.7). Through a graphical interface, the user first selects the parallel machine on which the application is to be compiled and run. Parameters and options for compiling and running are chosen through pull-down menus. Cosy automatically connects, if necessary, to the remote machine, executes the appropriate commands, and displays the resulting output in a scrollable window.

The program and performance analysis environment is shown in the right side of Figure 15.1. It includes the TAU tool set, instrumentation, profiling, tracing, and breakpointing support, and interfaces to performance analysis tools developed by other groups [Arnold *et al.* 1995, Herrarte & Lusk 1991, Mohr 1992, Reed *et al.* 1991]. The TAU tools are described in more detail in Section 15.4.

15.3.2   TAU Implementation

The TAU architecture defines how the tools interoperate and fit into the pC++ programming system. This section discusses two components of TAU that support this: global features and well-defined internal tool interfaces.

Global Features   Global features are a natural extension to the "click-for-source" feature found in some other parallel program analysis tools. But whereas these tools only allow users to find the source code of elements in the performance views (e.g., show the code containing the **send** or **receive** function call for a message transmission), TAU allows users to click on anything which represents a function or class in any tool, and automatically updates all tool displays to show information about the selected object (Figure 15.2).

For example, suppose a user is looking at the execution profile for her application, and wonders why a specific function is taking so much time. Clicking either on the function's name label or on the colored bar showing the execution time used by the function will invoke the global feature **select-function**. This calls the Tcl/Tk function **globalSelectFunc**, shown in the middle of Figure 15.2, with the unique identifier of the selected function as a parameter. This then calls **localSelectFunc**, which causes the tool to show more specific information about the selected function. Next, each of the tools known to implement the global feature is checked to see if it is running. If it is, a message is sent to invoke **localSelectFunc** with the same function identifier as an argument. In Figure 15.2, this causes the file browser to show the source code of the selected function, and the callgraph browser to show all of its call sites. The same effect would have been achieved if the user had clicked on a function in either the source code browser or the callgraph display.

This implementation has several strengths:

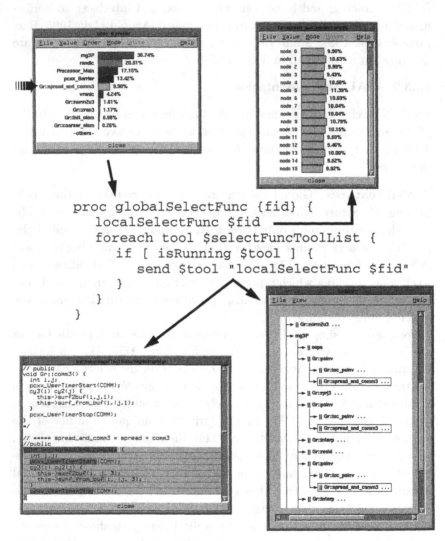

```
proc globalSelectFunc {fid} {
  localSelectFunc $fid
  foreach tool $selectFuncToolList {
    if [ isRunning $tool ] {
      send $tool "localSelectFunc $fid"
    }
  }
}
```

Figure 15.2
Global Feature Implementation

- The use of global features makes it possible to implement the TAU environment as *hypertools*, instead of as a single huge program. Hence, the individual tools can be kept small, which simplifies maintenance and debugging. It also makes tools easier to re-use in different contexts or environments.

- The environment can easily be extended. A new tool only has to implement those global features it needs or is able to support, then bind invocation of those features to appropriate elements of its graphical user interface and add itself to the global list of tools supporting that feature.

- The use of high-level interprocess communication (e.g., Tk's **send**) allows a very simple implementation. It is also quite portable, as there are now Tk modules for Scheme and Perl, and a C interface for writing libraries.

Other global features include **select-class**, **switch-application**, and **exit**.

Internal Tool Interfaces   Figure 15.3 shows the internal implementation of the TAU's static analysis tools: the source code browser Fancy, the callgraph browser Cagey, and the class hierarchy browser Classy (not shown in Figure 15.3). If a browser is started or switched to another user application, it invokes the object manager (**om**) and reads its output. Command line switches (e.g., **-txt** or **-cg**) are used to specify the type of the requested information. The object manager uses the Sage++ interface to access the program database describing the current user application, then prints the requested information in an easy-to-parse ASCII format. The object manager reduces dependence on a particular language system by producing the necessary information in a generic format where possible, and enhances tool interoperability by making inter-tool communication more robust. For example, this architecture of information servers makes it easy to use TAU on a workstation to control a pC++ application running on remote parallel computer. In this case, instead of launching the object manager directly, the TAU tools use a standard TCP/IP remote shell command.

TAU's dynamic analysis tools are implemented in much the same way. Racy and Easy invoke programs much like the object manager to read profile data and event traces respectively, then parse their ASCII output.

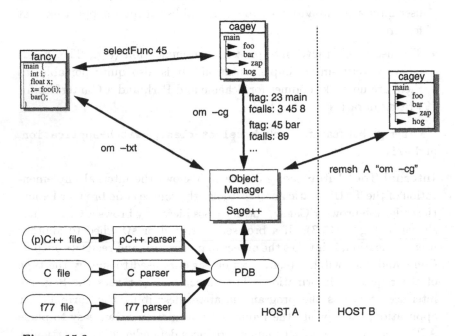

Figure 15.3
TAU Internal Tool Interfaces

This allows TAU to be ported to other language systems in any of four different ways:

1. Change the compiler of the new target environment to produce a program data base in the format used by Sage++.

2. Implement the part of the Sage++ function interface which is necessary for the object manager to access the program data base used in the new language environment.

3. Implement new information servers that understand the same command line options, and output information in the same format, as the TAU object manager.

4. Change the TAU tool interfaces to the information servers so that they work with the new language environment.

As an example, TAU was ported recently to work with the HPF compiler of the Portland Group Inc. We used the third approach—write a new object manager—to port the source code and the callgraph browser, and the first approach—implement routines to generate TAU-compatible profile data files—to adapt the profile data browser. The whole port required less than one person-week, and shows the benefits of TAU's modular design.

15.4 TAU Tools

In this section, we describe the tools in the current TAU tool set.[1] These tools are available as part of the pC++ distribution and operate in any environment where pC++ runs. Some tools are pC++ specific, while others are also applicable to other language systems. As TAU was designed to support extensions to the tool set, new tools are continually being developed and incorporated into the TAU architecture.

15.4.1 Static Analysis Tools

Some material in this section is revised from [Mohr *et al.* 1994], and appears with the permission of Springer-Verlag.

---

[1]All TAU tools have adjectives as names, so that the answer to "What is TAU?" is "TAU is Cosy, Fancy, Cagey, Classy, Easy, Racy, Speedy, and Breezy!"

A major motivation for using C++ as the base for new parallel languages is its ability to support the development and maintenance of large, complex applications. However, if they are to use C++'s capabilities effectively, users must be given support tools which can access source code at the level of programming abstractions.

TAU currently provides three tools to enable users to navigate through large pC++ programs: a global function and method browser called Fancy, a static callgraph display called Cagey, and a class hierarchy display called Classy. Since these tools are integrated with TAU's dynamic analysis tools, it is easy for users to find object-level execution information. To locate dynamic results after a measurement has been made, a user only has to click on the object of interest, such as a function name in a callgraph display.

File and Source Code Browser   Fancy (File ANd Class displaY) lets a user browse through the files and classes making up her application. The main window displays listboxes showing the source files used and the classes defined (Figure 15.8 on page 612). Selecting an item in either listbox displays all global functions defined for the selected file, or all methods of the selected class.

Selecting a global function or a class method causes the corresponding source code to be displayed in a separate viewer window (Figure 15.9 on page 613). The header and body of the currently selected routine, as well as functions and methods which are called from that routine, are highlighted using different colors. Routines and class definitions can be selected by clicking on the appropriate names.

Callgraph Browser   Cagey (CAll Graph Extended displaY) shows the static callgraph of the user's application (Figure 15.10 on page 613). Cagey helps users locate parts of their programs where parallelism is used by marking parallel routines with the string "||". As callgraphs can be quite large, Cagey allows users to control how far a callgraph is expanded.

Cagey supports two graph layout modes: *extended* and *compact*. In compact mode, each function or method is represented by a single node. If a function calls another function more than once, the connecting arc is labeled with the number of calls. This mode works well for structured or regular codes. In expanded mode, Cagey draws a node for each individual function or method call; the resulting graph is always a tree. Figure 15.10 shows a callgraph in compact mode.

Class Hierarchy Browser Classy (CLASS hierarchY browser) is a class hierarchy browser for programs written in C++ and derivative languages such as pC++. Classes which have no base class (called level 0 classes) are shown on the left side of the display window (Figure 15.11 on page 614). Subclasses derived from level 0 classes are shown in the next column to the right, and so on. Like Cagey, Classy lets the user choose the level of detail in the class hierarchy display by allowing folding or expansion of subtrees in the graph. Classy also allows quick access to key properties of a class, such as data members. Finally, Classy marks collections by putting the string "||" before their names.

15.4.2 Dynamic Analysis Tools

> Some material in this section is revised from [Mohr et al. 1994], and appears with the permission of Springer-Verlag.

Static analysis tools provide high-level views of a program's structure; dynamic analysis tools capture information about the program's execution and correlate it with those high-level views so that users can find correctness and performance problems. TAU supports dynamic analysis in three ways: *profiling*, which computes statistical information to summarize program behavior; *tracing*, which portrays execution behavior as a sequence of abstract *events* that can be used to determine various properties of time-based behavior; and *breakpoint debugging* which allows a user to stop the program at selected points and query the program's state. These are supported by an execution profile data browser called Racy, an event trace browser called Easy, and a barrier breakpoint debugger called Breezy.

Program Instrumentation

> Some material in this section is revised from [Malony et al. 1994b], and appears with the permission of the IEEE.

All three analysis modes use instrumentation to capture runtime data. The program transformations needed for this are done at the language level to ensure portability. One problem this approach faces is to ensure that code to profile function exits is executed as late as possible. Since a function can return an arbitrarily complex expression, correct profiling instrumentation is not straightforward. It must extract the expression from the return statement, compute its value, execute the profiling exit code, and only then return the expression result. Matters become even more complicated when we consider multiple exit points.

This is a good example of how we can leverage our language environment for tool implementation. The trick is very simple: we declare a special *Profiler* class that has a constructor and a destructor, but no other methods. A variable of this class is then declared in the first line of each function that has to be profiled, as shown below for function bar().

```
class Profiler {
 char* name;
 public:
 Profiler(char *n) {name=n; code_enter(n);}
 ~Profiler() {code_exit(name);}
};

void bar() {
  Profiler tr("bar"); // Profiler variable
  // body of bar
}
```

The variable tr is created and initialized by its constructor each time control flow reaches its definition, and destroyed by its destructor on exit from its block. The C++ compiler automatically rearranges the code and inserts destructor calls to ensure correct behavior no matter how the scope is exited.

We use the Sage++ toolkit to manipulate pC++ programs to insert such instrumentation at the beginning of each function. The user can selectively specify the set of functions to instrument using an instrumentation command file. Filenames, classes, and functions can be specified as regular expressions, and included or excluded based on their name, source file, or class. Functions can also be selected by their size (measured in number of statements and/or number of function calls), by whether they are inline functions, and by their position in the static callgraph. If an instrumentation command file is not given, every function in the pC++ input files is profiled by default. A graphical interface to control the instrumentation process for TAU is not yet available.

Portable Profiling for pC++ The data captured by the entry and exit instrumentation described above can be used to calculate the number of times a function is called and the execution time it consumes. For pC++, we capture performance profiles for thread-level functions, collection class methods, and runtime system routines. The data we capture includes activation counts, execution times, and, in the case of collections, referencing information.

Our approach to profiling has two basic advantages. First, instrumenting at the source code level makes it portable. Second, different implementations of the profiler can be easily created by providing different code for the constructor and destructor of the `Profiler` class. This makes instrumentation flexible. Currently, we have implemented two versions of the profiler: one based on direct profiling, and one which calls event logging functions from the pC++ library. Other profiling alternatives could be implemented in the same way. The instrumented version of the pC++ class library supports profiling of runtime system functions and collection access.

If a pC++ program is compiled for direct profiling, executing it produces a profile data file for each node. This profile data can be browsed using either Pprof, a parallel profile tool similar to Unix Prof, or Racy (Routine and data ACcess profile displaY). Racy, shown in Figure 15.12 on page 616, gives a quick overview of an applications' execution by summarizing both function and collection access performance. The function profile summary presents a bar graph with one line per processor, showing where program time was spent on that processor. In addition, the mean, maximum, and minimum values are shown on top of the graph. Detailed profiles for each node and each function can be displayed in a variety of formats (Figure 15.13, Figure 15.15, and Figure 15.16).

The collection access data profile summary shows access information for pC++ collections. A bar graph shows the percentage of collection accesses that were local or remote. By clicking on the collection name, the user can get a per-node profile of this data (Figure 15.17).

Event Tracing for pC++

Some material in this section is revised from [Malony *et al.* 1994b], and appears with the permission of the IEEE.

EC_BASIC	Basic runtime events like begin and end of the whole program and the user's main function.
EC_KERNEL	Creation and deletion of collections, collection element access.
EC_RUNTIME	Entry and exit of every pC++ runtime function including barriers, message send and receives, polling. Mainly used for debugging.
EC_TIMER	Calls to the pC++ timer and clock package.
EC_TRACER	Functions of the software event tracing package itself like Init, Close, and FlushBuffer.
EC_PROFILER	User function entry and exit points. Events of this class are automatically inserted by the pC++ instrumentor.
EC_USER1 ⋯ EC_USER4	Available to the user for manually inserted event recording calls.

Table 15.1
pC++ Event Classes

In addition to profiling, we have implemented a system for tracing pC++ program events. Events are stored in a buffer on each node, which is written to disk when it is full or when the program ends. Each event record includes the event type, the originating processor, a high-resolution timestamp, and an optional parameter. Each event is assigned an *event class* (Table 15.1); when a program compiled for tracing is executed, particular event classes can be activated or deactivated at runtime to allow selective recording. The instrumentation required by tracing is implemented in the same way as profiling instrumentation.

We have also implemented several utilities for merging event traces, for converting them to other formats, such as PARvis's PV [Arnold *et al.* 1995], Pablo's SDDF [Reed *et al.* 1991], or Upshot's ALOG [Herrarte & Lusk 1991], and for analyzing and visualizing traces using the Simple environment or other tools based on the Tdl/Poet interface [Mohr 1992].

Easy (Event And State displaY) is an Upshot-like event and state display tool. It displays states and events on an X-Y graph, allowing more detailed access to event data when necessary. The Y axis shows individual processors, while the X axis shows elapsed time. A particular event or state can be examined by clicking on the corresponding graphical object. States are displayed in such a way that they show when

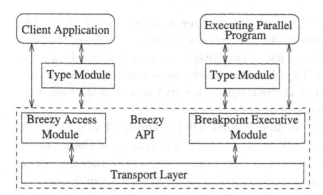

Figure 15.4
Breezy Architecture

states are nested. Figure 15.18 shows the major phases of the pC++ example program.

Barrier Breakpoint Debugging

> Some material in this section is revised from [Brown *et al.*
> 1995], and appears with the permission of Tata McGraw-Hill.

We have developed a program interaction system for pC++ called Breezy (BReakpoint Executive Environment for visualiZation and data DisplaY) [Brown *et al.* 1995]. Breezy provides the infrastructure for a client application to attach to a pC++ application at runtime. This partnership gives the client several capabilities:

- The client can control the execution of the program.

- The client can retrieve data from parallel data structures created in the program.

- The client can invoke functions or methods in the parallel program.

- The client can retrieve information about the program's execution state.

- The client can retrieve meta-information about the program, such as type descriptions.

- The client may communicate in a general way with the parallel program.

The Breezy architecture consists of three modules (Figure 15.4). The Breakpoint Executive Module maintains information about the program's state, including a list of currently instantiated parallel data objects. It consults the Type Module, which stores meta-information such as type descriptions of the parallel data structures or lists of all user-defined functions that can be called.

The Breezy Access Module is currently implemented as a library of C routines. It allows a client to control the execution of the program, to request information about the program state, and to access program data structures. For example, a client using the API can specify the program variable that holds the parallel data object of interest. If this object is a structured object with fields, such as a class, the client can further specify a particular field. The client can then retrieve this data from all of the distributed elements of the parallel data object, or from a single element in that object. To serve requests for parallel data, the Breakpoint Executive Module calls access functions in the executing program. These access functions reside in the (modified) user program in order to have access to the program variables and functions, and are generated automatically by the Breezy instrumentation phase of the pC++ compiler.

Important features of Breezy are:

- Its modular design allows for component re-use and clean substitution of new technologies (such as replacing the transport layer with CORBA/IDL [OMG 1993]).

- It allows the pC++ programmer to make functions available for calling by the client, giving the client the power to alter the course of the program or perform specific computations. This allows the user to implement more complex functionality in the client, such as computational steering.

- Almost all of the implementation is done in the target language making it as portable as the language itself. (There need to be some minor support from the runtime system).

This last point is particularly interesting because it allows client applications to reference data objects exactly as they were defined in the program, rather than at a lower level resulting from compiler transformation. Also, it means that a new implementation of Breezy is not required for each new architecture; because Breezy is implemented using the language, it runs everywhere the language does.

15.4.3   Performance Extrapolation for pC++

> Some material in this section is revised from [Shanmugam *et al.* 1995c], and appears with the permission of Springer-Verlag.

The dynamic analysis tools already discussed enable users to investigate the execution behavior of pC++ programs. However, because pC++ programs are portable, users may want to develop and analyze programs that will run across platforms or that will run in environments different from the development environment. To support this type of program analysis, we implemented a performance extrapolation system for pC++ called ExtraP, that has been integrated into TAU in the guise of the Speedy tool [Shanmugam *et al.* 1995c]. The ExtraP/Speedy combination allows users to predict the performance of pC++ programs in the target execution environments.

The technique that we developed extrapolates the performance of a n-thread pC++ program from a 1-processor execution to a n-processor execution. The pC++ language system is used to build a n-thread program which is executed on a single processor using a non-preemptive threads package. Important high-level events including remote accesses and barriers are recorded along with timestamps during the program run in a trace file.

Events are then sorted on a per-thread basis, and their timestamps adjusted to reflect concurrent execution. This is done by treating remote accesses and barrier events as taking place instantaneously. This is possible because threads are only switched at synchronization points by the non-preemptive thread package, and because global barriers are the only form of synchronization used by pC++ programs. Thus, the behavior of threads between barriers is independent, and the sorted trace files look as if they were obtained from an n-thread, n-processor run. The only features these traces lack are timings for remote accesses and barriers. A trace-driven simulation attempts to model such features and predict when events would have occurred in a real n-processor execution environment. These extrapolated trace files are then used to obtain performance metrics for the pC++ program. The technique is depicted in

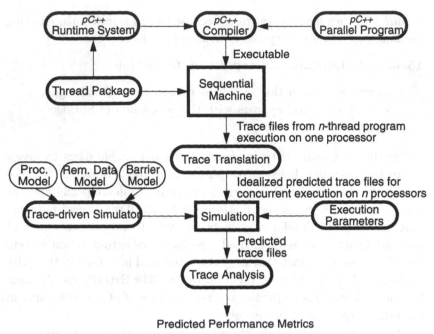

Figure 15.5
A Performance Extrapolation Technique for pC++

Figure 15.5, and described in more detail in [Shanmugam 1994, Shanmugam & Malony 1995a, Shanmugam *et al.* 1995b].

ExtraP uses pC++'s built-in event tracing system to generate the
traces needed for the simulation. These traces can be analyzed using
TAU's event trace browsers, and compared and validated against traces
from real parallel executions. Actual extrapolation experiments can be
controlled using Speedy (Speedup and Parallel Execution Extrapolation DisplaY), shown in Figure 15.20. Speedy lets users control the
compilation of pC++ programs, specify parameters for the extrapolation model and the experiment, execute the experiment, and view the
experiment results. Speedy uses Cosy to perform the necessary compilation, execution, trace processing, and extrapolation commands. Speedy
also automatically keeps track of parameters by storing them in *experiment description files* and manages all trace and experiment control files.
Users can re-execute experiments, or re-use parameter specifications, by
loading a former experiment description file into Speedy.

The experiment and extrapolation model parameters can be entered and viewed through the ExtraP parameter file viewer (see Figure 15.21 on page 623). Numerical parameters can either be entered directly into the input fields or manipulated through increment/decrement buttons and a slider bar. Parameters with discrete values can be specified through a pull-down menu (like **ProcessMsgType** in the picture). In Figure 15.21, the viewer displays the parameters associated with the modeling of the processor of the target machine. Other modeling parameter groups can be displayed by pressing one of the buttons in the top of the viewer window. Besides the five parameter groups describing the simulated parallel machine, the group **General** allows the setting of parameters controlling the generation and post-processing of the execution traces.

15.5   Tour de TAU: The Polygon Overlay Example

In this section, we show how the TAU environment was used to analyze the pC++ implementation of the polygon overlay problem described in Section 13.5.

15.5.1   Utility Tools

When TAU is started from the command line, the TAU main control panel appears (Figure 15.6). The first line shows the host name and architecture of the parallel machine on which compilation and execution of the pC++ program will take place. The second line displays the directory where the program files and program database are stored. The other fields show information about the currently-selected user application. The last line only shows information when a program was compiled for profiling. The buttons at the bottom are used to invoke TAU's static and dynamic tools.

The compilation and execution of pC++ programs can be controlled using Cosy (Figure 15.7). Cosy automatically connects to the remote machine (if necessary), executes the appropriate commands, and displays the resulting output. It allows users to build, run, and stop pC++ programs, to set compilation and execution parameters, and to do standard tasks like cleaning up or listing the current directory.

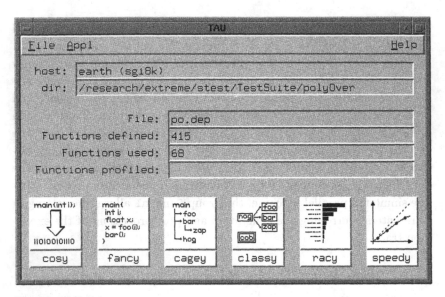

Figure 15.6
TAU Main Control Panel

Figure 15.7 shows the compilation and execution of the polygon overlay example. The version shown is being compiled for tracing; the generated event traces can then be viewed with Easy. As the pC++ polygon overlay program re-uses the original ANSI C reference program, we have to specify a list of extra objects in the **Build Parameters** window before we can **build**. In this case, the user must supply a makefile for these objects. We then supply the necessary extra command line parameters in the **Run Parameters** window as well as the number of processors we want to use and the event classes we want to be activated. Pressing the **run** button finally executes the program and, in Figure 15.7, we can see the actual command executed and the output of the program.

15.5.2 Static Analysis Tools

Figure 15.8 shows the main window of the Fancy file and class browser. The lists of all files and classes are shown on the left. The file list includes the pC++ main program (**po.pc**), and pC++-specific header files like **kernel.h**, as well as the files making up the ANSI C reference implementation. The classes list includes pC++'s predefined collection classes (**Kernel** and **SuperKernel**) the pC++-supplied classes for describing

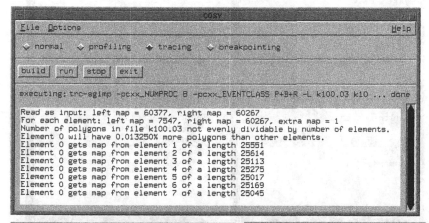

Figure 15.7
Cosy

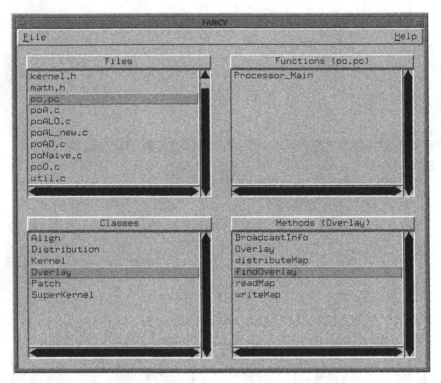

Figure 15.8
Fancy Main Window

the alignment and distribution of collections, and the user-defined collection (`Overlay`) and element (`Patch`) classes. Selecting a file shows all global functions defined in the file, selecting a class shows all its defined methods. Selecting a function or method (like `findOverlay()` in the example) shows the source code of this routine in the Fancy file viewer (see Figure 15.9).

Figure 15.10 shows a Cagey callgraph view of the polygon overlay code with `Overlay::findOverlay()` expanded. In addition to allowing users to check the static structure of their programs, these displays are convenient navigation aids. As can be seen, the overlay example has a fairly simple structure, with the bulk of the data-parallel computation in the expanded routine.

The class hierarchy browser, Classy, allows quick access to key properties of a class. pC++ collections are marked with a "‖" before the

```
void Overlay::findOverlay()
{
  double time;
  pcxx_UserTimerClear(index1);
  pcxx_UserTimerStart(index1);

  if (useLnArea && useOrder){
    outVec = overlayAreaLinkedOrder(leftVec, rightVec);
  } else if (useLnArea){
    outVec = overlayAreaLinked(leftVec, rightVec);
  } else if (useArea && useOrder){
    outVec = overlayAreaOrder(leftVec, rightVec);
  } else if (useArea){
    outVec = overlayArea(leftVec, rightVec);
  } else if (useOrder){
    outVec = overlayOrder(leftVec, rightVec);
  } else {
    outVec = overlay(leftVec, rightVec);
  }

  pcxx_UserTimerStop(index1);
  time = pcxx_UserTimerElapsed(index1);
  printf("Time for element %d : %lf\n", index1, time);
```

Figure 15.9
Fancy File Viewer Window

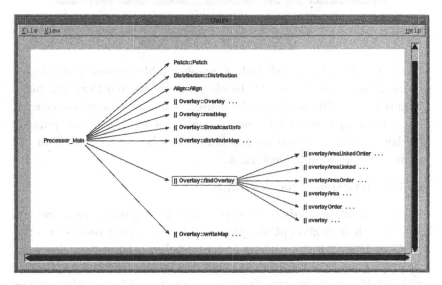

Figure 15.10
Cagey

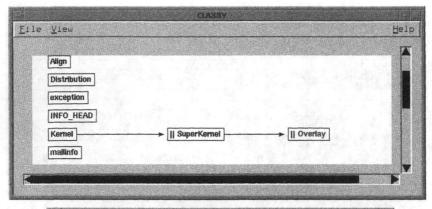

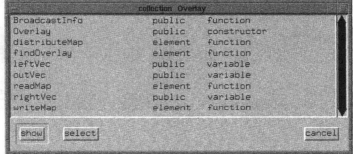

Figure 15.11
Classy

name. When a class is selected, a member table window is displayed,
which shows a detailed list of the class's members and their attributes
(Figure 15.11). The word `element` is used to indicate the pC++ concept
of a *method of element* function. As can be seen, the pC++ polygon
overlay algorithm defines its collection class by subclassing from the
predefined collection `SuperKernel`.

15.5.3   Dynamic Analysis Tools

TAU's dynamic analysis tools help users relate dynamic measurement
results to their original pC++ programs by presenting results in terms
of pC++ language objects. To demonstrate how, this section shows the
results of some experiments done on an 8-processor SGI PowerChallenge
with 512 Mbyte of memory. As stated in Section 13.5, the pC++ implementation of the polygon overlay problem is embarrassingly parallel, so

a dynamic analysis of it is not particularly exciting. We therefore show the dynamic behavior of the whole application, including its input and output phases.

The main window of the Racy profiling tool (Figure 15.12) gives a quick overview of the application's performance by summarizing both function and collection access profile data. These summary displays allow us to make three important observations about the pC++ polygon overlay program:

1. Processor 0 has a different behavior than all the other nodes. A closer look using the function legend reveals that this is because node 0 is doing all of the program's I/O (in `Overlay::readMap()` and `Overlay::writeMap()`).

2. The other processors spent about two thirds of their time waiting (in pC++ runtime system functions `pcxx_Barrier()` and `pcxx_Poll()`).

3. The good speedup of the main algorithm (`Overlay::findOverlay()`) has a simple explanation: from the collection summary we can see that processes make only local accesses to the distributed collection X, which holds the map data. This means that there is no communication or synchronization in this part of the program.

To investigate the program further, we bring up node profiles for node 0 and node 1 (as a representative for the other nodes) by clicking on the labels in the function summary display (Figure 15.13). As the behavior of node 0 is different from that of the others, comparing the functions implementing polygon overlay is misleading if we display the execution times as percentages. We therefore configure the displays using the **Mode** and **Units** menus to show the time spent in the functions in seconds. Comparing the functions that actually implement overlay (`overlayAreaLinked()`, `polyArea()`, `polyVec2AreaLn()`, `polyLnCons()`, and `polyLn2Vec()`), we can now see that they use approximately the same time on the different nodes.

We can make this observation even easier if we use the **Value** menu to configure the displays[2] to show the execution time including all children (Figure 15.14). We now only have to compare the execution time for `Overlay::findOverlay()`.

---

[2]Note that we do not have to do this for every node profile window. In using the **Configure** menu in the Racy main window, we can change all displays at once.

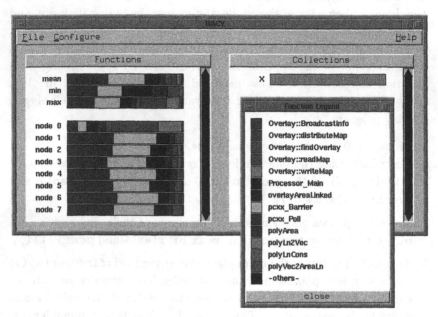

Figure 15.12
Racy Main Window

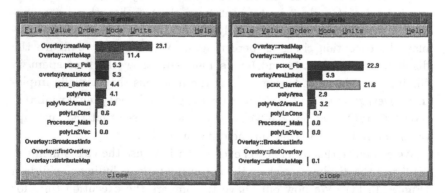

Figure 15.13
Racy Node Profile (showing seconds)

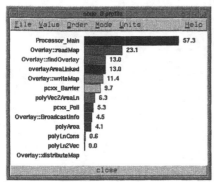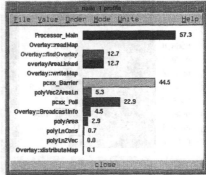

Figure 15.14
Racy Node Profile (showing total seconds)

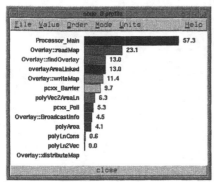

Figure 15.15
Racy Text Node Profile

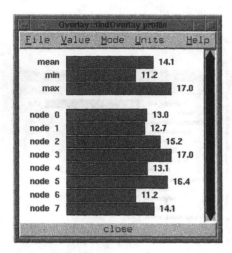

Figure 15.16
Racy Function Profile

We can also use a function profile display to compare the performance of a specific function on all nodes simply by clicking on a function name or the bar representing the function. Figure 15.16 shows the time spent in Overlay::findOverlay() and its children on the different nodes used for the execution of the program.

This information lets us hypothesize that most of the waiting on processors 1 to 7 happens during the I/O phase on processor 0. Simple profiling does not allow us to verify our hypothesis, but we can do this very easily using event tracing.

After recompiling the program for tracing and executing it, we have an event trace for each node. Once these are merged, we can use Easy to look at the dynamic execution behavior of our application (Figure 15.18). We easily see that processors 1 to 7 are waiting in a barrier while node 0 is performing I/O (in Overlay::readMap() and Overlay::writeMap()). This confirms the hypothesis we made after profiling. We can also see the typical SPMD behavior of pC++ programs. Execution of a compiler-inserted barrier after each call to a MethodOfElement method can be spotted by the vertical alignment of the right ends of the arrows representing the pC++ runtime system function pcxx_Barrier().

It is interesting to note that we measured the same performance behavior for input sizes ranging from 100 to 100,000 polygons. The ratio

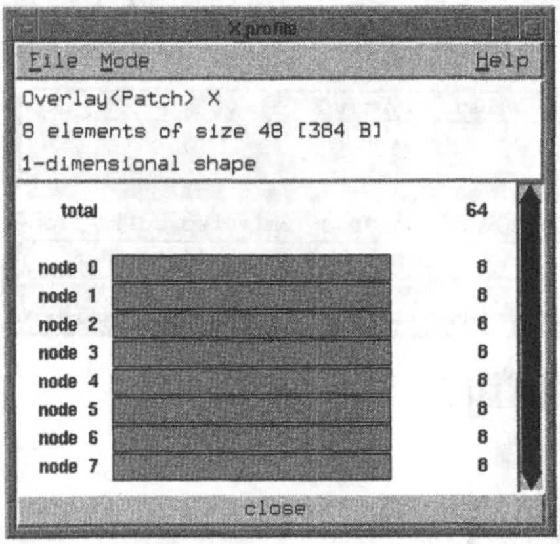

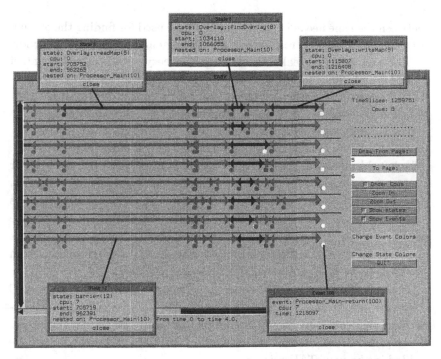

Figure 15.17
Racy Collection Profile

Figure 15.18
Easy

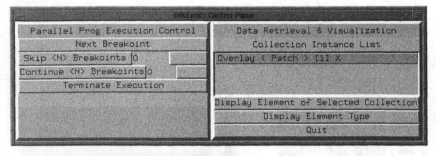

Figure 15.19
Breezy

between the time needed for I/O and the time used for finding the overlay was roughly constant, resulting in the same general execution behavior.

The TAU barrier breakpoint debugger, Breezy, allows users to control a pC++ program running on a parallel machine from a remote workstation. Unfortunately, the polygon overlay example is too simple to allow a full demonstration of Breezy's functionality.

Having used Cosy to compile the program for breakpointing, executing it automatically launches the Breezy main control panel (Figure 15.19). The left side allows the user to select the next breakpoint (i.e., barrier) or to terminate execution. Every time the program is stopped at a barrier, the display of active collections is updated. In our example, there is only one active collection instance, **Overlay<Patch> X**. Selecting the collection results in a window showing the type of an element. Users can select one or more fields of the element class, and retrieve data from these fields to pipe into a visualization program.

Because the pC++ polygon overlay program re-uses the original C code to perform local node calculations, the (**Overlay<Patch> X**) collection elements only contain pointers to locally-allocated map data. Breezy is currently unable to reference such data; this feature will be added in the next TAU release.

15.5.4   Performance Extrapolation

The use of ExtraP/Speedy to estimate the performance of the polygon overlap problem proved to be more interesting than trace analysis. We used a Hewlett-Packard workstation to predict the performance of the polygon overlay code on our SGI PowerChallenge machine. We ran an n-threaded version of the code ($n = 1, 2, 4, 8, 16$) on our workstation, collecting event traces as described in Section 15.4.3. We then set execution environment parameters to correspond to the SGI machine and observed the performance behavior. The maps used in these experiments had approximately 25,000 polygons.

The Speedy main control window (Figure 15.20) is launched by clicking the Speedy button on the TAU main control panel. We build a trace-generating pC++ executable by selecting the Compile button of the main Speedy window; Speedy then uses Cosy to execute the necessary commands. We then specify the parameters for the experimental run. Clicking on varying parameter 1 gives us a parameter menu, from which we select and modify Number of Processors.

The Speedy parameter viewer (Figure 15.21) is used to specify the necessary parameters for the ExtraP simulation phase of the experiment. As the Overlay:findOverlay() code in the pC++ implementation does not involve any communication or synchronization, the only significant one of the 25 ExtraP parameters is MipsRatio, which is the relative speed of the CPU of the target machine (SGI) to that of the simulation machine (HP). We ran the sequential polygon overlay code on both platforms to determine this ratio. Because the polygon overlay code involves only integer arithmetic, the time on the 99 MHz HP-PA chip (1.68 sec) was close to that on the 75 MHz R8000 (1.53 sec). We therefore set MipsRatio to 0.91.

Clicking Speedy's Run Experiment button starts the experiment. After each iteration of the extrapolation, the execution time graph in the Speedy main window is updated, which allows the user to see, and control, the evolution of the experiment. This is important for long-running experiments: if something goes wrong, it can be stopped early. Clicking on the data points in the graph displays individual values. A table can also be generated (Figure 15.22b). If the varying parameter is Number of Processors, as in our example, a speedup display is also available (Figure 15.22a).

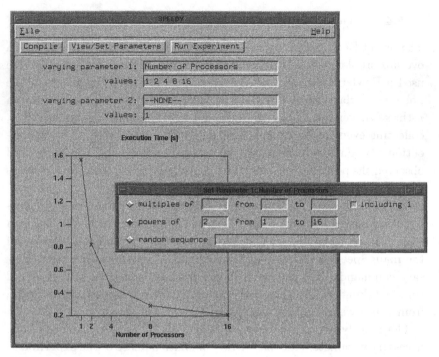

Figure 15.20
Speedy Main Window

Speedy uses one of the pC++ runtime system timers to determine
which part(s) of the program to measure. This allows the user to choose
whether to measure the whole program or only parts of it during a
performance extrapolation experiment. In our example, we put timer
calls around the `Overlay::findOverlay()` method only. The results
show almost linear speedup for this part of the code.

As Speedy is fully integrated with TAU, users can employ other TAU
tools to verify extrapolation results, or compare them with actual measurements. Table 15.2 lists both measured and estimated execution
times for our SGI PowerChallenge. As can be seen, the two sets of
values are reasonably close. We also used the extrapolation to estimate
the performance of the code on a 16 processor machine, twice as large
as actually available.

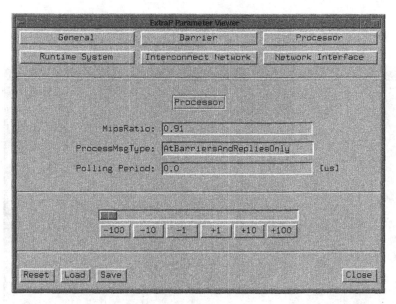

Figure 15.21
Speedy Parameter Viewer

	Number of Processors				
	1	2	4	8	16
estimated	1.56	0.83	0.46	0.29	0.21
measured	1.38	0.84	0.51	0.39	–

Table 15.2
Execution Time in Seconds

15.6   Critique

In this section, we evaluate TAU based on its implementation on a large number of parallel platforms.

First, a parallel programming environment should support the full development circle. The TAU environment currently supports compilation and execution control, static and dynamic program and performance analysis, debugging, and performance extrapolation. One area which is not yet supported is program development. Currently, we are working on an editor which would be integrated with the other TAU tools. One would use the static browsers to "jump" to a function, method, or class

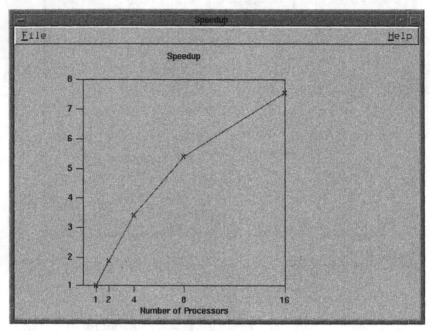

(a) Speedup Display

(b) Result Values Viewer

Figure 15.22
Speedy Result Values Windows

in the editor. If an error occurred during compilation with Cosy, clicking on the error message would jump to the corresponding source code line.

Also, TAU currently only supports function and class symbol lookup. We are planning to enhance the TAU browsers to support generic symbol browsing. This will require support for portable access to symbol table information, and tracking symbols between the parallel language level and the intermediate (compiler-generated) language representations.

Second, debugging for parallel programs is very important. The functionality of the Breezy debugger is too restricted. We are currently implementing a new event- and state-based debugging interface. It will form the basis for a number of high-level debugging tools, including traditional debuggers, data extraction and visualization tools, and interactive profiling tools, as well as for novel application-specific debuggers. It will be realized as a very-high-level multithreaded language on top of a simple but general event-based debugging API.

Third, portability is a design issue. Portability is difficult to achieve, especially on parallel machines, where operating systems and C++ compilers are not as standard as they appear. Even simple things like getting a program to start executing in parallel is different on all machines. Portability must be considered from the very beginnings of a design; it cannot be achieved by first implementing a prototype for a specific platform, and then trying to port that prototype to different platforms. We believe we have solved these problem in TAU, which, like pC++, runs on every major commercial parallel computer and Unix workstation and works with every major C++ compiler. This was achieved through a combination of software engineering methods and meticulous attention to detail in our initial designs.

Finally, C++ is a very complex language. Writing commercial-quality tools for a C++-based parallel language as a university research project is almost impossible. For example, even simple things like a generation of the application's callgraph is complex, in comparison to older languages like Fortran or C because of the need to handle constructors and destructor hierarchies, operators, virtual functions, etc.

15.7   Conclusion and Future Work

The current TAU system has been highly successful in meeting the program analysis requirements of the pC++ language system. However, TAU also established a methodology and architecture for building program analysis environments that we hope to extend in three ways:

Support a wider range of programming models. At present, the TAU tools focus on the data-parallel style of programming embodied in pC++ and HPF. That style makes program analysis relatively easy: data-parallel programs typically have simple, uniform communication patterns and frequent, global synchronization points. Once the model is relaxed to allow task parallelism or concurrent composition of data-parallel operations, program analysis becomes harder. Tools must contend with asynchrony, irreproducible behavior, the lack of consistent, global states, and complex patterns of process interaction.

To support these programming models, TAU will be extended to incorporate a replay mechanism. This will make it possible to repeat executions, instrumenting the code to any required level of detail. It will also make it possible to decide post mortem whether more sophisticated models of observability are needed. All existing TAU tools will be modified to work transparently during replay.

Replay, however, is only one approach, and is quite expensive in terms of tracing overhead. TAU should also support more limited models of observability, giving users a choice of a range of tools. For example, one level of support might provide tracing facilities sufficient for replay, another sufficient for animation of specified data structures, another for logging procedure calls, etc. As a consequence, Breezy (or its successor) will have to be updated to support multiple notions of a breakpoint. The user's choice of tools and options will determine the requirements for observability that are automatically supported with instrumentation.

Increase functionality. The generalization of the programming model will require new, more powerful tools, particularly for debugging. Programs with complex inter-process interactions will require a multi-level debugging strategy, in which event-based techniques are initially used to find gross patterns of process interactions, and state-based techniques predominate after the focus of attention has been narrowed to a single process or small set of processes [Kundu & Cuny 1995]. Initial use of event-based techniques focuses the user's attention on manageable portions of the state space and provides the basis for establishing consistent, meaningful, global breakpoints. Event-based techniques can incorporate replay mechanisms that support reproducible execution and logical time transformations to filter out perturbations due to asynchrony.

State-based techniques, on the other hand, allow the user to examine an execution to an arbitrary level of detail, and often make it easier to relate errors to source code. The event- and state-based tools that we are developing will be interoperable. Our current prototype demonstrates that this interaction can be quite powerful: it allows the user to set consistent breakpoints that are meaningful in the context of her ongoing event-based analysis. Often, these breakpoints would have been difficult or even impossible to set with conventional mechanisms [Kundu & Cuny 1995].

We will need to develop appropriate abstractions to include event-based tools in our environment. Most existing tools operate at a very low level, basing their models on explicit read and write operations that are not meaningful to the pC++ or HPF programmer.

Maintain tight integration with the language system despite increasingly aggressive program transformations and optimizations. Trying to find appropriate abstractions for event-based tools is just one instance of a more general problem for parallel program analysis environments: the trend toward higher levels of programming abstraction coupled with generation of ever-more-efficient target code, means that tools must become increasingly sophisticated if they are to relate execution to source code. The current implementation of pC++ does not optimize aggressively, but as the next generation parallel C++ language system, HPC++, is developed, TAU will have to provide more assistance in maintaining the source/execution correspondence. Our approach will be similar to that of [Adve et al. 1995], in which the compiler provides performance tools with extensive information on the mapping between source and SPMD codes. For debugging, however, we will have to go further, enabling the tools to interpret not just performance statistics, but detailed data manipulations and control flow in terms of the initial, high-level program.

Acknowledgments

This work is supported by ARPA under Rome Labs contract AF 30602-92-C-0135 and Fort Huachuca contract ARMY DABT63-94-C-0029, and in part by the National Science Foundation under grant NSF ASC92-13500, by a grant from OACIS, and by IBM R&D contract MHVU3704.

16 UC++

Russel Winder, Graham Roberts, Alistair McEwan,
Jonathan Poole, and Peter Dzwig

16.1 Introduction

The development of UC++ (University College C++) is a continuing investigation into the description of parallel and distributed computations using the C++ programming language. The main aim of the work is to provide "low-cost parallelism for the masses", i.e., to develop a language that is easy to use and provides the ability to create parallel applications on commonly available hardware as well as specialized parallel machines. The work, initially started at University College London (UCL), is currently a collaboration between UCL and the London Parallel Applications Centre (LPAC).

Our work has been influenced, directly and indirectly, by Concurrent C++ [Gehani & Roome 1988], CC++ (Chapter 3), CHARM++ (Chapter 5), Panda [Assenmacher *et al.* 1991], pC++ (Chapter 13), and the work reported in [Adamo 1991] and [Seliger 1990]. UC++ is different from all other work we are aware of on parallel and distributed variants of C++ in that it does not use the type system to embed parallel programming concepts into the programming language. Instead, UC++ uses a strategy based on object allocation. This approach has led us to what we believe is a minimal extension of C++ that incorporates active objects directly into the computational model of C++.

The goal of low-cost parallelism, and the desire to make use of C++ to effectively and efficiently develop parallel and distributed applications on a wide range of target architectures, can be expressed better in the following guiding principles of our work. UC++ should be:

- easy to use;
- as similar to standard C++ as possible;
- provide a uniform parallel programming model regardless of target system;
- allow a single parallel program to work across a heterogeneous system;
- be quickly ported to new machines or operating systems; and

- generate parallel applications with acceptable performance gains over sequential versions.

One of the significant motivations behind the work on UC++ came from the requirements of an industrial organization (ICL plc) which wanted to develop applications for their range of parallel machines, including the DRS (a shared-memory architecture) and Goldrush (a distributed-memory architecture) ranges. Recent work on UC++ is looking to extend the domain of applicability to include data-parallel computations and fine-grain (expression level) parallelism.

Section 16.2 below presents some of the history of UC++ and also gives more details of the design ideals that guide the work. Section 16.3 presents the computational model that UC++ implements. It also gives details of the syntactic additions to C++ provided by UC++. Section 16.4 presents an overview of the implementation strategy. Section 16.5 presents a UC++ implementation of the Polygon Overlay program. Section 16.6 is a critique of the UC++ system. We finish with a summary of some of the current applications of UC++ and some future directions.

Further information on UC++ can be obtained from:

`http://www.cs.ucl.ac.uk/coside/ucpp/`

The UC++ system is available via `ftp` from:

`ftp://ftp.lpac.ac.uk/pub/`

16.2 History and Philosophy

Work on UC++ started in 1990 and has progressed via a series of funded projects: the COOTS Project;[1] the UC++ Project;[2] and Extending UC++.[3]

---

[1] Concurrent Object-Oriented Languages Targetting parallel Systems (COOTS) was a collaboration between UCL, Defense Research Establishment (DRA Malvern) and Harlequin Ltd., in the period 1990–3, DTI/EPSRC project IED3/1/1059 (GR/F37955).

[2] The UC++ Project was collaboration between UCL and ICL plc under the auspices of LPAC; Phase 1 during 1993; Phase 2 during 1994, DTI PAP project IED3/95/91/015-CTA8.

[3] Extending UC++ is a collaborative project between UCL and LPAC, started in 1994 and due to finish in 1996, EPSRC project GR/J82423.

16.2.1   The Ancient Period

The COOTS project investigated the implementation of a number of parallel object-oriented programming languages. In particular, it looked at: the properties of various programming and implementation models (principally functional and object-oriented) when used for describing parallel computations; and the pros and cons of shared and distributed memory.

UCL's role was to develop a parallel version of C++, UC++ [Winder *et al.* 1992c, Winder *et al.* 1991, Roberts *et al.* 1990, Roberts & Winder 1994], targetted at a variety of MIMD architectures, one of which was the parallel version of a target independent description language called TDF.[4]

This research produced a compiler for a subset—all the control structures, functions, and the core features of classes and inheritance—of the UC++ language integrated into a programming environment called Co-SIDE [Winder *et al.* 1992b, Winder *et al.* 1992a, Roberts *et al.* 1992, Roberts *et al.* 1991]. CoSIDE supported incremental compilation of UC++ and allowed easily re-targetable code generation. This first version of UC++ had the following properties:

- An active object model, in which a program was decomposed into a set of active objects each encapsulating a process. Each active object could receive and process member functions calls asynchronously from its peers.

- A global shared address space, so that all pointers were valid wherever they were used.

- A new class construct introduced with the `activeclass` keyword instead of the `class` keyword. All instances of active class types (which could have only function in the public part, all data had to be private) were active objects.

- A keyword `active`, which provided a second, separate mechanism for declaring active objects, allowing any class instance to be made active.

- Explicit location of active objects using an optional `on` keyword during active object definition.

---

[4]TDF is the name for the ANDF (architecture neutral distribution format) system adopted by OSF. For further information on TDF and ANDF please contact andf-tech-request@osf.org.

- Sender-side parallelism, using the `split` keyword, which allowed an expression to be executed in parallel with the main thread. This was provided as a mechanism for calling member functions asynchronously.

- Receiver-side parallelism, using `retcont` instead of `return`. With this, a member function could return a value to a calling process without terminating. This feature was later deprecated in favor of using the expression:

  ```
  split return;
  ```

- Library classes to provide synchronization mechanisms such as semaphores.

An important feature of this version of UC++ was the use of an extension of the type mechanism to define active objects; active objects were created by instantiating a class defined using an `activeclass` definition. This new keyword, `activeclass`, was introduced so that rules regarding active object types could be enforced—in particular, that there should be no public data members and that a passive class could not inherit from an active class. This extra compilation checking cannot be achieved using a class library approach. The `activeclass` keyword, combined with the need to implement all pointers as global, required the implementation of a compiler. By the end of the COOTS project, we had developed the design for an incremental UC++ compiler and implemented sufficient of it to run test UC++ programs.

16.2.2 The Early Period

Following the COOTS project, funding for the UC++ work was provided by the UC++ Project. This brought a new industrial partner (ICL plc), one interested in building parallel applications for their MIMD machines (typically used as servers and database engines). At the outset of the UC++ Project, the intention was to continue the existing work and complete the implementation of the UC++ compiler and CoSIDE environment. However, a reassessment of the existing UC++ definition and CoSIDE identified the following issues.

UC++ did not have a single underpinning philosophy regarding active objects; it had both a type-based mechanism (`activeclass`) and an allocation-based mechanism (`active`). It is obvious to us now (it should perhaps have been obvious much earlier) that only a single system should be supported: the programming language should offer only one mechanism for each of the features of the computational model. Following this idea means that active objects should only have one, not two, mechanisms for creation. The question then is which of the models to follow up? We chose to use a variant of the **active** keyword, allocation-based mechanism by providing an additional version of the **new** keyword.

The global shared address space was both complicated and a significant performance bottleneck. While constructing the UC++ compiler for CoSIDE, we investigated implementing the parallel constructs entirely within a class library. This was promising but, although it pointed the way for possible future work, it foundered because there was no practical way to transform all pointers into the global format. However, the investigation did cause us to focus on using minimal extensions to C++ (for active object creation and asynchronous function call) internally implemented by calls to a library. We intend to re-investigate the library approach with all the new features of the C++ standard.

The language was too complex for the kind of parallel applications we intended to develop. The option of redefining certain C++ constructs to embody full parallel semantics was also investigated briefly but the result appeared to be leading into considerable and possibly excessive complexity. Also, the result of such work would, to all intents and purposes, have been a new language. If the goal of the work had been to construct a new language, then C++ is not an appropriate starting point: the development of a new language should not be constrained by the syntax and semantics of an extant language. As one of the goals of the UC++ work is actually to *extend* C++ keeping standard C++ as a proper sub-set it was, and is, inconsistent to contemplate changing standard C++; it is an axiom of our current work that C++ should remain unchanged from the standard.

Finally, the CoSIDE environment was large and would be difficult to port to the large range of architectures that would be required.

The results of the COOTS project convinced us that implementing a large part of the parallel behavior of UC++ via a library was viable, providing that minor syntactic and semantic extensions were made to C++ to control the library—in particular, to designate active objects. This combination seemed to provided the right set of facilities, was relatively easy to implement and, importantly, provided the kind of features that applications programmers were looking for.[5]

16.2.3   The Middle Period

Before presenting the details of the UC++ language as it is at the time of writing, it is important to summarize a few more lessons that are important in shaping UC++.

A question we regularly find ourselves debating is which approach is the best approach for specifying active objects: a mechanism based on the type system or a mechanism based on an allocation strategy.

In the type system approach to parallelism there are two possibilities: a new class definition mechanism, e.g., `activeclass`, can be introduced, or the class inheritance mechanism can be used. Using inheritance, a possible strategy is to encapsulate all the features and functionality associated with controlling parallelism into a class. For example, if we assume the existence of a class `Process`, which abstracts all the details of parallel processing, and the class `Demo` which is some application related type, then a new type `ActiveDemo` can be defined by inheritance from `Demo` and `Process`, instances of which are active objects. In such a scheme, the type of an active object is different and distinct from the type of a passive object even though the application-oriented functionality is the same. This follows the "build what you need using classes" philosophy of C++.

In the allocation approach, the activeness or passiveness of each object is not encoded in the type system, it is a runtime property of the object; the type of the object is the same whether it is active or passive. To implement this strategy requires either a new storage-class-specifier `active`, used in the same way as `static` is used when defining variables within a function[6] or a variant of the heap allocation operator specifically for creating active objects. This latter approach, which is the one followed in UC++, introduces a new operator to deal with creating active objects: in the same way that an operator `persistentnew` could be

---

[5]Although the current version of UC++ has two language extensions, we are currently investigating mechanisms whereby the functionality can be achieved entirely within the C++ standard language.

[6]Note that `static` has a meaning to do with scope and not allocation when it is used at the global level.

introduced as the operator for creating persistent objects, `activenew` is introduced to create active objects.

The `activenew` mechanism enables the creation of the potential for parallelism, setting up the active objects so that more than one thread of control can be executing concurrently.[7] How then should the multiple threads be controlled?

Although there is a very consistent semantics using a `split` keyword to specify expression level parallelism and employing this as the mechanism for specifying asynchronous function call, our implementation strategy had some significant inconsistencies. Since we were more interested in coarse- and medium-grain parallelism, we chose to separate the functionality (at least temporarily). The `split` keyword was reserved for later consideration of fine-grain parallelism and a new mechanism for specifying asynchronous function call was specified.

As stated previously, the earlier version of UC++ had resulted in the decision to express sender-side parallelism directly in the language and to construct receiver-side parallelism from the sender-side tools, i.e., using the expression `split return`. In looking for an alternative mechanism for specifying asynchronous function call, the philosophy under which UC++ was evolving meant that the mechanism for constructing new threads must be consistent with the inherent C++ computational model. In C++, expression evaluation and (synchronous) function call are the execution mechanisms. We therefore decided that thread creation using asynchronous function call was still the correct way forward, we just needed a new implementation mechanism.

Asynchronous function calls can be implemented in a number of ways (global state variables, extra function parameters, etc.) but we felt that whichever we chose must minimize the impact on the programming language and hence the programmer. We chose therefore to introduce a new function call operator (Section 16.3.3) to abstract away from any particular implementation mechanism.

Thus, with only two pieces of additional syntax and a runtime library, UC++ is a self-consistent and minimalistic, parallel C++. However, constructing receiver-side parallelism has not proved quite so easy as was the case with the earlier version of the language. In particular, an

---

[7]Note that we define a thread as a sequence of function calls which may pass between active objects as required.

implementation of receiver-side parallelism requires either multithreaded objects or at the very least a mechanism whereby return messages can interrupt an active object. Thus, current UC++ does not support receiver-side parallelism. We believe receiver-side parallelism to be important so we are likely to investigate it's re-introduction. We are, however, trying to avoid introducing multithreaded objects if at all possible.

During the ongoing design of UC++, the aim of ensuring that C++ is a proper subset of UC++ and maintaining as much consistency of style between the UC++ extensions and C++ was, and continues to be, a central issue. In particular, we believe it is important to avoid creating a variant of C++ that has syntactic differences and requires large amounts of existing code to be rewritten. The object-oriented approach to parallelism is particularly significant in this regard, as a well-written object based C++ program is likely to maintain much of its structure when parallelized.

Other issues include the fact that, we wish to provide a language that gives a consistent and understandable model and language syntax for developing parallel systems and that is suitable for programming a wide range of parallel architectures. Furthermore, we want the UC++ system itself to be as portable as possible.

16.3   Overview of Current UC++

The current UC++ takes a pragmatic and minimalistic approach to adding parallel features to C++. It does not aim to be a comprehensive, safe parallel language—security, checkpointing, synchronization checking, shared objects, persistence, attachment to running objects, and CORBA are not handled in the definition of UC++. Instead, UC++ provides two principal features: active objects, and asynchronous function calls (or message passing). This allows active object member functions to be called without the caller being blocked, providing the programmer with the basic facilities to write parallel applications. Anything more sophisticated must be programmed explicitly or, ideally, embedded in classes from a class library.

16.3.1 Active Objects—Overview

The unit of parallelism in UC++ is the *active object*. Any class instance can be made active. A parallel program is, therefore, a collection of communicating active objects, where communication takes place by calling the public member functions of the active objects. This coarse- and medium-grain (object level) style of parallelism is directly derived from the standard object-oriented model and fits well with C++ [Winder 1994].

An active object is only accessible by calling its public member functions, enforced by the fact that an object defines its own local address space. Pointers to active objects may be passed between active object, but all other pointers and all data they point at are local to the active object they were created by. This treatment of pointers is a compromise between providing a full global address space and redefining C++ so that pointers are not memory addresses. As pointers in C++ are already unsafe, which places onus for correct use fully on the programmer, this is believed to be an acceptable compromise.

UC++ supports active objects using an allocation-based mechanism; an object is active if it was allocated using the **activenew** operator. No distinction is made between the type of an active object and the type of an ordinary passive object. Thus, an array of pointers to objects of type T can include pointers to both active and passive instances of T.

An important cornerstone of the UC++ philosophy is that the programmer takes full responsibility for using an active object correctly once it has been created. UC++ does not provide any static compiler-based checking of the use of parallelism.

A UC++ program consists of a set of interconnected active objects with each active object capable of executing its member functions in parallel with those of other active objects (see Figure 16.1). Typically, only a small number of objects are active, providing the parallel structure of the program. The majority of objects are standard passive objects, existing as members of active objects or in data structures managed by active objects. As each active object provides its own local address space, passive objects (and any other variables) are local to a particular active object. There is no way to access a local value from another active object except by calling member functions or passing a copy to that active object.

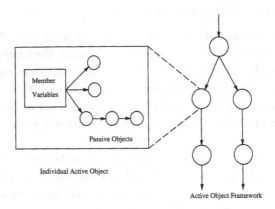

Figure 16.1
UC++ program framework

Thus, UC++ supports coarse- and medium-grain parallelism. Further, the underlying unit of parallel execution (invariably a process) is provided by the underlying operating system or supporting library such as PVM or MPI. UC++ makes no attempt to provide its own process creation or process scheduling. This makes the system portable to a wide range of machines and avoids building in assumptions about process structure or interprocess communication.

UC++ supports both synchronous and asynchronous member function calls between active objects. A synchronous call behaves in the same way as a standard C++ member function call, in that the caller is suspended until the called function returns. With an asynchronous call, the caller does not wait for the result of a function call to be returned and may continue processing. Asynchronous member function calls provide the mechanism for initiating parallelism in a UC++ program.

An active object becomes active when it receives a member function call. A thread of control is therefore a sequence of function calls passing from one active object to another. Each active object executes one member function call at any one time, there is no internal multitasking. Once started, a member function is executed to completion: whilst a member function is being processed, all other incoming calls are queued, the next call in the queue will not be processed until the current call terminates. This single-thread policy requires application programmers to be aware of any potential deadlock situations.

The single-thread model of UC++ has been chosen deliberately but is continually being reviewed. Allowing only a single active thread per active object keeps the implementation simple, while providing a level of parallelism that allows a wide range of useful programs to be written. It has the advantage of avoiding the need for language-implemented facilities such as critical sections and exclusive access to variables. Other mechanisms for dealing with parallelism, if needed, can be created using classes without the need to provide underlying primitive (language-level) features.

16.3.2 Active Objects—The Execution Model

The UC++ active object model is based on an abstract machine consisting of a networked collection of virtual processing elements (i.e., processor/memory pairs), each supporting an active object. The model assumes that each virtual processor supports only a single active object and that the object has only a single thread of control. This abstract machine provides a way of describing and reasoning about the behavior of UC++ programs which is independent of any particular hardware platform.

The mapping of active objects to real processors depends on the process allocation mechanism of the operating system on the target system, and on any information specified in the program using the on clause (Section 16.3.3). By default, (i.e., if the on clause is not used) each request to create an active object is sent to the next processor in the program's configuration file—a simple round-robin strategy. The request is served by the operating system of the target machine which allocates a virtual processor. In the case of multiprocessor machines, the physical processor on which the virtual processor is created is often irrelevant—the operating system effectively acts as a load balancer. On such multiprocessor machines, UC++ does not attempt to control physical processor allocation.

Where the on clause is used, it is mapped via the program's configuration file, i.e., if the clause 'on N' is used (N being an integer) then the virtual processor is created on the machine specified in the Nth entry of the configuration file. For values larger than the number of entries in the configuration file, simple modulo division is used to keep the resource

allocation valid—i.e., within the scope of the configuration file. Thus, if
N is a single processor Unix workstation, a request is made to create a
virtual processor on the real processor. If it is a multiprocessor machine
then the request is for a virtual processor to be created on any of the
available physical processors.

The abstract machine defines two address spaces: the virtual processor
addresses and the local memory addresses within a virtual processor.
Conceptually there is a global address space in which each address has
a two part representation of the form *processor_address.local_address*.
processor_address identifies a particular processor and *local_address* is an
address within the local address space defined by the memory directly
available to the processor. However, there is no access by one processor
into the address space of another. The global address space is not real;
a processor can only access memory within its local address space.

Pointers to active objects point to proxy objects, located in the local address space, which provide the interface to the communications
runtime system that gives the illusion that the pointer actually points
at the active object. Each active object contains a proxy for each of
the other active objects that it can send messages to. To reference the
data within another active object, a copy of that data must be available
within the address space of the active object into which the reference is
made. The policy of not providing a global address space means that
there is no guarantee that the local copy of a remote active object data
member is correct or up-to-date.

In fact, in the current version of UC++, there is no support for public data members of active objects. The proxy does not provide any
automatic access or any storage for such data members. It is up to
the programmer to design the class to have accessor functions for data
items and to access values only via these functions. We are investigating
providing default accessor and update functions and a copy coherence
strategy but we are not convinced that such is needed or should be provided in the language. We feel that this attitude is entirely consistent
with the beliefs that active objects should not have public data members (even though C++ allows classes to have public data members)
and that, like C++, UC++ should not attempt to protect against all
'faulty' activities of the programmer.

Thus, all pointers in a UC++ program appear and behave in the
same way as in C++, except for the following: de-referencing a pointer

apparently referring to an address within another active object is actually a reference to a proxy object within the local address space of the current 'calling' active object; and pointer arithmetic only generates pointers in the local address space of an active object (which may be invalid)—pointer arithmetic cannot manipulate processor addresses.—Apart from these restrictions, pointers to active objects and pointers to any other values are not distinguished and standard C++ pointer syntax and semantics apply. However, we must emphasize that the physical representation of an address is dependent on the runtime system provided for a particular target architecture.

The execution model has all virtual processors connected to a common communication subsystem. Data may be passed between any two processors. Communication between active objects is built on top of this basic mechanism. The actual communication medium is dependent on what is provided by the selected target system.

As we discovered after having defined our model, this is essentially the same architecture model as that provided by PVM [Geist *et al.* 1994]. The equivalence of the models means that a PVM implementation of the runtime system has been relatively easy. Moreover, it means that using UC++ to construct systems that will run using PVM are essentially as efficient as programming with PVM directly: the overhead of using UC++ compared to PVM directly amounts to one binary selection at each function call.

The abstract machine presented by UC++ spans four major types of computer architectures: sequential machines, shared-memory multiprocessors, distributed-memory multicomputers, and distributed computer systems. By providing a suitable runtime library, UC++ programs can be run on any of these architectures. To be executed on a different architecture, a UC++ program only needs to be re-compiled in order to generate object code using the correct instruction set and to link the appropriate run time libraries. No source code needs to be changed.

When an active object member function is invoked, the caller and called object do not (necessarily) share a common address space, might not reside on the same system and may even be executing on different types of hardware. For these reasons, a modified form of parameter passing is used, called *pass-by-copy*. This differs from normal C++ parameter passing in two ways:

1. The parameters are marshalled by the UC++ runtime library and formed into a message. This message is transmitted to the target process and the parameters unmarshalled before the target function is called.

2. Reference and pointer parameters within a called function refer to copies in the address space of the target active object. The data pointed at by a pointer or reference parameter is marshalled and copied into the address space of the target active object. Hence any modification of the data in the caller will have no effect on the data visible to the callee and vice versa.

Parameters are marshalled by means of the input and output operators, >> and <<, defined in the iostream library (see Section 16.4.2 for details). This library defines suitable functions for primitive data types only. The application developer is *required* to provide appropriate functions for all application specific data types.[8] This is all that is required of them though. The UC++ system takes care of all buffering and actual calling of the input/output operators: the marshalling and unmarshalling is essentially transparent to the programmer.

Active objects are normally terminated as a result of the delete operator. The associated destructor is executed synchronously, which gives a guarantee on return that all processing by the target object is complete.

When the application's main function returns, the runtime system terminates any remaining active objects. It is preferable to avoid this action, as termination will occur in an arbitrary order without regard to any dependencies between active objects.

16.3.3 Language Elements

As mentioned earlier, an active object is created in UC++ by using the keyword activenew. The syntax is similar to the C++ keyword new:

activenew *class-id* [(*constructor-parameters*)] [on *resource-id*]

When executed, this expression creates a virtual processor and constructs an active object in that processor. The local address of the active object (in fact the address of its proxy) is returned. This expression may be used in any context where an object address is expected

---

[8]We are currently reviewing the strategy to enable some default behavior.

such as the initialization value in a pointer declaration or the right hand of an assignment to a pointer.

The following shows the comparison between new and activenew:

```
class Demo { ... };
Demo * passiveObject = new Demo;
Demo * activeObject = activenew Demo;
```

Deleting an active object is no different from deleting a passive object:

```
delete passiveObject;  // points to passive object
delete activeObject;    // points to active object
```

Unless the pointer points at an active object, delete behaves exactly as in standard C++. If the pointer points at an active object, the effect is similar: the destructor, if defined, is called synchronously and the virtual processor containing the object is terminated. In addition, any resources associated with the object, including any local data or passive objects, are released and any open files are closed. (In the case of a passive object, store would not be released and files would remain open unless a destructor took appropriate action.)

An active object member function may be called either synchronously or asynchronously. The normal C++ syntax is used where a synchronous call is required. Implicit member function calls, i.e., of constructors and destructors, are made synchronously.[9] An asynchronous call is specified by the asynchronous function call operator (@@). (@@) may be used to indicate asynchronous calls of constructors and destructors as well as any member function:

```
X * p = activenew X(a, b, c);  // implied synch. call of X::X(a, b, c)
r = p->f(i, j, k);             // synch. call of X::f(i,j,k)
p->g(@ p, q, r @);             // asynch. call of X::g(p,q,r)
delete p;                      // implied synch. call of destructor
```

The on resource-id clause provides a means of controlling the allocation of active objects to real processors. resource-id is an integer that is an index into the file containing a list of processor information that controls execution of the program (default name UCConfig). If this clause

---

[9]Currently, this means that operator expressions such as a+b where a and b are active objects will always be synchronous, a.operator+(@b@) must be used to obtain an asynchronous call. We are working to remove this restriction.

is omitted, the effect is to leave allocation to the runtime system, which currently employs a round-robin allocation strategy by default. Clearly, the effect of this clause must be implementation dependent. For example, on a shared-memory multiprocessor, such as the ICL DRS 6000 MPU, the process scheduler is normally free to swap a given process from one CPU to another as CPUs become available. There is usually no means or any need to control which CPU is used to execute a particular process. In such systems the UC++ library will ignore any resource information provided; however it may be useful to provide the information if migration to some other environment is envisaged.

On a distributed-memory multicomputer, such as an ICL Goldrush server, the process scheduler normally does not swap processes from one processing element to another after they have been started. (If this is required a process migration system is normally used instead.) On systems such as this, active objects are allocated to resources with reference to the configuration file and to the on *resource-id* clause.

Finally, on networked workstations, the UC++ library will interpret the *resource-id* with reference to a configuration file and select the corresponding machine. The configuration file may be application specific or may be a system wide file.

16.3.4 Compiling and Running Programs

The UC++ system consists of three components:

The controller scripts control the compilation of a user program for the multiple architectures that may be used. This compiler driver deals with the command line arguments and the multiple machine architecture compilation control.

The source translator operates on the output of the C++ preprocessor and transforms UC++ source into normal C++ source, incorporating suitable calls to the appropriate UC++ runtime library. The resulting C++ is compiled by an unmodified C++ compiler. An application may comprise one or more source files, resulting in one or more object files which are linked together with the runtime library to produce an executable file in the normal way.

The runtime library provides the means to create new active objects, communicate between active objects and tidily close down the application. In some environments, the library is responsible for processing a configuration file and allocating processes to processors accordingly.

It is assumed that a C++ compiler system is already installed. With a fully installed UC++ system, the command:

uc++ *filename*

can be used to generate executable programs for the target machines. The normal compiler flags (-o, -c, etc.) may be used, and are passed directly to the C++ compiler. UC++ source files must end with the suffix .uc++, files with any other suffix are assumed not to be UC++ source code and are passed direct to the C++ compiler without translation.

It is important to note that #include statements in UC++ source code files lead to the processing of all code so included. This is not always what is wanted, for example it is unlikely that processing of iostream library classes is wanted. A mechanism to allow inclusion of header files which must not be processed by the UC++ filter in files that are to be processed by the UC++ filter is clearly required. We have instituted the 'feature' that a file called header.h, which should contain only #include directives and which exist in the same directory from which compilation was started (usually the directory containing the UC++ source code) is included after UC++→C++ translation and before C++ compilation (see Figure 16.2).

A configuration file (default UCConfig) is required for compilation. This file must exist in the same directory from which compilation is started and should contain information for each of the nodes for which executables are required. An executable will be produced for each differing kernel architecture (i.e., non-binary-compatible system). If the configuration file does not exist, the compiler driver will create one based on the machine from which it was started.

Executables resulting from compilation are placed in a subdirectory, <*filename*>.binaries, of the current working directory, and are named <*architecture-string*>, which is a compiler generated string used to identify the target kernel architecture of each individual executable. An executable shell script called <*filename*> is created in the current directory which selects a binary to start depending on the architecture of the host machine. This mechanism is essential as the compiler can be used to generate executables from the same source code for a variety

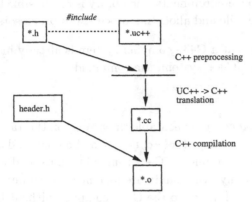

Figure 16.2
The UC++ compilation process

of differing non-binary-compatible architectures all of which share the same filestore.

For further details about the use of the compiler, UC++ flags, error handling and reports, and output produced by the compiler, the reader is referred to the UC++ User Manual [O'Brien *et al.* 1995].

In the current implementation of UC++, all classes used to create active objects must have at least one constructor and a destructor. A class with no constructors will lead to a program which will not compile. A class with no destructor will lead to "active object leakage", a phenomena analogous to memory leakage. In addition, the **main** function can only include **argc** and **argv** parameters. The **envp** parameter is not currently supported.

At the time of writing, the UC++ compilation system has been tested on the following systems: ICL DRS 6000 MPU; DEC Alpha workstations; Sun SPARC workstations; Silicon Graphics Indy workstations; ICL Goldrush servers; and heterogeneous workstation farms (i.e., any combination of the above).

16.3.5   An Example: The Sieve of Eratosthenes

The Sieve of Eratosthenes is a pipeline algorithm for finding prime numbers. The algorithm constructs a pipeline of filter objects, representing the prime numbers, along which flows the stream of all numbers. Non-

```
const int MAXSIZE = 1000;
class  Filter {
 public:
  Filter(int, int, int, int);
  ~Filter();
  void process(int);
  int print();
 private:
  int nactive;     // Number of active nodes when this was created.
  int size;        // Size of this node.
  int small;       // Size of small node.
  int normal;      // Size of normal node.
  int number[MAXSIZE];
  int count;
  Filter * next;
};
```

Program 16.1
Sieve of Eratosthenes (Prototype)

prime numbers are removed from the stream by one of the filters. Any other numbers are prime and are thus added to a filter object.

An initial implementation of the sieve might represent each prime number by a filter object which exists as a separate active object, preferably on its own real processor. However, this is not a good match with the coarse- and medium-grain parallelism of UC++; it creates far too many small active objects, each of which does very little processing for each message received.

To address this issue, each node in the pipeline can hold an array of primes, thus decreasing the number of active objects needed and increasing the processing done by each object. Further, nodes at the start of the pipeline hold fewer primes, in order to pass messages through more quickly and balance queue lengths.

A version of the program is shown in Programs 16.1 and 16.2, which exhibits real parallelism while avoiding excessive queues. The best results are obtained when searching for very large numbers of primes.

This example serves to illustrate two important features of UC++: parallelism is easily achieved by giving proper attention to grain size and message traffic; and testing is important for monitoring the behavior

```
Filter::Filter(int newPrime, int n, int s, int l)
:  nactive(n), count(0), next(0), small(s), normal(l){
  // Determine number of primes to store in this node
  if (nactive < 5) size = small;
  else              size = normal;
  number[count++] = newPrime;
}
Filter::~Filter() { delete next; }
void Filter::process(int newNumber){
  for (int i = 0; i < count; i++){
    if ((newNumber % number[i]) == 0) // Failed test, so reject.
      return;
  }
  // Got a new prime number
  if (count < size) number[count++] = newNumber;
  else {
    if (next != 0)
      next->process(@ newNumber @);  // Async call
    else
      next = activenew Filter(newNumber, nactive+1, small,
                              normal);
  }
}
int Filter::print(){
  for (int i = 0; i < count; i++) cout << number[i] << " ";
  if (next != 0) next->print();
  return number[0];
}
int main(){
  Filter *startPoint = activenew Filter (3, 1, 5, 50);
  for (int i = 5; i < Search; i += 2){
    startPoint->process(@ i @);  // Async call
  }
  cout << "Prime numbers in range 1 to " << Search
       << " are: " << endl;
  startPoint->print();
  delete startPoint;
  return 0;
}
```

Program 16.2
Sieve of Eratosthenes (Implementation)

of programs and balancing loads—good testing and profiling tools are needed.

Grain size (the amount of real work an active object does) needs to be judged carefully. Currently, an active object requires a full process and so should either perform a significant amount of processing or be required to respond to large numbers of simpler message requests.

Programming with UC++ requires the programmer to judge grain size and the amount of message traffic, and to verify any assumptions by testing. However, it is envisaged that class libraries and frameworks will be provided to encapsulate common parallel design patterns and so reduce the effort required. Testing will still be important to gain best performance. This approach to application development is aimed at giving an acceptable performance boost but does not attempt to optimize programs to the limits of the hardware available. We are looking for a trade-off between ease of development, development time (exploitation of existing programming skills), grain size and performance.

A further issue connected to grain size is the speed of modern processors compared to the speed of processor-to-processor communications. We believe that using fine-grain parallelism is far less portable across machines and a poor use of resources when matched to modern processor speeds. Hence, UC++ uses coarse-grain parallelism with optimization relying on standard compiler technology for the code at each node.

16.4 Implementation

As stated in the previous section, the UC++ implementation comprises two major components other than the compiler driver: a translator from UC++ syntax to standard C++; and a runtime library to provide process management and message passing.

The UC++ translator produces C++, with calls to the runtime system, so that the language can be used on any system which supports a C++ compiler. Furthermore, this has the advantage of avoiding any issues to do with full C++ compilation (which is complex) and needing to consider target code generation.

Currently, two runtime system implementations are supported, one based on PVM and the other hosted on our 'homegrown messaging sys-

tem' library.[10] Like the translator, the 'homegrown messaging system'
library is written in C++, with a generic interface to the output from the
translator and a back end that can be customized to different operating
systems. All process management and message transport is assumed to
be provided by the host operating system.

We support a PVM version of our runtime system since:

- there are many PVM implementations covering a large range of machines and architectures;
- there are a large number of tools for PVM, including the xpvm program monitor and Condor task scheduler; and
- the UC++ model maps very closely onto the PVM model of tasks, so that one UC++ active object becomes one PVM task.

We support the 'homegrown messaging system' library since it allows us
to experiment with architectures for which no PVM implementation exists. We can port this library quickly to perform experiments, and move
to a PVM implementation as it becomes available on that architecture.

16.4.1   The Translator

UC++ is translated to C++ by textual manipulation using a flex program; no compilation of UC++ is undertaken. The translator is inserted
as an extra pass within the resident C++ system: the uc++ compiler
driver manages the calling of the C preprocessor, the UC++ translator and then the C++ compiler proper—including a further call to the
preprocessor (see Figure 16.2).

The task of the translator is to delete non-C++ constructs from the
UC++ source code and replace them with extra C++ code. In the first
prototype of the translator, C++ code for the 'homegrown messaging
system' library was inserted directly by the translator. This proved
to be inflexible, a serious problem as one of the goals of the project
is to allow quick and easy portability. This was brought starkly to
light in creating the PVM version. The current translator therefore
inserts markers, actually preprocessor macro calls, rather than C++
code. Appropriate macros are included at C++ compilation stage which
provide the relevant C++ code.

For a class, the translator generates code as follows:

---

[10] At the time of writing an MPI-based version is being planned.

1. All classes that are to be UC++ classes have UCPP added as a virtual, public base class. This enables us to include any state variables, or member functions, into each and every class that could be instantiated to create an active object.

2. Each constructor has a macro inserted as the first line of its body in order to manage communication between active objects, if it is needed:

   CONSTRUCTOR_*N*(*id*, *class*, *paramtype*, *paramname*, ···)

   where *N* is the number of parameters *id* is a unique integer identifier for this function (used to distinguish between overloaded constructors or functions) *class* is the name of the class, and the following arguments are alternately the type and name of the parameters to the constructor, according to how many parameters the constructor has.

3. Each function has a macro inserted as the first line of its body as above to link with the message-passing system. If the return type is void, this is:

   FUNCTION_VOID_*N*(*id*, *classname*, *functionname*, *paramtype*, *paramname*, ···)

   If the return type is non-void, this is:

   FUNCTION_*N*(*id*, *classname*, *functionname*, *return-type*, *paramtype*, *paramname*, ···)

   where the meanings are as for the constructor, but with the addition of the return type for the non-void function.

4. Each UC++ class has the macro UCPP_CLASS(*class*) declared at file scope (outside the class body).

5. For each constructor and function of the class, there is a HOOK function called at file scope with the form:

   HOOK_*macro-form-in-class*

   These hooks are required in an active object in order to receive messages and dispatch the appropriate member function.

The easiest way to illustrate this is with an example. The program:

```
class MyClass {
 public:
  MyClass() { ... }
  MyClass(int i) { ... }
  void doWork();
  myType somethingElse(const char * x, double d) { ... }
 private:
  ...
};
void MyClass::doWork() { ... }
```

would be transformed into:

```
class MyClass : public virtual UCPP {
 public:
  MyClass(){
    CONSTRUCTOR_0(1, MyClass);
    ...
  }
  MyClass(int i){
    CONSTRUCTOR_1(2, MyClass, int, i);
    ...
  }
  void doWork();
  myType somethingElse(const char * x, double d){
    FUNCTION_2(4, MyClass, somethingElse, myType, const char *,
               x, double, d);
    ...
  }
 private:
  ...
};
void MyClass::doWork(){
  FUNCTION_VOID_0(3, MyClass, doWork);
  ...
}
UCPP_CLASS(MyClass)
HOOK_CONSTRUCTOR_0(1, MyClass)
HOOK_CONSTRUCTOR_1(2, MyClass, int, i)
HOOK_FUNCTION_VOID_0(3, MyClass, doWork)
HOOK_FUNCTION_2(4, MyClass, somethingElse, myType,
               const char *, x, double, d)
```

The source presented in one or more files to the translator must comprise a complete program, in particular it must define a **main** function. When the translator sees the definition of **main**, it renames the function to **ApplicationMain**. The UC++ library defines its own **main** function, this is used to initialize the message subsystem in each process when the process is started.

16.4.2 The Abstract Message Passing Interface

A UC++ application is started in the same way as any application, i.e., by issuing the name of the executable as a command, with or without parameters. On loading the application, the **main** function defined by the UC++ library is entered (the application's **main** function having been renamed **ApplicationMain** by the translator). The UC++ **main** function initializes the message subsystem and then calls the **ApplicationMain** function. After initialization of the message subsystem, new processes start listening for messages, acting on them as they arrive, until requested to terminate.

When the **ApplicationMain** function returns, the message system is closed down and any outstanding processes (active objects with associated message subsystems) are terminated before the UC++ **main** function returns.

All communication between processes is by means of message passing. Message passing makes use of two classes **OutputMessage** and **InputMessage** which are derived from **ostream** and **istream** respectively. Messages are used by the **Message** subsystem to handle creation and destruction of processes and in translator-generated code to invoke member functions of active objects.

To send a message, a variable of type **OutputMessage** is constructed, giving the destination process, transmission mode (synchronous or asynchronous) and the name of the function that will action the message on receipt. If further parameters are required these are added to the message using the output operator **<<**. Finally, the message is handed over to the message subsystem by invoking the **Transmit** member function. If the message is synchronous, a pointer to an **InputMessage** may be supplied, to receive a reply.

When the addressed process receives the message, an **InputMessage** is constructed which is passed to the appropriate function. This function may extract parameters using the input operator **>>**. A further

OutputMessage is supplied to the function which may be used to return a value to the original caller. When the function exits, a reply message is sent to the original caller. If the caller provided an InputMessage object, it is used to extract the value of the reply, otherwise any reply is discarded.

It is important for the applications programmers to remember that the operators << and >> are defined in the library only for the primitive data types. User-defined data types require an overload of these operators to be supplied by the application.

16.5 The Polygon Overlay Example

16.5.1 An Initial Solution

At first sight, the most straightforward way of creating a parallel implementation of the polygon overlay problem is to add parallelism to the sequential implementation (Appendix C).

Given that UC++ is a language which supports coarse- to medium-grain parallelism, a simple way to parallelize the code is to split the whole set of polygons into a set of discreet sub-maps,and treat each sub-map as if it were its own polygon map. The overlay for each sub-map can then be calculated concurrently (using the active object notation) and the results gathered together at the end to produce the full polygon map.

The problem then becomes straightforward—create one active object per sub-map that is to be calculated, and send each active object the coordinates of one of the sub-maps. The main function can call the required overlay function asynchronously in each active object, thus allowing multiple sub-map calculations. Once each active object has finished its own sub-map, the main function can then collate their output.

This scatter/gather method is a potentially useful way of parallelizing this problem in UC++ because we can implement it in such as way that there is very little interprocess communication, and it is quick and easy to implement.

The mesh Class The mesh class (the data structure for a sub-map) is relatively simple to implement. Given that each sub-map is effectively an individual overlay, we can use the C implementation of Appendix C

```
class mesh {
 public:
  mesh();
  ~mesh();
  // I/O functions
  void polyVecRdFmtLeft(char_p FnLeft);
  ...
  void polyLn2Vec();
  // Overlay functions
  void overlayAreaLinkedOrder();
  ...
  void overlay();
 private:
  // coordinates and private data go here
};
```

Program 16.3
The mesh Class from the Simple Polygon Overlay Implementation

in the implementation of this class, as shown in Program 16.3. This is done simply by declaring all of the overlay functions as public members and the associated sub-map areas as private data. By putting this into a class, it then becomes possible to construct a sub-map as an active object. This then gives us the simple class declaration for a mesh shown in Program 16.3.

The definitions of the member functions of the class can remain essentially unchanged from the sequential C code. Using this simple class mechanism we are able to parallelize the code while still maintaining the benefits of some of the optimizations gained from the sequential version.

The main Function Instead of the main function reading in the input files and passing pointers to the structure into which the input is read, each active object reads the input file into its own address space. This is necessitated by the fact that UC++ does not support a global address space. Each active object is then sent one set of coordinates, and begins calculating the required overlay. This is the scatter part of the scatter/gather algorithm.

Having presented, at least in sketch form, this possible solution, it must be noted that semi-literal translation of a procedural (e.g., C) program into an object-oriented (e.g., UC++) program, is rarely the

```
int main(int argc, char * argv[]){
   ··· variable definitions as in sequential version ···
   ··· argument handling as in sequential version ···
   // create active objects
   const int total = 5;
   mesh * ao_list[total];
   for (a = 0; a < total; a++) {
      ao_list[a] = activenew mesh ();
   }
   // input section
   if (ioFormatted){
      // send call to each active object to read in polygons
      for (a = 0; a < total; a++){
         ao_list[a]->polyVecRdFmtLeft(@ leftFn @);
         ao_list[a]->polyVecRdFmtRight(@ rightFn @);
      }
   } else {
      ··· invoke unformatted I/O methods ···
   }
   // do the overlay
   if (useLnArea && useOrder){
   for (a = 0; a < total; a++){
      ao_list[a]->overlayAreaLinkedOrder(@@);
      ao_list[a]->polyLn2Vec(@@);
      }
   } else if (···){
      ··· as above, invoking other overlay methods ···
   }
   // output
   if (ioFormatted){
      for (a = 0; a < total; a++){
         ao_list[a]->polyVecWrFmt(@ outFn @);
      }
   } else {
      ··· invoke unformatted I/O methods ···
   }
   return 0;
}
```

Program 16.4
The main Function from the Simple Polygon Overlay Implementation

way to proceed to achieve a good solution to a problem. Furthermore semi-literal translation of a sequential solution is hardly ever the correct way to proceed to a parallel solution to a problem. It is usually best to reflect carefully on the algorithm first and then the program.

As we shall see in the next few sections, it is fairly easy to design an efficient algorithm for the polygon overlay problem that can be made efficiently parallel—indeed the algorithm we use here might be seen to be embarrassingly parallel. Despite this, it is harder to get a substantial speed-up on the hardware that UC++ typically uses, Unix worksta-tions on Ethernet, because the algorithm complexity is actually quite low resulting in object creation time and message latency dominating execution time.

16.5.2 An Embarrassingly Parallel Algorithm

There is often a tension between the efficiency of an algorithm and the ease with which it can be implemented in parallel. In the case of the polygon overlay problem, the naïve algorithm can be fairly easily made parallel (as noted above). However the difference in efficiency between the naïve algorithm and an algorithm with even simple optimizations is large: the 'list-deletion' optimization is described as being 20 times as fast as the naïve algorithm (Appendix C). However, this particular optimization is less easy to use in a parallel algorithm as it would require a global list of the area of each polygon accounted for, and polygons that need not be considered further.

For these reasons, none of the methods described in Appendix C are actually good starting points for building the parallel algorithm. We require an approach as efficient as the list deletion method but more amenable to parallel implementation. It happens that for this problem it is not too difficult to design an algorithm that satisfies these criteria. In this section we present such a method.

We call the two input maps M_1 and M_2. We shall go through all the polygons $p_1 \in M_1$. For each p_1 the goal is to find all the intersections with any polygon in M_2. The key to efficiency is to limit the part of M_2 that we have to look at to find these overlaps.

To enable this, we sort the polygons in M_2 so that they are in order of their high x values. A polygon p_1 from M_1 can only possibly overlap a polygon p_2 from M_2 if the high x value of p_2 is greater than the low x value of p_1. Thus, we need only compare p_1 to the polygons in the ordered list of polygons in M_2 starting from those with high x just above the low x of p_1.

We also need an index into the polygon list of M_2 which will give us the starting point for a particular x value. We use a second array for this, which given an x value x_1 returns the array index i of the first polygon in the sorted polygon array for M_2 with a high x value x_2 equal to (or greater than if none are equal) x_1. All polygons with high x above x_1 are in the polygon array after array index i, as the array has been sorted according to high x value.

In addition, we keep track of the area of p_1 accounted for by the overlaps. We start the overlap process for p_1 from the polygon array index for M_2 given by the x value index we described above, and go upwards in that array. As the polygons that p_1 overlaps are more likely to have high x values only just greater than the low x of p_1 than much greater, it is likely that all the overlap polygons will be found quickly. Preliminary empirical tests seem to confirm this: with 60,000 polygon maps for example, less than 1% of the polygon array of M_2 was looked at for each polygon from M_1.

The interesting properties of this method are:

1. It is efficient: more efficient than the list-deletion method. In timings for 60,000 polygon maps on a serial machine we had timings of about 80% that of the list-deletion method; this with simple code that was not built for speed.

2. It is embarrassingly parallel: the steps in the outer loop, choosing polygons from M_1, are completely independent. Thus the polygons from M_1 can be split up into groups and sent off to separate processors for calculation with, in theory, no loss of efficiency (though in practice, as we shall see, the communication costs for our hardware tend to dominate in practice).

The method we use to make this a parallel algorithm is to build a processor farm. Because we use networks with heterogeneous machines and heterogeneous communication speeds, this is a typical programming approach for this sort of problem. We have a set of workers which do the actual polygon overlaying, a farmer that, on request, gives pieces of work to the workers, and a gatherer that is sent the work by the workers.

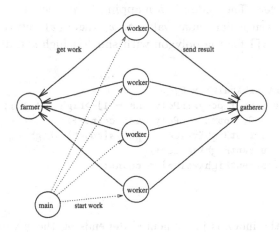

Figure 16.3
The Communication Structure at Run-time

The communication pattern among the active object structure is shown in Figure 16.3

The farmer, gatherer and workers are all made active objects.

The UC++ Code The actual overlay calculations are done in the workers, so we present the code for these first. The prototype for a worker is:

```
class Worker {
 public:
  Worker(string mapfile, Farmer * f, Gatherer * g);
  void startWork();
 private:
  Farmer * farmer;
  Gatherer * gatherer;
  Map * map;
};
```

The constructor is not shown in full: essentially what happens is that the map is read from the file named by `mapfile` into an array of polygons (in the `Map` data structure), and then an index is built in a second array, which has index values from the minimum to the maximum x values.

The code to build the index, taken from the constructor, is shown below: the array `polys[nPolygons]` holds pointers to the polygon, sorted

in high x order. The `index` is a mapping from x values to indexes in
`polys[]`. Given a particular value of x, `index[x]` returns the array
index in `polys[]` for the polygon with smallest high x that is equal to
or above x.

```
int currentHighXvalue = 0;
index = new int [(polys[nPolygons - 1]->high.x + 1)];
for (count = 0; count < nPolygons; count++){
  for ( ; currentHighXvalue <= polys[count]->high.x;
          currentHighXvalue++){
    index[currentHighXvalue] = count;
  }
}
```

The way the index is implemented depends on the x values forming
a relatively small, discrete set of integer values from 0 upwards. The
method could easily be adapted for larger ranges of values or for real
values by using a stepped value as the index instead of all possible values
of x.

Below we present the function `startWork` in full. This is the function
called by `main` on workers immediately after constructing them. It is
called asynchronously, and it is here that the parallelism of the algorithm
arises, as this function is executed on each worker in parallel.[11]

```
void Worker::startWork(){
  list<Polygon> results;
  for (;;){
    list<Polygon> * L = farmer->getWork();
    if (L->empty()){
      gatherer->blockWait();
      return;
    }
    Polygon * intersection;
    Polygon P1;
    forall(P1, (*L)){
      int areaLeft = P1.area();
      for (int i = map->index[P1.low.x];
           i < map->nPolys();
           i++){
        if ((intersection = P1.overlay((*map)[i])) != 0){
          results.append(*intersection);
```

---

[11]We use the template class `list` from the LEDA library.

```
            areaLeft -= intersection->area();
            if (areaLeft == 0) break;
          }
        }
      }
      delete L;
      gatherer->send(@ results @);
      results.clear();
    }
  }
```

Worker::startWork() is built around a loop, which starts with a blocking call to farmer->getWork() to obtain a list of polygons from map 1 to be overlaid onto the polygons on map 2. After processing the list of polygons, they are sent to the gatherer using a non-blocking function call. The forall statement is a macro that iterates through the elements of the list.

Finally, when an empty list is returned by the farmer, the worker makes the minimal blocking call to the gatherer, blockWait, before returning from startWork. Since messages between the same hosts are guaranteed to keep their relative ordering, this blockWait function call cannot return until after the gatherer has dealt with *all* the results sent by *this* worker, so startWork will only return after all the work requested from the farmer has been dealt with and all the results have been received by the gatherer.

Next we present the code for the farmer class. This is the class that handles the allocation of work units to workers requesting them.

```
class Farmer {
 public:
  Farmer(string mapFileName, int worksize);
  list<Polygon> * getWork();
 private:
  int lastPolySent;
  int workSize;
  Map * map;
};
```

The code for the constructor is not shown: it just reads in the map from the file named into an array based data structure called map. The integer worksize represents the number of polygons to be sent back as a unit of work: it is passed in as a command line parameter.

We present the code for the key function getWork in full below. This returns lists of polygons from M_1 to be overlaid onto M_2 by the workers.

```
list<Polygon> * Farmer::getWork(){
  list<Polygon> * work = new list<Polygon>;
  for (int i = (lastPolySent + 1);
       i<(lastPolySent + workSize + 1) && (i<map->nPolys());
       i++){
    work->append((*map)[i]);
  }
  lastPolySent = i - 1;
  return work;
}
```

An empty list is returned if all the polygons have already been allocated. The return value is a pointer in order to reduce unnecessary copying of the list and use of temporaries (this function could be improved further).

The gatherer class is shown below, with the **send** function that actually does the gathering included:

```
class Gatherer {
 public:
  Gatherer();
  void send(list<Polygon> send_result){
    results.conc(send_result);
  }
  bool printResults(string outputFileName);
 private:
  list<Polygon> results;
  string fileName;
};
```

The function printResults sorts the results list and outputs it to the file named by outputFileName. There is an opportunity here for parallelism not taken by this code: the results received by **send** could be inserted in sorted order as they are received rather than being sorted after the workers have all finished. In practice however, with 10 workers or more the gatherer becomes very heavily loaded with work already. To support more workers it would be necessary to devise a scheme with multiple gatherers.

Finally we present the main function which initiates and then manages the synchronization of the active objects. It is:

```
int main(int argc, char ** argv){
  ... code to parse parameters omitted ...
  Farmer * f = activenew Farmer (map1FileName, worksize) on 1;
  Gatherer * g = activenew Gatherer on 2;
  Worker* workers[nWorkers];
  for (int i = 0; i < nWorkers; i++){
    workers[i] = activenew Worker(map2FileName, f, g)
      on (i + 3);
    workers[i]->startWork(@@);
  }
  for (i = 0; i < nWorkers; i++) { workers[i]->blockWait(); }
  g->printResults(outputFileName);
}
```

Each worker is given the name of the file to read in and pointers to the farmer and worker. A non-blocking function call to `startWork` is then made on each active object, which starts them requesting work from the farmer. A blocking function call to `blockWait` is done on each of them; this will return only after the `startWork` calls finish, and so all the results have been received by the gatherer. The request to the gatherer to print the results is thus guaranteed to be sent after the gatherer has received all the results.

Evaluation and Efficiency We have an efficient and embarrassingly parallel algorithm, that can easily be implemented in UC++. The parallel version requires only the creation of a few helper classes, that follow a very well defined pattern for processor farm algorithms. In theory we should be able to get towards linear speedup as the data sets grow large, if we assume that the communication costs scale linearly while the computation costs scale superlinearly.

In practice however, this is hard to demonstrate simply, as the computation costs of this problem actually scale very slowly. For maps with 60,000, polygons the parallel version with 5 workers is only just faster than the serial version. It is clear that to get a significant speed-up much larger polygon maps would be needed, at which point the limitations of the standard hardware we have been using (Sun SPARCStations with 16 or 32 Mbyte main memory, connected by Ethernet) would become more apparent.

To get a reasonable speed-up on this (relatively) low-end hardware would require very careful optimization of the code to optimize start up times and reduce communication. In particular it would be necessary to design the algorithm so that it is not necessary to hold the entirety of one map at each worker. The algorithms to deal with this are more complicated.

In addition, the serial algorithm itself could be optimized given time, and get closer and closer to linear time. Indeed for this problem it appears that the serial version would be easier to speed-up than the parallel version, certainly for the coarse-grain hardware we target.

In conclusion, we can see that "coarse-grain architectures" such as these are more appropriate for problems where each active object can be given a large computational load and a limited amount of message passing.

16.6   Critique of UC++

The design of UC++ has focused on the issues of simplicity and portability. This has led to a trade-off between ease of implementation versus features supporting parallel computation.

By keeping extensions to C++ to a minimum we have avoided the need to implement a UC++ compiler and can potentially use UC++ with any system that supports a standard C++ compiler. This has proved to be an important decision, both for the practicality of development by a small team and with the many changes to C++ brought by the recent standardization effort.

While the parallel features in the language appear simple they have proved to be adequate for writing useful programs (as the polygon overlay examples demonstrate). Although the single-thread active object model seems limiting it does have the advantage of guaranteeing the order of message processing and avoids the need for critical regions. We have found that re-designing a parallel algorithm with UC++ in mind is often quite straight forward, especially if a strong object-oriented design is applied (such as the farmer/worker pattern).

The question of extensions to C++ versus implementing a parallel class library has already been addressed (see Section 16.2) but remains an issue. At one time we had the idea of parallelizing sequential C++ code simply by annotating it with UC++ syntactic extensions. In hindsight this is problematic (although a strong original object-oriented design makes it easier) and most programs need at least a degree of rewriting to get an acceptable parallel solution. During the re-write, a UC++ sympathetic design can be put in place.

UC++ has some weaknesses, notably in relying on the underlying operating system and the programmer writing safe parallel programs. Portability means that efficiency and performance are less optimal on some machines than code developed specifically for such machines. Debugging can be problematic as the UC++ source code is translated to C++ code before compilation.

Perhaps the most important issue is that the safety of programs is not automatically checked, so that avoiding problems such as deadlock is left to the programmer. This requires both careful design work and good runtime testing. Also, achieving good performance depends to a large extent on testing and fine-tuning code (although this is true of many parallel programming systems).

The coarse- to medium-grain object-based parallelism is biased towards machines with standard fast sequential processors and large memories (such as networked workstations). UC++ will only take advantage of more specialized features if either the standard C++ compiler on a machine is optimized for the architecture or the runtime library can be easily mapped to the operating system features. However, as there is a strong trend towards powerful processor/large memory configured machines, this seems to be a reasonable bias.

Work is currently underway on a number of amendments and improvements to UC++. Some of these changes will alter the language specification (in particular to address the implementation specific weaknesses highlighted above), while others are just improvements to the portability, efficiency and ease of use of the language.

16.7 Applications of UC++

UC++ is already being used by a number of other projects. London Integrated Management Information Toolkit (LIMIT)[12] is an integrated approach to tool building which is based on UC++. It consists of an object-oriented environment comprising a series of application modules, a database of module characteristics, management tools, and end-user development tools. The aim of LIMIT is to build object-oriented sys-

---

[12]LIMIT is a trademark of the London Parallel Applications Centre.

tems in areas as diverse as real-time financial modelling or analysis of large databases. UC++'s portability and flexibility make it ideal for application in this area.

Parallel Software Components (PSC)[13] aims to develop facilities to aid non-expert users in the management of new and existing software libraries for parallel systems. The project is developing software library management systems and graphical editing tools which will be encapsulated within an object-oriented system. UC++ offers the seamless and transparent inter-systems interface, and coordination model needed to do this within a single programming environment. A leading UK retail bank is involved with LPAC in determining the best user tools and environments for the typical user-base of these facilities, and to develop suitable data sets on which trial applications may be run.

Non-linear Tools for Financial Modelling (NLTFM)[14] has developed literate programming techniques to coordinate and clarify source code documentation, and to enhance maintainability and cross-architecture porting. These literate techniques, or derivatives of them, will eventually be integrated with those of PSC. NLTFM applications are written in a number of languages, which vary according to the specific area involved and range from numerical routines to database applications and GUIs. UC++ is being used to encapsulate such disparate applications, and to provide an object-oriented environment within which to integrate them in a re-targetable, portable manner.

LPAC is also the lead partner of the EUROPA Working Group,[15] a project aiming to standardize the approaches being made to parallel C++ work by researchers and other involved parties across Europe. The working group comprises users, developers and implementors, all of whom are seeking to create an environment building upon the work being carried out in Europe and elsewhere—in particular, the EUROPA Working Group is in discussion with the HPC++ Group—to define a framework for parallel C++. EUROPA will not produce a language definition *per se*; instead, EUROPA aims to set down a standard framework for parallel C++ systems on MIMD, SPMD, and SIMD systems. The aim being to ensure that the developer and end-user will see a standard

---

[13]PSC is an EPSRC funded project; EPSRC Portable Software Tools for Parallel Applications Program, grant reference GR/K40734.

[14]NLTFM is a project funded by LPAC, grant number /CTA7.

[15]ESPRIT Project Number 9502

framework within which to work, including the standard C++ language and a proxy model for inter-object/process/processor communication. It is not anticipated that SIMD parallelism will play a large part in the EC++ standard, as internal studies by EUROPA partners—including SIMD implementors—have shown that the most effective way to integrate SIMD parallelism is through the supply of class libraries. Clustered SIMD parallelism, where SIMD engines are clustered together to form a "MSIMD" architecture, will however enter into the EC++ framework and will be addressed appropriately.

The work being done by EUROPA is still in its early stages. Up-to-date information is available at:

http://www.lpac.ac.uk/europa

The "EC++ Roadmap" is available from EUROPA at:

http://www.lpac.ac.uk/europa/public_document/Roadmap.html

The "EC++ Standard Document" will be available at the end of 1995.

16.8 Conclusions and Future Work

In this chapter, we have given a summary introduction to UC++, the language, its philosophy and its implementation. What is reported here is the state at the time of writing. Work is currently underway to remove the two syntactic additions that UC++ makes to C++. Experience of developing UC++ and taking into account the features of the draft C++ standard, we feel that the future of UC++ is as layers on top of standard C++ with no syntactic extensions or added keywords: UC++ will, in the future, be C++ with a proxy generator program and a library of classes. The expression of parallelism will be in terms of expressions in standard C++; all issues to do with parallelism become part of the library, with support from the proxy model and generator program, not ad hoc alterations to C++.

There is, however, a conflict here: Using the operator (@@) for asynchronous message passing makes it clear to the reader of the source code what is happening; having the operator is good for program comprehension. Using the object state to determine things means that standard C++ can be used, no syntactic extensions are required. This is a very difficult conflict to resolve but on balance we believe that not having any syntactic extensions over C++ is actually preferable.

Another piece of work that is being contemplated is to construct an MPI port of UC++. This requires more work that the PVM version as under MPI there is no direct support for multiple tasks to run on one processor. However, when this is available, the advantage will be that the active objects will be light-weight, and will not require the spawning of a new task when created.

More substantial extensions to UC++ being considered concern data parallelism. It is expected that the means of dealing with data parallelism will be:

That there will be no specific extensions to deal with SIMD machines: it is assumed that all operations on such machines will be encapsulated inside C++ classes, such as the **valarray** class in the draft ISO/ANSI standard. As UC++ allows the use of all of standard C++ these off-the-shelf class libraries will be able to be used unchanged with UC++. The active object framework will indeed allow a SIMD machine using such classes to become a node in a heterogeneous network of machines.

To enable data parallel programming on MIMD machines we are incorporating a multicast message operator to allow a single message to be sent efficiently to a large group of distributed objects. In addition we shall provide parallel containers (based on the Standard Template Library (STL) and **valarray** containers in the draft standard) which will transparently manage large sets of distributed data.

Acknowledgments

We would like to thank a number of people who, whilst not authors of this paper, have contributed to the development of UC++. Mian Wei worked with Graham Roberts and Russel Winder at UCL during the COOTS project and the UC++ Project; his contribution to the development of UC++ cannot be overstated. Terry O'Brien worked from within ICL plc on the UC++ Project, he developed the first few prototypes of the "homegrown messaging system" library. Matthew Wahab, David Titcombe and Matthew Plaxton contributed both ideas and bits of implementation over the years.

We also wish to thank EPSRC for funding most of our work and Bill O'Riordan and Malcolm Rigg of ICL plc for being interested in the work, sufficiently so that ICL plc became a full partner in the UC++ Project.

Contributors

Susan R. Atlas
Parallel Solutions Inc.
Santa Fe, NM
susie@parasol.com

Subhankar Banerjee
New Mexico State University
Las Cruces, NM
sbanerje@cs.nmsu.edu

Purushotham V. Bangalore
Mississippi State University
Department of Computer Science and
NSF Engineering Research Center
for Computational Field Simulation
Mississippi State, MS 39762, USA
puri@cs.msstate.edu

Peter Beckman
Department of Computer Science
Indiana University
Bloomington, IN 47401, USA

Fabrice Belloncle
I3S—CNRS—University of Nice
INRIA Sophia Antipolis
650 Rte des Colles, B.P. 145
06903 Sophia Antipolis—France
belloncl@unice.fr

Denis Caromel
I3S—CNRS—University of Nice
INRIA Sophia Antipolis
650 Rte des Colles, B.P. 145
06903 Sophia Antipolis—France
caromel@unice.fr

Rohit Chandra
Silicon Graphics Computer Systems, 10U-178
2011 N. Shoreline Blvd
Mountain View, CA 94043, USA
rohit@sgi.com

Chialin Chang
Institute for Advanced Computer Studies and
Department of Computer Science
University of Maryland
College Park, MD 20742, USA
chialin@cs.umd.edu

Andrew A. Chien
Department of Computer Science,
Department of Electrical and Computer Engineering,
and the National Center for Supercomputing Applications
University of Illinois at Urbana-Champaign
Urbana, IL 61801, USA
achien@cs.uiuc.edu

Julian C. Cummings
Los Alamos National Laboratory
Los Alamos, NM
julianc@acl.lanl.gov

Janice E. Cuny
Department of Computer and Information Science
University of Oregon, Eugene, OR 97493, USA
cuny@cs.uoregon.edu

Julian T. Dolby
Department of Computer Science
University of Illinois at Urbana-Champaign
Urbana, IL 61801, USA
dolby@cs.uiuc.edu

Nathan Doss
Mississippi State University
Department of Computer Science and
NSF Engineering Research Center
for Computational Field Simulation
Mississippi State, MS 39762, USA
doss@cs.msstate.edu

Peter Dzwig
London Parallel Applications Centre
Queen Mary and Westfield College
Mile End Road, London E1 4NS, UK
P.E.Dzwig@lpac.ac.uk

Frank Ch. Eigler
IBM Canada
1150 Eglinton Avenue
Toronto, ON M3C 1H7, Canada

Adam Ferrari
Department of Computer Science
University of Virginia, VA, USA
ajf2j@virginia.edu

Dennis Gannon
Department of Computer Science
Indiana University
Bloomington, IN 47401, USA
gannon@cs.indiana.edu

Jacob Gotwals
Department of Computer Science
Indiana University
Bloomington, IN 47401, USA

Andrew S. Grimshaw
Department of Computer Science
University of Virginia, VA, USA
grimshaw@virginia.edu

Anoop Gupta
Department of Computer Science
Stanford University
Stanford, CA 94305, USA
gupta@cs.stanford.edu

John L. Hennessy
Department of Computer Science
Stanford University
Stanford, CA 94305, USA
jlh@cs.stanford.edu

Paul J. Hinker
Dakota Software Systems, Inc.
Rapid City, SD
phinker@scisoft.com

Atsushi Hori
Real World Computing Partnership
16F 1-6-1 Takezono, Tsukuba
Ibaraki, Japan 305

William F. Humphrey
University of Illinois at Urbana-Champaign
Urbana, IL, USA
billh@ks.uiuc.edu

Yutaka Ishikawa
Real World Computing Partnership
16F 1-6-1 Takezono, Tsukuba
Ibaraki, Japan 305

Laxmikant V. Kalé
Department of Computer Science
University of Illinois at Urbana-Champaign
Urbana, IL 61801, USA
kale@cs.uiuc.edu

Steve R. Karmesin
California Institute of Technology
Pasadena, CA
ssr@ccsf.caltech.edu

Katarzyna Keahey
Indiana University
Bloomington, IN
kksiazek@cs.indiana.edu

Carl Kesselman
Center for Computational Biology
California Institute of Technology
Pasadena, CA 91125, USA
carl@compbio.caltech.edu

Hiroki Konaka
Real World Computing Partnership
16F 1-6-1 Takezono, Tsukuba
Ibaraki, Japan 305

Sanjeev Krishnan
Department of Computer Science
University of Illinois at Urbana-Champaign
Urbana, IL 61801, USA
sanjeev@cs.uiuc.edu

James R. Larus
Computer Sciences Department
University of Wisconsin–Madison
1210 West Dayton Street
Madison, WI 53706, USA
larus@cs.wisc.edu

Ziyang Lu
Mississippi State University
Department of Computer Science and
NSF Engineering Research Center
for Computational Field Simulation
Mississippi State, MS 39762, USA
lu@cs.msstate.edu

Munenori Maeda
Real World Computing Partnership
16F 1-6-1 Takezono, Tsukuba
Ibaraki, Japan 305

Allen D. Malony
Department of Computer and Information Science
University of Oregon
Eugene, OR 97493, USA
malony@cs.uoregon.edu

Motohiko Matsuda
Real World Computing Partnership
16F 1-6-1 Takezono, Tsukuba
Ibaraki, Japan 305

Alistair McEwan
London Parallel Applications Centre
Queen Mary and Westfield College
Mile End Road, London E1 4NS, UK
A.McEwan@lpac.ac.uk

Bernd Mohr
Department of Computer and Information Science
University of Oregon, Eugene, OR 97493, USA

Current address:
Central Institute for Applied Mathematics
Research Centre Juelich (KFA)
D-52425 Juelich, Germany
b.mohr@kfa-juelich.de

Jörg Nolte
Real World Computing Partnership
16F 1-6-1 Takezono, Tsukuba
Ibaraki, Japan 305

William G. O'Farrell
IBM Canada
1150 Eglinton Avenue
Toronto, ON M3C 1H7, Canada
billo@vnet.ibm.com

Jonathan Poole
Information Systems Research Group
Department of Computer Science
University College London
Gower Street, London WC1E 6BT, UK
J.Poole@cs.ucl.ac.uk

S. David Pullara
IBM Canada
1150 Eglinton Avenue
Toronto, ON M3C 1H7, Canada

John V. W. Reynders
Los Alamos National Laboratory
Los Alamos, NM
reynders@acl.lanl.gov

Brad Richards
Computer Sciences Department
University of Wisconsin–Madison
1210 West Dayton Street
Madison, WI 53706, USA
richards@cs.wisc.edu

Graham Roberts
Information Systems Research Group
Department of Computer Science
University College London
Gower Street, London WC1E 6BT, UK
G.Roberts@cs.ucl.ac.uk

Yves Roudier
I3S—CNRS—University of Nice
INRIA Sophia Antipolis
650 Rte des Colles, B.P. 145
06903 Sophia Antipolis—France
roudier@unice.fr

Joel Saltz
Institute for Advanced Computer Studies and
Department of Computer Science
University of Maryland
College Park, MD 20742, USA
saltz@cs.umd.edu

Mitsuhisa Sato
ElectroTechnical Laboratory
1-1-4 Umezono, Tsukuba
Ibaraki, Japan 305

Thomas J. Sheffler
Rambus Inc.
sheffler@rambus.com

Anthony Skjellum
Mississippi State University
Department of Computer Science and
NSF Engineering Research Center
for Computational Field Simulation
Mississippi State, MS 39762, USA
tony@cs.msstate.edu

M. Srikant
New Mexico State University
Las Cruces, NM
srikant@cs.nmsu.edu

Bjarne Stroustrup
AT&T Bell Laboratories
Murray Hill, NJ 07974

Neelakantan Sundaresan
Department of Computer Science
Indiana University
Bloomington, IN 47401, USA

Current address:
IBM Santa Teresa
San Jose, CA

Alan Sussman
Institute for Advanced Computer Studies and
Department of Computer Science
University of Maryland
College Park, MD 20742, USA
als@cs.umd.edu

Hiroshi Tezuka
Real World Computing Partnership
16F 1-6-1 Takezono, Tsukuba
Ibaraki, Japan 305

MaryDell Tholburn
Los Alamos National Laboratory
Los Alamos, NM
marydell@acl.lanl.gov

Takashi Tomokiyo
Real World Computing Partnership
16F 1-6-1 Takezono, Tsukuba
Ibaraki, Japan 305

Guhan Viswanathan
Computer Sciences Department
University of Wisconsin–Madison
1210 West Dayton Street
Madison, WI 53706, USA
gviswana@cs.wisc.edu

Emily A. West
Department of Computer Science
University of Virginia, VA, USA
west@virginia.edu

Gregory V. Wilson
IBM Canada
844 Don Mills Rd.
North York, ON M3C 1V7, Canada
gvwilson@vnet.ibm.com

Russel Winder
Information Systems Research Group
Department of Computer Science
University College London
Gower Street, London WC1E 6BT, UK
R.Winder@cs.ucl.ac.uk

Shelby X. Yang
Department of Computer Science
Indiana University
Bloomington, IN 47401, USA

Current address:
Array Operation Center 301
National Radio Astronomy Observatory
P.O. Box O
Socorro, NM 87801

A An Overview of C++

This appendix is a brief overview of the basic concepts and terminology of C++. For brevity's sake, many aspects of the language are not discussed, and familiarity with ANSI C is assumed. For more information about C++ and object-oriented design, we recommend:

[Stroustrup 1991]: An introduction to C++ by its creator.

[Ellis & Stroustrup 1990]: The authoritative reference manual for C++.

[Stroustrup 1994]: A discussion of the motivation for, and evolution of, the features of C++. Some recent developments, such as RTTI, are not discussed in the reference manual, but are discussed here.

[Budd 1991]: An introduction to object-oriented design and programming using Smalltalk, Object Pascal, Objective-C, and C++.

A *class* is a definition of a type of object, including both its data and functions acting on that data. Classes implement abstract data types, and can represent such things as queues and multi-dimensional arrays. An *object* is a particular instance of a class, such as a particular printer queue, or the current temperature distribution in a metal plate.

C++ extends C to support object-oriented programming through encapsulation, inheritance and polymorphism. *Encapsulation* is a mechanism by which the behavior of an abstract data type is defined through a high-level interface in order to hide implementation details. *Inheritance* is a mechanism for interface and code re-use; if one data type is defined by inheritance from another, the newly-defined type can have all the properties of the previously-defined type, plus some more of its own. Finally, *polymorphism* is a mechanism for selectively and dynamically changing the behavior of objects.

Languages that support encapsulation, inheritance, and polymorphism are said to be *object-oriented*; languages that support encapsulation alone are generally said to be *object-based*. Different object-oriented languages support these mechanisms in different ways [Budd 1991]; the discussion below focuses on C++.

```
//  Defining a (useless) class
class Example {
  //  Member variables/data
  int     data1;
  //  Member functions/Methods (interfaces only)
  //  Implementations (i.e., code) specified elsewhere
  int     method();
  int     anothermethod(int par1);
};

//  Creating instances (i.e., objects) of the class
Example    obj;            //  Declarative object instantiation
Example * objPtr;
objPtr = new Example;    //  Imperative object instantiation
```

Program A.1
Simple Example of a C++ class

A.1 Encapsulation

Encapsulation is the tight coupling of data with functions that access that data. All objects are instances of some class; all objects of a class share the same interface. The benefit of encapsulation is the ability to hide the implementation of an object behind an interface, so that the implementation may be changed without affecting code that uses the class.

By using C++'s class construct, programmers can create, and enforce, a high-level interface to the data which store the state of an instance of the class, and the functions which inspect and alter that state. Data items within a class are called *member variables*, or *member data*, while functions within a class are called *member functions*, or *methods*. Collectively, they are both referred to as *members*.

Program A.1 shows how a class is defined, and how objects of a class are instantiated. Note that C++'s class construct is similar to C's struct construct, and that C++ uses // to start a comment, which then extends to the end of the line.

Given an object obj with a member function method(), the function can be called using obj.method(). If objPtr is a pointer to the object, the member function is called using objPtr->method(). Another term

```
class ClassA {
 private:
  int     data1;
  int     method();
 protected:
  double data2;
 public:
  int     anothermethod(int par1);
  ClassA();           // Constructor
  ~ClassA();          // Destructor
  friend int genericfunc();
};
```

Program A.2
More Complex Example of a C++ class

for a method function call is a *method invocation*. Data members are accessed using the same notation.

Access to class members is controlled by *member access control* rules, which are enforced by the compiler. `private` members are only accessible to other members of that class. `protected` members are accessible to members of that class, and members of derived classes (Section A.2). `public` members are universally accessible. Classes and functions that are explicitly qualified using the keyword `friend` can also access `private` or `protected` members of a class.

When an object is created, one of its *constructors* is implicitly called to handle initialization chores (if any). When an object is destroyed, its *destructor* method is implicitly called to handle any clean-up chores. The name of the constructor method is the same as the class name; a class may have any number of constructors, which are distinguished by the number and types of their parameters (Section A.4). The name of the destructor method is the same as the class name, but with a tilde (~) prefix. Constructors and destructors are optional.

Program A.2 shows `ClassA`, with member access controls, a constructor, and a destructor.

```
class ClassB : public ClassA {
  // data1, data2, anothermethod() are inherited (i.e., re-used)
  private:
    int    data3;      // New member data
  public:
    int    method();   // Redefines this method
    int    method3();  // New method
};
```

Program A.3
Simple Example of Inheritance

A.2   Inheritance

Instead of creating every class from scratch, programmers can use inheritance to *derive* new classes. A *derived class* inherits the interface and implementation of a *base class*. The new class can define new member variables or member functions, redefine existing member functions, or re-use the existing members. The benefit of inheritance is that it supports code re-use between base and derived classes. For example, derived class ClassB of base class ClassA can be created through inheritance, as in Program A.3.

The phrase public ClassA specifies that the protected and public members of ClassA have the same access controls in ClassB as they did in ClassA. The re-definition of method() in ClassB *hides* the original definition in ClassA. The *scope resolution operator* (::) can be used to refer to a specific class's definition of a member. For example, ClassA::method() explicitly refers to the member function method() of ClassA. When the scope resolution operator is not used, the member being referred to depends on various rules discussed below in Section A.3.

Inheritance allows a pointer to an object of a derived class to be used wherever a pointer to an object of the base class is expected. This works because an instance of a derived class is also an instance of the base class. In the absence of polymorphism (Section A.3), the method that is invoked is determined at compile-time (i.e., statically). Therefore, even if a method of a derived class hides a method of a base class, the method of the base class is invoked when using a pointer to an object of the base class. This is true even if the pointer is (legally) to an object of the derived class. Virtual functions (Section A.3) must be used to make the method invoked depend on whether the object is of the derived class or base class at run time.

A.3 Polymorphism

Polymorphism allows the behavior of instances of a class to change dynamically. The benefit of polymorphism is that the behavior of an object can be determined by context.

C++ supports polymorphism through *virtual functions*. When a method is declared **virtual**, the method in the derived class can *override* the method of the base class. Consequently, the method in the derived class is always invoked for objects of the derived class, even if the invocation is through a pointer to an object of the base class. This behavior is different from hiding the definition of a method: without virtual functions, a method invocation via the base class always invokes the method of the base class.

To summarize, the invocation of non-virtual functions depends on the static type of the object through which the call is made, while the invocation of virtual functions depends on the dynamic type of the object. The virtual function approach to polymorphism is an example of *dynamic binding* of function calls.

Consider Program A.4. The result of **func(&objBase)** is as expected, because virtual functions do not change the semantics of normal method invocation. On the one hand, through a virtual function, **Derived** overrides **method1()** such that **func(&objDerived)** invokes **Derived::method1()**. This happens even though **func()** is expecting a parameter of type **Base * obj**. On the other hand, **func()** always invokes **Base::method2()** because the virtual function mechanism is not used. An expression of the form **objPtrDerived->method2()** is required to invoke **Derived::method2()**.

A.4 Overloading

As well as supporting classes, C++ allows programmers to *overload* functions and operators. An overloaded function is one having several

```
class Base {
public:
  virtual int method1();   // Virtual function
  int method2();           // Non-Virtual function
};

class Derived : public Base {
public:
  int     method1();       // Overrides Base::method1()
  int     method2();       // Hides Base::method2() in Derived
                           //   (but not in Base)
};

// A function for both class Base and its derived classes
//   (i.e., this code can be re-used for Derived)
void func(Base * obj)
{
  obj->method1();
  obj->method2();
}

void main()
{
  Base        objBase;         // Instantiate object
  Derived     objDerived;      // Instantiate object
  Derived * objPtrDerived;     // Pointer to object

  // Invokes Base::method1() and Base::method2()
  func(&objBase);

  // Invokes Derived::method1() and Base::method2()
  func(&objDerived);

  objPtrDerived = &objDerived;
  objPtrDerived->method2();   // Invokes Derived::method2()
}
```

Program A.4
Example of Inheritance with Polymorphism and Virtual Functions

forms, which differ in the number or types of their parameters. For example, if a program contained the following function definitions:

```
int     max(int    i, int    j){return i > j ? i : j;}
float   max(float  i, float  j){return i > j ? i : j;}
char * max(char * i, char * j){return strcmp(i, j) > 0 ? i : j;}
```

then `max()` could be called with two `int`s, two `float`s, or two null-terminated strings, and the compiler would sort out which particular function to call.

Overloading is often used in the definition of constructors, to allow instances of a class to be created in a variety of ways. A class `Complex` with data members `real` and `imag` could, for example, have one constructor for creating a complex number from a pair of real numbers, and another for creating a complex number with the default value of $(0, 0)$:

```
class Complex {
  private :
   float real, imag;
  public :
   Complex(float r, float i){ real = r; imag = i; }
   Complex(){ real = imag = 0.0; }
   friend
      const int operator==(const Complex & a, const Complex & b);
};
```

Programmers can also re-define the behavior of most of the standard operators of C to handle user-defined data types. For example, equality for complex numbers could be defined using:

```
const int operator==(const Complex & a, const Complex & b)
{
   return ((a.real == b.real) && (a.imag == b.imag));
}
```

A.5 Templates

A *template class* is a prototype whose instantiation is translated by the compiler into an actual class. Templates are often used to create containers, such as vectors, queues, and trees. Their use allows type-independent code—accessing a vector element, testing whether a queue is empty, or traversing a tree—to be re-used in a type-safe manner.

For example, suppose a program needs to create pairs of integers, pairs of strings, and so on. Rather than define one class for each, a programmer can create a single template, such as:

```
template<class T>
class Pair {
 private :
  T myLeft, myRight;              // Elements in pair
 public :
  Pair(T left, T right){ myLeft = left; myRight = right; }
  T left(){ return myLeft; }
  T right(){ return myRight; }
  void setLeft(T left){ myLeft = left; }
  void setRight(T right){ myRight = right; }
};
```

The header **template<class T>** signals that this class is a template, with one class argument called T. When the compiler encounters a use of this template, such as:

```
Pair<int> aPair(5, 10);
```

it "expands" the template class to create an actual class for storing pairs of integers. If another use of **Pair** with a different type argument is encountered, the compiler expands **Pair** again for that type.

As well as template classes, C++ provides *template functions*. As might be expected, a template function takes one or more type names as template arguments, and is expanded when and as needed by the compiler. Thus, the function:

```
template<class T>
void swap(T a, T b)
{
  T tmp;
  tmp = a; a = b; b = tmp;
}
```

can be used to swap any two items of a type for which the assignment operator = has been defined.

— GVW & PL

B An Overview of Parallel Computing

This appendix is a brief overview of the theory and practice of parallel computing. For more depth, we recommend:

[Andrews 1991]: introduces the theory of concurrency, and includes extensive notes on the historical development of key ideas in the field.

[Foster 1994]: looks at the mechanics of parallel programming; an on-line version can be found at http://www.mcs.anl.gov/dbpp/.

[Kumar et al. **1993]:** describes a wide variety of algorithms for practical parallel architectures, and analyzes their behavior using the iso-efficiency metric developed by its authors.

[Quinn 1994]: a re-working of the author's 1987 textbook, and still one of the best undergraduate-level introductions to the subject around.

[Wilson 1995]: surveys and criticizes parallel programming paradigms from an application developer's point of view. Much of the material below is taken from its first chapter.

B.1 Basic Architectural Ideas

Parallel computer architecture can vary from distributed-memory multicomputers, in which the memory of other processors cannot be directly accessed, to shared-memory multiprocessors, in which load and store instructions can access other processors' memory. For example, a cluster of workstations (COW) is a distributed-memory multicomputer, while a bus-based symmetric multiprocessor (SMP) is a shared-memory multiprocessor. Of course, when the hardware does not support a shared-memory environment, the software can simulate a shared-data model, usually with some performance penalty. Such systems are called *distributed shared memory* systems.

B.2 Flynn's Taxonomy

The most influential paper on architectural taxonomy was [Flynn 1966]. It classified machines according to the number of instruction streams they could process at a time, and the number of data elements on which they could operate simultaneously. In a traditional von Neumann architecture, for example, a single processor steps through a single instruction stream, executing each instruction on a single datum. Architectures of this kind are accordingly classified as SISD, for *single instruction, single data*.

The next class in Flynn's taxonomy includes those machines which take advantage of the fact that many programs apply the same operation to many different data in succession. While the traditional way to do this is to pipeline execution, some machines accomplish the same end by combining a very large number of slow, simple processors. In this style of machine, the whole of each operation is carried out by one processor, but each of the many processors applies the operation to a different datum. The most common example of this is found in processor arrays, in which most processors contain only the hardware needed to execute instructions, and cannot fetch or decode instructions themselves. Instead, a single master processor fetches instructions, executes branches, and so on, while broadcasting simple commands to the many execution processors.

Both pipelined computers and processor arrays are classified as *single instruction, multiple data*, or SIMD, because they apply a single instruction to multiple data values before moving on to the next instruction. The utility of such designs is limited by the fact that what a program does to its data often depends on the values of those data. Since the instructions broadcast by the control processor to the data processors are different in each case, conditional calculations must be done in two steps. In the first, only the data processors taking the first conditional branch are busy, while in the second, only those taking the second branch are busy. As programs become more complicated, a SIMD machine's efficiency necessarily decreases.

The usual solution is to build a multiprocessor or multicomputer in which each processor executes its own instruction stream, and works on its own data. This type of architecture is called *multiple instruction, multiple data*, or MIMD. It is now the most popular supercomputer architecture because of its flexibility, and because manufacturers can take advantage of economies of scale by building such machines out of tens, hundreds, or thousands of standard, and relatively cheap, microprocessors. Unfortunately, their greater flexibility also makes MIMD computers more difficult to program than their SISD or SIMD counterparts.

In practice, the boundaries between Flynn's SIMD and MIMD categories are often blurred. Many programmers implement an application by writing one program, and then replicating it many times across different processors. This model is often called *single program, multiple data*, or SPMD. Each instance of the program works on it own data, and may follow different conditional branches or execute loops a different number of times, but basically performs the same operations. Since the different processors are executing the same basic instructions, SPMD can be viewed as an extension of SIMD. However, since the processors are not synchronized on a per-instruction basis, SPMD can also be viewed as a restriction of MIMD. A key benefit of SPMD is that it makes it easier to program MIMD computers by simplifying the semantics of the multiple instruction streams.

B.3   Programming Paradigms

The greatest shortcoming of Flynn's taxonomy is that it describes architectures in terms of what hardware they contain, rather than what that hardware looks like to programmers. In practice, one of the most important characteristics of a parallel computer is how memory is organized. A computer with a shared-memory architecture has a single address space, from which all processors read data, and to which they all write. In a distributed-memory architecture, on the other hand, there are many disjoint address spaces, usually (but not always) organized so that each processor has exactly one private memory. Processors only have direct access to their own memories, and must interact with others by sending messages or making requests in some way to access values in other address spaces.

Most programmers find shared memory easier to work with than distributed memory for two reasons. First, it is much easier to emulate distributed memory on shared memory than vice versa. Second, many of the techniques developed since the 1960s for implementing multi-user operating systems can be re-used directly on shared-memory computers. These techniques are well-known to computer scientists and application programmers, and have been tested and refined over several working generations.

In practice, most large machines have distributed memory because as a machine's size grows, the relative cost of providing or emulating shared memory also grows. A compromise which many architectures exploit is to provide a shared memory, but to implement it hierarchically. Thus, the key distinction between different shared-memory machines is whether access times for different parts of memory can differ. Architectures in which any part of memory can be accessed in the same time are called UMA, for *uniform memory access*; ones in which access times vary are called NUMA, for *non-uniform memory access*.

Locality—whether the data being accessed is local or remote—is important to achieving high performance on NUMA multiprocessors. Programmers working with shared-memory systems (whether machines or languages) can delay worrying about where each value lives until the time comes to tune their programs; programmers writing for distributed-memory platforms must include explicit code to handle non-locality from the start.

Another way to think about parallel programming paradigms is to look at how many different things can be going on at once, and how many different things an individual operation can be applied to. The four most important models are:

task parallel: a model in which many different operations may be executed concurrently.

method parallel: A model in which all objects which are members of an aggregate execute the same method (which may or may not be overloaded) at the same time. Method parallelism and task parallelism are both examples of *control parallelism*.

dataflow: a model in which programs are represented as dependence graphs, and each operation is automatically blocked until the values on which it depends are available.

data parallel: a model in which a single operation can be applied to many elements of an aggregate structure at once.

B.4   Decomposition Techniques

There are a few general problem decomposition techniques which can be exploited to parallelize many applications. The sections below discuss five of these in turn.

B.4.1 Geometric Decomposition

Programs which simulate the behavior of physical systems often contain data structures whose organization is similar to that of the system being simulated. The temperature and humidity at each point on a map, for example, are most naturally represented as dense arrays of real numbers, while the stress coupling between points in a metal object may be represented in a sparse array. The simplest way to parallelize operations on such structures is often to decompose the structures along physical lines, i.e., to divide up the data structures in the same way that the physical object being represented might be sub-divided. This process is called tiling; the parallelization method based on it is called geometric decomposition.

Geometric decomposition works best when the calculation to be done at each point in the data structure depends only on points within a relatively small radius around it. These points are called the halo; the larger the halo is, the more data must be moved around as calculations are done.

B.4.2 Iterative Decomposition

A second common decomposition strategy is to take advantage of the fact that many serial programs contain loops, each iteration of which may do a different amount of work, or different work entirely. If the description of what a particular iteration is to do, and the values it needs, are stored in a central pool of tasks, then each processor can get its next job as soon as it finishes its previous one. Such iterative decomposition is often supported directly on multiprocessors, which maintain a central queue of runnable tasks, and hand them out to processors on a demand-driven basis. If the work done in each loop is roughly the same, then loops may be pre-allocated to processors reduces administration costs.

Iterative decomposition is most effective when the number of iterations to be done is much larger than the number of available processors. It is also commonly used on distributed-memory machines, where it is usually called *task farming* (because tasks are farmed out to processors on a demand-driven basis by a central source). The classic example of this is the parallelization of Monte Carlo simulations, but many other problems lend themselves to this approach.

B.4.3   Recursive Decomposition

A third decomposition strategy, recursive decomposition, starts by breaking the original problem into two or more sub-problems and solving these
sub-problems concurrently. Each of these sub-problems may in turn be
decomposed recursively. This technique is used in many sequential algorithms, such as quicksort and numerical quadrature; on a parallel system
it may be implemented as a generalization of task farming, with each
process acting as both a source of new jobs and a sink for results from
previously-generated jobs.

One potential problem with recursive decomposition is that there is
often an inverse relationship in a problem between the degree of parallelism and the amount of work. In the quicksort algorithm, for example,
one process must initially partition the input vector V into two portions
V_{lo} and V_{hi}. Two processes may then start to work in parallel, but each
has only half as much to do as the first process. Their four children will
each only have one-quarter as much to do, and so on.

B.4.4   Speculative Decomposition

In some applications, such as symbolic integration, many different ways
of finding a solution may be run in parallel, with only the result of the
first to finish being kept. This technique is called speculative decomposition, and its benefit comes from the expectation that trying N solution
techniques simultaneously, and throwing away the effort of $N-1$ of them
as soon as one returns an answer, will result in a shorter overall solution
time.

B.4.5   Functional Decomposition

The final parallelization strategy in common use is functional decomposition. Suppose that an application can be broken down into many
distinct phases, each of which interacts with some or all of the others.
In some conventional computing systems, the most natural way to implement such an application would be to write several co-routines. Each
of these would execute as long as it could, then invoke another one,
remaining suspended until it was in turn invoked again. If the calculations of such co-routines can be overlapped, it may be simplest to use
one processor for each, in the same way that each member of a team of
builders specializes in one task.

B.5 Terms and Measures

This section describes some of the concepts which are commonly used in parallel computing. A complete list of terms and definitions is given in [Wilson 1993].

B.5.1 Locality

If processors have local memory, then access to it will usually be faster than access to other parts of memory. We define the locality of a computation as the proportion of memory references which can be satisfied locally. Perfect locality means that no processor needs to communicate with any other; this clearly cannot be achieved in any real computation (unless processors are running completely separate programs). Zero locality, on the other hand, means that all memory references are made to remote memory.

Most decomposition strategies are used because they increase or exploit locality. Geometric decomposition tends to deliver very high locality, since each processor only accesses the values in its own patch, and the values on the boundaries of its neighbors' patches. With iterative and speculative decomposition, once a processor has a task, it only communicates when it needs another task or has a result. Finally, functional decomposition is effective because it keeps all the data relevant to one portion of the overall algorithm (i.e., the variables which would be declared local to a particular subroutine in a serial program) in the memory most easily accessed by the processor executing that part of the algorithm.

B.5.2 Granularity

The granularity of a computation is the number of operations which are executed between communication or synchronization events. Granularity may also be defined as the number of operations done between context switches, or between references to non-local memory in systems in which the memory hierarchy is visible to programmers. Programs with large grains are usually called *coarse-grained*, while those in which grains are only a few instructions long are *fine-grained*.

The granularity of a program decomposition is important because it influences how easily that program can be load-balanced. The quickest way to complete a fixed amount of work given a fixed number of equally-fast processors is to give each processor an even share of the work (since if two processors have different amounts of work, one may finish before the other, and be idle for some time). If the amount of work done by each processor is roughly equal, that program is well-balanced; if the amount of work varies, the program is poorly balanced.

If a program is fine-grained, and its grains can be executed by any processor in any order with no set-up overhead, then it is relatively easy to load balance the computation by allocating grains to processors on a demand-driven basis, i.e., by task-farming. If the amount of work to be done for each element of the computation cannot be known in advance, and the amount of data which would have to be moved around in order to do task farming is prohibitively large, then an alternative strategy is to use a scattered decomposition, in which the work to be done is divided into many more fragments than there are processors, and each processor made responsible for many fragments. The disadvantage of a fine-grained scattered decomposition is that if the values on the boundaries of patches must be communicated between processors, the amount of interprocessor communication which must be done is greater than that which would be done in a coarse-grained decomposition, since the ratio of total boundary to total area increases as the number of patches increases and the size of each patch decreases. In general, there will be some optimal tradeoff between load balance and communication cost.

Another influence on program efficiency is the startup latency of performing remote operations. The time to send a message, for example, is normally the sum of a constant term representing setup costs, and a second term dependent on the length of the message. In many multicomputers, the startup latency is as great as the cost of sending hundreds of bytes of data. As a result, there is often an incentive to make fine-grained operations more coarse-grained.

By itself, knowing an application's granularity is not particularly useful, since a program could perform any amount of communication between grains. A measure which is therefore often associated with granularity is the *computation-to-communication ratio* of an application. This is simply the ratio of the number of operations a processor performs (measured in arithmetic instructions, total instructions, or whatever else is appropriate) to the volume of data that processor communicates. If this is large, the processors running the application perform many operations for each value they send or receive; if it is low, then the number of operations being done is roughly equal to the amount of data being exchanged. \

B.5.3 Speedup and Efficiency

One simple quantitative measure of the benefit of parallelism is the speedup of an application. If $T(P)$ is the time required to run a program on P processors, then the speedup on P processors is:

$$S(P) \;=\; \frac{T(1)}{T(P)}$$

i.e., the ratio of the time taken to run the program on one processor to the time taken to run it on P processors. Many programs have good speedup characteristics if measured against a sequential implementation of their algorithms, but do very poorly when compared with optimal sequential algorithms.

While speedup measures how much faster a program runs on a parallel computer than on a uniprocessor, it does not measure whether the processors in that parallel computer are being used effectively. The efficiency of a program on P processors is $e(P)$, and is defined as the ratio of the speedup achieved and the number of processors used to achieve it:

$$e(P) \;=\; \frac{S(P)}{P}$$
$$=\; \frac{T(1)}{PT(P)}$$

In all real programs, the law of diminishing returns eventually applies to processor utilization, and the speedup is sub-linear. In fact, for any given problem, the speedup will eventually level off, as the time required to perform intrinsically serial parts of the program starts to dominate the program's total execution time.

This rule was first formulated in [Amdahl 1967]. According to Amdahl's Law, a program contains two types of calculation: those which must be done serially, and those which can be parallelized to run on an arbitrary number of processors. Let the time taken to do the serial calculations be some fraction σ of the total T, $0 < \sigma \le 1$, so that the parallelizable portion is $1 - \sigma$ of the total. If we suppose that the parallelizable portion achieves linear speedup, i.e., that it runs P times faster on P processors than it does on one, then the speedup on P processors will be:

$$S(P) \;=\; \frac{T(1)}{T(P)}$$

$$=\; \frac{T(1)}{\sigma T(1) + (1 - \sigma)\frac{T(1)}{P}}$$

$$=\; \frac{1}{\sigma + \frac{1-\sigma}{P}}$$

No matter how many processors are used, the speedup in this problem will be limited to $1/\sigma$. For example, even if only 1% of a program is sequential, the greatest possible speedup which can be achieved is 99. Therefore, the efficiency, which is given by:

$$e(P) \;=\; \frac{1}{P\sigma + (1 - \sigma)}$$

will drop off to zero for large numbers of processors.

There are several ways to avoid the ugly conclusion of Amdahl's Law. One is to recognize that good serial algorithms are not necessarily good parallel algorithms, and to concentrate on parallelizing algorithms with small serial fractions. A more successful technique is to realize that Amdahl's formulation is incomplete, as it does not take the size of the problem into account. The amount of calculation done in the serial fraction of an algorithm is often independent of, or grows slowly with, the problem size, but the amount of calculation done in the parallel fraction usually increases in direct proportion to the size of the problem. One way to achieve higher efficiency is therefore to use parallel computers to solve larger problems.[1]

This line of argument leads to the notion of scaled speedup, which takes account of both the number of processors used and the size of the problem being solved. The most illuminating way to think about scalability and efficiency seems to be to ask how the size of a problem must be scaled up, relative to the increase in the number of processors, in order to maintain some specified efficiency. This approach has led to the

---

[1] This is sometimes called "cheating".

notion of isoefficiency functions [Grama *et al.* 1993, Kumar *et al.* 1993], which measure how the size of the problem being solved must grow as a function of the number of processors used in order to maintain efficiency.

— GVW & PL

C An Overview of Polygon Overlay

In order to facilitate comparison of the programming systems presented in this book, each group was asked to implement one problem—polygon overlay—in their system. This appendix describes the problem, several sequential algorithms for solving it, and some possible parallelization strategies. It also describes the code and sample data files given to each group as a starting point, and critiques the choice of polygon overlay as a reference problem.

C.1 The Problem

Suppose we have with two maps, A and B. Each map covers the same geographical area, and is decomposed into a set of non-overlapping polygons (Figure C.1). Our aim is to overlay the maps, i.e., to generate a new map consisting of the non-empty elements in the geometric intersection of A and B. This problem frequently arises in geographical information systems, in which the first map might represent soil type, and the second, vegetation. Their overlay then shows how combinations of soil type and vegetation are distributed [White 1978].

In the general case, polygons in the original maps may be non-convex; their overlay may then contain polygons which consist of multiple disjoint patches. This is often dealt with by representing each non-convex polygon as the union of two or more convex polygons. A post-processing stage then re-labels disjoint patches which are to be treated as a single polygon.

In order to simplify our implementations of this problem, we require that all polygons be non-empty rectangles, with vertices on a rectangular integer grid $[0\ldots N]\times[0\ldots M]$. We also require that input maps have

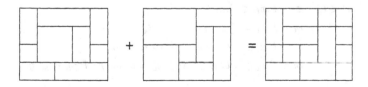

Figure C.1
Example of Polygon Overlay

identical extents, that each be completely covered by its rectangular decomposition, and that the data structures representing the maps be small enough to fit into physical memory. We do not require the output map to be sorted, although all of the input maps used in this book are sorted by the lower-left corner.

C.2 Overview of Sequential Implementation

All contributors were given a sequential C implementation of polygon overlay as a starting point. This included:

- a program **mapgen** to generate random maps;
- a program **mapchk** to check the correctness of maps;
- an overlay program implementing both the naïve and optimized algorithms described below; and
- several map files (called **k100.00**, **k100.01**, and so on) containing approximately 60,000 polygons each.

C.2.1 Map File Format

Maps are stored in either formatted or unformatted files. A formatted file contains the number of polygons in the file, followed by that number of polygons. Each polygon is represented by its lowest X co-ordinate, its lowest Y co-ordinate, and its highest X and Y coordinates (in that order). An unformatted file consists of a single field, whose value is the number of polygons in the file, followed by a machine-dependent representation of that many polygons.

By default, polygons in formatted map files are stored in sorted order. For two polygons P and Q with lower-left and upper-right coordinates (x_ℓ, y_ℓ) and (x_h, y_h), this order is defined by:

$$
\begin{aligned}
P < Q \quad &\equiv \quad P.x_\ell < Q.x_\ell \\
&or \quad P.x_\ell = Q.x_\ell \ \wedge\ P.x_h < Q.x_h \\
&or \quad P.x_{\ell,h} = Q.x_{\ell,h} \ \wedge\ P.y_\ell < Q.y_\ell \\
&or \quad P.x_{\ell,h} = Q.x_{\ell,h} \ \wedge\ P.y_\ell = Q.y_\ell \ \wedge\ P.y_h < Q.y_h
\end{aligned}
$$

C.2.2   Map Generation

mapgen begins by creating a rectangular grid containing $(X-1) \times (Y-1)$ cells, and setting each cell's value to **false**. Cell (i, j) is re-set to **true** to show that a polygon covers the area $[i, i+1] \times [j, j+1]$. Initially, npt cells are filled to create 1×1 "seed" polygons (where npt is specified by the user). The program then cycles through these seed polygons. On each pass, it expands each polygon by one size unit in one of the four cardinal directions, unless such expansion is blocked by an adjacent polygon.

Once all seed polygons have been expanded as far as possible, the map may contain uncovered "holes". mapgen searches through the map to find these, fills them using a greedy algorithm, and then sorts and outputs the resulting polygons.

C.3   Sequential Algorithms

The program po implements polygon overlay using a naïve algorithm, and is used to drive the more sophisticated versions described later. The naïve algorithm generates the overlay of its inputs by comparing each polygon in the first vector to each polygon in the vector. When an intersection occurs, the program adds a new polygon to an internal linked list. Once both input maps have been exhausted, this list is converted to a vector and returned to the main program. po then sorts this vector (unless unsorted I/O has been specified), and writes it to the output stream.

The most obvious way to improve this algorithm is to make use of the sorted order of the entries in each input vector. If a polygon's high-X coordinate is X, then no polygon whose low-X coordinate is greater than or equal to X can possibly overlap it. This fact can be used to limit the sweep of the inner overlay loop.

A second optimization is to keep track of how much of the area of each polygon has not yet been accounted for. Suppose, for example, that a polygon P from one map overlaps exactly two polygons Q_1 and Q_2 from a second map. Once the two output polygons have been generated, all of the area of P has been "used up"; the program no longer needs to consider it when calculating overlaps with other polygons from the second map. This is implemented by using an auxiliary integer vector

	naïve	ordered	area+ordered	area	list+ordered	list
1	0.78	0.50	0.20	0.14	0.05	0.05
2	0.77	0.48	0.19	0.14	0.05	0.05
3	0.76	0.49	0.20	0.15	0.05	0.05
4	0.78	0.50	0.19	0.14	0.05	0.05
5	0.78	0.49	0.21	0.15	0.05	0.04

Table C.1
Overlay Times (sec)

to keep track of the unaccounted-for area of each polygon in the second input vector, and a scalar integer to do the same job for the currently-selected polygon from the first input vector. When the area of the first polygon is exhausted, the outer loop is terminated; if the remaining area of a polygon from the second vector is zero, it is not examined.

A further refinement on this area-tracking optimization is to create a linked list of intermediate structures which "shadows" one of the input vectors. Each element of this list records the area of its corresponding polygon. Instead of looping through the whole of that vector, this variation repeatedly traverses this list. Once a polygon's area has been exhausted, its shadow is deleted from the linked list. so that successive iterations need not consider it at all. Combinations of these optimizations are of course possible.

C.3.1   Sequential Performance

The overlay implementations described above were compiled using xlc (Version 1.3.5) with the -O3 option, and run on a 50 MHz RS6000/970 with 256 Mbyte of memory under AIX (Version 3.2.5). Randomly-generated maps on 64×64 grids, containing approximately 1050 polygons each, were used as input. (Note that a more realistic map size is 10^5–10^6 polygons; maps of this size were used to measure the speed of parallel implementations.) Sample timings are given in Table C.1.

On its own, the sorted-order optimization reduced processing time by approximately half, which is what one would expect. The area-tracking optimization was much more effective, while the list-deletion optimization executed in approximately one-twentieth the time of the naïve algorithm.

Surprisingly, combining the sorted-order optimization with either of area tracking or list deletion produces a *slower* program. This may be attributable to the cost of an extra test in the control of the inner loop, but the profiling tools available do not have the resolution required to verify this.

C.4   Parallel Algorithms

Parallel implementations of this problem can take one of (at least) three forms. Each of these can be viewed as using either irregular geometric decomposition or iterative decomposition (Appendix B).

In a pure *data-parallel* version, the whole of one map is read into a parallel structure in memory, or, equivalently, associated with a single virtual processor (Figure C.2). Polygons from the second map are then read in one at a time, and the intersection of each with each polygon in the first map calculated simultaneously. The reading of polygons from the second map can be done via parallel I/O or by having one process read the entire second map and then broadcast individual polygons to the other processes. Non-empty intersections are collected using a scan or gather operation, and written to a file.

In a *pipelined* control-parallel implementation, each of P processes, $1 \leq P \leq N_A$, is allocated one of the N_A polygons in the first map. The polygons of the second map are then streamed through the pipeline; results are either passed through the same pipeline, stored locally for collection upon termination, or "bled off" as the pipeline executes (Figure C.3).

Finally, a *control-parallel* implementation may also construct the same $M \times M$ mesh used in the serial implementation outlined earlier, and associate a process with each mesh patch. As polygons from the second map are read in, they are either broadcast to all processes, or multicast to those processes responsible for patches within which intersections might lie. Results may be collected from each patch as the program executes, or upon termination.

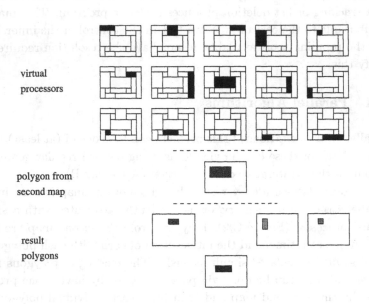

virtual
processors

polygon from
second map

result
polygons

Figure C.2
Data-Parallel Overlay

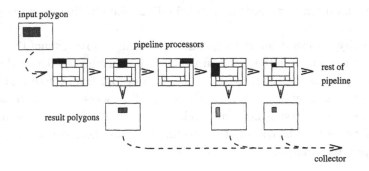

input polygon

pipeline processors

rest of
pipeline

result polygons

collector

Figure C.3
Pipelined Overlay

C.5   Critique

In retrospect, polygon overlay was not a good choice as a reference problem. First, since each polygon-to-polygon comparison is independent, the problem is embarrassingly parallel; a problem with more complex parallelism would have been better for highlighting the strengths and weaknesses of different systems.

Second, polygon overlay is I/O-limited for all but the largest data sets. Performance and speedup figures which include I/O times are therefore disappointing, while ones which do not are not representative of real-world performance on problems of this sort.

Third, as several chapters discuss, the performance of geometrically-decomposed polygon overlay is critically dependent on the way the input maps are partitioned. As the performance figures in Section C.3.1 show, keeping track of polygon areas, and discarding polygons whose unaccounted-for area is zero, dramatically improves performance. If one or both input maps are partitioned, however, it is possible that the area of some polygons in some partitions may never be completely accounted for. As a result, the near-linear behavior of the area-tracking algorithm is reduced to the quadratic behavior of the naïve algorithm. As [Bailey 1991] pointed out, this makes speedup look good, but only by reducing real performance.

Finally, surprisingly little work has been done on comparing the features and usability, as opposed to semantics or performance, of parallel programming languages. [Babb 1988] used numerical approximation of π to compare more than a dozen parallel programming systems; this example appears in Section 2.4.1. [Feo 1992] used four problems—solution of a skyline matrix equation, isomer generation, Hamming's problem, and a simple discrete event simulation—for similar purposes. This work inspired one of the editors to construct a similar set of problems [Wilson 1994, Wilson & Bal 1995], which were later revised to test the ability of various systems to support programming-in-the-large [Wilson & Irvin 1995].

— GVW & PL

Bibliography

[Abelson & Sussman 1985] H. Abelson, G.J. Sussman, and J. Sussman. *Structure and Interpretation of Computer Programs*. The MIT Press, 1985. (page 55)

[Ackerman 1982] W.B. Ackerman. Data Flow Languages. *IEEE Computer*, 15(2):15–25, February 1982. (pages 92, 101)

[Adamo 1991] J.-M. Adamo. Extending C++ with Communicating Sequential Processes. In P. Welch, D. Stiles, T. Kunii, and A. Bakkers, editors, *Proc. Transputing'91*, volume 1, pages 431–448. ISO Press, 1991. ISBN 90-5199-045-6. (page 629)

[Adams et al. 1992] J.C. Adams, W.S. Brainerd, J.T. Martin, B.T. Smith, and J.L. Wagener. *Fortran 90 Handbook*. McGraw-Hill, 1992. (pages 299, 301)

[Adve & Gharachorloo 1995] S.V. Adve and K. Gharachorloo. Shared Memory Consistency Models: A Tutorial. Technical Report 95/7, DEC Western Research Laboratory, September 1995. (page 25)

[Adve et al. 1995] V.S. Adve, J. Mellor-Crummey, M. Anderson, K. Kennedy, J.-C. Wang, and D.A. Reed. An Integrated Compilation and Performance Analysis Environment for Data Parallel Programs. In *Proc. Supercomputing 1995*, December 1995. (page 627)

[Agarwal et al. 1990] A. Agarwal, B.-H. Lim, D. Kranz, and J. Kubiatowicz. APRIL: A Processor Architecture for Multiprocessing. In *Proc. 17th International Symposium on Computer Architecture*, pages 104–114, Seattle, WA, May 1990. (page 217)

[Agarwal et al. 1995] A. Agarwal, R. Bianchini, D. Chaiken, K.L. Johnson, D. Kranz, J. Kubiatowicz, B.-H. Lim, K. Mackenzie, and D. Yeung. The MIT Alewife Machine: Architecture and Performance. In *Proc. 22nd International Symposium on Computer Architecture*, pages 2–13, Santa Margherita Ligure, Italy, June 1995. (page 217)

[Agha 1986] G. Agha. *Actors: A Model of Concurrent Computation in Distributed Systems*. MIT Press, 1986. (pages 1, 92, 178, 180, 262, 379)

[Agha 1990] G. Agha. Concurrent Object-Oriented Programming. *Communications of the ACM*, 33(9):125–141, September 1990. (page 349)

[Agha et al. 1993] G. Agha, S. Frølund, W.Y. Kim, R. Panwar, A. Patterson, and D. Sturman. Abstraction and Modularity Mechanisms for Concurrent Computing. *IEEE Parallel and Distributed Technology*, May 1993. (page 267)

[Agrawal et al. 1994] G. Agrawal, A. Sussman, and J.H. Saltz. Efficient Runtime Support for Parallelizing Block Structured Applications. In D.W. Walker and J.J. Dongarra, editors, *Proc. Scalable High Performance Computing Conference (SHPCC-94)*, pages 158–167. IEEE Computer Society Press, May 1994. (page 138)

[Agrawal et al. 1995] G. Agrawal, A. Sussman, and J.H. Saltz. An Integrated Runtime and Compile-Time Approach for Parallelizing Structured and Block Structured Applications. *IEEE Transactions on Parallel and Distributed Systems*, 6(7):747–754, July 1995. (page 138)

[Alpern 1995] B. Alpern. Private conversation (November 30, 1995). (page 82)

[Altschul et al. 1990] S.F. Altschul, W. Miller, E.W. Myers, and D.J. Lipman. Basic Local Alignment Search Tool. *Journal of Molecular Biology*, 215:403–410, 1990. (page 407)

[Amdahl 1967] G. Amdahl. Validity of the Single Processor Approach to Achieving Large-Scale Computer Capabilities. In *Proc. AFIPS Conference*, volume 30, 1967. (page 697)

[America 1987] P. America. POOL-T: A Parallel Object-Oriented Language. In A. Yonezawa and M. Tokoro, editors, *Object-Oriented Concurrent Programming*, pages 199–220. MIT Press, 1987. (page 349)

[America 1988] P. America. Definition of POOL2, a Parallel Object-Oriented Language. Technical Report 364, Philips Research Laboratories, April 1988. ESPRIT Project 415. (page 267)

[America 1990] P. America. A Parallel Object-Oriented Language with Inheritance and Subtyping. In *Proc. ECOOP/OOPSLA'90*, pages 161–168, 1990. (page 379)

[Andersen 1994] B. Andersen. A General, Fine-Grained, Machine Independent, Object-Oriented Language. *ACM SIGPLAN Notices*, pages 17–26, May 1994. (page 379)

[Anderson *et al.* 1992] E. Anderson, Z. Bai, C. Bischof, J. Demmel, J.J. Dongarra, J. Du Croz, A. Greenbaum, S. Hammarling, A. McKenney, S. Ostrouchov, and D. Sorensen. *LAPACK Users' Guide*. Society for Industrial and Applied Mathematics, 1992. (page 45)

[Andrews 1991] G.R. Andrews. *Concurrent Programming: Principles and Practice*. Benjamin/Cummings, 1991. (page 689)

[Arjomandi *et al.* 1994] E. Arjomandi, W. O'Farrell, and I. Kalas. Concurrency Suppport for C++: An Overview. *C++ Report*, 5(10):44–50, January 1994. (page 42)

[Arnold *et al.* 1995] A. Arnold, U. Deter, and W.E. Nagel. Performance Optimization of Parallel Programs: Tracing, Zooming, Understanding. In R. Winget and K. Winget, editors, *Proc. Cray User Group Meeting, Spring 1995*, pages 252–58, Denver, CO, March 1995. (pages 595, 604)

[Arpaci *et al.* 1995] R.H. Arpaci, D.E. Culler, A. Krishnamurthy, S.G. Steinberg, and K. Yelick. Empirical Evaluation of the CRAY-T3D: A Compiler Perspective. In *22nd International Symposium on Computer Architecture*, pages 320–332, June 1995. (page 339)

[Arvind & Brobst 1993] Arvind and S. Brobst. The Evolution of Dataflow Architectures: From Static Dataflow to P-RISC. *International Journal of High Speed Computing*, 5(2), 1993. (page 180)

[Assenmacher *et al.* 1991] H. Assenmacher, T. Breitbach, P. Buhler, V. Hübsch, and R. Schwarz. PANDA—Supporting Distributed Programming in C++. In O.M. Nierstrasz, editor, *ECOOP'93—Object-Oriented Programming*, volume 707 of *Lecture Notes in Computer Science*, pages 361–383. Springer-Verlag, 1991. (pages 42, 629)

[Athas & Boden 1989] W. Athas and N. Boden. Cantor: An Actor Programming System for Scientific Computing. In *Proc. ACM SIGPLAN Workshop on Object Based Concurrent Programming, ACM SIGPLAN Notices*, pages 66–68, April 1989. (page 186)

[AT&T 1989] AT&T. *C++ Language System Release 2.0: Product Reference Manual*, 1989. (page 42)

[Attali & Caromel 1995] I. Attali, D. Caromel, and A. Wendelborn. A Formal Semantics and an Interactive Environment for Sisal. In A. Zaky, editor, *Tools and Environments for Parallel and Distributed Systems*, pages 231–258. Kluwer, 1995. to appear. (page 295)

[Attali *et al.* 1993] I. Attali, D. Caromel, and M. Oudshoorn. A Formal Definition of the Dynamic Semantics of the Eiffel Language. In G. Gupta, G. Mohay, and R. Topor, editors, *Sixteenth Australian Computer Science Conference (ACSC-16)*, pages 109–120. Griffith University, February 1993. (page 295)

[Babb 1988] R.G. Babb, editor. *Programming Parallel Processors.* Addison-Wesley, 1988. (page 707)

[Backus 1978] J.W. Backus. Can Programming be Liberated from the von Neumann Style? A Functional Style and its Algebra of Programs. *Communications of the ACM*, 21(8):613–641, August 1978. (page 299)

[Bailey 1991] D.H. Bailey. Twelve Ways to Fool the Masses When Giving Performance Results on Parallel Computers. *Supercomputing Review*, 4(8), August 1991. (page 707)

[Bailey *et al.* 1994] D.H. Bailey, E. Barszcz, L. Dagum, and H.D. Simon. NAS Parallel Benchmark Results October 1994. Technical Report NAS-94-001, NASA Ames Research Center, 1994. (page 82)

[Bal 1991] H.E. Bal. *Programming Distributed Systems.* Prentice Hall, 1991. (page 42)

[Bal *et al.* 1992] H.E. Bal, M.F. Kaashoek, and A.S. Tanenbaum. Orca: A Language for Parallel Programming of Distributed Systems. *IEEE Transactions on Software Engineering*, 18(3), March 1992. (pages 1, 42, 349)

[Bangalore *et al.* 1994] P. Bangalore, N.E. Doss, and A. Skjellum. MPI++ : Issues and Features. In *Proc. OONSKI'94*, January 1994. (pages 465, 472)

[Barnes & Hut 1986] J.E. Barnes and P. Hut. A Hierarchical O(N log N) Force Calculation Algorithm. *Nature*, 324(4):446–449, December 1986. (page 314)

[Beazley *et al.* 1995] D.M. Beazley, P.S. Lomdahl, N. Grønbech-Jensen, R. Giles, and P. Tamayo. Parallel Algorithms for Short-Range Molecular Dynamics. In *Annual Review in Computational Physics*. World Scientific, 1995. (page 555)

[Beguelin *et al.* 1991] A. Beguelin, J.J. Dongarra, A. Geist, R. Manchek, and V.S. Sunderam. A Users' Guide to PVM (Parallel Virtual Machine). Technical Report ORNL/TM-11826, Oak Ridge National Laboratory, 1991. (page 430)

[Beguelin *et al.* 1994] A. Beguelin, E. Seligman, and M. Starkey. Dome: Distributed Object Migration Environment. Technical Report CMU-CS-94-153, School of Computer Science, Carnegie-Mellon University, May 1994. (page 378)

[Beltrametti *et al.* 1988] M. Beltrametti, K. Bobey, and J.R. Zorbas. The Control Mechanism for the Myrias Parallel Computer System. *Computer Architecture News*, 16(4):21–30, September 1988. (page 321)

[Bennet *et al.* 1995] R. Bennett, K. Bryant, A. Sussman, R. Das, and J.H. Saltz. Collective I/O: Models and Implementation. Technical Report CS-TR-3429 and UMIACS-TR-95-29, University of Maryland, Department of Computer Science and University of Maryland Institute for Advanced Computer Studies, February 1995. (page 168)

[Bennett *et al.* 1990] J.K. Bennett, J.B. Carter, and W. Zwaenepoel. Munin: Distributed Shared Memory Based on Type-Specific Memory Coherence. In *Proc. 1990 Conference on Principles and Practice of Parallel Programming*. ACM Press, 1990. (page 1)

[Bennett *et al.* 1994] R. Bennett, K. Bryant, A. Sussman, R. Das, and J.H. Saltz. Jovian: A Framework for Optimizing Parallel I/O. In A. Skjellum and D.S. Reese, editors, *Proc. Scalable Parallel Libraries Conference*, pages 10–20. IEEE Computer Society Press, October 1994. (page 167)

[Bershad *et al.* 1988] B.N. Bershad, E.D. Lazowska, and H.M. Levy. Presto: A System for Object-oriented Parallel Programming. *Software: Practice and Experience*, 18(8):713–732, August 1988. (pages 42, 378)

[Binau 1993] U. Binau. Distributed Diners: From UNITY Specification to CC++ Implementation. Technical Report CS-TR-93-20, California Institute of Technology, 1993. (page 94)

[Birdsall & Langdon 1985] C.K. Birdsall and A.B. Langdon. *Plasma Physics Via Computer Simulation*. McGraw-Hill, New York, 1985. (page 548)

[Birrell *et al.* 1995] A. Birrell, G. Nelson, S. Owicki, and E. Wobber. Network Objects. Technical Report SRC-RR-115, DEC Systems Research Center, 1995. (page 289)

[Blelloch 1990] G.E. Blelloch. *Vector Models for Data-Parallel Computing*. MIT Press, 1990. (pages 55, 62)

[Blelloch 1993] G.E. Blelloch. NESL: A Nested Data-Parallel Language. Technical Report CMU-CS-92-103, School of Computer Science, Carnegie-Mellon University, April 1993. (pages 304, 543)

[Blelloch *et al.* 1993] G.E. Blelloch, S. Chatterjee, J.C. Hardwick, M. Reid-Miller, J.M. Sipelstein, and M. Zagha. CVL: A C Vector Library Manual, Version 2. Technical Report CMU-CS-93-114, Carnegie Mellon University, February 1993. (pages 48, 83, 84)

[Bobrow *et al.* 1988] D.G. Bobrow, L.G. DiMichiel, R.P. Gabriel, S.E. Keen, G. Kiczales, and D.A. Moon. Common Lisp Object System Specification: X3J13 document 88-002R. *SIGPAN Notices*, 23, September 1988. (page 289)

[Boden *et al.* 1995] N.J. Boden, D. Cohen, R.E. Felderman, A.E. Kulawik, C.L. Seitz, J.N. Seizovic, and W. Su. Myrinet—A Gigabit-per-Second Local-Area Network. *IEEE Micro*, 15(1):29–36, February 1995. (pages 429, 454)

[Bodin 1993a] F. Bodin, P. Beckman, D. Gannon, S. Narayana, and S. Yang. Distributed pC++: Basic Ideas for an Object Parallel Language. *Scientific Programming*, 2(3), 1993. (pages 51, 421, 508)

[Bodin 1993b] F. Bodin, P. Beckman, D. Gannon, S. Yang, K. Shanmugam, A. Malony, and B. Mohr. Implementing a Parallel C++ Runtime System for Scalable Parallel Systems. In *Proc. Supercomputing 1993*, pages 588–597, November 1993. (pages 83, 84)

[Böhm *et al.* 1992] A.P.W. Böhm, R.R. Oldehoeft, D.C. Cann, and J.T. Feo. SISAL Reference Manual, Language Version 2.0. Technical report, Lawrence Livermore National Laboratory, 1992. (page 92)

[Booch 1986] G. Booch. Object-Oriented Development. *IEEE Transaction on Software Engineering*, February 1986. (page 275)

[Booch 1987] G. Booch. *Software Engineering with Ada*. Benjamin/Cummings, Second edition, 1987. (page 275)

[Boyle *et al.* 1987] J. Boyle, R. Butler, T. Disz, B. Glickfield, E. Lusk, R. Overbeek, J. Patterson, and R. Stevens. *Portable Programs for Parallel Processors*. Holt, Rinehart and Winston, Inc., New York, NY, 1987. (pages 222, 236)

[Bozkus et al. 1993] Z. Bozkus, A. Choudhary, G.C. Fox, T. Haupt, and S. Ranka. Fortran 90D/HPF Compiler for Distributed Memory MIMD Computers: Design, Implementation and Performance Results. In Proc. Supercomputing 1993, pages 351–360. IEEE Computer Society Press, November 1993. (page 138)

[Brown et al. 1995] D. Brown, A. Malony, and B. Mohr. Language-based Parallel Program Interaction: the Breezy Approach. In Proc. International Conference on High Performance Computing (HiPC'95), New Delhi, India, December 1995. IEEE Computer Society, Tata McGraw–Hill. (page 605)

[Budd 1991] T. Budd. An Introduction to Object-Oriented Programming. Addison-Wesley, 1991. (page 681)

[Burns 1985] A. Burns. Concurrent Programming in ADA. Cambridge University Press, 1985. (page 267)

[Buschmann et al. 1992] F. Buschmann, K. Kiefer, F. Paulish, and M. Stal. The Meta-Information-Protocol: Run-Time Type Information for C++. In A. Yonezawa and B.C. Smith, editors, Proc. International Workshop on Reflection and Meta-Level Architecture, pages 82–87, 1992. (page 289)

[Butler & Lusk 1992] R. Butler and E. Lusk. A User's Guide to the P4 Parallel Programming System. Technical Report ANL 92/17, Argonne National Laboratory, Argonne, Illinois, October 1992. (page 465)

[Calkin et al. 1994] R. Calkin, H.H.-C. Hempel, and P. Wypior. Portable Programming with the PARMACS Message-Passing Library. Parallel Computing, 20(4):615–32, 1994. (page 465)

[Campbell & Haberman 1974] R.H. Campbell and A.N. Haberman. The Specification of Process Synchronization by Path Expression. In Colloque sur les Aspects Théoriques et Pratiques des Systèmes d'Exploitation, Paris, 1974. (page 267)

[Campbell & Kolstad 1980] R.H. Campbell and R.B. Kolstad. An Overview of PATH PASCAL. SIGPLAN Notices, 15:13–14, September 1980. (page 424)

[Carey et al. 1994] M.J. Carey, D.J. DeWitt, M.J. Franklin, N.E. Hall, M.L. McAuliffe, J.F. Naughton, D.T. Schuh, M.H. Solomon, C.K. Tan, O.G. Tsatalos, S.J. White, and Y. Zwilling. Shoring Up Persistent Applications. In Proc. 1994 ACM-SIGMOD Conference on the Management of Data, May 1994. (page 518)

[Caromel 1989] D. Caromel. Service, Asynchrony and Wait-by-necessity. Journal of Object-Oriented Programming, 2(4):12–22, November 1989. (page 258)

[Caromel 1990a] D. Caromel. Concurrency: an Object Oriented Approach. In J. Bezivin, B. Meyer, and J.-M. Nerson, editors, Technology of Object-Oriented Languages and Systems (TOOLS'90), pages 183–197. Angkor, June 1990. (pages 270, 289)

[Caromel 1990b] D. Caromel. Concurrency and Reusability: From Sequential to Parallel. Journal of Object-Oriented Programming, 3(3):34–42, September 1990. (page 259)

[Caromel 1990c] D. Caromel. Programming Abstractions for Concurrent Programming. In J. Bezivin, B. Meyer, J. Potter, and M. Tokoro, editors, Technology of Object-Oriented Languages and Systems (TOOLS Pacific'90), pages 245–253. TOOLS Pacific, November 1990. (pages 268, 272)

[Caromel 1991] D. Caromel. A Solution to the Explicit/Implicit Control Dilemma. *Object-Oriented Programming Systems Messenger*, 2(2), April 1991. (page 272)

[Caromel 1993a] D. Caromel. Towards a Method of Object-Oriented Concurrent Programming. *Communications of the ACM*, 36(9):90–102, September 1993. (pages 258, 267)

[Caromel 1993b] D. Caromel and M. Rebuffel. Object Based Concurrency: Ten Language Features to Achieve Reuse. In R. Ege, M. Singh, and B. Meyer, editors, *Technology of Object-Oriented Languages and Systems (TOOLS USA '93)*, pages 205–214. Prentice Hall, August 1993. (pages 258, 289)

[Caromel 1993c] D. Caromel. Abstract Control Types for Concurrency (Position Statement for the panel : *How could object-oriented concepts and parallelism cohabit ?*). In L. O'Conner, editor, *International Conference on Computer Languages (IEEE ICCL'94)*, pages 205–214. IEEE Computer Society Press, August 1993. (page 272)

[Carriero & Gelernter 1989] N. Carriero and D. Gelernter. Linda in Context. *Communications of the ACM*, 32(4), April 1989. (page 194)

[Carroll & Pollock 1994] M.C. Carroll and L. Pollock. Composites: Trees for Data Parallel Programming. In *Proc. 1994 International Conference on Computer Languages*, pages 43–54. IEEE Computer Society Press, May 1994. (page 172)

[Carson 1985] M. Carson and J. Hermans. *Molecular Dynamics and Protein Structure*, chapter The Molecular Dynamics Workshop Laboratory, pages 165–166. University of North Carolina, Chapel Hill, NC, 1985. (page 380)

[Casavant & Kuhl 1988] T.L. Casavant and J.G. Kuhl. A Taxonomy of Scheduling in General Purpose Distributed Computing Systems. *IEEE Transactions on Software Engineering*, 14:141–54, February 1988. (page 403)

[Chandra 1995] R. Chandra. *The COOL Parallel Programming Language: Design, Implementation and Performance*. PhD thesis, Department of Computer Science, Stanford University, Stanford, CA, January 1995. Also published as CSL-TR-95-676. (page 242)

[Chandra et al. 1994] R. Chandra, A. Gupta, and J.L. Hennessy. COOL: An Object-Based Language for Parallel Programming. *IEEE Computer*, 27(8):14–26, August 1994. (page 86)

[Chandy & Kesselman 1992a] K.M. Chandy and C. Kesselman. The Derivation of Compositional Programs. In *Proc. 1992 Joint International Conference and Symposium on Logic Programming*. MIT Press, 1992. (page 94)

[Chandy & Kesselman 1992c] K.M. Chandy and C. Kesselman. Compositional C++: Compositional Parallel Programming. In *Proc. Fourth Workshop on Parallel Computing and Compilers*. Springer-Verlag, 1992. (page 91)

[Chandy & Kesselman 1993] K.M. Chandy and C. Kesselman. CC++: A Declarative Concurrent Object-oriented Programming Notation. In G. Agha, P. Wegner, and A. Yonezawa, editors, *Research Directions in Concurrent Object-Oriented Programming*, pages 281–313. MIT Press, 1993. ISBN 0-272-01139-5. (pages 379, 507)

[Chandy & Taylor 1992] K.M. Chandy and S. Taylor. *An Introduction to Parallel Programming*. Jones and Bartlett, 1992. (page 91)

[Chang et al. 1995] C. Chang, A. Sussman, and J.H. Saltz. Object-Oriented Runtime Support for Complex Distributed Data Structures. Technical Report CS-TR-3438 and UMIACS-TR-95-35, University of Maryland, Department of Computer Science and University of Maryland Institute for Advanced Computer Studies, March 1995. (page 155)

[Chase et al. 1989] J.S. Chase, F.G. Amador, E.D. Lazowska, H.M. Levy, and R.J. Littlefield. The Amber System: Parallel Programming on a Network of Multiprocessors. In Proc. 12th ACM Symposium on Operating System Principles, pages 147–158. ACM, 1989. (page 42)

[Chatterjee et al. 1991] A. Chatterjee, A. Khanna, and Y. Hung. ES-Kit: An Object-Oriented Distributed System. Concurrency: Practice and Experience, 3(6):525–539, 1991. (page 42)

[Chiba & Masuda 1992] S. Chiba and T. Masuda. Designing an Extensible Distributed Language with Meta-Level Architecture. In O. Nierstrasz, editor, Proc. 7th European Conference on Object-Oriented Programming (ECOOP'93), volume 707 of Lecture Notes in Computer Science, pages 482–501, Kaiserslautern, July 1993. Springer-Verlag. (page 289)

[Chiba 1995] S. Chiba. A Metaobject Protocol for C++. In Proc. OOPSLA'95, pages 285–99, Austin, Texas, October 1995. ACM Press. (page 289)

[Chien & Dally 1990] A.A. Chien and W.J. Dally. Concurrent Aggregates. In Second ACM SIGPLAN Symposium on Principles and Practice of Parallel Programming, pages 187–196, February 1990. (pages 86, 349, 358, 378–380)

[Chien & Dolby 1994] A.A. Chien and J. Dolby. The Illinois Concert System: A Problem-solving Environment for Irregular Applications. In Proc. DAGS'94, The Symposium on Parallel Computation and Problem Solving Environments, 1994. (page 380)

[Chien & Reddy 1995] A.A. Chien and U. Reddy. ICC++ Language Definition. Concurrent Systems Architecture Group Memo, February 1995. (page 380)

[Chien 1990] A.A. Chien. Application Studies for Concurrent Aggregates. Technical report, Artificial Intelligence Laboratory, Massachusetts Institute of Technology, Cambridge, Massachusetts, 1990. (page 380)

[Chien 1993] A.A. Chien. Concurrent Aggregates: Supporting Modularity in Massively-Parallel Programs. MIT Press, 1993. (pages 186, 193, 349, 369, 378, 380)

[Chien et al. 1994] A.A. Chien, M. Straka, J. Dolby, V. Karamcheti, J. Plevyak, and X. Zhang. A Case Study in Irregular Parallel Programming. In DIMACS Workshop on Specification of Parallel Algorithms, May 1994. Also available as Springer-Verlag LNCS. (page 380)

[Choi et al. 1994] J. Choi, J.J. Dongarra, and D.W. Walker. The Design of Scalable Software Libraries for Distributed Memory Concurrent Computers. In H.J. Siegel, editor, Proc. Eighth International Parallel Processing Symposium. IEEE Computer Society Press, April 1994. (page 507)

[Cohn 1990] E.R. Cohn. Implementing the Multiprefix Operation Efficiently. Journal of Parallel and Distributed Computing, 10:29–34, 1990. (page 69)

[Conery 1987] J.S. Conery. Parallel Execution of Logic Programs. Kluwer Academic Publishers, Boston, 1987. (page 180)

[Connor 1986] J. Connor. Transport Due to Ion Pressure Gradient Turbulence. *Nuclear Fusion*, 26:193, 1986. (page 577)

[Convex 1994] Convex Computer Corporation, 3000 Waterview Parkway, Richardson, TX 75083-3851. *Convex Exemplar: System Overview*, 1994. Order No. 080-002293-000. (page 217)

[Coplien 1992] J.O. Coplien. *Advanced C++: Programming Styles and Idioms*. Addison–Wesley, 1992. (pages 482, 489, 502, 503, 556, 560)

[Coulaud & Dillon 1995] O. Coulaud and E. Dillon. PARA++ C++ Bindings for Message Passing Libraries: User Guide. Technical Report INRIA RT-0174, National Research Institute in Software Engineering and Automatism, Lorraine, France, June 1995. (page 465)

[Cray 1993] Cray Research, Inc. *Cray Standard C Programmer's Reference Manual*, SR-2074 4.0 edition, 1993. (page 47)

[CRI 1993] Cray Research, Inc. *Cray T3D System Architecture Overview*, March 1993. (page 380)

[Culler *et al.* 1993] D.E. Culler, A. Dusseau, S.C. Goldstein, A. Krishnamurthy, S. Lumetta, T. von Eicken, and K. Yelick. Parallel Programming in Split-C. In *Proc. Supercomputing 1993*, 1993. (pages 142, 434)

[Dahl 1990] E.D. Dahl. Mapping and Compiled Communication on the Connection Machine System. Technical report, Thinking Machines Corporation, 1990. (page 69)

[Das *et al.* 1992] R. Das, R. Ponnusamy, J.H. Saltz, and D.J. Mavriplis. Distributed Memory Compiler Methods for Irregular Problems – Data Copy Reuse and Runtime Partitioning. In J.H. Saltz and P. Mehrotra, editors, *Languages, Compilers and Runtime Environments for Distributed Memory Machines*, pages 185–220. Elsevier, 1992. (page 139)

[Das *et al.* 1994a] R. Das, D.J. Mavriplis, J.H. Saltz, S. Gupta, and R. Ponnusamy. The Design and Implementation of a Parallel Unstructured Euler Solver Using Software Primitives. *AIAA Journal*, 32(3):489–496, March 1994. (page 131)

[Das *et al.* 1994b] R. Das, M. Uysal, J.H. Saltz, and Y.-S. Hwang. Communication Optimizations for Irregular Scientific Computations on Distributed Memory Architectures. *Journal of Parallel and Distributed Computing*, 22(3):462–479, September 1994. (pages 132, 138, 152, 153)

[Dave *et al.* 1992] A. Dave, M. Sefika, and R.H. Campbell. Proxies, Application Interfaces and Distributed Systems. In *Proc. 2nd International Workshop on Object-Orientation in Operating Systems (OOOS)*. IEEE Computer Society Press, September 1992. (page 289)

[Decouchant *et al.* 1989] D. Decouchant, S. Krakowiak, M. Meysembourg, M. Riveill, and X. Rousset de Pina. A Synchronization Mechanism for Typed Objects. *SIGPLAN Notices*, 24(4):105–107, April 1989. (page 266)

[Decouchant *et al.* 1991] D. Decouchant, P. Le Dot, M. Riveill, C. Roisin, and X. Rousset de Pina. A Synchronization Mechanism for an Object-Oriented Distributed System. In *IEEE Eleventh International Conference on Distributed Computing Systems*, 1991. (page 267)

[Decyk 1995] V. Decyk. Skeleton PIC codes for parallel computers. *Computer Physics Communications*, 87:87–94, 1995. (page 548)

[DoD 1982] United States Department of Defense, Ada Joint Program Office. *Reference Manual for the Ada Programming Language*, July 1982. (page 399)

[Doeppner & Gebele 1987] T.W. Doeppner Jr. and A.J. Gebele. C++ on a Parallel Machine. Technical report, Computer Science, Brown University, July 1987. CS-87-26. (page 42)

[Doss et al. 1993] N.E. Doss, W.D. Gropp, E. Lusk, and A. Skjellum. A Model Implementation of MPI. Technical Report MCS-P393-1193, Mathematics and Computer Science Division, Argonne National Laboratory, Argonne, IL, 1993. (page 499)

[Doulas & Ramkumar 1994] N. Doulas and B. Ramkumar. Efficient Task Migration for Message-Driven Parallel Execution on Nonshared Memory Architectures. In *Proc. International Conference on Parallel Processing*, August 1994. (page 186)

[Duff et al. 1989] I. Duff, R. Grimes, and J. Lewis. Sparse Matrix Problems. *ACM Transactions on Mathematical Software*, 15(1):1–14, March 1989. (page 252)

[Eager et al. 1986] D.L. Eager, E.D. Lazowska, and J. Zahorjan. Adaptive Load Sharing in Homogeneous Distributed Systems. *IEEE Transactions on Software Engineering*, 12:662–675, May 1986. (page 404)

[Edelson 1992] D. Edelson. Smart Pointers: They're Smart, but They're Not Pointers. In *Proc. Usenix C++ Conference*, August 1992. (page 289)

[Ellis & Stroustrup 1990] M. Ellis and B. Stroustrup. *The Annotated C++ Reference Manual*. Addison-Wesley, 1990. (page 681)

[Evripidou & Gaudiot 1990] P. Evripidou and J.L. Gaudiot. A Decoupled Data-Driven Architecture with Vectors and Macro Actors. In *Proc. Joint International Conference on Vector and Parallel Processing*. Springer-Verlag, September 1990. (page 180)

[Falgout et al. 1992] R.D. Falgout, A. Skjellum, S.G. Smith, and C.H. Still. The Multicomputer Toolbox Approach to Concurrent BLAS and BLACS. In J.H. Saltz, editor, *Proc. Scalable High Performance Computing Conf. (SHPCC)*, pages 121–28, Los Alamitos, CA, 1992. IEEE Press. (page 472)

[Feeley & Levy 1992] M.J. Feeley and H.M. Levy. Distributed Shared Memory with Versioned Objects. Technical report, Department of Computer Science, University of Washington, 1992. 92-03-01. (page 42)

[Fenton et al. 1991] W. Fenton, B. Ramkumar, V. Saletore, A.B. Sinha, and L.V. Kalé. Supporting Machine-Independent Parallel Programming on Diverse Architectures. In *Proc. 1991 International Conference on Parallel Processing*, 1991. (pages 177, 203)

[Feo 1992] J.T. Feo, editor. *A Comparative Study of Parallel Programming Languages: The Salishan Problems*. North-Holland, 1992. (page 707)

[Ferrari 1995] A.J. Ferrari, A. Filipi-Martin, and S. Viswanathan. The NAS Parallel Benchmark Kernels in MPL. Technical Report CS-95-39, University of Virginia, 1995. (page 406)

[Ferrell & Bertschinger 1993] R. Ferrell and E. Bertschinger. Particle-Mesh Methods on the Connection Machine. *International Journal of Modern Physics C*, 1993. (page 538)

[Fink & Baden 1995] S.J. Fink and S.B. Baden. Run-time Data Distribution for Block-Structured Applications on Distributed Memory Computers. In D.H. Bailey, P.E. Bjorstad, J.R. Gilbert, M.V. Mascagni, R.S. Shreiber, H.D. Simon, V.J. Torczon, and L.T. Watson, editors, *Proc. Seventh SIAM Conference on Parallel Processing for Scientific Computing*, pages 762–767. Society for Industrial and Applied Mathematics, 1995. (page 87)

[Flynn 1966] M.J. Flynn. Very High-Speed Computing Systems. *Proc. IEEE*, 54(12):1901–1909, 1966. (pages 297, 689)

[Forslund *et al.* 1990] D.W. Forslund, C. Wingate, P. Ford, J. Junkins, J. Jackson, and S. Pope. Experiences in Writing a Distributed Particle Simulation Code in C++. In *Proc. 1990 USENIX C++ Conference*, 1990. (page 548)

[Foster 1994] I. Foster. *Designing and Building Parallel Programs*. Addison–Wesley, 1994. ISBN 0-201-57594-9. (page 689)

[Foster *et al.* 1994a] I. Foster, B. Avalani, A. Choudhary, and M. Xu. A Compilation System that Integrates High Performance Fortran and Fortran M. In *Proc. 1994 Scalable High-Performance Computing Conference*, pages 293–300. IEEE Press, 1994. (page 95)

[Foster *et al.* 1994b] I. Foster, C. Kesselman, R. Olson, and S. Tuecke. Nexus: An interoperability toolkit for parallel and distributed computer systems. Technical Report ANL/MCS-TM-189, Argonne National Laboratory, 1994. (page 124)

[Fox 1988] G.C. Fox. What Have We Learnt from Using Real Parallel Machines to Solve Real Problems. In G.C. Fox, editor, *Proc. Third Conference on Hypercube Concurrent Computers and Applications*, volume 2, pages 897–955, January 1988. (page 299)

[Fox 1993] G.C. Fox. Fortran D Language Specification. Technical Report SCCS 42c, Northeast Parallel Architectures Center, Syracuse University, 1993. (page 421)

[Fox *et al.* 1990] G.C. Fox, S. Hiranandani, K. Kennedy, C.H. Koelbel, U. Kremer, C.-W. Tseng, and M.-Y. Wu. Fortran D Language Specification. Technical Report CRPC-TR900749, Centre for Research on Parallel Computation, Rice University, December 1990. (page 315)

[Fox *et al.* 1994] G.C. Fox, R.D. Williams, and P.C. Messina. *Parallel Computing Works*. Morgan Kaufman, 1994. (page 131)

[Frolund 1992] S. Frølund. Inheritance of Synchronization Constraints in Concurrent Object-Oriented Programming. In *Proc. ECOOP'92*, June 1992. (page 267)

[Furmento & Baude 1995] N. Furmento and F. Baude. Design and Implementation of Communications for the C++// System. Technical Report RR 95-50 I3S, CNRS I3S - Univ. de Nice - INRIA Sophia Antipolis, 1995. (page 288)

[Gamma *et al.* 1995] E. Gamma, R. Helm, R. Johnson, and J. Vlissides. *Design Patterns: Elements of Reusable Object-Oriented Software*. Addison–Wesley, 1995. (pages 482, 557, 565)

[Gannon & Lee 1991] D. Gannon and J.-K. Lee. Object Oriented Parallelism: pC++ Ideas and Experiments. In *Japan Society for Parallel Processing*, pages 13–23, 1991. (page 508)

[Gannon & Lee 1992] D. Gannon and J.-K. Lee. On Using Object Oriented Parallel Programming to Build Distributed Algebraic Abstractions. In Bourge and Cosnard, editors, *Proc. CONPAR 92-VAPP V*, pages 769–774. Springer Verlag, 1992. (page 508)

[Gannon 1993] D. Gannon. Libraries and Tools for Object Parallel Programming. In *Advances in Parallel Computing: CNRS-NSF Workshop on Environments and Tools for Parallel Scientific Computing, Saint Hilaire du Touvet*, volume 6, pages 231–246. Elsevier Science Publisher, 1993. (page 508)

[Gannon et al. 1989] D. Gannon, V. Guarna, and J.-K. Lee. Static Analysis and Runtime Support for Parallel Execution of C. In *Languages and Compilers for Parallel Computing*, pages 254–274. MIT Press, 1993. (page 508)

[Gannon et al. 1994a] F. Bodin, P. Beckman, D. Gannon, J. Gotwals, S. Narayana, S. Srinivas, and B. Winnicka. Sage++: An Object Oriented Toolkit and Class Library for Building Fortran and C++ Restructuring Tools. In M. Chapman and A. Vermeulen, editors, *Proc. Second Annual Object-Oriented Numerics Conference*, Corvallis, OR, 1994. Rogue Wave Software. (pages 508, 593)

[Gannon et al. 1994b] D. Gannon, S. Yang, P. Bode, and V. Menkov. Object Oriented Methods for Parallel Execution of Astrophysics Simulations. In *Mardigras Teraflops Grand Challenge Conference*. Lousiana State University, 1994. (page 533)

[Gannon et al. 1994c] D. Gannon, N. Sundaresan, and P. Beckman. pC++ Meets Multithreaded Computation. In J.J. Dongarra and B. Tourancheau, editors, *Second Workshop on Environments and Tools for Parallel Scientific Computing*, pages 76–85. SIAM Press, 1994. (page 508)

[Gautron 1991] P. Gautron. Porting and Extending the C++ Task System with the Support of Lightweight Processes. In *USENIX C++ Conference*. USENIX, 1991. (page 42)

[Gehani & Roome 1988] N.H. Gehani and W.D. Roome. Concurrent C++: Concurrent Programming with Classes. *Software—Practice and Experience*, 18(12):1157–1177, 1988. (pages 42, 629)

[Gehani & Roome 1989] N.H. Gehani and W.D. Roome. *The Concurrent C Programming Language*. Silicon Press, 1989. (page 267)

[Gehani 1984a] N.H. Gehani. Concurrent Programming in the ADA Language: the Polling Bias. *Software–Practice and Experience*, 14(5), 1984. (page 270)

[Gehani 1984b] N.H. Gehani. *ADA Concurrent Programming*. Prentice-Hall, 1984. (page 267)

[Geist et al. 1993] A. Geist, A. Beguelin, J.J. Dongarra, J. Weicheng, R. Manchek, and V.S. Sunderam. PVM 3 User's' Guide and Reference Manual. ORNL/TM 12187, Oak Ridge National Laboratories, Oak Ridge, TN, 1993. (page 465)

[Geist et al. 1994] A. Geist, A. Beguelin, J.J. Dongarra, W. Jiang, R. Manchek, and V.S. Sunderam. *PVM (Parallel Virtual Machine): A Users' Guide and Tutorial for Network Parallel Computing*. MIT Press, 1994. (pages 387, 641)

[Gerndt 1990] M. Gerndt. Updating Distributed Variables in Local Computations. *Concurrency: Practice and Experience*, 2(3):171–193, September 1990. (page 139)

[Goldberg & Robson 1983] A. Goldberg and D. Robson. *Smalltalk-80: The Language and Its Implementation.* Addison-Wesley, Reading, MA, 1983. (page 44)

[Gotwals *et al.* 1995] J. Gotwals, S. Srinivas, and D. Gannon. pC++/streams: a Library for I/O on Complex Distributed Data Structures. In *Symposium on the Principles and Practice of Parallel Programming.* ACM, 1995. (page 516)

[Grama *et al.* 1993] A. Grama, A. Gupta, and V. Kumar. Isoefficiency: Measuring the Scalability of Parallel Algorithms and Architectures. *IEEE Parallel & Distributed Technology,* 1(3), August 1993. (page 699)

[Gray & Reuter 1993] J. Gray and A. Reuter. *Transaction Processing: Concepts and Techniques.* Morgan Kaufmann, San Mateo, California, 1993. (page 353)

[Grimshaw 1993] A.S. Grimshaw. Easy-to-Use Object-Oriented Parallel Processing with Mentat. *IEEE Computer,* 26(5):39–51, May 1993. (pages 85, 180, 349)

[Grimshaw 1993] A.S. Grimshaw. Easy to Use Object-Oriented Parallel Programming with Mentat. *IEEE Computer,* pages 39–51, May 1993. (pages 383, 387, 391)

[Grimshaw 1993] A.S. Grimshaw. The Mentat Computation Model – Data-Driven Support for Object-Oriented Parallel Processing. Technical Report CS-94-45, University of Virginia, 1994. (page 401)

[Grimshaw 1994] A.S. Grimshaw, W.A. Wulf, J.C. French, A.C. Weaver, and P.F. Reynolds Jr. Legion: The Next Logical Step Toward a Nationwide Virtual Computer. Technical Report CS-94-21, University of Virginia, 1994. (page 426)

[Grimshaw 1995] A.S. Grimshaw. Mentat – Applying the Object-Oriented Paradigm to Parallel Processing. In J.J. Dongarra, L Grandinetti, G. Joubert, and J. Kowalik, editors, *High Performance Computing: Issues, Methods and Applications.* Elsevier Science, Amsterdam, 1995. (pages 405, 425)

[Grimshaw *et al.* 1993a] A.S. Grimshaw, W.T. Strayer, and P. Narayan. Dynamic Object-Oriented Parallel Processing. *IEEE Parallel & Distributed Technology,* pages 34–47, May 1993. (page 387)

[Grimshaw *et al.* 1993b] A.S. Grimshaw, E.A. West, and W.R. Pearson. No Pain and Gain! - Experiences with Mentat on Biological Application. *Concurrency—Practice & Experience,* 4:309–328, July 1993. (pages 387, 406, 409)

[Grimshaw *et al.* unpub.] A.S. Grimshaw, J.B. Weissman, and W.T. Strayer. Portable Run-Time Support for Dynamic Object-Oriented Parallel Processing. *ACM Transactions on Computer Systems,* to appear. (pages 384, 387)

[Gropp & Smith 1993] W.D. Gropp and B. Smith. Chameleon Parallel Programming Tools User's Manual. Technical Report ANL-93/23, Argonne National Laboratory, March 1993. (page 465)

[Gropp *et al.* 1994] W.D. Gropp, E. Lusk, and A. Skjellum. *Using MPI: Portable Parallel Programming with the Message-Passing Interface.* MIT Press, 1994. (page 466)

[Grunwald 1991] D. Grunwald. A User's Guide to AWESIME. Technical report, University of Colorado at Boulder, 1991. CU-CS-552-91. (page 42)

[Gupta 1992] R. Gupta. SPMD Execution of Programs with Pointer-Based Data Structures on Distributed-Memory Machines. *Journal of Parallel and Distributed Computing*, 16:92–107, 1992. (page 172)

[Gupta *et al.* 1995] A. Gupta, V. Kumar, and A. Sameh. Performance and Scalability of Preconditioned Conjugate Gradient Methods on Parallel Computers. *IEEE Transactions on Parallel and Distributed Systems (to appear)*, 1995. (page 565)

[Gursoy 1994] A. Gursoy. *Simplified Expression of Message-Driven Programs and Quantification of Their Impact on Performance*. PhD thesis, Department of Computer Science, University of Illinois, Urbana-Champaign, June 1994. (pages 180, 207)

[Haines *et al.* 1994] M. Haines, D. Cronk, and P. Mehrotra. On the Design of Chant: A Talking Threads Package. In *Proc. Supercomputing 1994*, Washington D.C., November 1994. (page 182)

[Halbert & O'Brien 1987] D.C. Halbert and P.D. O'Brien. Using Types and Inheritance in Object-Oriented Languages. In *European Conference on Object-Oriented Programming*, June 1987. (page 275)

[Halstead 1985] R. Halstead. Multilisp: A Language for Concurrent Symbolic Computation. *ACM Transactions on Programming Languages and Systems*, October 1985. (pages 18, 228, 263)

[Halton 1960] J. Halton. On the Efficienty of Certain Quasi-Random Sequences of Points in Evaluating Multi-Dimensional Integrals. *Numerische Mathematik*, 2:84–90, 1960. (page 577)

[Hatcher & Quinn 1991] P.J. Hatcher and M.J. Quinn. *Data-Parallel Programming on MIMD Computers*. MIT Press, 1991. (pages 85, 300)

[Hatcher *et al.* 1991] P.J. Hatcher, M.J. Quinn, A.J. Lapadula, B.K. Seevers, R.J. Anderson, and R.R. Jones. Data-Parallel Programming on MIMD Computers. *IEEE Transactions on Parallel and Distributed Systems*, 2(3):377–83, July 1991. (page 421)

[Havlak & Kennedy 1991] P. Havlak and K. Kennedy. An Implementation of Interprocedural Bounded Regular Section Analysis. *IEEE Transactions on Parallel and Distributed Systems*, 2(3):350–360, July 1991. (page 138)

[Hernquist & Ostriker 1992] L. Hernquist and J.P. Ostriker. A Self-Consistent Field Method for Galactic Dynamics. *The Astrophysical Journal*, 386:375–397, 1992. (page 534)

[Hernquist *et al.* 1995] L. Hernquist, S. Sigurdsson, and G.L. Bryan. A Parallel Self-Consistent Field Code. *Astrophysical Journal*, 446:717, June 1995. (page 534)

[Herrarte & Lusk 1991] V. Herrarte and E. Lusk. Studying Parallel Program Behavior with Upshot. Technical Report ANL-91/15, Mathematics and Computer Science Division, Argonne National Laboratory, August 1991. (pages 595, 604)

[Hewitt 1977] C. Hewitt. Viewing Control Structures as Patterns of Passing Messages. *Journal of Artificial Intelligence*, 8(3):323–364, 1977. (page 262)

[Hill *et al.* 1994] M.D. Hill, J.R. Larus, and D.A. Wood. The Wisconsin Wind Tunnel Project: An Annotated Bibliography. *Computer Architecture News*, 22(5):19–26, December 1994. Frequently updated at http://www.cs.wisc.edu/~wwt). (page 339)

[Hill et al. 1995] M.D. Hill, J.R. Larus, and D.A. Wood. Tempest: A Substrate for Portable Parallel Programs. In *COMPCON'95*, pages 327–332, San Francisco, CA, March 1995. IEEE Computer Society. (page 298)

[Hillis & Steele 1986] W.D. Hillis and G.L. Steele Jr. Data Parallel Algorithms. *Communications of the ACM*, 29(12):1170–1183, December 1986. (pages 299, 549)

[Hillis 1985] W.D. Hillis. *The Connection Machine*. MIT Press, 1985. (page 300)

[Hoare 1974] C.A.R. Hoare. Monitors: an Operating System Structuring Concept. *Communications of the ACM*, 17(10):549–557, October 1974. (pages 216, 219, 389)

[Hoare 1978] C.A.R. Hoare. Communicating Sequential Processes. *Communications of the ACM*, 21(8), August 1978. (page 267)

[Hoare 1985] C.A.R. Hoare. *Communicating Sequential Processes*. Prentice-Hall, 1985. (page 267)

[Hori et al. 1993] A. Hori, Y. Ishikawa, H. Konaka, M. Maeda, and T. Tomokiyo. Overview of Massively Parallel Operating System Kernel SCore. Technical Report TR–93003, Real World Computing Partnership, 1993. (page 464)

[Houck & Agha 1992] C. Houck and G. Agha. HAL: A High Level Actor Language and its Distributed Implementation. In *Proc. International Conference on Parallel Processing*, August 1992. (page 186)

[Howard et al. 1989] W. Horwat, A.A. Chien, and W.J. Dally. Experience with CST: Programming and Implementation. In *Proc. SIGPLAN Conference on Programming Language Design and Implementation*, pages 101–109. ACM SIGPLAN, ACM Press, 1989. (page 360)

[Hsieh & Sotelino 1994] S.-H. Hsieh and E.D. Sotelino. PPI++: An Object-Oriented Parallel Portability Interface in C++. Technical report, School of Civil Engineering, Purdue University, West Lafayette, IN, 1994. (page 465)

[Hwang et al. 1995] Y.-S. Hwang, R. Das, J.H. Saltz, M. Hodoscek, and B.R. Brooks. Parallelizing Molecular Dynamics Programs for Distributed Memory Machines. *IEEE Computational Science & Engineering*, 2(2):18–29, Summer 1995. (page 131)

[IBM 1993] IBM. *Optimization and Tuning Guide for Fortran, C and C++*, first edition, 1993. (pages 47, 83)

[ICC 1995] Concurrent Systems Architecture Group. The ICC++ Reference Manual. Technical report, University of Illinois, Department of Computer Science, 1304 W. Springfield Avenue, Urbana, Illinois, 1995. Also available from http://www-csag.cs.uiuc.edu/. (pages 355, 357, 379, 380)

[Ichbiah et al. 1979] J.D. Ichbiah. ADA Reference Manual and Rationale for the Design of the ADA Programming Language. *SIGPLAN Notices*, 14(6), 1979. (page 267)

[Inmos 1988] Inmos Ltd. *Occam 2 Reference Manual*. Prentice Hall, 1988. (page 267)

[Ishikawa 1994] Y. Ishikawa. The MPC++ Programming Language V1.0 Specification with Commentary Document Version 0.1. Technical Report TR–94014, Real World Computing Partnership, June 1994. (page 429)

[Ishikawa 1995] Y. Ishikawa. Meta-Level Architecture for Extendable C++. Technical Report TR–94024, Real World Computing Partnership, January 1995. (pages 429, 431, 451)

[Ishikawa et al. 1994] Y. Ishikawa, A. Hori, H. Konaka, M. Munenori, and T. Takashi. Implementation of Parallel Programming Language MPC++. In JSPP'94, pages 105–12, 1994. In Japanese; an English version may be found at http://www.rwcp.or.jp/people/mpslab/mpc++/mpc++.html. (pages 429, 440)

[Ishikawa et al. 1995] Y. Ishikawa, A. Hori, M. Sato, M. Matsuda, J. Nolte, H. Tezuka, H. Konaka, M. Maeda, and T. Tomokiyo. RWC Massively Parallel Software Environment and An Overview of MPC++. In Proc. Workshop on Parallel Symbolic Languages and Systems, 1995. (pages 379, 544)

[Jones 1979] A.K. Jones. The Object Model: A Conceptual Tool for Structuring Software. In R. Bayer, R.M. Graham, and G. Seegmuller, editors, Operating Systems: An Advanced Course, pages 199–220. Springer-Verlag, 1979. (page 384)

[Kafura & Lee 1989] D.G. Kafura and K.H. Lee. Inheritance in Actor Based Concurrent Object-Oriented Languages. The Computer Journal, 32(4), 1989. (page 267)

[Kafura & Lee 1990] D.G. Kafura and K.H. Lee. ACT++: Building a Concurrent C++ with Actors. Journal of Object-Oriented Programming, 3(1), May 1990. (pages 42, 267)

[Kalé & Krishnan 1993] L.V. Kalé and S. Krishnan. CHARM++: A Portable Concurrent Object Oriented System Based on C++. In A. Paepcke, editor, Proc. OOPSLA'93, pages 91–108. ACM Press, 1993. (pages 86, 178, 349, 379)

[Kalé & Shu 1988] L.V. Kalé and W. Shu. The Chare-Kernel Language for Parallel Programming: A Perspective. Technical Report UIUCDCS-R-88-1451, Department of Computer Science, University of Illinois, Urbana-Champaign, August 1988. (page 175)

[Kalé & Sinha 1993] L.V. Kalé and A.B. Sinha. Projections: A Scalable Performance Tool. In Parallel Systems Fair, International Parallel Processing Symposium, April 1993. (pages 201, 210)

[Kalé 1987] L.V. Kalé. Parallel Execution of Logic Programs: The REDUCE-OR Process Model. In Proc. International Conference on Logic Programming, pages 616–632, Melbourne, May 1987. (page 180)

[Kalé 1990] L.V. Kalé. The Chare Kernel Parallel Programming Language and System. In D.A. Padua, editor, Proc. 19th International Conference on Parallel Processing, pages II–17–II–25, August 1990. (page 177)

[Kalé 1992] L.V. Kalé. A Tutorial Introduction to CHARM, December 1992. (page 177)

[Kalé et al. 1995a] L.V. Kalé, B. Ramkumar, A.B. Sinha, and A. Gursoy. The Charm Parallel Programming Language and System: Part I – Description of Language Features. Technical Report 95-2, Parallel Programming Laboratory, Department of Computer Science, University of Illinois, Urbana-Champaign, 1995. (pages 178, 190, 194)

[Kalé et al. 1995b] L.V. Kalé, M. Bhandarkar, N. Jagathesan, and S. Krishnan. Converse: An Interoperable Framework for Parallel Programming. Technical Report 95–12, Parallel Programming Laboratory, Department of Computer Science, University of Illinois, Urbana-Champaign, March 1995. (pages 178, 183, 203)

[Karamcheti & Chien 1993] V. Karamcheti and A.A. Chien. Concert—Efficient Runtime Support for Concurrent Object-Oriented Programming Languages on Stock Hardware. In *Proc. Supercomputing 1993*, 1993. (page 380)

[Karpovich et al. 1993] J.F. Karpovich, M. Judd, W.T. Strayer, and A.S. Grimshaw. A Parallel Object-Oriented Framework for Stencil Algorithms. In *Proc. Second Symposium on High-Performance Distributed Computing*, pages 233–249, Spokane, WA, July 1993. IEEE Press. (pages 411, 412)

[Keller et al. 1984] R.M. Keller, F.C.H. Lin, and J. Tanaka. Rediflow Multiprocessing. *Digest of Papers COMPCON, Spring'84*, pages 410–417, February 1984. (page 180)

[Kennedy (ed.) 1992] K. Kennedy, editor. *Proc. First CRPC Workshop on Standards for Message Passing in a Distributed Memory Environment*. CRPC, April 1992. (page 466)

[Kiczales et al. 1991] G. Kiczales, J. des Rivières, and D.G. Bobrow. *The Art of the Metaobject Protocol*. MIT Press, 1991. (pages 289, 294)

[Koelbel et al. 1994] C.H. Koelbel, D.B. Loveman, R.S. Schreiber, G.L. Steele Jr., and M.E. Zosel. *The High Performance Fortran Handbook*. MIT Press, 1994. (pages 43, 138, 177, 299, 301, 302, 430, 507, 589)

[Kohn & Baden 1994] S.R. Kohn and S.B. Baden. A Robust Parallel Programming Model for Dynamic Non-Uniform Scientific Computations. In *Proc. Scalable High Performance Computing Conference (SHPCC-94)*, pages 509–517. IEEE Computer Society Press, May 1994. (page 171)

[Konaka 1993] H. Konaka. An Overview of OCore: A Massively Parallel Objectbased Language. Technical Report TR-P-93-002, Tsukuba Research Center, Real World Computing Partnership, Tsukuba Mitsui Building 16F, 1-6-1 Takezono, Tsukuba-shi, Ibaraki 305, Japan, 1993. (page 379)

[Kornkven & Kalé 1994] E. Kornkven and L.V. Kalé. Efficient Implementation of High Performance Fortran via Adaptive Scheduling – An Overview. In V.K. Prasanna, V.P. Bhatkar, L.M. Patnaik, and S.K. Tripathi, editors, *Proc. 1st International Workshop on Parallel Processing*. Tata McGraw-Hill, New Delhi, India, December 1994. (pages 205, 212)

[Kranz et al. 1993] D. Kranz, K.L. Johnson, A. Agarwal, J. Kubiatowicz, and B.-H. Lim. Integrating Message-Passing and Shared-Memory: Early Experience. In *Fourth ACM SIGPLAN Symposium on Principles & Practice of Parallel Programming (PPOPP)*, pages 54–63, May 1993. (page 320)

[Kumar et al. 1993] V. Kumar, A. Grama, A. Gupta, and G. Karypis. *Introduction to Parallel Computing: Design and Analysis of Algorithms*. Benjamin-Cummings, 1994. (pages 565, 689, 699)

[Kundu & Cuny 1995] J. Kundu and J.E. Cuny. The Integration of Event- and State-Based Debugging in Ariadne. In C. Polychronopoulos, editor, *Proc. 1995 International Conference on Parallel Processing (ICPP)*, pages 130–134. CRC Press, August 1995. (page 627)

[Larus 1993] J.R. Larus. C**: a Large-Grain, Object-Oriented, Data-Parallel Programming Language. In U. Banerjee, D. Gelernter, A. Nicolau, and D. Padua, editors, *Languages And Compilers for Parallel Computing (5th International Workshop)*, pages 326–341. Springer-Verlag, August 1993. (pages 85, 297, 303, 304)

[Larus 1994] J.R. Larus. Compiling for Shared-Memory and Message-Passing Computers. *ACM Letters on Programming Languages and Systems*, 2(1-4):165–180, March-December 1994. (page 319)

[Larus et al. 1994] J.R. Larus, B. Richards, and G. Viswanathan. LCM: Memory System Support for Parallel Language Implementation. In *Proc. Sixth International Conference on Architectural Support for Programming Languages and Operating Systems (ASPLOS VI)*, pages 208–218, October 1994. (pages 297, 298, 319)

[Lawson 1979] C.L. Lawson, R.J. Hanson, D.R. Kincaid, and F.T. Krogh. Basic Linear Algebra Subprograms for FORTRAN Usage. *ACM Transactions on Mathematical Software*, 5:308–323, 1979. (page 45)

[Lee & Gannon 1991] J.-K. Lee and D. Gannon. Object Oriented Parallel Programming: Experiments and Results. In *Proc. Supercomputing 1991*. IEEE Computer Society and ACM SIGARCH, 1991. (pages 193, 302, 358)

[Lee 1987] W.W. Lee. Gyrokinetic Particle Simulation Model. *Journal of Computational Physics*, 72:243, 1987. (page 548)

[Lemke & Quinlan 1992] M. Lemke and D. Quinlan. P++, a C++ Virtual Shared Grids Based Programming Environment for Architecture-Independent Development of Structured Grid Applications. In *Proc. CONPAR 92–VAPP V*. Springer-Verlag, September 1992. (pages 127, 553)

[Lemke & Quinlan 1993] M. Lemke and D. Quinlan. P++, a Parallel C++ Array Class Library for Architecture-Independent Development of Numerical Software. In *Proc. First Annual Object-Oriented Numerics Conference*, pages 268–269, 1993. (pages 86, 507)

[Lenoski et al. 1992a] D. Lenoski, J. Laudon, K. Gharachorloo, W.-D. Weber, A. Gupta, J.L. Hennessy, M. Horowitz, and M. Lam. The Stanford Dash Multiprocessor. *IEEE Computer*, 25(3):63–79, March 1992. (page 217)

[Lenoski et al. 1992b] D. Lenoski, J. Laudon, T. Joe, D. Nakahira, L. Stevens, A. Gupta, and J.L. Hennessy. The DASH Prototype: Implementation and Performance. In *Proc. 19th International Symposium on Computer Architecture*, pages 92–103, Gold Coast, Australia, May 1992. (page 243)

[Li & Hudak 1989] K. Li and P. Hudak. Memory Coherence in Shared Virtual Memory Systems. *ACM Transactions on Computer Systems*, 7(4), November 1989. (pages 1, 134)

[Lieberman 1987] H. Lieberman. Concurrent Object-Oriented Programming in Act 1. In A. Yonezawa and M. Tokoro, editors, *Object-Oriented Concurrent Programming*. The MIT Press, 1987. (page 263)

[Lin & Snyder 1994] C. Lin and L. Snyder. ZPL: An Array Sublanguage. In *Languages and Compilers for Parallel Computing (Proc. Sixth International Workshop)*, pages 96–114. Springer-Verlag, 1994. (page 301)

[Liskov 1988a] B. Liskov. Data Abstraction and Hierarchy. *ACM SIGPLAN Notices*, 23(5):17–34, May 1988. (page 349)

[Liskov 1988b] B. Liskov. Distributed Programming in Argus. *Communications of the ACM*, 31(3):300–313, March 1988. (page 353)

[Lohr 1992] K.-P. Lohr. Concurrency Annotations Improve Reusability. In *TOOLS USA '92*, August 1992. (page 267)

[Loveman 1993] D.B. Loveman. High Performance Fortran. *IEEE Parallel and Distributed Technology*, 1(1):25–42, February 1993. (page 421)

[Lucassen & Gifford 1988] J.M. Lucassen and D.K. Gifford. Polymorphic Effect Systems. In *Conference Record of the Fifteenth Annual ACM Symposium on Principles of Programming Languages*, pages 47–57, January 1988. (page 314)

[MacCallum & Grimshaw 1994] L. MacCallum and A.S. Grimshaw. A Parallel Object-Oriented Linear Algebra Library. In M. Chapman and A. Vermeulen, editors, *Proc. Second Annual Object-Oriented Numerics Conference*, pages 233–249, Corvallis, OR, 1994. Rogue Wave Software. (page 406)

[Madany et al. 1992] P. Madany, N. Islam, P. Kougiouris, and R.H. Campbell. Practical Examples of Reification and Reflection in C++. In A. Yonezawa and B.C. Smith, editors, *Proc. International Workshop on Reflection and Meta-Level Architecture*, pages 76–81, 1992. (page 289)

[Makpangou et al. 1994] M. Makpangou, Y. Gourhant, J.-P. Le Narzul, and M. Shapiro. Fragmented Objects for Distributed Abstractions. In T.L. Casavant and M. Singhal, editors, *Readings in Distributed Computing Systems*. IEEE Computer Society Press, 1994. (page 289)

[Mallet & Mussi 1993] L. Mallet and P. Mussi. Object Oriented Parallel Discrete Event Simulation: The PROSIT Approach. In A. Pave, editor, *Modelling and Simulation FSM 93*. Society for Computer Simulation, June 1993. (page 258)

[Malony et al. 1994b] A. Malony, B. Mohr, P. Beckman, D. Gannon, S. Yang, and F. Bodin. Performance Analysis of pC++: A Portable Data-Parallel Programming System for Scalable Parallel Computers. In H.J. Siegel, editor, *Proc. Eighth International Parallel Processing Symposium*. IEEE Computer Society Press, April 1994. (pages 601, 603)

[Martin 1985] A.J. Martin. The Probe: An Addition to Communication Primitives. *Information Processing Letters*, 20:125–130, April 1985. (page 93)

[Matsuoka & Yonezawa 1993] S. Matsuoka and A. Yonezawa. Analysis of Inheritance Anomaly in Object-Oriented Concurrent Languages. In G. Agha, P. Wegner, and A. Yonezawa, editors, *Research Directions in Object-Based Concurrency*. MIT Press, 1993. (pages 41, 375)

[Matsuoka et al. 1990] S. Matsuoka, K. Wakita, and A. Yonezawa. Synchronization Constraints With Inheritance: What is Not Possible—So What Is? Technical Report Technical Report 10, The University of Tokyo, Department of Information Science, 1990. (page 267)

[McAffer 1995] J. McAffer. Meta-level Programming with CodA. In *Proc. Ninth European Conference on Object-Oriented Programming (ECOOP'95)*, Aarhus, Denmark, August 1995. (page 289)

[McDonald 1991] J.D. McDonald. Particle Simulation in a Multiprocessor Environment. In *Proc. 26th Thermophysics Conference*, June 1991. AIAA Paper No. 91-1366. (page 223)

[McHale et al. 1990] C. McHale, B. Walsh, S. Baker, A. Donnelly, and N. Harria. Extending Synchronisation Counters. Technical Report TCD-Pub-0011, University of Dublin, Trinity College, July 1990. ESPRIT Project Comandos, number 834 and 2071. (page 267)

[Mehrotra & Haines 1994] P. Mehrotra and M. Haines. An Overview of the Opus Language and Runtime System. In *Proc. 7th Workshop on Languages and Compilers for Parallel Computing*, August 1994. (page 183)

[Mentat 1994] A.S. Grimshaw. *The Mentat Users Manual.* University of Virginia, 1994. (pages 384, 387, 393)

[Meyer 1988] B. Meyer. *Object-Oriented Software Construction.* Prentice-Hall, 1988. (pages 258, 275)

[Meyer 1992] B. Meyer. *Eiffel: The Language (Version 3).* Prentice–Hall, 1992. (page 258)

[Mirchandaney et al. 1988] R. Mirchandaney, J.H. Saltz, R.M. Smith, K. Crowley, and D.M. Nicol. Principles of Runtime Support for Parallel Processors. In *Proc. 1988 International Conference on Supercomputing*, pages 140–152. ACM Press, July 1988. (page 135)

[Mohr 1992] B. Mohr. Standardization of Event Traces Considered Harmful or Is an Implementation of Object-Independent Event Trace Monitoring and Analysis Systems Possible? In J.J. Dongarra and B. Tourancheau, editors, *Proc. CNRS-NSF Workshop on Environments and Tools For Parallel Scientific Computing*, volume 6 of *Advances in Parallel Computing*, pages 103–124. Elsevier, September 1992. (pages 595, 604)

[Mohr et al. 1994] B. Mohr, D. Brown, and A. Malony. TAU: A Portable Parallel Program Analysis Environment for pC++. In B. Buchberger and J. Volkert, editors, *Proc. CONPAR 94–VAPP VI*, volume 854 of *Lecture Notes in Computer Science*, pages 29–40. Springer-Verlag, September 1994. (pages 591, 592, 599, 601)

[Moon & Saltz 1994] B. Moon and J.H. Saltz. Adaptive Runtime Support for Direct Simulation Monte Carlo Methods on Distributed Memory Architectures. In D.W. Walker and J.J. Dongarra, editors, *Proc. Scalable High Performance Computing Conference (SHPCC-94)*, pages 176–183. IEEE Computer Society Press, May 1994. (pages 131, 163, 165)

[MPI 1994] Message Passing Interface Forum. *MPI: A Message-Passing Interface Standard*, May 1994. (pages 46–48, 194, 314, 430, 465, 466, 474, 489)

[MPI2 1995] Message Passing Interface Forum. *Draft Document for the MPI-2 Standard*, October 1995. (pages 465, 468)

[Mueller 1993] F. Mueller. A Library Implementation of POSIX Threads under UNIX. In *USENIX Winter Conference*, pages 29–41, 1993. (page 455)

[Mukherjee et al. 1995] S.S. Mukherjee, S.D. Sharma, M.D. Hill, J.R. Larus, A. Rogers, and J.H. Saltz. Efficient Support for Irregular Applications on Distributed-Memory Machines. In *Fifth ACM SIGPLAN Symposium on Principles & Practice of Parallel Programming (PPOPP)*, 1995. (pages 312, 313)

[Murer et al. 1993] S. Murer, J.A. Feldman, C.-C. Lim, and M.-M. Seidel. pSather: Layered Extensions to an Object-Oriented Language for Efficient Parallel Computation. Technical Report TR-93-028, International Computer Science Institute, Berkeley, CA, June 1993. (page 379)

[Nelson et al. 1995] M. Nelson, W. Humprey, A. Gursoy, A. Dalke, L.V. Kalé, R. Skeel, K. Schulten, and R. Kufrin. MDScope: A Visual Computing Environment for Structural Biology. *Computer Physics Communications*, 91, October 1995. (page 211)

[Neusius 1991] C. Neusius. Synchronizing Actions. In *Proc. ECOOP'91*, June 1991. (page 267)

[Nierstrasz 1987] O.M. Nierstrasz. Active Objects In Hybrid. In *ACM Conference on Object-Oriented Programming Systems, Languages and Applications*, October 1987. (page 265)

[Nikhil & Pingali 1989] R.S. Nikhil and K.K Pingali. I–Structure: Data Structures for Parallel Computing. *ACM Transactions on Programming Languages and Systems*, 11(4):598–639, 1989. (pages 439, 449)

[Nitzberg & Lo 1991] W. Nitzberg and V. Lo. Distributed Shared Memory: A Survey of Issues and Algorithms. *IEEE Computer*, 24(8):52–60, August 1991. (page 134)

[Numrich 1994] R.W. Numrich. The Cray T3D Address Space and How to Use It. Technical report, Cray Research, Inc., August 1994. (page 380)

[O'Brien et al. 1995] T. O'Brien, G. Roberts, M. Wei, R. Winder, D. Titcombe, M. Plaxton, A. McEwan, and J. Poole. UC++ V1.4 Language and Compiler Documentation. Technical Report TR/95/8, Department of Computer Science, University College London, 1995. (page 646)

[OMG 1993] Object Management Group. *The Common Object Request Broker: Architecture and Specification*, Version 1.2 edition, December 1993. (pages 212, 568, 606)

[Ousterhout 1994] J. Ousterhout. *Tcl and the Tk Toolkit*. Addison-Wesley, 1994. (pages 580, 593)

[Padua & Wolfe 1986] D.A. Padua and M.J. Wolfe. Advanced Compiler Optimizations for Supercomputers. *Communications of the ACM*, 29(12):829–842, dec 1986. (page 177)

[Parker & Lee 1992] S.E. Parker and W.W. Lee. A Fully Nonlinear Characteristic Method for Gyokinetic Simulation. *Physics of Fluids B*, 5:77–86, 1992. (page 577)

[Parson & Quinlan 1994] R. Parsons and D. Quinlan. A++/P++ Array Classes for Architecture Independent Finite Difference Calculations. In *Proc. Second Annual Object-Oriented Numerics Conference*, April 1994. (page 562)

[Parsons & Quinlan 1993] R. Parsons and D. Quinlan. Run-time Recognition of Task Parallelism Within the P++ Class Library. In A. Skjellum and D.S. Reese, editors, *Proc. Scalable Parallel Libraries Conference*, pages 77–86. IEEE Computer Society Press, October 1993. (page 171)

[Parulekar et al. 1994] R. Parulekar, L. Davis, R. Chellappa, J.H. Saltz, A. Sussman, and J. Townshend. High Performance Computing for Land Cover Dynamics. In *Proc. International Joint Conference on Pattern Recognition*, September 1994. (page 166)

[Pearson & Lipman 1988] W.R. Pearson and D.J. Lipman. Improved Tools for Biological Sequence Analysis. In *Proc. National Academy of Science*, volume 85, pages 2444–2448, 1988. (page 407)

[Peyton Jones 1987] S.L. Peyton Jones. *The Implementation of Functional Programming Languages*. Prentice-Hall International (UK), 1987. (pages 55, 304)

[Plevyak & Chien 1994] J. Plevyak and A.A. Chien. Precise Concrete Type Inference of Object-Oriented Programs. In *Proc. OOPSLA*, 1994. (pages 369, 380)

[Plevyak & Chien 1995] J. Plevyak and A.A. Chien. Type Directed Cloning for Object-Oriented Programs. In *Proc. Workshop for Languages and Compilers for Parallel Computing*, 1995. (page 369)

[Plevyak et al. 1995a] J. Plevyak, X. Zhang, and A.A. Chien. Obtaining Sequential Efficiency in Concurrent Object-Oriented Programs. In *Proc. ACM Symposium on the Principles of Programming Languages*, pages 311–321, January 1995. (pages 369, 380)

[Plevyak et al. 1995b] J. Plevyak, V. Karamcheti, X. Zhang, and A.A. Chien. A Hybrid Execution Model for Fine-Grained Languages on Distributed Memory Multicomputers. In *Proc. Supercomputing 1995*, 1995. (page 380)

[Ponnusamy et al. 1995] R. Ponnusamy, Y.-S. Hwang, R. Das, J.H. Saltz, A. Choudhary, and G.C. Fox. Supporting Irregular Distributions using Data-Parallel Languages. *IEEE Parallel & Distributed Technology*, 3(1):12–24, Spring 1995. (page 136)

[Pthreads 1994] Draft Standard for Information Technology—Portable Operating Systems Interface (Posix), September 1994. (page 127)

[Quinn 1994] M.J. Quinn. *Parallel Computing: Theory and Practice*. McGraw-Hill, 1994. (page 689)

[Ramkumar & Banerjee 1994] B. Ramkumar and P. Banerjee. ProperCAD: A Portable Object-Oriented Parallel Environment for VLSI CAD. *IEEE Transactions on Computer Aided Design*, 13(7):829–842, July 1994. (page 211)

[Ramkumar 1995] B. Ramkumar. Intrepid: An Environment for Debugging Concurrent Object-Oriented Programs. In *Proc. International Conference on High-Performance Computing*, December 1995. to appear. (page 210)

[Ramkumar et al. 1995] B. Ramkumar, A.B. Sinha, V. Saletore, and L.V. Kalé. The Charm Parallel Programming Language and System: Part II – The Runtime System. Technical Report 95–3, Parallel Programming Laboratory, Department of Computer Science, University of Illinois, Urbana-Champaign, 1995. (pages 178, 203)

[Rault & Woronowicz 1993] D.F.G. Rault and M.S. Woronowicz. Spacecraft Contamination Investigation by Direct Simulation Monte Carlo – Contamination on UARS/HALOE. In *Proc. AIAA 31th Aerospace Sciences Meeting and Exhibit*, Reno, Nevada, January 1993. American Institute of Aeronautics and Astronautics. (page 163)

[Reed et al. 1991] D.A. Reed, R.D. Olson, R.A. Aydt, T.M. Madhyasta, T. Birkett, D.W. Jensen, A.A. Nazief, and B.K. Totty. Scalable Performance Environments for Parallel Systems. In *Proc. 6th Distributed Memory Computing Conference*, pages 562–569. IEEE Computer Society Press, 1991. (pages 595, 604)

[Reinhardt et al. 1994] S.K. Reinhardt, J.R. Larus, and D.A. Wood. Tempest and Typhoon: User-Level Shared Memory. In *Proc. 21st Annual International Symposium on Computer Architecture*, pages 325–337, April 1994. (pages 320, 321, 332)

[Reynders et al. 1994] J.V.W. Reynders, D.W. Forslund, P.J. Hinker, M. Tholburn, D.G. Kilman, and W.F. Humphrey. Object-Oriented Particle Simulation on Parallel Computers. In M. Chapman and A. Vermeulen, editors, *Proc. Second Annual Object-Oriented Numerics Conference*, Corvallis, OR, 1994. Rogue Wave Software. (page 548)

[Reynders *et al.* 1995] J.V.W. Reynders, D.W. Forslund, P.J. Hinker, M. Tholburn, D.G. Kilman, and W.F. Humphrey. OOPS: An Object-Oriented Particle Simulation Class Library for Distributed Architectures. *Computational Physics Communications*, to appear. (page 548)

[Roache 1972] P.J. Roache. *Computational Fluid Dynamics*, volume 1. Hermosa Publishers, Albuquerque, New Mexico, 1972. (page 163)

[Robert & Verjus 1977] P. Robert and J.-P. Verjus. Towards Autonomous Descriptions of Synchronization Modules. In B. Gilchrist, editor, *Proc. IFIP Congress*, pages 981–986, North-Holland, 1977. (page 267)

[Roberts & Winder 1994] G. Roberts and R. Winder. UC++: Parallel and Distributed Programming with C++. Research Note RN/94/34, Department of Computer Science, University College London, 1994. Poster Paper presented at OOPSLA'94. (page 631)

[Roberts *et al.* 1990] G. Roberts, R. Winder, and M. Wei. UC++: Concurrent Object Oriented C++. In *Proc. 2nd Workshop on Parallel Object Oriented Programming*. BCS Object-Oriented Programming Systems and BCS Parallel Processing Specialist Groups, 1990. (page 631)

[Roberts *et al.* 1991] G. Roberts, M. Wei, and R. Winder. COOTS Project Subtask 1.1 Deliverable – UC++ and CoSIDE Design and Implementation. Technical Report TR/92/8, Department of Computer Science, University College London, 1991. (page 631)

[Roberts *et al.* 1992] G. Roberts, M. Wei, and R. Winder. COOTS Deliverable 1.2— UC++ compiler and CoSIDE. Technical Report TR/92/30, Department of Computer Science, University College London, 1992. (page 631)

[Rodríguez 1994] C. Rodríguez. An Appearance-Based Approach to Object Recognition in Aerial Images. Master's thesis, Computer Science Department, University of Maryland, College Park, 1994. (page 168)

[Rogers *et al.* 1995] A. Rogers, M.C. Carlisle, J.H. Reppy, and L.J. Hendren. Supporting Dynamic Data Structures on Distributed-Memory Machines. *ACM Transactions on Programming Languages and Systems*, 17(2):233–263, March 1995. (page 172)

[Rose & Steele 1987] J.R. Rose and G.L. Steele Jr. C*: An Extended C Language for Data Parallel Programming. In *Proc. Second International Conference on Supercomputing*, volume III, pages 2–16, May 1987. (pages 85, 297, 300)

[Rose 1988] J.S. Rose. LocusRoute: A Parallel Global Router for Standard Cells. In *Proc. 25th ACM/IEEE Design Automation Conference*, pages 189–195, June 1988. (page 247)

[Rothberg & Gupta 1990] E. Rothberg and A. Gupta. Techniques for Improving the Performance of Sparse Matrix Factorization on Multiprocessor Workstations. In *Proc. Supercomputing 1990*, pages 232–243, New York, NY, November 1990. (pages 235, 250)

[Sabot 1988] G.W. Sabot. *The Paralation Model: Architecture-Independent Parallel Programming*. MIT Press, 1988. (pages 302, 316, 378)

[Sakai *et al.* 1994] S. Sakai, H. Matsuoka, K. Okamoto, T. Yokota, H. Hirono, Y. Kodama, and M. Sato. RWC-1 Massively Parallel Architecture. In *Proc. High Performance Computing Conference*, pages 33–38, 1994. (page 429)

[Saletore & Kalé 1990] V. Saletore and L.V. Kalé. Consistent Linear Speedups for a First Solution in Parallel State-Space Search. In *Proc. AAAI*, pages 227–233. AAAI Press / MIT Press, August 1990. (page 186)

[Saltz et al. 1991] J.H. Saltz, R. Mirchandaney, and K. Crowley. Run-Time Parallelization and Scheduling of Loops. *IEEE Transactions on Computers*, 40(5):603–612, May 1991. (pages 131, 135, 324)

[Saltz et al. 1995] J.H. Saltz, R. Ponnusamy, S.D. Sharma, B. Moon, Y.-S. Hwang, M. Uysal, and R. Das. A Manual for the CHAOS Runtime Library. Technical Report CS-TR-3437 and UMIACS-TR-95-34, University of Maryland, Department of Computer Science and University of Maryland Institute for Advanced Computer Studies, March 1995. (pages 134, 136, 140)

[Sandhu et al. 1993] H.S. Sandhu, B. Gamsa, and S. Zhou. The Shared Regions Approach to Software Cache Coherence. In *Proc. Symposium on Principles and Practices of Parallel Programming*, pages 229–238, May 1993. (page 1)

[Sato et al. 1994a] M. Sato, Y. Kodama, S. Sakai, and Y. Yamaguchi. EM-C: Programming with Explicit Parallelism and Locality for EM-4 Multiprocessor. In *International Conference on Parallel Architecture and Compilation Techniques'94*, pages 3–14. IFIP A-50, North–Holland, 1994. (page 434)

[Sato et al. 1994b] M. Sato, Y. Kodama, S. Sakai, and Y. Yamaguchi. Programming with Distributed Data Structures for EM-X Multiprocessor. In *Theory and Practice of Parallel Programming*, number 907 in Lecture Notes in Computer Science, pages 472–83. Springer-Verlag, 1994. (page 449)

[Schoinas et al. 1994] I. Schoinas, B. Falsafi, A.R. Lebeck, S.K. Reinhardt, J.R. Larus, and D.A. Wood. Fine-grain Access Control for Distributed Shared Memory. In *Proc. Sixth International Conference on Architectural Support for Programming Languages and Operating Systems (ASPLOS VI)*, pages 297–307, October 1994. (pages 320, 321)

[Seevers et al. 1992] B.K. Seevers, M.J. Quinn, and P.J. Hatcher. A Parallel Programming Environment Supporting Multiple Data-Parallel Modules. *International Journal of Parallel Programming*, 21(5), 1992. (page 300)

[Seliger 1990] R. Seliger. Extending C++ to Support Remote Procedure Call, Concurrency, Exception Handling and Garbage Collection. In *Proc. Usenix C++ Conference*, pages 241–264, 1990. (page 629)

[Shanmugam et al. 1995c] H. Beilner and F. Bause, editors. *Speedy: An Integrated Performance Extrapolation Tool for pC++ Programs*, number 977 in Lecture Notes in Computer Science. Springer–Verlag, September 1995. (page 607)

[Shanmugam & Malony 1995a] K. Shanmugam and A. Malony. Performance Extrapolation of Parallel Programs. In C. Polychronopoulos, editor, *Proc. 1995 International Conference on Parallel Processing (ICPP)*, volume II Software, pages 117–120. CRC Press, August 1995. (page 608)

[Shanmugam 1994] K. Shanmugam. Performance Extrapolation of Parallel Programs. Master's thesis, University of Oregon, Department of Computer and Information Science, June 1994. (page 608)

[Shanmugam et al. 1995b] K. Shanmugam, A. Malony, and B. Mohr. Performance Extrapolation of Parallel Programs. Technical Report CIS-TR-95-14, University of Oregon, Department of Computer and Information Science, May 1995. (page 608)

[Shapiro 1986] M. Shapiro. Structure and Encapsulation in Distributed Systems: the Proxy Principle. In *Proc. 6th International Conference on Distributed Computing Systems, Cambridge, Mass. (USA)*, pages 198–204. IEEE, May 1986. (page 289)

[Sharma *et al.* 1994] S.D. Sharma, R. Ponnusamy, B. Moon, Y.-S. Hwang, R. Das, and J.H. Saltz. Run-time and Compile-time Support for Adaptive Irregular Problems. In *Proc. Supercomputing 1994*, pages 97–106, November 1994. (pages 69, 87, 135, 311, 312)

[Sheffler & Chatterjee 1995] T.J. Sheffler and S. Chatterjee. An Object-Oriented Approach to Nested Data Parallelism. In *Proc. Frontiers'95: The Fifth Symposium on the Frontiers of Massively Parallel Computation*, pages 203–210, February 1995. (page 358)

[Sheffler 1992] T.J. Sheffler. *Match and Move, an Approach to Data Parallel Computing*. PhD thesis, Carnegie Mellon University, 1992. (page 69)

[Sheffler 1993] T.J. Sheffler. Implementing the Multiprefix Operation on Parallel and Vector Computers. In *Proc. 1993 Fifth Annual ACM Symposium on Parallel Algorithms and Architectures*, June 1993. (page 69)

[Sheffler 1995] T.J. Sheffler. A Portable MPI-Based Parallel Vector Template Library. Technical Report RIACS TR-95.04, Research Institute for Advanced Computer Science, 1995. (page 84)

[Shibayama 1991] E. Shibayama. Reuse of Concurrent Object Descriptions. In A. Yonesawa and T. Ito, editors, *Concurrency: Theory, Language, and Architecture*. Springler Verlag, 1991. (page 267)

[Shock *et al.* 1995] C.T. Shock, C. Chang, L. Davis, S. Goward, J.H. Saltz, and A. Sussman. A High Performance Image Database System for Remote Sensing. In *Proc. 24th Automatic Image and Pattern Recognition Workshop on Tools and Techniques for Modeling and Simulation*, Washington, D.C., October 1995. Society for Photogrammetric and Industrial Engineers. (page 167)

[Shopiro 1987] J.E. Shopiro. Extending the C++ Task System for Real-Time Control. In *Proc. USENIX C++ Conference*, Santa Fe, NM, November 1987. (page xxviii)

[Singh & Hennessy 1992] J.P. Singh and J.L. Hennessy. Finding and Exploiting Parallelism in an Ocean Simulation Program: Experience, Results, and Implications. *Journal of Parallel and Distributed Computing*, 15(1):27–48, May 1992. (page 243)

[Singh *et al.* 1992] J.P. Singh, W.-D. Weber, and A. Gupta. SPLASH: Stanford Parallel Applications for Shared Memory. *Computer Architecture News*, 20(1):5–44, March 1992. (pages 217, 223, 226, 242)

[Singh *et al.* 1993] J.P. Singh, T. Joe, J.L. Hennessy, and A. Gupta. An Empirical Comparison of the Kendall Square Research KSR-1 and Stanford DASH Multiprocessors. In *Proc. Supercomputing 1993*, pages 214–225. IEEE Computer Society Press, November 1993. (page 134)

[Sinha & Kalé 1993] A.B. Sinha and L.V. Kalé. A Load Balancing Strategy for Prioritized Execution of Tasks. In *Proc. 7th International Parallel Processing Symposium*, pages 230–237, April 1993. (page 185)

[Sinha & Kalé 1994] A.B. Sinha and L.V. Kalé. Information Sharing Mechanisms in Parallel Programs. In H.J. Siegel, editor, *Proc. 8th International Parallel Processing Symposium*, pages 461–468, April 1994. (page 194)

[Sinha 1995] A.B. Sinha. *Performance Analysis of Object Based and Message Driven Programs.* PhD thesis, Department of Computer Science, University of Illinois, Urbana-Champaign, January 1995. (page 210)

[Sipelstein & Blelloch 1991] J.M. Sipelstein and G.E. Blelloch. Collection-Oriented Languages. *Proc. IEEE*, 79(4):504–523, April 1991. (page 43)

[Sivilotti 1994] P. Sivilotti. A Verified Integration of Parallel Programming Paradigms in CC++. In *Proceeding of the International Parallel Processing Symposium*, 1994. (page 94)

[Skjellum & Baldwin 1991] A. Skjellum and C. Baldwin. The Multicomputer Toolbox: Scalable Parallel Libraries for Large-Scale Concurrent Applications. Technical Report UCRL-JC-109251, Lawrence Livermore National Laboratory, December 1991. (page 472)

[Skjellum et al. 1994] A. Skjellum, S.G. Smith, N.E. Doss, A.P. Leung, and M Morari. The Design and Evolution of Zipcode. *Parallel Computing*, 20:565–96, 1994. (page 465)

[Smith & Chatterjee 1990] K. Smith and A. Chatterjee. A C++ Environment for Distributed Application Execution. Technical Report ACT-ESP-015-91, Microelectronics and Computer Technology Corporation (MCC), November 1990. (page 378)

[Smith & Waterman 1981] T.F. Smith and M.S. Waterman. Identification of Common Molecular Subsequences. *Journal of Molecular Biology*, 147:195–197, 1981. (page 406)

[Srinivasan 1994] S. Srinivasan and J.H. Aylor. Digital Circuit Testing on a Network of Workstations. In *Proc. 1994 International Conference on Parallel Processing (ICPP)*, August 1994. (page 406)

[Steele & Hillis 1986] G.L. Steele Jr. and W.D. Hillis. Connection Machine LISP: Fine-Grained Parallel Symbolic Processing. In *Proc. 1986 ACM Conference on LISP and Functional Programming*, pages 279–297, August 1986. (page 302)

[Steele 1990a] G.L. Steele Jr. Making Asynchronous Parallelism Safe for the World. In *Proc. 17th ACM Symposium on the Principles of Programming Languages*, pages 218–31, January 1990. (page 315)

[Steele 1990b] G.L. Steele Jr. *Common Lisp, The Language.* Digital Press, second edition, 1990. (page 55)

[Stepanov 1994] A. Stepanov and M. Lee. The Standard Template Library. Technical Report HPL-95-11, Hewlett-Packard Laboratories, 1501 Page Mill Road, Palo Alto, CA 94304, October 1994. (pages 35, 44, 83)

[Stroustrup 1980] B. Stroustrup. A Set of C Classes for Co-routine Style Programming. Technical Report CSTR-90, Bell Laboratories, November 1980. (page xxviii)

[Stroustrup 1988] B. Stroustrup. Parameterized Types for C++. In *USENIX C++ Conference, Denver*, October 1988. (page 509)

[Stroustrup 1991] B. Stroustrup. *The C++ Programming Language, Second Edition.* Addison-Wesley, 1991. (pages 44, 94, 216, 681)

[Stroustrup 1994] B. Stroustrup. *The Design and Evolution of C++.* Addison–Wesley, 1994. (pages xxix, 292, 681)

[Sun 1990] Sun Microsystems, Inc. *SunOS Reference Manual Vol. II*, 1990. (page 455)

[Sunderam 1990] V.S. Sunderam. PVM: A Framework for Parallel Distributed Computing. *Concurrency: Practice and Experience*, 2(4), December 1990. (pages 177, 194)

[Sussman et al. 1993] A. Sussman, G. Agrawal, and J.H. Saltz. A Manual for the Multiblock PARTI Runtime Primitives, Revision 4.1. Technical Report CS-TR-3070.1 and UMIACS-TR-93-36.1, University of Maryland, Department of Computer Science and University of Maryland Institute for Advanced Computer Studies, December 1993. (pages 134, 138)

[Taura et al. 1993] K. Taura, S. Matsuoka, and A. Yonezawa. An Efficient Implementation Scheme of Concurrent Object-Oriented Languages on Stock Multicomputers. In *Proc. Fifth ACM SIGPLAN Symposium on the Principles and Practice of Parallel Programming*, 1993. (page 380)

[TMC 1991] Thinking Machines Corporation, 245 First Street, Cambridge, MA 02154-1264. *The Connection Machine CM-5 Technical Summary*, October 1991. (page 380)

[von Eicken et al. 1992] T. von Eicken, D.E. Culler, S.C. Goldstein, and K.E. Schauser. Active Messages: a Mechanism for Integrated Communication and Computation. In *Proc. 19th International Symposium on Computer Architecture*, Gold Coast, Australia, May 1992. (page 180)

[Watanabe & Yonezawa 1998] T. Watanabe and A. Yonezawa. Reflection in an Object-Oriented Concurrent Language. In *ACM Conference on Object-Oriented Programming Systems, Languages and Applications (OOPSLA)*, September 1988. (page 289)

[Wegner 1987] P. Wegner. Dimensions of Object-Based Language Design. In *Proc. 1987 Object-Oriented Programming Systems, Languages and Applications Conference*, pages 169–182. ACM Press, 1987. (page 384)

[Wei et al. 1993a] M. Wei, R. Winder, and G. Roberts. UC++ Definition. Internal Note IN/93/8, Department of Computer Science, University College London, 1993. (page 86)

[Weinand et al. 1989] A. Weinand, E. Gamma, and R. Marty. Design and Implementation of ET++, a Seamless Object-Oriented Application Framework. *Structured Programming*, 10(2), 1989. (page 477)

[Weissman & Grimshaw 1995] J.B. Weissman and A.S. Grimshaw. A Framework for Partitioning Parallel Computations in Heterogeneous Environments. *Concurrency—Practice and Experience*, 7(5):455–478, August 1995. (page 405)

[Weissman 1995] J.B. Weissman. *Scheduling Parallel Computations in Heterogeneous Environments*. PhD thesis, University of Virginia, 1995. (page 405)

[Weissman et al. 1994] J.B. Weissman, A.S. Grimshaw, and R. Ferraro. Parallel Object-Oriented Computation Applied to a Finite Element Problem. *Scientific Computing*, 2(4):133–144, February 1994. (page 406)

[West & Grimshaw 1995] E.A. West and A.S. Grimshaw. Braid: Integrating Task and Data Parallelism. In *Proc. Frontiers'95: The Fifth Symposium on the Frontiers of Massively Parallel Computation*, pages 211–219, February 1995. (page 422)

[West 1994b] E.A. West. Combining Control and Data Parallelism: Data Parallel Extensions to the Mentat Programming Language. Technical Report CS-94-16, University of Virginia, 1994. (page 422)

[White 1978] D. White. A Design for Polygon Overlay. In G. Dutton, editor, *Harvard Papers on Geographic Information Systems: Volume 6—Spatial Algorithms: Efficiency in Theory and Practice.* Laboratory for Computer Graphics and Spatial Analysis, Harvard University, 1978. (page 701)

[Wilson & Bal 1995] G.V. Wilson and H.E. Bal. Experiences with the Orca Programming Language. Technical Report 320, Computer Systems Research Institute, University of Toronto, March 1995. (page 707)

[Wilson & Irvin 1995] G.V. Wilson and R.B. Irvin. Assessing and Comparing the Usability of Parallel Programming Systems. Technical Report 321, Computer Systems Research Institute, University of Toronto, March 1995. (page 707)

[Wilson 1993] G.V. Wilson. A Glossary of Parallel Computing Terminology. *IEEE Parallel & Distributed Technology,* February 1993. (page 695)

[Wilson 1994] G.V. Wilson. Assessing the Usability of Parallel Programming Systems: The Cowichan Problems. In *Proceedings of the IFIP Working Conference on Programming Environments for Massively Parallel Distributed Systems.* Birkhäuser Verlag AG, April 1994. (page 707)

[Wilson 1995] G.V. Wilson. *Practical Parallel Programming.* MIT Press, 1995. (page 689)

[Wilson et al. 1994] G.V. Wilson, B. Gorda, and P. Lu. Twelve Ways to Make Sure Your Parallel Programming System Doesn't Make Others Look Bad. *IEEE Computer,* 27(10), October 1994. (page xxxiii)

[Winder 1994] R. Winder. Is Object-oriented the Answer? In D. Gilmore, R. Winder, and F. Détienne, editors, *User-centred Requirements for Software Engineering Environments,* volume 123 of *NATO ASI Series F: Computer and Systems Science.* Springer-Verlag, 1994. Proc. NATO Advanced Research Workshop, 5-11 September 1991, Bonas, France. (page 637)

[Winder et al. 1991] R. Winder, M. Wei, and G. Roberts. Harnessing Parallelism with UC++. In *Proc. ECUG'91,* pages 101–114. European C++ User Group Conference, 1991. (page 631)

[Winder et al. 1992a] R. Winder, G. Joly, and A. Kamalati. Applications in Co-SIDE. *OOPS Messenger,* 4(2):215–216, 1992. (page 631)

[Winder et al. 1992b] R. Winder, G. Roberts, and M. Wei. CoSIDE and Parallel Object Oriented Languages. *OOPS Messenger,* 4(2):211–213, 1992. Poster paper presented at OOPSLA'92. (page 631)

[Winder et al. 1992c] R. Winder, M. Wei, and G. Roberts. UC++: An Active Object Model for Parallel C++. Research Note RN/92/115, Department of Computer Science, University College London, 1992. (page 631)

[Wirth & Gutknecht 1992] N. Wirth and J. Gutknecht. *Project Oberon: The Design of an Operating System and Compiler.* Addison–Wesley, 1992. (page 349)

[Wood et al. 1993] D.A. Wood, S. Chandra, B. Falsafi, M.D. Hill, J.R. Larus, A.R. Lebeck, J.C. Lewis, S.S. Mukherjee, S. Palacharla, and S.K. Reinhardt. Mechanisms for Cooperative Shared Memory. In *Proc. 20th Annual International Symposium on Computer Architecture,* pages 156–168, May 1993. (page 299)

[Wulf 1974] W.A. Wulf. Hydra: The Kernel of a Multiprocessor Operating System. *Communications of the ACM,* 17(96):337–345, June 1974. (page 384)

[Wulf 1981] W.A. Wulf. Compilers and Computer Architecture. *IEEE Computer*, 14(7):41–47, July 1981. (page 299)

[Wyllie 1979] J.C. Wyllie. *The Complexity of Parallel Computation*. PhD thesis, Cornell University, 1979. (page 55)

[Yang *et al.* 1994] B. Yang, J. Webb, J.M. Stichnoth, D.R. O'Hallaron, and T. Gross. Do&Merge: Integrating Parallel Loops and Reductions. In *Languages and Compilers for Parallel Computing (Proc. Sixth International Workshop)*, pages 169–183. Springer Verlag, 1994. (page 317)

[Yang *et al.* 1994] S. Yang, D. Gannon, S. Bodin, P. Bode, and S. Srinivas. High Performance Fortran Interface to the Parallel C++. In *Scalable High Performance Computing Conference*. IEEE, 1994. (pages 533, 535)

[Yokote & Tokoro 1986] Y. Yokote and M. Tokoro. The Design and Implementation of ConcurrentSmalltalk. In *Proc. ACM Conference on Object-Oriented Programming Systems, Languages, and Applications*, pages 331–340, 1986. (page 289)

[Yokote & Tokoro 1987] Y. Yokote and M. Tokoro. Concurrent Programming in ConcurrentSmalltalk. In A. Yonezawa and M. Tokoro, editors, *Object-Oriented Concurrent Programming*. The MIT Press, 1987. (page 263)

[Yonezawa 1990] A. Yonezawa, editor. *ABCL: An Object-Oriented Concurrent System*. MIT Press, 1990. (pages 186, 349, 379)

[Yonezawa *et al.* 1987] A. Yonezawa, E. Shibayama, T. Takada, and Y. Honda. Modelling and Programming in an Object-Oriented Concurrent Language ABCL/1. In A. Yonezawa and M. Tokoro, editors, *Object-Oriented Concurrent Programming*. The MIT Press, 1987. (pages 263, 267)

Citation Author Index

Abelson, H., 55, 709
Ackerman, W.B., 92, 101, 709
Adamo, J.-M., 629, 709
Adams, J.C., 299, 301, 709
Adve, S.V., 25, 709
Adve, V.S., 627, 709
Agarwal, A., 217, 320, 709, 724
Agha, G., 1, 92, 178, 180, 186,
    262, 267, 349, 379, 709, 722
Agrawal, G., 134, 138, 709, 734
Alpern, B., 82, 709
Altschul, S.F., 407, 709
Amador, F.G., 42, 715
Amdahl, G., 697, 710
America, P., 267, 349, 379, 710
Andersen, B., 379, 710
Anderson, E., 45, 710
Anderson, M., 627, 709
Anderson, R.J., 421, 721
Andrews, G.R., 689, 710
Arjomandi, E., 42, 710
Arnold, A., 595, 604, 710
Arpaci, R.H., 339, 710
Arvind, 180, 710
Assenmacher, H., 42, 629, 710
Athas, W., 186, 710
Attali, I., 295, 710, 711
Avalani, B., 95, 718
Aydt, R.A., 595, 604, 729
Aylor, J.H., 406, 733

Backus, J.W., 299, 711
Baden, S.B., 87, 171, 718, 724
Bai, Z., 45, 710
Bailey, D.H., 82, 707, 711
Baker, S., 267, 726
Bal, H.E., 1, 42, 349, 707, 711,
    735
Baldwin, C., 472, 733
Banerjee, P., 211, 729
Bangalore, P., 465, 472, 711
Barnes, J.E., 314, 711
Barszcz, E., 82, 711
Baude, F., 288, 718
Beazley, D.M., 555, 711

Beckman, P., 51, 83, 84, 421, 508,
    593, 601, 603, 712, 719, 726
Beguelin, A., 378, 387, 430, 465,
    641, 711, 719
Beltrametti, M., 321, 711
Bennett, J.K., 1, 711
Bennett, R., 167, 168, 711, 712
Bershad, B.N., 42, 378, 712
Bertschinger, E., 538, 717
Bhandarkar, M., 178, 183, 203,
    724
Bianchini, R., 217, 709
Binau, U., 94, 712
Birdsall, C.K., 548, 712
Birkett, T., 595, 604, 729
Birrell, A., 289, 712
Bischof, C., 45, 710
Blelloch, G.E., 43, 48, 55, 62, 83,
    84, 304, 543, 712, 733
Bobey, K., 321, 711
Bobrow, D.G., 289, 294, 712, 724
Bode, P., 533, 535, 719, 736
Boden, N., 186, 710
Boden, N.J., 429, 454, 712
Bodin, F., 51, 83, 84, 421, 508,
    593, 601, 603, 712, 719, 726
Bodin, S., 533, 535, 736
Böhm, A.P.W., 92, 712
Booch, G., 275, 712
Boyle, J., 222, 236, 712
Bozkus, Z., 138, 713
Brainerd, W.S., 299, 301, 709
Breitbach, T., 42, 629, 710
Brobst, S., 180, 710
Brooks, B.R., 131, 722
Brown, D., 591, 592, 599, 601,
    605, 713, 727
Bryan, G.L., 534, 721
Bryant, K., 167, 168, 711, 712
Budd, T., 681, 713
Buhler, P., 42, 629, 710
Burns, A., 267, 713
Buschmann, F., 289, 713
Butler, R., 222, 236, 465, 712, 713

Calkin, R., 465, 713

Campbell, R.H., 267, 289, 424, 713, 716, 726

Cann, D.C., 92, 712

Carey, M.J., 518, 713

Carlisle, M.C., 172, 730

Caromel, D., 258, 259, 267, 268, 270, 272, 289, 295, 710, 711, 713, 714

Carriero, N., 194, 714

Carroll, M.C., 172, 714

Carson, M., 380, 714

Carter, J.B., 1, 711

Casavant, T.L., 403, 714

Chaiken, D., 217, 709

Chandra, R., 86, 242, 714

Chandra, S., 299, 735

Chandy, K.M., 91, 94, 379, 507, 714

Chang, C., 155, 167, 715, 732

Chase, J.S., 42, 715

Chatterjee, A., 42, 378, 715, 733

Chatterjee, S., 48, 83, 84, 358, 712, 732

Chellappa, R., 166, 728

Chiba, S., 289, 715

Chien, A.A., 86, 186, 193, 349, 358, 360, 369, 378–380, 715, 722, 724, 728, 729

Choi, J., 507, 715

Choudhary, A., 95, 136, 138, 713, 718, 729

Cohen, D., 429, 454, 712

Cohn, E.R., 69, 715

Concurrent Systems Architecture Group, 355, 357, 379, 380, 722

Conery, J.S., 180, 715

Connor, J., 577, 716

Coplien, J.O., 482, 489, 502, 503, 556, 560, 716

Coulaud, O., 465, 716

Cronk, D., 182, 721

Crowley, K., 131, 135, 324, 727, 731

Culler, D.E., 142, 180, 339, 434, 710, 716, 734

Cuny, J.E., 627, 724

Dagum, L., 82, 711

Dahl, E.D., 69, 716

Dalke, A., 211, 727

Dally, W.J., 86, 349, 358, 360, 378–380, 715, 722

Das, R., 69, 87, 131, 132, 134–136, 138–140, 152, 153, 167, 168, 311, 312, 711, 712, 716, 722, 729, 731, 732

Dave, A., 289, 716

Davis, L., 166, 167, 728, 732

Decouchant, D., 266, 267, 716

Decyk, V., 548, 716

Demmel, J., 45, 710

des Rivières, J., 289, 294, 724

Deter, U., 595, 604, 710

DeWitt, D.J., 518, 713

Dillon, E., 465, 716

DiMichiel, L.G., 289, 712

Disz, T., 222, 236, 712

Doeppner Jr., T.W., 42, 717

Dolby, J., 380, 715

Dongarra, J.J., 45, 387, 430, 465, 507, 641, 710, 711, 715, 719

Donnelly, A., 267, 726

Doss, N.E., 465, 472, 499, 711, 717, 733

Doulas, N., 186, 717

Du Croz, J., 45, 710

Duff, I., 252, 717

Dusseau, A., 142, 434, 716

Eager, D.L., 404, 717

Edelson, D., 289, 717

Ellis, M., 681, 717

Evripidou, P., 180, 717

Falgout, R.D., 472, 717

Falsafi, B., 299, 320, 321, 731, 735

Feeley, M.J., 42, 717

Felderman, R.E., 429, 454, 712

Feldman, J.A., 379, 727
Fenton, W., 177, 203, 717
Feo, J.T., 92, 712
Ferrari, A.J., 406, 717
Ferraro, R., 406, 734
Ferrell, R., 538, 717
Filipi-Martin, A., 406, 717
Fink, S.J., 87, 718
Flynn, M.J., 297, 689, 718
Ford, P., 548, 718
Forslund, D.W., 548, 718, 729, 730
Foster, I., 95, 124, 689, 718
Fox, G.C., 131, 136, 138, 299, 315, 421, 713, 718, 729
Franklin, M.J., 518, 713
French, J.C., 426, 720
Frølund, S., 267, 709, 718
Furmento, N., 288, 718

Gabriel, R.P., 289, 712
Gamma, E., 477, 482, 557, 565, 718, 734
Gamsa, B., 1, 731
Gannon, D., 51, 83, 84, 193, 302, 358, 421, 508, 516, 533, 535, 593, 601, 603, 712, 718–720, 725, 726, 736
Gaudiot, J.L., 180, 717
Gautron, P., 42, 719
Gebele, A.J., 42, 717
Gehani, N.H., 42, 267, 270, 629, 719
Geist, A., 387, 430, 465, 641, 711, 719
Gelernter, D., 194, 714
Gerndt, M., 139, 719
Gharachorloo, K., 25, 217, 709, 725
Gifford, D.K., 314, 726
Giles, R., 555, 711
Glickfield, B., 222, 236, 712
Goldberg, A., 44, 720
Goldstein, S.C., 142, 180, 434, 716, 734

Gorda, B., xxxiii, 735
Gotwals, J., 508, 516, 593, 719, 720
Gourhant, Y., 289, 726
Goward, S., 167, 732
Grama, A., 565, 689, 699, 720, 724
Gray, J., 353, 720
Greenbaum, A., 45, 710
Grimes, R., 252, 717
Grimshaw, A.S., 85, 180, 349, 383, 384, 387, 391, 393, 401, 405, 406, 409, 411, 412, 422, 425, 426, 720, 724, 726, 727, 734
Grønbech-Jensen, N., 555, 711
Gropp, W.D., 465, 466, 499, 717, 720
Gross, T., 317, 736
Grunwald, D., 42, 720
Guarna, V., 508, 719
Gupta, A., 86, 134, 217, 223, 226, 235, 242, 243, 250, 565, 689, 699, 714, 720, 721, 724, 725, 730, 732
Gupta, R., 172, 721
Gupta, S., 131, 716
Gursoy, A., 178, 180, 190, 194, 207, 211, 721, 723, 727
Gutknecht, J., 349, 735

Haberman, A.N., 267, 713
Haines, M., 182, 183, 721, 727
Halbert, D.C., 275, 721
Hall, N.E., 518, 713
Halstead, R., 18, 228, 263, 721
Halton, J., 577, 721
Hammarling, S., 45, 710
Hanson, R.J., 45, 725
Hardwick, J.C., 48, 83, 84, 712
Harria, N., 267, 726
Hatcher, P.J., 85, 300, 421, 721, 731
Haupt, T., 138, 713
Havlak, P., 138, 721
Helm, R., 482, 557, 565, 718

Hempel, H.H.-C., 465, 713
Hendren, L.J., 172, 730
Hennessy, J.L., 86, 134, 217, 243,
    714, 725, 732
Hermans, J., 380, 714
Hernquist, L., 534, 721
Herrarte, V., 595, 604, 721
Hewitt, C., 262, 721
Hill, M.D., 298, 299, 312, 313,
    339, 721, 722, 727, 735
Hillis, W.D., 299, 300, 302, 549,
    722, 733
Hinker, P.J., 548, 729, 730
Hiranandani, S., 315, 718
Hirono, H., 429, 730
Hoare, C.A.R., 216, 219, 267, 389,
    722
Hodoscek, M., 131, 722
Honda, Y., 263, 267, 736
Hori, A., 379, 429, 440, 464, 544,
    722, 723
Horowitz, M., 217, 725
Horwat, W., 360, 722
Houck, C., 186, 722
Hsieh, S.-H., 465, 722
Hübsch, V., 42, 629, 710
Hudak, P., 1, 134, 725
Humphrey, W.F., 548, 729, 730
Humprey, W., 211, 727
Hung, Y., 42, 715
Hut, P., 314, 711
Hwang, Y.-S., 69, 87, 131, 132,
    134–136, 138, 140, 152, 153,
    311, 312, 716, 722, 729, 731,
    732

Ichbiah, J.D., 267, 722
Inmos Ltd., 267, 722
Irvin, R.B., 707, 735
Ishikawa, Y., 379, 429, 431, 440,
    451, 464, 544, 722, 723
Islam, N., 289, 726

Jackson, J., 548, 718
Jagathesan, N., 178, 183, 203, 724

Jensen, D.W., 595, 604, 729
Jiang, W., 387, 641, 719
Joe, T., 134, 243, 725, 732
Johnson, K.L., 217, 320, 709, 724
Johnson, R., 482, 557, 565, 718
Joly, G., 631, 735
Jones, A.K., 384, 723
Jones, R.R., 421, 721
Judd, M., 411, 412, 724
Junkins, J., 548, 718

Kaashoek, M.F., 1, 42, 349, 711
Kafura, D.G., 42, 267, 723
Kalas, I., 42, 710
Kalé, L.V., 86, 175, 177, 178, 180,
    183, 185, 186, 190, 194, 201,
    203, 205, 210–212, 349, 379,
    717, 723, 724, 727, 729, 731,
    732
Kamalati, A., 631, 735
Karamcheti, V., 380, 715, 724,
    729
Karpovich, J.F., 411, 412, 724
Karypis, G., 565, 689, 699, 724
Keen, S.E., 289, 712
Keller, R.M., 180, 724
Kennedy, K., 138, 315, 627, 709,
    718, 721
Kesselman, C., 91, 94, 124, 379,
    507, 714, 718
Khanna, A., 42, 715
Kiczales, G., 289, 294, 712, 724
Kiefer, K., 289, 713
Kilman, D.G., 548, 729, 730
Kim, W.Y., 267, 709
Kincaid, D.R., 45, 725
Kodama, Y., 429, 434, 449, 730,
    731
Koelbel, C.H., 43, 138, 177, 299,
    301, 302, 315, 430, 507, 589,
    718, 724
Kohn, S.R., 171, 724
Kolstad, R.B., 424, 713
Konaka, H., 379, 429, 440, 464,
    544, 722–724

Kornkven, E., 205, 212, 724
Kougiouris, P., 289, 726
Krakowiak, S., 266, 716
Kranz, D., 217, 320, 709, 724
Kremer, U., 315, 718
Krishnamurthy, A., 142, 339, 434, 710, 716
Krishnan, S., 86, 178, 183, 203, 349, 379, 723, 724
Krogh, F.T., 45, 725
Kubiatowicz, J., 217, 320, 709, 724
Kufrin, R., 211, 727
Kuhl, J.G., 403, 714
Kulawik, A.E., 429, 454, 712
Kumar, V., 565, 689, 699, 720, 721, 724
Kundu, J., 627, 724

Lam, M., 217, 725
Langdon, A.B., 548, 712
Lapadula, A.J., 421, 721
Larus, J.R., 85, 297–299, 303, 304, 312, 313, 319–321, 332, 339, 721, 722, 725, 727, 729, 731, 735
Laudon, J., 217, 243, 725
Lawson, C.L., 45, 725
Lazowska, E.D., 42, 378, 404, 712, 715, 717
Le Dot, P., 267, 716
Le Narzul, J.-P., 289, 726
Lebeck, A.R., 299, 320, 321, 731, 735
Lee, J.-K., 193, 302, 358, 508, 718, 719, 725
Lee, K.H., 42, 267, 723
Lee, M., 35, 44, 83, 733
Lee, W.W., 548, 577, 725, 728
Lemke, M., 86, 127, 507, 553, 725
Lenoski, D., 217, 243, 725
Leung, A.P., 465, 733
Levy, H.M., 42, 378, 712, 715, 717
Lewis, J., 252, 717
Lewis, J.C., 299, 735

Li, K., 1, 134, 725
Lieberman, H., 263, 725
Lim, B.-H., 217, 320, 709, 724
Lim, C.-C., 379, 727
Lin, C., 301, 725
Lin, F.C.H., 180, 724
Lipman, D.J., 407, 709, 728
Liskov, B., 349, 353, 725
Littlefield, R.J., 42, 715
Lo, V., 134, 728
Lohr, K.-P., 267, 726
Lomdahl, P.S., 555, 711
Loveman, D.B., 43, 138, 177, 299, 301, 302, 421, 430, 507, 589, 724, 726
Lu, P., xxxiii, 735
Lucassen, J.M., 314, 726
Lumetta, S., 142, 434, 716
Lusk, E., 222, 236, 465, 466, 499, 595, 604, 712, 713, 717, 720, 721

MacCallum, L., 406, 726
Mackenzie, K., 217, 709
Madany, P., 289, 726
Madhyasta, T.M., 595, 604, 729
Maeda, M., 379, 464, 544, 722, 723
Makpangou, M., 289, 726
Mallet, L., 258, 726
Malony, A., 83, 84, 591, 592, 599, 601, 603, 605, 607, 608, 712, 713, 726, 727, 731
Manchek, R., 387, 430, 465, 641, 711, 719
Martin, A.J., 93, 726
Martin, J.T., 299, 301, 709
Marty, R., 477, 734
Masuda, T., 289, 715
Matsuda, M., 379, 544, 723
Matsuoka, H., 429, 730
Matsuoka, S., 41, 267, 375, 380, 726, 734
Mavriplis, D.J., 131, 139, 716
McAffer, J., 289, 726

McAuliffe, M.L., 518, 713
McDonald, J.D., 223, 726
McEwan, A., 646, 728
McHale, C., 267, 726
McKenney, A., 45, 710
Mehrotra, P., 182, 183, 721, 727
Mellor-Crummey, J., 627, 709
Menkov, V., 533, 719
Messina, P.C., 131, 718
Meyer, B., 258, 275, 727
Meysembourg, M., 266, 716
Miller, W., 407, 709
Mirchandaney, R., 131, 135, 324, 727, 731
Mohr, B., 83, 84, 591, 592, 595, 599, 601, 603–605, 607, 608, 712, 713, 726, 727, 731
Moon, B., 69, 87, 131, 134–136, 140, 163, 165, 311, 312, 727, 731, 732
Moon, D.A., 289, 712
Morari, M, 465, 733
Mueller, F., 455, 727
Mukherjee, S.S., 299, 312, 313, 727, 735
Munenori, M., 429, 440, 723
Murer, S., 379, 727
Mussi, P., 258, 726
Myers, E.W., 407, 709

Nagel, W.E., 595, 604, 710
Nakahira, D., 243, 725
Narayan, P., 387, 720
Narayana, S., 51, 421, 508, 593, 712, 719
Naughton, J.F., 518, 713
Nazief, A.A., 595, 604, 729
Nelson, G., 289, 712
Nelson, M., 211, 727
Neusius, C., 267, 728
Nicol, D.M., 135, 727
Nierstrasz, O.M., 265, 728
Nikhil, R.S., 439, 449, 728
Nitzberg, W., 134, 728
Nolte, J., 379, 544, 723

Numrich, R.W., 380, 728

O'Brien, P.D., 275, 721
O'Brien, T., 646, 728
O'Farrell, W., 42, 710
O'Hallaron, D.R., 317, 736
Okamoto, K., 429, 730
Oldehoeft, R.R., 92, 712
Olson, R., 124, 718
Olson, R.D., 595, 604, 729
Ostriker, J.P., 534, 721
Ostrouchov, S., 45, 710
Oudshoorn, M., 295, 711
Ousterhout, J., 580, 593, 728
Overbeek, R., 222, 236, 712
Owicki, S., 289, 712

Padua, D.A., 177, 728
Palacharla, S., 299, 735
Panwar, R., 267, 709
Parker, S.E., 577, 728
Parsons, R., 171, 562, 728
Parulekar, R., 166, 728
Patterson, A., 267, 709
Patterson, J., 222, 236, 712
Paulish, F., 289, 713
Pearson, W.R., 387, 406, 407, 409, 720, 728
Peyton Jones, S.L., 55, 304, 728
Pingali, K.K, 439, 449, 728
Plaxton, M., 646, 728
Plevyak, J., 369, 380, 715, 728, 729
Pollock, L., 172, 714
Ponnusamy, R., 69, 87, 131, 134–136, 139, 140, 311, 312, 716, 729, 731, 732
Poole, J., 646, 728
Pope, S., 548, 718

Quinlan, D., 86, 127, 171, 507, 553, 562, 725, 728
Quinn, M.J., 85, 300, 421, 689, 721, 729, 731

Ramkumar, B., 177, 178, 186, 190, 194, 203, 210, 211, 717, 723, 729
Ranka, S., 138, 713
Rault, D.F.G., 163, 729
Rebuffel, M., 258, 289, 714
Reddy, U., 380, 715
Reed, D.A., 595, 604, 627, 709, 729
Reid-Miller, M., 48, 83, 84, 712
Reinhardt, S.K., 299, 320, 321, 332, 729, 731, 735
Reppy, J.H., 172, 730
Reuter, A., 353, 720
Reynders, J.V.W., 548, 729, 730
Reynolds Jr., P.F., 426, 720
Richards, B., 297, 298, 319, 725
Riveill, M., 266, 267, 716
Roache, P.J., 163, 730
Robert, P., 267, 730
Roberts, G., 86, 631, 646, 728, 730, 734, 735
Robson, D., 44, 720
Rodríguez, C., 168, 730
Rogers, A., 172, 312, 313, 727, 730
Roisin, C., 267, 716
Roome, W.D., 42, 267, 629, 719
Rose, J.R., 85, 297, 300, 730
Rose, J.S., 247, 730
Rothberg, E., 235, 250, 730
Rousset de Pina, X., 266, 267, 716

Sabot, G.W., 302, 316, 378, 730
Sakai, S., 429, 434, 449, 730, 731
Saletore, V., 177, 178, 186, 203, 717, 729, 731
Saltz, J.H., 69, 87, 131, 132, 134–136, 138–140, 152, 153, 155, 163, 165–168, 311–313, 324, 709, 711, 712, 715, 716, 722, 727–729, 731, 732, 734
Sameh, A., 565, 721
Sandhu, H.S., 1, 731
Sato, M., 379, 429, 434, 449, 544, 723, 730, 731

Schauser, K.E., 180, 734
Schoinas, I., 320, 321, 731
Schreiber, R.S., 43, 138, 177, 299, 301, 302, 430, 507, 589, 724
Schuh, D.T., 518, 713
Schulten, K., 211, 727
Schwarz, R., 42, 629, 710
Seevers, B.K., 300, 421, 721, 731
Sefika, M., 289, 716
Seidel, M.-M., 379, 727
Seitz, C.L., 429, 454, 712
Seizovic, J.N., 429, 454, 712
Seliger, R., 629, 731
Seligman, E., 378, 711
Shanmugam, K., 83, 84, 607, 608, 712, 731
Shapiro, M., 289, 726, 732
Sharma, S.D., 69, 87, 134–136, 140, 311–313, 727, 731, 732
Sheffler, T.J., 69, 84, 358, 732
Shibayama, E., 263, 267, 732, 736
Shock, C.T., 167, 732
Shopiro, J.E., xxviii, 732
Shu, W., 175, 723
Sigurdsson, S., 534, 721
Simon, H.D., 82, 711
Singh, J.P., 134, 217, 223, 226, 242, 243, 732
Sinha, A.B., 177, 178, 185, 190, 194, 201, 203, 210, 717, 723, 729, 732, 733
Sipelstein, J.M., 43, 48, 83, 84, 712, 733
Sivilotti, P., 94, 733
Skeel, R., 211, 727
Skjellum, A., 465, 466, 472, 499, 711, 717, 720, 733
Smith, B., 465, 720
Smith, B.T., 299, 301, 709
Smith, K., 378, 733
Smith, R.M., 135, 727
Smith, S.G., 465, 472, 717, 733
Smith, T.F., 406, 733
Snyder, L., 301, 725

Solomon, M.H., 518, 713
Sorensen, D., 45, 710
Sotelino, E.D., 465, 722
Srinivas, S., 508, 516, 533, 535,
    593, 719, 720, 736
Srinivasan, S., 406, 733
Stal, M., 289, 713
Starkey, M., 378, 711
Steele Jr., G.L., 43, 55, 85, 138,
    177, 297, 299–302, 315, 430,
    507, 549, 589, 722, 724, 730,
    733
Steinberg, S.G., 339, 710
Stepanov, A., 35, 44, 83, 733
Stevens, L., 243, 725
Stevens, R., 222, 236, 712
Stichnoth, J.M., 317, 736
Still, C.H., 472, 717
Straka, M., 380, 715
Strayer, W.T., 384, 387, 411, 412,
    720, 724
Stroustrup, B., xxviii, xxix, 44,
    94, 216, 292, 509, 681, 717,
    733
Sturman, D., 267, 709
Su, W., 429, 454, 712
Sundaresan, N., 508, 719
Sunderam, V.S., 177, 194, 387,
    430, 465, 641, 711, 719, 734
Sussman, A., 134, 138, 155,
    166–168, 709, 711, 712, 715,
    728, 732, 734
Sussman, G.J., 55, 709
Sussman, J., 55, 709

Takada, T., 263, 267, 736
Takashi, T., 429, 440, 723
Tamayo, P., 555, 711
Tan, C.K., 518, 713
Tanaka, J., 180, 724
Tanenbaum, A.S., 1, 42, 349, 711
Taura, K., 380, 734
Taylor, S., 91, 714
Tezuka, H., 379, 544, 723
Tholburn, M., 548, 729, 730

Titcombe, D., 646, 728
Tokoro, M., 263, 289, 736
Tomokiyo, T., 379, 464, 544, 722,
    723
Totty, B.K., 595, 604, 729
Townshend, J., 166, 728
Tsatalos, O.G., 518, 713
Tseng, C.-W., 315, 718
Tuecke, S., 124, 718

Uysal, M., 132, 134, 136, 138,
    140, 152, 153, 716, 731

Verjus, J.-P., 267, 730
Viswanathan, G., 297, 298, 319,
    725
Viswanathan, S., 406, 717
Vlissides, J., 482, 557, 565, 718
von Eicken, T., 142, 180, 434,
    716, 734

Wagener, J.L., 299, 301, 709
Wakita, K., 267, 726
Walker, D.W., 507, 715
Walsh, B., 267, 726
Wang, J.-C., 627, 709
Watanabe, T., 289, 734
Waterman, M.S., 406, 733
Weaver, A.C., 426, 720
Webb, J., 317, 736
Weber, W.-D., 217, 223, 226, 242,
    725, 732
Wegner, P., 384, 734
Wei, M., 86, 631, 646, 728, 730,
    734, 735
Weicheng, J., 465, 719
Weinand, A., 477, 734
Weissman, J.B., 384, 387, 405,
    406, 720, 734
Wendelborn, A., 295, 710
West, E.A., 387, 406, 409, 422,
    720, 734
White, D., 701, 735
White, S.J., 518, 713
Williams, R.D., 131, 718

Wilson, G.V., xxxiii, 689, 695,
    707, 735
Winder, R., 86, 631, 637, 646,
    728, 730, 734, 735
Wingate, C., 548, 718
Winnicka, B., 508, 593, 719
Wirth, N., 349, 735
Wobber, E., 289, 712
Wolfe, M.J., 177, 728
Wood, D.A., 298, 299, 320, 321,
    332, 339, 721, 722, 729, 731,
    735
Woronowicz, M.S., 163, 729
Wu, M.-Y., 315, 718
Wulf, W.A., 299, 384, 426, 720,
    735, 736
Wyllie, J.C., 55, 736
Wypior, P., 465, 713

Xu, M., 95, 718

Yamaguchi, Y., 434, 449, 731
Yang, B., 317, 736
Yang, S., 51, 83, 84, 421, 508,
    533, 535, 601, 603, 712, 719,
    726, 736
Yelick, K., 142, 339, 434, 710, 716
Yeung, D., 217, 709
Yokota, T., 429, 730
Yokote, Y., 263, 289, 736
Yonezawa, A., 41, 263, 267, 289,
    375, 380, 726, 734, 736

Zagha, M., 48, 83, 84, 712
Zahorjan, J., 404, 717
Zhang, X., 369, 380, 715, 729
Zhou, S., 1, 731
Zorbas, J.R., 321, 711
Zosel, M.E., 43, 138, 177, 299,
    301, 302, 430, 507, 589, 724
Zwaenepoel, W., 1, 711
Zwilling, Y., 518, 713

Index

A++, 507, 553
ABC++ (Chapter 1), 1–42, 376
ABCL/1, 186, 263, 267, 379
ACT++, 42
Act1, 263
active message, 516
active object, 1–10, 15, 16, 22, 33,
    40, 41, 179, 259–261, 264, 265,
    276, 430, 629, 631, 634,
    636–639, 642, 643, 668
  allocation-based, 260, 632–635,
    637
  class, 5, 7, 19, 27, 260, 266,
    276–278, 631, 632, 634
actor, 1, 178, 180, 190, 379
Actors, 178, 180, 194, 262, 378,
    379
Ada, 267, 270, 275, 399
  Ada-95, 504
Advanced Research Projects
    Agency, 130, 174, 340, 506,
    545, 628
affinity, 234–236
aggregate, 85, 193, 298–301, 304,
    305, 340, 358, 378, 507, 508,
    513, 692
  operation, 44, 51, 299, 305–307
aggregate parallelism, see
    parallelism, aggregate
Agrawal, Avneesh, 255
Agrawala, Maneesh, 255
Alewife, see Massachusetts
    Institute of Technology
    Alewife
Alpha, see Digital Equipment
    Corporation Alpha
Amber, 42
Amdahl's Law, 697
Amelia Vector Template Library
    (Chapter 2), 43–89, 340, 507
ANL, see Argonne National
    Laboratory
Argonne National Laboratory,
    155, 174, 466

Arjomandi, Eshrat, 4, 42
ARPA, see Advanced Research
    Projects Agency
asynchronous operation, 17, 18,
    21, 101, 116, 125, 126, 179,
    183, 190, 195, 205, 207, 210,
    216, 220, 262, 297, 350, 395,
    433, 515, 631, 632, 635, 638,
    643
AT&T, 42
Atlas, Susan R., 547
atomic
  base class, 126
  data, 314
  function, 103, 106, 107, 126, 221,
    308, 379
  operation, 8, 32, 92, 93, 106,
    116, 120, 126, 349
atomic operation, 186, 207, 294
AVTL, see Amelia Vector
    Template Library
AWESIME, 42
Aylor, James, 427

Banerjee, Prith, 382
Banerjee, Subhankar, 547
Bangalore, Purushotham V., 465
barrier synchronization, 222, 322,
    351, 360, 513, 514, 526, 605
Baude, Françoise, 296
BBN, see Bolt Beranek and
    Newman
Beckman, Peter, 507
Belloncle, Fabrice, 257
Bennet, Karen, xxxiv, 42
Bermond, Jean-Claude, 296
Bhandarkar, Milind, 213
BLAS, 45
Blelloch, Guy, 61
blocking operation, 6, 7, 9, 10, 18,
    19, 25, 34, 101, 103, 105, 221,
    262, 265, 272, 395, 402, 432,
    433, 467
Bodin, François, 545
Bohm, Denis, 255

Bolt Beranek and Newman
  Butterfly, 386
  TC2000, 84
broadcast, 40, 191, 205, 220, 221
Bryan, Greg, 534
busy wait, 239, 240
Butterfly, *see* Bolt Beranek and
  Newman Butterfly

C*, 85, 297, 300, 301
C** (Chapter 8), 85, 171,
  297–341, 378, 507
C++ (Appendix A), 681–688
  base class, 684, 685
  class, 681, 682, 684, 687
  constructor method, 683, 687
  derived class, 683–685
  destructor method, 683
  dynamic binding, 681, 685
  encapsulation, 681, 682
  inheritance, 681, 684
  member access control, 683, 684
  member function, 682, 684, 685
  member function call, 683–685,
    687
  member variable, 682, 684
  name hiding, 684
  object, 681–685
  object-based system, 681
  object orientation, 681
  overloading, 685, 687
  overriding, 685
  polymorphism, 681, 684, 685
  scope resolution operator (: :),
    684
  template, 687, 688
  virtual function, 685
C++// (Chapter 7), 186, 257–296
CA, 186
Cantor, 186
Cantor-Adams, Deborah, xxxiv
Carnegie-Mellon University, 83,
  84, 543
Caromel, Denis, 257

CC++ (Chapter 3), 42, 91–130,
  142, 171, 186, 187, 379, 434,
  507, 544, 629
CEDAR, 380
Center for Supercomputing
  Research and Development,
  508
CenterLine, 419
chained-expression optimization,
  557, 559
Chameleon, 465
Chandra, Rohit, 215
Chandy, K. Mani, 130
Chang, Chialin, 131
CHAOS++ (Chapter 4), 87,
  131–174
  CHAOS, 87, 422
CHARM++ (Chapter 5), 42, 86,
  175–213, 378, 379, 587, 629
  Chare Kernel, 177, 178, 203,
    206, 207, 210
  CHARM, 92, 171
  DP, 205, 212
  Projections, 201, 210
  Visual Dagger, 207, 208
Cheek, Gorrell, 427
Chien, Andrew A., 343, 382
Choo, Young-il, 42
CLOS, 289
cluster of workstations, 1, 47, 84,
  87, 121, 175, 381, 386, 409,
  414, 418, 426, 429, 430, 454,
  455, 463, 465, 513, 551, 558,
  559, 569, 581, 644, 658, 665,
  689
CM-1, *see* Thinking Machines
  Corporation CM-1
CM-2, *see* Thinking Machines
  Corporation CM-2
CM-5, *see* Thinking Machines
  Corporation CM-5
CMU, *see* Carnegie-Mellon
  University

CM Fortran, 534, 537, 538, 542, 543, 553
coarse-grained, *see* granularity, coarse
collection, 43–46, 51, 54, 83–86, 89, 193, 298, 299, 305, 306, 318, 344, 355–358, 362, 378, 381, 507–509, 511–513, 516, 518, 543, 592, 593, 603, 610
  class, 43, 47, 49, 355, 356, 375, 509, 510, 513
  performance, 603, 615
Common Object Request Broker Architecture, 212, 375, 545, 568, 569, 606, 636
computation-to-communication ratio, 394, 696
Concurrent Aggregates, 86, 193, 349, 354, 369, 379, 380
ConcurrentSmalltalk, 263
Concurrent C, 42, 267
  Concurrent C++, 629
Condor, 650
consistency, 376
  of memory, 186
  of objects, 1, 21, 25, 195, 344, 350, 352, 354, 378
  release, 25
continuation, 172, 399, 437, 454
control parallelism, *see* parallelism, control
Converse, 178, 183, 203, 205, 206, 212
Convex
  Exemplar, 89, 175, 217, 232, 386, 513, 515
COOL (Chapter 6), 42, 86, 186, 215–255, 378, 544
Cooper, Nick, 42
COOTS, 630–633, 668
copying
  deep, 136, 148, 173, 264, 480
  shallow, 422, 480, 482, 560

CORBA, *see* Common Object Request Broker Architecture
Cornell Theory Center, 155, 174
CoSIDE, 631–633
COW, *see* cluster of workstations
Cray Research Incorporated, 371, 551
  T3D, 89, 371, 380–382, 513, 516, 529, 537, 538, 542, 551, 559, 564, 575, 581
  Y-MP, 84, 86
CS-2, *see* Meiko CS-2
CSP, 267
CSRD, *see* Center for Supercomputing Research and Development
Cummings, Julian C., 547
Cuny, Janice E., 589
CVL, 48, 83, 84

Dalle, Olivier, 296
DARPA, *see* Defense Advanced Research Projects Agency
DASH, *see* Stanford DASH
data dependence, 187, 207, 300, 345–349, 356, 379, 384, 385, 401, 417, 418
data distribution, 61, 97, 134, 137, 138, 232–235, 237, 246, 247, 253, 333, 343, 355, 357–359, 381, 430, 509, 510, 548, 555, 556, 558, 563, 564, 567, 612
dataflow, 92, 180, 379, 384, 467, 470, 692
  macro-dataflow, 180, 187, 207, 396
  runtime detection, 401, 402
  single-assignment variable, 101, 187
data layout, *see* data distribution
data parallelism, *see* parallelism, data
Dataparallel C, 85
Davis, Larry, 174

deadlock, 106, 183, 221–223, 375,
    482, 502
DEC, see Digital Equipment
    Corporation
decomposition
  functional, 694
  geometric, 693
  iterative, 693
  recursive, 694
  speculative, 694
deep copying, see copying, deep
Defense Advanced Research
    Projects Agency, 255
Defense Research Establishment,
    630
Delmas, Olivier, 296
Department of Energy, 340, 506
Digital Equipment Corporation,
    340
  Alpha, 47, 646
  AlphaStation, 288
  DEC Unix, 288
distributed memory, 2, 21, 43, 44,
    47, 89, 91, 95, 99, 112, 120,
    131, 178, 181, 194, 381, 431,
    509, 512, 513, 644, 691
distributed shared memory, 689
DOE, see Department of Energy
Dolby, Julian T., 343
DOME, 378
Doss, Nathan, 465
Dzwig, Peter, 629

EC++, 667
efficiency, 697
Eiffel, 258
Eiffel//, 258, 267, 289
Eigler, Frank Ch., 1
element-wise parallelism, see
    parallelism, element-wise
EM-C, 434
embarrassing parallelism, see
    parallelism, embarrassing
Encore
  Multimax, 175, 217

ES-Kit, 42
  ES-Kit++, 378
EUROPA Working Group, 666
executor, 135, 138, 139, 144
Exemplar, see Convex Exemplar
ExtraP, 607–609, 621

FALCON, 403, 404
false sharing, 1, 21, 332
Fenton, Wayne, 213
Ferrari, Adam, 383, 427
Ferraro, Robert, 427
fine-grained, see granularity, fine
Flynn's taxonomy, 689
  MIMD, 175, 205, 257, 258, 293,
    294, 297, 300, 302, 507, 590,
    631, 632, 666, 668, 690
  MSIMD, 667
  SIMD, 51, 297, 300–302, 314,
    337, 666–668, 690
  SISD, 690
  SPMD, 40, 131, 172, 176, 179,
    180, 205, 294, 318, 319, 474,
    507, 513, 514, 543, 587, 618,
    627, 666, 691
Forslund, David, 587
Fortran, 2, 47, 165, 346, 406, 510,
    535, 536, 544, 545, 560, 574,
    586, 593, 625
  Fortran-77, 465, 467, 502, 503,
    534, 538
  Fortran-90, 86, 139, 299, 301,
    348, 349, 357, 504, 507, 508,
    510, 512, 551
  Fortran-90D, 138
  Fortran D, 315
functional parallelism, see
    parallelism, functional
Furmento, Nathalie, 296
future, 18, 20, 37, 116, 117, 228,
    263
  return-to-future, 388, 396, 425

Gamsa, Ben, xxxiv
Gannon, Dennis, 507

Garnett, John, 130
gather, 63, 139–141, 148, 562, 578, 654
Gaujal, Bruno, 296
Gharachorloo, Kourosh, 255
Ghobadpour, Ali, 42
global pointer, 114, 115, 125, 126, 130, 142, 151, 183, 207, 434, 447, 512, 515
GNU, 155, 288, 452, 454, 488
Gotwals, Jacob, 507
Goward, Samuel, 174
granularity, 50, 51, 82, 83, 210, 250, 295, 300, 329, 334, 379, 381, 394, 425, 647, 649, 695
  coarse, 186, 215, 218, 247, 300, 302–304, 313, 316, 378, 394, 426, 635, 637, 638, 647, 649, 654, 665, 695
  fine, 172, 180, 182, 186, 218, 244, 297, 298, 300–302, 312, 314, 320, 321, 343, 369, 380, 381, 394, 425, 630, 635, 649, 695
  large, 297, 300, 303, 304, 339
  medium, 182, 183, 470, 635, 637, 638, 647, 654, 665
Grimshaw, Andrew S., 383
guard, 37, 41, 399
Guide, 266
Gupta, Anoop, 215
Gursoy, Attila, 213

HAL, 186
Harlequin, 630
Hasker, Rob, 382
Hatcher, Philip J., 300
Hennessy, John L., 215
Hernquist, Lars, 534
heterogeneous
  architecture, 206, 383, 386, 387, 420, 426, 551, 629, 658, 668
  collections, 44, 54
  parallelism, 96, 108
Hewlett-Packard, 386, 621
  HP-PA, 621

High Performance Fortran, 43, 47, 56, 68, 138, 173, 177, 206, 212, 299, 301–303, 314, 430, 507, 509, 510, 513, 553, 589, 591, 599, 626, 627
Hinker, Paul J., 547
homogeneous
  collection, 54
Hori, Atsushi, 429
HP, see Hewlett-Packard
HPC++, 627, 666
HPF, see High Performance Fortran
Huang, Howard, 382
Humphrey, William F., 547
Hybrid, 265, 266

I-structure, 439, 440, 449
I/O, 187–189, 201, 394, 395, 516, 518
I3S-CNRS, 257
IBM, see International Business Machines Corporation
ICC++ (Chapter 9), 86, 171, 186, 187, 343–382, 507, 544
ICL, 630, 632, 668, 669
  DAP, 300
  DRS, 630, 644, 646
  Goldrush, 630, 644, 646
Indiana University, 508
inheritance anomaly, 41, 354, 375, 378
INRIA Sophia Antipolis, 257
inspector, 135, 138–140, 144
instance, see C++, object
Intel, 87
  iPSC/2, 386, 408
  iPSC/860, 134, 155, 168–170, 174, 386
  Paragon, 47, 84, 89, 121, 134, 175, 201, 386, 513, 516, 526, 529, 537, 542
International Business Machines Corporation, 38, 42, 71, 82, 83, 87, 130, 155, 488, 628

Center for Advanced Studies, 1,
   2
RS6000, 83, 386, 581
SP-1, 134, 155, 168–170, 174, 386
SP-2, 34, 38, 47, 74, 89, 124,
   134, 154, 155, 175, 386, 427,
   488, 499, 513, 515, 516, 529,
   537, 542, 551, 559, 575, 581
T.J. Watson Research
   Laboratory, 42
interrupt-driven execution, 181,
   424, 516
iPSC/2, see Intel iPSC/2
iPSC/860, see Intel iPSC/860
Ishikawa, Yutaka, 429

Jagathesan, Narain, 213
Jones, David M., xxxiv
Jovian, 167, 168

Kalé, Laxmikant V., 175, 382
Kalas, Ivan, 42
Kamin, Sam, 382
Karamcheti, Vijay, 381
Karmesin, Steve R., 547
Karpovich, John, 427
Keahey, Katarzyna, 547
Kendall Square Research
   KSR-1, 84
Kesselman, Carl, 91
Kilman, David, 587
Konaka, Hiroki, 429
Krishnan, Sanjeev, 175
KSR, see Kendall Square
   Research
KSR-1, see Kendall Square
   Research KSR-1
Kumar, Pankaj, 42

Lakshman, T. K., 382
Lancaster, Tal, 130
LANL, see Los Alamos National
   Laboratory
LAPACK, 45

large-grained, see granularity,
   large
Larus, James R., 297
latency, 696
LCM, see Loosely Coherent
   Memory
LEDA, 660
Lee, Henry, 4, 42
Legion, 426, 427
Lewis, Mike, 427
Lin, Calvin, 301
Linda, 194, 411
Linux, 288
Lisp, 55
Livermore Kernels, 380
locality, 692, 695
London Parallel Applications
   Centre, 629, 630, 666
loop parallelism, see parallelism,
   loop
Loosely Coherent Memory, 298,
   320–325
Los Alamos National Laboratory,
   86, 548, 553, 587
Loyot, Ed, 427
LPAC, see London Parallel
   Applications Centre
LPARX, 87, 171
Lu, Ziyang, 465
Lui, Cassandra, 42

MacCallum, Laurie, 427
Mack, Dave, 427
Maeda, Munenori, 429
Malony, Allen D., 589
marshalling, 4, 7, 136, 212, 264,
   292, 393, 422, 642
MasPar
   MP-1, 84
Massachusetts Institute of
   Technology
   Alewife, 217, 232
Matsuda, Motohiko, 429
Maui High Performance
   Computing Center, 506, 587

McCracken, Nancy, 42
McEwan, Alistair, 629
McGill University, 1
medium-grained, see granularity,
    medium
Meiko
  CS-2, 513, 516, 551, 559
member data, see C++, member
    variable
Menezes, Arul, 255
Mentat (Chapter 10), 42, 85, 86,
    92, 171, 186, 187, 378, 383–427
message-driven execution, 177,
    178, 431
Message-Passing Interface, see
    MPI
meta-object protocol, 289, 290,
    293, 294, 431, 440
method, see C++, member
    function
method invocation, see C++,
    member function call
method parallelism, see
    parallelism, method
Milley, Peter, 42
MIMD, see Flynn's taxonomy,
    MIMD
Ministry of International Trade
    and Industry, 464
MIPS
  R8000, 621
Mississippi State University, 466,
    506
MIT, see Massachusetts Institute
    of Technology
MITI, see Ministry of
    International Trade and
    Industry
Mohr, Bernd, 589
monitor, 217, 219, 349, 389, 423
Moon, Bongki, 174
Morgan, Mark, 427
MP-1, see MasPar MP-1

MPC++ (Chapter 11), 379,
    429–464, 544
MPI, 46, 47, 84, 182, 183, 194,
    212, 314, 430, 465–506, 551,
    559, 638, 650, 668
  MPI-1, 467, 503
  MPI-2, 465, 468, 470, 473, 483,
    494, 500, 501, 503, 504
  MPICH, 466, 488, 499, 500, 538
  MPI Forum, 465, 466, 501, 503,
    504
MPI++ (Chapter 12), 465–506
MPL, 155, 384, 388, 393, 396,
    399, 400, 405, 414, 421, 422
MSIMD, see Flynn's taxonomy,
    MSIMD
Multilisp, 228
Multimax, see Encore Multimax
Mussi, Philippe, 296
Myricom
  Myrinet, 429, 454, 455
Myrinet, see Myricom Myrinet

Narayan, Padmini, 427
NAS, see Numerical Aerodynamic
    Simulation
NASA, see National Aeronautics
    and Space Administration
Nasser, Fernando, 42
National Aeronautics and Space
    Administration, 89, 174, 382,
    427
  Jet Propulsion Laboratory, 382
National Center for
    Supercomputing Applications,
    534, 538
National Energy Research
    Supercomputer Center, 587
National Institutes of Health, 155
National Science Foundation, 130,
    174, 340, 382, 427, 506–508,
    545, 628
NCSA, see National Center for
    Supercomputer Applications
nCUBE

nCUBE/2, 175
NERSC, *see* National Energy
    Research Supercomputer
    Center
NESL, 304, 543
network of workstations, *see*
    cluster of workstations
Nexus, 124–126
Nguyen-Tuong, Ahn, 427
NIH, *see* National Institutes of
    Health
Nolte, Jörg, 429
Nomura, Kevin, 213
non-blocking operation, 20, 93,
    101, 105, 179, 185, 392, 393,
    432, 467, 468, 483, 515, 636
non-determinism, 92, 179, 210,
    221, 273, 399, 400
non-uniform memory access, 692
NOW, *see* cluster of workstations
NSF, *see* National Science
    Foundation
NUMA, *see* non-uniform memory
    access
Numerical Aerodynamic
    Simulation, 89
NAS Benchmarks, 43, 50, 71, 82,
    88, 406

O'Brien, Terry, 668
O'Carroll, Francis, 464
O'Farrell, William G., 1, 2
O'Riordan, Bill, 669
OACIS, 628
Objective-C, 681
Object Management Group, 545
object parallelism, *see*
    parallelism, object
Object Pascal, 681
Occam, 267
Office of Naval Research, 174, 382
Olden, 172
OMG, *see* Object Management
    Group

ONR, *see* Office of Naval
    Research
Open Systems Foundation, 631
Operowsky, Howard, 42
Orca, 42
OSF, *see* Open Systems
    Foundation

P++, 86, 127, 171, 553
P4, 411, 465
Pablo, 604
Panda, 42, 629
Paragon, *see* Intel Paragon
parallelism, *see* Appendix B
  aggregate, 44, 85
  control, 86, 379, 383, 429, 431,
    438, 494, 507, 589, 692, 705
  data, 40, 43, 45, 47, 50–52, 69,
    70, 83, 85, 94, 95, 138, 172,
    176, 177, 193, 206, 212,
    297–304, 309–313, 315, 317,
    318, 325, 339, 355, 356, 378,
    379, 404, 405, 415, 421, 426,
    429–431, 463, 467, 468, 470,
    507–509, 521, 543, 544, 549,
    551–553, 556, 587, 589, 612,
    626, 630, 692, 705
  element-wise, 44, 84
  embarrassing, 526, 584, 614, 657,
    658, 663
  functional, 94
  loop, 177, 215, 693
  method, 190, 692
  object, 94
  task, 94, 95, 124, 125, 215, 378,
    379, 470, 589, 692
parallel prefix, 45, 48, 55, 64, 210,
    313
  multiprefix, 69
Parallel Scheme, 314
Parallel Virtual Machine, *see*
    PVM
Parkes, Steven, 382
PARMACS, 465
Parti, 87

Multiblock Parti, 134, 138–140, 173
PARvis, 604
Pascal, 346, 425
Path Pascal, 424
Patton, James, 130
pC++ (Chapter 13), 42, 51, 83–85, 142, 171, 193, 302, 339, 355, 356, 378, 507–545, 590–595, 597, 599–610, 612, 614, 615, 618, 620–622, 625–627, 629
PCN, 91
Pearson, William, 427
Perennes, Stéphane, 296
Perl, 339, 597
Pittsburgh Supercomputing Center, 382, 538
Plaxton, Matthew, 668
Plevyak, John, 381
polling, 10, 516
polygon overlay, see Appendix C
POOL2, 267
Poole, Jonathan, 629
POOMA (Chapter 14), xxxii, 507, 547–587
Portland Group, 599
POSIX, 127
PowerChallenge, see Silicon Graphics Incorporated PowerChallenge
prefix, see parallel prefix
PRESTO, 42, 378
Prior, Bob, xxxiv
probe, 93
process group, 470, 480
programming-in-the-large, 91, 384, 707
PSC, see Pittsburgh Supercomputer Center
Pullara, S. David, 1
PVM, 84, 177, 194, 205, 212, 288, 289, 387, 411, 430, 465, 551, 559, 581, 638, 641, 649, 650, 668

Q-structure, 449
Quinlan, Dan, 86, 587
Quinn, Michael, 300

race condition, 3, 98, 297, 300, 302, 389, 423, 438
Ramkumar, Balkrishna, 213
Real World Computing Program, 429, 464, 544
RWC-1, 429, 440, 452, 464
Reconcilable Shared Memory, 320
Reddy, Ujay, 382
reduction operation, 46, 55, 64, 183, 192, 298, 302, 309–311, 313–318
reification, 289, 290, 294
remote procedure call, 7, 8, 399, 433, 515
replication, 21, 52, 135, 137, 138, 152, 194, 294, 365
Research Institute for Advanced Computer Science, 89
return-to-future, see future
Reynders, John V. W., 547
RIACS, see Research Institute for Advanced Computer Science
Rice University, 174
Richards, Brad, 297
Rigg, Malcolm, 669
Roberts, Graham, 629, 668
Rodríguez, Claudia, 174
Roudier, Yves, 257
RPC, see remote procedure call
RS6000, see International Business Machines Corporation RS6000
RSM, see Reconcilable Shared Memory
RTTI, see runtime type information
runtime type information, 260, 289, 291, 293, 681

Rutter, Michael, xxxiv
RWCP, *see* Real World
    Computing Program

Sage++, 508, 593, 597, 599, 602
Sakai, Shuichi, 464
Saletore, Vikram, 213
Saltz, Joel, 131
Saltzman, Jeff, 587
Sandhu, Harjinder, xxxiv, 42
Sato, Mitsuhisa, 429
Sayre, Steven, 425
SCALAPACK++, 507
scan, *see* parallel prefix
scatter, 63, 139, 140, 148, 562,
    578, 654
Scheme, 55, 597
Science Applications International
    Corporation, 425
Seelemann, Ilene, 42
Sequent
  Symmetry, 84, 175
serialization, 219, 220, 240, 313,
    344–346, 350, 352, 354
SGI, *see* Silicon Graphics
    Incorporated
shallow copying, *see* copying,
    shallow
shared memory, 2, 4, 10, 21, 47,
    94, 99, 119, 182, 186, 216, 298,
    319, 320, 395, 439, 514, 644,
    691
Sheffler, Thomas J., 43
Shiflet, David, 427
Shimada, Junichi, 464
Shock, Carter T., 174
SHORE, 518, 519
Shu, Wennie, 213
Siegel, Günther, 296
Silicon Graphics Incorporated,
    217, 237, 386, 621
  4D, 217
  Indy, 646

PowerChallenge, 386, 513, 515,
    526, 529, 533, 537, 538, 542,
    551, 614, 621, 622
Sim, Susan, 42
SIMD, *see* Flynn's taxonomy,
    SIMD
Simple, 604
Simula, xxviii
Singh, J.P., 255
single-assignment variable, *see*
    dataflow
Sinha, Amitabh, 213
Skjellum, Anthony, 465
Slonim, Jacob, 42
Smalltalk, 681
Smoot, Sherry, 427
Snyder, Lawrence, 301
SP-1, *see* International Business
    Machines Corporation SP-1
SP-2, *see* International Business
    Machines Corporation SP-2
SPARC, *see* Sun SPARC
SPARCStation, *see* Sun
    SPARCStation
speedup, 697
SPLASH, 217, 224, 242
Split-C, 142, 434
split-phase
  communication, 207
  control, 182
  operation, 179
SPMD, *see* Flynn's taxonomy,
    SPMD
Srikant, M., 547
Standard Template Library, 35,
    43, 44, 47, 55, 60, 61, 83, 88,
    89, 544, 668
Stanford University, 217
  DASH, 217, 232, 236–238, 240,
    243, 246, 253
stencil, 301–303, 308, 323, 411,
    412, 414, 553, 563, 566, 567,
    580

STL, *see* Standard Template
    Library
Strayer, Tim, 427
Stroustrup, Bjarne, xxvii, xxxiv
Su, Mei-Hui, 130
Sun, 340, 488
  IPC, 409, 414
  Solaris, 288
  SPARC, 454
  SPARCStation, 288, 370, 386,
      418, 429, 454, 455, 529, 646,
      663
  SPARCworks, 488
  SunOS, 288, 419, 455
Sundaresan, Neelakantan, 507
Sussman, Alan, 131
Symmetry, *see* Sequent Symmetry
synchronous operation, 6, 51, 101,
    103, 126, 190, 205, 217, 219,
    221, 222, 264, 272, 449, 467,
    480, 638, 643
Syracuse University, 1, 42
Syska, Michel, 296

T3D, *see* Cray Research
    Incorporated T3D
Takahashi, Toshiyuki, 464
task farming, 693
task parallelism, *see* parallelism,
    task
TAU (Chapter 15), 508, 589–628
  Breezy, 599, 601, 605–607, 620,
      625, 626
  Cagey, 597, 599–601, 612
  Classy, 597, 599–601, 612
  Cosy, 594, 599, 608, 609, 620,
      621, 625
  Easy, 597, 599, 601, 604, 610,
      618
  Fancy, 597, 599, 600, 610, 612
  Racy, 597, 599, 601, 603, 615
  Speedy, 599, 607, 608, 621, 622
TC2000, *see* Bolt Beranek and
    Newman TC2000
Tcl/Tk, 339, 580, 593, 595, 597

Tdl/Poet, 604
Tezuka, Hiroshi, 429
Thinking Machines Corporation,
    534, 542
  CM-1, 300
  CM-2, 52, 300
  CM-5, 47, 52, 84, 87, 89, 134,
      175, 313, 318, 321, 332, 333,
      380, 381, 513, 534, 537, 538,
      542
Tholburn, MaryDell, 547
Titcombe, David, 668
TMC, *see* Thinking Machines
    Corporation
Tomokiyo, Takashi, 429
Tsukuba Research Center, 464
Tulip, 514, 516
two-phase communication, 68

U.S. Air Force, 340
UC++ (Chapter 16), 42, 86, 186,
    629–669
Uchida, Kaoru, 255
UCL, *see* University College
    London
UMA, *see* uniform memory access
UMIACS, *see* University of
    Maryland Institute for
    Advanced Computer Science
uniform memory access, 692
Universities Space Research
    Association, 89
University College London,
    629–631, 668
University of Illinois, 213, 508,
    573
University of Iowa, 210
University of Maryland Institute
    for Advanced Computer
    Studies, 155, 174
University of Nice, 257
University of Tokyo, 464
University of Toronto, xxxiv, 1, 42
University of Virginia, 406, 426
University of Waterloo, 42

Unix, 59, 94, 238, 288, 388, 515,
    533, 551, 559, 603, 625, 640,
    657
Upshot, 604
Urushibara, Shigeru, 255

Versioned Objects, 42
virtual shared memory, 1, 5, 134,
    171, 321, 332, 381
Viswanathan, Guhan, 297
Vivas, Virgil, 427
VPC, 508

Wahab, Matthew, 668
wait-by-necessity, 262, 294
Wei, Mian, 668
Weissman, Jon, 427
West, Emily A., 383, 427
Wilmoth, Richard, 174
Wilson, Gregory V., 1
Wilson, Robert, 255
Winder, Russel, 629, 668

Y-MP, see Cray Research
    Incorporated Y-MP
Yang, Shelby X., 507
Yelon, Josh, 213
Yonezawa, Akinori, 464
York University, 1, 42

Zhang, Xingbin, 381
Zhou, Songnian, xxxiv
Zipcode, 465, 472, 487
ZPL, 301